Android Programming with Kotlin for Beginners

Build Android apps starting from zero programming experience with the new Kotlin programming language

John Horton

BIRMINGHAM - MUMBAI

Android Programming with Kotlin for Beginners

Commissioning Editor: Pavan Ramchandani
Acquisition Editor: Larissa Pinto
Content Development Editor: Smit Carvalho
Technical Editor: Surabhi Kulkarni
Copy Editor: Safis Editing
Project Coordinator: Kinjal Bari
Proofreader: Safis Editing
Indexers: Pratik Shirodkar
Graphics: Alishon Mendonsa
Production Coordinator: Arvindkumar Gupta

First published: April 2019

Production reference: 1260419

Published by Packt Publishing Ltd.
Livery Place
35 Livery Street
Birmingham B3 2PB, UK.

ISBN 978-1-78961-540-1

www.packtpub.com

I think that everybody has an app inside of them, and all you need do is work hard enough to get it out of you.

For Jo, Jack, James, Ray, Rita, and Missy.

mapt.io

Mapt is an online digital library that gives you full access to over 5,000 books and videos, as well as industry leading tools to help you plan your personal development and advance your career. For more information, please visit our website.

Why subscribe?

- Spend less time learning and more time coding with practical eBooks and Videos from over 4,000 industry professionals
- Learn better with Skill Plans built especially for you
- Get a free eBook or video every month
- Mapt is fully searchable
- Copy and paste, print, and bookmark content

Packt.com

Did you know that Packt offers eBook versions of every book published, with PDF and ePub files available? You can upgrade to the eBook version at `www.Packt.com` and as a print book customer, you are entitled to a discount on the eBook copy. Get in touch with us at `customercare@packtpub.com` for more details.

At `www.Packt.com`, you can also read a collection of free technical articles, sign up for a range of free newsletters, and receive exclusive discounts and offers on Packt books and eBooks.

Contributors

About the author

John Horton is a programming and gaming enthusiast based in the UK. He has a passion for writing apps, games, books, and blog articles. He is the founder of Game Code School.

About the reviewers

Ashok Kumar S has been working in the mobile development domain for about six years. In his early days, he was a JavaScript and Node developer. With his strong web development skills, he mastered web and mobile development. He is a Google-certified engineer, a speaker at global conferences, such as DroidCon Berlin and MODS, and he also runs a YouTube channel called AndroidABCD for Android developers. He also contributes heavily to open source to improve his e-karma.

He has written books on WearOS programming and the Firebase toolchain. Ashok has also reviewed books on mobile and web development, namely *Mastering Junit5*, *Android Programming for Beginners*, and *Developing Enterprise Applications Using JavaScript*.

Mitchell Wong Ho was born in Johannesburg, South Africa, where he completed his national diploma in electrical engineering. Mitchell's software development career started on embedded systems and then moved to Microsoft desktop/server applications.

Mitchell has been programming in Java since 2000 on J2ME, JEE, desktop, and Android applications, and has more recently been advocating Kotlin for Android.

Packt is searching for authors like you

If you're interested in becoming an author for Packt, please visit `authors.packtpub.com` and apply today. We have worked with thousands of developers and tech professionals, just like you, to help them share their insight with the global tech community. You can make a general application, apply for a specific hot topic that we are recruiting an author for, or submit your own idea.

Table of Contents

Preface

Are you trying to start a career in Android programming, but haven't found the right way in? Do you have a great idea for an app, but don't know how to make it a reality? Or maybe you're just frustrated that to learn Android, you must already know Kotlin. If so, then this book is for you.

Android Programming with Kotlin for Beginners will be your guide to creating Android applications from scratch. We will introduce you to all the fundamental concepts of programming in an Android context, from the basics of Kotlin to working with the Android API. All examples are created within Android Studio, the official Android development environment, which helps supercharge your application development process. After this crash course, we'll dive deeper into Android programming, and you'll learn how to create applications with a professional-standard UI through fragments and store your user's data with SQLite. In addition, you'll see how to make your apps multilingual, draw on the screen with a finger, and work with graphics, sound, and animations too.

By the end of this book, you'll be ready to start building your own custom applications in Android and Kotlin.

Who this book is for

This book is for you if you are completely new to Kotlin, Android, or programming and want to make Android applications. This book also acts as a refresher for those who already have some basic experience of using Kotlin on Android to advance their knowledge and make fast progress through the early projects.

What this book covers

Chapter 1, Getting Started with Android and Kotlin, welcomes you to *the exciting world of Android and Kotlin*. In this first chapter, we won't waste any time before getting started developing Android apps. We will look at what is so great about Android, what Android and Kotlin are, how they work and complement each other, and what that means to us as future developers. Moving on, we will set up the required software so that we can build and deploy a simple first app.

Chapter 2, Kotlin, XML, and the UI Designer, discusses how, at this stage, we have a working Android development environment and we have built and deployed our first app. It is obvious, however, that code autogenerated by Android Studio is not going to make the next top-selling app on Google Play. We need to explore this autogenerated code so that we can begin to understand Android and then learn how to build on this useful template.

Chapter 3, Exploring Android Studio and the Project Structure, takes us through creating and running two more Android projects. The purpose of these exercises is to explore Android Studio and the structure of Android projects more deeply. When we build our apps ready for deployment, the code and the resource files need to be packed away in the APK file - just as they are. Therefore, all the layout files and other resources, which we will be looking at soon, need to be in the correct structures. Fortunately, Android Studio handles this for us when we create a project from a template. However, we still need to know how to find and amend these files, how to add our own and sometimes remove the files created by Android Studio, and how the resource files are interlinked - sometimes with each other and sometimes with the Kotlin code (that is, the autogenerated Kotlin code as well as our own). Along with understanding the composition of our projects, it will also be beneficial to make sure that we get the most from the emulator.

Chapter 4, Getting Started with Layouts and Material Design, builds on what we have already seen; that is, the Android Studio UI designer and a little bit more Kotlin in action. In this hands-on chapter, we will build three more layouts - still quite simple, yet a step up from what we have done so far. Before we get to the hands-on part, we will have a quick introduction to the concept of **material design**. We will look at another type of layout called `LinearLayout` and walk through it, using it to create a usable UI. We will take things a step further using `ConstraintLayout` both to understand constraints and design more complex and precise UI designs. Finally, we will use `TableLayout` to lay data out in an easily readable table. We will also write some Kotlin code to switch between our different layouts within one app/project. This is the first major app that links together multiple topics into one neat parcel. The app is called *Exploring Layouts*.

Chapter 5, Beautiful Layouts with CardView and ScrollView, is the last chapter on layouts before we spend some time focusing on Kotlin and object-oriented programming. We will formalize our learning on some of the different attributes we have already seen, and we will also introduce two more cool layouts, `ScrollView` and `CardView`. To finish the chapter off, we will run the `CardView` project on a tablet emulator.

Chapter 6, The Android Lifecycle, will familiarize us with the lifecycle of an Android app. The idea that a computer program has a lifecycle might sound strange at first, but it will soon make sense. The lifecycle is the way that all Android apps interact with the Android OS. In the same way that the lifecycle of humans enables them to interact with the world around them, we have no choice but to interact with the Android lifecycle, and we must be prepared to handle numerous unpredictable events if we want our apps to survive. We will explore the phases of the lifecycle that an app goes through, from creation to destruction, and how this helps us know *where* to put our Kotlin code, depending on what we are trying to achieve.

Chapter 7, Kotlin Variables, Operators, and Expressions, along with the following chapter, explains the core fundamentals of Kotlin. In fact, we will explore the topics that are the main principles of programming in general. In this chapter, we will focus on the creation and understanding of the data itself, and in the next chapter, we will explore how to manipulate and respond to it.

Chapter 8, Kotlin Decisions and Loops, moves on from variables, and we now understand how to change the values that they hold with expressions, but how can we take a course of action that is dependent upon the value of a variable? We can certainly add the number of new messages to the number of previously unread messages, but how can we, for example, trigger an action within our app when the user has read all their messages? The first problem is that we need a way to test the value of a variable, and then respond when the value falls within a range of values or is equal to a specific value. Another problem that is common in programming is that we need sections of our code to be executed a certain number of times (more than once, or sometimes not at all) depending on the value of variables. To solve the first problem, we will look at making decisions in Kotlin with `if`, `else`, and `when`. To solve the latter, we will look at loops in Kotlin with `while`, `do - while`, `for`, `continue`, and `break`. Furthermore, we will learn that, in Kotlin, decisions are also expressions that produce a value.

Chapter 9, Kotlin Functions, explains that functions are the building blocks of our apps. We write functions that do specific tasks, and then call them when we need to execute that specific task. As the tasks we need to perform in our apps will be quite varied, our functions need to cater to this and be very flexible. Kotlin functions are very flexible, more so than the functions of other Android-related languages. We therefore need to spend a whole chapter learning about them. Functions are intimately related to object-oriented programming, and once we understand the basics of functions, we will be in a good position to take on the wider learning of object-oriented programming.

Chapter 10, Object-Oriented Programming, explains that, in Kotlin, classes are fundamental to just about everything and, in fact, just about everything is a class. We have already talked about reusing other people's code, specifically the Android API, but in this chapter, we will really get to grips with how this works and learn about object-oriented programming (OOP) and how to use it.

Chapter 11, Inheritance in Kotlin, shows inheritance in action. In fact, we have already seen it, but now we will examine it more closely, discuss the benefits, and write classes that we inherit from. Throughout the chapter, I will show you several practical examples of inheritance, and at the end of the chapter we will improve our naval battle simulation from the previous chapter and show how we could have saved lots of typing and future debugging by using inheritance.

Chapter 12, Connecting Our Kotlin to the UI and Nullability, fully reveals, by the end of the chapter, the missing link between our Kotlin code and our XML layouts, leaving us with the power to add all kinds of widgets and UI features to our layouts as we have done before, but this time we will be able to control them through our code. In this chapter, we will take control of some simple UI elements, such as `Button` and `TextView`, and, in the next chapter, we will take things further and manipulate a whole range of UI elements. To enable us to understand what is happening, we need to find out a bit more about the memory in an app, and two areas of it in particular – the **Stack** and the **Heap**.

Chapter 13, Bringing Android Widgets to Life, discusses that since we now have a good overview of both the layout and coding of an Android app, as well as our newly acquired insight into object-oriented programming (OOP) and how we can manipulate the UI from our Kotlin code, we are ready to experiment with more widgets from the Android Studio palette. At times, OOP is a tricky thing, and this chapter introduces some topics that can be awkward for beginners. However, by gradually learning these new concepts and practicing them repeatedly, they will, over time, become our friend. In this chapter, we will diversify a lot by going back to the Android Studio palette and looking at half a dozen widgets that we have either not seen at all or have not used fully yet. Once we have done so, we will put them all into a layout and practice manipulating them with our Kotlin code.

Chapter 14, Android Dialog Windows, explains how to present the user with a pop-up dialog window. We can then put all that we know into the first phase of our first multi-chapter app, *Note to self*. We will then learn about new Android and Kotlin features in this chapter and the four following chapters (up to *Chapter 18, Localization*), and then use our newly-acquired knowledge to enhance the Note to self app.

Chapter 15, Handling Data and Generating Random Numbers, shows that we are making good progress. We have a rounded knowledge of both the Android UI options and the basics of Kotlin. In the previous few chapters, we started bringing these two areas together and we have manipulated the UI, including some new widgets, using Kotlin code. However, while building the Note to self app, we have stumbled upon a couple of gaps in our knowledge. In this chapter, we will fill in the first of these blanks, and then, in the next chapter, we will use this new information to progress with the app. We currently have no way of managing large amounts of related data. Aside from declaring, initializing, and managing dozens, hundreds, or even thousands of properties or instances, how will we let the users of our app have more than one note? We will also take a quick diversion to learn about random numbers.

Chapter 16, Adapters and Recyclers, first takes us through the theory of adapters and lists. We will then look at how we can use a `RecyclerAdapter` instance in Kotlin code and add a `RecyclerView` widget to the layout, which acts as a list for our UI, and then, through the apparent magic of the Android API, bind them together so that the `RecyclerView` instance displays the contents of the `RecyclerAdapter` instance and allows the user to scroll through the contents of an `ArrayList` instance full of `Note` instances. You have probably guessed that we will be using this technique to display our list of notes in the Note to self app.

Chapter 17, Data Persistence and Sharing, goes through a couple of different ways to save data to an Android device's permanent storage. Also, for the first time, we will add a second `Activity` instance to our app. It often makes sense when implementing a separate "screen", such as a "Settings" screen, in our app to do so in a new `Activity` instance. We could go to the trouble of hiding the original UI and then showing the new UI in the same `Activity`, as we did in *Chapter 4, Getting Started with Layouts and Material Design*, but this would quickly lead to confusing and error-prone code. So, we will see how to add another `Activity` instance and navigate the user between them.

Chapter 18, Localization, is quick and simple, but what we will learn to do can make your app accessible to millions of potential users. We will see how to add additional languages, and we will see why adding text the correct way via String resources benefits us when it comes to adding multiple languages.

Chapter 19, Animations and Interpolations, explores how we can use the `Animation` class to make our UI a little less static and a bit more interesting. As we have come to expect, the Android API will allow us to do some quite advanced things with relatively straightforward code, and the `Animation` class is no different.

Chapter 20, Drawing Graphics, is about the Android `Canvas` class and some related classes, such as `Paint`, `Color`, and `Bitmap`. When combined, these classes have great power when it comes to drawing on the screen. Sometimes, the default UI provided by the Android API isn't what we need. If we want to make a drawing app, draw graphs, or perhaps make a game, we need to take control of every pixel that the Android device has to offer.

Chapter 21, Threads and Starting the Live Drawing App, gets us started on our next app. This app will be a kid's-style drawing app where the user can draw on the screen using their finger. The drawing app that we create will be slightly different, however. The lines that the user draws will be comprised of particle systems that explode into thousands of pieces. We will call the project Live Drawing.

Chapter 22, Particle Systems and Handling Screen Touches, builds on our real-time system that we implemented in the previous chapter using a thread. In this chapter, we will create the entities that will exist and evolve in this real-time system as if they have a mind of their own and form the appearance of the drawings that the user can create. We will also see how the user implements these entities by learning how to respond to interaction with the screen. This is different to interacting with a widget in a UI layout.

Chapter 23, Android Sound Effects and the Spinner Widget, explores the SoundPool class and the different ways we use it depending on whether we just want to play sounds or go further and keep track of the sounds we are playing. At this point, we can then put everything we have learned into producing a cool sound demo app, which will also introduce us to a new UI widget; the Spinner.

Chapter 24, Design Patterns, Multiple Layouts, and Fragments, shows just how far we have come the start, when we were just setting up Android Studio. Back then, we went through everything step by step, but as we have proceeded, we have tried to show not just how to add x to y, or feature a to app b, but to enable you to use what you have learned in your own way in order to bring your own ideas to life. This chapter is more about your future apps than anything in the book so far. We will look at a few aspects of Kotlin and Android that you can use as a framework or template for making ever more exciting and complex apps at the same time as keeping the code manageable.

Chapter 25, Advanced UI with Paging and Swiping, explains that **paging** is the act of moving from page to page, and, on Android, we do this by swiping a finger across the screen. The current page then transitions in a direction and speed to match the finger movement. It is a useful and practical way to navigate around an app, but perhaps even more than this, it is an extremely satisfying visual effect for the user. Also, as with `RecyclerView`, we can selectively load just the data required for the current page and perhaps the data for the previous and next pages in anticipation. The Android API, as you would have come to expect, has a few solutions for achieving paging in a quite simple manner.

Chapter 26, Advanced UI with Navigation Drawer and Fragment, explores what is (arguably) the most advanced UI. `NavigationView`, or the navigation drawer (because of the way it slides out its content), can be created simply by choosing it as a template when you create a new project. We will do just that, and then we will examine the auto-generated code and learn how to interact with it. We will then use everything we know about the `Fragment` class to populate each of the "drawers" with different behaviors and views. Then, in the next chapter, we will learn about databases to add some new functionality to each `Fragment`.

Chapter 27, Android Databases, explains that if we are going to make apps that offer our users significant features, then almost certainly we are going to need a way to manage, store, and filter significant amounts of data. It is possible to efficiently store very large amounts of data with JSON, but when we need to use that data selectively rather than simply restricting ourselves to the options of "save everything" and "load everything," we need to think about which other options are available. As so often, it makes sense to use the solutions provided in the Android API. As we have seen, `JSON` and `SharedPreferences` classes have their place but at some point, we need to move on to using real databases for real-world solutions. Android uses the SQLite database management system and, as you would expect, there is an API to make it as easy as possible.

Chapter 28, A Quick Chat Before You Go, contains a few ideas and pointers that you might like to look at before rushing off and making your own apps.

To get the most out of this book

To succeed with this book, you don't need any experience whatsoever. If you are confident with your operating system of choice (Windows, Mac, or Linux), you can learn to make Android apps while learning the Kotlin programming language. Learning to develop professional quality apps is a journey that anybody can embark upon and stay on for as long as they want.

If you do have previous programming (Kotlin, Java, or any other language), Android, or other development experience, then you will make faster progress with the earlier chapters.

Download the example code files

You can download the example code files for this book from your account at `http://www.packtpub.com`. If you purchased this book elsewhere, you can visit `http://www.packtpub.com/support` and register to have the files emailed directly to you.

You can download the code files by following these steps:

1. Log in or register at `http://www.packtpub.com`.
2. Select the **SUPPORT** tab.
3. Click on **Code Downloads & Errata**.
4. Enter the name of the book in the **Search** box and follow the on-screen instructions.

Once the file is downloaded, please make sure that you unzip or extract the folder using the latest version of:

- WinRAR / 7-Zip for Windows
- Zipeg / iZip / UnRarX for Mac
- 7-Zip / PeaZip for Linux

The code bundle for the book is also hosted on GitHub at `https://github.com/PacktPublishing/Android-Programming-with-Kotlin-for-Beginners`. In case there's an update to the code, it will be updated on the existing GitHub repository.

We also have other code bundles from our rich catalog of books and videos available at `https://github.com/PacktPublishing/`. Check them out!

Download the color images

We also provide a PDF file that has color images of the screenshots/diagrams used in this book. You can download it here: `https://www.packtpub.com/sites/default/files/downloads/9781789615401_ColorImages.pdf`.

Conventions used

There are a number of text conventions used throughout this book.

`CodeInText`: Indicates code words in text, database table names, folder names, filenames, file extensions, pathnames, dummy URLs, user input, and Twitter handles. For example; "Mount the downloaded `WebStorm-10*.dmg` disk image file as another disk in your system."

A block of code is set as follows:

```
<TextView
 android:id="@+id/textView"
 android:layout_width="match_parent"
 android:layout_height="wrap_content"
 android:text="TextView" />
```

When we wish to draw your attention to a particular part of a code block, the relevant lines or items are set in bold:

```
<?xml version="1.0" encoding="utf-8"?>
<LinearLayout
xmlns:android="http://schemas.android.com/apk/res/android"
  android:orientation="vertical"
  android:layout_width="match_parent"
  android:layout_height="match_parent">
</LinearLayout>
```

Bold: Indicates a new term, an important word, or words that you see on the screen, for example, in menus or dialog boxes, also appear in the text like this. For example: "If not, click on the **Logcat** tab"

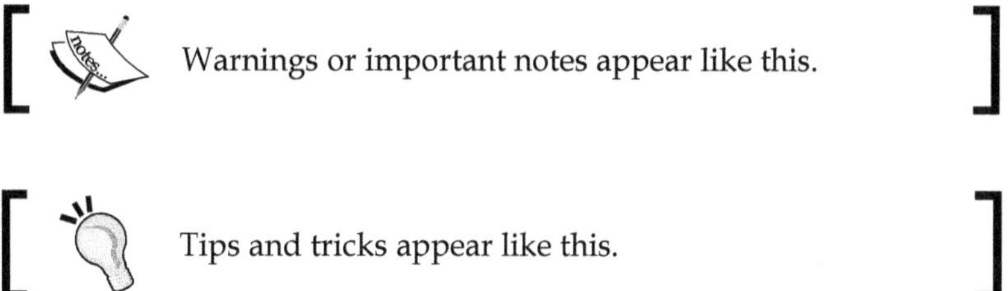

Warnings or important notes appear like this.

Tips and tricks appear like this.

Get in touch

Feedback from our readers is always welcome.

General feedback: Email feedback@packtpub.com, and mention the book's title in the subject of your message. If you have questions about any aspect of this book, please email us at questions@packtpub.com.

Errata: Although we have taken every care to ensure the accuracy of our content, mistakes do happen. If you have found a mistake in this book we would be grateful if you would report this to us. Please visit, http://www.packtpub.com/submit-errata, selecting your book, clicking on the Errata Submission Form link, and entering the details.

Piracy: If you come across any illegal copies of our works in any form on the Internet, we would be grateful if you would provide us with the location address or website name. Please contact us at copyright@packtpub.com with a link to the material.

If you are interested in becoming an author: If there is a topic that you have expertise in and you are interested in either writing or contributing to a book, please visit http://authors.packtpub.com.

Reviews

Please leave a review. Once you have read and used this book, why not leave a review on the site that you purchased it from? Potential readers can then see and use your unbiased opinion to make purchase decisions, we at Packt can understand what you think about our products, and our authors can see your feedback on their book. Thank you!

For more information about Packt, please visit packtpub.com.

1
Getting Started with Android and Kotlin

Welcome to *the exciting world of Android and Kotlin*! In this first chapter, we won't waste any time before getting started developing Android apps.

We will look at what is so great about Android, what Android and Kotlin are, how they work and complement each other, and what that means to us as future developers. Moving on, we will set up the required software, so that we can build and deploy a simple first app.

In this chapter, we will cover the following topics:

- Learning how Kotlin and Android work together
- Setting up our development environment, Android Studio
- Learning what makes an android app
- Learning about Kotlin
- Building our very first Android app
- Deploying an Android emulator
- Running our app on an Android emulator and a real device

This is a lot to get through, so let's get started.

Why use Kotlin and Android?

When Android first arrived in 2008, it was a bit drab compared to the much more stylish iOS on the Apple iPhone/iPad. But, quite quickly, through a variety of handset offers that struck a chord with practical, price-conscious consumers, as well as those who are fashion-conscious and tech-savvy, Android user numbers exploded.

For many, myself included, developing for Android is the most rewarding pastime and business, bar none.

Quickly putting together a prototype of an idea, refining it, and then deciding to run with it and wire it up into a fully-fledged app, is such an exciting and rewarding process. Any programming can be fun - I have been programming all my life - but creating for Android is somehow extraordinarily rewarding.

Defining exactly why this is the case is quite difficult. Perhaps it is the fact that the platform is free and open. You can distribute your apps without needing the permission of a big controlling corporation - nobody can stop you. And, at the same time, you have well-established, corporate-controlled mass markets, such as Amazon Appstore and Google Play.

It is more likely, however, that the reason that developing for Android gives such a good feeling is the nature of the devices themselves. They are deeply personal. You can develop apps that interact with people's lives, which educate, entertain, tell a story, and so on, and it is there in their pocket ready to go - in the home, in the workplace, or on holiday.

You can certainly build something bigger for the desktop but knowing that thousands (or millions) of people are carrying your work in their pockets and sharing it with friends is more than just a buzz.

No longer is developing apps considered geeky, nerdy, or reclusive. In fact, developing for Android is considered highly skillful, and the most successful developers are hugely admired, even revered.

If all this fluffy, spiritual stuff doesn't mean anything to you, then that's fine too; developing for Android can make you a living, or even make you wealthy. With the continued growth of device ownership, the ongoing increase in CPU and GPU power, and the non-stop evolution of the Android operating system itself, the need for professional app developers is only going to grow.

In short, the best Android developers - and, more importantly, the Android developers with the best ideas and the most determination - are in greater demand than ever. Nobody knows who these future Android app developers are, and they might not even have written their first line of code yet.

So, why isn't everybody an Android developer? Obviously, not everybody will share my enthusiasm for the thrill of creating software that can help make people's lives better, but I am guessing that, because you are reading this, you might.

The beginner's first stumbling block

Unfortunately, for those who do share my enthusiasm, there is a kind of glass wall on the path of progress that frustrates many aspiring Android developers.

Android asks aspiring developers to choose from three programming languages to make apps. Every Android book, even those aimed at so-called beginners, assumes that readers have at least an intermediate level of Kotlin, C++, or Java, and most need an advanced level. So, good-to-excellent programming knowledge is considered a prerequisite for learning Android.

Unfortunately, learning these languages in a completely different context to Android can sometimes be a little dull, and much of what you learn is not directly transferable into the world of Android either. You can see why beginners to Android are often put off.

It doesn't need to be like this. In this book, I have carefully placed all the Kotlin topics that you would learn in a thick and weighty Kotlin-only beginner's tome, and reworked them into three multi-chapter apps and more than a dozen quick mini-apps, starting from a simple memo app, progressing to a cool drawing app and a database app.

If you want to become a professional Android developer, or just want to have more fun when learning Kotlin and Android, this book will help.

How Kotlin and Android work together

The **Android Software Development Kit (SDK)** is largely written in Java, because Kotlin is the new kid on the block; but when we tell Android Studio to turn our Kotlin code into a working app, it is merged together with the Java from the SDK in an intermediate form before being converted into a format called DEX code, which the Android device uses to convert into a running app. This is seamless to us as developers, but it is worth knowing (and, perhaps, is quite interesting) to know what is going on behind the scenes.

Whether you have programmed your app in Kotlin or Java, the resulting DEX code is the same. However, there are some significant advantages to working with Kotlin.

Kotlin is named after an island near St Petersburg, Russia. Kotlin is very similar to Apple's Swift language, so learning Kotlin now will stand you in very good stead for learning iPhone/iPad development.

Kotlin is the most succinct language, and therefore is the least error-prone, which is great for beginners. Kotlin is also the most fun language, mainly because the succinctness means you can get results faster and with less code. Google considers Kotlin an official (first-class) Android language. There are some other advantages to Kotlin that make it less error-prone and less likely to make mistakes that cause crashes. We will discover the details of these advantages as we proceed.

Loads of the most advanced, innovative, and popular apps were coded using Kotlin. Just a few examples include Kindle, Evernote, Twitter, Expedia, Pinterest, and Netflix.

Before we start our Android quest, we need to understand how Android and Kotlin work together. After we write a program for Android, either in Java or Kotlin, we click a button and our code is transformed into another form, a form that is understood by Android. This other form is called **Dalvik Executable,** or **DEX** code, and the transformation process is called **compiling**. When the app is installed on a device, the DEX code is transformed again by the operating system into an optimized executable state.

> We will see this process in action right after we set up our development environment later on in the chapter.

Android is a complex system, but you do not need to understand it in depth to be able to start making amazing apps.

> A full understanding will come after using and interacting with it over time.

To get started, we only need to understand the basics. Android runs on a specially adapted version of the Linux operating system. So, what the user sees of Android is just an app running on yet another operating system.

Android is a system within a system. The typical Android user doesn't see the Linux operating system, and most probably doesn't even know it is there.

One purpose of this is to hide the complexity and diversity of the hardware and software that Android runs on, but, at the same time, exposing all its useful features. The exposure of these features works in two ways:

- First, the operating system itself must have full access to the hardware, which it does.
- Second, this access must be programmer-friendly and easy to use, and it is because of the Android **application programming interface** (**API**).

Let's continue by looking further into the Android API.

The Android API

The Android API is code that makes it easy to do exceptional things. A simple analogy could be drawn with a machine, perhaps a car. When you press on the accelerator, a whole bunch of things happen under the hood. We don't need to understand combustion or fuel pumps, because some smart engineer has made an **interface** for us; in this case, a mechanical interface - the accelerator pedal.

For example, the following line of code probably looks a little intimidating at this stage in the book, but it serves as a good example of how the Android API helps us:

```
locationManager.getLastKnownLocation(LocationManager.GPS_PROVIDER)
```

Once you learn that this single line of code searches for available satellites in space, communicates with them in their orbits around the Earth, and then retrieves your precise latitude and longitude on the surface of the planet, it becomes easy to glimpse the power and depth of the Android API.

That code does look a little challenging, even mind-boggling at this stage of the book, but imagine trying to talk to a satellite some other way!

The Android API has a whole bunch of code that has already been written for us to use as we like.

The question we must ask, and the one this book tries to answer, is as follows: how do we use all this code to do cool stuff? Or, to frame the question to fit the earlier analogy: how do we find and manipulate the pedals, steering wheel, and, most importantly, the sunroof of the Android API?

The answer to this question is the Kotlin programming language, and the fact that Kotlin was designed to help programmers handle complexity, avoid mistakes, and make fast progress. Let's look deeper into Kotlin and **object-oriented programming** (**OOP**).

Kotlin is object-oriented

Kotlin is an **object-oriented** language. This means that it uses the concept of reusable programming objects. If this sounds like technical jargon, another analogy will help. Kotlin enables us and others (like the Android API development team) to write code that can be structured based on real-world things, and here is the important part - it can be **reused**.

So, using the car analogy, we could ask the following question: if a manufacturer makes more than one car in a day, do they redesign every part for every car that comes off the production line?

The answer, of course, is no. They get highly skilled engineers to develop exactly the right components, honed, refined, and improved over years. Then, those same components are reused again and again, as well as being occasionally improved.

If you are going to be fussy about my analogy, then you can point out that each of the car's components must still be built from the raw materials using real-life engineers or robots. This is true.

What software engineers do when they write their code is build a blueprint for an object. We then create an object from their blueprint using code and once we have that object, we can configure it, use it, combine it with other objects, and more besides.

Furthermore, we can design blueprints ourselves and make objects from them. The compiler then transforms (manufactures) our bespoke creation into DEX code. Hey presto! We have an Android app.

In Kotlin, a blueprint is called a **class.** When a class is transformed into a real working "thing," we call it an **object** or an **instance** of the class.

Objects in short.

We could go on making analogies all day long. As far as we care at this point, Kotlin (and most modern programming languages) is a language that allows us to write code once that can then be used repeatedly.

This is very useful because it saves us time, and allows us to use other people's code to perform tasks we might otherwise not have the time or knowledge to write for ourselves. Most of the time, we do not even need to see this code, or even know how it does its work!

One last analogy. We just need to know how to use that code, just as we need to learn how to drive a car.

So, some smart software engineers up at Android HQ write a desperately complex program that can talk to satellites, and as a result of this, in a single line of code, we can get our location on the surface of the planet. Nice.

Most of the Android API is written in another language (Java), but this doesn't matter to us as we have full access to the functionality (coded in Java) while using the more succinct Kotlin. Android Studio and the Kotlin compiler handle the complexities behind the scenes.

The software engineers have considered how they can make this code useful to all Android programmers who want to make amazing apps that use users' locations to do cool things. One of the things they will do is make features, such as getting the device's location in the world into a simple one-line task.

So, the single line of code we saw previously sets in action many more lines of code that we don't see, and don't need to see. This is an example of using somebody else's code to make our code infinitely simpler.

If the fact that you don't have to see all the code is a disappointment to you, then I understand how you feel. Some of us, when we learn about something, want to learn every intricate detail. If this is you, then be reassured that the best place to start learning how the Android API works internally is to use it as the API programmers intended. And, throughout the book, I will regularly point out further learning opportunities where you can find out the inner workings of the Android API. Also, we will be writing classes that are themselves reusable, kind of like our own API, except that our classes will focus on what we want our app to do.

Welcome to the world of **OOP**. I will constantly refer to OOP in every chapter, and there will be a big reveal in *Chapter 10, Object-Oriented Programming*.

Run that by me again – what, exactly, is Android?

To get things done on Android, we write code of our own, which also uses the code of the Android API. This is then compiled into DEX code, and the rest is handled by the Android device, which, in turn, runs on an underlying operating system called Linux, which handles the complex and extremely diverse range of hardware that is the different Android devices.

The manufacturers of Android devices and of the individual hardware components obviously know this too, and they write advanced software called **drivers** that ensure that their hardware (for example, CPU, GPU, GPS receivers, memory chips, and hardware interfaces) can run on the underlying Linux operating system.

The DEX code (along with some other resources) are placed in a bundle of files called an **Android application package** (**APK**), and this is what the device needs to run our app.

It is not necessary to remember the details of the steps that our code goes through when it interacts with the hardware. It is enough just to understand that our code goes through some automated processes to become the app that we will publish to the Google Play store.

The next question is: where exactly does all this coding and compiling into DEX code, along with APK packaging, take place? Let's look at the development environment that we will be using.

Android Studio

A **development environment** is a term that refers to having everything you need to develop, set up and ready to go in one place.

There is an entire range of tools needed to develop for Android, and we also need the Android API, of course. This whole suite of requirements is collectively known as the SDK. Fortunately, downloading and installing a single application will give us these things all bundled together. The application is called Android Studio.

Android Studio is an **integrated development environment** (**IDE**) that will take care of all the complexities of compiling our code and linking with the Android API. Once we have installed Android Studio, we can do everything we need inside this single application, and put to the back of our minds many of the complexities we have been discussing.

Over time, these complexities will become second nature. It is not necessary to master them immediately to make further progress.

So, we had better get our hands on Android Studio.

Setting up Android Studio

Setting up Android Studio is quite straightforward, if a little time-consuming. Grab some refreshments and get started with the following steps:

1. Visit `developer.android.com/studio/index.html`. Click the big **DOWNLOAD ANDROID STUDIO** button to proceed:

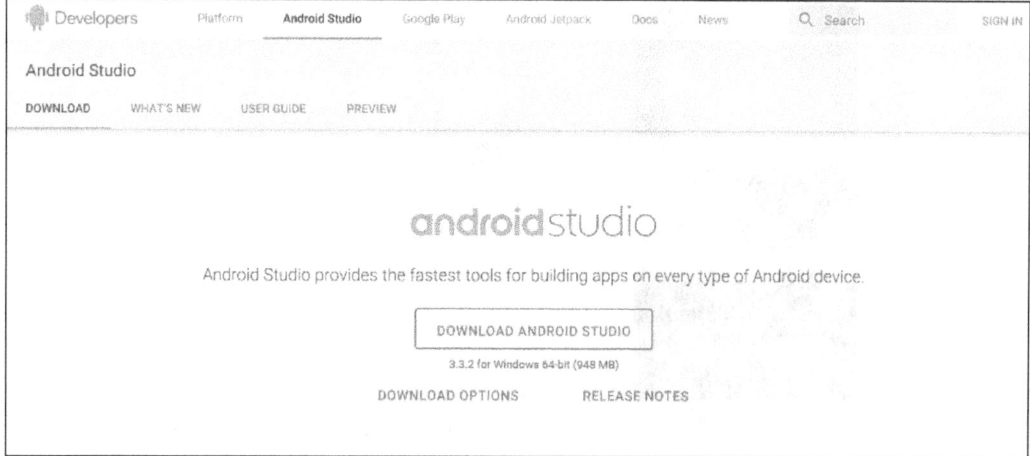

2. Accept the terms and conditions by checking the checkbox, and then click the **DOWNLOAD ANDROID STUDIO FOR WINDOWS** button:

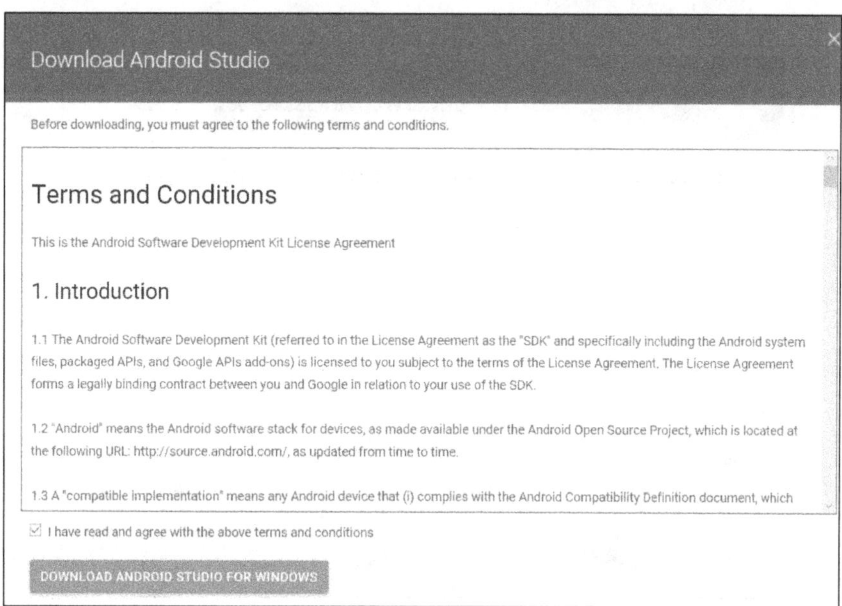

3. When the download is complete, run the file you just downloaded. It has a name that starts `android-studio-ide...`, while the end of the name of the file will vary based on the current version at the time of reading.
4. Click the **Next >** button to proceed:

5. Leave the default options selected, as shown in the following screenshot, and click the **Next >** button:

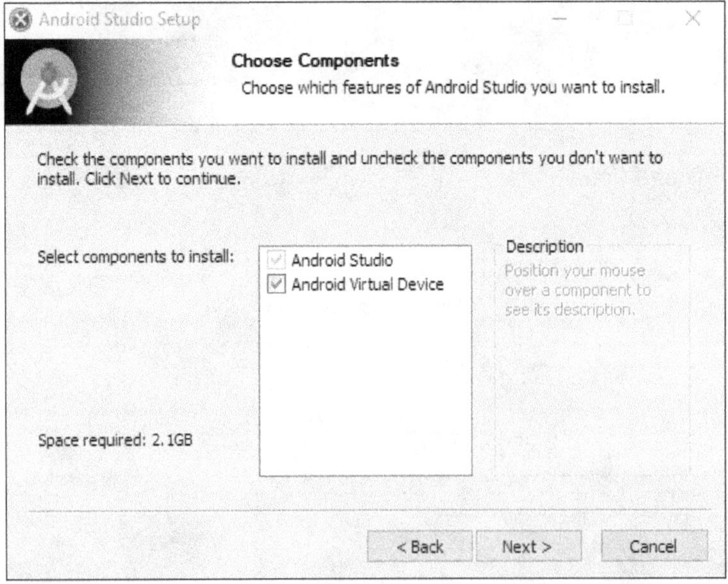

6. Next, we need to choose where to install Android Studio, as shown in the following screenshot:

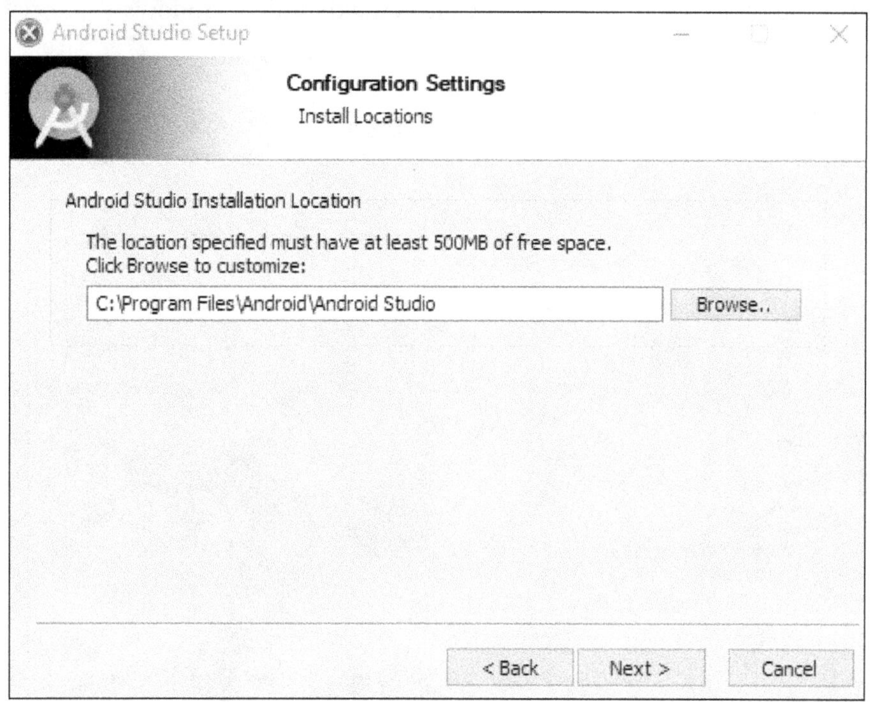

The install wizard recommends **500 MB of free space**, but you probably noticed from the previous screen that 2.1 GB was suggested. However, there are even more requirements later in the installation process. Furthermore, it is much easier if you have all your Android Studio parts, as well as your project files, on the same hard drive.

For these reasons, I recommend having at least 4 GB of free space. If you need to switch drives to accommodate this, then use the **Browse..** button to browse to a suitable place on your hard drive.

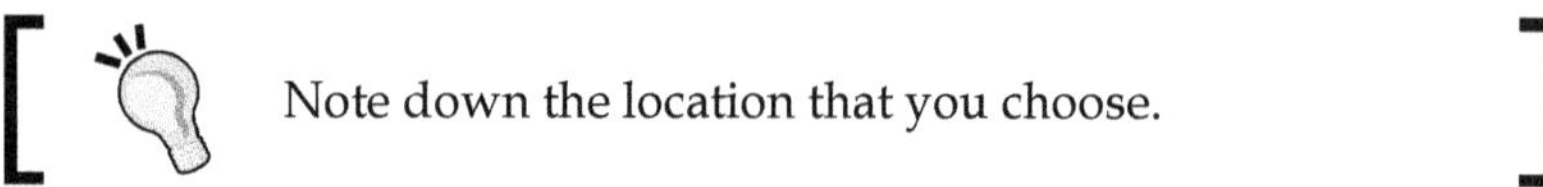

Note down the location that you choose.

7. When you are ready, click the **Next >** button.
8. In this next window, choose the folder in your start menu where **Android Studio** will appear. You can leave it as the default, as follows:

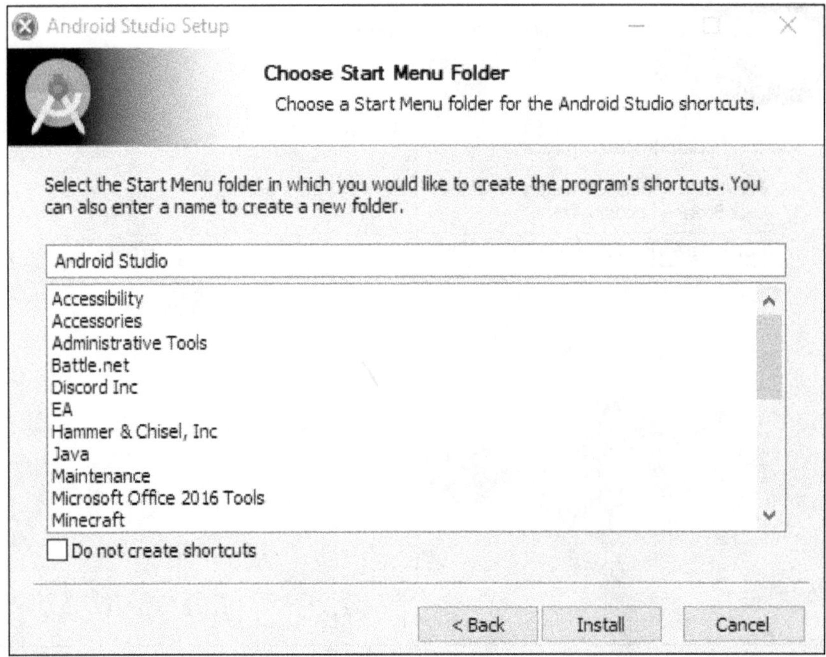

9. Click **Install**. This step might take some time, especially on older machines or if you have a slow internet connection. When this stage is done, you will see the following screen:

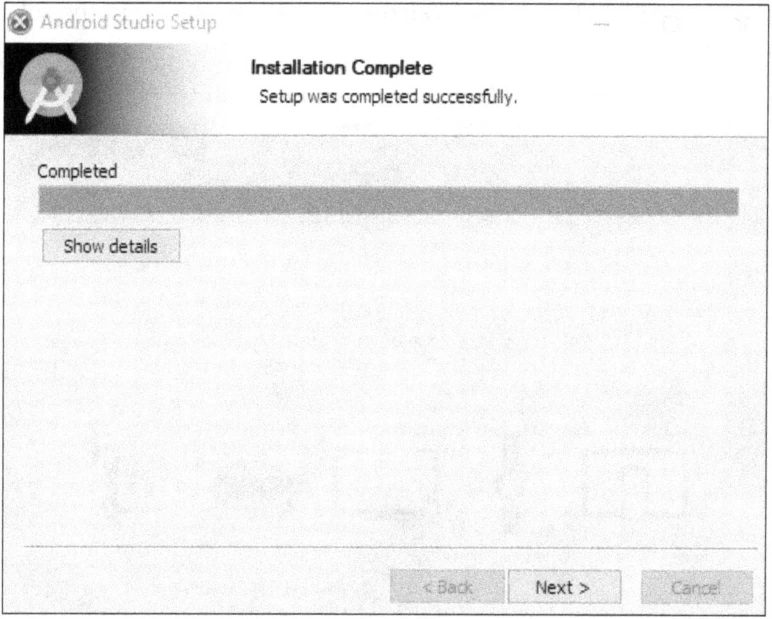

10. Click **Next >**.
11. Android Studio is now installed – kind of. Check the **Start Android Studio** checkbox and click the **Finish** button:

12. You will be greeted with the **Welcome** screen, as shown in the following screenshot:

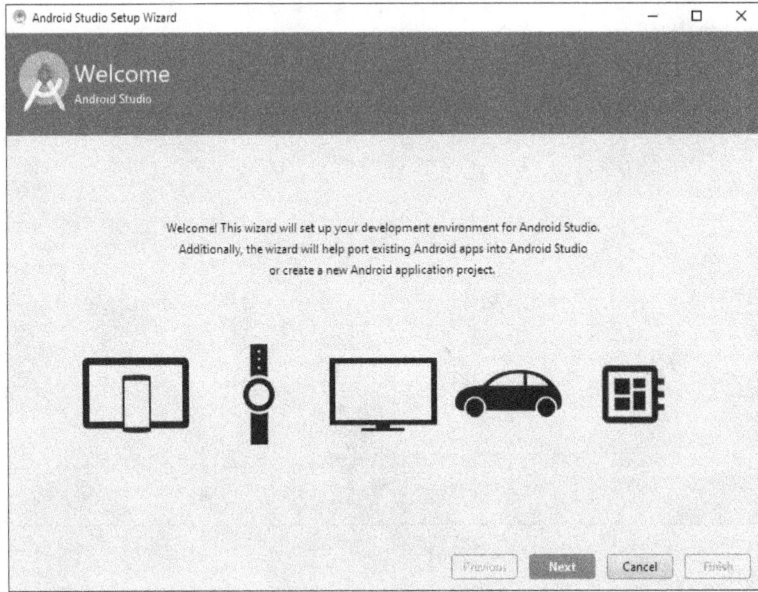

13. Click the **Next** button.
14. Choose the **Standard** install type, as shown in the following screenshot:

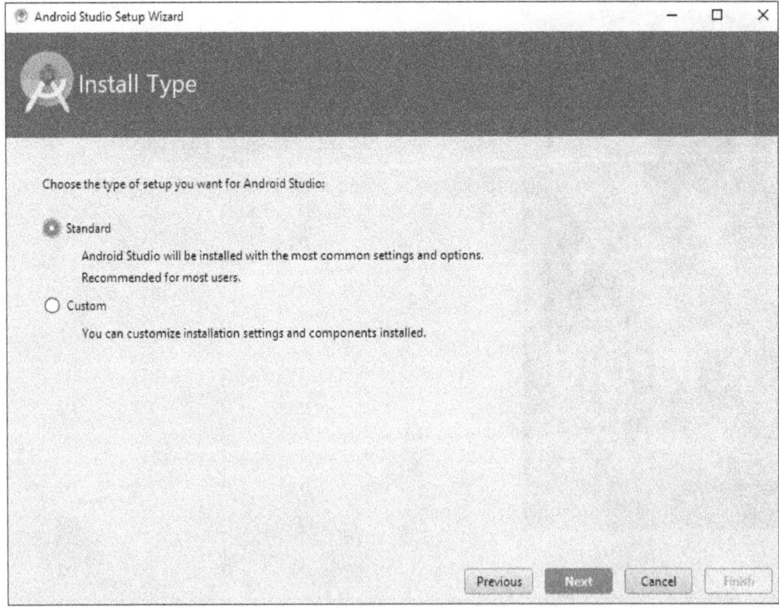

15. Click the **Next** button.
16. Choose whichever color scheme looks nice to you. I chose **IntelliJ**, as shown in the following screenshot:

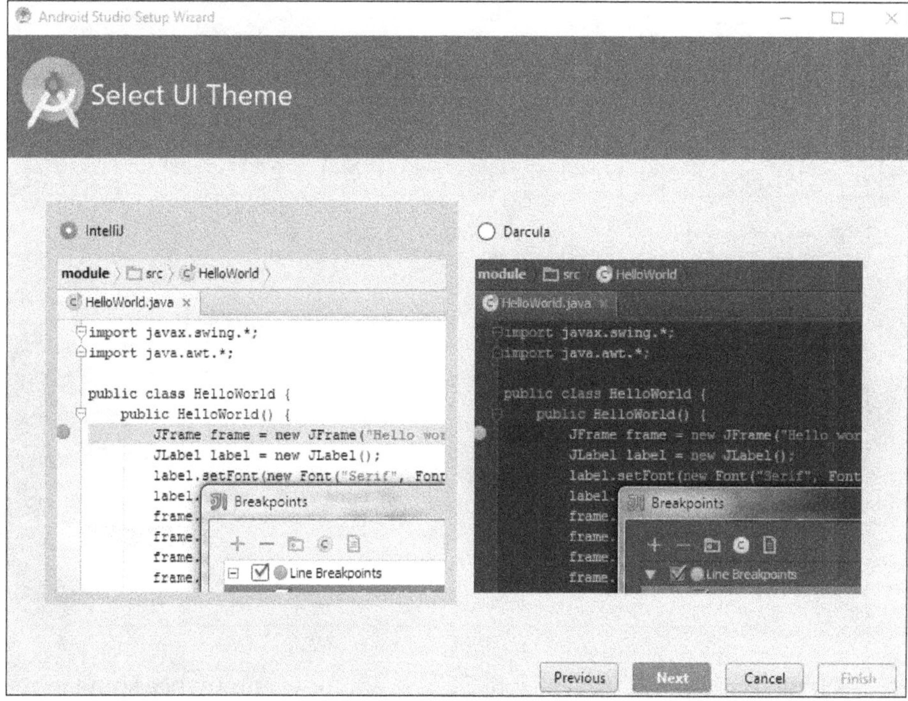

17. Click **Next**.

18. Now you will see the **Verify Settings** screen:

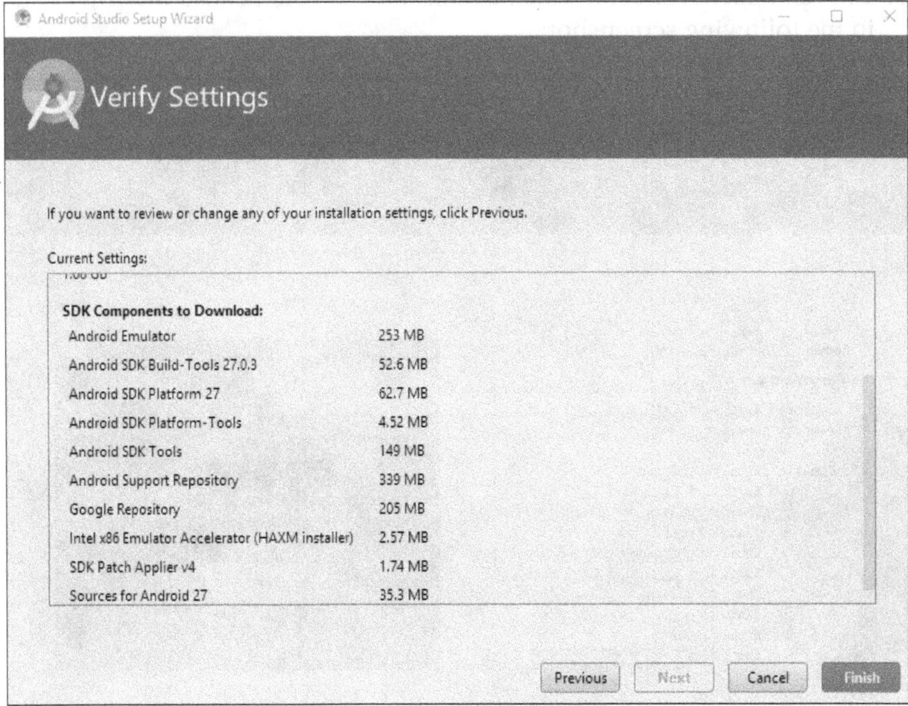

19. Click the **Finish** button. Android Studio will now commence some more downloads, which could take some time.
20. When Android Studio is ready, you will have the option to run it. At this point, click the **Finish** button. Android Studio is most likely ready. You can leave it open if you are carrying straight on with the next section, or you can close it and then reopen it when instructed to in the next section.

Final step – for now

Using your preferred file manager software, perhaps Windows Explorer, create a folder called `AndroidProjects`. Make it at the root of the same drive where you installed Android Studio. So, if you installed Android Studio at `C:/Program Files/Android`, then create your new folder at `C:/AndroidProjects`.

Or, if you installed Android Studio at `D:/Program Files/Android`, then create your new folder at `D:/AndroidProjects`.

> Note that the screenshots in the next section show the `AndroidProjects` folder on the `D:` drive. This is because my `C:` drive is a bit full up. Either is fine. I did the install tutorial screen captures on a borrowed PC with plenty of space on the C: drive, because that is the default for Android Studio. Keeping it on the same drive as the Android installation is neater and could avoid future problems, so do so if you can.
>
> Notice that there is no space between the words `Android` and `Projects`, and that the first letter of both words is capitalized. The capitalization is for clarity, and the omission of a space is required by Android Studio.

Android Studio and the supporting tools that we need are installed and ready to go. We are now really close to building our first app.

Now, let's look a little bit at the composition of an Android app.

What makes an Android app?

We already know that we will write Kotlin code that will use other people's code, and that will be compiled into DEX code that is used on our users' Android devices. In addition to this, we will also be adding and editing other files that get included in the final APK. These files are known as **Android resources**.

Android resources

As mentioned earlier in this chapter, our app will include resources, such as images, sound, and user interface layouts, that are kept in separate files from the Kotlin code. We will slowly introduce ourselves to them over the course of the book.

They will also include files that have the textual content of our app. It is convention to refer to the text in our app through separate files because it makes them easy to change, and easy to create apps that work for multiple different languages and geographical regions.

Furthermore, the actual **User Interface** (**UI**) layout of our apps, despite the option to implement them with a visual designer, are read from text-based files by Android.

Android (or any computer) cannot read and recognize text in the same way that a human can. Therefore, we must present our resources in a highly organized and predefined manner. To do so, we will use **Extensible Markup Language** (**XML**). XML is a huge topic; fortunately, its whole purpose is to be both human- and machine- readable. We do not need to learn this language; we just need to note (and then conform to) a few rules. Furthermore, most of the time, when we interact with XML, we will do so through a neat visual editor provided by Android Studio. We can tell when we are dealing with an XML resource because the filename will end with the `.xml` extension.

You do not need to memorize this, as we will constantly be returning to this concept in the book.

The structure of Android's code

In addition to these resources, it is worth noting that Android has a structure to its code. There are many millions of lines of code that we can take advantage of. This code will obviously need to be organized in a way that makes it easy to find and refer to. It is organized into **packages** that are specific to Android.

Packages

Whenever we create a new Android app, we will choose a unique name, known as a **package**. We will see how we do this very soon, in the section titled *Our first Android app*. Packages are often separated into **sub-packages** so that they can be grouped together with other similar packages. We can simply think of these as folders and sub-folders, which is almost exactly what they are.

We can think of all the packages that the Android API makes available to us as code from a code library. Some common Android packages that we will use include the following:

- `android.graphics`
- `android.database`
- `android.view.animation`

As you can see, they are arranged and named to make what is in them as obvious as possible.

If you want to get an idea of the sheer depth and breadth of the Android API, then look at the Android package index at `https://developer.android.com/reference/packages`

Classes

Earlier, we learned that the reusable code blueprints that we can transform into objects are called **classes**. Classes are contained in these packages. We will see in our very first app how we can easily **import** other people's packages, along with specific classes from those packages for use in our projects. A class will usually be contained in its own file with the same name as the class.

Functions

In Kotlin, we further break up our classes into sections that perform the different actions of our class. We call these action-oriented sections **functions**. It is the functions of the class that we will use to access the functionality provided within all the millions of lines of Android code.

We do not need to read the code. We just need to know which class has what we need, which package it is in, and which function from within the class gives us precisely the result we are after.

We can think of the structure of the code we will write ourselves in the same way, although we will usually have just one package per app.

Of course, because of the object-oriented nature of Kotlin, we will only be using selected parts from this API. Note also that each class has its own distinct **data**. Typically, if you want access to the data in a class, you need to have an object of that class.

You do not need to memorize this, as we will constantly be returning to this concept in the book.

By the end of this chapter, we will have imported multiple packages, as well as some classes from them. By the end of *Chapter 2, Kotlin, XML, and the UI Designer*, we will have even written our very own functions.

Our first Android app

Now we can get started on our first app. In programming, it is tradition for the first app of a new student to use whatever language/OS they are using to say hello to the world. We will quickly build an app that does just that, and, in *Chapter 2, Kotlin, XML, and the UI Designer*, we will go beyond that and add some buttons that respond to the user when they are clicked.

The complete code as it stands at the end of this chapter is in the download bundle in the `Chapter01` folder for your reference. You can't simply copy and paste this code, however. You still need to go through the project creation phase explained in this chapter (and at the beginning of all projects) as Android Studio does lots of work behind the scenes. Once you become familiar with these steps and understand which code is typed by you, the programmer, and which code/files are generated by Android Studio, you will then be able to save time and typing by copying and pasting from the files I supply in the download bundle.

Follow these steps to start the project:

1. Run Android Studio in the same way you run any other app. On Windows 10, for example, the launch icon appears in the start menu.

If you are prompted to **Import Studio settings from...:**, choose **Do not import settings**.

2. You will be greeted with the Android Studio welcome screen, as shown in the following screenshot. Locate the **Start a new Android Studio project** option and left-click it:

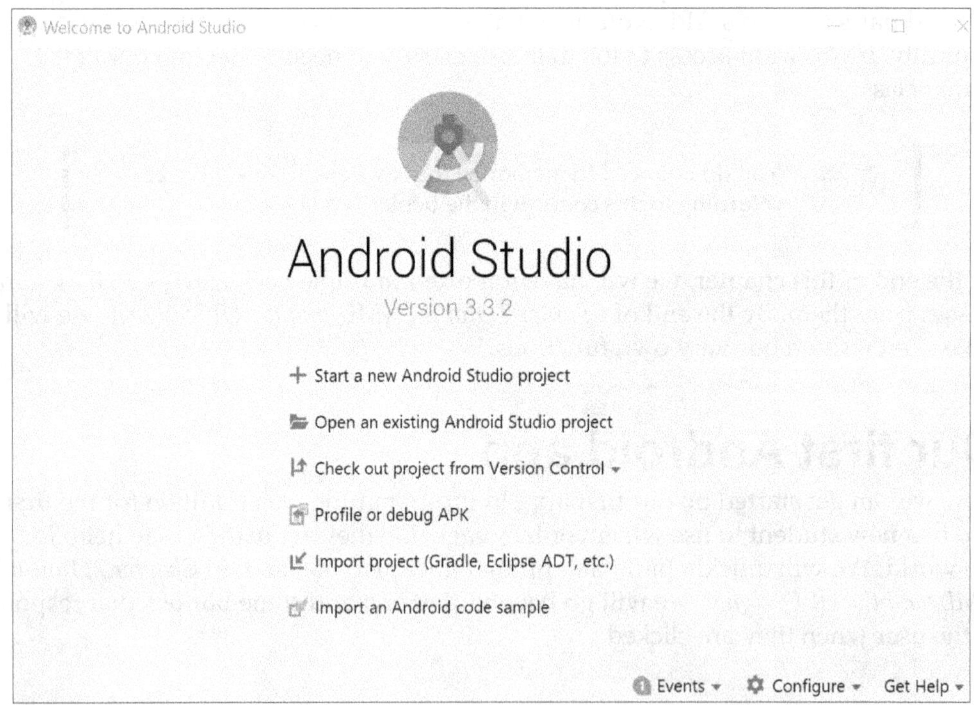

3. After this, Android Studio will bring up the **Choose your project** window, as follows:

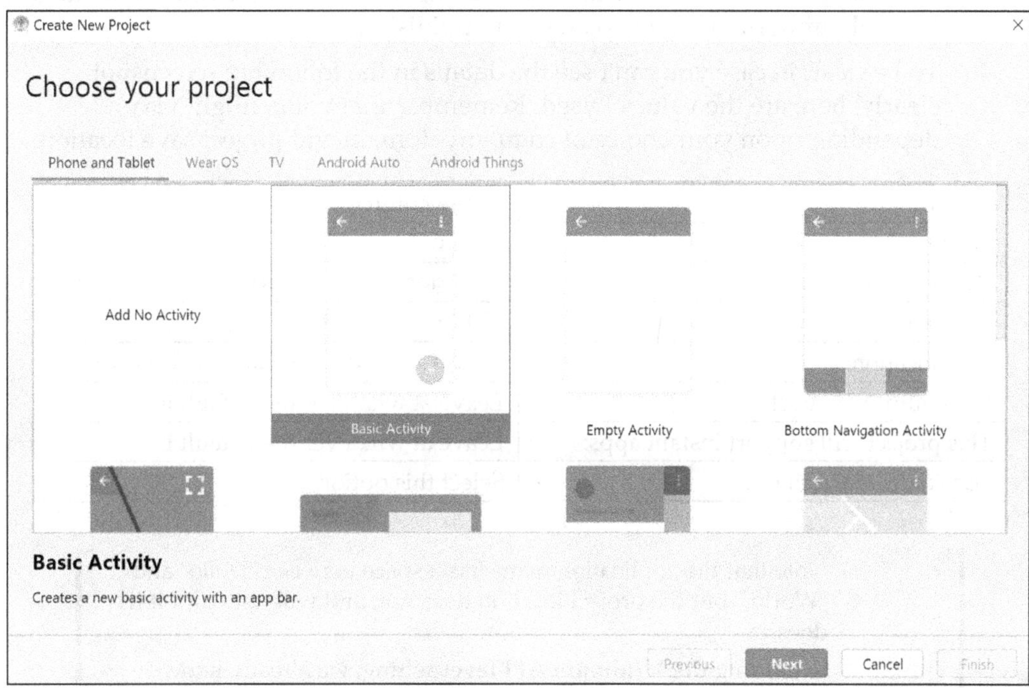

4. We will use the **Basic Activity** option, as selected in the previous screenshot. Android Studio will autogenerate some code and a selection of resources to get our project started. We will discuss the code and the resources in detail in the next chapter. Select **Basic Activity** and click **Next**.
5. This next screen is the **Configure your project** screen, where we will perform the following steps and a few more things as well:
    1. Name the new project
    2. Provide a company domain as a package name to distinguish our project from any others, in case we should ever decide to publish it on the Play Store
    3. Choose where on our computer the project files should go
    4. Select our preferred programming language
6. The name of our project is going to be `Hello World`, and the location for the files will be your `AndroidProjects` folder that we created in the *Setting up Android Studio* section.

7. The package name can be almost anything you like. If you have a website, you could use the `com.yourdomain.helloworld` format. If not, feel free to use `com.gamecodeschool.helloworld`, or something that you just make up. It is only important when you come to publish it.
8. To be clear, in case you can't see the details in the following screenshot clearly, here are the values I used. Remember that yours might vary depending upon your choice of company domain and project save location:

Option	**Value entered**
Name:	`Hello World`
Package Name:	`com.gamecodeschool.helloworld`
Language:	Kotlin
Save location:	`D:\AndroidProjects\HelloWorld`
Minimum API Level:	Leave at whatever the default is
This project will support instant apps:	Leave at whatever the default is
Use AndroidX artifacts:	Select this option

Note that the application name has a space between "Hello" and "World," but the project location does not, and will not work if it does.

Regarding the **Minimum API level** setting, we already know that the Android SDK is the collection of packages of code that we will be using to develop our apps. Like any good SDK, the Android SDK is regularly updated, and each time it gets a significant update, the version number is increased. Simply put, the higher the version number, the newer the features you get to use; the lower the version number, the more devices our app will work on. For now, the default **API 15, Android 4.0.3 (IceCreamSandwich)** version will give us lots of great features and near 100% compatibility with the Android devices currently in use. If, at the time of reading, Android Studio is suggesting a newer API, then go with that.

If you are reading this some years in the future, then the **Minimum API** option will probably default to something different, but the code in this book will still work.

The following screenshot shows the **Configure your project** screen once you have entered all the information:

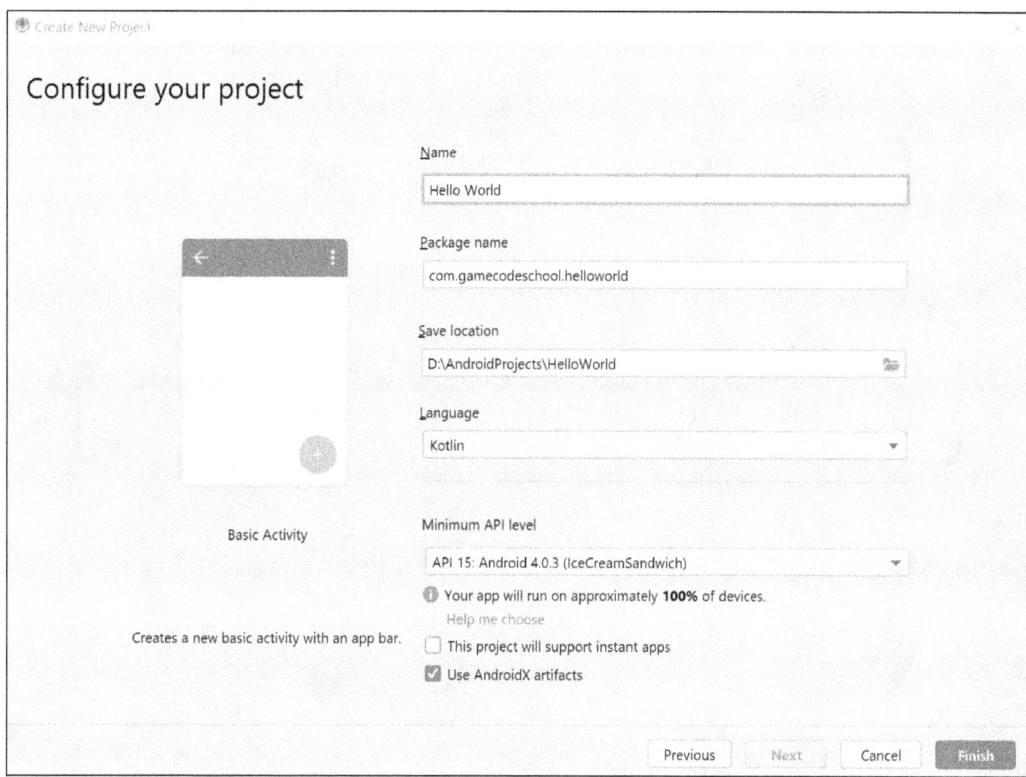

You can write Android apps in a few different languages, including C++ and Java. There are various advantages and disadvantages to each compared to using Kotlin. Learning Kotlin will be a great introduction to other languages, and Kotlin is also the newest (and arguably best) official language of Android.

9. Click the **Finish** button and Android Studio will prepare our new project for us. This might take a few seconds or a few minutes, depending upon how powerful your PC is.

   At this stage, you might be ready to proceed but, depending on the install process, you might need to click a couple of extra buttons.

   [This is why I mentioned that we are only *probably* finished installing and setting up.]

   Look in the bottom window of Android Studio and see if you have the following message:

[Note that if you do not see a horizontal window at the bottom of Android Studio like the one shown in the following screenshot, you can skip these two extra steps.]

Possible extra step 1

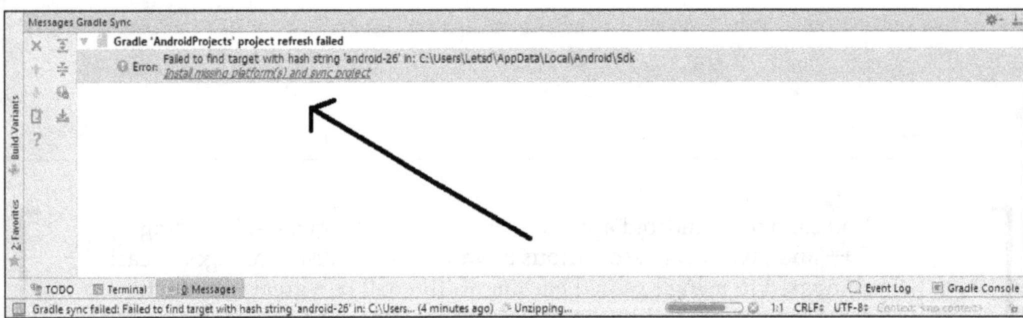

If you do, click **Install missing platform(s) and sync project**, accept the license agreement, and then click **Next**, followed by **Finish**.

Possible extra step 2

You may get another message like this:

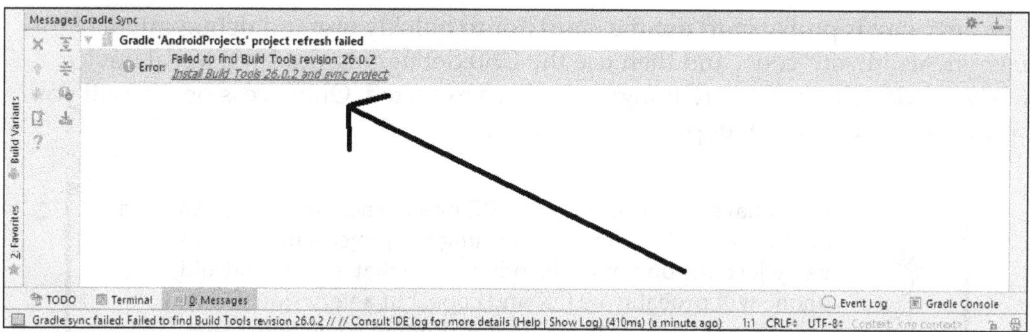

If the preceding message appears, click **Install Build tools....** and then click **Finish**.

You can tidy up the screen a bit and close this bottom horizontal window by clicking the **Messages** tab at the very bottom of Android Studio, but this isn't compulsory.

Deploying the app so far

Before we explore any of the code and learn our first bit of Kotlin, you might be surprised to learn that we can already run our project. It will be a fairly featureless screen, but as we will be running the app as often as possible to check our progress, let's see how to do that now. You have three options:

- Run the app on the emulator on your PC (part of Android Studio) in debug mode
- Run the app on a real Android device in USB debugging mode
- Export the app as a full Android project that can be uploaded to the Play Store

The first option (debug mode) is the easiest to set up, because we did it as part of setting up Android Studio. If you have a powerful PC, you will hardly see the difference between the emulator and a real device. However, screen touches are emulated by mouse clicks, and proper testing of the user experience is not possible in some of the later apps, such as the drawing app. Furthermore, you might just prefer to test out your creations on a real device – I know I do.

The second option, using a real device, has a couple of additional steps, but, once set up, is as good as option one, and the screen touches are for real.

The final option takes about five minutes (at least) to prepare, and then you need to manually put the created package onto a real device and install it (every time you make a change to the code).

The best way is probably to use the emulator to quickly test and debug minor increments in your code, and then use the USB debugging mode on a real device fairly regularly to make sure things are still as expected. Only occasionally will you want to export an actual deployable package.

If you have an especially slow PC or a particularly aging Android device, you will be fine just running the projects in this book using just one option or the other. Note that a slow Android phone will probably be OK and cope, but a very slow PC will probably not handle the emulator running some of the later apps, and you will benefit from running them on your phone/tablet.

For these reasons, I will now go through how to run the app using the emulator and USB debugging on a real device.

Running and debugging the app on an Android emulator

Follow these simple steps to run the app on the default Android emulator:

1. On the Android Studio main menu bar, select **Tools** | **AVD Manager**. AVD stands for Android Virtual Device (an emulator). You will see the following window:

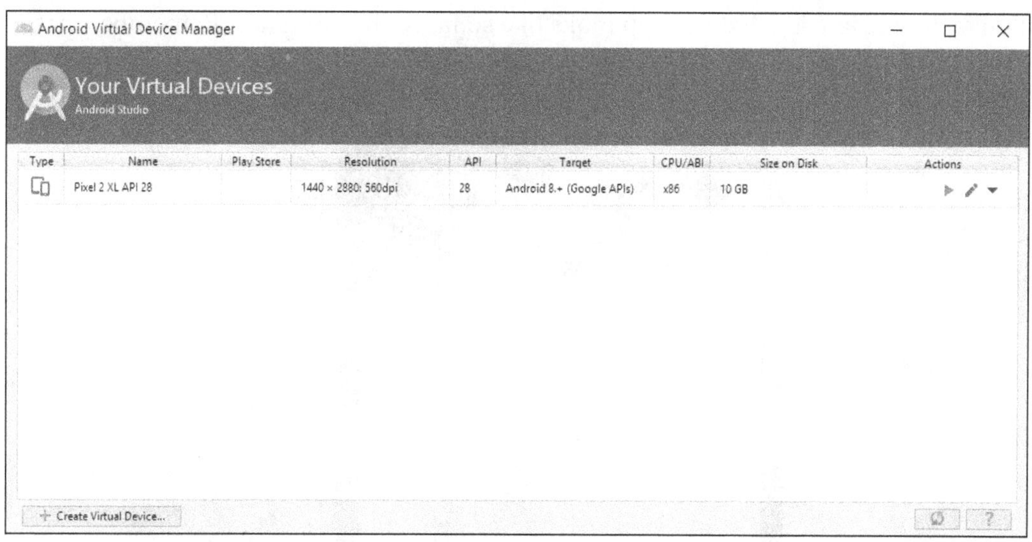

2. Notice that there is an emulator in the list. In my case, it is **Pixel 2 XL API 28**. If you are following this sometime in the future, it will be a different emulator that was installed by default. It won't matter. Click the green play icon (to the right) shown in the following screenshot, and wait while the emulator boots up:

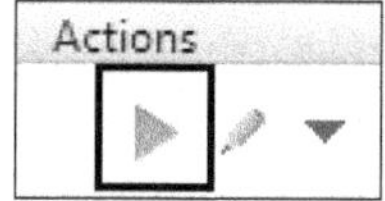

3. Now you can click the play icon on the Android Studio quick-launch bar as shown in the following screenshot and, when prompted, choose **Pixel 2 XL API 28** (or whatever your emulator is called) and the app will launch on the emulator:

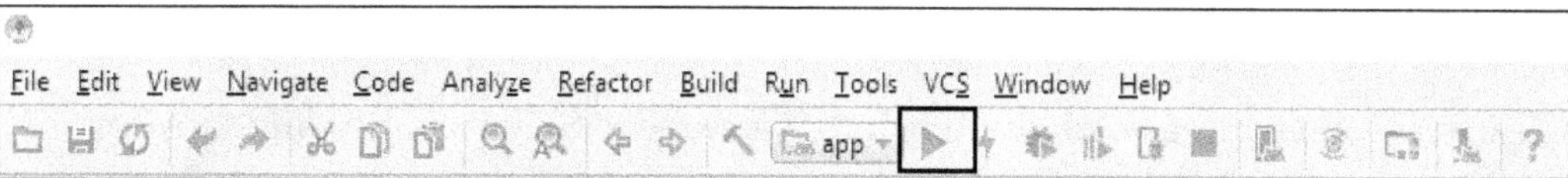

You're done. Here is what the app looks like so far in the emulator. Remember that you might (probably do) have a different emulator, which is fine:

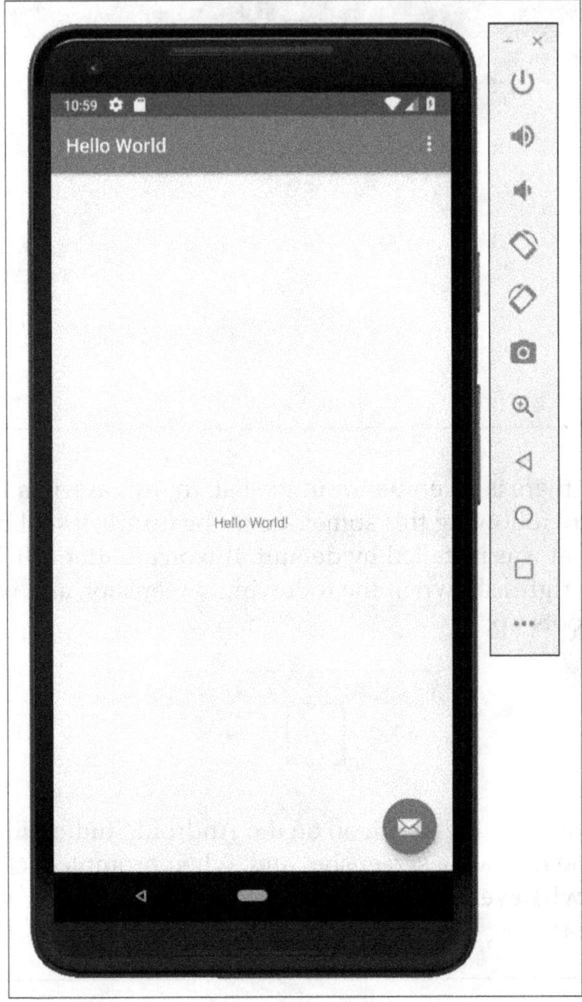

Clearly, we have more work to do before we move to Silicon Valley and look for financial backing, but it is a good start.

We need to test and debug our apps often throughout development to check for any errors, crashes, or anything else unintended.

We will see how we get errors and other feedback for debugging from our apps in the next chapter.

It is also important to make sure it looks good and runs correctly on every device type/size that you want to target. Obviously, we do not own one of each of the many thousands of Android devices. This is where emulators come in.

Emulators, however, are sometimes a bit slow and cumbersome, although they have improved a lot recently. If we want to get a genuine feel for the experience our user will get, then you can't beat deploying to a real device. So, we will want to use both real devices and emulators while developing our apps.

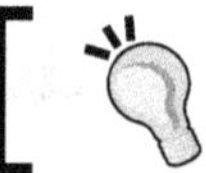

If you are planning on using the emulator again soon, leave it running to avoid having to wait for it to start again.

If you want to try out your app on a tablet, you're going to need a different emulator.

Creating a new emulator

It is simple to create an emulator for a different Android device. From the main menu, select **Tools** | **AVD Manager**. In the **AVD Manager** window, left-click **Create New Virtual Device**. Now left-click on the type of device you want to create - **TV**, **Phone**, **Wear OS**, or **Tablet**. Now simply left-click **Next** and follow the instructions to create your new AVD. Next time you run your app, the new AVD will appear as an option to run the app on.

Now we can look at how we can get our app onto a real device.

Running the app on a real device

The first thing to do is to visit your device manufacturer's website and obtain and install any drivers that are needed for your device and operating system.

Most newer devices won't need a driver, so you may want to just try the following steps first.

The next few steps will set up the Android device for debugging. Note that different manufacturers structure the menu options slightly differently to others. But the following sequence is probably very close, if not exact, for enabling debugging on most devices:

1. Tap the **Settings** menu option or the **Settings** app on your phone/tablet.

2. This next step will vary slightly for different versions of Android. The **Developer options** menu is hidden away so as not to trouble regular users. You must perform a slightly odd task to unlock the menu option. Tap the **About device** or **About Phone** option. Find the **Build Number** option and repeatedly tap it until you get a message informing you that **You are now a developer!**

Some manufacturers have different, obscure methods for achieving this step. If this step doesn't work, do a web search for your device and "unlocking developer options."

3. Go back to the **Settings** menu.
4. Tap **Developer options.**
5. Tap the checkbox for **USB Debugging.**
6. Connect your Android device to the USB port of your computer.
7. Click the play icon from the Android Studio toolbar, as shown in the following screenshot:

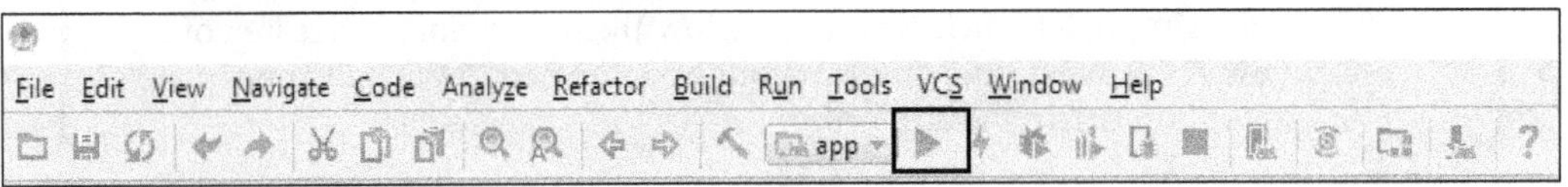

8. When prompted, click OK to run the app on your chosen device.

We are now ready to learn some Kotlin and add our own Kotlin code to the Hello World project.

Frequently asked question

Q) So, Android isn't really an operating system; it is just a virtual machine and all Android phones and tablets are really Linux machines?

A) No, all the different subsystems of an Android device, which include Linux, the libraries, and the drivers, are what make up the Android operating system.

Summary

So far, we have set up an Android development environment, and created and deployed an app on both an emulator and a real device. If you still have unanswered questions (and you probably have more than at the start of the chapter), don't worry, because as we dig deeper into the world of Android and Kotlin, things will become clearer.

As the chapters progress, you will build a very rounded understanding of how everything fits together, and then success will just be a matter of practice and digging even deeper into the Android API.

In the next chapter, we will edit the UI using the visual designer and raw XML code, as well as writing our first Kotlin functions, and we will get to use some of the functions provided for us by the Android API.

2
Kotlin, XML, and the UI Designer

At this stage, we have a working Android development environment and we have built and deployed our first app. It is obvious, however, that code autogenerated by Android Studio is not going to make the next top-selling app on Google Play. We need to explore this autogenerated code so that we can begin to understand Android and then learn how to build on this useful template. With this aim in mind, we will do the following in this chapter:

- See how to get technical feedback from our apps.
- Examine the Kotlin code and **User Interface** (**UI**) XML code from our first app.
- Get our first taste of using the Android UI designer.
- Write our first Kotlin code.
- Learn some core Kotlin fundamentals and how they relate to Android.

First, let's see how to get feedback from our apps.

Examining the log output

In the previous chapter, we mentioned that our app was running in debug mode on the emulator or real device; this is so that we can monitor it and get feedback when things go wrong. So, where is all this feedback?

You might have noticed a lot of scrolling text at the bottom of the Android Studio window. If not, click on the **logcat** tab, as shown by the highlighted area labeled as **1** in the following screenshot:

Note that the emulator must be running, or a real device must be attached in debugging mode, for you to see the following window. Furthermore, if you restarted Android Studio for some reason and have not yet executed the app, then the **logcat** window will be empty. Refer to the first chapter to get the app running on an emulator or a real device:

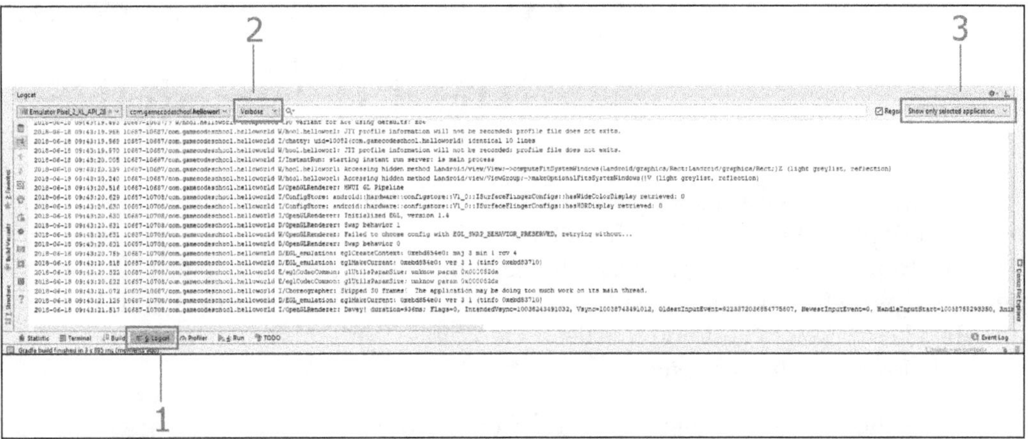

You can drag the window to make it taller, just as you can in most other Windows applications, if you want to see more.

This window is called **logcat**, or, sometimes, it is referred to as **console**. It is our app's way of telling us what is going on underneath what the user sees. If the app crashes or has errors, the reason or clues will appear here. If we need to output debugging information, we can do so here as well.

If you just cannot work out why your app is crashing, copying and pasting a bit of the text from logcat into Google will often reveal the reason.

Filtering the logcat output

You might have noticed that most, if not all, of the content of logcat is almost unintelligible. That's OK; right now, we are only interested in errors that will be highlighted in red and the debugging information that we will learn about next. In order to see less of the superfluous text in our **logcat** window, we can turn on some filters to make things clearer.

In the previous screenshot, I highlighted two more areas, as **2** and **3**. Area **2** is the drop-down list that controls the first filter. Left-click on it now and change it from **Verbose** to **Info**. We have cut down the text output significantly. We will see how this is useful when we have made some changes to our app and redeployed it. We will do this after we have explored the code and the assets that make up our project. Also, double-check that the area labeled as **3** says **Show only the selected application**. If it doesn't, left-click on it and change it to **Show only the selected application**.

Now we can look at what Android Studio has automatically generated for us, and then we can set about changing and adding to the code to personalize it beyond what we got from the project creation phase.

Exploring the project's Kotlin code and the main layout's XML code

We are going to look at the resource files containing the code that defines our simple UI layout and the file that has our Kotlin code. At this stage, we won't try to understand it all, as we need to learn some more basics before it makes sense to do so. What we will see, however, is the basic content and structure of both files, so we can reconcile their content with what we already know about Android resources and Kotlin.

Examining the MainActivity.kt file

Let's take a look at the Kotlin code first. You can see this code by left-clicking on the `MainActivity.kt` tab, as shown in the following screenshot:

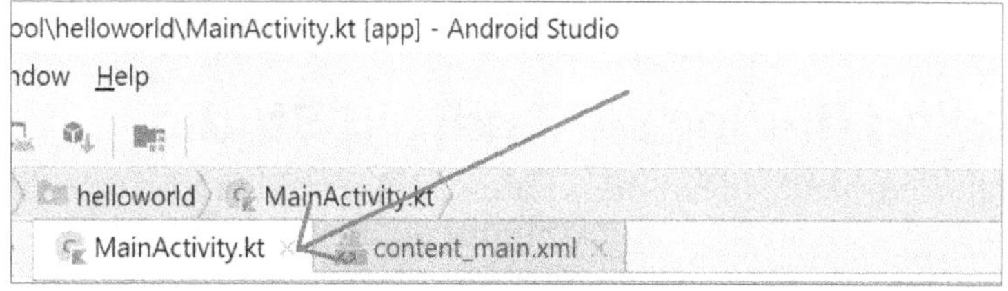

As we are not looking at the intricate details of the code, an annotated screenshot is more useful than reproducing the actual code in text form. Regularly refer to the following screenshot while reading this section:

```
package com.gamecodeschool.helloworld                1

import android.os.Bundle
import com.google.android.material.snackbar.Snackbar
import androidx.appcompat.app.AppCompatActivity;              2
import android.view.Menu
import android.view.MenuItem

import kotlinx.android.synthetic.main.activity_hello_world.*

class HelloWorldActivity : AppCompatActivity() {  3

    override fun onCreate(savedInstanceState: Bundle?) {  5
        super.onCreate(savedInstanceState)
        setContentView(R.layout.activity_hello_world)
        setSupportActionBar(toolbar)                          9
        fab.setOnClickListener { view ->
            Snackbar.make(view, text: "Replace with your own action",
                    Snackbar.LENGTH_LONG)
                    .setAction( text: "Action", listener: null).show()
        }
    }6

    override fun onCreateOptionsMenu(menu: Menu): Boolean {...}  7

    override fun onOptionsItemSelected(item: MenuItem): Boolean {...}  8
}4
```

The first thing to note is that I have added a few empty lines in among the code to space things out and present a clearer image.

Code folding (hiding) in Android Studio

Now, look at the left-hand side of the window in Android Studio (not the preceding screenshot) and observe all the **+** and **-** buttons on the left-hand side of the editor that can collapse and expand parts of the code:

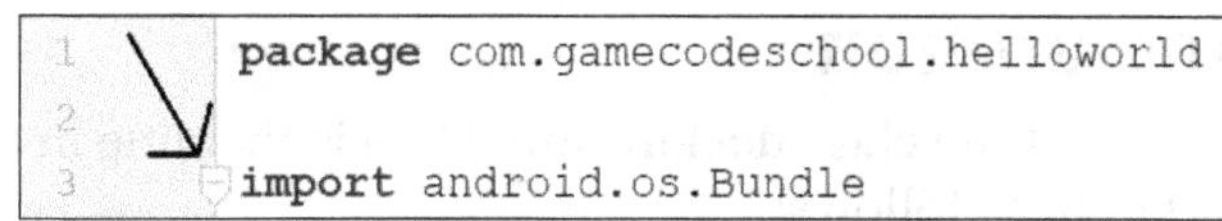

I have collapsed some parts of the code, and have left other parts visible. So, what you can see on your screen is slightly different to what you will see if you look at the preceding screenshot. In Android Studio, play with the **+** and **-** buttons for a while to practice hiding and unhiding sections of the code. You might be able to get your screen to look like the preceding screenshot, but this is not a requirement to continue. The technical term for hiding code like this is called **folding**.

The package declaration

Part **1** is called the **package declaration** and, as you can see, it is the package name that we chose when we created the project, preceded by the word `package`. Every Kotlin file will have a package declaration at the top.

Importing classes

Part **2** is six lines of code that all begin with `import`. After `import`, we can see there are various dot-separated words. The last word of each line is the name of the class that line imports into our project, and all the earlier words in each line are the packages and subpackages that contain these classes.

For example, this next line imports the `AppCompatActivity` class from the `androidx.appcompat.app` package and subpackages:

```
import androidx.appcompat.app.AppCompatActivity
```

This means that in our project, we will have access to these classes. In fact, it is these classes that the autogenerated code uses to make our simple app, which we saw in action in the previous chapter.

We will not discuss all of these classes in this chapter. It is just the idea that we can do this importing of classes that gives us access to more functionality that is significant right now. Note that we can add extra classes from any package at any time, and we will do so when we improve upon our app shortly.

The class declaration

Part **3** of our code is called the **class declaration**. Here is that line in full; I have highlighted one part of it, as follows:

```
class MainActivity : AppCompatActivity() {
```

The class declaration is the start of a class. Notice that the highlighted part, `MainActivity`, is the name that was autogenerated when we created the project and is also the same as the `MainActivity.kt` filename. This is as we would expect, having discussed Kotlin classes previously.

The colon (`:`) means that our class called `MainActivity` will be of the type `AppCompatActivity`. This indicates that although there are not that many lines of code in this file, we are also using more code that we don't see that comes from the `AppCompatActivity` class. All this and more will become clear in *Chapter 10, Object-Oriented Programming*.

Finally, for part **3**, look at the opening curly brace at the end of the line: `{`. Now look at the bottom of the screenshot at part **4** of our code. This closing curly brace (`}`) denotes the end of the class. Everything in between the opening and closing curly braces, `{...}`, is part of the class.

Functions inside the class

Now look at part **5** of the code. Here is that line of code in full, with the key part for our current discussion highlighted:

```
override fun onCreate(savedInstanceState: Bundle?) {
```

This is a function **signature**. The highlighted part, `onCreate`, is the function **name**. The Kotlin `fun` keyword makes it clear that this is the start of a function. We make a function execute its code by using its name. We say we are **calling** a function when we do this.

Although we will not concern ourselves now with the parts of the code on either side of the function name, you might have noticed `Bundle`, one of the classes that we imported in part **2** of our code. If we remove that related `import` line, Android Studio will not know what the `Bundle` class is, and it will be unusable and highlighted in red underline as an error.

Our code will then not compile and run. Notice that the very last thing in the line of the preceding code is an opening curly brace ({). This denotes the start of the code contained within the `onCreate` function. Now jump to part **6** of our code and you will see a closing curly brace (}). You might have guessed that this is the end of the function. Everything in between the opening and closing curly braces of the `onCreate` function is the code that executes when the function is called.

We do not need to go into what this code does yet but, as an overview, it sets up the appearance and layout of the app by referring to some resource files that were autogenerated by Android Studio when we created the project. I have highlighted these resource files with an outline in the previous screenshot labeled **9**.

Parts **7** and **8** are also functions that I have collapsed to make the screenshot and this discussion more straightforward. Their names are `onCreateOptionsMenu` and `onOptionsItemSelected`.

We know enough about our Kotlin code to make some progress. We will see this code again and change it later in this chapter.

A summary of the Kotlin code so far

It is true that, contained within the preceding code, there is some complex syntax. However, what we are doing is building up just enough knowledge about this code, so that we can work within it and begin to make rapid progress in learning Kotlin and Android without having to read hundreds of pages of Kotlin theory first. By the end of the book, all the code will make sense. But in order to make quick progress now, we just need to accept that some of the details will remain a mystery for a little while longer.

Examining the main layout file

Now we will look at just one of the many `.xml` files. There are several different layout files and we will meet them all throughout the course of this book, but let's start with the most significant one that decides the appearance of our app.

Left-click on the `content_main.xml` tab next to the `MainActivity.kt` tab that we have been discussing.

In the main window on the right-hand side, you will see the **Design** view of our app, as shown in the following screenshot:

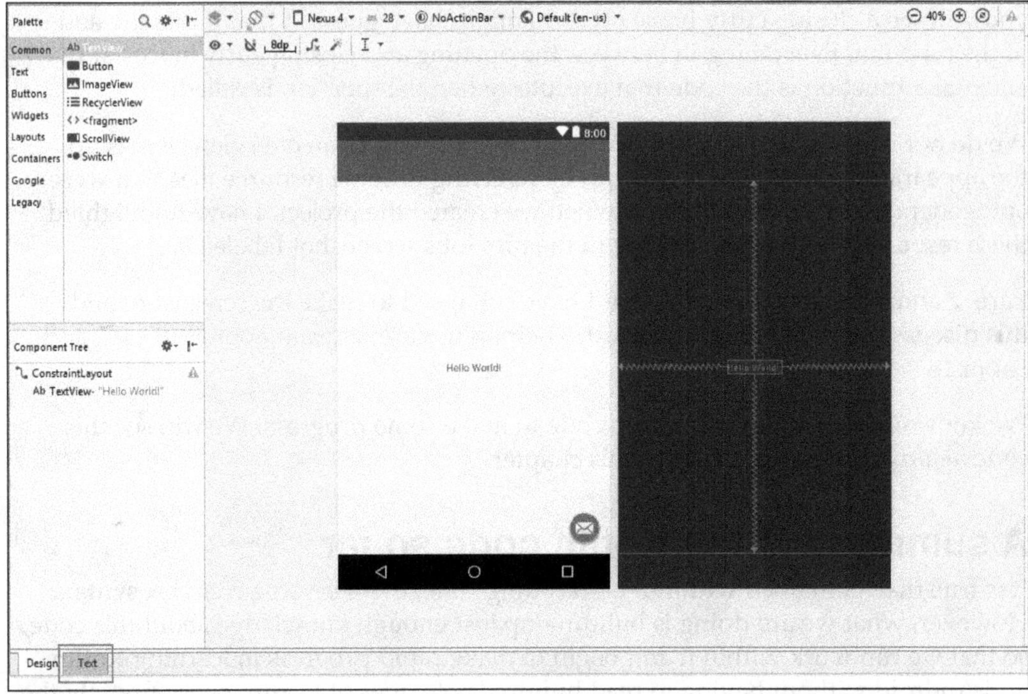

Most of the work that we do throughout the book when we design apps will be done in this design view. It is important, however, to know what is going on behind the scenes.

The design view is a graphical representation of the XML code contained in the `content_main.xml` file. Click on the **Text** tab (as outlined near the bottom-left in the previous screenshot) to see the XML code that forms the layout. I have annotated a screenshot of the XML text so that we can discuss it next:

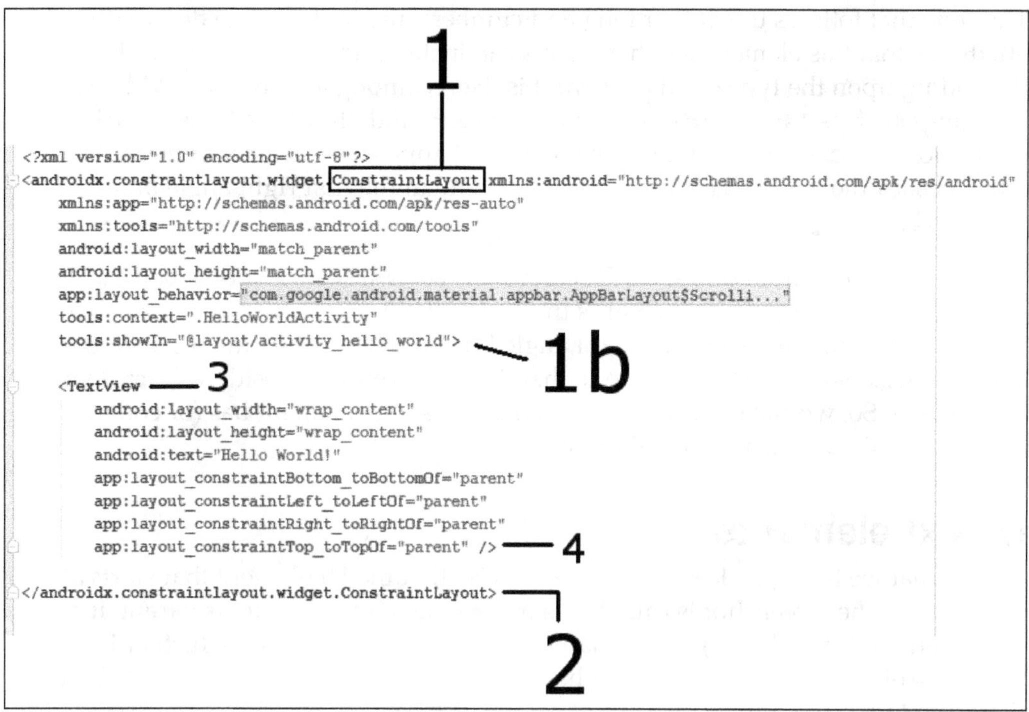

The first thing to note is that this file does not represent the entire layout. It does, however, represent most of the surface area and the **Hello World** message in the center. Also, on the left-hand side, we can see the now familiar **+** and **-** icons so that we can fold and unfold sections of the code.

UI layout elements

If we first look at the part of the code labeled **1**, we can see that the very first thing is ...`ConstraintLayout....` A `ConstraintLayout` element is a UI element that is used to wrap other parts of the UI.

> There are more technical and specific ways to refer to the different "elements" of our user interface designs. As we progress, we will introduce terminology such as widget, view, and view-group, as well.

When we add a new element to a UI in Android, we always start a line with a left angle bracket (<) followed by the element's name.

The code that follows this rather long and cumbersome-looking line defines the **attributes** that this element will have. This can include dozens of different things, depending upon the type of UI element it is. Here, among a bit of other XML, we can see things such as layout_width, layout_height, and showIn. All these attributes define how the ConstraintLayout element will appear on the user's screen. The attributes for the ConstraintLayout element end at the first right angle bracket (>), labeled **1b**.

If we look at the bottom of our XML screenshot, we will see the code labeled **2**. This code, </...ConstraintLayout>, marks the end of the ConstraintLayout element Anything in between the closing right angle bracket (>) of the element's attributes and the </...ConstraintLayout> code that defines its end is considered a **child** of the element. So, we can see that our ConstraintLayout element has (or contains) a child. Let's take a look at that child now.

UI text elements

Using what we have just learned, we can devise that the UI element that starts at position **3** in the screenshot is called a TextView element. Just like its parent, it starts with a left angle bracket (<) and its name: <TextView.... If we look further into our TextView element, we can see that it has several attributes. It has a text attribute that is set to "Hello world!". This, of course, is the exact text that our app shows to the user. It also has layout_width and layout_height attributes that are both set to "wrap_content". This tells the TextView element that it can take up as much space as the content it has needs, but no more. As we will see throughout the book, there are many more attributes available for this and other UI elements.

Notice that the code at the **4** position on our XML screenshot is />. This marks the end of the TextView element. This is slightly different to how the end of the ConstraintLayout element was written. When an element in XML has no children, we can just end it like this: />. When the element has children and its end comes further on in the code from where its attributes are defined, it is much clearer to end the element by repeating its name like this: </...ConstraintLayout>.

You might be wondering why the element name for the TextView element is short and concise (simply, TextView), yet the full name for the ConstraintView element is preceded by apparent complicated clutter (androidx.constraintlayout.widget.ConstraintLayout). This ConstraintLayout element is a special version of the layout that is used to ensure our app's compatibility with older versions of Android. As we will see in a minute, when we add buttons to the app, most elements have simple and concise names.

We will edit this code in the next section and learn more about the attributes, as well as explore another type of UI element - that is, a `Button` element.

Adding buttons to the main layout file

Here, we will add a couple of buttons to the screen and will then explore a quick way to make them do something. We will add a button in two different ways; first, using the visual designer, and second, by adding to and editing the XML code directly.

Adding a button via the visual designer

To get started adding our first button, switch back to the design view by clicking on the **Design** tab underneath the XML code that we have just been discussing. The button is highlighted in the following screenshot:

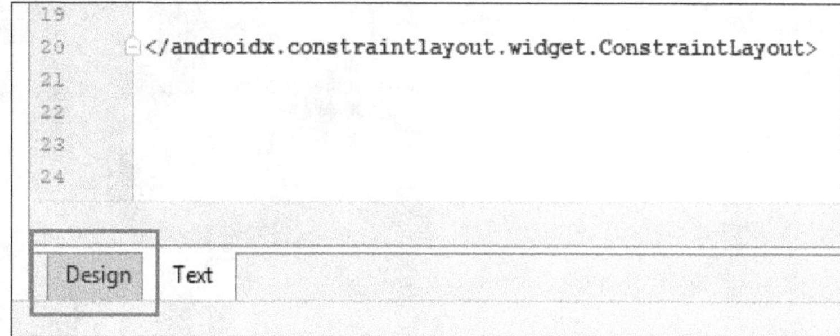

Notice that in the left-hand side of the layout, we have a window that is called **Palette**:

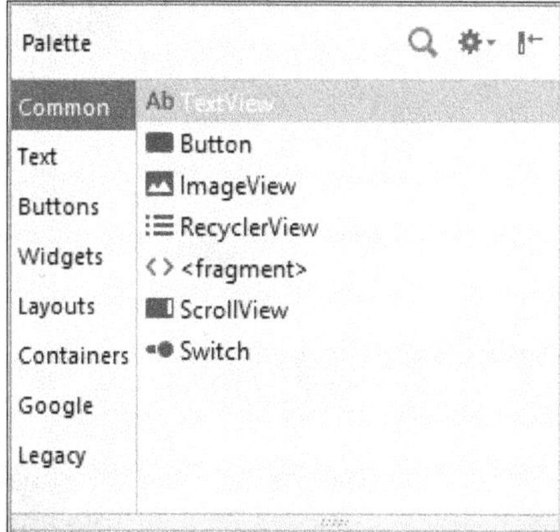

The palette window is divided into two parts. The left-hand list has the categories of the UI elements and allows you to select a category, while the right-hand side shows you all the available UI elements from the currently selected category.

Make sure that the **Common** category is selected, as shown in the previous screenshot. Now, left-click and hold on the **Button** widget, and then drag it onto the layout somewhere near the top and center.

It doesn't matter if it is not exact; however, it is good to practice to get it right. So, if you are not happy with the position of your button, then you can left-click on it to select it on the layout and then tap the *Delete* key on the keyboard to get rid of it. Now you can repeat the previous step until you have one neatly placed button that you are happy with, as demonstrated in the following diagram:

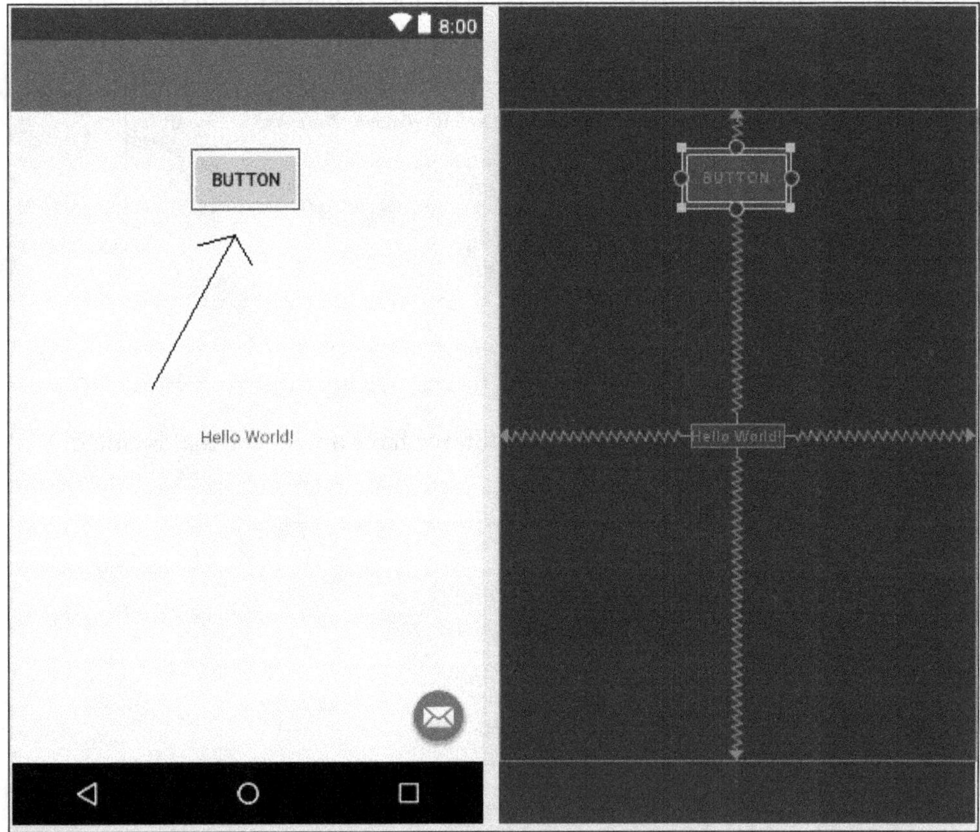

At this point, we can run the app on the emulator or on a real device, and the button will be there. If we click on it, there will even be a simple animation to represent the button being pressed and released. Feel free to try this now if you like.

To start making the app more interesting, we are going to edit the attributes of our button using the **Attributes** window.

Editing the button's attributes

Make sure the button is selected by left-clicking on it. Now find the **Attributes** window to the right of the editing window, as follows:

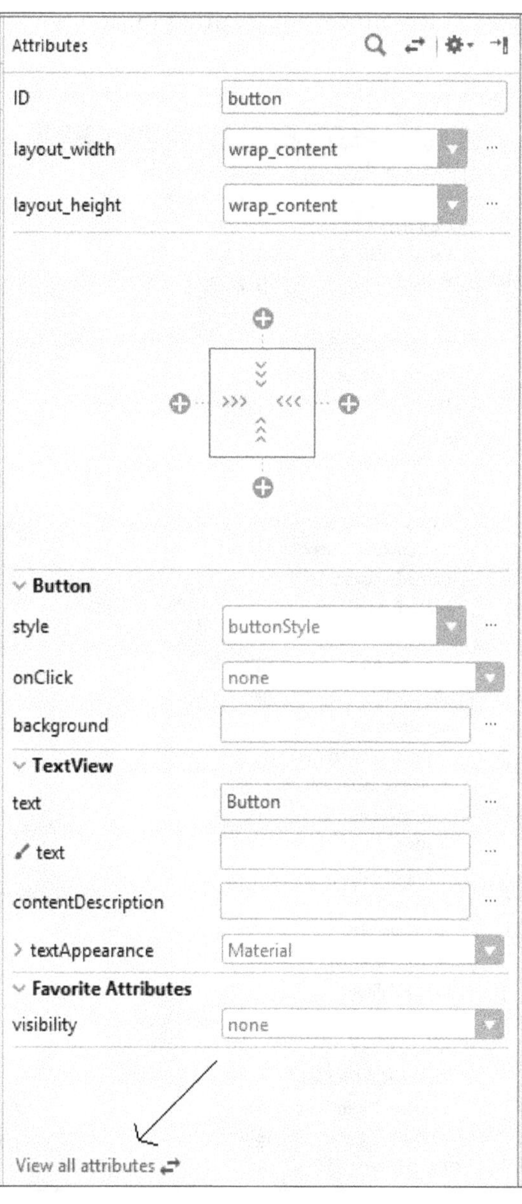

In the preceding screenshot, you can see that we have access to some, although not all, of the button's attributes. To reveal more of the attributes, click on the **View all attributes** link (indicated in the preceding screenshot).

Now you can see the full details of the button and we can set about editing it. It might seem surprising to see the substantial number of attributes that something as apparently simple as a button has. This is a sign of the versatility and power that the Android API provides for UI manipulation. Look at the following screenshot that shows the full attributes list for our recently added button:

Furthermore, notice that even the previous screenshot doesn't show everything, and you can use the scroll bar on the right of the **Attributes** window to reveal even more attributes.

As you can see, there is a large array of different attributes that we can edit right here in the UI designer. In *Chapter 12, Connecting our Kotlin to the UI and Nullability,* we will also edit and manipulate these attributes using our Kotlin code. For now, we will edit just one attribute. Scroll down the **Attributes** window until you see the **onClick** attribute and then left-click on it to select it for editing, as shown in the following screenshot:

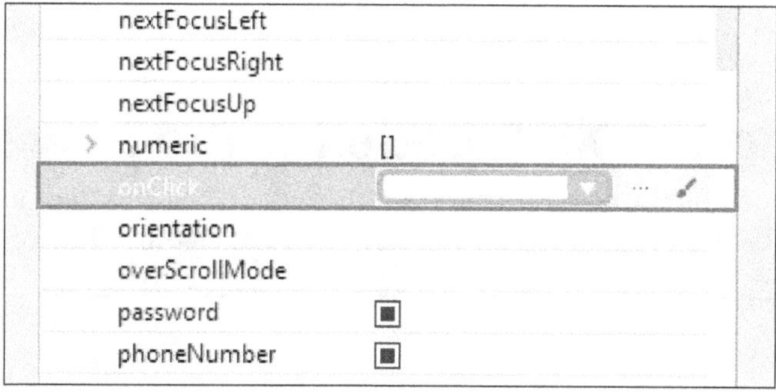

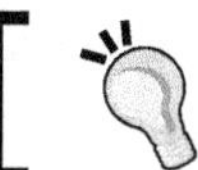

The attributes are in alphabetical order and **onClick** can be found about two thirds of the way down the lengthy list.

Type `topClick` in the **onClick** attribute's edit box and press *Enter* on the keyboard. Be sure to use the same case, including the slightly counterintuitive lowercase `t` and upper-case `C`.

The **Attributes** window will look like the next screenshot when you are done:

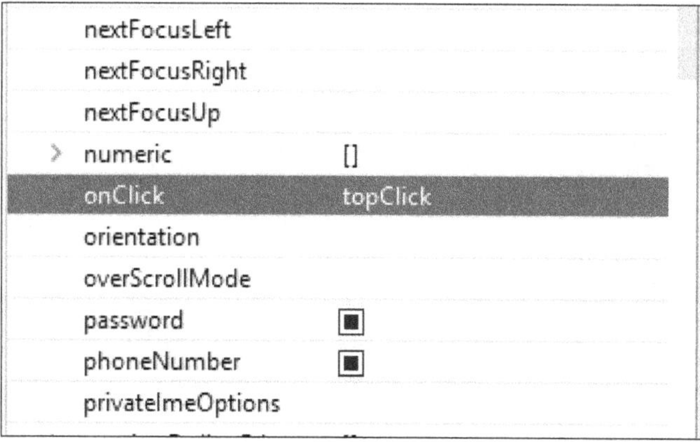

What we have done here is named the Kotlin function in our code that we want to call (or execute) when this button is clicked on by the user. The name is arbitrary but, as this button is on the top part of the screen, the name seems meaningful and easy to remember. The odd casing that we used is a convention that will help us to keep our code clear and easy to read. We will see the benefits of this as our code gets longer and more complicated.

Of course, the `topClick` function doesn't exist yet. Android Studio is very helpful, but there are some things that we need to do for ourselves. We will write this function using Kotlin code after we have added a second button to our UI. You can run the app at this point, and it will still work, but if you click on the button, the app will crash and you will get an error message, because the function does not exist.

Examining the XML code for the new button

Before we add our final button for this project, click on the **Text** tab underneath the editor to switch back to seeing the XML code that makes our UI:

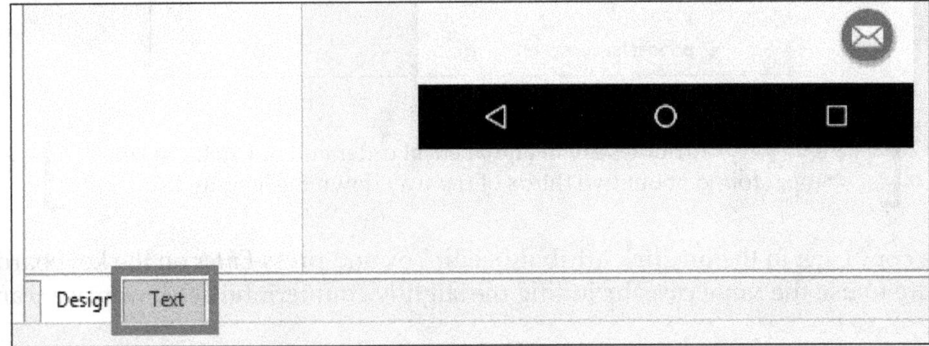

Notice that there is a new block of code amongst the XML code that we examined earlier. Here is a screenshot of the new block of code:

```
<Button
    android:id="@+id/button"
    android:layout_width="wrap_content"
    android:layout_height="wrap_content"
    android:onClick="topClick"
    android:text="Button"
    tools:layout_editor_absoluteX="147dp"
    tools:layout_editor_absoluteY="30dp" />
```

Notice the following details, which should correspond to what we know about XML and Android UI elements:

- The new code starts with the `<Button` text and ends with `/>`.
- The new code has a range of attributes that define the button, including `layoutWidth` and `layoutHeight`.
- The code includes the `onClick` attribute that we added with a value of `"topClick"`.
- The `topClick` value of the `onClick` attribute is underlined in red, showing an error because the function does not exist yet.
- The start and end of the code representing the button is enclosed within the `ConstraintLayout` element.

[The dp is a unit of measurement/distance and will be discussed in more depth in *Chapter 5, Beautiful Layouts with CardViewand ScrollView.*]

Hover the mouse cursor over the underlined `topClick` value to reveal the details of the problem, as shown in the following screenshot:

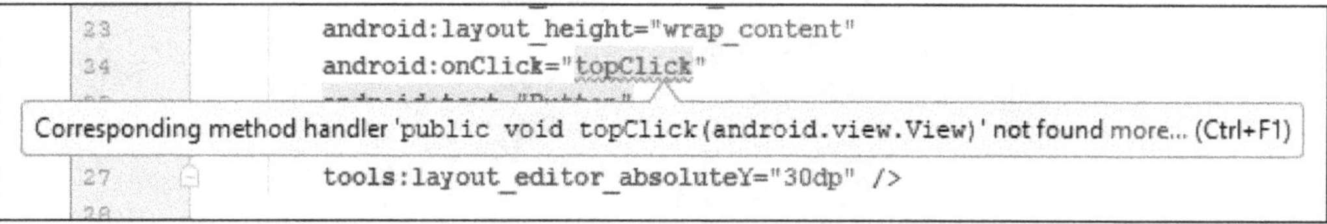

We can confirm that the issue is that Android Studio expects a function called `topClick` to be implemented within our code. We will do this as soon as we have added that second button.

Adding a button by editing the XML code

Just for variety, and to prove that we can, we will now add another button using only the XML code, and not the UI designer. Most of the time, we will use the UI designer, but this quick exercise should cement the relationship between the UI designer and the underlying XML code in your mind.

We will achieve this by copying and pasting the code for the existing button. We will then make some minor edits to the pasted code.

Left-click just before the button code that starts <Button. Notice that the beginning and end of the code now has a slight highlight:

```
<Button
    android:id="@+id/button"
    android:layout_width="wrap_content"
    android:layout_height="wrap_content"
    android:onClick="topClick"
    android:text="Button"
    tools:layout_editor_absoluteX="147dp"
    tools:layout_editor_absoluteY="30dp" />
```

This has identified the part of the code that we want to copy. Now, left-click and drag to select all the button code, including the highlighted start and end, as shown in the next screenshot:

```
<Button
    android:id="@+id/button"
    android:layout_width="wrap_content"
    android:layout_height="wrap_content"
    android:onClick="topClick"
    android:text="Button"
    tools:layout_editor_absoluteX="147dp"
    tools:layout_editor_absoluteY="30dp" />
```

Press the *Ctrl* + *C* keyboard combination to copy the highlighted text. Place the cursor below the existing button code and tap the *Enter* key a few times to leave some additional empty lines.

Press the *Ctrl* + *V* keyboard combination to paste the button code. At this point, we have two buttons; however, there are a couple of problems:

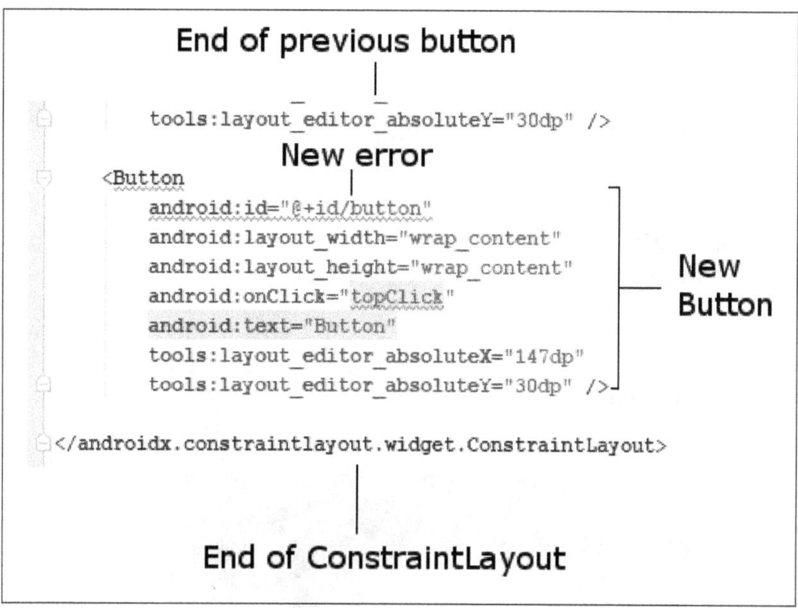

We have an additional error in both blocks of code that represent our buttons. The `id` attribute (in both blocks) is underlined in red. The reason for this error is that both buttons have an `id` attribute that is the same. The `id` attribute is supposed to distinguish a UI element from all other UI elements, so they must not be the same. Let's try and fix that.

Giving the buttons unique id attributes

We could solve the problem by calling the second button as `button2`, but it will be more meaningful to change them both. Edit the code in the first button to give it an `id` attribute of `buttonTop`. To do so, identify this following line of code (in the first button):

```
android:id="@+id/button"
```

Then, change the line of code to the following:

```
android:id="@+id/buttonTop"
```

Notice the lowercase `b` in `button` and the uppercase `T` in `Top`.

Now identify this line of code in the second button:

```
android:id="@+id/button"
```

Then, change the line of code to the following:

```
android:id="@+id/buttonBottom"
```

The errors on the `id` attribute lines are gone. At this point, you might think that we can move on to solving our missing function problem.

However, if you run the app and take a quick glance at it, you will see that we only appear to have one button. Not only that, but the buttons are not in the places that we expected them to be in, either:

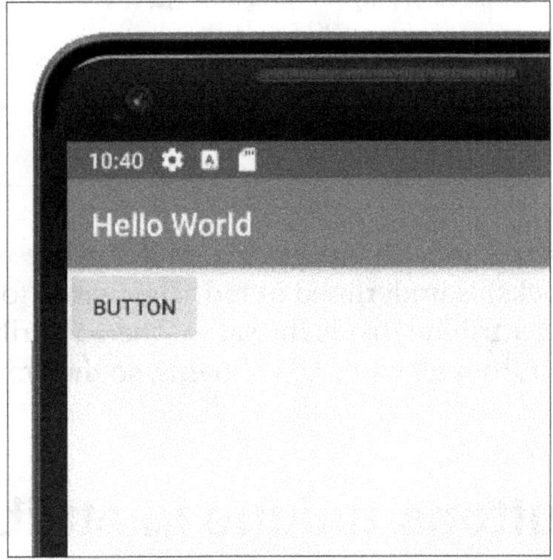

The reason for this is that we haven't explicitly positioned them, so they have defaulted to the top-left of the screen. The position we see on the **Design** tab is just a design-time position. So, let's change that now.

Positioning the two buttons in the layout

The reason we can only see one button is that both buttons are in the same position. The second button is exactly covering the first button. So, even in the **Design** tab (feel free to take a look), the buttons are still sat on top of each other, although they are in the middle of the screen:

> You might be wondering why the UI layout tool was designed in this apparently counterintuitive way; the reason is flexibility. As you will see in the next two chapters, not only is it possible to position UI elements differently at design time to when the app is running, but there is also a range of different layout schemes that the app designer (that's you) can choose from to suit their plans. This flexibility results in a little awkwardness while learning about Android, and great design power once you have got past this awkwardness. But don't worry, we will move a step at a time until you have this thing beaten.

We will make Android Studio solve the problem for us automatically by first adding to our code, and then using the UI designer. First, let's get the design time layout right. In the code for the second button, locate this line of code:

```
tools:layout_editor_absoluteY="30dp" />
```

Now edit it to be the same as the following line of code:

```
tools:layout_editor_absoluteY="100dp" />
```

> Depending upon exactly where you positioned your first button, the values in Android Studio will likely be different to the values just discussed. If the second button is around 70dp higher than the first button, then you can proceed with this exercise.

This subtle change will move the second button down a little, but only for design time. If you look in the **Design** tab, the button is positioned neatly underneath the first button, but if you run the app on the emulator, they are both still in the top-left corner of the screen and are on top of one another.

Switch to the **Design** tab and find the **Infer Constraints** button that is shown in the following screenshot:

Click on the **Infer Constraints** button. Android Studio will edit the XML code. Let's take a brief look at what has happened behind the scenes. From the end of both of the sections of code representing the buttons, the following lines of code were removed:

```
tools:layout_editor_absoluteX="147dp"
tools:layout_editor_absoluteY="30dp" />
```

These two lines of code were what positioned the buttons horizontally (...`absoluteX`) and vertically (...`absoluteY`).

Android Studio also added four lines of code to the first button, and three lines of code to the second button. Here is the code that was added near the start of the first button:

```
android:layout_marginTop="30dp"
```

Exact values of dp might vary depending on precisely where you placed your buttons.

This code causes the button to have a margin of `30` on the top. But on the top of what exactly? Look at the following three lines of code that were added at the end of the first button:

```
app:layout_constraintEnd_toEndOf="parent"
app:layout_constraintStart_toStartOf="parent"
app:layout_constraintTop_toTopOf="parent" />
```

Notice the new attributes of `layout_constraintEnd_toEndOf`, `layout_constraintStart_toStartOf`, and `layout_constraintTop_toTopOf`. The value that is assigned to each of these attributes is `"parent"`. This causes the first button to be positioned relative to the parent UI element. The parent is the layout that contains everything else; in this case, the parent is the `ConstraintLayout` element.

Now look at the three lines of code added to the second (bottom) button.

Near the start of the code, we see the following:

```
android:layout_marginTop="22dp"
```

[Again, exact values of dp might vary depending on precisely where you placed your buttons.]

At the end of the code for the second button, we see the following two extra lines of code:

```
app:layout_constraintStart_toStartOf="@+id/buttonTop"
app:layout_constraintTop_toBottomOf="@+id/buttonTop" />
```

This means that the second button is positioned with a margin of 22 relative to `buttonTop`.

Now run the app and you will see that we have two distinct buttons. One has an `id` attribute of `buttonTop`, and it is above the other button with an `id` attribute of `buttonBottom`:

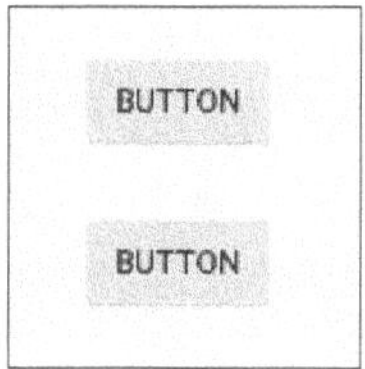

Clearly, there is more to layouts than I have alluded to so far, but you have had your first glance at the options provided by Android Studio to design the UI of our apps. We will be taking a closer look at `ConstraintLayout`, as well as exploring more layout options in *Chapter 4, Getting Started with Layouts and Material Design*.

We want to make one more alteration to our XML code.

Making the buttons call different functions

Switch back to the **Text** tab and identify this next line of code in the second (`buttonBottom`) button:

```
android:onClick="topClick"
```

Next, edit the code as follows:

```
android:onClick="bottomClick"
```

Now we have two buttons, one above the other. The top one has an `id` attribute of `buttonTop` and an `onClick` attribute with a value of `topClick`. The other has an `id` attribute of `buttonBottom` and an `onClick` attribute with a value of `bottomClick`.

These last XML code changes now mean we need to supply two functions (`topClick` and `bottomClick`) in our Kotlin code.

It is technically OK for two buttons to call the same function when they are clicked on - it is not a syntax error. However, most buttons do have distinct purposes, so this exercise will be more meaningful if our buttons do different things.

We will do that soon, but before we do, let's learn a little bit more about Kotlin comments and look at some Kotlin code that we can write to send messages to the user, and to ourselves for debugging purposes.

Leaving comments in our Kotlin code

In programming, it is always a clever idea to write messages known as code comments, and sprinkle them liberally amongst your code. This is to remind us what we were thinking at the time we wrote the code. To do this, you simply append a double forward slash and then type your comment, as follows:

```
// This is a comment and it could be useful
```

In addition, we can use comments to comment out a line of code. Suppose we have a line of code that we temporarily want to disable; we can do so by adding two forward slashes, as follows:

```
// The code below used to send a message
// Log.i("info","our message here")
// But now it doesn't do anything
// And I am getting ahead of where I should be
```

Using comments to comment out code should only be a temporary measure. Once you have found the correct code to use, commented-out code should be cut to keep the code file clean and organized.

Let's take a look at two separate ways to send messages in Android, and then we can write some functions that will send messages when our UI buttons are pressed.

Coding messages to the user and the developer

In the introduction to this chapter and in the previous chapter, we talked a bit about using other people's code, specifically via the classes and their functions of the Android API. We saw that we could do some quite complex things with fairly insignificant amounts of code (such as talking to satellites).

To get us started on coding, we are going to use two different classes from the Android API that allow us to output messages. The first class, `Log`, allows us to output messages to the logcat window. The second class, `Toast`, is not a tasty breakfast treat, but it will produce a toast-shaped pop up message for our app's user to see.

Here is the code we need to write to send a message to logcat:

```
Log.i("info","our message here")
```

Exactly why this works will become clearer in *Chapter 10, Object-Oriented Programming*, but for now, we just need to know that whatever we put between the two sets of quote marks will be output to the logcat window. We will see where to put this type of code shortly.

Here is the code we need to write in order to send a message to the user's screen:

```
Toast.makeText(this, "our message",
    Toast.LENGTH_SHORT).show()
```

This is a very convoluted-looking line of code and exactly how it works, again, will not become clear until *Chapter 9, Kotlin Functions*. The important thing here is that whatever we put between the quote marks will appear in a pop-up message to our users.

Let's put some code (like we have just seen) into our app for real.

Writing our first Kotlin code

So, we now know the code that will output to logcat or the user's screen. However, where do we put the code? To answer this question, we need to understand that the `onCreate` function in `MainActivity.kt` executes as the app is preparing to be shown to the user. So, if we put our code at the end of this function, it will run just as the user sees it; that sounds good.

We know that to execute the code in a function, we need to **call** it. We have wired our buttons up to call a couple of functions, such as `topClick` and `bottomClick`. Soon, we will write these functions. But who or what is calling `onCreate`? The answer to this mystery is that Android itself calls `onCreate` in response to the user clicking on the app icon to run the app. In *Chapter 6, The Android Lifecycle,* we will look deeper, and it will be clear what exactly the code executes and when. You don't need to completely comprehend this now; I just wanted to give you an overview of what was going on.

Let's quickly try this out; switch to the `MainActivity.kt` tab in Android Studio.

We know that the `onCreate` function is called just before the app starts for real. Let's copy and paste some code into the `onCreate` function of our Hello World app and see what happens when we run it.

Adding message code to the onCreate function

Find the closing curly brace (`}`) of the `onCreate` function and add the highlighted code shown in the following code block. In the code, I haven't shown the complete content of the `onCreate` function, but instead, I have used ... to indicate a number of lines of code not being shown. The important thing is to place the new code (shown in full) right at the end, but before the closing curly brace (`}`):

```
override fun onCreate(savedInstanceState: Bundle?) {
…
…
…
        // Your code goes here
        Toast.makeText(this, "Can you see me?",
              Toast.LENGTH_SHORT).show()

        Log.i("info", "Done creating the app")
}
```

Notice that the instances of `Toast` and `Log` are highlighted in red in Android Studio. They are errors. We know that `Toast` and `Log` are classes and that classes are containers for code.

The problem is that Android Studio doesn't know about them until we tell it. We must add an `import` directive for each class. Fortunately, this is semi-automatic.

Left-click on `Toast`; now hold the *Alt* key and tap *Enter*. You need to do this step twice, once for `Toast`, and once for `Log`. Android Studio adds the `import` directives at the top of the code with our other imports, and the errors are gone.

Alt + *Enter* is just one of many useful keyboard shortcuts. The following is a keyboard shortcut reference for Android Studio. More specifically, it is for the IntelliJ Idea IDE, which Android Studio is based on. Bookmark this web page; it will be invaluable over the course of this book: `http://www.jetbrains.com/idea/docs/IntelliJIDEA_ReferenceCard.pdf`.

Scroll to the top of `MainActivity.kt` and look at the added `import` directives. Here they are for your convenience:

```
import android.util.Log
import android.widget.Toast
```

Run the app in the usual way and look at the output in the **logcat** window.

Examining the output

The following is a screenshot of the output in the logcat window:

```
com.gamecodeschool.helloworld W/hool.helloworl: Accessing hidden
com.gamecodeschool.helloworld W/hool.helloworl: Accessing hidden
com.gamecodeschool.helloworld I/info: Done creating the app
com.gamecodeschool.helloworld I/ConfigStore: android::hardware::
com.gamecodeschool.helloworld I/ConfigStore: android::hardware::
```

Looking at the logcat, you can see that our message - **Done creating the app** - was output, although it is mixed up amongst other system messages that we are currently not interested in. If you watched the emulator when the app first starts, you will also see the neat pop-up message that the user will see:

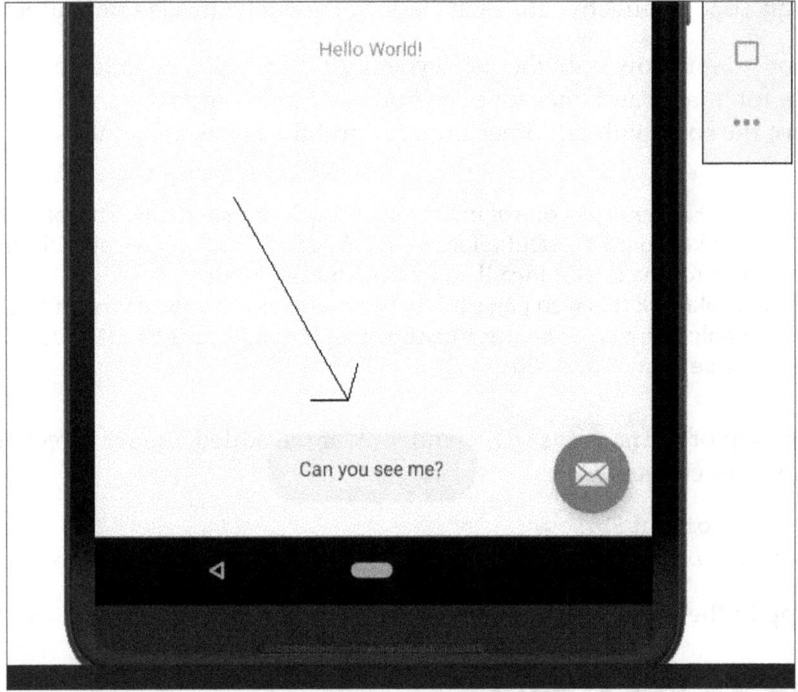

You might be wondering why the messages were output at the time that they were. The simple answer is that the `onCreate` function is called just before the app starts to respond to the user. It is common practice amongst Android developers to put code in this function to get their apps set up and ready for user input.

Now, we will go a step further and write our own functions that are called by our UI buttons. We will place similar `Log` and `Toast` messages inside them.

Writing our own Kotlin functions

Let's go straight on to writing our first Kotlin functions with some more `Log` and `Toast` messages inside them.

Now will be a good time, if you haven't done so already, to get the download bundle that contains all the code files. You can view the completed code for each chapter. For example, the completed code for this chapter can be found in the `Chapter02` folder. I have further subdivided the `Chapter02` folder into `kotlin` and `res` folders (for Kotlin and resource files). In chapters with more than one project, I will divide the folders further to include the project name. You should view these files in a text editor. My favorite is Notepad++, a free download from `https://notepad-plus-plus.org/download/`. Code viewed in a text editor is easier to read than directly from the book, especially the paperback version, and even more so where the lines of code are long. The text editor is also a great way to select sections of the code to copy and paste into Android Studio. You could open the code in Android Studio, but then you risk mixing up my code with the autogenerated code of Android Studio.

Identify the closing curly brace (}) of the `MainActivity` class.

Note that you are looking for the end of the entire class, not the end of the `onCreate` function, as in the previous section. Take your time to identify the new code and where it goes among the existing code.

Inside that curly brace, enter the following code that is highlighted:

```
override fun onCreate(savedInstanceState: Bundle?) {
...
...
...
...
}

...
...
...
fun topClick(v: View) {
    Toast.makeText(this, "Top button clicked",
      Toast.LENGTH_SHORT).show()

    Log.i("info", "The user clicked the top button")
}

fun bottomClick(v: View) {
```

```
        Toast.makeText(this, "Bottom button clicked",
          Toast.LENGTH_SHORT).show()

        Log.i("info", "The user clicked the bottom button")
    }

} // This is the end of the class
```

Notice that the two instances of `View` are in red, indicating an error. Simply use the *Alt* + *Enter* keyboard combination to import the `View` class and remove the errors.

Deploy the app to a real device or emulator in the usual way and start tapping the buttons so that we can observe the output.

Examining the output

At last, our app does something! We can see that the function names we defined in the button `onClick` attribute are indeed called when the buttons are clicked on; the appropriate messages are added to the **logcat** window; and the appropriate `Toast` messages are shown to the user.

Admittedly, we still don't understand why `Toast` and `Log` really work, nor do we fully comprehend the `(v: View)` parts of our function's syntax, or the rest of the autogenerated code. This will become clear as we progress. As stated previously, in *Chapter 10, Object-Oriented Programming,* we will take a deep dive into the world of classes and, in *Chapter 9, Kotlin Functions,* we will master the rest of the syntax associated with functions.

Take a look at the logcat output; you can see that a log entry was made from the `onCreate` function just as before, as well as from the two functions that we wrote ourselves, each time you clicked on a button. In the following screenshot, you can see that I clicked on each button three times:

```
com.gamecodeschool.helloworld I/info: The user clicked the top button
com.gamecodeschool.helloworld I/info: The user clicked the top button
com.gamecodeschool.helloworld I/info: The user clicked the top button
com.gamecodeschool.helloworld I/info: The user clicked the bottom button
com.gamecodeschool.helloworld I/info: The user clicked the bottom button
com.gamecodeschool.helloworld I/info: The user clicked the bottom button
```

As you are now familiar with where to find the **logcat** window, in future, I will present the logcat output as trimmed text as it is clearer to read:

```
The user clicked the top button
The user clicked the top button
The user clicked the top button
The user clicked the bottom button
The user clicked the bottom button
The user clicked the bottom button
```

In the following screenshot, you can see that the top button has been clicked on and that the `topClick` function was called, triggering the pop-up `Toast` message:

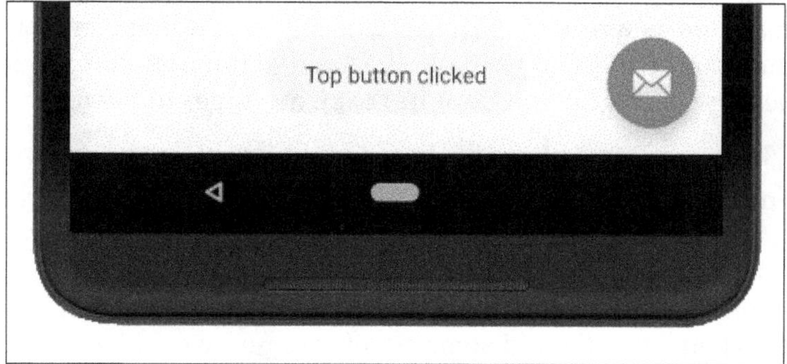

Throughout this book, we will regularly output to logcat, so that we can see what is going on behind the UI of our apps. `Toast` messages are more for notifying the user that something has occurred. This might be a download that has completed, a new email has arrived, or some other occurrence that needs their attention.

Frequently asked questions

Q.1) Can you remind me what functions are?

A) Functions are containers for our code that can be executed (called) from other parts of our code.

Q.2) Like the first, I found this chapter tough going. Do I need to re-read it?

A) No, if you managed to build the app, you have made enough progress to handle all of the next chapter. All the blanks in our knowledge will be steadily filled in and replaced with glorious moments of realization as the book progresses.

Summary

We have achieved a lot in this exercise. It is true that much of the XML code is still generally incomprehensible. That's OK, because in the next two chapters, we will be really getting to grips with the visual designer and learning more about the XML code, although, ultimately, our aim is to use the XML code as little as possible.

We have seen how, when we drag a button onto our design, the XML code is generated for us. Also, if we change an attribute in the **Attributes** window then, again, the XML code is edited for us. Furthermore, we can type (or, in our case, copy and paste) the XML code directly to create new buttons on our UI or edit existing ones.

We have seen as well as written our first Kotlin code, including comments that help us document our code, and we have even added our own functions to output debugging messages to logcat and pop-up `Toast` messages to the user.

In the next chapter, we will take a full guided tour of Android Studio to see exactly where different things get done. Additionally, we will gain an understanding of how our project's assets, such as files and folders, are structured and how we can manage them. This will prepare us for a more in-depth look at UI design in *Chapter 4, Getting Started with layouts and Material Design* and *Chapter 5, Beautiful Layouts with CardView and ScrollView*, when we will build some significant real-world layouts for our apps.

3
Exploring Android Studio and the Project Structure

In this chapter, we will create and run two more Android projects. The purpose of these exercises is to explore Android Studio and the structure of Android projects more deeply.

When we build our apps ready for deployment, the code and the resource files need to be packed away as they are in the APK file. Therefore, all the layout files and other resources, which we will be looking at soon, need to be in the correct structures.

Fortunately, Android Studio handles this for us when we create a project from a template. However, we still need to know how to find and amend these files, how to add our own and sometimes remove the files created by Android Studio, and how the resource files are interlinked - sometimes with each other, and sometimes with the Kotlin code (that is, the autogenerated Kotlin code, as well as our own).

Along with understanding the composition of our projects, it will also be beneficial to make sure that we get the most from the emulator.

Emulators are particularly useful when you want to make sure that your app will work on hardware that you don't own. Also, learning about some of the latest features (as we will in this book) often requires the latest handset, and an emulator is a cost-effective way of following along with all the mini-apps without buying the latest phone.

In this chapter, we will do the following:

- Explore the file and folder structure of the **Empty Activity** project template.
- See the difference between the **Empty Activity** and the **Basic Activity** templates.
- Find out how to get the most from the emulator.

This chapter will leave us in a good position to build and deploy multiple different layouts in the next chapter.

A quick guided tour of Android Studio

To get started, take a look at this annotated diagram of Android Studio. We will reacquaint ourselves with the parts that we have already seen, and learn about the parts that we have not yet discussed:

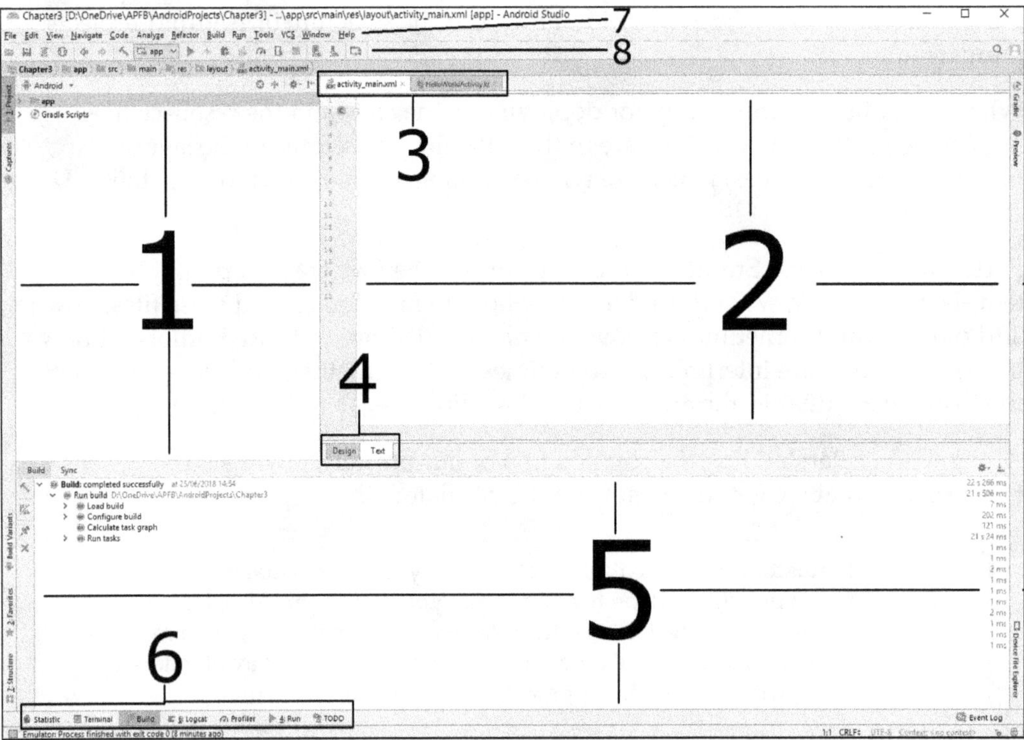

It will be useful to formally point out and name the various parts of the Android Studio **User Interface** (**UI**), so that I can refer to them by name, rather than describing their location and showing screenshots all the time. So, let's run through them from number **1**:

1. This is the **Project** window and will be the main focus of this chapter. It enables us to explore the folders, code, and resources of the project and is also referred to as the Project Explorer window. Double-click on a file here to open the file and add a new tab to area **3** on the diagram. The structure of the files and folders here closely resembles the structure that will eventually end up in the finished APK file.

As we will see, while the structure of folders for an Android project remains the same, the files, filenames, and contents of the files vary considerably. Therefore, we will explore two projects in this chapter, and then look at more projects as we progress through the book.

2. This is the **Editor** window. As we have already seen, the **Editor** window takes on a few different forms depending on what it is that we are editing. If we are editing Kotlin, then we can see our code neatly formatted and ready for editing; if we are designing a UI, then it offers us either a visual editing view or a text/XML code view. You can also view and edit graphics and other files in this window.
3. These tabs allow us switch between the different files in our project. The **Editor** window will display the file we select here. We can add another tab to this section by double-clicking on the file in the **Project** window.
4. This allows us to switch between the **Design** and **Text** (code) view on the file that is currently being edited.
5. This window varies depending upon the option selected in part **6** of the diagram. Typically, in this book, we will switch between the **Build** window to see that our project has been compiled and launched without errors, and the **Logcat** window to view the debugging output and any errors or crash reports from our apps.
6. This area of the UI is used to switch between the different displays described in part **5**.

There are even more tabs in Android Studio, but we won't need them in the context of this book.

Now that we know how to unambiguously refer to the various parts of the UI, let's turn our attention to the **Project/Project Explorer** window.

Project Explorer and project anatomy

When we create a new Android project, we most often do so with a project template, just as we did in *Chapter 1, Getting Started with Android and Kotlin*. The template that we use determines the exact selection and contents of the files that Android Studio will generate. While there are big similarities across all projects that are worth noting, seeing the differences can also help. Let's build two different template projects and examine the files, their contents, and how they are all linked together through the code (XML and Kotlin).

The Empty Activity project

The simplest project type with an autogenerated UI is the **Empty Activity** project. Here, the UI is empty, but it is ready to be added to. It is also possible to generate a project without a UI at all. When we create a project, even with an empty UI, Android Studio autogenerates the Kotlin code to display the UI. Therefore, when we add to it, it is ready to be displayed.

Let's create an **Empty Activity** project. This is almost the same process as we did in *Chapter 1, Getting Started with Android and Kotlin*, but with one slight difference that I will point out:

1. In Android Studio, select **File** | **New** | **New Project...**.
2. On the **Choose your project** screen, select the **Empty Activity** template and click on **Next**.
3. Change the **Name** field to `Empty Activity App`.
4. Choose the same package name and save location as the previous project.
5. Be sure to select **Kotlin** as the language.
6. Check the **Use AndroidX artifacts** checkbox as we did previously.
7. The remaining settings can be left to their default settings, so just click on **Next**.

Android Studio will generate all the code and other project resources. Now we can see what has been generated and compare it to what we expected in the project explorer window.

If the emulator is not already running, launch it by selecting **Tools** | **AVD Manager** and then start your emulator in the **Android Virtual Devices** window. Run the app on the emulator by clicking on the play button in the quick launch bar:

Take a look at the app and notice how it is a little bit different to that of the first project. It is, well, empty; there is no menu at the top, and no floating button at the bottom. It does, however, still have the **Hello World!** text:

Don't worry about referring to the first project; we will build another one just like it soon.

Now that we have a brand new **Empty Activity App** project, let's explore the files and folders that Android Studio has generated for us.

Exploring the Empty Activity project

Now, it is time to go on a deep dive into the files and folders of our app. This will save us lots of time and head-scratching later in the book. Please note, however, that there is no need to memorize where all these files go, and there is even less need to understand the code within the files. In fact, parts of the XML code will remain a mystery at the end of the book, but it will not stop you from designing, coding, and releasing amazing apps.

Take a look at the project explorer window after the project is created:

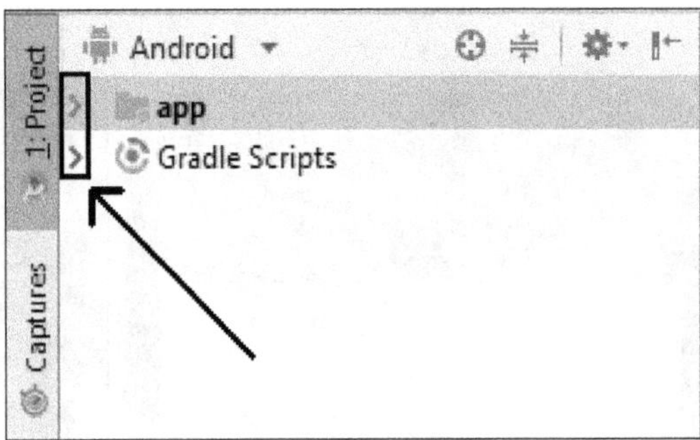

Notice the two arrows indicated in the previous screenshot. These, as you probably can guess, allow us to expand the `app` and `Gradle Scripts` folders.

> We do not need to explore the `Gradle Scripts` folder in the context of this book. Gradle is a significant part of Android Studio, but its role is to hide the quite-complicated processes that Android Studio performs from the user, such as adding resource files, and compiling and building projects. Therefore, we don't need to dig into this any further. If, however, you decide to take Android to the next level, then gaining a good understanding of Gradle and its relationship with Android Studio is time well invested.

We will explore the `app` folder in more detail. Click on the arrow next to the `app` folder to expand its contents and we will begin exploring. The first level of contents is displayed in the following screenshot:

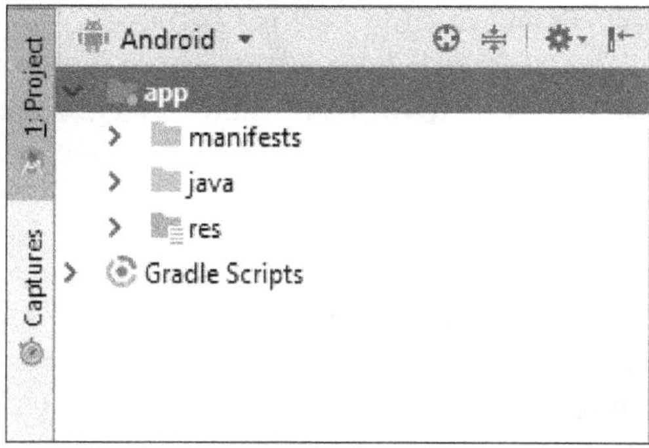

We have revealed three more folders: `manifests`, `java`, and `res`. Let's take a closer look in all three, starting at the top.

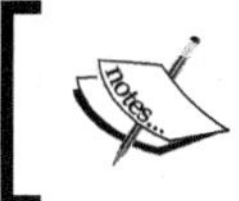

> We will keep our Kotlin code in the `java` folder. Additionally, since the release of Android Studio version 3.3, there is also a folder named `generatedjava` , but we don't need to explore it.

The manifests folder

The `manifests` folder has just one file inside it. Expand the `manifests` folder and double-click on the `AndroidManifest.xml` file. Notice that the file has been opened in the editor window and a tab has been added so that we can easily switch between this and other files. The following screenshot shows the new tab that has been added, as well as the XML code contained in the `AndroidManifest.xml` file within the `manifests` folder:

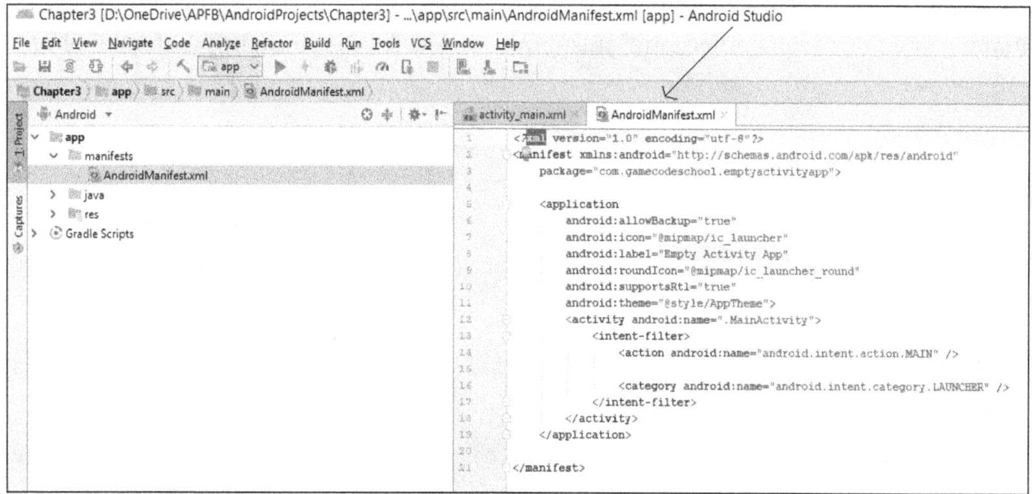

We don't need to understand everything in this file, but it is worth pointing out that we will make occasional amendments here, for example, when we need to ask the user for permission to access some features of their device, such as the messaging app or the images folder. We will also edit this file when we want to make a fullscreen app for immersion, such as for a game.

Notice that the structure of the file is very similar to the structure of the layout file that we saw in the previous chapter. For instance, there are clearly denoted sections that start with `<section name` and end with `</section name>`. Real examples of this are `<application` and `</application>`, and `<activity` and `</activity>`.

Indeed, the entire file contents, apart from the first line, are wrapped in `<manifest` and `</manifest>`.

In the same way that we enter the brackets of a calculation into a calculator, these opening and closing parts must match or the file will cause an error in our project. Android Studio indents (that is, places tabs) in front of the lines to make the sections and their depth in this structure clearer.

A number of specific parts of this code are worth noting, so I will point out some of the lines.

The following line tells Android that the icon that we want to show the user in their app drawer/home screen, and with which they can launch the app, is contained in the `mipmap` folder and is called `ic_launcher`:

```
android:icon="@mipmap/ic_launcher"
```

We will verify this for ourselves as we continue our exploration.

The next line has two aspects that are worth discussing. First, it denotes the name that we gave our app; and second, this name is contained as a **String** with a label of `app_name`:

```
android:label="@string/app_name"
```

In programming, including Kotlin and XML, a String can be any alphanumeric value. We will learn more about Strings throughout the book, starting in *Chapter 7, Kotlin Variables, Operators, and Expressions.*

We can, therefore, guess that the alphanumeric value of the label of `app_name` is `Empty Activity App`, because that is what we called the app when we created it.

This might sound unusual, but we will see this file shortly along with its label. And, in later projects, we will add more labels and values to it. We will also come to understand the reasons why we add text to our apps in what might, at this stage, seem like a convoluted manner.

We could discuss every line in the `AndroidManifest.xml` file, but we don't need to. Let's take a look at another two lines as they are related to each other. The following line indicates the name of our Activity, which was auto-generated when we created the project. I have highlighted the Activity name just to make it stand out:

```
<activity android:name=".MainActivity">
```

The following line, which appears within the `<activity` and `</activity>` tags, denotes that it is an attribute of the `activity` file. This tells us that this Activity is the one that should run when the app is started; it is the `LAUNCHER`:

```
<category android:name="android.intent.category.LAUNCHER" />
```

This implies that our apps can have more than one Activity. Very often, if you have an app with multiple screens, such as a home screen or settings screen, those screens are built from multiple Activity class **instances**.

In XML, such as the `AndroidManifest` file, `activity` is in lowercase; but in Kotlin, the `Activity` class has an uppercase `A`. This is just convention and it is nothing to be concerned about.

As you have just seen, `activity` in XML has a `name` attribute with a value that refers to an instance of a Kotlin `Activity`.

Let's now dig into the `java` folder.

The java folder

Here, we will find all the Kotlin code. To begin with, this consists of just one file, but as our projects grow further, we will add more. Expand the `java` folder and you will find three more folders, as shown in the following screenshot:

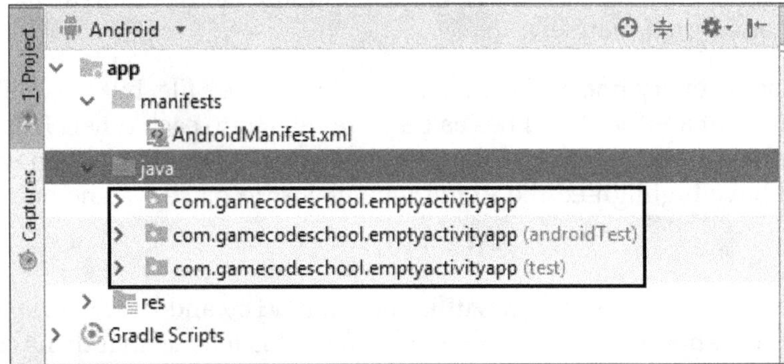

For this book, we will only need one of these three folders; that is, the top one. The names of these folders are composed of the package name (chosen when we created the app), and the app name, presented in lowercase and with no spaces (this was also chosen when we created the app).

> The reason there is more than one folder with the same name is due to automated testing, which is beyond the scope of this book. Therefore, you can safely ignore the folders that end with `(androidTest)` and `(test)`.

The only folder that we are interested in for this book is the top folder, which for this app (on my screen) is `com.gamecodeschool.emptyactivityapp`. Depending on your chosen package name and the name of the app that we are currently working on, the folder name will change, but it will always be the top folder that we need to access and add or edit the contents of.

Expand the `com.gamecodeschool.emptyactivityapp` (or whatever yours is called) folder now to view its contents. In the following screenshot, you can see that the folder has just one file:

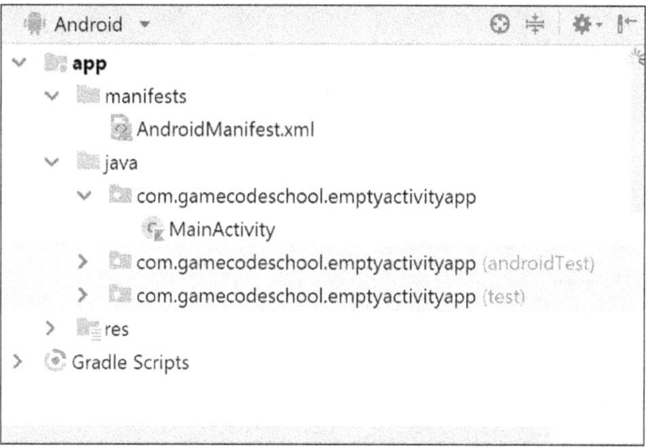

It is the `MainActivity.kt` file, although the file extension isn't shown in the project window, even though it is in the tab above the editor window. In fact, all the files in the `java/packagename.appname` folder for this book will have the `.kt` extension.

If you double-click on the `MainActivity.kt` file, it will open in the editor window, although we could have just clicked on the `MainActivity.kt` tab above the editor window. As we add more Kotlin files to our project, knowing where they are kept will be useful.

Examine the `MainActivity.kt` file and you will see that it is a simplified version of the Kotlin file that we worked with in the first project. It is the same, except that there are fewer functions and less code in the `onCreate` function. The functions are missing because the UI is simpler, and they are not needed; therefore, Android Studio didn't generate them.

For reference, take a look at the contents of the `MainActivity.kt` file in the following screenshot:

```
package com.gamecodeschool.emptyactivityapp

import androidx.appcompat.app.AppCompatActivity
import android.os.Bundle

class MainActivity : AppCompatActivity() {

    override fun onCreate(savedInstanceState: Bundle?) {
        super.onCreate(savedInstanceState)
        setContentView(R.layout.activity_main)
    }
}
```

The file still has the `onCreate` function, which runs when the app is run, but there is much less code in it, and `onCreate` is the only function. Take a look at the last line of code in the `onCreate` function, which we will discuss before moving on to explore the `res` folder. Here is the line of code under discussion:

```
setContentView(R.layout.activity_main)
```

The code is calling a function named `setContentView` and is passing some data into `setContentView` for the code in the `setContentView` function to make use of. The data being passed to `setContentView` is `R.layout.activity.main`.

For now, I will just mention that the `setContentView` function is provided by the Android API and is the function that prepares and displays the UI to the user. So, what exactly is `R.layout.activity_main`?

Let's find out by exploring the `res` folder.

The res folder

The `res` folder is where all the resources go. Left-click to expand the `res` folder and we will examine what's inside. Here is a screenshot of the top level of folders inside the `res` folder:

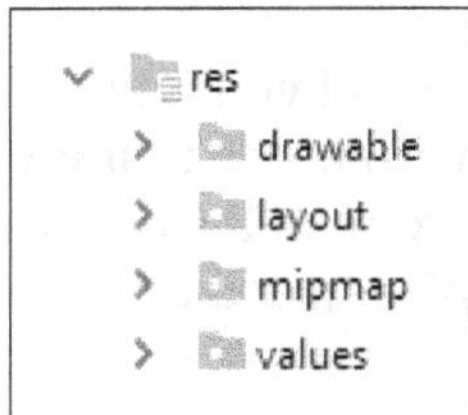

Let's begin with the top of the list; that is, the `drawable` folder.

The res/drawable folder

The name gives things away a little bit, but the `drawable` folder holds much more than just graphics. As we progress through this book, we will indeed add graphics to this folder; however, for now, it holds just two files.

These files are `ic_launcher_foreground` and `ic_launcher_background`. We will not examine these files because we will never need to alter them, but I will quickly mention what they are.

If you open the files, you will see that they are quite long and technical. They include lists of coordinates, colors, and more. They are what is known as a **graphical mask**.

They are used by Android to adapt or mask other graphics; in this case, the launcher icon of the app. The files are instructions to Android on how to adapt the app launcher icon.

This system is made available so that different device manufacturers can create their own masks to suit their own Android devices. The masks, which are in the `drawable` folder by default (`ic_launcher_foreground` and `ic_launcher_background`), are default adaptive masks that add visually pleasing shadows and depth to the launcher icon.

> If the concept of adaptive icons is interesting to you, then you can refer to a full and a very visual explanation on the Android developer's website at `https://developer.android.com/guide/practices/ui_guidelines/icon_design_adaptive`.

Now that we know enough about `drawable`, let's move on to `layout`.

The res/layout folder

Expand the `layout` folder and you will see our familiar layout file that we edited in the previous chapter. There is less in it this time because we generated an Empty Activity project. It is not entirely empty, as it still holds a `ConstraintLayout` layout wrapping a `TextView` widget that says `Hello World!`.

Be sure to look at the contents - you should find that it looks as you might expect, but it is not the contents that are of interest here. Take a closer look at the name of the file (without the XML file extension): `activity_main`.

Now think back to the Kotlin code in the `MainActivity.kt` file. Here is the line of code that sets up the UI; I have highlighted a portion of the code:

```
setContentView(R.layout.activity_main);
```

The `R.layout.activity_main` code is indeed a reference to the `activity_main` file within the `res/layout` folder. This is the connection between our Kotlin code and our XML layout/design.

There is a difference in the first project; in the `layout` folder of the first project, there is an additional file. Later in this chapter, we will build another project using the same template (Basic Activity) that we used in the first chapter to understand why.

Before doing that, let's explore the final two folders and all their subfolders, starting with the next in the list, `mipmap`.

The res/mipmap folder

The `mipmap` folder is straightforward - that is, *fairly* straightforward. Expand the folder to see its contents, as shown in the following screenshot:

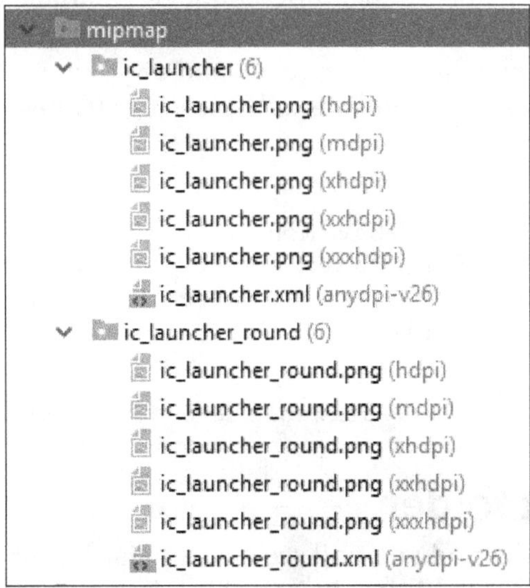

Here, you can see two subfolders; they are `ic_launcher` and `ic_launcher_round`. The contents of `ic_launcher` include the graphics for the regular launcher icon we see in the app drawer/home screen of the device, while `ic_launcher_round` holds the graphics for the devices that use round icons, as opposed to square icons. Double-click on one of the `.png` files from each folder to have a look. I have photoshopped one of each side by side in this screenshot to aid our discussion:

You are probably also wondering why there are five `ic_launcher....png` files in each folder. The reason for this is that it is good practice to provide icons that are suitably scaled for different sizes and resolutions of the screen. Providing an image with the `hdpi`, `mdpi`, `xhdpi`, `xxhdpi`, and `xxxhdpi` qualifications allows different Android devices to choose the icon that will look best for the user.

The letters `dpi` stands for **dots-per-inch**, and the `h`, `m`, `xh`, `xxh`, and `xxxh` prefixes stand for high, medium, extra high, extra extra high, and so on. These are known as **qualifiers** and you will see as you progress throughout this book that Android has lots of qualifiers, which help us to build our apps to suit the wide range of different devices available for users to choose from.

The final conundrum from the `mipmap` folder is that there is also an XML file in each of the two subfolders. Open one of them up and you will see that they refer to the `ic_launcher_foreground` and `ic_launcher_background` files that we looked at in the `drawable` folder. This tells the Android device where to get the details for the adaptive icons. These files are not required, but they make the icons look better, as well as add flexibility to the appearance.

We have one more folder and all its files to explore, and then we will finally understand the structure of an Android app.

The res/values folder

Open the `res/values` folder to reveal three files that we will talk about briefly in turn. All these files interlink and refer to each other and other files that we have seen already.

For the sake of completeness, here is a screenshot of the three files in the `res/values` folder:

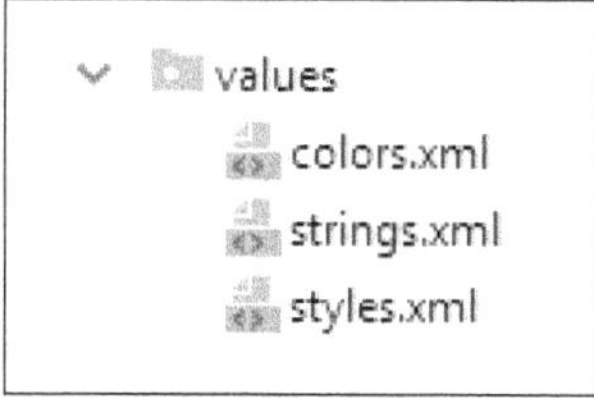

The key to understanding is not in memorizing the connections, and certainly not in trying to memorize or even understand the code in the files, but rather to get an appreciation of the interlinked nature of all the files and code we have seen so far.

Let's glance inside the files one at a time.

The colors.xml file

Next, take a look at the contents of the `colors.xml` file:

```
<?xml version="1.0" encoding="utf-8"?>
<resources>
    <color name="colorPrimary">#008577</color>
    <color name="colorPrimaryDark">#00574B</color>
    <color name="colorAccent">#D81B60</color>
</resources>
```

Notice that the starting and closing tags take the usual pattern we have come to expect from XML files. There is an opening `<resources>` tag and a closing `</resources>` tag. As children of resources, there are three pairs of `<color>` ... `</color>` tags.

Within each `color` tag is contained a `name` attribute and some curious-looking code consisting of numbers and letters. The `name` attribute is the name of a color. We will see, in another file that follows, that the various names in this file are referred to from another file.

The code is what defines an actual color itself. Therefore, when the name is referred to, the color defined by the related code is what is produced on the screen.

The code is called a hexadecimal code, because in each position of the code, the values `0` through `9` and the letters `a` through to `f` can be used, giving 16 possible values. If you want to find out more about hex `colors`, visit `http://www.color-hex.com/color-wheel/`. If you are intrigued about number bases, such as hexadecimal (base 16), binary (base 2), and others, then look at this article, which explains them and discusses why humans typically use base 10: `https://betterexplained.com/articles/numbers-and-bases/`.

We will see where these names are referred to later.

The strings.xml file

Most modern apps are made for as wide an audience as possible. Furthermore, if the app is of significant size or complexity, then the roles in the software company are often divided up into many different teams. For example, the person writing the Kotlin code for an Android app very possibly had little to do with designing the layout of the UI.

By separating the content of the app from the programming of the app, it is easier to make changes at any time, and it is also possible to create content for multiple different languages without altering the Kotlin code for each.

Take a look at the following contents of the `strings.xml` file:

```
<resources>
    <string name="app_name">Empty Activity App</string>
</resources>
```

You can see that, within the now familiar `<resources>...</resources>` tags, there is a `<string>...</string>` tag. Within the `string` tag, there is an attribute called `name` with an `app_name` value and then a further value of `Empty Activity App`.

Let's look at one more line from the `AndroidManifest.xml` file that we explored earlier in *The manifests folder* section. The line in question is displayed in the following code, but refer to the file itself in Android Studio if you want to see the line in its full context:

```
android:label="@string/app_name"
```

The `android:label` attribute is being assigned a value of `@string/app_name`. In Android, `@string` refers to all the strings in the `strings.xml` file. In this specific app, the `string` attribute with the `app_name` label has the `Empty Activity App` value.

Therefore, the line of code in the `AndroidManifest.xml` file shown previously has the following effect on the screen when the app is running:

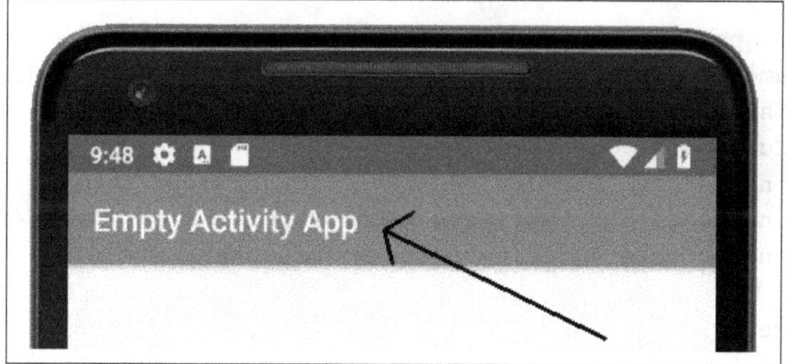

While this system might seem convoluted at first, in practice, it separates design and content from coding, which is very efficient to do. If the designers want to change the name of the app, they simply edit the `strings.xml` file. There is no need to interact with the Kotlin programmers, and, if all the text in an app is provided as string resources, then all of it can be easily altered and adapted as the project proceeds.

Android takes the flexibility further by allowing developers to use different files for string resources for each language and locale. This means that a developer can cater to a planet full of happy users with exactly the same Kotlin code. The Kotlin programmer just needs to refer to the `name` attribute of a string resource instead of **hardcoding** the text itself, and then the other departments can design the text content and handle tasks such as translation. We will make an app multilingual in *Chapter 18, Localization*.

It is possible to hardcode the actual text directly into the Kotlin code, instead of using string resources, and most of the time, we will do so for the sake of easily demonstrating some Kotlin code without getting bogged down with editing or adding to the `strings.xml` file.

We know enough about `strings.xml` to move on to the final file that we will explore for the Empty project template.

The styles.xml file

Here, you can see the pieces of the interconnectivity puzzle for this project template finally come together. Study the code in the `styles.xml` file and we can then discuss it:

```
<resources>
<!-- Base application theme. -->
<style name="AppTheme"
parent="Theme.AppCompat.Light.DarkActionBar">
    <!-- Customize your theme here. -->
    <item name="colorPrimary">@color/colorPrimary</item>
    <item name="colorPrimaryDark">@color/colorPrimaryDark</item>
    <item name="colorAccent">@color/colorAccent</item>
</style>
</resources>
```

This is yet another resource file, but it is referring to the `colors.xml` file that we saw earlier. Notice that there is a `style` tag, which is enclosing multiple `item` tags; each `item` tag has a name, such as `colorPrimary`, `colorPrimaryDark`, or `colorAccent`. Then, each of these names is assigned a value, such as `@color/colorPrimary`.

You are probably wondering what is going on; `@color` refers to the `colors.xml` file, and `colorPrimary`, `colorPrimaryDark`, and `colorAccent` refer to the actual colors defined with their hexadecimal values in that file. But why bother to create the colors and give them names, and then in another file define `item` instances and assign those colors to `item` instances? Why not just assign hexadecimal color values directly to each `item`?

Take a look at the top of the code block to understand the reason behind this apparently unnecessary convolutedness. I have shown the relevant lines of code again, so that we can discuss them more easily:

```
<style name="AppTheme"
parent="Theme.AppCompat.Light.DarkActionBar">
```

What is going on is that items have been defined and the items are contained within a `style` element. As you can see, the style is called `AppTheme`. Furthermore, the style has a parent called `Theme.AppCompat.Light.DarkActionBar`.

The system allows designers to choose a selection of colors and then define them in the `colors.xml` file. They can then further build up styles that use those colors in different combinations - there will often be more than one style per app. A style can further be associated with a theme (`parent = "..."`). This parent theme can be one completely designed by the styles and colors of the app designers, or it can be one of the default themes of Android, such as `Theme.AppCompat.Light.DarkActionBar`.

The UI designers can then simply refer to a style in the `AndroidManifest.xml` file, like in this line:

```
android:theme="@style/AppTheme"
```

UI designers can then happily tweak the colors and where they are used (items) without interfering with the Kotlin code. This also allows for different styles to be created for different regions of the world without any changes to the actual layout file (in this case, `activity_main.xml`).

For example, in Western culture, green can represent themes such as nature and correctness; and in many Middle Eastern countries, green represents fertility and is the color associated with Islam. While you might just get away with distributing green in both of these regions, your app will be perceived very differently.

If you then roll your app out in Indonesia, you will find that green is culturally despised among many (although not all) Indonesians. Next, if you launch in China, you will find that green has potential negative connotations to do with unfaithful spouses. It is a minefield that the typical programmer will never learn to navigate. And, fortunately, because of the way we can divide up responsibilities in Android Studio, they don't need to learn.

Therefore, colors, styles, and themes are very specialized topics. While we won't be exploring any more deeply than that quick foray into green, hopefully you can see the benefit of a system that separates responsibility for programming, layout, color, and textual content.

I thought it is also worth mentioning at this point that images can also be divided up into different locales so that users in different regions see different images within the same app. And, if you are wondering, yes, that will mean supplying different resolutions (such as `hdpi` and `xhdpi`, and so on) for each locale as well.

It is also worth mentioning that it is entirely possible to produce a fantastic app that is enjoyed by thousands or even millions of users without catering individually to every region. However, even if we are not going to employ teams of designers, translators, and cultural experts, we must still work within this system that was designed to enable them, and that is why we are going into such depth.

At this stage, we have a good grasp of what goes in an Android project and how it all links together. Let's now build one more app to see the differences that different app templates make to the underlying files that Android Studio generates.

The Basic Activity project

The next simplest project type with an autogenerated UI is the Basic Activity project. This is the same type of project that we created in *Chapter 1, Getting Started with Android and Kotlin*. Feel free to open that project up now, but it is recommended to generate a new one so that we can examine it without any of our alterations and additions clouding the discussions.

Let's create a Basic Activity project, as follows:

1. In Android Studio, select **File** | **New** | **New Project...**.
2. On the **Choose your project** screen, select the **Basic Activity** template and click on **Next**.
3. Change the **Name** field to `Basic Activity App`.
4. Choose the same package name and save the location as in the previous project.
5. Be sure to select **Kotlin** as the language.
6. Check the **Use AndroidX artifacts** checkbox as we did previously.
7. The rest of the settings can be left at their defaults, so just click on **Next**.

Now we can dig into the files. We won't look at everything in the same detail that we did for the Empty Activity project; we will just look at the differences and extra bits.

Exploring the Basic Activity project

Let's compare the Kotlin code first. Take a look at the `MainActivity.kt` tab in the code editor. They both contain a class called `MainActivity`. The difference is in the number of functions and the content of the `onCreate` function.

As already stated, the Basic Activity project has more to it than the Empty Activity project.

You can open as many instances of Android Studio as you like. If you want to compare projects side by side, select **File** | **Open** and choose the project, then when prompted, select **New Window** to open the project without closing any that are already open.

The first difference is that there is some extra code in the `onCreate` function.

The MainActivity.kt file

I mentioned very briefly, back in *Chapter 2, Kotlin, XML, and the UI Designer*, the interconnections that exist in the Kotlin code and the XML code. Let's look through the resources files and point out the XML files that this Kotlin code points to.

Here is the relevant Kotlin code from the `onCreate` function; I have slightly reformatted it to make it more readable in a book:

```
setSupportActionBar(toolbar)

fab.setOnClickListener { view ->
   Snackbar.make(view, "Replace with your own action",
               Snackbar.LENGTH_LONG)
               .setAction("Action", null).show()
}
```

Understanding this code fully will take quite a few more chapters, but to point out where this code uses files in the resources will only take a moment, and will then leave us even more aware of the components that make up our projects.

The code refers to two more resources compared to the Empty Activity project. The first is `toolbar`, the second is `fab`, and both refer to an XML file that we will see next.

If you open the `res/layout` folder in the project window, you can see that things look slightly differently to how they did in the Empty Activity project:

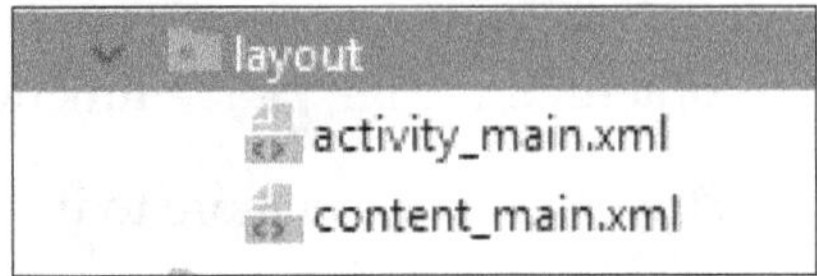

There are now two files that were autogenerated. We will explore the `content_main.xml` file and gain an understanding of why it is required shortly.

The activity_main.xml file

For now, open up the `activity_main.xml` file and you will see there are some elements to represent both `toolbar` and `fab`. By referring to these elements, the Kotlin code is setting up the toolbar and the floating action bar ready for use. The XML code, as we have come to expect, describes what they look like.

Here is the XML code for the toolbar:

```
<androidx.appcompat.widget.Toolbar
    android:id="@+id/toolbar"
    android:layout_width="match_parent"
    android:layout_height="?attr/actionBarSize"
    android:background="?attr/colorPrimary"
    app:popupTheme="@style/AppTheme.PopupOverlay" />
```

Notice that it refers to a `Toolbar`, a color, and a style, as well as some others. It is the line that starts with `android:id...`, which declares a widget of type `Toolbar` and its `@+id/toolbar` value, which makes it accessible via the `toolbar` instance name in the Kotlin code.

For clarity, this is the toolbar in the actual working app:

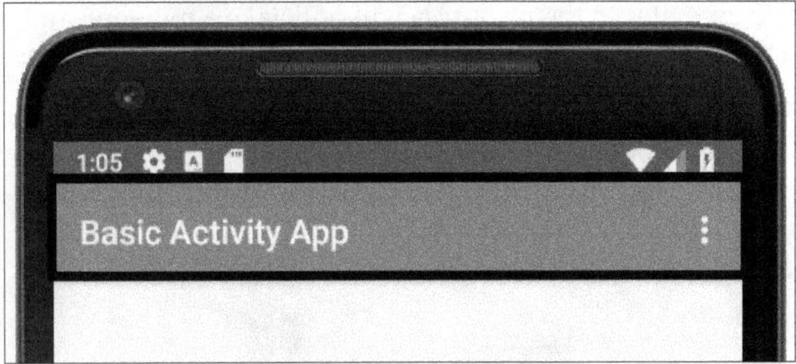

Here is the XML code for the floating action button. I have slightly reformatted the first line of the code onto two lines:

```
<com.google.android.material.floatingactionbutton.
        FloatingActionButton

    android:id="@+id/fab"
    android:layout_width="wrap_content"
    android:layout_height="wrap_content"
    android:layout_gravity="bottom|end"
    android:layout_margin="@dimen/fab_margin"
    app:srcCompat="@android:drawable/ic_dialog_email" />
```

Notice that it has an `id` attribute of `fab`. It is through this `id` attribute that we gain access to the floating action button in our Kotlin code.

Now, `fab` in our Kotlin code can directly control the floating action button and all its attributes. In *Chapter 13, Bringing Android Widgets to Life*, we will learn how to do this in detail.

Here is the floating action button in the actual app:

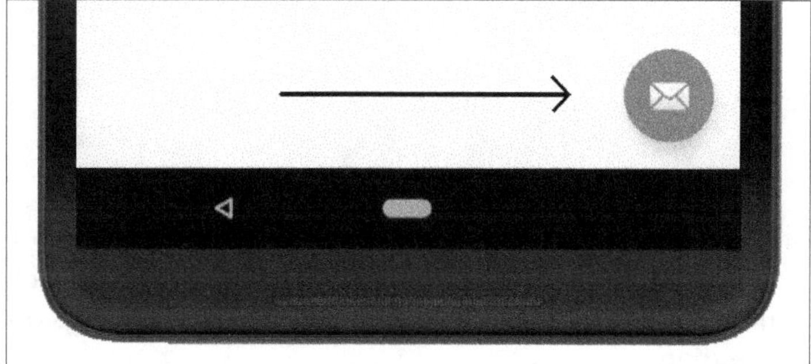

It is evident that I haven't explained the code in detail; there is no point at this stage. Instead, make a mental note of the interconnections, as follows:

- XML files can refer to other XML files.
- Kotlin can refer to XML files (and, as we will see soon, other Kotlin files).
- In Kotlin, we can grab control of a specific part of the UI in an XML file via its `id` attribute.

We have seen enough from this file; let's move on and dip into the remaining files.

The extra functions in MainActivity.kt

So, what do the functions do, when are they called, and who exactly calls them?

The next difference is this extra function, as follows:

```
override fun onCreateOptionsMenu(menu: Menu): Boolean {
  // Inflate the menu; this adds items to
  // the action bar if it is present.
  menuInflater.inflate(R.menu.menu_main, menu)
  return true
}
```

This code prepares (inflates) the menu that is defined in the `menu_main.xml` file. And, just as with `onCreate`, the function is overridden and it is called by the operating system directly.

Then there is yet another function, as follows:

```
override fun onOptionsItemSelected(item: MenuItem): Boolean {
  // Handle action bar item clicks here. The action bar will
  // automatically handle clicks on the Home/Up button, so long
  // as you specify a parent activity in AndroidManifest.xml.
  return when (item.itemId) {
        R.id.action_settings -> true
        else -> super.onOptionsItemSelected(item)
  }
}
```

This function is also overridden and is called directly by the operating system. It handles what happens `when` an item (or option) from the menu is selected by the user. At the moment, it handles just one option, which is the settings option, and it currently takes no action.

The preceding code determines whether the settings menu option was clicked on; if it was, then the `return` when code executes, and control is returned to whatever part of the app was executing before it was interrupted by the user clicking on the **Settings** menu option. We will learn more about the Kotlin `when` keyword in *Chapter 8, Kotlin Decisions and Loops*.

We nearly know enough for now; don't worry about memorizing all these connections. We will be coming back to each connection, investigating more deeply, and cementing our understanding of each.

So, why do we need that second file in the `res/layout` folder?

The content_main.xml file

The `MainActivity.kt` file calls `setContentView` on `R.layout.activity_main`. Then, in turn, `activity_main` has this line of code highlighted:

```
...
</com.google.android.material.appbar.AppBarLayout>

<include layout="@layout/content_main" />

<com.google.android.material.floatingactionbutton
  .FloatingActionButton
...
```

The highlighted line of code does `include` the `content_main` file. So, just after the app bar is added to the layout, the execution branches to `content_main`, where all its XML code is turned into the UI; then, the execution goes back to `activity_main` and the floating action bar is added to the layout. We will use `include` in *Chapter 5, Beautiful Layouts with CardView and ScrollView*, when we build some neat scrolling `CardView` layouts and separate the code that defines `CardView` from the actual contents of `CardView`.

Exploring the Android emulator

As we progress, it helps to be familiar with exactly how to use the Android emulator. If you haven't used the latest version of Android, some of the ways to achieve even simple tasks (such as viewing all the apps) can be different to how your current device works. In addition, we want to know how to use the extra controls that come with all emulators.

The emulator control panel

You probably noticed the mini control panel that appears beside the emulator when you run it. Let's go through some of the most useful controls. Take a look at this screenshot of the emulator control panel. I have annotated it to aid the discussion:

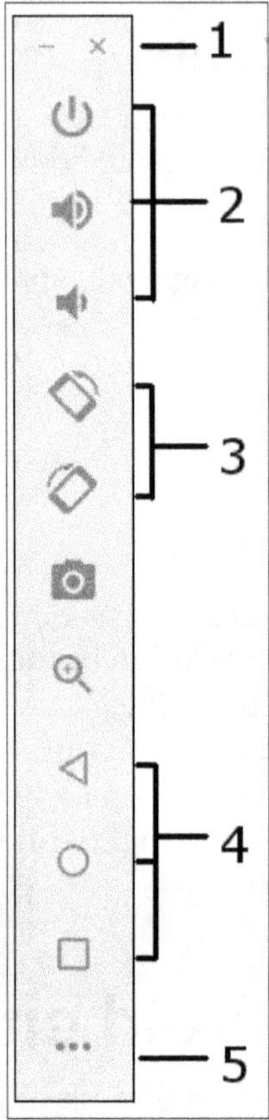

I will just mention the more obvious controls and go into a bit more depth when necessary:

1. These are the window controls. They minimize or close the emulator window.

2. From top to bottom, the first button is used to power-off the emulator, to simulate powering off the actual device. The next two icons raise and lower the volume.
3. These two buttons allow you to rotate the emulator both left and right. This means that you can test what your app looks like in all orientations, as well as how it handles orientation changes while the app is running. The icons immediately underneath these take a screenshot and zoom in, respectively. Here is the emulator after being rotated horizontally:

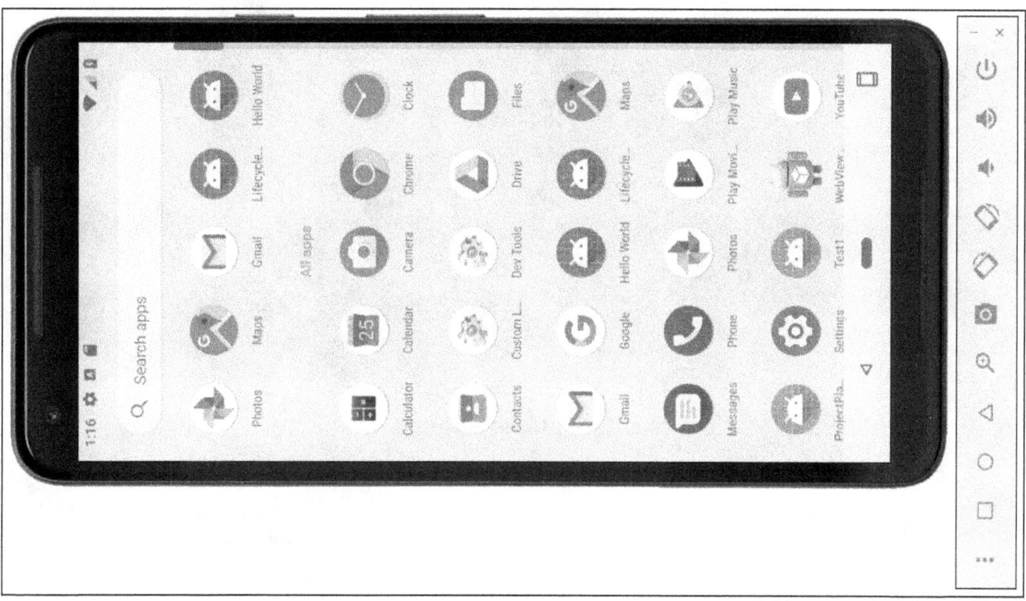

4. These icons simulate the back button, home button, and view running apps button. Have a play with these buttons - we will need to use them from time to time, including in *Chapter 6, The Android Lifecycle*.

5. Press the button labelled **5** in the annotated image to launch the advanced settings menu, where you can interact with things such as sensors, GPS, the battery, and the fingerprint reader. Have a play around with some of these settings if you are curious:

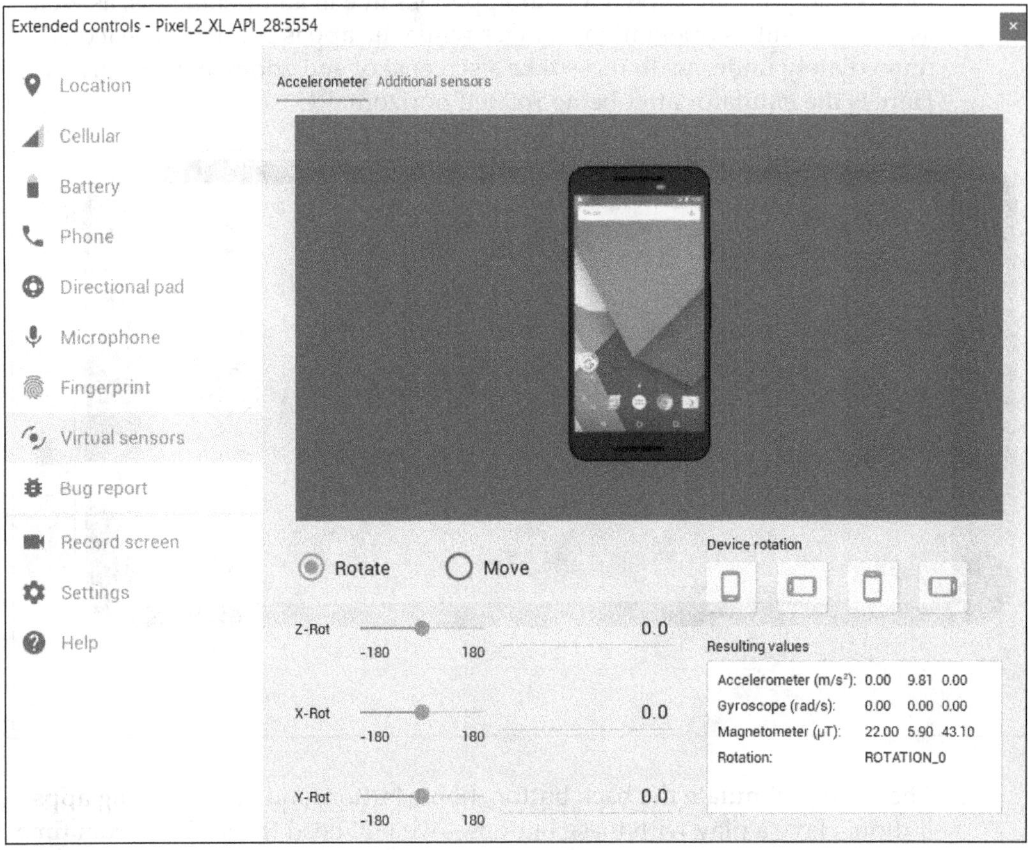

Let's play around with the emulator itself.

Using the emulator as a real device

The emulator can emulate every feature of a real phone, so it is possible to write a whole book on it alone. If you want to write apps that your users love, then understanding a whole range of Android devices is well worth taking the time to do. I just want to point out a few of the most basic features here, because without these basic interactions, it will be hard to follow along with the book. Furthermore, if you have an old Android device, then some essential basics (such as accessing the app drawer) have changed and you might be left a little baffled.

Accessing the app drawer

Hold the mouse cursor on the bottom of the home screen and drag upward to access the app drawer (with all the apps); the following screenshot shows this action halfway through:

Now you can run any app installed on the emulator. Note that when you run one of your apps through Android Studio, it remains installed on the emulator and, therefore, is runnable from the app drawer. However, every change you make to the app in Android Studio will require you to run or install the app again by clicking on the play button on the Android Studio quick launch bar, as we have been doing.

Viewing active apps and switching between apps

To view active apps, you can use the emulator control panel, that is, the square labelled as number **4** on the screenshot of the emulator control panel. To access the same option using the phone screen (as you will have to do on a real device), swipe up, just as with accessing the app drawer, but do so only for about one quarter of the length of the screen, as shown in following screenshot:

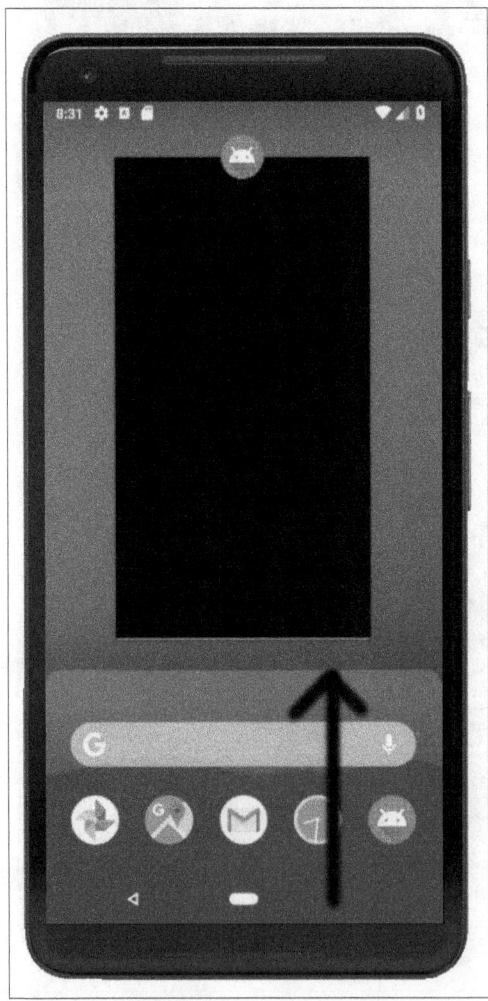

You can now swipe left and right through the recent apps, swipe an app up to close it, or tap the back button to return to what you were doing before you viewed this option. Do try this out, as we will use these basic features quite often in this book.

Summary

Remember that the goal of this chapter was to familiarize ourselves with the system and structure of Android and an Android project. Android projects are an elaborate interweaving of Kotlin and a multitude of resource files. Resource files can contain XML to describe our layouts, textual content, styles, and colors, as well as images. Resources can be produced to target different languages and regions of the world. Other resource types that we will see and use throughout the book include themes and sound effects.

It is not important to remember all the different ways in which the different resource files and Kotlin files are interconnected. It is only important to realize that they *are* interconnected, and also be able to examine files of various types and realize when they are dependent on code in another file. Whenever we create connections from our Kotlin code to the XML code, I will always point out the details of the connection again.

We do not need to learn XML in addition to Kotlin, but we will become a little bit familiar with it over the next 25 chapters. Kotlin will be the focus of this book, but our Kotlin code will frequently refer to the XML code, so understanding and having seen some examples of the interconnections will put you in good stead to make quicker progress.

We have also explored the emulator to get the most out of it when testing our apps.

In the next chapter, we will build three custom layouts using three different Android layout schemes. We will also write some Kotlin code so that we can switch between them with the tap of a button.

4

Getting Started with Layouts and Material Design

We have already seen the Android Studio UI designer, as well as a little bit more of Kotlin in action. In this hands-on chapter, we will build three more layouts - still quite simple, yet a step up from what we have done so far.

Before we get to the hands-on part, we will have a quick introduction to the concept of **Material Design**.

We will look at another type of layout, called `LinearLayout`, and walk through it, using it to create a usable UI. We will take things a step further using `ConstraintLayout`, both to understand constraints and to design more complex and precise UI designs. Finally, we will meet the `TableLayout` to lay data out in an easily readable table.

We will also write some Kotlin code to switch between our different layouts within one app/project. This is the first major app that links together multiple topics into one neat parcel. The app is called Exploring Layouts.

In this chapter, we will cover the following topics:

- Material Design
- Building a `LinearLayout` and learning when it is best to use this type
- Building another, slightly more advanced, `ConstraintLayout` and finding out a bit more about using constraints
- Building a `TableLayout` and filling it with data to display
- Linking everything together in a single app called Exploring Layouts

First on the list is material design.

Material design

You might have heard of material design, but what exactly is it? The objective of material design is, quite simply, to achieve beautiful user interfaces. It is also, however, about making these user interfaces consistent across Android devices. Material design is not a new idea. It is taken straight from the design principles used in pen-and-paper design, like having visually pleasing embellishments such as shadows and depth.

Material design uses the concept of layers of materials that you can think of in the same way you would think of layers in a photo-editing app. Consistency is achieved with a set of principles, rules, and guidelines. It must be stressed that material design is entirely optional, but it also must be stressed that material design works, and, if you are not following it, there is a good chance your design will be disliked by the user. The user, after all, has become used to a certain type of UI, and that UI was most likely created using material design principles.

So, material design is a sensible standard to strive for, but while we are learning the details of material design, we mustn't let it hold us back from learning how to get started with Android.

This book will focus on getting things done, while occasionally pointing out when material design is influencing how we do it, as well as pointing you to further resources for those who want to look at material design in more depth right away.

Exploring Android UI design

We will see with Android UI design that so much of what we learn is context-sensitive. The way that a given widget's x attribute will influence its appearance might depend on a widget's y attribute, or even on an attribute on another widget. It isn't easy to learn this verbatim. It is best to expect to gradually achieve better and faster results with practice.

For example, if you play with the designer by dragging and dropping widgets onto the design, the XML code that is generated will vary considerably depending upon which layout type you are using. We will see this as we proceed through this chapter.

This is because different layout types use different means to decide the position of their children. For example, the `LinearLayout`, which we will explore next, works very differently to `ConstraintLayout`, which was added by default to our project in *Chapter 1, Getting Started with Android and Kotlin.*

This information might initially seem like a problem, or even a bad idea, and it certainly can be a little awkward. What we will begin to learn, however, is that this clear abundance of layout options and their individual quirks are a good thing, because they give us almost unlimited design potential. There are very few layouts you can imagine that are not possible to achieve.

As implied, however, this almost unlimited potential comes with a bit of complexity. The best way to start to get to grips with this is to build some working examples of several types. In this chapter, we will see three – a `LinearLayout`, a `ConstraintLayout`, and a `TableLayout`. We will see how to make things easier using the distinctive features of the visual designer, and we will also pay some attention to the XML that is auto-generated to make our understanding more rounded.

Layouts

We have already seen `ConstraintLayout`, but there are more. Layouts are the building blocks that group together the other UI elements/widgets. Layouts can, and often do, contain other layouts themselves.

Let's look at some commonly used layouts in Android, because knowing the different layouts and their pros and cons will make us more aware of what can be achieved, and therefore will expand our horizons of what is possible.

We have already seen that, once we have designed a layout, we can put it into action using the `setContentView` function in our Kotlin code.

Let's build three designs with different layout types and then put `setContentView` to work and switch between them.

Creating the Exploring Layouts project

One of the toughest things in Android is not just finding out how to do something, but finding out how to do something amongst other things. That is why, throughout this book, as well as showing you how to do some neat stuff, we will link lots of topics together into apps that span multiple topics and often chapters. The **Exploring Layouts** project is the first app of this type. We will learn how to build multiple types of layout while linking them all together in one handy app:

1. Create a new project in Android Studio. If you already have a project open, select **File | New Project**. When prompted, choose **Open in same window**, as we do not need to refer to our previous project.

If you are on the start screen of Android Studio, you can create a new project simply by clicking the **Start a new Android Studio project** option.

2. Select the **Empty Activity** project template, as we will build most of the UI from scratch. Click the **Next** button.
3. Enter `Exploring Layouts` for the name of the project.
4. All the rest of the settings are the same as we have used for the previous three projects.
5. Click the **Finish** button.

Look at the `MainActivity.kt` file. Here is the entirety of the code, excluding the `import...` statements:

```
class MainActivity : AppCompatActivity() {

    override fun onCreate(savedInstanceState: Bundle?) {
        super.onCreate(savedInstanceState)
        setContentView(R.layout.activity_main)
    }
}
```

Locate the call to `setContentView` and delete the entire line. The line is shown highlighted in the previous code.

This is just what we want, because now we can build our very own layouts, explore the underlying XML, and write our own Kotlin code to display these layouts. If you run the app now, you will just get a blank screen with a title; not even a Hello World! message.

The first type of layout we will explore is the `LinearLayout`.

Building a menu with LinearLayout

`LinearLayout` is probably the simplest layout that Android offers. As the name suggests, all the UI items within it are laid out linearly. You have just two choices - vertical and horizontal. By adding the following line of code (or editing via the Attribute window), you can configure a `LinearLayout` to lay things out vertically:

```
android:orientation="vertical"
```

You can then (as you could probably have guessed) change `"vertical"` to `"horizontal"` to lay things out horizontally.

Before we can do anything with `LinearLayout`, we need to add one to a layout file. And, as we are building three layouts in this project, we also need a new layout file.

Adding a LinearLayout to the project

In the project window, expand the `res` folder. Now right-click the `layout` folder and select **New**. Notice that there is an option for **Layout resource file,** as shown in the following screenshot:

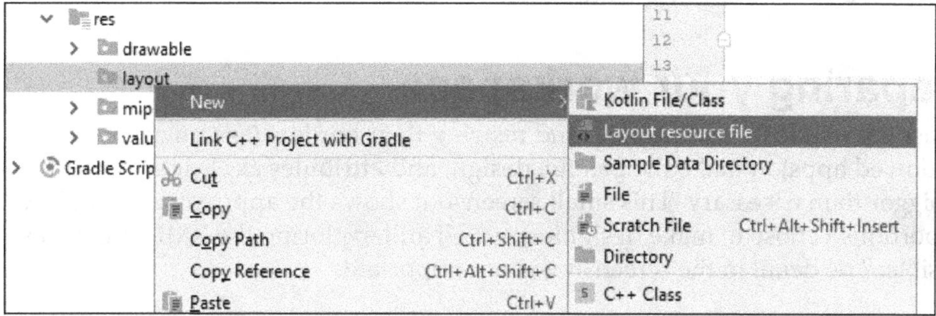

Select **Layout resource file** and you will see the **New Resource File** dialog window:

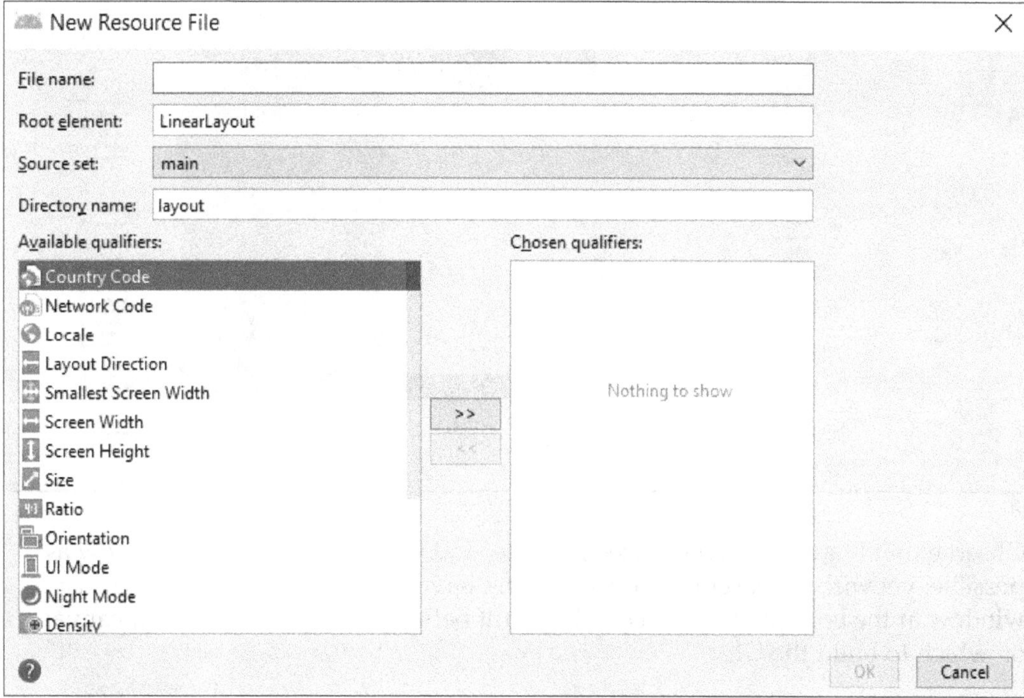

In the **File name** field, enter `main_menu`. The name is arbitrary, but this layout is going to be our "main" menu that is used to select the other layouts, so the name seems appropriate.

Notice that it has already selected **LinearLayout** as the **Root element** option.

Click the **OK** button, and Android Studio will generate a new `LinearLayout` in an XML file called `main_menu` and place it in the `layout` folder ready for us to build our new main menu UI. Android Studio will also open the UI designer with the palette on the left and the attributes window on the right.

Preparing your workspace

Adjust the windows by dragging and resizing their borders (as you can in most windowed apps) to make the palette, design, and attributes as clear as possible, but no bigger than necessary. This small screenshot shows the approximate window proportions I chose to make designing our UI and exploring the XML as clear as possible. The detail in the screenshot is not important:

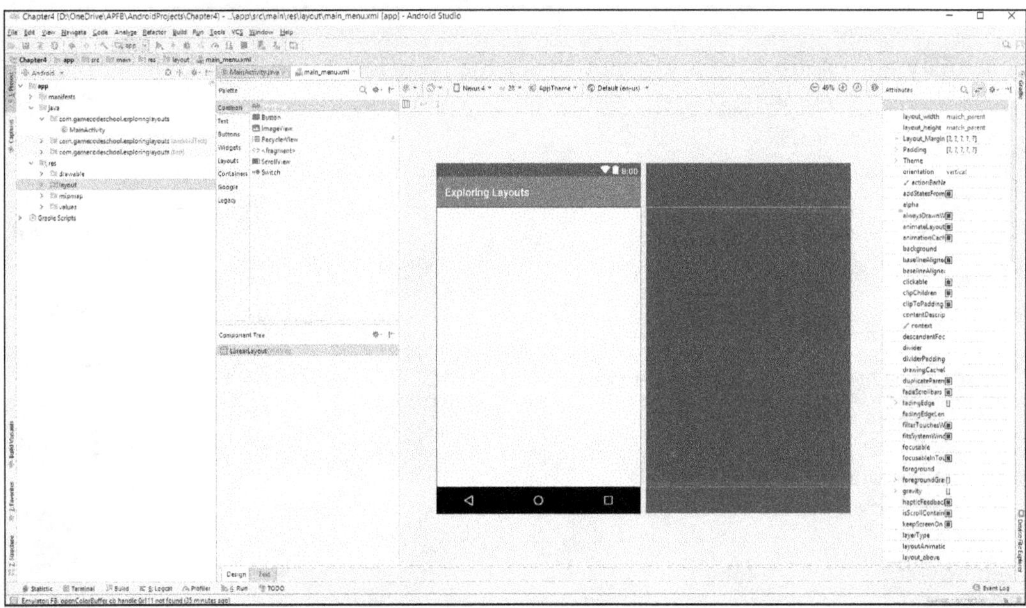

Observe that I have made the project, palette, and attribute windows as narrow as possible, yet without obscuring any content. I have also closed the build/logcat window at the bottom of the screen, the result being that I have a nice clear canvas on which to build the UI.

Examining the generated XML

Click on the **Text** tab and we will have a look at the current state of the XML code that forms our design at this stage. Here is the code so that we can discuss this further:

```
<?xml version="1.0" encoding="utf-8"?>
<LinearLayout
   xmlns:android="http://schemas.android.com/apk/res/android"

      android:orientation="vertical"
      android:layout_width="match_parent"
      android:layout_height="match_parent">

</LinearLayout>
```

We have the usual starting and closing tags and, as we could have predicted, they are `<LinearLayout` and `</LinearLayout>`. There is no child element yet, but there are three attributes. We know they are attributes, and not children, of the `LinearLayout`, because they appear before the first closing `>`. The three attributes that define this `LinearLayout` have been highlighted in the previous code for clarity.

The first attribute is `android:orientation`, or, more succinctly, we will just refer to the attributes without the `android:` part. The `orientation` attribute has a value of `vertical`. This means that, when we start to add items to this layout, it will arrange them vertically from top to bottom. We could change the value from `vertical` to `horizontal` and it would lay things out from left to right.

The next two attributes are `layout_width` and `layout_height`. These determine the size of the `LinearLayout`. The value given to both attributes is `match_parent`. The parent of a layout is the entire available space. By matching the parent horizontally and vertically, therefore, the layout will fill the entire space available.

Adding a TextView to the UI

Switch back to the **Design** tab and we will add some elements to the UI.

First, find the **TextView** in the palette. This can be found in both the **Common** and **Text** categories. Left-click and drag the **TextView** onto the UI, and notice that it sits neatly at the top of the `LinearLayout`.

Look at the XML on the **Text** tab and confirm that it is a child of the `LinearLayout` and that it is indented by one tab to make this clear. Here is the code for the `TextView` without the surrounding code for the `LinearLayout`:

```
<TextView
    android:id="@+id/textView"
    android:layout_width="match_parent"
    android:layout_height="wrap_content"
    android:text="TextView" />
```

Notice that it has four attributes: `id`, in case we need to refer to it from another UI element or from our Kotlin code; `layout_width` is set to `match_parent`, which means the that `TextView` stretches across the whole width of the `LinearLayout`; a `layout_height` attribute is set to `wrap_content`, which means the that `TextView` is precisely tall enough to contain the text within it; and finally, for now, it has a `text` element that determines the actual text it will display, and this is currently just set to `TextView`.

Switch back to the design tab and we will make some changes.

We want this text to be the heading text of this screen, which is the main menu screen. In the attributes window, click the search icon, type `text` into the search box, and change the **text** attribute to `Menu`, as shown in the following screenshot:

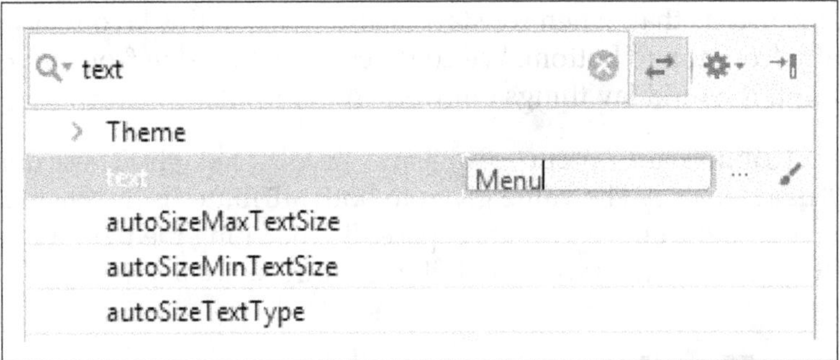

You can find any attribute by searching or just by scrolling through the options. When you have found the attribute you want to edit, left-click it to select it and then press the *Enter* key on the keyboard to make it editable.

Next, find the `textSize` attribute using your preferred search technique and set `textSize` to `50sp`. When you have entered this new value, the text size will increase.

The `sp` stands for scalable pixels. This means that when the user changes the font size settings on their Android device, the font will dynamically rescale itself.

Now, search for the **gravity** attribute and expand the options by clicking the little arrow indicated in the following screenshot:

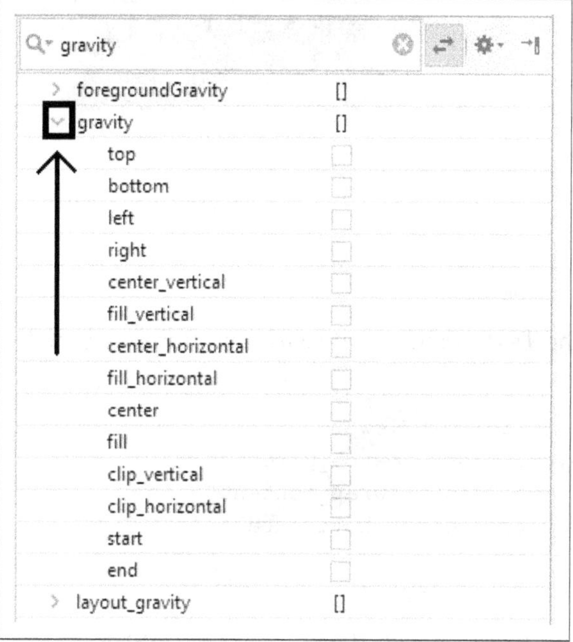

Set **gravity** to **center_horizontal,** as shown in the following screenshot:

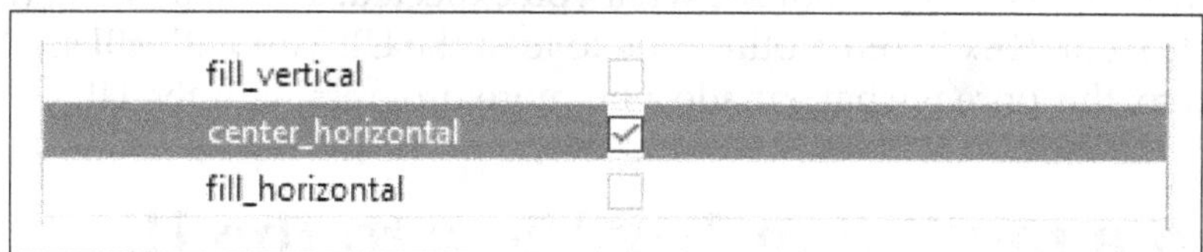

The `gravity` attribute refers to the gravity within the `TextView` itself, and our change has the effect of moving the actual text inside the `TextView` to the center.

Note that `gravity` is different to `layout_gravity`. The `layout_gravity` property sets the gravity within the layout: in this case, the parent `LinearLayout`. We will use `layout_gravity` later in this project.

At this point, we have changed the text of the TextView, increased its size, and centered it horizontally. The UI designer should now look like the following diagram:

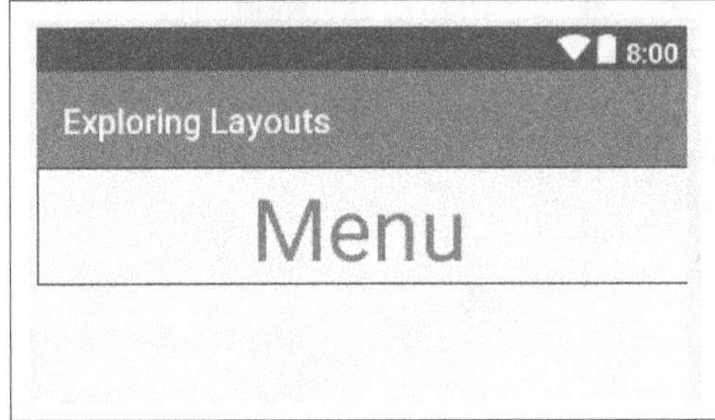

A quick glance at the **Text** tab to see the XML would reveal the following code:

```
<TextView
    android:id="@+id/textView"
    android:layout_width="match_parent"
    android:layout_height="wrap_content"
    android:gravity="center_horizontal"
    android:text="Menu"
    android:textSize="50sp" />
```

You can see the new attributes as follows: `gravity`, which is set to `center_horizontal`; text, which has changed to `Menu`; and `textSize`, which is set to `50sp`.

If you run the app, you might not see what you expected. This is because we haven't called `setContentView` in our Kotlin code to load the UI. You will still see the blank UI. We will fix this once we have made a bit more progress with the UI.

Adding a multi-line TextView to the UI

Switch back to **Design** tab, find the **Multiline Text** in the **Text** category of the palette, and drag it onto the design just below the `TextView` we added a moment ago.

Using your preferred search technique, set **text** to `Select a layout type to view an example. The onClick attribute of each button will call a function which executes setContentView to load the new layout.`

Your layout will now look like the following screenshot:

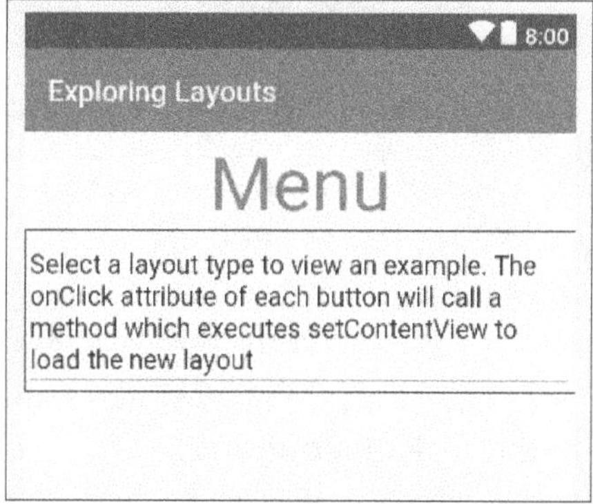

Your XML will be updated with another child in the `LinearLayout`, after the `TextView`, that looks like the following code:

```
<EditText
   android:id="@+id/editText"
   android:layout_width="match_parent"
   android:layout_height="wrap_content"
   android:ems="10"
   android:inputType="textMultiLine"
   android:text="Select a layout type to view an example.
         The onClick attribute of each button will call a function
         which executes setContentView to load the new layout" />
```

You can see the details of the UI item and it turns out that the description on the palette of **Multiline Text** was not entirely obvious as to exactly what this would be. A look at the XML reveals that we have an `inputType` attribute, indicating that this text is editable by the user. There is also another attribute that we haven't seen before, and that is `ems`. The `ems` attribute controls how many characters can be entered per line, and the value of `10` was chosen automatically by Android Studio. However, another attribute, `layout_width="match_parent"`, overrides this value because it causes the element to expand to fit its parent; in other words, to cover the whole width of the screen.

When you run the app (in the next section), you will see that the text is, indeed, editable - although, for the purposes of this demo app, it serves no practical purpose.

Wiring up the UI with the Kotlin code (part 1)

To achieve an interactive app, we will do the following three things:

1. We will call `setContentView` from the `onCreate` function to show the progress of our UI when we run the app.
2. We will write two more functions of our own and each one will call `setContentView` on a different layout (that we have yet to design).
3. Then, later in this chapter, when we design two more UI layouts, we will be able to load them at the click of a button.

As we will be building a `ConstraintLayout` and a `TableLayout`, we will call our new functions, `loadConstraintLayout` and `loadTableLayout`, respectively.

Let's do that now, and then we'll see how we can add some buttons that call these functions alongside some neatly formatted text.

Inside the `onCreate` function, add the following highlighted code:

```
override fun onCreate(savedInstanceState: Bundle?) {
   super.onCreate(savedInstanceState)

      setContentView(R.layout.main_menu)
}
```

The code uses the `setContentView` function to load the UI we are currently working on. You can now run the app to see the following results:

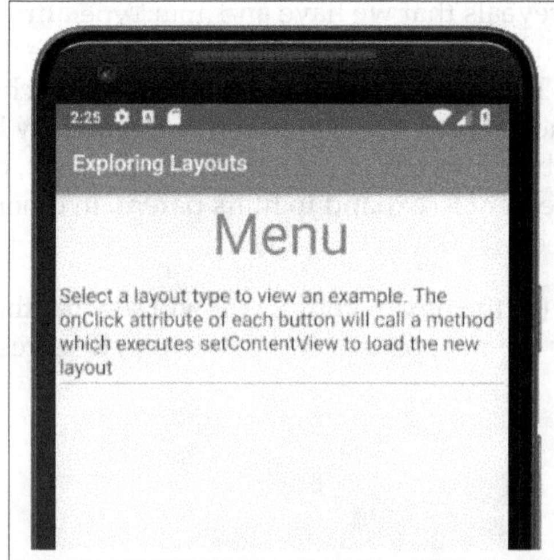

Add these two new functions inside the `MainActivity` class after the `onCreate` function:

```
fun loadConstraintLayout(v: View) {
  setContentView(R.layout.activity_main)
}

fun loadTableLayout(v: View) {
  setContentView(R.layout.my_table_layout)
}
```

There is one error with the first function and two with the second. The first we can fix by adding an `import` statement so that Android Studio is aware of the `View` class. Left-click the word `View` to select the error. Hold down the *Alt* key and then tap the *Enter* key. You will see the following popup:

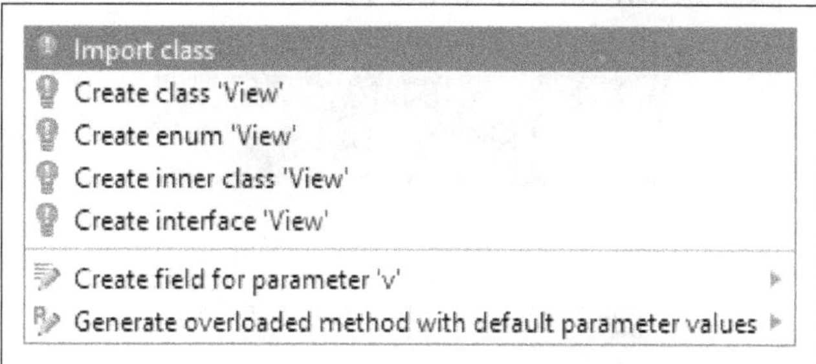

Chose **Import class**. The error is now gone. If you scroll to the top of the code, you will see that a new line of code has been added by that shortcut we just performed. Here is the new code:

```
import android.view.View
```

Android Studio no longer considers the `View` class an error.

The second function still has an error, however. The problem is that the function calls the `setContentView` function to load a new UI (`R.layout.my_table_layout`). As this UI layout does not exist yet, it produces an error. You can comment out this call to remove the error until we create the file and design the UI layout later this chapter. Add the double forward slash (//), as highlighted in the following code:

```
fun loadTableLayout(v: View) {
  //setContentView(R.layout.my_table_layout)
}
```

Now we can add some buttons that we can click to call our new functions and load the new layouts we will be building soon. But adding a couple of buttons with some text on is too easy - we have done that before. What we want to do is line up some text with a button to the right of it. The problem is that our `LinearLayout` has the `orientation` attribute set to `vertical` and, as we have seen, all the new parts we add to the layout will be lined up vertically.

Adding layouts within layouts

The solution to laying out some elements with a different orientation to others is to nest layouts within layouts. Here is how to do it.

From the **Layouts** category of the palette, drag a **LinearLayout (Horizontal)** onto the design, placing it just below the **Multiline Text**. Notice that there is a blue border occupying all the space below the **Multiline Text**:

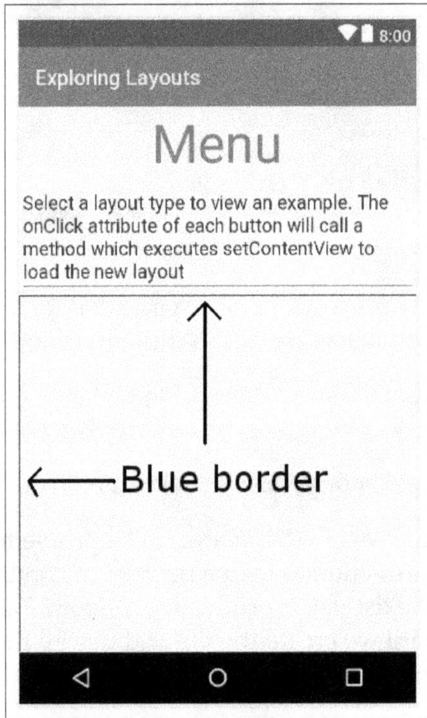

This indicates that our new **LinearLayout (Horizontal)** is filling the space. Keep this blue border area in mind, as it is where we will put the next item on our UI.

Now, go back to the **Text** category of the palette and drag a **TextView** onto the new `LinearLayout` we just added. Notice how the `TextView` sits snuggly in the top left-hand corner of the new `LinearLayout`:

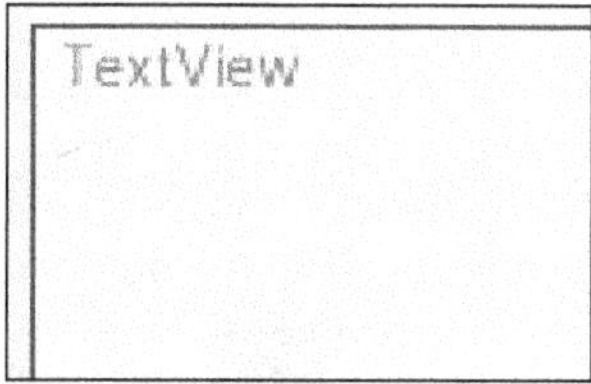

At first, this seems no different to what happened with the previous vertical `LinearLayout` that was part of our UI from the start. But watch what happens when we add our next piece of the UI.

> The term used to refer to adding layouts within layouts is **nesting**. The Android term applied to any item that appears on the UI (buttons and text, for example) is **view**, and anything that contains views is a **view group.** As the terms **view** and **view group** do not always make their meanings clear in certain contexts, I will usually refer to parts of the UI either specifically (such as `TextView`, `Button`, and `LinearLayout`) or more broadly (UI element, item, or widget).

From the **Button** category, drag a **Button** onto the right-hand side of the previous `TextView`. Notice that the button sits to the right of the text, as shown in the following screenshot:

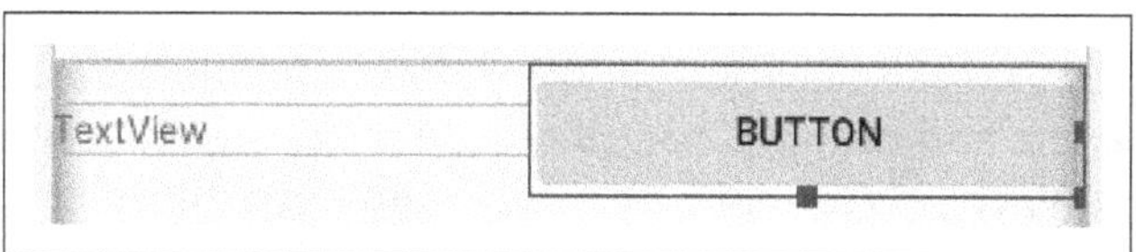

Next, select the `LinearLayout` (the horizontal one) by clicking on an empty part of it. Find the `layout_height` attribute and set it to `wrap_content`. Observe that the `LinearLayout` is now taking up only as much space as it needs:

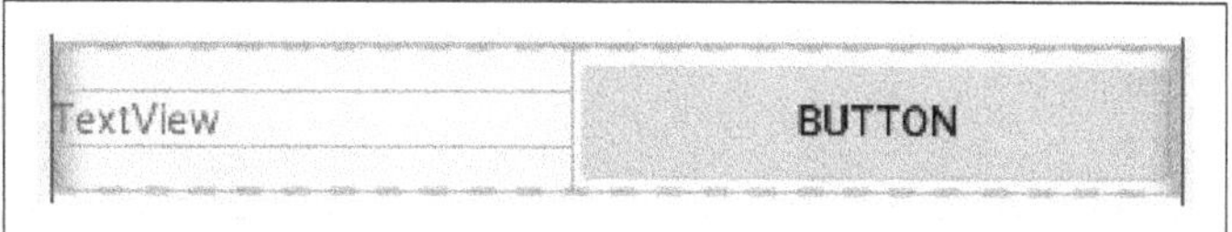

Let's configure the text attribute of the `TextView` and the `Button` before we add the next part of the UI. Change the `text` attribute of the `Button` to `LOAD`. Change the text attribute of our new `TextView` to `Load ConstraintLayout`.

Did you work out how to achieve the previous instruction for yourself? Yes? Excellent! You are now familiar with editing attributes of Android views. No? Left-click the item you want to edit (in this case, the `TextView`), search using the search icon or scroll to find the attribute you want to edit in the **Attributes** window (in this case, the `text` attribute), select the attribute, and press *Enter* to edit it. I can now give more succinct instructions on how to build future UI projects, and this makes your journey to becoming an Android ninja much quicker.

Now we can repeat ourselves and add another `TextView` and `Button` attribute within another **LinearLayout (Horizontal)** just below the one we have just finished. To do so, follow these steps in order:

1. Add another **LinearLayout (Horizontal)**, just below the previous one
2. Add a **TextView** to the new `LinearLayout`
3. Change the `text` attribute of the `TextView` to `Load TableLayout`
4. Add a `Button` on the right-hand side of the `TextView`
5. Change the `text` attribute of the `Button` to `LOAD`
6. Resize the `LinearLayout` by changing the `layout_height` attribute to `wrap_content`

Now we have two neatly (and horizontally) aligned texts and buttons.

Just for fun, and for the sake of exploring the palette a bit more, find the **Widgets** category of the palette and drag a **RatingBar** onto the design just below the final `LinearLayout`. Now, your UI should look very similar to this next screenshot:

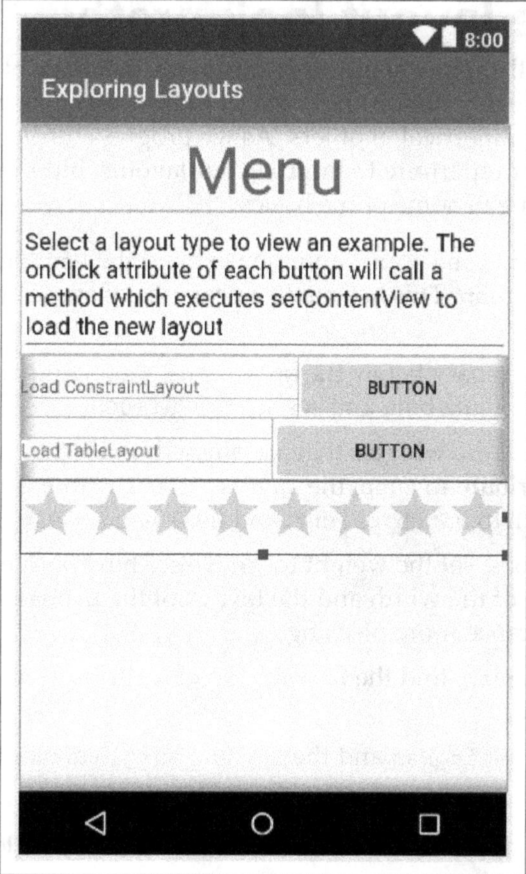

In the previous two screenshots, I hadn't yet changed the `text` attribute of the two `Button` elements. Everything else should be the same as yours.

Let's add some visual finishing touches to the layout.

Making the layout look pretty

In this section, we will explore some more attributes that control the finer details of our UI. You have probably noticed how the UI looks a bit squashed in some places, and wonky and unsymmetrical in others. As we progress through the book, we will continually add to our repertoire to improve our layouts, but these short steps will introduce and take care of some of the basics:

1. Select the `Multiline Text`, and then expand the `Padding` attribute. Set the `all` option to `15sp`. This has made a neat area of space around the outside of the text.
2. To make a nice space below the `Multiline text`, find and expand the `Layout_Margin` attribute and set `bottom` to `100sp`.
3. On both `TextView` widgets that are aligned/related to the buttons, set the `textSize` attribute to `20sp`, the `layout_gravity` to `center_vertical`, the `layout_width` to `match_parent`, and the `layout_weight` to `.7`.
4. On both buttons, set the weight to `.3`. Notice how both buttons now take up exactly `.3` of the width and the text `.7` of the `LinearLayout`, making the whole appearance more pleasing.
5. On the `RatingBar`, find the `Layout_Margin` attribute, and then set `left` and `right` to `15sp`.
6. Still with the `RatingBar` and the `Layout_Margin` attribute, change `top` to `75sp`.

You can now run the app and see our first full layout in all its glory:

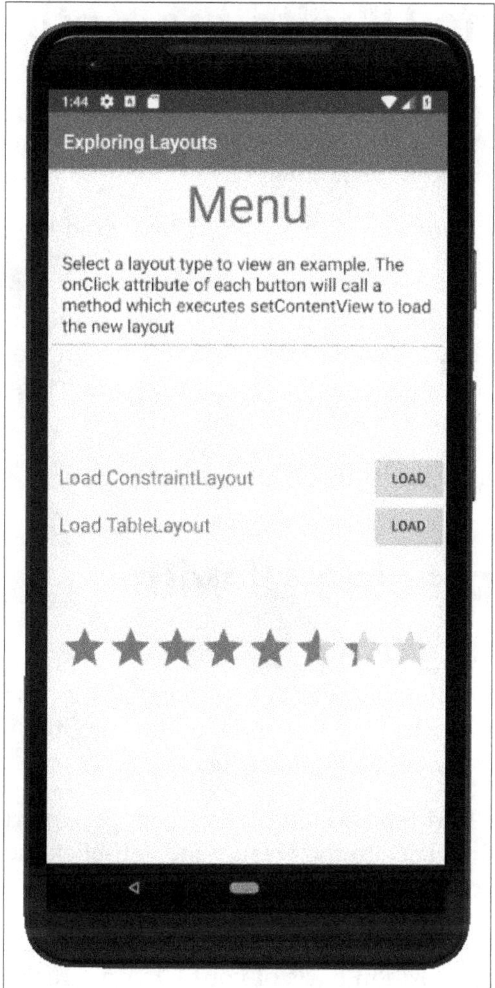

Notice that you can play with the `RatingBar`, although the rating won't persist when the app is turned off.

By way of a reader challenge, find an attribute or two that could further improve the appearance of the `LoadConstraintLayout` and `LoadTableLayout` text. They look a little bit close to the edges of the screen. Refer to the section Attributes – a quick summary at the start of *Chapter 5, Beautiful Layouts with CardView and ScrollView*.

Unfortunately, the buttons don't do anything yet. Let's fix that.

Wiring up the UI with the Kotlin code (part 2)

Select the button next to the `Load ConstraintLayout` text. Find the `onClick` attribute and set it to `loadConstraintLayout`.

Select the button next to the `Load TableLayout` text. Find the `onClick` attribute and set it to `loadTableLayout`.

Now, the buttons will call the functions, but the code inside the `loadTableLayout` function is commented out to avoid errors. Feel free to run the app and see that you can switch to the `ConstraintLayout` by clicking the `loadConstraintLayout` button. But all it has is a **Hello World** message.

We can now move on to building this `ConstraintLayout`.

Building a precise UI with ConstraintLayout

Open the `ConstraintLayout` that was auto-generated when we created the project. It is probably already in a tab at the top of the editor. If not, it will be in the `res/layout` folder. Its name is `activity_main.xml`.

Inspect the XML in the **Text** tab and note that it is empty, apart from a `TextView` that says `Hello World`. Switch back to the **Design** tab, left-click the `TextView` to select it, and tap the *Delete* key to get rid of it.

Now we can build ourselves a simple, yet intricate, UI. `ConstraintLayout` is very useful when you want to position parts of your UI very precisely and/or relative to the other parts.

Adding a CalenderView

To get started, look in the **Widgets** category of the palette and find the `CalenderView`. Drag and drop the `CalenderView` near the top and horizontally central. As you drag the `CalenderView` around, notice that it jumps/snaps to certain locations.

Also notice the subtle visual cues that show when the view is aligned. I have highlighted the horizontally central visual cue in the following screenshot:

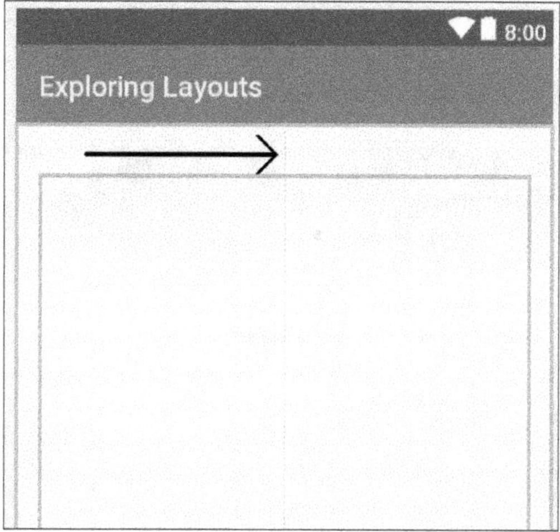

Let go when it is horizontally central, as it is in the screenshot. Now, we will resize it.

Resizing a view in a ConstraintLayout

Left-click and hold one of the corner squares that are revealed when you let go of the `CalenderView`, and drag inwards to decrease the size of the `CalenderView`:

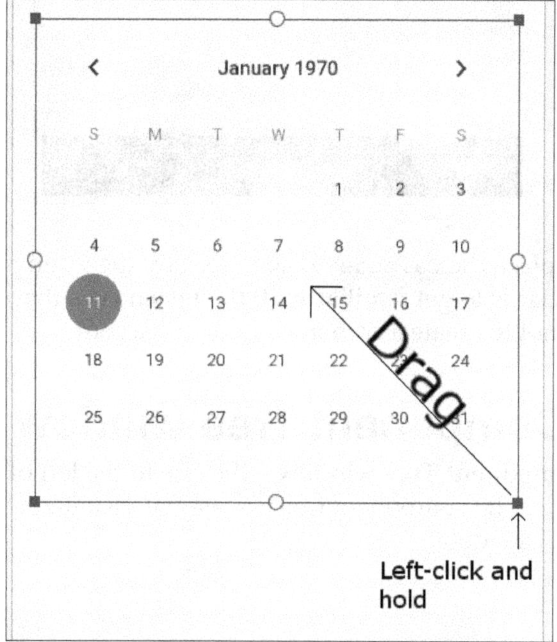

Reduce the size by about half and leave the `CalenderView` near the top, horizontally centered. You might need to reposition it a little after you have resized it, a bit like the following diagram:

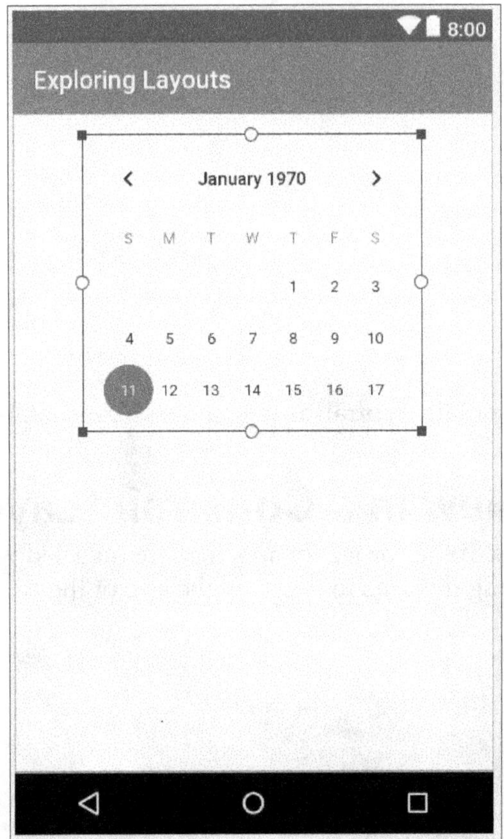

You do not need to place the `CalenderView` in exactly the same place as me. The purpose of the exercise is to get familiar with the visual cues that inform you where you have placed it, not to create a carbon copy of my layout.

Using the Component Tree window

Now look at the **Component Tree** window – the one to the left of the visual designer and below the palette. The component tree is a way of visualizing the layout of the XML, but without all the details.

In the following screenshot, we can see that the `CalenderView` is indented to the right of the `ConstraintLayout`, and is therefore a child. In the next UI we build, we will see that we sometimes need to take advantage of the **Component Tree** to build the UI.

For now, I just want you to observe that there is a warning sign by our `CalenderView`. I have highlighted it in the following screenshot:

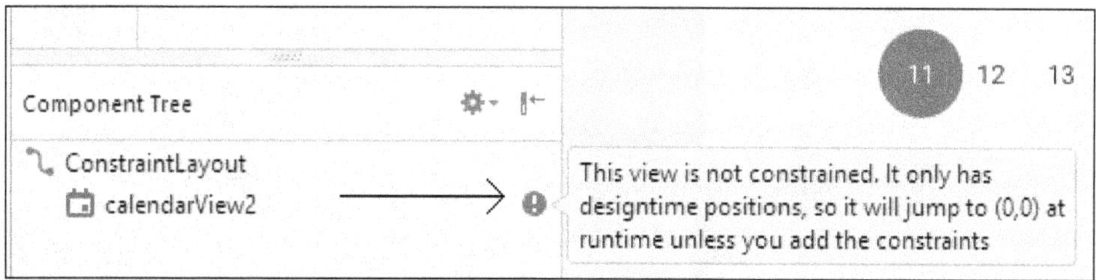

The error says **This view is not constrained. It only has designtime positions, so it will jump to (0,0) at runtime unless you add the constraints**. Remember when we first added buttons to the screen in *Chapter 2, Kotlin, XML, and the UI Designer*, that they simply disappeared off to the top-left corner?

Run the app now and click on the **Load ConstraintLayout** button if you want to be reminded of this problem.

Now, we could fix this by clicking the **Infer constraints** button that we used in *Chapter 2, Kotlin, XML, and the UI Designer*. Here it is again as a reminder:

But learning to add the constraints manually is worthwhile because it offers us more options and flexibility. And, as your layouts become more complex, there is always an item or two that doesn't behave as you want it to, and fixing it manually is nearly always necessary.

Adding constraints manually

Make sure that the `CalenderView` is selected and observe the four small circles at the top, bottom, left, and right:

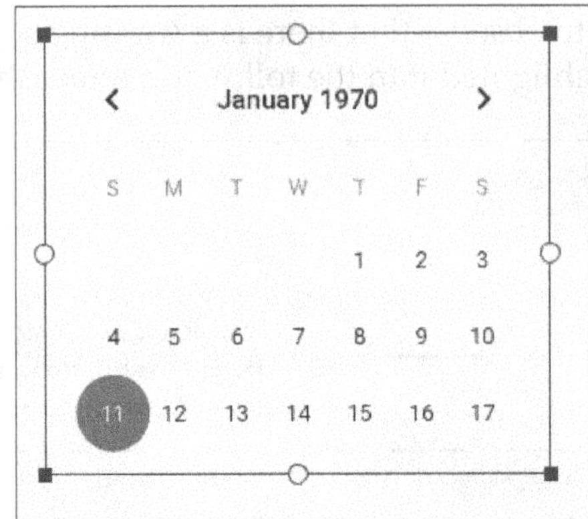

These are the constraint handles. We can click and drag them to anchor them with other parts of the UI or the sides of the screen. By anchoring the `CalenderView` with the four edges of the screen, we can lock it into position when the app is run.

One at a time, click and drag the top handle to the top of the design, the right to the right of the design, the bottom to the bottom of the design, and the left to the left of the design.

Observe that the `CalenderView` is now constrained in the center. Left-click and drag the `CalenderView` back to the upper part of the screen somewhere, as in the following diagram. Use the visual cues (also shown in the following screenshot) to make sure the `CalenderView` is horizontally centered:

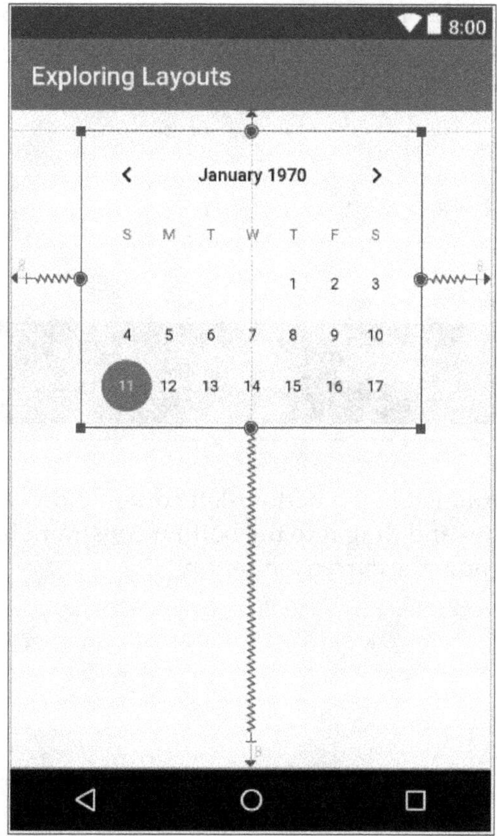

At this stage, you could run the app and the `CalenderView` would be positioned as shown in the preceding screenshot.

Let's add a couple more items to the UI and see how to constrain them.

Adding and constraining more UI elements

Drag an `ImageView` from the **Widgets** category of the palette and position it below and to the left of the `CalenderView`. When you place the `ImageView`, a pop-up window will prompt you to choose an image. Select **Project** | **ic_launcher,** and then click **OK**.

Constrain the left-hand side of the `ImageView` and the bottom of the `ImageView` to the left and bottom of the UI, respectively. Here is the position you should be in now:

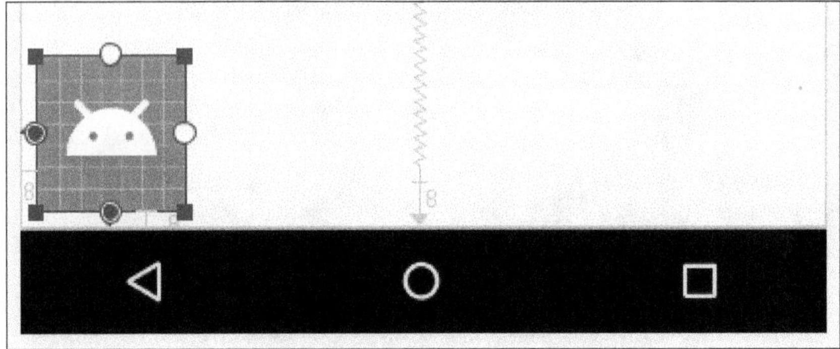

The `ImageView` is constrained in the bottom-left corner. Now, grab the top constraint handle on the `ImageView` and drag it to the bottom constraint handle of the `CalenderView`. This is now the current situation:

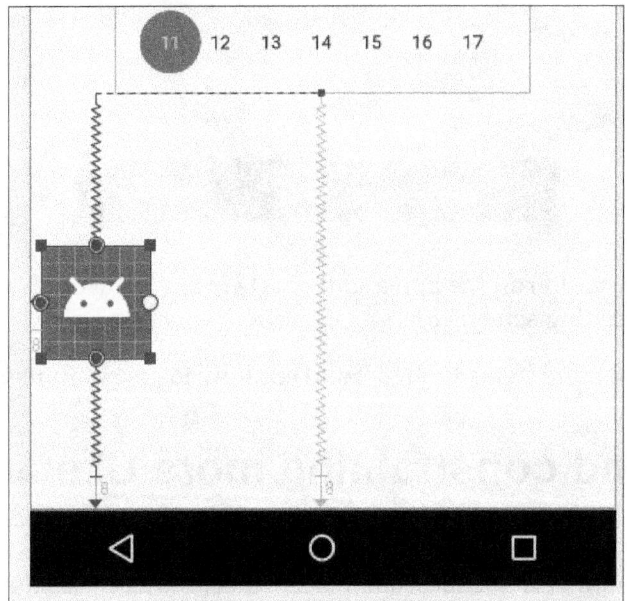

The `ImageView` is only constrained horizontally on one side, so is pinned/ constrained to the left. It is also constrained vertically and equally between the `CalenderView` and the bottom of the UI.

Next, add a `TextView` to the right of the `ImageView`. Constrain the right of the `TextView` to the right of the UI and constrain the left of the `TextView` to the right of the `ImageView`. Constrain the top of the `TextView` to the top of the `ImageView` and constrain the bottom of the `TextView` to the bottom of the UI. Now you will be left with something resembling the following diagram:

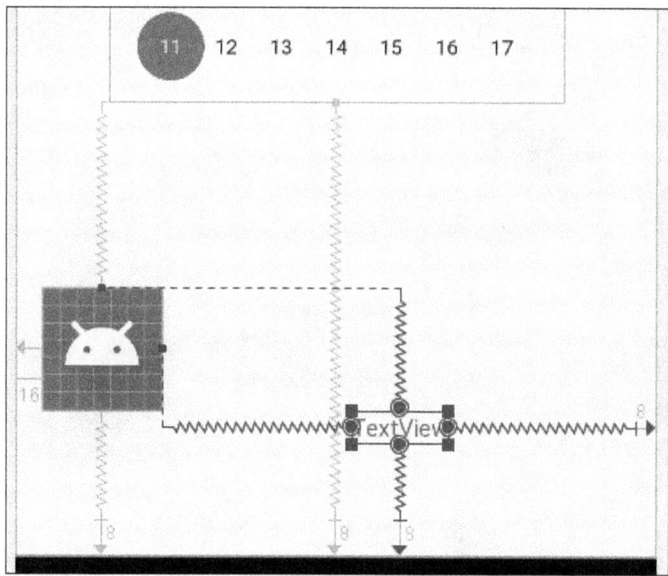

Notice that all the warnings in the **Component Tree** window about unconstrained items are gone.

> There are warnings about hardcoded strings because we are adding text directly to the layout instead of the `strings.xml` file and a warning about missing the **contentDescription** attribute. The **contentDescription** attribute should be used to add a textual description so that visually impaired users can get a spoken description of images in the app. For the sake of making rapid progress with the `ConstraintLayout`, we will ignore these two warnings. We will look at adding string resources correctly in *Chapter 18, Localization*, and you can read about accessibility features in Android Studio on the Android developer's website, at `https://developer.android.com/studio/intro/accessibility`.

You can move the three UI elements around and line them up neatly, just how you want them. Notice that when you move the `ImageView`, the `TextView` moves with it because the `TextView` is constrained to the `ImageView`. But also notice that you can move the `TextView` independently, and wherever you drop it, this represents its new constrained position relative to the `ImageView`. Whatever an item is constrained to, its position will always be relative to that item. And, as we have seen, the horizontal and vertical constraints are distinct from each other. I positioned mine as shown in the following diagram:

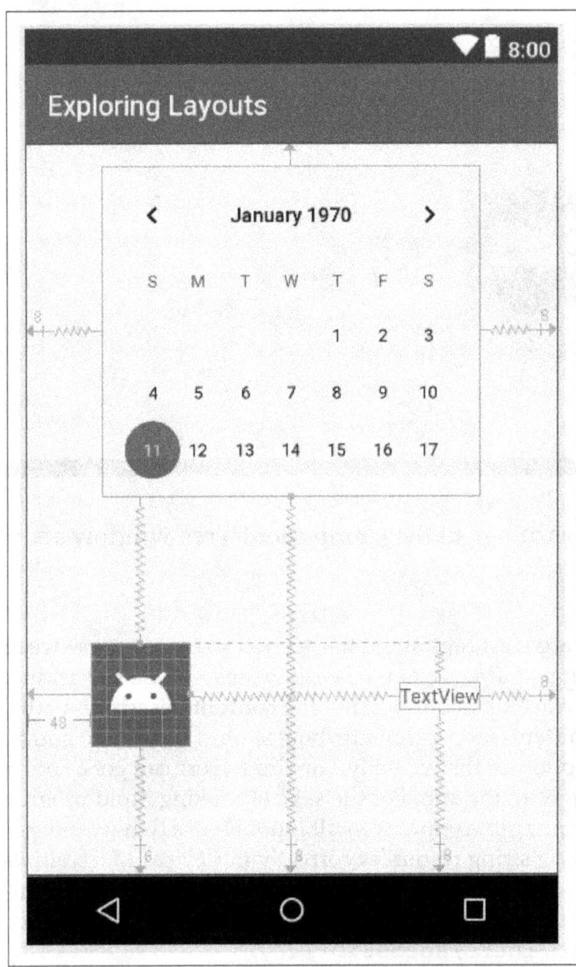

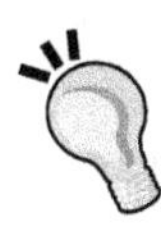

ConstraintLayout is the newest layout type, and, while it is more complex than the other layouts, it is the most powerful, as well as the one that runs the best on our user's device. It is worth spending more time looking at some more tutorials about ConstraintLayout. Especially look on YouTube, as video is a great medium to learn about tweaking ConstraintLayout. We will return to ConstraintLayout throughout the book, and you do not need to know any more than we have covered already to be able to move on.

Making the text clickable

We are nearly done with our ConstraintLayout. We just want to wire up a link back to the main menu screen. This is a good opportunity to demonstrate that TextView (and most other UI items) are also clickable. In fact, clickable text is probably more common in modern Android apps than conventional-looking buttons.

Change the text attribute of the TextView to Back to the menu. Now, find the onClick attribute and enter loadMenuLayout.

Now, add the following function to the MainActivity.kt file just after the loadTableLayout function, as highlighted here:

```
fun loadTableLayout(v: View) {
  //setContentView(R.layout.my_table_layout)
}

fun loadMenuLayout(v: View) {
  setContentView(R.layout.main_menu)
}
```

Now, whenever the user clicks the Back to the menu text, the loadMenuLayout function will be called and the setContentView function will load the layout in main_menu.xml.

You can run the app, and click back and forth between the main menu (LinearLayout) and the CalenderView widget (ConstraintLayout).

Let's build the final layout for this chapter.

Laying out data with TableLayout

In the project window, expand the `res` folder. Now, right-click the `layout` folder and select **New**. Notice that there is an option for **Layout resource file**.

Select **Layout resource file**, and you will see the **New Resource File** dialog window.

In the **File name** field, enter `my_table_layout`. This is the same name we used in the call to `setContentView` within the `loadTableLayout` function.

Notice that it has already selected **LinearLayout** as the **Root** element option. Delete `LinearLayout` and type `TableLayout` in its place.

Click the **OK** button and Android Studio will generate a new `TableLayout` in an XML file called `my_table_layout` and place it in the `layout` folder ready for us to build our new table-based UI. Android Studio will also open the UI designer (if it isn't already) with the palette on the left and the attributes window on the right.

You can now uncomment the `loadTableLayout` function:

```
fun loadTableLayout(v: View) {
  setContentView(R.layout.my_table_layout)
}
```

You can now switch to the `TableLayout`-based screen when you run the app, although currently, it is blank.

Adding a TableRow to TableLayout

Drag a `TableRow` element from the `Layouts` category on to the UI design. Notice that the appearance of this new `TableRow` is virtually imperceptible, so much so that it is not worth inserting a diagram in the book. There is just a thin blue line at the top of the UI. This is because the `TableRow` has collapsed itself around its content, which is currently empty.

It is possible to drag and drop our chosen UI elements onto this thin blue line, but it is also a little awkward, even counter intuitive. Furthermore, once we have multiple `TableRow` elements next to each other, it gets even harder. The solution lies in the **Component Tree** window, which we introduced briefly when building the `ConstraintLayout`.

Using the Component Tree when the visual designer won't do

Look at the **Component Tree** and notice how you can see the `TableRow` as a child of the `TableLayout`. We can drag our UI directly onto the `TableRow` in the **Component Tree**. Drag three `TextView` objects onto the `TableRow` in the **Component Tree** and that should leave you with the following layout. I have photoshopped the following screenshot to show you the **Component Tree** and the regular UI designer in the same diagram:

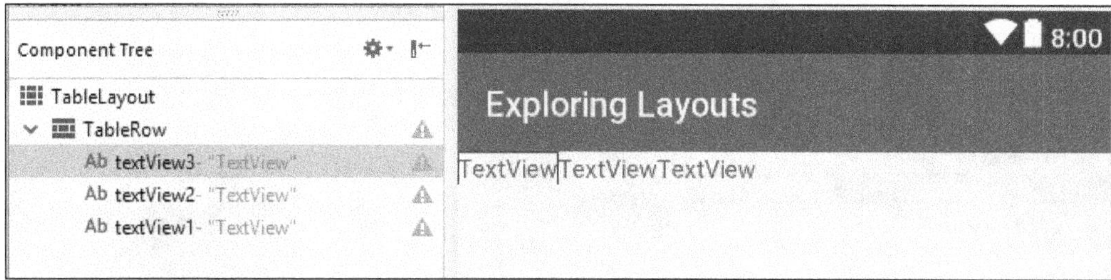

Now add another two `TableRow` objects (from the **Layouts** category). You can add them via the **Component Tree** window or the UI designer.

> You need to drop them on the far-left of the window, otherwise the new `TableRow` will become a child of the previous `TableRow`. This will leave the whole table a bit of a muddle. If you accidentally add a `TableRow` as a child of the previous `TableRow`, you can either select it, then tap the *Delete* key, use the *Ctrl* + Z keyboard combination to undo it, or drag the mispositioned `TableRow` to the left (in the **Component Tree**) to make it a child of the Table - as it should be.

Now, add three `TextView` objects to each of the new `TableRow` items. This will be most easily achieved by adding them via the **Component Tree** window. Check your layout to make sure it is as in the following screenshot:

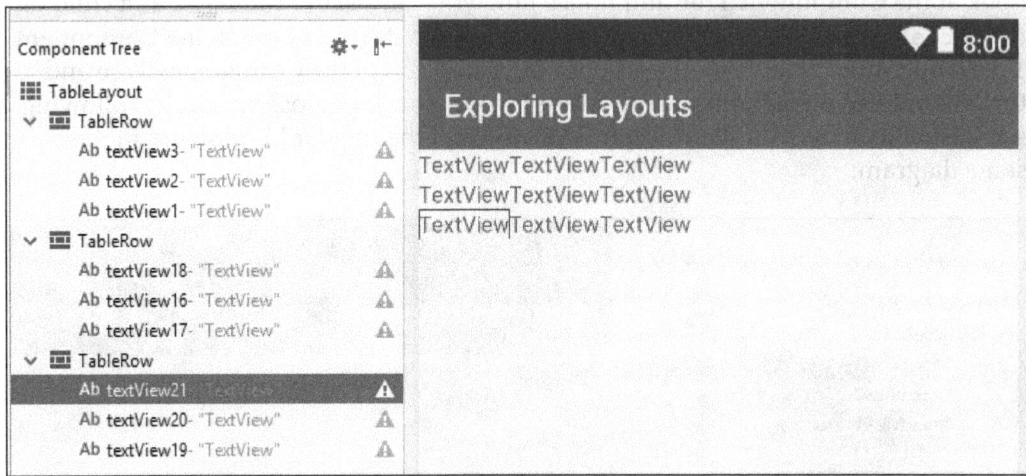

Let's make the table look more like a genuine table of data that you might get in an app by changing some attributes.

On the `TableLayout`, set the `layout_width` and `layout_height` attributes to `wrap_content`. This gets rid of extra cells.

Change the color of all the outer (along the top and down the left-hand side) `TextView` objects to black by editing the `textColor` attribute. You achieve this by selecting the first `TextView`, searching for its `color` attribute, and then typing `black` in the `color` attribute values field. You will then be able to select `@android:color/black` from a drop-down list. Do this for each of the outer `TextView` elements.

Edit the `padding` of each `TextView` and change the `all` attribute to `10sp`.

Organizing the table columns

It might seem at this point that we are done, but we need to organize the data better. Our table, like many tables, will have a blank cell in the top-left to divide the column and row titles. To achieve this, we need to number all the cells. For this, we need to edit the `layout_column` attribute.

Cell numbers are numbered from zero from the left.

Start by deleting the top-left TextView. Notice that the TextView from the right has moved into the top-left position.

Next, in the new top-left TextView, edit the layout_column attribute to be 1 (this assigns it to the second cell, because the first is 0 and we want to leave the first one empty) and, for the next cell along, edit the layout_column attribute to be 2.

For the next two rows of cells, edit their layout_column attributes from 0 to 2 from left to right.

If you want clarification on the precise code for this row after editing, here is a snippet, and remember to look in the download bundle in the Chapter04/LayoutExploration folder to see the whole file in context:

```
<TableRow
    android:layout_width="wrap_content"
    android:layout_height="wrap_content">

    <TextView
            android:id="@+id/textView2"
            android:layout_width="wrap_content"
            android:layout_height="wrap_content"
            android:layout_column="1"
            android:padding="10sp"
            android:text="India"
            android:textColor="@android:color/black" />

    <TextView
            android:id="@+id/textView1"
            android:layout_width="wrap_content"
            android:layout_height="wrap_content"
            android:layout_column="2"
            android:padding="10sp"
            android:text="England"
            android:textColor="@android:color/black" />

</TableRow>
```

Try to complete this exercise, however, using the **Attributes** window if possible.

Linking back to the main menu

Finally, for this layout, we will add a button that links back to the main menu. Add another `TableRow` via the **Component Tree**. Drag a button onto the new `TableRow`. Edit its `layout_column` attribute to `1` so that it is in the middle of the row. Edit its `text` attribute to `Menu` and edit its `onClick` attribute to match our already existing `loadMenuLayout` function.

You can now run the app and switch back and forth between the different layouts.

If you want to, you can add some meaningful titles and data to the table by editing all the `text` attributes of the `TextView` widgets, as I have done in this following screenshot, showing the `TableLayout` running in the emulator:

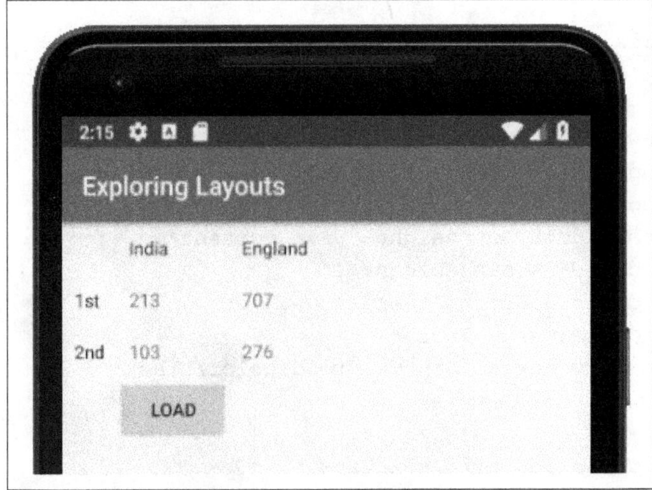

As a final thought, think about an app that presents tables of data. Chances are that data will be added to the table dynamically, not by the developer at design time as we have just done, but more likely by the user or from a database on the web. In *Chapter 16, Adapters and Recyclers,* we will see how to dynamically add data to different types of layout using adapters, and, in *Chapter 27, Android Databases,* we will also see how to create and use databases in our apps.

Summary

We have covered many topics in just a few dozen pages. We have not only built three different types of layout, including `LinearLayout` with nested layouts, `ConstraintLayout` with manually configured constraints, and `TableLayout` (albeit with fake data), but we have also wired all the layouts together with clickable buttons and text that trigger our Kotlin code to switch between all these different layouts.

In the next chapter, we will stick with the topic of layouts. We will review the many attributes we have seen, and we will build our most aesthetically pleasing layout so far by incorporating multiple `CardView` layouts, complete with depth and shadow, into a smooth-scrolling `ScrollView` layout.

5

Beautiful Layouts with CardView and ScrollView

This is the last chapter on layouts before we spend some time focusing on Kotlin and object-oriented programming. We will formalize our learning on some of the different attributes we have already seen, and we will also introduce two more cool layouts: `ScrollView` and `CardView`. To finish the chapter off, we will run the `CardView` project on a tablet emulator.

In this chapter, we will cover the following topics:

- Compiling a quick summary of UI attributes
- Building our prettiest layout so far using `ScrollView` and `CardView`
- Switching and customizing themes
- Creating and using a tablet emulator

Let's start by recapping some attributes.

Attributes – a quick summary

In the last few chapters, we have used and discussed quite a few different attributes. I thought it would be worth a quick summary and further investigation of a few of the more common ones.

Sizing using dp

As we know, there are thousands of different Android devices. Android uses **density-independent pixels**, or **dp**, as a unit of measurement to try and have a system of measurement that works across different devices. The way this works is by first calculating the density of the pixels on the device an app is running on.

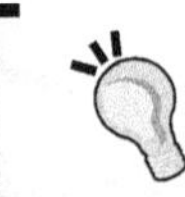

We can calculate density by dividing the horizontal resolution by the horizontal size, in inches, of the screen. This is all done on the fly on the device on which our app is running.

All we have to do is use `dp` in conjunction with a number when setting the size of the various attributes of our widgets. Using density-independent measurements, we can design layouts that scale to create a uniform appearance on as many different screens as possible.

So, problem solved then? We just use `dp` everywhere and our layouts will work everywhere? Unfortunately, density independence is only part of the solution. We will see more of how we can make our apps look great on a range of different screens throughout the rest of the book.

As an example, we can affect the height and width of a widget by adding the following code to its attributes:

```
...
android:height="50dp"
android:width="150dp"
...
```

Alternatively, we can use the attributes window and add them through the comfort of the appropriate edit boxes. Which option you use will depend on your personal preference, but sometimes one way will feel more appropriate than another in a given situation. Either way is correct and, as we go through the book making apps, I will usually point out if one way is *better* than another.

We can also use the same `dp` units to set other attributes, such as margin and padding. We will look more closely at margins and padding in a minute.

Sizing fonts using sp

Another device-dependent unit of measurement used for sizing Android fonts is **scalable pixels**, or **sp**. The `sp` unit of measurement is used for fonts, and is pixel density-dependent in the exact same way that `dp` is.

The extra calculation that an Android device will use when deciding how big your font will be based on the value of `sp` you use is the user's own font size settings. So, if you test your app on devices and emulators with normal-size fonts, then a user who has a sight impairment (or just likes big fonts) and has their font setting set to large will see something different to what you saw during testing.

If you want to try playing with your Android device's font size settings, you can do so by selecting **Settings | Display | Font size**:

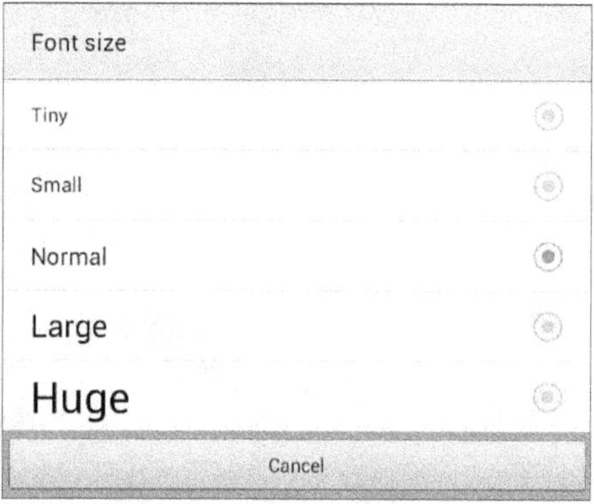

As we can see in the preceding screenshot, there are quite a few settings, and if you try it on **Huge**, the difference is, well, huge!

We can set the size of fonts using `sp` in any widget that has text. This includes `Button`, `TextView`, and all the UI elements under the **Text** category in the palette, as well as some others. We do so by setting the `textSize` property as follows:

```
android:textSize="50sp"
```

As usual, we can also use the attributes window to achieve the same thing.

Determining size with wrap or match

We can also decide how the size of UI elements, and many other UI elements, behave in relation to the containing/parent element. We can do so by setting the `layoutWidth` and `layoutHeight` attributes to either `wrap_content` or `match_parent`.

For example, say we set the attributes of a lone button on a layout to the following:

```
...
android:layout_width="match_parent"
android:layout_height="match_parent"
....
```

Then, the button will expand in both height and width to **match** the **parent**. We can see that the button in the next image fills the entire screen:

More common for a button is `wrap_content`, as shown in the following code:

```
....
android:layout_width="wrap_content"
android:layout_height="wrap_content"
....
```

This causes the button to be as big as it needs to be to **wrap** its **content** (width and height in `dp` and text in `sp`).

Using padding and margin

If you have ever done any web design, you will be very familiar with the next two attributes. **Padding** is the space from the edge of the widget to the start of the content in the widget. The **margin** is the space outside of the widget that is left between other widgets - including the margin of other widgets, should they have any. Here is a visual representation:

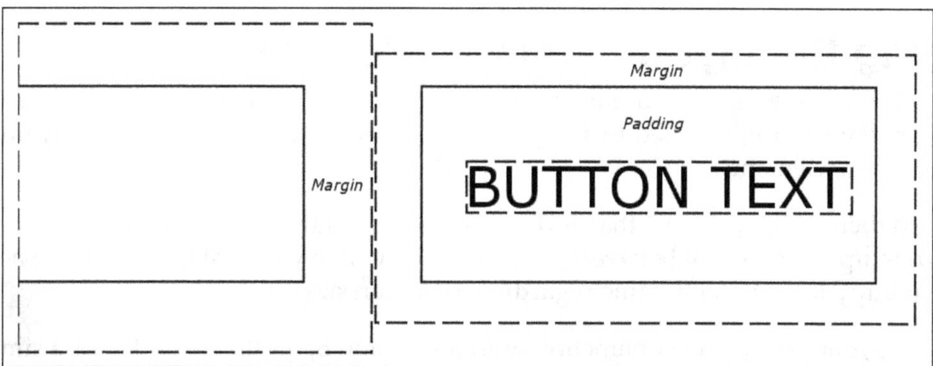

We can set padding and margin in a straightforward way, equally for all sides, like this:

```
...
android:layout_margin="43dp"
android:padding="10dp"
...
```

Look at the slight difference in naming convention for margin and padding. The padding value is just called `padding`, but the margin value is referred to as `layout_margin`. This reflects the fact that padding only affects the UI element itself, but margin can affect other widgets in the layout.

Or, we can specify different top, bottom, left, and right margins and padding, as follows:

```
android:layout_marginTop="43dp"
android:layout_marginBottom="43dp"
android:paddingLeft="5dp"
android:paddingRight="5dp"
```

Specifying the margin and padding values for a widget is optional, and a value of zero will be assumed if nothing is specified. We can also choose to specify some of the different side's margins and padding but not others, as in the earlier example.

It is probably becoming obvious that the way we design our layouts is extremely flexible, but also that it is going to take some practice to achieve precise results with these many options. We can even specify negative margin values to create overlapping widgets.

Let's look at a few more attributes, and then we will go ahead and play around with a stylish layout, `CardView`.

Using the layout_weight property

Weight refers to a relative amount compared to other UI elements. So, for `layout_weight` to be useful, we need to assign a value to the `layout_weight` property on two or more elements.

We can then assign portions that add up to 100% in total. This is especially useful for dividing up screen space between parts of the UI where we want the relative space they occupy to remain the same regardless of screen size.

Using `layout_weight` in conjunction with the `sp` and `dp` units can make for a simple and flexible layout. For example, look at this code:

```
<Button
        android:layout_width="match_parent"
        android:layout_height="0dp"
        android:layout_weight="0.10"
        android:text="one tenth" />

<Button
        android:layout_width="match_parent"
        android:layout_height="0dp"
        android:layout_weight="0.20"
        android:text="two tenths" />

<Button
        android:layout_width="match_parent"
        android:layout_height="0dp"
        android:layout_weight="0.30"
        android:text="three tenths" />

<Button
        android:layout_width="match_parent"
        android:layout_height="0dp"
        android:layout_weight="0.40"
        android:text="four tenths" />
```

Here is what this code will do:

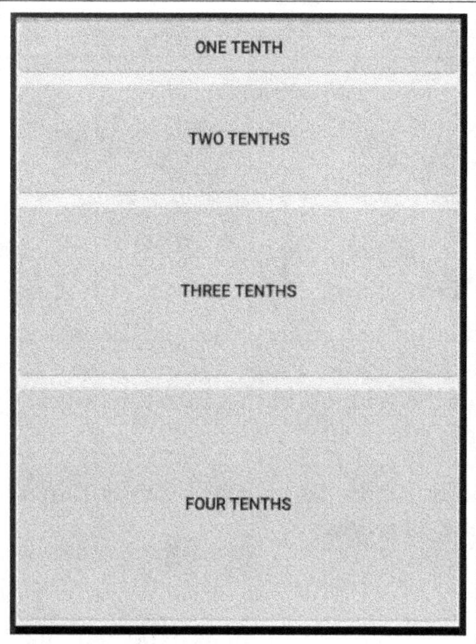

Notice that all the `layout_height` attributes are set to `0dp`. Effectively, the `layout_weight` attribute is replacing the `layout_height` property. The context in which we use `layout_weight` is important (or it won't work), and we will see this in a real project soon. Also note that we don't have to use fractions of one; we can use whole numbers, percentages, and any other number. As long as they are relative to each other, they will probably achieve the effect you are after. Note that `layout_weight` only works in certain contexts, and we will get to see where as we build more layouts.

Using gravity

Gravity can be our friend, and can be used in so many ways in our layouts. Just like gravity in the solar system, it affects the position of items by moving them in a given direction as if they were being acted upon by gravity. The best way to see what gravity can do is to look at some example code and diagrams:

```
android:gravity="left|center_vertical"
```

If the `gravity` property on a button (or another widget) is set to `left|center_vertical` as shown in the preceding code, it will have an effect that looks like this:

Notice that the content of the widget (in this case the button's text) is indeed aligned left and centrally vertical.

In addition, a widget can influence its own position within a layout element with the `layout_gravity` element, as follows:

```
android:layout_gravity="left"
```

This would set the widget within its layout, as expected, like this:

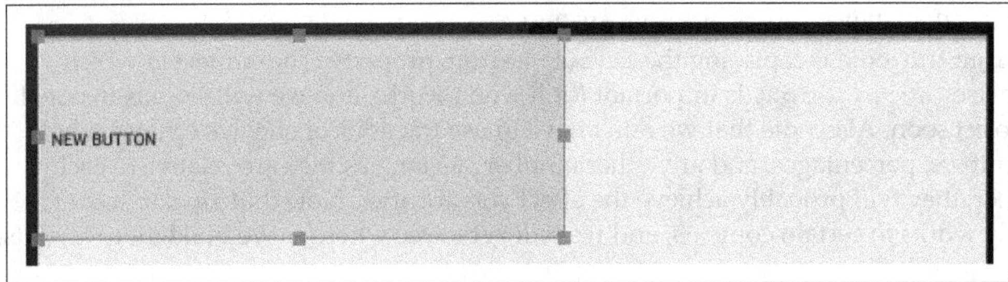

The previous code allows different widgets within the same layout to be affected as if the layout has multiple different gravities.

The content of all the widgets in a layout can be affected by the `gravity` property of their parent layout by using the same code as a widget:

```
android:gravity="left"
```

There are, in fact, many more attributes than those we have discussed. Many we won't need in this book, and some are quite obscure, so you might never need them in your entire Android career. But others are quite commonly used and include `background`, `textColor`, `alignment`, `typeface`, `visibility`, and `shadowColor`. Let's explore some more attributes and layouts now.

Building a UI with CardView and ScrollView

Create a new project in the usual way. Name the project `CardView Layout` and choose the **Empty Activity** project template. Leave all the rest of the settings the same as all the previous projects.

To be able to edit our theme and properly test the result, we need to generate our layout file and edit the Kotlin code to display it by calling the `setContentView` function from the `onCreate` function. We will design our `CardView` masterpiece inside a `ScrollView` layout, which, as the name suggests, allows the user to scroll through the content of the layout.

Right-click the `layout` folder and select **New**. Notice that there is an option for **Layout resource file**. Select **Layout resource file** and you will see the **New Resource File** dialog window.

In the **File name** field, enter `main_layout`. The name is arbitrary, but this layout is going to be our main layout, so the name makes that plain.

Notice that it is set to **LinearLayout** as the **Root** element option. Change it to `ScrollView`. This layout type appears to work just like `LinearLayout`, except that, when there is too much content to display on screen, it will allow the user to scroll the content by swiping with their finger.

Click the **OK** button and Android Studio will generate a new `ScrollView` layout in an XML file called `main_layout` and place it in the `layout` folder ready for us to build our `CardView`-based UI.

You can see our new file in this next screenshot:

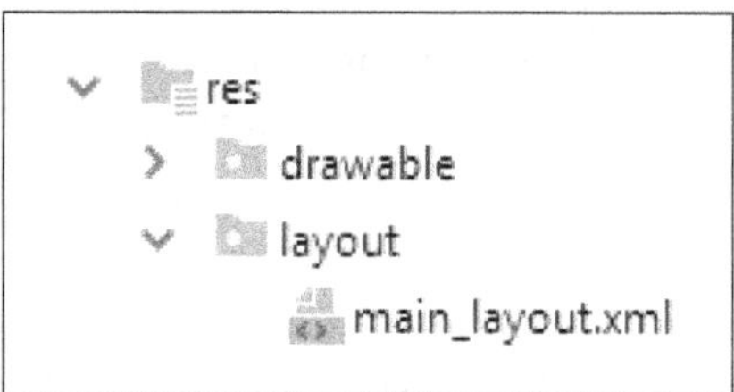

Android Studio will also open the UI designer ready for action.

Setting the view with Kotlin code

As we have done previously, we will now load the `main_layout.xml` file as the layout for our app by calling the `setContentView` function in the `MainActivity.kt` file.

Select the `MainActivity.kt` tab. In the unlikely event the tab isn't there by default, you can find it in the project explorer under `app/java/your_package_name`, where `your_package_name` is equal to the package name that you chose when you created the project.

Amend the code in the `onCreate` function to look exactly like this next code. I have highlighted the line that you need to add:

```
override fun onCreate(savedInstanceState: Bundle?) {
   super.onCreate(savedInstanceState)
   setContentView(R.layout.main_layout);
}
```

You could now run the app, but there is nothing to see except an empty `ScrollView` layout.

Adding image resources

We are going to need some images for this project. This is so we can demonstrate how to add them into the project (this section) and neatly display and format them in a `CardView` layout (next section).

It doesn't really matter where you get your images from. It is the practical hands-on experience that is the purpose of this exercise. To avoid copyright and royalty issues, I am going to use some book images from the Packt Publishing website. This also makes it easy for me to provide you with all the resources you need to complete the project should you not want to go to the bother of acquiring your own images. Feel free to swap the images in the `Chapter05/CardViewLayout/res/drawable` folder.

There are three images: `image_1.png`, `image_2.png`, and `image_3.png`. To add them to the project, follow these steps.

1. Find the image files using your operating system's file explorer.
2. Highlight them all and press *Ctrl* + *C* to copy them.
3. In the Android Studio project explorer, select the `res/drawable` folder by left-clicking it.
4. Right-click the `drawable` folder and select **Paste.**

5. In the pop-up window that asks you to **Choose Destination Directory**, click **OK** to accept the default destination, which is the `drawable` folder.
6. Click **OK** again to **Copy Specified Files.**

You should now be able to see your images in the `drawable` folder along with a couple of other files that Android Studio placed there when the project was created, as shown in this next screenshot:

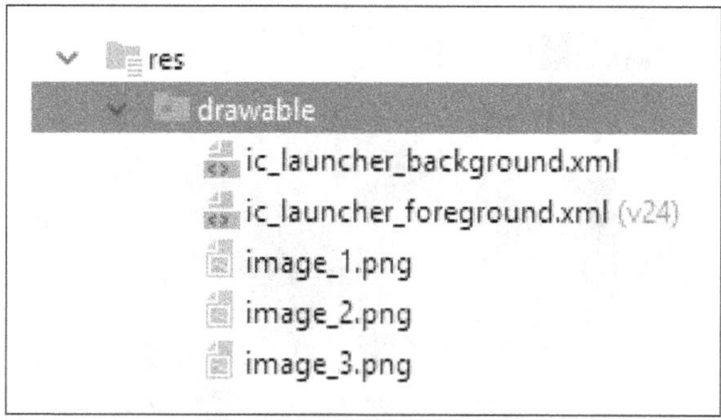

Before we move on to `CardView`, let's design what we will put inside them.

Creating the content for the cards

The next thing we need to do is create the content for our cards. It makes sense to separate the content from the layout. What we will do is create three separate layouts, called `card_contents_1`, `card_contents_2`, and `card_contents_3`. They will each contain a `LinearLayout`, which will contain the actual image and text.

Let's create three more layouts with `LinearLayout` at their root:

1. Right-click the `layout` folder and select **New layout resource file**.
2. Name the file `card_contents_1` and make sure that **LinearLayout** is selected as the **Root element**
3. Click **OK** to add the file to the `layout` folder
4. Repeat steps one through three two more times, changing the filename each time to `card_contents_2` and then `card_contents_3`

Now, select the `card_contents_1.xml` tab and make sure you are in design view. We will drag and drop some elements to the layout to get the basic structure and then we will add some `sp`, `dp`, and gravity attributes to make them look nice:

1. Drag a `TextView` widget on to the top of the layout.
2. Drag an `ImageView` widget on to the layout below `TextView` widget.

3. In the **Resources** pop-up window, select **Project** | **image_1** and then click **OK.**
4. Drag another two **TextView** widgets below the image.
5. This is how your layout should now appear:

Now, let's use some material design guidelines to make the layout look more appealing.

> It is possible that, as you proceed through these modifications, the UI elements on the bottom of the layout might disappear from the bottom of the design view. If this happens to you, remember you can always select any UI element from the **Component Tree** window underneath the palette. Or, refer to the next tip.

Another way of minimizing the problem is to use a bigger screen, as explained in the following instructions:

I changed the default device for the design view to **Pixel 2 XL** to create the previous screenshot. I will leave this setting for the rest of the book unless I specifically mention that I am changing it. It allows a few more pixels on the layout and means this layout is easier to complete. If you want to do the same, look at the menu bar above the design view, click the device dropdown, and choose your design view device, as shown in the following screenshot:

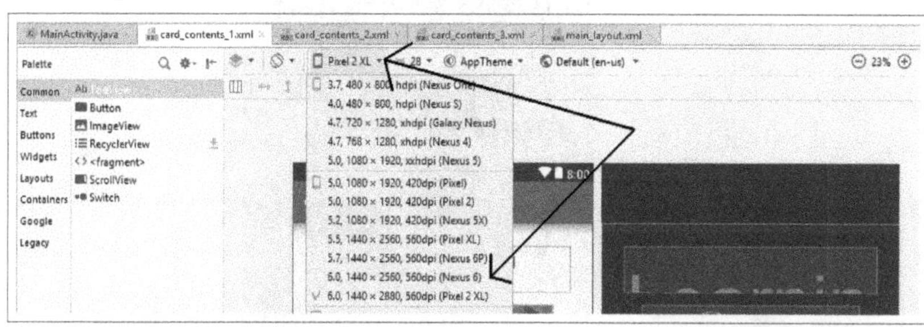

1. Set the `textSize` attribute for the `TextView` widget at the top to `24sp`.
2. Set the **Layout_Margin** | **all** attribute to `16dp`.
3. Set the `text` attribute to **Learning Java by Building Android Games** (or whatever title suits your image).
4. On the `ImageView`, set `layout_width` and `layout_height` to `wrap_content`.
5. On the `ImageView`, set `layout_gravity` to `center_horizontal`.
6. On the `TextView` beneath the `ImageView`, set `textSize` to `16sp`.
7. On the same `TextView`, set **Layout_Margin** | **all** to `16dp`.
8. On the same `TextView`, set the `text` attribute to `Learn Java and Android from scratch by building 6 playable games` (or something that describes your image).
9. On the bottom `TextView`, change the `text` attribute to `BUY NOW`.
10. On the same `TextView`, set **Layout_Margin** | **all** to `16dp`.
11. On the same `TextView`, set the `textSize` attribute to `24sp`.
12. On the same `TextView`, set the `textColor` attribute to `@color/colorAccent`.
13. On the `LinearLayout` holding all the other elements, set `padding` to `15dp`. Note that it is easiest to select `LinearLayout` from the **Component Tree** window.

14. At this point, your layout will look very similar to the following screenshot:

Now, lay out the other two files (`card_contents_2` and `card_contents_3`) with the exact same dimensions and colors. When you get the **Resources** popup to choose an image, use `image_2` and `image_3` respectively. Also, change all the `text` attributes on the first two `TextView` elements so that the titles and descriptions are unique. The titles and descriptions don't really matter; it is layout and appearance that we are learning about.

> Note that all the sizes and colors were derived from the material design website at `https://material.io/design/introduction`, and the Android specific UI guideline at `https://developer.android.com/guide/topics/ui/look-and-feel`. It is well worth studying alongside this book, or soon after you complete it.

We can now move on to `CardView`.

Defining dimensions for CardView

Right-click the `values` folder and select **New** | **Values resource file**. In the **New Resource File** pop-up window, name the file `dimens.xml` (short for dimensions) and click **OK**. We will use this file to create some common values that our `CardView` object will use by referring to them.

To achieve this, we will edit the XML directly. Edit the `dimens.xml` file to be the same as the following code:

```
<?xml version="1.0" encoding="utf-8"?>
<resources>
    <dimen name="card_corner_radius">16dp</dimen>
    <dimen name="card_margin">10dp</dimen>
</resources>
```

Be sure to make it exactly the same because a small omission or mistake could cause an error and prevent the project from working.

We have defined two resources, the first called `card_corner_radius`, with a value of `16dp`, and the second called `card_margin`, with a value of `10dp`.

We will refer to these resources in the `main_layout` file and use them to consistently configure our three `CardView` elements.

Adding CardView to our layout

Switch to the `main_layout.xml` tab and make sure you are in the design view. You probably recall that we are now working with a `ScrollView` that will scroll the content of our app, rather like a web browser scrolls the content of a web page that doesn't fit on one screen.

`ScrollView` has a limitation – it can only have one direct child layout. We want it to contain three `CardView` elements.

To overcome this problem, drag a `LinearLayout` from the `Layouts` category of the palette. Be sure to pick **LinearLayout (vertical),** as represented by this icon in the palette:

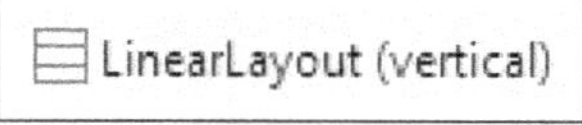

We will add our three `CardView` objects inside `LinearLayout` and then the whole thing will scroll nice and smoothly without any errors.

`CardView` can be found in the **Containers** category of the palette, so switch to that and locate `CardView`.

Drag a `CardView` object onto the `LinearLayout` on the design and you will get a pop-up message in Android Studio. This is the message pictured here:

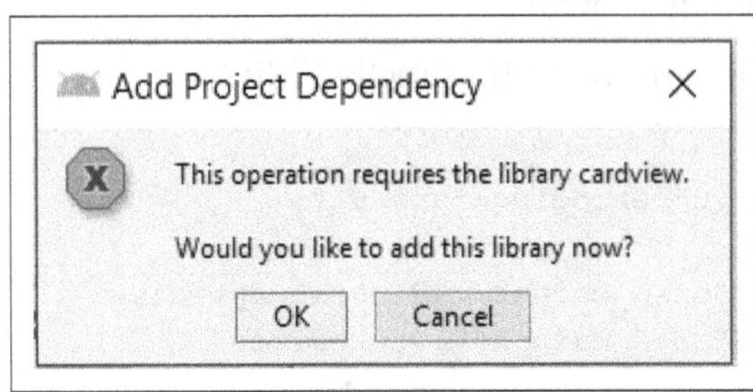

Click the **OK** button, and Android Studio will do some work behind the scenes and add the necessary parts to the project. Android Studio has added some more classes to the project, specifically, classes that provide `CardView` features to older versions of Android that wouldn't otherwise have them.

You should now have a `CardView` object on the design. Until there is some content in it, the `CardView` object is only easily visible in the **Component Tree** window.

Select the `CardView` object via the **Component Tree** window and configure the following attributes:

- Set `layout_width` to `wrap_content`
- Set `layout_gravity` to `center`
- Set **Layout_Margin | all** to `@dimens/card_margin`
- Set `cardCornerRadius` to `@dimens/card_corner_radius`
- Set `cardEleveation` to `2dp`

Now, switch to the **Text** tab and you will find you have something very similar to this next code:

```
<androidx.cardview.widget.CardView
   android:layout_width="wrap_content"
   android:layout_height="wrap_content"
   android:layout_gravity="center"
   android:layout_margin="@dimen/card_margin"
   app:cardCornerRadius="@dimen/card_corner_radius"
   app:cardElevation="2dp" />
```

The previous code listing only shows the code for the `CardView` object.

The current problem is that our `CardView` object is empty. Let's fix that by adding the content of `card_contents_1.xml`. Here is how to do it.

Including layout files inside another layout

We need to edit the code very slightly, and here is why. We need to add an `include` element to the code. The `include` element is the code that will insert the content from the `card_contents_1.xml` layout. The problem is that, to add this code, we need to slightly alter the format of the `CardView` XML. The current format starts and concludes the `CardView` object with one single tag, as follows:

```
<androidx.cardview.widget.CardView
...
.../>
```

We need to change the format to a separate opening and closing tag like this (don't change anything just yet):

```
<androidx.cardview.widget.CardView
...
...
</androidx.cardview.widget.CardView>
```

This change in format will enable us to add the `include...` code, and our first `CardView` object will be complete. With this in mind, edit the code of `CardView` to be exactly the same as the following code. I have highlighted the two new lines of code, but also note that the forward slash that was after the `cardElevation` attribute has also been removed:

```
<androidx.cardview.widget.CardView
   android:layout_width="wrap_content"
   android:layout_height="wrap_content"
   android:layout_gravity="center"
   android:layout_margin="@dimen/card_margin"
   app:cardCornerRadius="@dimen/card_corner_radius"
   app:cardElevation="2dp" >

   <include layout="@layout/card_contents_1" />

</androidx.cardview.widget.CardView>
```

You can now view the `main_layout` file in the visual designer and see the layout inside the `CardView` object. The visual designer does not reveal the real aesthetics of `CardView`. We will see all the `CardView` widgets scrolling nicely in the completed app shortly. Here is a screenshot of where we are up to so far:

Add two more `CardView` widgets to the layout and configure them the same as the first, with one exception. On the second `CardView` object, set `cardElevation` to `22dp` and, on the third `CardView` object, set `cardElevation` to `42dp`. Also, change the `include` code to reference `card_contents_2` and `card_contents_3` respectively.

You could do this very quickly by copying and pasting the `CardView` XML and simply amending the elevation and the `include` code, as mentioned in the previous paragraph.

Now we can run the app and see our three beautiful, elevated `CardView` widgets in action. In this next screenshot, I have photoshopped two screenshots to be side by side, so you can see one full `CardView` layout in action (on the left) and, in the image on the right, the effect the elevation setting has, which creates a very pleasing depth with a shadow effect:

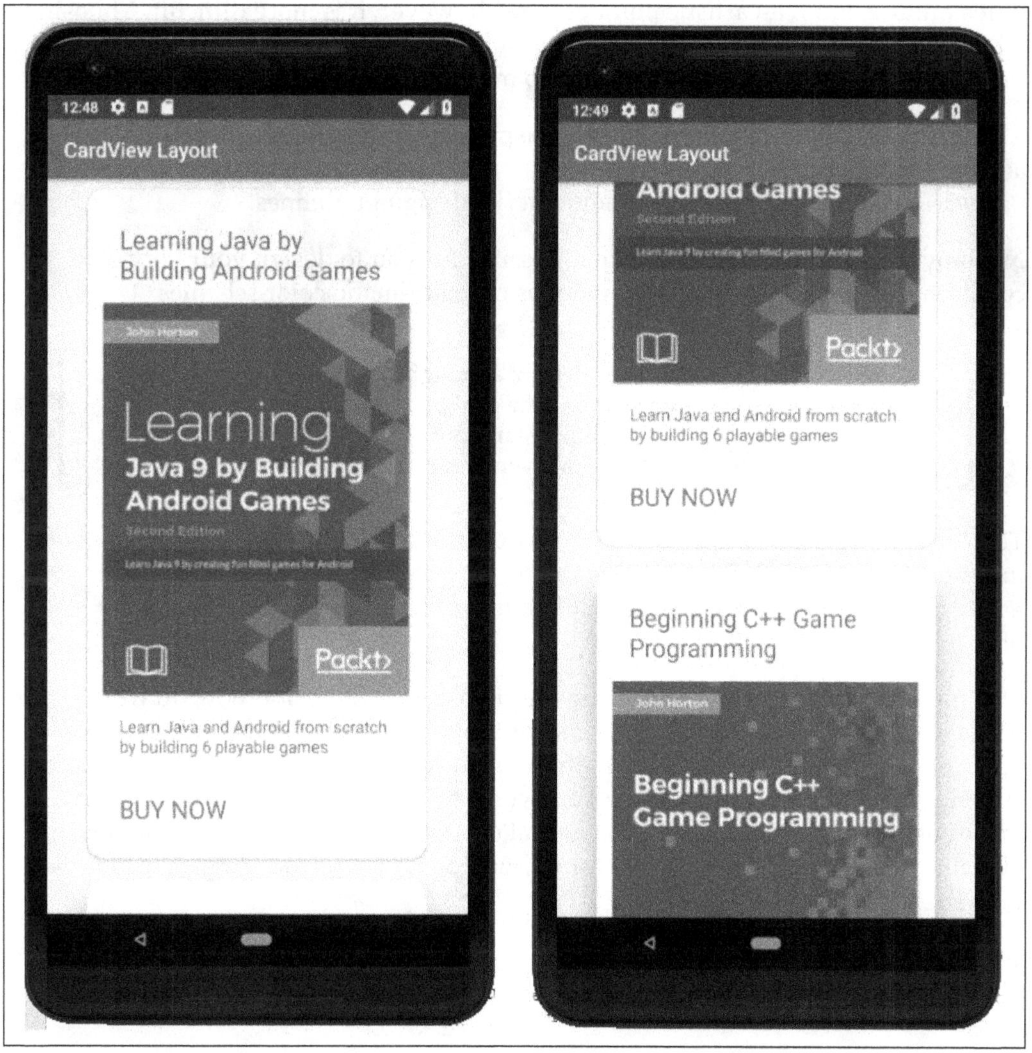

The image will likely be slightly unclear in the black and white printed version of this book. Be sure to build and run the app for yourself to see this cool effect.

Now we can play around with editing the theme of the app.

Themes and material design

Creating a new theme, technically speaking, is very easy, and we will see how to do it in a minute. From an artistic point of view, however, it is more difficult. Choosing which colors work well together, let alone suit your app and the imagery, is much more difficult. Fortunately, we can turn to material design for help.

Material design has guidelines for every aspect of UI design and all the guidelines are very well documented. Even the sizes for text and padding that we used for the `CardView` project were all taken from material design guidelines.

Not only does material design make it possible for you to design your very own color schemes, but it also provides palettes of ready-made color schemes.

This book is not about design, although it is about implementing design. To get you started, the goal of our designs might be to make our UI unique and to stand out at the exact same time as making it comfortable for, even familiar to, the user.

Themes are constructed from XML `style` items. We saw the `styles.xml` file in *Chapter 3, Exploring Android Studio and the Project Structure*. Each item in the `styles` file defined the appearance and gave it a name such as `colorPrimary` or `colorAccent`.

The questions that remain are, how do we choose our colors and how do we implement them in our theme? The answer to the first question has two possible options. The first answer is to enroll on a design course and spend the next few years studying UI design. The more useful answer is to use one of the built-in themes and make customizations based on the material design guidelines, discussed in depth for every UI element at `https://developer.android.com/guide/topics/ui/look-and-feel/`.

We will do the latter now.

Using the Android Studio theme designer

From the Android Studio main menu, select **Tools** | **Theme Editor**. On the left-hand side, notice the UI examples that show what the theme will look like, and on the right are the controls to edit aspects of the theme:

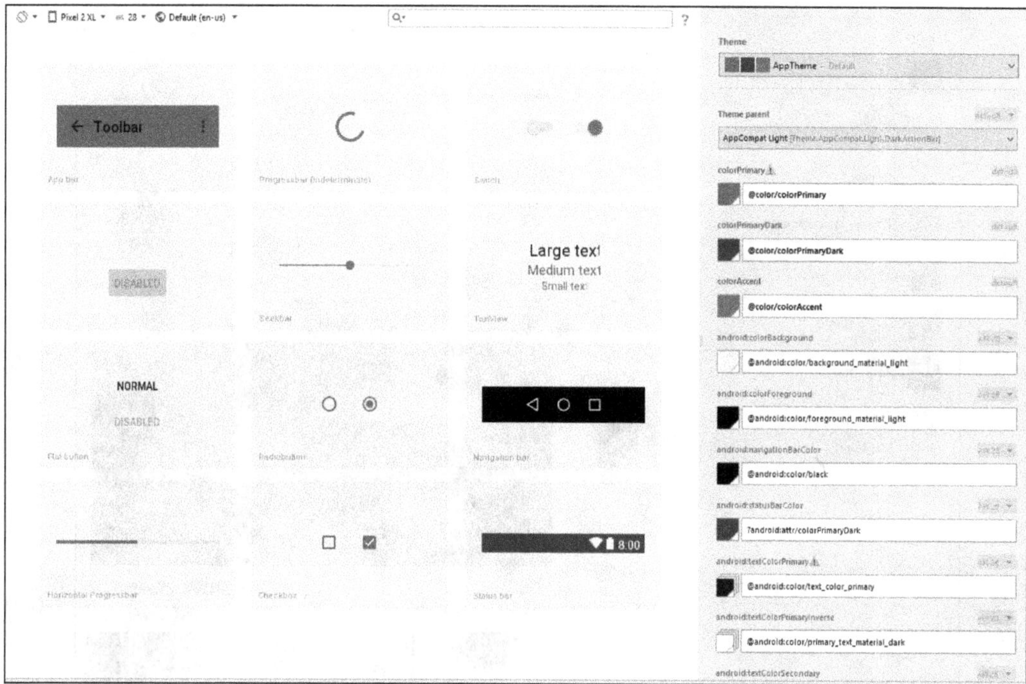

As mentioned, the easiest way to create your own theme is to start with, and then edit, an existing theme. In the **Theme** dropdown, select a theme you like the look of. I chose **AppCompat Dark**:

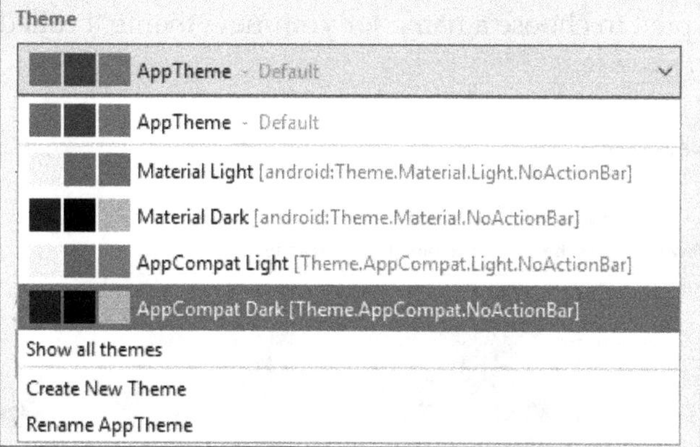

Select any items on the right-hand side that you want to change the color of, and choose a color in the screen that follows:

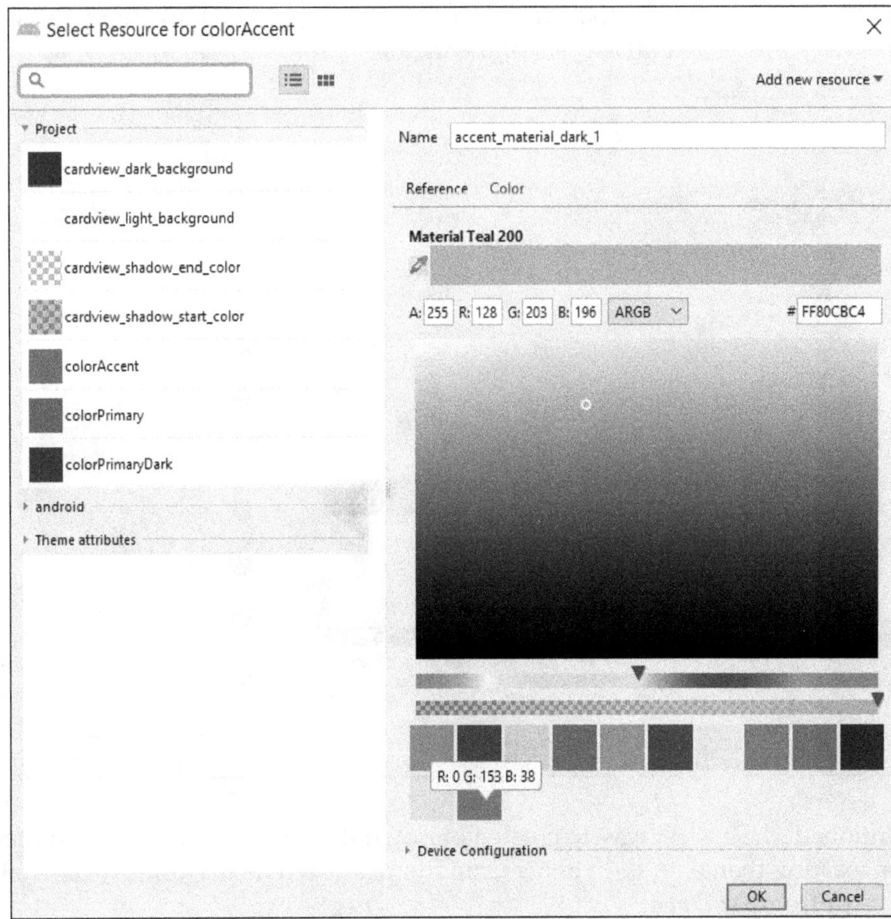

You will be prompted to choose a name for your new theme. I called mine `Theme.AppCompat.MyDarkTheme`:

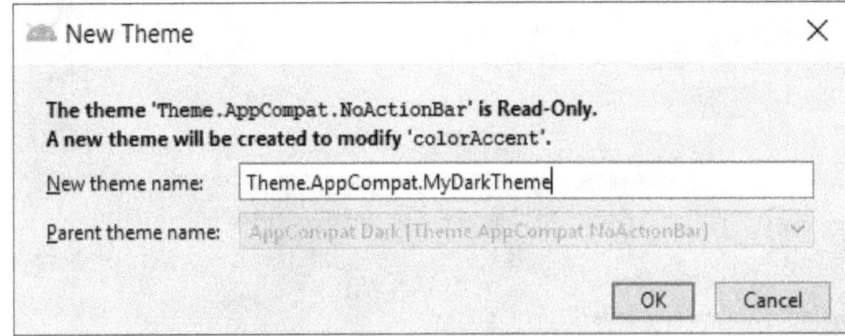

Now, click the **fix** text to apply your theme to the current app, as indicated in the following screenshot:

You can then run your app on the emulator to see the theme in action:

So far, all our apps have been run on a phone. Obviously, a huge part of the Android device ecosystem is tablets. Let's see how we can test our apps on a tablet emulator, as well as get an advanced look at some of the problems this diverse ecosystem is going to cause us, and then we can begin to learn to overcome these problems.

Creating a tablet emulator

Select **Tools** | **AVD Manager** and then click the **Create Virtual Device...** button on the **Your Virtual Devices** window. You will see the **Select Hardware** window in the following screenshot:

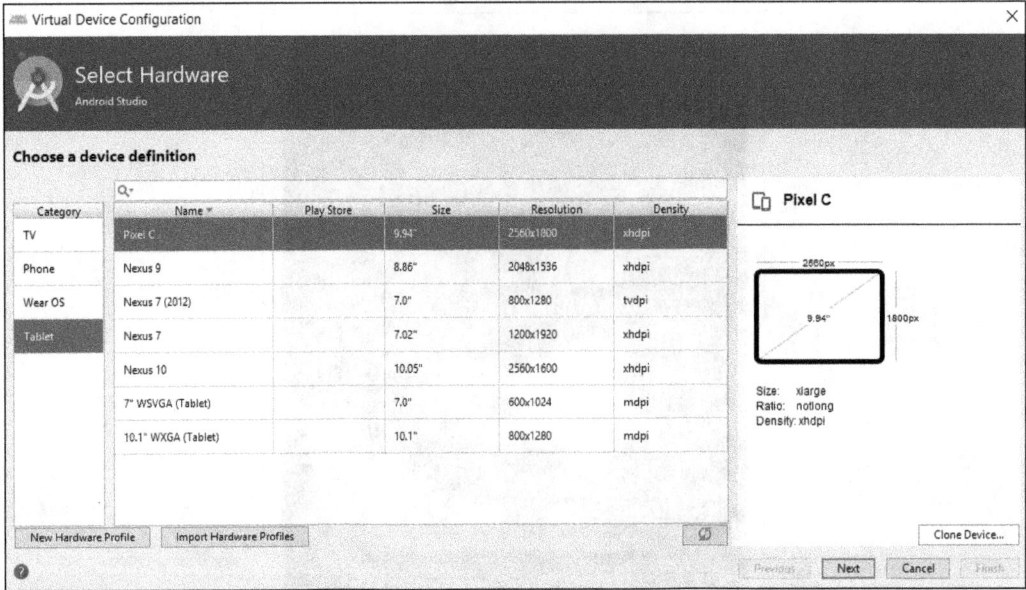

Select the **Tablet** option from the **Category** list and then highlight the **Pixel C** tablet from the choice of available tablets. These choices are highlighted in the previous screenshot.

If you are reading this sometime in the future, the Pixel C option might have been updated. The choice of tablet is less important than practicing this process of creating a tablet emulator and then testing your apps.

Click the **Next** button. On the **System Image** window that follows, just click **Next**, because this will select the default system image. It is possible that choosing your own image will cause the emulator not to work properly.

Finally, on the **Android Virtual Device** screen, you can leave all the default options as they are. Feel free to change the **AVD Name** for your emulator or the **Startup Orientation** (portrait or landscape) if you want to:

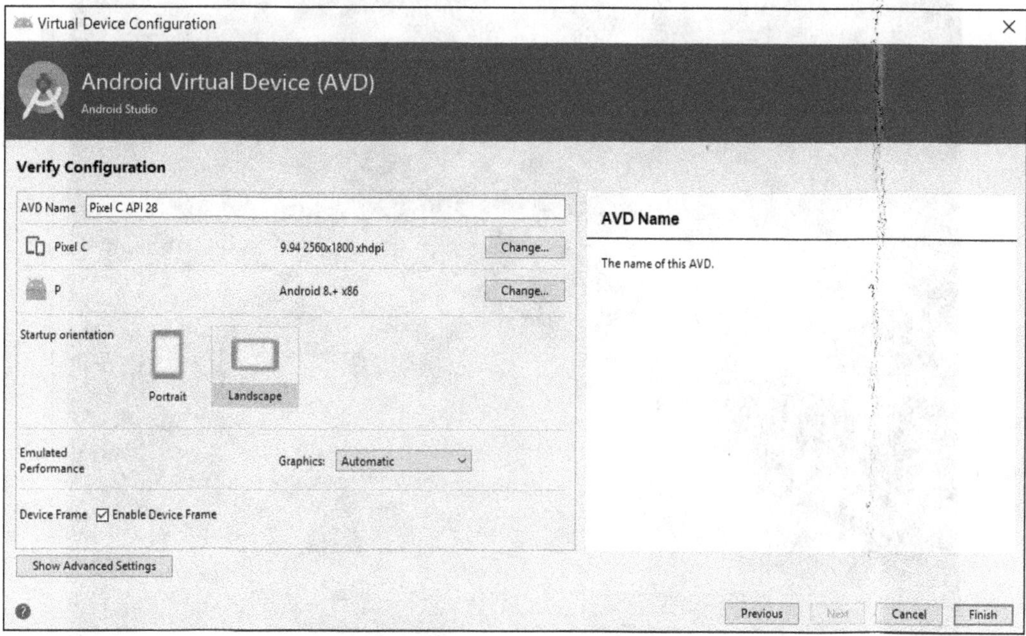

Click the **Finish** button when you are ready.

Now, whenever you run one of your apps from Android Studio, you will be given the option to choose **Pixel C** (or whatever tablet you created). Here is a screenshot of my Pixel C emulator running the `CardView` app:

Not too bad, but there is quite a large amount of wasted space and it looks a bit sparse. Let's try it in landscape mode. If you try running the app with the tablet in landscape mode, the results are worse. What we can learn from this is that we are going to have to design our layouts for different size screens and for different orientations. Sometimes, these will be clever designs that scale to suit different sizes or orientations, but often they will be completely different designs.

Frequently asked question

Q) Do I need to master all this stuff about material design?

A) No. Unless you want to be a professional designer. If you just want to make your own apps and sell them or give them away on the Play store, then knowing just the basics is good enough.

Summary

In this chapter, we built aesthetically pleasing `CardView` layouts and put them in a `ScrollView` layout so that the user can swipe through the content of the layout a bit like browsing a web page. To conclude the chapter, we launched a tablet emulator and saw that we are going to need to get smart with how we design our layouts if we want to cater for different device sizes and orientations. In *Chapter 24, Design Patterns, Multiple Layouts, and Fragments*, we will begin to take our layouts to the next level and learn how to cope with such a diverse array of devices by using Android Fragments.

Before we do so, however, it will serve us well to learn more about Kotlin and how we can use it to control our UI and interact with the user. This will be the focus of the next seven chapters.

Of course, the elephant in the room at this point is that, despite learning lots about layouts, project structure, the connection between Kotlin and XML, and much more besides, our UIs, no matter how pretty, don't actually do anything! We need to seriously upgrade our Kotlin skills while also learning more about how to apply them in an Android context.

In the next chapter, we will do exactly that. We will look at how we can add Kotlin code that executes at exactly the moment we need it to by working with the **Android Activity lifecycle**.

6
The Android Lifecycle

In this chapter, we will familiarize ourselves with the lifecycle of an Android app. The idea that a computer program has a lifecycle might sound strange at first, but it will soon make sense.

The lifecycle is the way that all Android apps interact with the Android OS. In the same way that the lifecycle of humans enables them to interact with the world around them, we have no choice but to interact with the Android lifecycle and we must be prepared to handle numerous unpredictable events if we want our apps to survive.

We will explore the phases of the lifecycle that an app goes through, from creation to destruction, and how this helps us know *where* to put our Kotlin code, depending on what we are trying to achieve.

In this chapter, we will explore the following topics:

- The life and times of an Android app
- The process of overriding and the `override` keyword
- The phases of the Android lifecycle
- What exactly we need to know and do to code our apps
- A lifecycle demonstration app
- How Android code is structured, and preparation for going deeper into Kotlin coding in the next chapter

Let's start learning about the Android lifecycle.

The life and times of an Android app

We have talked a bit about the structure of our code; we know that we can write classes, and within those classes we have functions, and these functions contain our code, which gets things done. We also know that when we want the code within a function to run (that is, be **executed**), we **call** that function by using its name.

Additionally, in *Chapter 2, Kotlin, XML, and the UI Designer*, we learned that Android itself calls the `onCreate` function just before the app is ready to start. We saw this when we output to the logcat window and used the `Toast` class to send a pop-up message to the user.

In this chapter, we will examine what happens throughout the lifecycle of every app that we write; that is, when it starts, ends, and the stages in between. What we will see is that Android interacts with our app on numerous occasions each time that it is run.

How Android interacts with our apps

Android interacts with our apps by calling functions that are contained within the `Activity` class. Even if the function is not visible within our Kotlin code, it is still being called by Android at the appropriate time. If this doesn't appear to make any sense, then read on.

Have you ever wondered why the `onCreate` function has the unusual `override` keyword just before it? Consider the following line of code:

```
override fun onCreate(…
```

When we override a function such as `onCreate`, we are saying to Android that when you call `onCreate`, please use our overridden version because we have some code in it that we want to execute.

Furthermore, you might remember the unusual-looking first line of code in the `onCreate` function:

```
super.onCreate(savedInstanceState)
```

This is telling Android to call the original version of `onCreate` before proceeding with our overridden version.

There are also many other functions that we can optionally override, and they allow us to add our code at appropriate times within the lifecycle of our Android app. In the same way that `onCreate` is called just before the app is shown to the user, there are also other functions that are called at other times. We haven't seen them or overridden them yet, but they are there, they are called, and their code executes.

The reason we need to know and understand the functions of *our* app that Android calls whenever it wants is because these functions control the very life and death of our code. For instance, what if our app allows the user to type an important reminder, then, halfway through typing the reminder, their phone rings, our app disappears, and the data (that is, the user's important reminder) is gone?

It is vital and, thankfully, quite straightforward to learn when, why, and which functions Android will call as part of the lifecycle of our app. We can then understand where we need to override functions to add our own code, and where to add the real functionality (code) that defines our app.

Let's examine the Android lifecycle. We can then move on to the ins and outs of Kotlin and gain an understanding of exactly where to put the code that we write.

A simplified explanation of the Android lifecycle

If you have ever used an Android device, you have probably noticed that it works quite differently to many other operating systems. For example, you can be using an app on your device, perhaps checking what people are doing on Facebook.

Then, you get an email notification and you tap the notification to read it. Halfway through reading the email, you might get a Twitter notification and, because you are waiting on important news from someone you follow, you interrupt your email reading and change apps to Twitter with a touch.

After reading the tweet, you fancy a game of *Angry Birds*; however, halfway through the first fling, you suddenly remember the Facebook post. So, you quit *Angry Birds* and tap on the Facebook icon.

You will likely resume Facebook at the exact same point that you left it. Afterward, you could then go back to reading the email, decide to reply to the tweet, or start an entirely new app.

All this toing and froing takes quite a lot of management on the part of the operating system, and is independent from the individual apps themselves.

The difference between, for example, a Windows PC and Android in the context of what we have just discussed is notable. With Android, although the user decides which app they are using, the OS decides when to close down (or destroy) an application and our user's data (such as the hypothetical note) along with it. We need to consider this when coding our apps; just because we might write code to do something interesting with our user's input doesn't mean that Android will let the code execute.

The lifecycle phases demystified

The Android system has a number of distinct phases that any given app can be in. Depending upon the phase, the Android system decides how the app is viewed by the user, or whether it is viewed at all.

Android has these phases so that it can decide which app is in current use, and can then allocate the correct amount of resources, such as memory and processing power, to the app.

In addition, as the user interacts with the device (for example, touches the screen), Android must give the details of that interaction to the correct app. For instance, a drag-and-release movement in *Angry Birds* means take a shot, but in a messaging app, it might mean delete a text message.

We have already raised the issue of when the user quits our app to answer a phone call; will they lose their progress, data, or important note?

Android has a system that, when simplified a little for the purposes of explanation, means that every app on an Android device is in one of the following phases:

- Being created
- Starting
- Resuming
- Running
- Pausing
- Stopping
- Being destroyed

This list of phases will hopefully appear logical. As an example, the user presses the Facebook app icon and the app is **being created**; then, it is **started**. This is all straightforward so far, but the next phase in the list is **resuming**.

This is not as illogical as it might first appear. If, for a moment, we can just accept that the app resumes after it starts, then all will become clear as we continue.

After **resuming,** the app is **running**. This is when the Facebook app has control of the screen and has the greater share of system memory and processing power, and is receiving the details of the user's input.

Now, what about our example where we switch from the Facebook app to the email app?

As we tap to go to read our email, the Facebook app will have entered the **paused** phase, followed by the **stopping** phase, and the email app will enter the **being created** phase, followed by **resuming**, and then **running**.

If we decide to revisit Facebook, as in the previous scenario, the Facebook app will probably skip **being created** and go straight to **resume** and then be **running** again (most likely at the exact same place that we left it).

Note that at any time, Android can decide to **stop** and then **destroy** an app, in which case, when we run the app again, it will need to be **created** at the first phase all over again.

So, had the Facebook app been inactive long enough, or perhaps *Angry Birds* had needed so many system resources that Android had **destroyed** the Facebook app, then our experience of finding the exact post that we were previously reading might have been different. The point is that it is within the control of the app and how it interacts with the lifecycle to determine the user's experience.

If all this is starting to get confusing, then you will be pleased to know that the only reason to mention these phases is due to the following:

- You know they exist
- We will occasionally need to interact with them
- We will take things step by step when we do

How we handle the lifecycle phases

When we are programming an app, how do we interact with this complexity? The good news is that the Android code that was autogenerated when we created our first project does most of it for us.

As we have discussed, we just don't see the functions that handle this interaction, but we do have the opportunity to override them and add our own code to that phase if we need to.

This means that we can get on with learning Kotlin and making Android apps until we come to one of the occasional instances where we need to do something in one of the phases.

If our app has more than one activity, they will each have their own lifecycle. This doesn't have to complicate things and, overall, it will make things easier for us.

The following list offers a quick explanation of the functions provided by Android to manage the lifecycle phases. To clarify our discussion of lifecycle functions, they are listed next to their corresponding phases that we have been discussing. However, as you will see, the function names make it clear on their own where they fit in.

In the list, there is also a brief explanation or suggestion for why we might use each function to interact during each phase. We will meet most of these functions as we progress through the book; we have, of course, already seen `onCreate`:

- `onCreate`: This function is executed when the Activity is *being created.* Here, we get everything ready for the app, including the UI (such as calling `setContentView`), graphics, and sound.
- `onStart`: This function is executed when the app is in the *starting* phase.
- `onResume`: This function runs after `onStart`, but can also be entered (most logically) after our Activity is resuming after being previously paused. We might reload the previously saved user data (such as an important note) from when the app had been interrupted, perhaps by a phone call or the user running another app.
- `onPause`: This occurs when our app is *pausing*. Here, we might save unsaved data (such as the note) that could be reloaded in `onResume`. Activities always transition into a paused state when another UI element is displayed on top of the current Activity (for example, a pop-up dialog) or when the Activity is about to stopped (for example, when the user navigates to a different Activity).
- `onStop`: This relates to the *stopping* phase. This is where we might undo everything we did in `onCreate`, such as releasing system resources or writing information to a database. If we reach here, the Activity is probably going to get destroyed sometime soon.
- `onDestroy`: This is when our Activity is finally being *destroyed*. There is no turning back at this phase. This is our last chance to dismantle our app in an orderly manner. If the Activity reaches this stage, it will need to go through the lifecycle phases from the beginning the next time the app is used.

The following diagram shows the likely flows of execution between the functions:

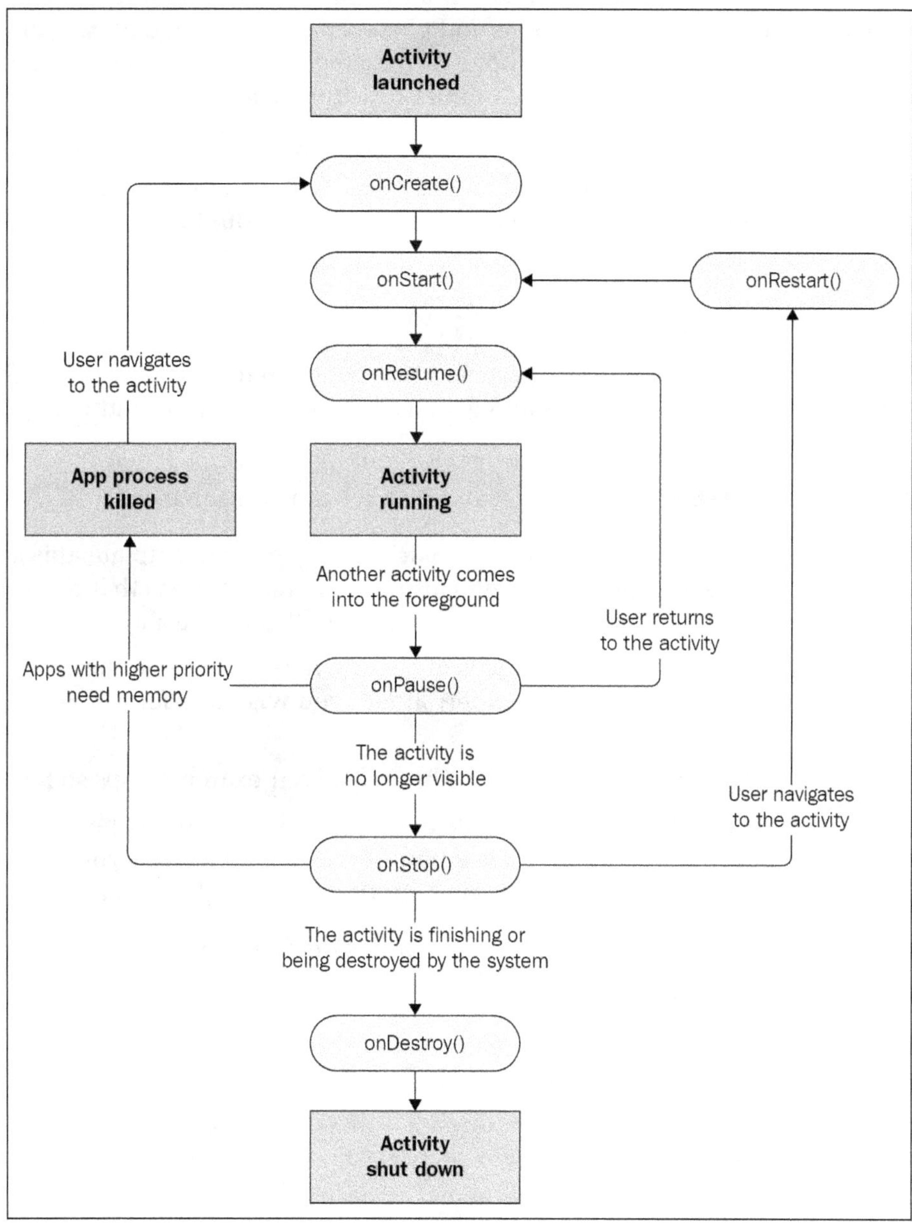

All the function descriptions and their related phases should appear straightforward. The only real question is: what about the running phase? As you will see when we write our code in the other functions and phases, the `onCreate`, `onStart`, and `onResume` functions will prepare the app, which then persists, forming the running phase. Then, the `onPause`, `onStop`, and `onDestroy` functions will occur afterward.

Now we can look at these lifecycle functions in action with a mini-app. We will do so by overriding them all and adding a `Log` message and a `Toast` message to each. This will visually demonstrate the phases that our app passes through.

The lifecycle demo app

In this section, we will do a quick experiment that will help to familiarize us with the lifecycle functions that our app uses and give us a chance to play around with a bit more Kotlin code.

Follow these steps to start a new project and then we can add some code:

1. Start a new project and choose the **Basic Activity** project template; this is because during this project, we will also look at the functions that control the app menu and the **Empty Activity** option doesn't generate a menu.
2. Call it **Lifecycle Demo**. The code is in the download bundle in the `Chapter06/Lifecycle Demo` folder, should you wish to refer to it or copy and paste it.
3. Keep the other settings as they have been in all our example apps so far.
4. Wait for Android Studio to generate the project files and then open the `MainActivity.kt` file in the code editor (if it is not opened for you by default) by left-clicking on the **MainActivity** tab above the editor.

We will only need the `MainActivity.kt` file for this demonstration as we will not be building a UI.

Coding the lifecycle demo app

In the `MainActivity.kt` file, find the `onCreate` function and add two lines of code just before the closing curly brace (`}`), which marks the end of the `onCreate` function:

```
Toast.makeText(this, "In onCreate",
            Toast.LENGTH_SHORT).show()

Log.i("info", "In onCreate")
```

Remember that you will need to use the *Alt* + *Enter* keyboard combination twice to import the classes needed for `Toast` and `Log`.

After the closing curly brace (}) of the `onCreate` function, leave one clear line and add the following five lifecycle functions and their contained code. Note that it doesn't matter in what order we add our overridden functions; Android will call them in the correct order, regardless of the order in which we type them:

```
override fun onStart() {
  // First call the "official" version of this function
  super.onStart()

  Toast.makeText(this, "In onStart",
        Toast.LENGTH_SHORT).show()

  Log.i("info", "In onStart")
}

override fun onResume() {
  // First call the "official" version of this function
  super.onResume()

  Toast.makeText(this, "In onResume",
              Toast.LENGTH_SHORT).show()

  Log.i("info", "In onResume")
}

override fun onPause() {
  // First call the "official" version of this function
  super.onPause()

  Toast.makeText(this, "In onPause",
               Toast.LENGTH_SHORT).show()

  Log.i("info", "In onPause")
}

override fun onStop() {
  // First call the "official" version of this function
  super.onStop()

  Toast.makeText(this, "In onStop",
```

```
                Toast.LENGTH_SHORT).show()

    Log.i("info", "In onStop")
  }

  override fun onDestroy() {
    // First call the "official" version of this function
    super.onDestroy()

    Toast.makeText(this, "In onDestroy",
                Toast.LENGTH_SHORT).show()

    Log.i("info", "In onDestroy")
  }
```

First, let's talk about the code itself. Notice that the function names all correspond to the lifecycle functions and their related phases, which we discussed earlier in this chapter. Notice that all the function declarations are preceded by the `override` keyword. Also, see that the first line of code inside each function is `super.on....`

The following explains exactly what is going on:

- Android calls our functions at the various times that we have already discussed.
- The `override` keyword shows that these functions replace or override the original version of the function that is provided as part of the Android API. Note that we don't see these replaced functions, but they are there, and if we didn't override them, these original versions will be called by Android instead of ours.
- The `super.on...` code, which is the first line of code within each of the overridden functions, then calls these original versions. So, we don't simply override these original functions in order to add our own code; we also call them, and their code is executed too.

For the eager reader, the `super` keyword is for super-class. We will explore function overriding and super-classes more as we progress through this book.

Finally, the code that you added will make each of the functions output one `Toast` message and one `Log` message. However, the messages that are output vary, as can be seen with the text that is in between the double speech marks (`""`). The messages that are output will make it clear which function produced them.

Running the lifecycle demo app

Now that we have looked at the code, we can play with our app and learn about the lifecycle from what happens:

1. Run the app on either a device or an emulator.
2. Watch the screen of the emulator and you will see the following appear one after the other as `Toast` messages: **In onCreate**, **In onStart**, and **In onResume**.
3. Notice the following messages in the logcat window; if there are too many messages, remember that you can filter them by setting the **Log level** dropdown to **Info**:

```
info:in onCreate
info:in onStart
info:in onResume
```

4. Now tap the back button on the emulator or the device. Notice that you get the following three `Toast` messages in this exact order: **In onPause**, **In onStop**, and **In onDestroy**. Verify that we have matching output in the logcat window.
5. Next, run a different app. Perhaps run the Hello World app from *Chapter 1, Getting Started with Android and Kotlin* (but any app will do), by tapping its icon on the emulator or device screen.
6. Now try opening the task manager on the emulator.

You can refer to *Chapter 3, Exploring Android Studio and the Project Structure*, and the *Using the emulator as a real device* section for how to do this on the emulator if you are unsure.

7. You should now see all the recently run apps on the device.
8. Tap on the lifecycle demo app and notice that the usual three starting messages are shown; this is because our app was previously destroyed.
9. Now tap the task manager button again and switch to the Hello World app. Notice that this time, only the **In onPause** and **In onStop** messages are shown. Verify that we have matching output in the logcat window; this should tell us that the app has **not** been destroyed.
10. Now, again using the task manager button, switch to the lifecycle demo app. You will see that only the **In onStart** and **In onResume** messages are shown, indicating that `onCreate` was not required to get the app running again. This is as expected because the app was not previously destroyed, but merely stopped.

Next, let's talk about what we saw when we ran the app.

Examining the lifecycle demo app output

When we started the lifecycle demo app for the first time, we saw that the `onCreate`, `onStart`, and `onResume` functions were called. Then, when we closed the app using the back button, the `onPause`, `onStop`, and `onDestroy` functions were called.

Furthermore, we know from our code that the original versions of all these functions are also called because we are calling them ourselves with the `super.on...` code, which is the first thing we do in each of our overridden functions.

The quirk in our app's behavior came when we used the task manager to switch between apps and, when switching away from the lifecycle demo app, it was not destroyed and, subsequently, when switching back, it was not necessary to run `onCreate`.

> **Where's my Toast?**
> The opening three and closing three `Toast` messages are queued by the operating system and the functions have already completed by the time they are shown. You can verify this by running the experiments again and see that all three starting and closing log messages are output before the second `Toast` message is even shown. However, the `Toast` messages do reinforce our knowledge about the order, if not the timing.

It is entirely possible (but not that likely) that you got slightly different results when you followed the preceding steps. What is for sure is that when our apps are run on thousands of different devices by millions of different users who have different preferences for interacting with their devices, Android will be calling the lifecycle functions at unpredictable times.

For example, what happens when the user exits the app by pressing the home button? If we open two apps one after the other, and then use the back button to switch to the earlier app, will that destroy or just stop the app? What happens when the user has a dozen apps in their task manager and the operating system needs to destroy some apps that were previously only stopped; will our app be one of the victims?

You can, of course, test out all the preceding scenarios on the emulator. But the results will only be true for the one time you test it. It is not guaranteed that the same behavior will be exhibited every time, and certainly not on every different Android device.

At last, there is some good news; the solution to all of this complexity is to follow a few simple rules:

- Set up your app so that it is ready to run in the `onCreate` function.
- Load your user's data in the `onResume` function.
- Save your user's data in the `onPause` function.
- Tidy up your app and make it a good Android citizen in the `onDestroy` function.
- Watch out for a couple of occasions in this book where we might like to use `onStart` and `onStop`.

If we follow the preceding rules, we will see that, over the course of the book, we can simply stop worrying about the lifecycle and let Android handle it.

There are a few more functions that we can override as well; so, let's take a look at them.

Some other overridden functions

You may have noticed that there are two other autogenerated functions in the code of all our projects using the Basic Activity template. They are `onCreateOptionsMenu` and `onOptionsItemSelected`. Many Android apps have a pop-up menu, so Android Studio generates one by default when using the Basic Activity template, including the outline of the code to make it work.

You can see the XML that describes the menu in `res/menu/menu_main.xml` from the project explorer. The key lines of XML code are as follows:

```
<item
      android:id="@+id/action_settings"
      android:orderInCategory="100"
      android:title="@string/action_settings"
      app:showAsAction="never" />
```

This describes a menu **item** with the **Settings** text. If you run any of our apps built with the Basic Activity template, you will see the button as shown in the following screenshot:

If you tap the button, you can see it in action as follows:

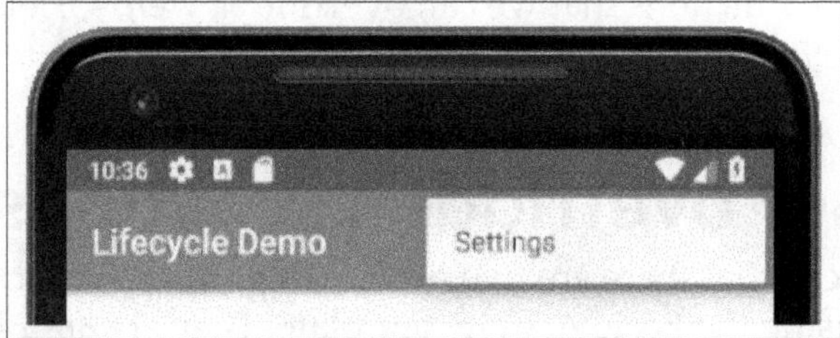

So, how do the `onCreateOptionsMenu` and `onOptionsItemSelected` functions produce these results?

The `onCreateOptionsMenu` function loads the menu from the `menu_main.xml` file with this line of code:

```
menuInflater.inflate(R.menu.menu_main, menu)
```

It is called by the default version of the `onCreate` function, which is why we don't see it happen.

> We will use the pop-up menu in *Chapter 17, Data Persistence and Sharing,* to switch between the different screens of our app.

The `onOptionsItemSelected` function is called when the user taps on the menu button. This function handles what will happen when an item is selected. Now, nothing happens; it just returns `true`.

Feel free to add `Toast` and `Log` messages to these functions to test out the order and timing I have just described.

Now that we have seen how the Android lifecycle works and have been introduced to a number of overridable functions to interact with this lifecycle, we had better learn the fundamentals of Kotlin so that we can write some more useful code to go in these functions and write our own functions too.

The structure of Kotlin code – revisited

We have already seen that each time we create a new Android project, we also create a new **package**; this is a kind of container for the code that we write.

We have also learned about and played around with **classes**. We have imported and taken direct advantage of classes from the Android API, such as `Log` and `Toast`. We have also used the `AppCompatActivity` class but in a different manner to that of `Log` and `Toast`. You might recall that the first line of code in all our projects so far, after the `import` statements, used the `:` notation to inherit from a class:

```
class MainActivity : AppCompatActivity() {
```

When we inherit from a class, as opposed to just importing it, we are making it our own. In fact, if you take another look at the line of code, you can see that we are making a new class, with a new name, `MainActivity`, but basing it on the `AppCompatActivity` class from the Android API.

`AppCompatActivity` is a modified version of `Activity`. It gives extra features for older versions of Android that would otherwise not be present. Everything we have discussed about `Activity`, such as the lifecycle, is equally true for `AppCompatActivity`. If the name ends in `...Activity`, it doesn't matter because everything we have discussed and will discuss is equally true. I will usually just refer to this class simply as `Activity`.

We can summarize our use of classes as follows:

- We can import classes to use them
- We can inherit from classes to use them and to extend their functionality
- We can eventually make our own classes (and will do so soon)

Our own classes, and those that are written by others, are the building blocks of our code, and the functions within the classes wrap the functional code - that is, the code that does the work.

We can write functions within the classes that we extend as we did with `topClick` and `bottomClick` in *Chapter 2, Kotlin, XML, and the UI Designer*. Furthermore, we overrode functions that are already part of classes written by others, such as `onCreate` and `onPause`.

The only code, however, that we put in these functions was a few calls using `Toast` and `Log`. Now we are ready to take some more steps with Kotlin.

Summary

In this chapter, we have learned that it is not only us that can call our code; the operating system can also call the code contained within the functions that we have overridden. By adding the appropriate code to the various overridden lifecycle functions, we can be sure that the right code will be executed at the right time.

What we need to do now is to learn how to write some more Kotlin code. In the next chapter, we will start to focus on Kotlin and, because we have such a good grounding already in Android, we will have no problem practicing and using everything we learn.

7
Kotlin Variables, Operators, and Expressions

In this chapter and the next, we are going to learn and practice the core fundamentals of Kotlin. In fact, we will explore the main principles of programming in general. In this chapter, we will focus on the creation and understanding of data itself, and in the next chapter, we will explore how to manipulate and respond to it.

This chapter will focus on the simplest type of data in Kotlin - variables. We will revisit more complex and powerful types of data in *Chapter 15, Handling Data and Generating Random Numbers*.

The core Kotlin fundamentals that we'll learn about apply when working within classes that we inherit from (such as `Activity` and `AppCompatActivity`) and the classes that we write ourselves (as we will start to do in *Chapter 10, Object-Oriented Programming*).

As it is more logical to learn the basics before we write our own classes, we will learn the basics and then use the extended `Activity` class, `AppCompatActivity`, to put this new theory into practice. We will use `Log` and `Toast` again to see the results of our coding. In addition, we will use more functions that we will write ourselves (called from buttons) as well as the overridden functions of the `Activity` class to trigger the execution of our code. We will save studying the full details on functions, however, until *Chapter 9, Kotlin Functions*.

When we move onto *Chapter 10, Object-Oriented Programming*, and start to write our own classes, as well as gain an understanding about how classes that are written by others work, everything we have learned here will still apply then too.

By the end of the chapter, you will be comfortable writing Kotlin code that creates and uses data within Android. This chapter will take you through the following topics:

- Learning the jargon
- Learning some more about code comments
- What are variables?
- Types of variables
- The different ways to declare variables
- Initializing variables
- Operators and expressions
- The express yourself demo app

Let's start by finding out exactly what a variable is.

Learning the jargon

Throughout this book, I will use simple English to explain a number of technical concepts. I will not ask you to read the technical explanation of a Kotlin or Android concept that has not been previously explained in non-technical language.

A note to Java programmers who are new to Kotlin: if you have done some Java programming, then things are about to get weird! You might even swear that I have made some errors; perhaps you might even think that I have forgotten to add semicolons to the ends of all the lines of code! I urge you to keep reading because I think you will discover that Kotlin has some advantages over Java because it is more succinct and expressive. Learning Java still has its place because most of the Android API is still Java, and even if the entire Android community were to drop Java immediately (and they haven't), there would still be legacy Java code for years to come. I won't continually point out the differences between Java and Kotlin because there are so many and such an analysis is unnecessary. If you are interested, I recommend this article: `https://yalantis.com/blog/kotlin-vs-java-syntax/`. Ultimately, Kotlin and Java compile to the exact same Dalvik-compatible Java byte code. In fact, Java and Kotlin are 100% interoperable and can even be mixed together in a project. You can even paste Java code into a Kotlin project, and it will be instantly converted to Kotlin.

The Kotlin and Android communities are full of people who speak in technical terms; therefore, to join in and learn from these communities, you need to understand the terms that they use.

So, the approach that this book takes is to learn a concept or get a rough outline using entirely simple language, but at the same time introduce the jargon or technical terms as part of the learning.

Kotlin syntax is the way that we put together the language elements of Kotlin to produce code that executes. The Kotlin syntax is a combination of the words that we use and the formation of those words into sentence-like structures that is our code.

These Kotlin "words" are many in number but, taken in small chunks, they are certainly easier to learn than any human language. We call these words **keywords**.

I am confident that if you can read plain English then you can learn Kotlin, because learning Kotlin is much easier than learning to read English. So, what then separates someone who has finished an elementary Kotlin course such as this one and an expert programmer?

The answer is the exact same things that separate a student of language and a master poet. Expertise in Kotlin comes not in the number of Kotlin keywords we know how to use, but in the way that we use them. Mastery of the language comes through practice, further study, and using the keywords more skillfully. Many consider programming an art as much as a science, and there is some truth to this.

More on code comments

As you become more advanced at writing Kotlin programs, the solutions that you use to create your programs will become longer and more complicated. Furthermore, as we will see in later chapters, Kotlin was designed to manage complexity by having us divide up our code into separate classes, usually across multiple files.

Code comments are a part of the Kotlin files that do not have any function in the program execution itself; that is, the compiler ignores them. They serve to help the programmer to document, explain, and clarify their code to make it more understandable to themselves later, or to other programmers who might need to use or change it.

We have already seen a single-line comment:

```
// this is a comment explaining what is going on
```

The preceding comment begins with the two forward slash characters, `//`. The comment ends at the end of the line. So, anything on that line is for people only, whereas anything on the next line (unless it's another comment) needs to be syntactically correct Kotlin code:

```
// I can write anything I like here
but this line will cause an error
```

We can use multiple single-line comments, as follows:

```
// Below is an important note
// I am an important note
// We can have as many single line comments like this as we like
```

Single-line comments are also useful if we want to temporarily disable a line of code. We can put `//` in front of the code and it will not be included in the program. Refer back to this code, which tells Android to load our layout:

```
// setContentView(R.layout.activity_main)
```

In this situation, the layout will not be loaded, and the app will have a blank screen when run as the entire line of code is ignored by the compiler.

We saw this in *Chapter 5, Beautiful Layouts with CardView and ScrollView* when we temporarily commented out one of the lines of code in a function.

There is another type of comment in Kotlin known as the **multiline comment**. The multiline comment is useful for longer comments that span across multiple lines and for adding things such as copyright information at the top of a code file. Like the single-line comment, a multiline comment can be used to temporarily disable code; in this case, usually across multiple lines.

Everything in between the leading `/*` character and the ending `*/` character is ignored by the compiler. Take a look at the following examples:

```
/*
   You can tell I am good at this because my
   code has so many helpful comments in it.
*/
```

There is no limit to the number of lines in a multiline comment; the type of comment that is best to use will depend upon the situation. In this book, I will always explain every line of code explicitly in the text, but you will often find liberally sprinkled comments within the code itself that add further explanation, insight, or context. So, it's always a good idea to read all the code thoroughly:

```
/*
   The winning lottery numbers for next Saturday are
   9,7,12,34,29,22
   But you still want to make Android apps?
*/
```

All the best programmers liberally sprinkle their code with comments!

Variables

We can think of a **variable** as a named storage box. We choose a name, perhaps `variableA`. These names are the programmer's access into the memory of the user's Android device.

Variables are values in memory that are ready to be used when necessary by referring to them with their name.

Computer memory has a highly complex system of addresses that, fortunately, we do not need to directly interact with. Kotlin variables allow us to devise our own convenient names for all the data that we need our app to work with. The operating system will, in turn, interact with the physical (hardware) memory.

So, we can think of our Android device's memory as a huge warehouse waiting for us to add our variables. When we assign names to our variables, they are stored in the warehouse, ready for when we need them. When we use our variable's name, the device knows exactly what we are referring to. We can then tell it to do things, such as the following:

- Assign a value to `variableA`
- Add `variableA` to `variableB`
- Test the value of `variableB` and take an action based on the result

In a typical app, we might have a variable named `unreadMessages`; perhaps to hold the number of unread messages that the user has. We can add to it when a new message arrives, take away from it when the user reads a message, and show it to the user somewhere in the app's layout, so that they know how many unread messages they have.

Situations that might arise can include the following:

- The user gets three new messages, so add three to the value of `unreadMessages`.
- The user logs into the app, so use `Toast` to display a message along with the value stored in `unreadMessages`.
- The user sees that a couple of the messages are from someone they don't like and deletes two messages. We could then subtract two from `unreadMessages`.

Variable names are arbitrary, and if you don't use any of the characters or keywords that Kotlin restricts, you can call your variables whatever you like.

In practice, however, it is best to adopt a **naming convention** so that your variable names will be consistent. In this book, we will use a simple convention of variable names starting with a lowercase letter. When there is more than one word in the variable's name, the second word will begin with an uppercase letter. This is called **camel casing**.

Here are some examples of camel-case variable names:

- `unreadMessages`
- `contactName`
- `isFriend`

Before we take a look at some real Kotlin code that uses some variables, we need to first look at the **types** of variables that we can create and use.

Types of variables

It is not hard to imagine that even a simple app will have quite a few variables. In the previous section, we introduced the `unreadMessages` variable as a hypothetical example. What if the app has a list of contacts and needs to remember each of their names? Then, we might need variables for each contact.

And what about when an app needs to know whether a contact is also a friend, or just a regular contact? We might need code that tests for friend status and then adds messages from that contact into an appropriate folder, so that the user knows whether they were messages from a friend or not.

Another common requirement in a computer program, including Android apps, is the right or wrong test. Computer programs represent right or wrong calculations using **true** and **false**.

To cover these and many other types of data that you might want to store or manipulate, Kotlin uses variables of different **types**.

There are many types of variables, and we can even invent our own types as well. But, for now, we will look at the most commonly-used Kotlin types, and these will cover just about every situation that we are likely to run into. The best way to explain types is through a number of examples.

We have already discussed the hypothetical `unreadMessages` variable. This variable is, of course, a number.

On the other hand, the hypothetical `contactName` variable will hold the characters or letters that make up a contact's name.

The type that holds a regular number is called an **Int** (an abbreviation of integer) type, and the type that holds name-like data is called a **String**.

Here is a list of the types of variables that we will use in this book:

- `Int`: The `Int` type is for storing integers and whole numbers. This type can store values with a size that is in excess of 2 billion, including negative values too.
- `Long`: As the name suggests, `Long` data types can be used when even larger numbers are needed. A `Long` variable can store numbers up to 9,223,372,036,854,775,807. That's a lot of unread messages. There are plenty of uses for `Long` variables, but if a smaller variable will do, we should use it because our app will use less memory.
- `Float`: This variable is used for floating point numbers. That is, numbers where there is precision beyond the decimal point. As the fractional part of a number takes memory space just as the whole number part, the range of a number that is possible in a `Float` variable is, therefore, decreased compared to non-floating-point numbers. So, unless our variable will use the extra precision, `Float` will not be our data type of choice.
- `Double`: When the precision in a `Float` variable is not enough, we have `Double`.

- `Boolean`: We will be using plenty of Booleans throughout the book. The `Boolean` variable type can be either `true` or `false`; nothing else. Booleans answer questions, such as the following:
    - Is the contact a friend?
    - Are there any new messages?
    - Are two examples of Booleans enough?
- `Char`: This stores a single alphanumeric character. It's not going to change the world on its own, but it could be useful if we put lots of them together.
- `String`: Strings can be used to store any keyboard character. It is similar to a `Char` variable but of almost any length. Anything from a contact's name to an entire book can be stored in a single `String`. We will be using Strings regularly, including in this chapter.
- `Class`: This is the most powerful data type and we have already discussed it a little. We will take a deep dive into classes in *Chapter 10, Object-Oriented Programming*.
- `Array`: This type comes in lots of different flavors and is key for handling and organizing large sets of data. We will explore the variations of `Array` in *Chapter 15, Handling Data and Generating Random Numbers.*

Now we know what variables are and that there is a wide selection of types, we are nearly ready to see some actual Kotlin code.

Declaring and initializing variables

Before we can use a variable type that we just discussed, we must **declare** them, so that the compiler knows they exist, and we must also **initialize** them, so they hold a value.

For each of the variable types in Kotlin, such as `Int`, `Float`, and `String`, there are two keywords that we can use to declare them: `val` and `var`.

The `val` type is for storing values that are decided by the programmer before the application starts or during initialization and cannot be changed again during execution. The `var` type is for values that can be manipulated and altered throughout execution.

Therefore, the `val` type is only readable. In technical terms, it is known as **immutable**. The `var` type is readable and writeable, and this is called **mutable**. Writing code that attempts to change the value of a `val` type during execution will cause Android Studio to show an error and the code will not compile. There are also rules for `var` that we will explore later.

There are the two ways that we can declare and initialize a `String` type; first, by using `val`, as follows:

```
val contactName: String = "Gordon Freeman"
```

In the preceding line of code, a new `val` variable named `contactName` and of type `String` is declared and now holds the `Gordon Freeman` value.

Furthermore, the `Gordon Freeman` text is now the only value that `contactName` can hold for the duration of the app's execution. You could attempt to change it with the following line of code:

```
contactName = "Apple Crumble" // Causes an error
```

Here is what you will see if you paste the preceding code into the `onCreate` function in an Android project:

```
val contactName: String= "Gordon Freeman"
contactName = "Apple Crumble" // Causes an error
```

Val cannot be reassigned

Android Studio is helping us to enforce our decision to make the variable **constant**. Of course, we will frequently need to change the value held by a variable. When we do, we will use `var` instead; take a look at the next two lines of code:

```
var contactName: String = "Gordon Freeman"
contactName = "Alyx Vance" // No problem
```

In the preceding code, we use `var` to declare a `String` type, and this time we successfully change the value held by `contactName` to `Alyx Vance`.

The point to take away here is that if the variable does not need to change during the execution of the app, then we should use `val`, because the compiler can help to protect us from making mistakes.

Let's declare and initialize some different types of variables:

```
val battleOfHastings: Int = 1066
val pi: Float = 3.14f
var worldRecord100m: Float = 9.63f
var millisecondsSince1970: Long = 1544693462311
// True at 9:30am 13/12/2018
val beerIsTasty: Boolean = true
var isItRaining: Boolean = false
```

```
val appName: String = "Express Yourself"
var contactName: String = "Geralt"

// All the var variables can be reassigned
worldRecord100m = 9.58f
millisecondsSince1970 = 1544694713072
// True at 9:51am 13/12/2018
contactName = "Vesemir"
```

Notice that in the previous code, I declared variables as `val` when they are unlikely to change and as `var` when it is likely that they will change. As you develop your app, you can guess whether to use `val` or `var` and, if necessary, you can change a `var` variable to a `val` variable, or the other way around. Also, in the preceding code notice that `String` types are initialized with the value between speech marks but `Int`, `Float`, `Long`, and `Boolean` are not.

Saving keystrokes with type inference

Kotlin was designed to be as succinct as possible. It was one of the aims of the JetBrains team to let developers get as much done with as little code as possible. We will see examples of this throughout the Kotlin language. If you have previously coded in another language, especially Java, you will notice a significant reduction in typing. The first example of this is **type inference**.

Kotlin can often infer the type you need from the context, and if this is the case, then you don't need to write the type explicitly; consider the following example:

```
var contactName: String = "Xian Mei"
```

In the preceding code, a `String` type called `contactName` is declared and initialized using "Xian Mei". If you think about it for a moment, it must be a `String`. Fortunately, this is obvious to the Kotlin compiler too. We could (and should) improve the preceding line of code using type inference, such as with this next code:

```
var contactName = "Xian Mei"
```

The colon and the type have been omitted, but the result is identical.

Java programmers will also notice that Kotlin code does not need to have a semicolon at the end of each line. If you like semicolons, however, the compiler will not complain if you do add one to the end of each line:

```
var contactName = "Xian Mei"; // OK but superfluous
```

We must remember, however, that although we haven't specified `String` explicitly, it is still a `String` type - and only a `String` type. If we try to do something unsuitable for a `String` type, then we will get an error; for example, as we do when we try to reinitialize it to a number value as in this code:

```
contactName = 3.14f // Error
```

The preceding code will be flagged in Android Studio and compilation won't work. Here are all the declarations and initializations from the previous section of code, but this time using type inference:

```
val battleOfHastings = 1066
val pi = 3.14f
var worldRecord100m = 9.63f
var millisecondsSince1970 = 1544693462311
// True at 9:30am 13/12/2018
val beerIsTasty = true
var isItRaining = false
val appName = "Express Yourself"
var contactName =  "Geralt"
```

We will see more type inference with variables in the next two sections, and in later chapters, we will use type inference with more complex types such as classes, Arrays, and Collections. Type inference will also become a good timesaver, by making our code shorter and more manageable.

It might sound obvious, but it is worth mentioning that if you are declaring a variable for initialization later then type inference is not possible, as shown in the following code:

```
var widgetCount // Error
```

The preceding line of code will cause an error and the app will not compile.

When using type inference, it will usually be obvious what type a variable is but, if there is ever any doubt, you can select a variable in Android Studio and press *Shift* + *Ctrl* + *P* simultaneously to get a handy onscreen hint:

Omitting the occasional `String`, `Int`, or colon (`:`) type isn't going to change much on its own, so let's learn how to make **expressions** with our variables by combining them with **operators**.

Operators and expressions

Of course, in almost any program, we are going to need to "do things" with these variables' values. We can manipulate and change variables with operators. When we combine operators and variables for a result, it is called an expression.

The following sections list the most common Kotlin operators that allow us to manipulate variables. You do not need to memorize them as we will look at every line of code as and when we use them for the first time.

We already saw the first operator when we initialized our variables in the previous section, but we will see it again being a bit more adventurous.

The assignment operator

This is the assignment operator:

```
=
```

It makes the variable to the left of the operator the same as the value to the right; for example, as in this line of code:

```
unreadMessages = newMessages
```

After the previous line of code has executed, the value stored in `unreadMessages` will be the same as the value stored in `newMessages`.

The addition operator

This is the addition operator:

```
+
```

It will add together values on either side of the operator. It's usually used in conjunction with the assignment operator. For example, it can add together two variables that have numeric values, as in this next line of code:

```
unreadMessages = newMessages + unreadMessages
```

Once the previous code has executed, the sum of the values held by `newMessages` and `unreadMessages` will be stored in `unreadMessages`. As another example of the same thing, take a look at this line of code:

```
accountBalance = yesterdaysBalance + todaysDeposits
```

Notice that it is perfectly acceptable (and quite common) to use the same variable simultaneously on both sides of an operator.

The subtraction operator

This is the subtraction operator:

```
-
```

It will subtract the value on the right side of the operator from the value on the left. This is usually used in conjunction with the assignment operator, as in this example:

```
unreadMessages = unreadMessages - 1
```

Another example of the subtraction operator is as follows:

```
accountBalance = accountBalance - withdrawals
```

After the previous line of code has executed, `accountBalance` will hold its original value minus whatever the value held in `withdrawals` is.

The division operator

This is the division operator:

```
/
```

It will divide the number on the left by the number on the right. Again, it's usually used in conjunction with the assignment operator; here is an example line of code:

```
fairShare = numSweets / numChildren
```

If, in the previous line of code, `numSweets` held nine and `numChildren` held three, then `fairShare` would now hold the value of three.

The multiplication operator

This is the multiplication operator:

```
*
```

It will multiply variables and numbers together and, as with many of the other operators, is usually used in conjunction with the assignment operator; for example, look at this line of code:

```
answer = 10 * 10
```

Another example of the multiplication operator is as follows:

```
biggerAnswer = 10 * 10 * 10
```

After the previous two lines of code have executed, `answer` holds the value 100, and `biggerAnswer` holds the value 1000.

The increment operator

This is the increment operator:

```
++
```

The increment operator is a quick way to add one to something. For example, take a look at this next line of code, which uses the addition operator:

```
myVariable = myVariable + 1
```

The previous line of code has the same result as this much more compact code:

```
myVariable ++
```

The decrement operator

This is the decrement operator:

```
--
```

The decrement operator (as you have you probably guessed) is a quick way to subtract one from something. For example, take a look at this next line of code, which uses the subtraction operator:

```
myVariable = myVariable -1
```

The previous line of code is the same as `myVariable --`.

Now we can put this new knowledge into a working app.

The express yourself demo app

Let's try using some declarations, assignments, and operators. When we bundle these elements together into some meaningful syntax, we call it an **expression**. Let's write a quick app to try some out. We will then use `Toast` and `Log` to check our results.

Create a new project called `Express Yourself`, use an **Empty Activity** project template, and leave all the other options in their usual settings. The completed code that we will write in this project can be found in the `Chapter07` folder of the download bundle.

Switch to the **MainActivity** tab in the editor and we will write some code. In the `onCreate` function, just before the closing curly brace (}), add this highlighted code:

```
class MainActivity : AppCompatActivity() {

    override fun onCreate(savedInstanceState: Bundle?) {
        super.onCreate(savedInstanceState)
        setContentView(R.layout.activity_main)

        val name = "Nolan Bushnell"
        val yearOfBirth = 1943
        var currentYear = 2019
        var age: Int
    }
}
```

We have just added four variables to the `onCreate` function. The first two are `val` variables that cannot be altered. They are a `String` type that holds a person's name and an `Int` type holding a year of birth. The types are not explicitly mentioned in the code; they are inferred.

The next two variables are `var` variables. We have an `Int` type to represent the current year, and an `Int` type that is uninitialized to represent the age of a person. As the `age` variable is uninitialized, its type cannot be inferred, and so we must specify it.

After the previous code, still inside `onCreate`, add the following lines:

```
age = currentYear - yearOfBirth
Log.i("info", "$age")
```

Run the app and notice the following output in the logcat window:

```
info: 76
```

The use of the `$` symbol in the speech marks of the `Log.i`... code indicates to the compiler that we want to output the *value stored in* the `age` variable, not the literal word "age".

The actual value itself (76), indicates that the value stored in `yearOfBirth` (1943) was subtracted from the value stored in `currentYear` (2019), and the result was used to initialize the `age` variable. As you will see, we can include as many `$` symbols in speech marks as we like and mix them with text and even Kotlin expressions. This feature is known as **String templates**. Let's try another String template.

Add these two lines of code after the previous code inside the `onCreate` function:

```
currentYear++
Log.i("info", "$name
was born in $yearOfBirth and is $age years old.
Next year he will be ${currentYear - yearOfBirth} years old)")
```

The first thing to explain about the code is that although it is formatted as four lines in this book, when you enter it into Android Studio it must be entered as two. The first line, `currentYear++`, increments (adds one) to the value stored in `currentYear`. All the rest of the code is one line.

Run the app and observe the following output in the logcat window:

```
Nolan Bushnell was born in 1943 and is 76 years old. Next year he will be
77 years old
```

The code works because of Kotlin String templates. Let's break down this rather long line of code. First, we call the `Log.i` function as we have done many times before. In the first String, we pass `"info"` and, in the second, we pass a selection of variable names preceded by the `$` symbol mixed up with some literal text. The most interesting part of the breakdown is the second to last part as we use an expression to form part of the String:

- `$name` prints Nolan Bushnell
- `Was born in` is literal text
- `$yearOfBirth` prints 1943
- The literal text, `and is`, follows next
- `$currentAge` prints 76
- Next, follows the literal text of `years old`
- The literal text, `Next year he will be`, follows next
- `${currentYear - yearOfBirth}` is an expression, and the result of the expression (77) is printed
- The final literal text, `years old`, is printed to conclude the output

This demonstrates that we can include any valid Kotlin expression inside a `String` type using the following form:

```
${expression}
```

We will see more complex and powerful expressions in the next chapter.

Summary

In this chapter, we have learned the fundamental building blocks of data in Kotlin. We have explored the different types and an overview of their different uses. We have also learned how to use String templates to build Strings from literal values, variables, and expressions. We also saw how we can and should use type inference to make our code more concise when possible.

We didn't see much of the Boolean variable type, but we will right that wrong in the next chapter when we learn about Kotlin decisions and loops.

8
Kotlin Decisions and Loops

We have just learned about variables and we now understand how to change the values that they hold with expressions, but how can we take a course of action that is dependent upon the value of a variable?

We can certainly add the number of new messages to the number of previously unread messages, but how can we, for example, trigger an action within our app when the user has read all their messages?

The first problem is that we need a way to test the value of a variable, and then respond when the value falls within a range of values or is equal to a specific value.

Another problem that is common in programming is that we need sections of our code to be executed a certain number of times (more than once or sometimes not at all) depending on the values of variables.

To solve the first problem, we will look at making decisions in Kotlin with `if`, `else`, and `when`. To solve the latter, we will look at loops in Kotlin with `while`, `do` - `while`, `for`, `continue`, and `break`.

Furthermore, we will learn that, in Kotlin, decisions are also expressions that produce a value. We will cover the following topics in this chapter:

- Making decisions with `if`, `else`, `else` - `if`, and `switch`
- The `when` demo app
- Kotlin `while` loops and `do` - `while` loops
- Kotlin `for` loops

Now let's learn more about Kotlin.

Making decisions in Kotlin

Our Kotlin code will constantly be making decisions. For example, we might need to know whether the user has new messages, or whether they have a certain number of friends. We need to be able to test our variables to see whether they meet certain conditions, and then execute a specific section of code depending upon whether they did or not.

In this section, as our code gets more in-depth, it helps to present the code in a way that makes it more readable. Let's take a look at code indenting to make our discussion about making decisions easier.

Indenting code for clarity

You have probably noticed that the Kotlin code in our project is indented. For example, the first line of code inside the `MainActivity` class is indented by one tab. Additionally, the first line of code is indented inside each function by another tab; here is an annotated diagram to make this clear:

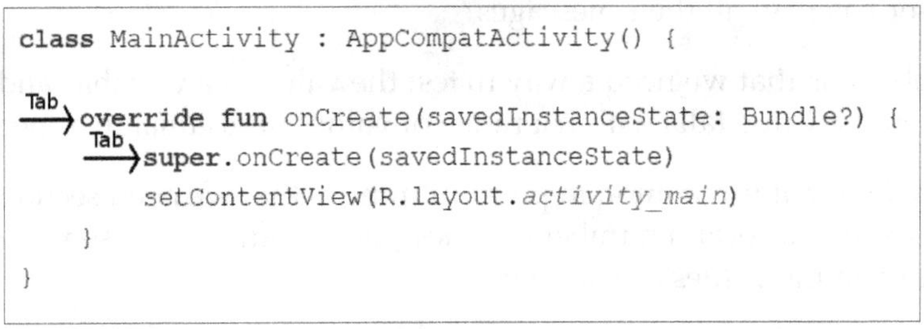

```
class MainActivity : AppCompatActivity() {

Tab
  ──>override fun onCreate(savedInstanceState: Bundle?) {
       Tab
       ──>super.onCreate(savedInstanceState)
          setContentView(R.layout.activity_main)
     }
}
```

Notice that when the indented block has ended, often with a closing curly brace (`}`), it is indented to the same extent as the line of code that began the block.

We do this to make the code more readable. It is not part of the Kotlin syntax, however, and the code will still compile if we don't bother to do this.

As our code gets more complicated, indenting, along with comments, helps to keep the meaning and structure of our code clear. I mention this now because when we start to learn the syntax for making decisions in Kotlin, indenting becomes especially useful and it is recommended that you indent your code the same way. Most of this indenting is done for us by Android Studio, but not all of it.

Now that we know how to present our code more clearly, we can learn about more operators, and then we can get to work by making decisions with Kotlin.

More Kotlin operators

We can already add (+), take away (-), multiply (*), divide (/), assign (=), increment (++), and decrement (--) with operators. Now we will explore some more useful operators, and then we will go straight onto learning about how to use them.

> Don't worry about memorizing each of the following operators. Glance over them and their explanations, and then move on to the next section. There, we will put a few operators to use and they will become much clearer as we see the examples of what they allow us to do. They are presented here in a list just to make the variety and scope of operators clear from the start. The list will also be more convenient to refer to later when not intermingled with the discussion about implementation that follows it.

We use operators to create an expression that is either true or false. We wrap that expression in parentheses or brackets like this: `(expression goes here)`.

The comparison operator

This is the comparison operator. It tests for equality and is either true or false; it is of the `Boolean` type:

```
==
```

An expression such as `(10 == 9)`, for example, is false. 10 is obviously not equal to 9. However, an expression such as `(2 + 2 == 4)` is obviously true.

> That is, except in *1984*, when 2 + 2 == 5 (`https://en.wikipedia.org/wiki/Nineteen_Eighty-Four`).

The logical NOT operator

This is the logical NOT operator:

```
!
```

It is used to test the negation of an expression. If the expression is false, then the NOT operator causes the expression to be true.

For instance, the expression `(!(2+2 == 5))` evaluates to true because 2 + 2 *is not* 5. But, a further example of `(!(2 + 2 = 4))` is false. This is because 2 + 2 *is* obviously 4.

The NOT equal operator

This is the NOT equal operator and it is another comparison operator:

```
!=
```

The NOT equal operator tests whether something is NOT equal; for example, the `(10 != 9)` expression is true because 10 is not equal to 9. On the other hand, `(10 != 10)` is false because 10 is equal to 10.

The greater-than operator

Another comparison operator (and there are a few more as well) is the greater-than operator:

```
>
```

This operator tests whether something is greater than something else. The expression `(10 > 9)` is true, but the expression `(9 > 10)` is false.

The less-than operator

You can probably guess that this operator tests for values that are less than others; here is what the operator looks like:

```
<
```

The expression `(10 < 9)` is false because 10 is not less than 9, while the expression `(9 < 10)` is true.

The greater-than-or-equal-to operator

This operator tests whether one value is greater than or equal to the other, and if either is true, the result is true. This is what the operator looks like:

```
>=
```

As an example, the expression `(10 >= 9)` is true, the expression `(10 >= 10)` is also true, but the expression `(10 >= 11)` is false because 10 is neither greater than nor equal to 11.

The less-than-or-equal-to operator

Like the previous operator, this one tests for two conditions, but this time, **less** than or equal to; take a look at the following operator:

```
<=
```

The expression `(10 <= 9)` is false, the expression `(10 <= 10)` is true, and the expression `(10 <= 11)` is also true.

The logical AND operator

This operator is known as logical AND. It tests two or more separate parts of an expression, and both or all parts must be true for the entire expression to be true:

```
&&
```

Logical AND is usually used in conjunction with the other operators to build more complex tests. The expression `((10 > 9) && (10 < 11))` is true because both parts are true. On the other hand, the expression `((10 > 9) && (10 < 9))` is false because only one part of the expression is true – `(10 > 9)`, while the other is false – `(10 < 9)`.

The logical OR operator

This operator is called logical OR and it is just like logical AND, except that only one of two or more parts of an expression needs to be true for the expression to be true:

```
||
```

Take another look at the previous example that we used for logical AND, but instead, replace `&&` with `||`. The expression `((10 > 9) || (10 < 9))` is now true because only one or more parts of the expression needs to be true.

Seeing these operators in a more practical context, in this chapter and throughout the rest of the book, will help to clarify their different uses. Now we know how to form expressions with operators, variables, and values. Next, we can look at a way of structuring and combining expressions to make several deep decisions.

How to use all these operators to test variables

All these operators are virtually useless without a way of properly using them to make real decisions that affect real variables and code.

Now that we have all the information we need, we can look at a hypothetical situation, and then actually examine some code for decision making.

Using the if expression

As you have seen, operators serve very little purpose on their own, but it is useful to see just part of the wide and varied range that is available to us. Now when we look at putting the most common operator, `==`, to use, we can start to see the powerful, yet fine, control that they offer us.

Let's make the previous examples less abstract. Meet the **if** expression by examining the following code:

```
val time = 9

val amOrPm = if(time < 12) {
  "am"
} else {
  "pm"
}

Log.i("It is ", amOrPm)
```

The preceding code starts by declaring and initializing an `Int` type called `time` to the value of `9`. The next line of code is quite interesting as it does two things. The `if(time < 12)` expression is a test; we know that time is less than `12` because we just initialized it to `9`. As the condition is true, the `if` expression returns the `"am"` value and the first part of the line of code before the `if` expression declares and initializes a new `String` type called `amOrPm` with that value.

Had we initialized the `time` variable to any value that was not less than 12 (that is, 12 or higher) then the value returned would have been `"pm"` from the `else` block. If you copy and paste the preceding code into a project, such as the `onCreate` function, the output in logcat will be as follows:

```
It is: am
```

The `if` expression is evaluated and, if the condition is true, then the code in the first set of curly braces ({...}) is executed; if the condition is false, then the code in the `else` {...} block is executed.

It is worth noting that `if` does not have to return a value, rather it could simply execute some code based on the result of the test; take a look at the following sample code:

```
val time = 13

if(time < 12) {
```

```
    // Execute some important morning task here
} else {
    // Do afternoon work here
}
```

In the preceding code, there is no returned value; we only care that the correct bit of code gets executed.

Technically, there is still a value returned (in this case, true or false), but we chose not to do anything with it.

Furthermore, our `if` expression can handle more than two outcomes, as we will see later.

We can also use `if` in a String template. We saw in the previous chapter that we can insert an expression into a `String` type by inserting the expression between curly brackets following the `$` symbol. Here is a reminder of the code from the previous chapter:

```
Log.i("info", "$name
was born in $yearOfBirth and is $age years old.
Next year he will be ${currentYear - yearOfBirth} years old)")
```

The highlighted part in the preceding code will cause the value of `yearOfBirth` that is subtracted from `currentYear` being printed amongst the rest of the message.

The following code sample shows how we can insert an entire `if` expression into a `String` template in the same way:

```
val weight = 30
val instruction =
  "Put bag in ${if (weight >= 25) "hold" else "cabin" }"

Log.i("instruction is ", instruction)
```

The preceding code uses `if` to test whether the `weight` variable was initialized to a value that was greater than or equal to 25. Depending upon whether the expression is true, it will add the word `hold` or the word `cabin` into the `String` initialization.

If you execute the preceding code, you will get the following output:

instruction is: Put this bag in the hold

If you change the initialization of `weight` to any value under 25 and execute the code, you will get the following output:

```
instruction is: Put this bag in the cabin
```

Let's take a look at a more complicated example.

If they come over the bridge, shoot them!

In the next example, we will use `if`, a few conditional operators, and a short story to demonstrate their use.

The captain is dying and, knowing that his remaining subordinates are not very experienced, he decides to write a Kotlin program (what else?) to convey his last orders after he has died. The troops must hold one side of a bridge while awaiting reinforcements, but with a few rules that determine their actions.

The first command the captain wants to make sure his troops understand is as follows:

If they come over the bridge, shoot them.

So, how do we simulate this situation in Kotlin? We need a `Boolean` variable – `isComingOverBridge`. The next bit of code assumes that the `isComingOverBridge` variable has been declared and initialized to either `true` or `false`.

We can then use `if` as follows:

```
if(isComingOverBridge){

    // Shoot them

}
```

If the `isComingOverBridge` Boolean is true, the code inside the opening and closing curly braces will execute. If `isComingOverBridge` is false, the program continues after the `if` block and without running the code within it.

Else do this instead

The captain also wants to tell his troops what to do if the enemy is not coming over the bridge. In this situation, he wants them to stay where they are and wait.

For this, we can use `else`. When we want to explicitly do something when the `if` expression does not evaluate to true, we use `else`.

For example, to tell the troops to stay put if the enemy is not coming over the bridge, we can write the following code:

```
if(isComingOverBridge){

   // Shoot them

}else{

   // Hold position

}
```

The captain then realizes that the problem isn't as simple as he first thought. What if the enemy comes over the bridge, but has too many troops? His squad will be overrun and slaughtered.

So, he comes up with the following code (this time, we'll use some variables as well):

```
var isComingOverBridge: Boolean
var enemyTroops: Int
var friendlyTroops: Int

// Code that initializes the above variables one way or another

// Now the if
if(isComingOverBridge && friendlyTroops > enemyTroops){

   // shoot them

}else if(isComingOveBridge && friendlyTroops < enemyTroops) {

   // blow the bridge

}else{

   // Hold position

}
```

The preceding code has three possible paths of execution. The first is for if the enemy is coming over the bridge and the friendly troops are greater in number:

```
if(isComingOverBridge && friendlyTroops > enemyTroops)
```

The second is for if the enemy troops are coming over the bridge but outnumber the friendly troops:

```
else if(isComingOveBridge && friendlyTroops < enemyTroops)
```

The third and final possible outcome that will execute if neither of the other two paths are true is captured by the final `else` statement without an `if` condition.

Reader challenge

Can you spot a flaw with the preceding code? One that might leave a bunch of inexperienced troops in complete disarray? The possibility of the enemy troops and friendly troops being exactly equal in number has not been handled explicitly and will, therefore, be handled by the final `else` statement, which is meant for when there are no enemy troops. Any self-respecting captain would expect his troops to fight in this situation, and he could have changed the first `if` statement to accommodate this possibility, as follows:

```
if(isComingOverBridge && friendlyTroops >=
enemyTroops)
```

Finally, the captain's last concern is that if the enemy comes over the bridge waving the white flag of surrender and are promptly slaughtered, then his men will end up as war criminals. The code required here is obvious; using the `wavingWhiteFlag` Boolean variable, he can write the following test:

```
if (wavingWhiteFlag){

   // Take prisoners

}
```

However, where to put this code is less clear. In the end, the captain opts for the following nested solution, and changing the test for `wavingWhiteFlag` to logical NOT, as follows:

```
if (!wavingWhiteFlag){

   // not surrendering so check everything else

   if(isComingOverBridge && friendlyTroops >= enemyTroops){

         // shoot them
   }else if(isComingOverBridge && friendlyTroops <
               enemyTroops) {
```

```
            // blow the bridge

        }

    }else{

        // this is the else for our first if
        // Take prisoners

    }

    // Holding position
```

This demonstrates that we can nest `if` and `else` statements inside one another in order to create deep and detailed decisions.

We could go on making more and more complicated decisions with `if` and `else`, but what we have seen here is more than enough as an introduction.

It is probably worth pointing out that, very often, there is more than one way to arrive at a solution to a problem. The *right* way will usually be the way that solves the problem in the clearest and simplest manner.

Now we will look at some other ways to make decisions in Kotlin, and then we can put them all together in an app.

Using when to make decisions

We have seen the vast and virtually limitless possibilities of combining the Kotlin operators with `if` and `else` statements. But, sometimes, a decision in Kotlin can be better made in other ways.

When we want to make decisions and execute different sections of code based on a range of possible outcomes, we can use `when`. The following code declares and initializes the `rating` variable and then outputs a different response to the logcat window based on the value of `rating`:

```
val rating:Int = 4
when (rating) {
  1 -> Log.i("Oh dear! Rating = ", "$rating stars")
  2 -> Log.i("Not good! Rating = ", "$rating stars")
  3 -> Log.i("Not bad! Rating = ", "$rating stars")
  4 -> Log.i("This is good! Rating = ", "$rating stars")
```

```
    5 -> Log.i("Amazing! Rating = ", "$rating stars")

    else -> {
      Log.i("Error:", "$rating is not a valid rating")
    }
}
```

If you copy and paste the preceding code into the `onCreate` function of an app, it will produce the following output:

```
This is good! Rating =: 4 stars
```

The code works by first initializing the `Int` variable, called `rating`, to `4`. The `when` block then uses `rating` as its condition:

```
val rating:Int = 4
when (rating) {
```

Next, five separate possibilities for the values that rating could be initialized to are handled. For each of the values, `1` through `5`, a different message is output to the logcat window:

```
1 -> Log.i("Oh dear! Rating = ", "$rating stars")
2 -> Log.i("Not good! Rating = ", "$rating stars")
3 -> Log.i("Not bad! Rating = ", "$rating stars")
4 -> Log.i("This is good! Rating = ", "$rating stars")
5 -> Log.i("Amazing! Rating = ", "$rating stars")
```

Finally, there is an `else` block that executes if none of the specified options are true:

```
else -> {
  Log.i("Error:", "$rating is not a valid rating")
}
```

Let's take a look at a slightly different usage of `when` by building a small demo app.

The When Demo app

To get started, create a new Android project called `When Demo`. Use an **Empty Activity** project template and leave all the other options in their usual settings. Switch to the `MainActivity.kt` file by left-clicking on the **MainActivity.kt** tab above the editor and we can start coding.

You can get the code for this app in the `Chapter08/When Demo` folder of the download bundle. The file also includes code that is related to our previous discussions on expressions and `if`. Why not play around with the code, run the app, and study the output?

Add the following code inside the `onCreate` function. The app demonstrates that multiple different values can trigger the same path of execution:

```
// Enter an ocean, river or breed of dog
val name:String = "Nile"
when (name) {
  "Atlantic","Pacific", "Arctic" ->
    Log.i("Found:", "$name is an ocean")

  "Thames","Nile", "Mississippi" ->
    Log.i("Found:", "$name is a river")

  "Labrador","Beagle", "Jack Russel" ->
    Log.i("Found:", "$name is a dog")

  else -> {
    Log.i("Not found:", "$name is not in database")
  }
}
```

In the preceding code, there are four possible paths of execution based on the value that the `name` variable is initialized to. If any of the `Atlantic`, `Pacific`, or `Arctic` values are used, then the following line of code is executed:

```
Log.i("Found:", "$name is an ocean")
```

If any of the `Thames`, `Nile`, or `Mississippi` values are used, then the following line of code is executed:

```
Log.i("Found:", "$name is a river")
```

If any of the = `Labrador`, `Beagle`, or `Jack Russel` values are used, then the following line of code is executed:

```
Log.i("Found:", "$name is a dog")
```

If none of the oceans, rivers, or dogs are used to initialize the `name` variable, then the app branches to the `else` block and executes this line of code:

```
Log.i("Not found:", "$name is not in database")
```

If you execute the app with `name` initialized to `Nile` (as the preceding code does), this is the output that you will see in the logcat window:

```
Found:: Nile is a river
```

Run the app a few times and, each time, change the initialization of `name` to something new. Notice that when you initialize `name` to something that is explicitly handled by a statement, we get the expected output. Otherwise, we get the default output handled by the `else` block.

If we have a lot of code to execute for an option in a `when` block, we can contain it all in a function and then call that function. I have highlighted the changed line in the following hypothetical code:

```
"Atlantic","Pacific", "Arctic" ->
      printFullDetailsOfOcean(name)
```

Of course, we will then need to write the new `printFullDetailsOfOcean` function. Then, when `name` is initialized to one of the oceans explicitly handled, the `printFullDetailsOfOcean` function will be executed. The execution will then return to the first line of code outside the `when` block.

You might be wondering about the significance of placing the `name` variable in the brackets of the `printFullDetailsOfOcean(name)` function call. What is happening is that we are passing the data stored in the `name` variable to the `printFullDetailsOfOcean` function. This then means that the `printFullDetailsOfOcean` function can use that data. This will be covered in more detail in the next chapter.

Of course, one of the things that this code seriously lacks is interaction with a GUI. We have seen how we can call functions from button clicks, but even that isn't enough to make this code worthwhile in a real app. We will see how we solve this problem in *Chapter 12, Connecting our Kotlin to the UI and Nullability*.

The other problem we have is that after the code has been executed, then that's it – the app won't do anything else! We need it to continually ask the user for instructions, not just once, but over and over. We will look at a solution to this problem next.

Repeating code with loops

Here, we will learn how to repeatedly execute portions of our code in a controlled and precise way by looking at several types of **loop** in Kotlin. These include `while` loops, `do-while` loops, and `for` loops. We will also learn about the most appropriate situations in which to use these different types of loops.

It is completely reasonable to ask what loops have to do with programming, but they are exactly what the name implies. They are a way of repeating the same part of the code more than once, or looping over the same part of code, although, potentially for a different outcome each time.

This can simply mean doing the same thing until the code being looped over (**iterated**) prompts the loop to end. It could be a predetermined number of iterations as specified by the loop code itself. It might be until a predetermined situation or **condition** is met. Or, it could be a combination of these things. Along with `if`, `else`, and `when`, loops are part of the Kotlin **control flow statements**.

We will look at all the major types of loop that Kotlin offers us to control our code, and we will use some of them to implement a working mini-app to make sure that we understand them completely. Let's take a look at the first and simplest loop type in Kotlin, the `while` loop.

while loops

Kotlin `while` loops have the simplest syntax. Think back to the `if` statements for a moment; we could use virtually any combination of operators and variables in the conditional expression of the `if` statement. If the expression evaluated to true, then the code in the body of the `if` block is executed. With the `while` loop, we also use an expression that can evaluate to true or false:

```
var x = 10

while(x > 0) {
  Log.i("x=", "$x")
  x--
}
```

Take a look at the preceding code; what happens here is as follows:

1. Outside of the `while` loop, an `Int` type named `x` is declared and initialized to 10.
2. Then, the `while` loop begins; its condition is `x > 0`. So, the `while` loop will execute the code in its body.
3. The code in its body will repeatedly execute until the condition evaluates to false.

So, the preceding code will execute 10 times.

On the first pass, x equals 10 on the second pass it equals 9, then 8, and so on. But once x is equal to 0, it is, of course, no longer greater than 0. At this point, the execution will exit the while loop and continue with the first line of code (if any) after the while loop.

In the same way as an if statement, it is possible that the while loop will not execute even once. Take a look at the following example, where the code in the while loop will not execute:

```
var x = 10

while(x > 10){
   // more code here.
   // but it will never run
  // unless x is greater than 10.
}
```

Moreover, there is no limit to the complexity of the conditional expression or the amount of code that can go in the loop body; here is another example:

```
var newMessages = 3
var unreadMessages = 0

while(newMessages > 0 || unreadMessages > 0){
   // Display next message
   // etc.
}

// continue here when newMessages and unreadMessages equal 0
```

The preceding while loop will continue to execute until both newMessages and unreadMessages are equal to, or less than, zero. As the condition uses the logical OR operator (||), either one of those conditions being true will cause the while loop to continue executing.

It is worth noting that once the body of the loop has been entered, it will always complete, even if the expression evaluates to false part of the way through. This is because it is not tested again until the code tries to start another pass:

```
var x = 1

while(x > 0){
   x--
   // x is now 0 so the condition is false
   // But this line still runs
```

```
    // and this one
    // and me!
}
```

The preceding loop body will execute exactly once. We can also set a `while` loop that will run forever! This is called an **infinite loop**; here is an example of an infinite loop:

```
var x = 0

while(true){
    x++ // I am going to get very big!
}
```

The preceding code will never end; it will loop round and round forever. We will see some solutions for controlling when to break out of a `while` loop shortly. Next, we will look at a variation on the `while` loop.

do-while loops

The `do` - `while` loop works in the same way as the ordinary `while` loop except that the presence of a `do` block guarantees that the code will execute at least once, even when the condition of the `while` expression does not evaluate to true:

```
var y = 10
do {
  y++
  Log.i("In the do block and y=","$y")
}
while(y < 10)
```

If you copy and paste this code into one of your apps in the `onCreate` function, and then execute it, the output might not be what you expect. Here is the output:

```
In the do block and y=: 11
```

This is a less-used but sometimes perfect solution for a problem. Even though the condition of the `while` loop is false, the `do` block executes its code, increments the `y` variable to 11, and prints a message to logcat. The condition of the `while` loop is `y < 10`, so the code in the `do` block is not executed again. If the expression in the `while` condition is true, however, then the code in the `do` block continues to execute as though it was a regular `while` loop.

Ranges

In order to continue our discussion on loops, it is necessary to briefly introduce the topic of ranges. Ranges are intimately connected to the Kotlin topic of arrays, which we will discuss more fully in *Chapter 15, Handling Data and Generating Random Numbers*. What follows is a quick introduction to ranges to enable us to then go on to cover `for` loops.

Take a look at the following line of code that uses a range:

```
val rangeOfNumbers = 1..4
```

What is happening is that we are using type inference to create a list of values that contains the values 1, 2, 3, and 4.

We can also explicitly declare and initialize a list, as in the following code:

```
val rangeOfNumbers = listOf(1, 2, 3, 4, 5, 6, 7, 8, 9, 10)
```

The preceding code uses the `listOf` keyword to explicitly create a list containing the numbers 1 through to 10 inclusively.

How these work under the hood will be explored in more depth when we learn about arrays in *Chapter 15, Handling Data and Generating Random Numbers*. Then, we will see that there is much more to ranges, arrays, and lists than we have covered here. It is just helpful to have this quick introduction to complete our discussion of loops by looking at the `for` loop.

For loops

To use a `for` loop, we need a range or list. We can then use a `for` loop to step through that list and execute some code in each step; take a look at the following example:

```
// We could do this...
// val list = listOf(1, 2, 3, 4, 5, 6, 7, 8, 9, 10)
// It is much quicker to do this...
val list = 1..10
for (i in list)
  Log.i("Looping through list","Current value is $i")
```

Take a look at the output this will produce if copied and pasted into an app:

```
Looping through list: Current value is 1
Looping through list: Current value is 2
Looping through list: Current value is 3
Looping through list: Current value is 4
Looping through list: Current value is 5
Looping through list: Current value is 6
Looping through list: Current value is 7
Looping through list: Current value is 8
Looping through list: Current value is 9
Looping through list: Current value is 10
```

You can see from the output that the `list` variable does indeed contain all the values from 1 through to 10. On each pass through the loop, the `i` variable holds the current value. You can also see that the `for` loop allows us to iterate through all those values and execute some code based on those values.

Furthermore, we can use the opening and closing curly braces with a `for` loop when we want the loop to contain multiple lines of code:

```
for (i in list){
  Log.i("Looping through list","Current value is $i")
   // More code here
  // etc.
}
```

In Kotlin, the `for` loop is extremely flexible and can handle much more than just simple `Int` values. We will not explore all the options in this chapter because we need to learn more about classes first. We will, however, be returning to the `for` loop in a number of places throughout the rest of the book.

Controlling loops with break and continue

Having just discussed all the ways that we can control looping through code, it is important to know that sometimes we need to break out of a loop earlier than the condition of the loop specifies.

For such occasions, Kotlin has the `break` keyword. Here is `break` in action with a `while` loop:

```
var countDown = 10
while(countDown > 0){

  if(countDown == 5)break

  Log.i("countDown =","$countDown")
  countDown --
}
```

In the preceding code, the condition of the `while` loop should make the code repeatedly execute while the `countDown` variable is greater than zero. However, inside the `while` loop, there is an `if` expression that checks to see whether `countDown` is equal to 5. If it is equal to 5, the `break` statement is used. Also, inside the `while` loop, the value of `countDown` is printed to the logcat window and is decremented (reduced by 1). Take a look at the following output when this code is executed:

```
countDown =: 10
countDown =: 9
countDown =: 8
countDown =: 7
countDown =: 6
```

You can see from the preceding output that when `countDown` equals 5, the `break` statement executes, and execution exits the `while` loop before it gets to print to the logcat window.

Sometimes, we might want to execute only a part of the code within a loop but not stop looping entirely. For this, Kotlin has the `continue` keyword. Take a look at the following code with a `while` loop, which demonstrates how we can make use of `continue` in our apps:

```
var countUp = 0
while(countUp < 10){
  countUp++

  if(countUp > 5)continue

  Log.i("Inside loop","countUp = $countUp")
}
Log.i("Outside loop","countUp = $countUp")
```

In the preceding code, we initialize a variable called `countUp` to zero. We then set up a `while` loop to keep executing while `countUp` is less than 10. Inside the `while` loop, we increment (increase by 1) `countUp`. The next line of code checks to see whether `countUp` is greater than 5 and, if it is, the `continue` statement is executed. The next line of code prints the value of `countUp` to the logcat window. The line of code that prints the value will only execute when `countUp` is 5 or lower because the `continue` statement sends the execution of the app back to the start of the loop. Take a look at the following output of code to verify what is happening:

```
Inside loop: countUp = 1
Inside loop: countUp = 2
Inside loop: countUp = 3
Inside loop: countUp = 4
Inside loop: countUp = 5
Outside loop: countUp = 10
```

You can see in the preceding output that `countUp` is printed while its value is 5 or lower. Once its value exceeds 5, the `continue` statement prevents the line of code that does the printing from being executed. However, the final line of code outside the loop prints the value of `countUp`, and you can see that its value is 10, indicating that the first line of code in the loop, which increments `countUp`, executed continuously through to the completion of the `while` loop condition.

The `break` and `continue` keywords can also be used in `for` loops and `do - while` loops.

Sample code

If you want to play around with loop code, you can create a new project called `Loops Demo` and copy any of the code from this chapter into the end of the `onCreate` function. I have placed the code that we have used throughout our discussion of loops in the `Chapter08/Loops Demo` folder.

Summary

In this chapter, we used `if`, `else`, and `when` to make decisions with expressions and branch our code. We saw and practiced with `while`, `for`, and `do- while` to repeat parts of our code. Furthermore, we used `break` for breaking out of a loop before the condition would otherwise allow, and we used `continue` to conditionally execute only part of the code in a loop.

It doesn't matter if you don't remember everything straight away, as we will constantly be using all these techniques and keywords throughout the book. We will also explore a number of more advanced ways to use some of these techniques.

In the next chapter, we will take a much closer look at Kotlin functions, which is where all our tests and loops code will go.

9
Kotlin Functions

Functions are the building blocks of our apps. We write functions that do specific tasks, and then call them when we need to execute that specific task. As the tasks we need to perform in our apps will be quite varied, our functions need to cater to this and be very flexible. Kotlin functions are very flexible, more so than the other Android-related languages. We therefore need to spend a whole chapter learning about them. Functions are intimately related to object-oriented programming, and once we understand the basics of functions, we will be in a good position to take on the wider learning of object-oriented programming.

This is what we have in store for this chapter:

- Function basics and recap
- Function return types and the return keyword
- Single-expression functions
- Default arguments
- More function-related topics

We know a little bit about functions already, so a recap is in order.

Function basics and recap

We have already seen and used functions. Some were provided for us by the Android API, such as `onCreate` and the other lifecycle functions.

We wrote others ourselves; for example, `topClick` and `bottomClick`. However, we haven't explained them properly, and there is more to functions than we have seen so far.

You will often hear another term that is closely related and almost synonymous with functions. This is especially the case if you have previously learned Java or another object-oriented language. The word I am referring to is **method**. The distinction between a method and a function is rarely important from a technical point of view, and the difference is, in part, where in our code the function/method is declared. If you want to be programmatically correct, you can read this article, which goes into some depth and provides multiple opinions:

`https://stackoverflow.com/questions/155609/whats-the-difference-between-a-method-and-a-function`

In this book, I will refer to all methods/functions as functions.

The basic function declaration

Here is an example of a very simple function:

```
fun printHello(){
  Log.i("Message=","Hello")
}
```

We could call the `printHello` function like this:

```
printHello()
```

The result would be this output in the logcat window:

```
Message=: Hello
```

The first line of the function is the **declaration**, and all the code contained within the opening and closing curly brackets is the function **body**. We use the `fun` keyword, followed by the name of the function, followed by an opening and closing bracket. The name is arbitrary, but it is good practice to use names that describe what the function does.

Function parameter lists

The declaration can take many forms, and this gives us lots of flexibility and power. Let's look at some more examples:

```
fun printSum(a: Int, b: Int) {
  Log.i("a + b = ","${a+b}")
}
```

The preceding `printSum` function could be called as follows:

```
printSum(2, 3)
```

The result of calling the `printSum` function is that the following message would be output to the logcat window:

```
a + b =: 5
```

Note that the `2` and `3` values that are passed to the function are arbitrary. We could pass any values we like, provided they are of the `Int` type.

This part of the declaration `(a: Int, b: Int)` is called the **parameter list**, or just **parameters**. It is a list of types that the function expects and needs in order to execute successfully. The parameter list can take many forms, and any Kotlin type can be part of the parameter list, including having no parameters at all (as we saw in the first example).

When we call a function with a parameter list, we must supply arguments that match whenever we call it. Here are a few other possible ways we could call the preceding `printSum` function example:

```
val number1 = 35
val number2 = 15
printSum(9, 1)// Prints a + b: = 10
printSum(10000, 1)// Prints a + b: = 10001
printSum(number1, number2)// Prints a + b: = 50
printSum(65, number1)// Prints a + b: = 100
```

As shown in the previous examples, any combination of values that amount to two `Int` values are acceptable as arguments. We can even use expressions as arguments, provided they are equal to an `Int` value. This call is also fine, for example:

```
printSum(100 - 50, number1 + number2)// Prints a + b = 100
```

In the previous example, 50 is subtracted from 100, the result (50) is passed as the first argument, and `number1` is added to `number2` and the result is passed as the second argument.

Here is another couple of functions with various parameters, followed by examples of how we might call them:

```
// These functions would be declared(typed)
// outside of other functions
// As we did for topClick and bottomClick
fun printName(first: String, second: String){
  Log.i("Joined Name =","$first $second")
```

```
}

fun printAreaCircle(radius: Float){
  Log.i("Area =","${3.14 * (radius *radius)}")
}
//...
// This code calls the functions
// Perhaps from onCreate or some other function
val firstName = "Gabe"
val secondName = "Newell"

// Call function using literal String
printName("Sid","Meier")

// Call using String variables
printName(firstName, secondName)

// If a circle has a radius of 3
// What is the area
printAreaCircle(3f)
```

Before we discuss the code, let's have a look at the output we get from it:

```
Joined Name =: Sid Meier
Joined Name =: Gabe Newell
Area =: 28.26
```

In the preceding code, we declare two functions. The first is called `printName`, and it has two `String` parameters. The declaration, along with highlighted parameter names, is shown again next. The names are arbitrary, but using meaningful names will make the code easier to understand:

```
fun printName(first: String, second: String){
  Log.i("Joined Name =","$first $second")
}
```

Attempting to call the function with anything other than two `String` values as arguments will result in an error. When we call this function, the `first` and `second` parameters are initialized as variables that we then use in a String template to print the joined-up name to the logcat window. The line of code that achieves this is shown again as follows, with the variables highlighted:

```
Log.i("Joined Name =","$first $second")
```

Note the space in between `$first` and `$second` in the code. Note that this space is also present in the output we saw previously.

The second function is `printAreaCircle`. It has one `Float` parameter called `radius`. Here it is again for easy reference:

```
fun printAreaCircle(radius: Float){
  Log.i("Area =","${3.14 * (radius * radius)}")
}
```

The function uses the `radius` variable, which is initialized when the function is called to calculate the area of a circle using the formula `3.14 * (radius * radius)`.

The code then proceeds to call the first function twice and the second function once. This is shown again in the following code snippet (with helpful comments removed for focus):

```
val firstName = "Gabe"
val secondName = "Newell"

printName("Sid","Meier")
printName(firstName, secondName)

printAreaCircle(3f)
```

Notice that we can call functions with literal values or variables, provided they are of the correct type that matches the declared parameters.

To be clear, the function declarations are outside of any other functions, but are inside the class opening and closing curly brackets. The function calls are inside the `onCreate` function. As our apps get more complex, we will call functions from all over our code (even other code files). The `onCreate` function is just a handy place to use while discussing these topics.

If you want to examine the code structure more closely, the file that contains this code is in the `Chapter09/Functions Demo` folder. Create a new Empty Activity project and you can copy and paste the code to play around with it.

Another point, which is perhaps obvious but is well worth mentioning, is that when we write functions for real apps, they can contain as much code as is practical; they won't just be a single line of code like these examples. Any code we learned about in the previous chapters can go into our functions.

Now, let's move on to another function-related topic that gives us even more options.

The return type and the return keyword

Very often, we will need to get a result from a function. It is not always enough just to have the function know the result. Functions can be declared to have a **return type**. Look at this next function declaration:

```
fun getSum(a: Int, b: Int): Int {
  return a + b
}
```

In the preceding code, look at the highlighted part after the closing bracket of the parameter list. The `: Int` code means the function can and must return a value of the `Int` type to the code that called it. The line of code inside the function body uses the `return` keyword to achieve this. The `return a + b` code returns the sum of `a` and `b`.

We can call the `getSum` function in the same way we do a function without a return type:

```
getSum(10, 10)
```

The preceding line of code will work, but is a little pointless because we don't do anything with the returned value. This next code shows a more likely call to the `getSum` function:

```
val answer = getSum(10, 10)
```

In the preceding function, the value returned from the function is used to initialize the `answer` variable. As the return type is `Int`, Kotlin infers that `answer` is also of type `Int`.

We could also use `getSum` in other ways - one such example is shown next:

```
// Print out the returned value
Log.i("Returned value =","${getSum(10, 10)}")
```

The preceding code uses the `getSum` function in another way, by printing the returned value using a String template to print to the logcat window.

Any type can be returned from a function. Here are a few examples; first the declarations, followed by some of the ways we might call them:

```
// Return the area of the circle to the calling code
fun getAreaCircle(radius: Float): Float{
  return 3.14f * (radius * radius)
}

// Return the joined-up String to the calling code
```

```
fun getName(first: String, second: String): String{
  return "$first $second"
}

// Now we can call them from elsewhere in the code
Log.i("Returned area =","${getAreaCircle(3f)}")
Log.i("Returned name =","${getName("Alan","Turing")}")
```

Here is the output that those two function calls would produce:

Returned area =: 28.26

Returned name =: Alan Turing

We can see that the area of a circle is retrieved and printed, and the first and last names joined together are retrieved and printed.

As a quick sanity check, it is worth pointing out that we don't actually need to write functions just to add numbers together or join Strings. It is just a useful way to demonstrate various aspects of functions.

It is also worth noting that the `return` keyword has its uses even when the function doesn't have a return type.

For example, we can use the `return` keyword to return from a function early. All our previous function examples (without return types) automatically returned to the calling code when the last line of code in the body had executed. Here is an example where we use the `return` keyword:

```
fun printUpTo3(aNumber: Int){ // No return type!
  if(aNumber > 3){
    Log.i("aNumber is","TOO BIG! - Didn't you read my name")
    return // Going back to the calling code
  }

  Log.i("aNumber is","$aNumber")
}

// And now we call it with a few different values
printUpTo3(1)
printUpTo3(2)
printUpTo3(3)
printUpTo3(4)
```

Look at the output when we run the preceding code, and then we will discuss how it works:

```
aNumber is: 1
aNumber is: 2
aNumber is: 3
aNumber is: TOO BIG! - Didn't you read my name
```

In the function body, the `if` expression checks whether `aNumber` is bigger than three, and, if it is, prints a disgruntled comment and uses the `return` keyword to go back to the calling code and avoid printing the value to the logcat. From the program output, we can see that when `aNUmber` was one, two, or three, it was dutifully printed by the `printUpTo3` function, but as soon as we passed in the value of four, we got the alternative result.

Function bodies and single-expression functions

The function body can be as complex or simple as we need it to be. All the examples I have shown so far were deliberately overly simplistic, so that we could concentrate on functions specifically rather than the code within them. As the book progresses through more real-world examples, we will see the code in the function bodies grow longer and more complex. However, function bodies should stick to performing one specific task. If you have a function that takes up a whole screen in Android Studio, it is likely a sign that it should be split into multiple functions.

When you have a function with a very simple body containing just a single expression, Kotlin allows us to shorten the code by using a single-expression syntax. As an example, the `getSum` function could be changed to the following code:

```
fun getSum(a: Int, b: Int) = a + b
```

In the preceding example, we have shed the curly brackets that usually wrap the code in the body, and we have inferred the return type, because adding `a` to `b` could only result in an `Int` variable because `a` and `b` are, themselves, `Int` variables.

Making functions flexible

As functions are the building blocks of our code, they need to be versatile to cater for anything we might need to do. We have already seen how we can create very varied parameter lists and return types, as well as deciding in code when to return to the calling code. As we progress, you will see that we need even more options. What follows is a quick glance at some more Kotlin function options that we will introduce now, and then get around to using for real at various points throughout the book.

Default and named arguments

A **default parameter** is where we the programmers provide a value (default) for a parameter that will be used if the code that calls the function does not provide it. A **named argument** is when the code calling a function specifies a name along with a value. Note that providing a value is optional. Just because a default value for a parameter is given does not prevent the calling code from overriding it by providing it. Have a look at the following example:

```
fun orderProduct(giftWrap: Boolean = false,
                 product: String,
                 postalService: String = "Standard") {

   var details: String = ""

   if (giftWrap) {
       details += "Gift wrapped "
   }

   details += "$product "
   details += "by $postalService postage"

   Log.i("Product details",details)
}

// Here are some ways we can call this function
orderProduct(product = "Beer")
orderProduct(true, product = "Porsche")
orderProduct(true, product = "Barbie (Jet-Set Edition)",
   postalService = "Next Day")

orderProduct(product = "Flat-pack bookcase",
   postalService = "Carrier Pigeon")
```

In the preceding code, we first declare a function called `orderProduct`. Observe that amongst the parameter list, we have declared two default values, as reprinted and highlighted next for clarity:

```
fun orderProduct(giftWrap: Boolean = false,
       product: String,
       postalService: String = "Standard") {
```

When we call the function, we can do so without specifying values for `giftwrap` and/or `postalService`. The first function call in the following code makes this clear:

```
orderProduct(product = "Beer")
```

Note that, when we do so, we need to specify the name of the argument, which must match the name in the parameter list as well as the type. In the second function call, we specify a value for `giftwrap` and `product`:

```
orderProduct(true, product = "Porsche")
```

In the third, we specify a value for all three arguments, as seen again in the following code:

```
orderProduct(true, product = "Barbie (Jet-Set Edition)",
   postalService = "Next Day")
```

Finally, in the fourth, we specify the final two arguments:

```
orderProduct(product = "Flat-pack bookcase",
   postalService = "Carrier Pigeon")
```

The code inside the function itself starts by declaring a `var` variable called `details`, which is a `String` value. If the value of `giftwrap` is true, then `Gift Wrapped` is appended to `Product details`. Next, the value of `product` is appended to `details`, and finally the value of `postalService` is appended with a literal `String` value on either side.

If we run the code, this is the output in the logcat window:

```
Product details: Beer by Standard postage
Product details: Gift wrapped Porsche by Standard postage
Product details: Gift wrapped Barbie (Jet-Set Edition)
      by Next Day postage
Product details: Flat-pack bookcase by Carrier Pigeon postage
```

The varied ways we can call the function are extremely useful. In other programming languages, when you want to be able to call the same named function in different ways, you must supply multiple versions of the function. While learning about named arguments and default parameters might add a little complexity, it certainly beats having to write four versions of the `orderProduct` function. This, along with type inference, are just two of the reasons you will often hear programmers extolling Kotlin's succinct nature.

Using named arguments and default parameters, we can choose to supply as much or as little data as the function allows. Simply put, if we provide values for all parameters without default values, it will work.

> If you want to play with this code, then all the examples from this chapter are in the `Chapter09` folder. Create an Empty Activity project, then copy and paste the functions into the `MainActivity` class and the function calls into the `onCreate` function.

There are some caveats when we do this, and we will see them as we progress with some more real-world examples throughout the book.

Even more on functions

There is more to functions, such as top-level functions, local functions, and variable argument functions, as well as function access levels, but these are best discussed alongside or after the topic of classes and object-oriented programming.

Summary

In this chapter, we made good progress with learning about functions. Although functions have been lurking in our code since the first chapter, we finally got to study and understand them formally. We learned about the different parts of a function: the name, the parameters, and the return type. We have seen that what the function actually does goes inside the opening and closing curly brackets, and is called the function body.

We also saw that we can return from a function at any time by using the `return` keyword, and that we can also use the return type in conjunction with the `return` keyword to make data from the function available to the code that called the function in the first place.

We learned how we can use default and named arguments to provide different versions of the same function without writing multiple functions. This makes our code more succinct and manageable.

We also discovered that there is even more to functions than we covered in this chapter, but that it is best to learn about these topics as they arise in the various projects sprinkled throughout this book.

Next, we will move on to the most trailed chapter. I have constantly referred and deferred to *Chapter 10, Object-Oriented Programming*. Finally, it is here, and we will see the real power of classes and objects combined with Kotlin. We will quickly see over the next few chapters that classes and objects are the key to unleashing the power of the Android API. We will soon be able to make our user interfaces come to life, and will build some real, usable apps that we can publish to the Play store.

10
Object-Oriented Programming

In this chapter, we will discover that, in Kotlin, classes are fundamental to just about everything and, in fact, just about everything is a class.

We have already talked about reusing other people's code, specifically the Android API, but in this chapter, we will really get to grips with how this works and learn about **object-oriented programming** (**OOP**) and how to use it.

In this chapter, we will cover the following topics:

- Introduction to OOP and the three key topics of encapsulation, polymorphism, and inheritance
- Basic classes, including how to write our first class including adding **properties** for data/variable encapsulation and functions to get things done
- Explore **visibility modifiers** that further aid and refine encapsulation
- Learn about **constructors** that enable us to quickly prepare our classes to be turned into usable objects/instances
- Code a Basic Classes mini app to put in to practice everything we have learned in this chapter

If you try to memorize this chapter (or the next), you will have to make a lot of room in your brain, and you will probably forget something really important in its place.

A good goal will be to try and just about get it. This way, your understanding will become more rounded. You can then refer to this chapter (and the next) for a refresher when needed.

It doesn't matter if you don't completely understand everything in this chapter or the next straight away! Keep on reading and be sure to complete all the apps.

Introducing OOP

In *Chapter 1, Getting Started with Android and Kotlin,* we mentioned that Kotlin was an object-oriented language. An object-oriented language requires us to use OOP; it isn't an optional extra, it's part of Kotlin.

Let's find out a little bit more.

What is OOP exactly?

OOP is a way of programming that involves breaking our requirements down into chunks that are more manageable than the whole.

Each chunk is self-contained, and potentially reusable, by other programs, while working together as a whole with the other chunks.

These chunks are what we have been referring to as objects. When we plan/code an object, we do so with a class. A class can be thought of as the blueprint of an object.

We implement an object of a class. This is called an **instance** of a class. Think about a house blueprint - you can't live in it, but you can build a house from it; so, you build an instance of it. Often, when we design classes for our apps, we write them to represent real-world things.

However, OOP is more than this. It is also a way of doing things - a methodology that defines best practices.

The three core principles of OOP are **encapsulation**, **polymorphism**, and **inheritance**. These might sound complex but, taken a step at a time, are reasonably straightforward.

Encapsulation

Encapsulation means keeping the internal workings of your code safe from interference from the code that uses it, by allowing only the variables and functions you choose to be accessed.

This means that your code can always be updated, extended, or improved without affecting the programs that use it, provided that the exposed parts are still accessed in the same way.

You may recall this line of code from *Chapter 1, Getting Started with Android and Kotlin*:

```
locationManager.getLastKnownLocation(LocationManager.GPS_PROVIDER)
```

With proper encapsulation, it doesn't matter if the satellite company or the Android API team need to update the way their code works. If the `getLastKnownLocation` function signature remains the same, we don't have to worry about what goes on inside. Our code, as written before the update, will still work after the update.

If the manufacturer of a car gets rid of the wheels and makes it an electrically-powered hover car, if it still has a steering wheel, accelerator, and brake pedal, driving it should not be a challenge.

When we use the classes of the Android API, we are doing so in the way the Android developers designed their classes to allow us to.

We will dig deeper into encapsulation in this chapter.

Polymorphism

Polymorphism allows us to write code that is less dependent on the types we are trying to manipulate, making our code clearer and more efficient. Polymorphism means **many forms**. If the objects that we code can be more than one type of thing, then we can take advantage of this. Some future examples will make this clear. An analogy will give you a more real-world perspective. If we have car factories that can make vans and small trucks just by changing the instructions given to the robots and the parts that go onto the production line, then the factory is polymorphic.

Wouldn't it be useful if we could write code that can handle different types of data without starting again? We will see some examples of this in *Chapter 11, Inheritance in Kotlin*.

We will also find out more about polymorphism in *Chapter 12, Connecting Our Kotlin to the UI and Nullability*.

Inheritance

Just like it sounds, **inheritance** means we can harness all the features and benefits of other peoples' classes (including encapsulation and polymorphism) while further refining their code specifically to our situation. Actually, we have done this already, every time we used the `:` operator as follows:

```
class MainActivity : AppCompatActivity() {
```

The `AppCompatActivity` class itself inherits from `Activity`. So, we inherited from `Activity` every time we created a new Android project. We can go further than this, and we will see how it is useful.

Imagine if the strongest man in the world gets together with the smartest woman in the world. There is a good chance that their children will have serious benefits from gene inheritance. Inheritance in Kotlin lets us do the same thing with another person's code and our own.

We will look at inheritance in action in the next chapter.

Why do it like this?

When used carefully, all this OOP allows you to add new features without worrying as much about how they interact with existing features. When you do have to change a class, its self-contained (encapsulated) nature means less, or perhaps even zero, consequences for other parts of the program. This is the encapsulation part.

You can use other people's code (such as the Android API) without knowing or perhaps even caring how it works. Think about the Android lifecycle, `Toast`, `Log`, all the UI widgets, listening to satellites, and so on. We don't know, and we don't need to know, how they work internally. As a more detailed example, the `Button` class has nearly 50 functions - do we really want to write all that ourselves, just for a button? It would be much better to use someone else's `Button` class.

OOP allows you to write apps for highly complex situations without breaking a sweat.

You can create multiple similar, yet different, versions of a class without starting the class from scratch by using inheritance, and you can still use the functions intended for the original type of object with your new object because of polymorphism.

It makes sense really. And Kotlin was designed from the start with all of this in mind, so we are forced into using all this OOP - however, this is a good thing. Let's have a quick class recap.

Class recap

A class is a container for a bunch of code that can contain functions, variables, loops, and all the other Kotlin syntax we have learned already. A class is part of a Kotlin package, and most packages will normally have multiple classes. Most often, although not always, each new class will be defined in its own `.kt` code file with the same name as the class, as with all of our activity-based classes so far.

Once we have written a class, we can use it to make as many objects from it as we want. Remember, the class is the blueprint, and we make objects based on the blueprint. The house isn't the plan, just as the object isn't the class - it is an object made from the class. An object is a reference variable, just like a string and, later, we will discover exactly what being a reference variable means. For now, let's look at some actual code.

Basic classes

There are two main steps involved with classes. First, we must declare our class, and then we can bring it to life by instantiating it into an actual useable object. Remember, the class is just a blueprint, and you must use the blueprint to build an object before you can do anything with it.

Declaring a class

Classes can be of varying sizes and complexities depending upon what its purpose is. Here is the absolute simplest example of a class declaration.

Remember that we most often declare a new class in a file of its own with the same name as the class.

We will cover some exceptions to the rule throughout the rest of the book.

Let's have a look at three examples of declaring a class:

```
// This code goes in a file named Soldier.kt
class Soldier

// This code would go in a file called Message.kt
class Message

// This code would go in a file called ParticleSystem.kt
class ParticleSystem
```

Note that we will do a full working project to practice at the end of this chapter. There are also completed classes for all the theoretical examples throughout this chapter in the `Chapter10/Chapter Example Classes` folder of the download bundle.

The first thing to note in the previous code is that I have lumped together three class declarations. In real code, each declaration would be contained in its own file with the same name as the class and the `.kt` file name extension.

To declare a class, we use the `class` keyword followed by the name of the class. Therefore, we can work out that, in the previous code, we declared a class called `Soldier`, a class called `Message`, and a class called `ParticleSystem`.

We already know that classes can, and often do, model real-world things. It would, therefore, be safe to assume that the three hypothetical classes will model a soldier (perhaps from a game), a message (perhaps from an email or text messaging app), and a particle system (perhaps from a scientific simulation app).

A particle system is a system that contains individual particles that act as a part of that system. In computing, they are used to model/simulate/visualize things such as chemical reactions/explosions and particle behavior, perhaps smoke. In *Chapter 21, Threads and Starting the Live Drawing App* we will build a cool drawing app that uses particle systems to make the user's drawings appear to come alive.

It is plain, however, that a simple declaration like the three we have just seen does not contain enough code to achieve any useful functionality. We will expand on class declarations in a moment. First, let's see how to go about using the classes that we have declared.

Instantiating a class

To build a usable object from our classes, we would turn to another code file. So far throughout the book we have used the `onCreate` function in the `AppCompatActivity` class to demonstrate different concepts. While you can instantiate a class from virtually anywhere in Android, because of the lifecycle functions, it is quite common to use `onCreate` to instantiate objects/instances of our classes.

Have a look at the following code. I have highlighted the new code to focus on:

```
class MainActivity : AppCompatActivity() {

    override fun onCreate(savedInstanceState: Bundle?) {
        super.onCreate(savedInstanceState)

         // Instantiating one of each of our classes
            val soldier = Soldier()
            val message = Message()
            val particleSystem = ParticleSystem()

    } // End of onCreate function

}// End of MainActivity class
```

In the preceding code we instantiated an instance (made a usable object) from each of our three previously declared classes. Let's examine the syntax more closely. Here is the line of code that instantiated an instance of the `Soldier` class:

```
val soldier = Soldier()
```

First, we decide whether we need to change our instance. As with regular variables, we then choose `val` or `var`. Next, we name our instance. In the preceding code, the object/instance is called `soldier`, but we could have called it `soldierX`, `marine`, `john117`, or even `squashedBanana`. The name is arbitrary, but, as with variables, it makes sense to call them something meaningful. Also, as with variables, it is convention, but not required, to use a lowercase letter at the start of the name and an uppercase letter for any subsequent words in the name.

> The distinction between `val` and `var` when using them to declare instances of classes is much more nuanced and significant. We will initially learn the details about classes, and in *Chapter 12, Connecting our Kotlin to the UI and Nullability* we will revisit `val` and `var` to see what is going on under the hood of our instances.

The final part of the code contains the assignment operator, `=`, followed by the class name, `Soldier`, and an opening and closing set of brackets `()`.

The assignment operator tells the Kotlin compiler to assign the result of the right-hand side of the code to the variable on the left. Type inference establishes that `soldier` is of the `Soldier` type.

The curious, but perhaps familiar looking `()` after the class name implies that we are calling a function. We are - and it is a special function called a **constructor** that is provided by the Kotlin compiler. There is much to discuss about constructors, so we will defer the conversation to a little later in the chapter.

For now, all we need to know is that this next line of code creates a usable object of the `Soldier` type, called `soldier`:

```
val soldier = Soldier()
```

Remember that one of the goals of OOP is that we get to reuse our code. We are not limited to just one object of the `Soldier` type. We can have as many as we choose. Have a look at this next block of code:

```
val soldier1 = Soldier()
val soldier2 = Soldier()
val soldier3 = Soldier()
```

The `soldier1`, `soldier2`, and `soldier3` instances are all separate, distinct instances. It is true they are all the same type - but that is their only connection. You and your neighbor might both be human, but you are not the same human. If we do something to, or change something about `soldier1`, that something is only done to/about `soldier1`. The `soldier2` and `soldier3` instances remain unaffected. It is, indeed, possible to instantiate a whole army of `Soldier` objects.

The power of OOP is slowly revealing itself, but the elephant in the room at this stage of our discussion is that our classes don't actually *do* anything at all. Furthermore, our instances hold no values (data), so there is nothing we can change about them either.

Classes have functions and variables (kind of)

I will explain the slightly cryptic **(kind of)** heading shortly when we get to the *Class variables are properties* section later in the chapter.

Any of the code that we learned about throughout our discussion on Kotlin can be used as part of a class. This is how we make our classes meaningful and our instances genuinely useful. Let's expand on the class declaration and add some variables and functions.

Using the variables of a class

First, we will add some variables to our empty `Soldier` class, like in this next code:

```
class Soldier{

    // Variables
    val name = "Ryan"
    val rank = "Private"
    val missing = true
}
```

Remember, all the preceding code would go in a file named `Soldier.kt`. Now that we have a class declaration with some member variables, we can use them as shown in this next code:

```
// First declare an instance of Soldier called soldier1
val soldier1 = Soldier()

// Now access and print each of the variables
Log.i("Name =","${soldier1.name}")
Log.i("Rank =","${soldier1.rank}")
Log.i("Missing =","${soldier1.missing}")
```

The code, if placed in the `onCreate` function, would produce the following output in the logcat window:

```
Name =: Ryan
Rank =: Private
Missing =: true
```

In the preceding code, we instantiated an instance of the `Soldier` class in the usual way. But now, because the `Soldier` class has some variables with values, we can access those values using **dot syntax**:

```
instanceName.variableName
```

Or, we could access the values by using this specific example:

```
soldier1.name
soldier1.rank
// Etc..
```

To be clear, we use the instance name, not the class name:

```
Soldier.name // ERROR!
```

As usual, there are some exceptions and variations that we will cover as we proceed.

If we want to change the value of a variable, we can use the exact same dot syntax. Of course, if you remember back to *Chapter 7, Kotlin Variables, Operators, and Expressions,* variables that can be changed need to be declared as `var`, not `val`. Here is the `Soldier` class reworked so that we can use it slightly differently:

```
class Soldier{

    // Member variables
    var name = "Ryan"
    var rank = "Private"
    var missing = true
}
```

Now, we can manipulate the value of the variables as if they are regular `var` variables by using the dot syntax:

```
// First declare an instance of Soldier called soldier1
val soldier1 = Soldier()

// Now access and print each of the variables
Log.i("Name =","${soldier1.name}")
Log.i("Rank =","${soldier1.rank}")
Log.i("Missing =","${soldier1.missing}")

// Mission to rescue Private Ryan succeeds
soldier1.missing = false;

// Ryan behaved impeccably
soldier1.rank = "Private First Class"

// Now access and print each of the variables
Log.i("Name =","${soldier1.name}")
Log.i("Rank =","${soldier1.rank}")
Log.i("Missing =","${soldier1.missing}")
```

The preceding code would produce the following output in the logcat window:

```
Name =: Ryan
Rank =: Private
Missing =: true
Name =: Ryan
Rank =: Private First Class
Missing =: false
```

In the preceding output, first we see the same three lines as before, and then we see three more lines indicating that Ryan is no longer missing, and has been promoted to `Private First Class`.

Using the functions and variables of a class

Now that we can give our classes data, it is time to make them even more useful by giving them things that they can do. To achieve this, we can give our classes functions. Have a look at this expanded code for the `Soldier` class. I have reverted the variables to `val` and highlighted the new code:

```
class Soldier{

    // members
    val name = "Ryan"
    val rank = "Private"
    val missing = true

    // Class function
    fun getStatus() {
        var status = "$rank $name"
        if(missing){
            status = "$status is missing!"
        }else{
            status = "$status ready for duty."
        }

        // Print out the status
        Log.i("Status",status)
    }
}
```

The code in the getStatus function declares a new String variable called status, and initializes it using the values contained in rank and name. It then checks the value in missing with an if expression, and appends either is missing or ready for duty depending upon whether missing is true or false.

We can then use this new function as demonstrated in the following code:

```
val soldier1 = Soldier()
soldier1.getStatus()
```

As before, we create an instance of the Soldier class and then use dot syntax on that instance to call the getStatus function. The preceding code would produce the following output in the logcat window:

```
Status: Private Ryan is missing!
```

If we changed the value of missing to false, the following output would be produced:

```
Status: Private Ryan ready for duty.
```

Note that functions in classes can take any form that we discussed in *Chapter 9, Kotlin Functions*.

If you are thinking that all this class stuff is great, but at the same time seems a little bit rigid and inflexible, you would be correct. What is the point of having multiple, hundreds, or thousands of Soldier instances if they are all called Ryan and they are all missing? Certainly, we have seen we can use var variables and then change them, but this could still be awkward and long-winded.

We need ways to better manipulate and initialize data in each instance. And, if we think back to the start of the chapter when we briefly discussed the topic of encapsulation, then we will also realize that we need to not only allow code to manipulate our data, but also control when and how this manipulation takes place.

To gain this knowledge, we need to learn more about variables in classes, then a little more detail about encapsulation and visibility, and finally reveal what is going on with those function-like brackets () that we have seen at the end of the code when we instantiate an instance of our class.

Class variables are properties

It turns out that in Kotlin class variables are more than just plain old variables that we have already learned about. They are **properties**. Everything we have learned about how to use variables so far still holds true, but a property has more to it than just a value. It has **getters**, **setters**, and a special class variable called a **field** hidden behind the scenes.

Getters and setters can be thought of as special functions that are automatically generated by the compiler. In fact, we have already used them without knowing it.

When we use the dot syntax on a property/variable declared in a class, Kotlin uses the getter to "get" the value. And when we use dot syntax to set the value, Kotlin uses the setter.

The field/variable itself isn't accessed directly when we use the dot syntax we have just seen. The reason for this abstraction is to aid encapsulation.

If you have previously done some programming in another object-oriented language (perhaps Java or C++) this could be confusing, but if you have used a more modern OOP language (perhaps C#), then this won't be entirely new to you. If Kotlin is your first language, then you are probably at an advantage compared to someone with previous experience, as you don't carry the baggage of previous learning.

And, as you might guess, if the variable is `var` then a getter and a setter is provided, but if it is `val`, then just a getter is provided. Therefore, when the variables (which we will call properties most of the time from now on) in the `Soldier` class were `var` we could get and set them, but when they were `val` we could only get them.

Kotlin gives us the flexibility to **override** these getters and setters in order to change what happens when we get and set the value of properties and their associated fields.

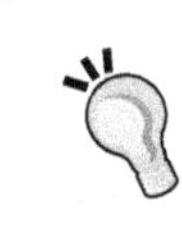

When a property uses a field, it is called a **backing field**. As we will see, some properties don't require a backing field, as they can rely on the logic of the code in the getters and setters to make them useful.

At this point, some examples using fields will make things clearer.

Examples using properties with their getters, setters, and fields

We can use the getters and setters to control the range of values that can be assigned to its backing field. For example, consider this next code being added to the `Soldier` class:

```
var bullets = 100
get() {
   Log.i("Getter being used","Value = $field")
   return field
}
set(value) {
   field = if (value < 0) 0 else value
   Log.i("Setter being used","New value = $field")
}
```

The preceding code adds a new `var` property called `bullets`, and initializes it to 100. Then we see some new code. The getter and the setter are overridden. Strip out the code from the getter and setter to see this in action in its simplest form:

```
get() {
   //.. Executes when we try to retrieve the value
}
set(value) {
   //.. Executes when we try to set the value
}
```

To be clear, the code in the getter and setter execute when we are accessing the value of bullet through an instance of the `Soldier` class. Take a look at how this might happen in this next code:

```
// In onCreate or some other function/class from our app
// Create a new instance of the Soldier class
val soldier = Soldier()
// Access the value of bullets
Log.i("bullets = ","${soldier.bullets}")// Getter will execute
// Reduce the number of bullets by one
soldier.bullets --
Log.i("bullets =","${soldier.bullets}")// Setter will execute
```

In the preceding code, we first create an instance of the `Soldier` class, and then we get the value stored in the `bullet` property and print the value. This triggers the getter code to execute.

Next, we decrement (reduce by one) the value stored by the `bullet` property. Any action that attempts to change the value held by the property will trigger the code in the setter.

If we execute the preceding four lines of code, we will get the following output in the logcat window:

```
Getter being used: Value = 100
bullets =: 100
Getter being used: Value = 100
Setter being used: New value = 99
Getter being used: Value = 99
bullets =: 99
```

After we create a `Soldier` instance called `soldier`, we use `Log.i` to print the value to the logcat window. As this code accesses the value stored by the property, the getter code runs and prints out the following:

```
Getter being used: Value = 100
```

The getter then returns the value to the `Log.i` function using this next line of code:

```
return field
```

When we created the property, Kotlin created a backing field. The way that we access the backing field in the getter or setter is to use the name `field`. Therefore, the preceding line of code works the same way it would in a function and returns the value allowing the `Log.i` call in the calling code to print the value, and we will get this next line of output:

```
bullets =: 100
```

The next line of code is perhaps the most interesting. Here it is again for easy reference:

```
soldier.bullets --
```

We might guess that this simply triggers the setter to execute, but if we examine the next two lines of output in the logcat, we can see that the following two lines of output have been generated:

```
Getter being used: Value = 100
Setter being used: New value = 99
```

The action of decrementing (or incrementing) requires the use of the getter (to know what to decrement) and then the setter to change the value.

Notice that the setter has a parameter named `value` that we can refer to in the setter's body just like a regular function parameter.

Next, the instance is used to output the value held by the `bullets` property, and we can see that again the getter is used, and the output is generated from both the getter code in the class followed by the code using the instance (outside the class). The final two lines of output are shown again next:

```
Getter being used: Value = 99
bullets =: 99
```

Now we can look at another example of using getters and setters.

As already mentioned, sometimes properties do not need a backing field at all. It is sometimes enough to allow the logic in the getters and setters to handle the value accessed via the property. Examine this following code that we could add to the `Soldier` class that demonstrates this:

```
var packWeight = 150
val gunWeight = 30
var totalWeight = packWeight + gunWeight
  get() = packWeight + gunWeight
```

In the preceding code, we create three properties: a `var` property called `packWeight`, which we will change using the instance we will soon create, a `val` property called `gunWeight`, which we will never need to change, and another `var` property called `totalWeight`, which is initialized to `packWeight + gunWeight`. The interesting part is that we override the getter for `totalWeight` so that it recalculates its value using `packWeight + gunWeight`. Next, look at how we might use these new properties with an instance of the `Soldier` class, and then we will look at the output:

```
// Create a soldier
val strongSoldier = Soldier()

// Print out the totalWeight value
Log.i("totalWeight =","${strongSoldier.totalWeight}")

// Change the value of packWeight
strongSoldier.packWeight = 300

// Print out the totalWeight value again
Log.i("totalWeight =","${strongSoldier.totalWeight}")
```

In the preceding code, we create a `Soldier` instance called `strongSoldier`. Next, we print the value of `totalWeight` to the logcat. The third line of code changes the value of `packWeight` to `300`, and then the final line of code prints out the value of `totalWeight`, which will use our overridden getter. Here is the output from those four lines of code:

```
totalWeight =: 180
totalWeight =: 330
```

We can see from the output that the `totalWeight` value is entirely dependent on the values stored in `packWeight` and `gunWeight`. The first line of output is the starting value of `packWeight` (`150`) added to the value of `gunWeight` (`30`), and the second line of output is equal to the new value of `packWeight` added to `gunWeight`.

Just like functions, this enormously flexible system of properties will raise some questions.

When to use overridden getters and setters

When to utilize these different techniques comes with practice and experience; there are no hard rules about exactly when it is appropriate for a specific technique. At this stage, it is just necessary to understand that variables declared in the body of a class (outside of a function) are actually properties, and properties are accessed via getters and setters. These getters and setters are not transparent to the user of the instance, and they are provided by default by the compiler unless overridden by the programmer of the class. This is the essence of encapsulation; the programmer of the class controls how that class works. Properties provide indirect access to its related value (called a backing field), although sometimes this backing field is not needed.

It is OK (and I sometimes do so) to simplify a discussion by referring to a property as a variable. This is especially so when the getters, setters, and field are not relevant to the discussion at hand.

In the next section we will see more ways that we can use getters and setters, so let's move on to discuss visibility modifiers.

Visibility modifiers

Visibility modifiers are used to control the access/visibility of variables, functions, and even whole classes. As we will see, it is possible to have variables, functions, and classes with different levels of access depending upon where in the code the access is being attempted from. This allows the designers of a class to practice good encapsulation and make just the functionality and data they choose available to users of the class. As a slightly contrived but useful example, the designers of a class used to talk to a satellite and get GPS data wouldn't allow access to the `dropOutOfTheSky` function.

These are the four access modifiers in Kotlin.

Public

Declaring classes, functions, and properties as `public` means that they are not hidden/encapsulated at all. In fact, the default visibility is `public` and everything we have seen and used so far is, therefore, public. We could make this explicit by using the `public` keyword before all our class, function, and property declarations, but it is not necessary. When something is declared `public` (or left at the default) no encapsulation is used. This is only occasionally what we want. Often the functions of a class that expose the core functionality of the class will be declared public.

Private

The next access modifier we will discuss is `private`. Properties, functions, and classes can be declared `private` by prefixing the `private` keyword before the declaration, as shown in this next hypothetical code:

```
private class SatelliteController {
   private var gpsCoordinates = "51.331958,0.029057"

   private fun dropOutOfTheSky() {
   }
}
```

The `SatelliteController` class is declared as `private`, which means that it is only available (can be instantiated) from within the same file. An attempt to instantiate an instance, perhaps from `onCreate`, would cause the following error:

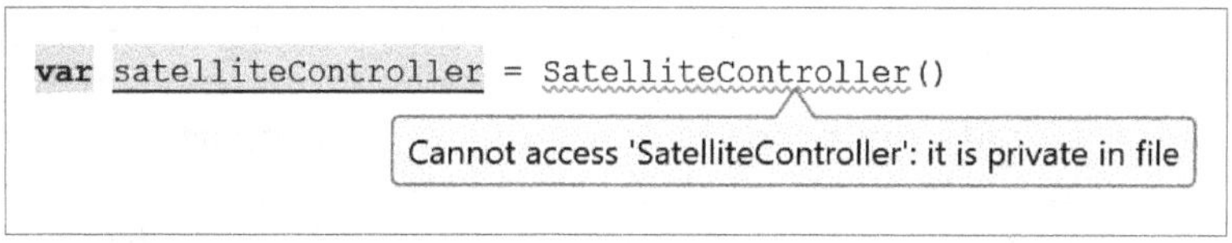

```
var satelliteController = SatelliteController()
```

Cannot access 'SatelliteController': it is private in file

This raises the question of whether the class can be used at all. Declaring a class as `private` is much less common than using one of the remaining modifiers that we will go on to discuss, but it does happen, and there are various techniques that make it a viable tactic. It is more likely, however, that a `SatelliteController` class would be declared with the much more accessible `public` visibility.

Moving on, we have a `private` property called `gpsCoordinates`. Assuming we change the `SatelliteController` class to public, we can then instantiate it and continue our discussion. Even when `SatelliteController` is declared (or left at the default) to be `public`, the private `gpsCoordinates` property is still not visible to instances of the class, as shown in this next screenshot:

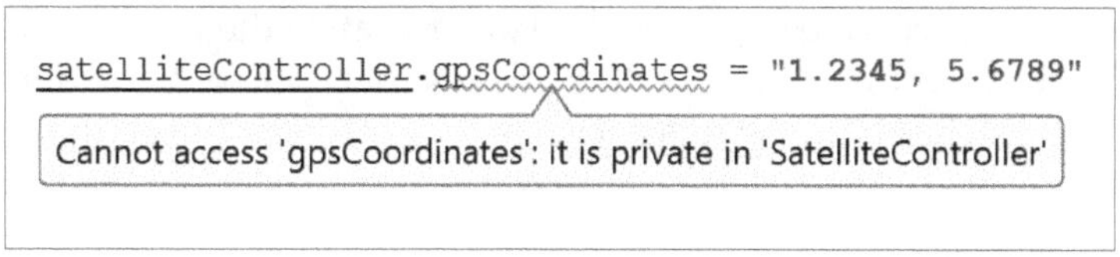

```
satelliteController.gpsCoordinates = "1.2345, 5.6789"
```

Cannot access 'gpsCoordinates': it is private in 'SatelliteController'

As we can see in the preceding screenshot, the `gpsCoordinates` property is inaccessible because it is `private`, and, as we saw from our discussion of properties earlier in this chapter, when the property is left at its default it is accessible. The point of these access modifiers is that the designer of the class can choose when and what to expose. It is likely that a GPS satellite would want to share GPS coordinates. However, it is also very likely that it wouldn't want users of the class to play any part whatsoever in calculating the coordinates. This suggests that we would want users of the class to be able to read the data but not write/change it. This is an interesting situation, because a first reaction might be to make the property a `val` property. This way the user could get the data but couldn't change it. The problem with this is that GPS coordinates obviously do change, and it needs to be a `var` property, just not a `var` property that is changeable from outside the class.

When we declare a property as `private`, Kotlin automatically makes the getter and the setter `private` too. We can change this behavior by overriding the getter and/or the setter. To solve our problem of needing a `var` property that is not changeable from outside the class, readable outside the class, and changeable from within the class, we would leave the default setter so it can never change externally, and override the getter so it can be read externally. Look at this re-writing of the `SatelliteController` class:

```
class SatelliteController {
    var gpsCoordinates = "51.331958,0.029057"
    private set

    private fun dropOutOfTheSky() {
    }
}
```

In the preceding code, the `SatelliteController` class and the `gpsCoordinates` property are `public`. Furthermore, `gpsCoordinates` is a `var` property, and therefore is mutable. However, look closely at the line of code after the property declaration, because it sets the setter to `private`, which means that code outside of the class can't access it to change it; but because it is a `var` property, code within the class can do whatever it likes to it.

We could now write the following code in the `onCreate` function to use the class:

```
// This still doesn't work which is what we want
// satelliteController.gpsCoordinates = "1.2345, 5.6789"

// But this will print the gpsCoordinates
Log.i("Coords=","$satelliteController.gpsCoordinates")
```

Now that the setter is made private by the code, we cannot change the value from an instance, but we can happily read it, as demonstrated in the preceding code. Note that setters cannot have their visibility changed, but can (as we saw when first discussing properties) have their functionality overridden.

Moving on to discuss the function of the `dropOutOfSky` function, this is `private` and totally inaccessible. Only code within the `SateliteController` class can call that function. If we want users of the class to have access to a function, as we have already seen, we would simply leave it at the default visibility. The `SatelliteController` class might have functions that look something like this next code:

```
class SatelliteController {
    var gpsCoordinates = "51.331958,0.029057"
```

```
        private set

        private fun dropOutOfTheSky() {
        }

        fun updateCoordinates(){
            // Recalculate coordinates and update
            // the gpsCoordinates property
            gpsCoordinates = "21.123456, 2.654321"

            // user can now access the new coordinates
            // but still can't change them
        }
    }
```

In the previous code, a public `updateCoordinates` function was added. This allows the instance of the class to use the following code:

```
satelliteController.updateCoordinates()
```

The previous code would then trigger the execution of the `updateCoordinates` function, which will cause the class to internally update the property, which can then be accessed and provide the new value.

This begs the question: what data should be private? The level of visibility that should be used can be learned partly with common sense, partly through experience, and partly by asking the question, "who really needs to access this data and to what extent?" We will be practicing these three things throughout the rest of the book. Here is some more hypothetical code that shows some private data and more private functions for the `SatelliteController` class:

```
class SatelliteController {
    var gpsCoordinates = "51.331958,0.029057"
    private set

    private var bigProblem = false

    private fun dropOutOfTheSky() {
    }

    private fun doDiagnostics() {
      // Maybe set bigProblem to true
      // etc
    }
```

```
        private fun recalibrateSensors(){
          // Maybe set bigProblem to true
          // etc
        }

        fun updateCoordinates(){
            // Recalculate coordinates and update
            // the gpsCoordinates property
            gpsCoordinates = "21.123456, 2.654321"

            // user can now access the new coordinates
            // but still can't change them
        }

        fun runMaintenance(){
            doDiagnostics()
            recalibrateSensors()

            if(bigProblem){
                dropOutOfTheSky()
            }

        }
    }
```

In the preceding code, there is a new private `Boolean` property called `bigProblem`. It can only be accessed internally. It cannot even be read externally. There are three new functions, one public property called `runMaintenance`, which runs the two private functions, `doDiagnostics` and `calibrateSensors`. These two functions could access and change the value of `bigProblem` if needed. In the `runMaintenance` function, a check is done to see if `bigProblem` is true, and, if so, the `dropOutOfTheSky` function is called.

Obviously, in the code for a real satellite, solutions other than dropping out of the sky would likely be sought first.

Let's look at the final two visibility modifiers.

Protected

When the `protected` visibility modifier is used, its effects are more nuanced than `public` and `private`. When a function or property is declared as `protected`, it is almost private - but not quite. The other key OOP topic of inheritance that we will explore in the next chapter allows us to write classes, and then write another class that inherits the functionality of that class. The `protected` modifier would allow functions and properties to be visible to such classes but hidden from all other code.

We will explore this further throughout the book.

Internal

The internal modifier is nearer to public than the others. It would expose the property/function to any code within the same package. If you consider that some apps only have one package, then this is quite a loose visibility. We won't use it much, I just wanted to let you know about it for the sake of completeness.

Visibility modifiers summary

What we have covered, despite being several pages long, is only scratching the surface of visibility modifiers. The point is that they exist, and their purpose is to aid encapsulation and make your code less prone to bugs and more reusable. Combined with properties, functions, getters, and setters, Kotlin is immensely flexible, and we could go on all day with more examples of when and where to use each visibility modifier and when, where, and how to override getters and setters in different ways. It is much more useful to use the techniques to build working programs. This is what we will do throughout the book, and I will often refer to why we use a specific visibility modifier or why we used a getter/setter in a specific way. I also encourage you to do the basic classes demo app at the end of this chapter.

Constructors

Throughout this chapter we have been instantiating objects (instances of classes) and we have gone into some depth about the various syntax. There is one small part of the code we have been ignoring until now. This next code we have seen several times before, but I have highlighted a small part of it so we can discuss it further:

```
val soldier = Soldier()
```

The brackets on the end of the code that initialize the object looks just like code from the previous chapter when we called a function (without any parameters). That is, in fact, exactly what is happening. When we declare a class, Kotlin provides (behind the scenes) a special function called a **constructor** that prepares the instance.

So far in this chapter, we have declared and initialized all our instances in a single line each. Often, we will need to use some more logic in initialization, and often we will need to allow the code that initializes an instance of a class to pass in some values (just like a function). This is the reason for constructors.

Often, this default constructor is all we need, and we can forget all about it, but sometimes we need to do more work to set up our instance so that it is ready for use. Kotlin allows us to declare our own constructors and gives us three main options: primary constructors, secondary constructors, and `init` blocks.

Primary constructors

A primary constructor is one that is declared with the class declaration. Look at this next code, which defines a constructor that allows the user of the class to pass in two values. As we have come to expect, this code would go in a file named `Book.kt`:

```
class Book(val title: String, var copiesSold: Int) {
    // Here we put our code as normal
    // But title and copiesSold are properties that
    // are already declared and initialized
}
```

In the preceding code, we have declared a class called `Book` and provided a constructor that takes two parameters. It requires an immutable `String` value and a mutable `Int` value passed to it when it is initialized. Providing a constructor like this and then using it to instantiate an instance declares and initializes the `title` and `copiesSold` properties. There is no need to declare or initialize them in the usual way.

Look at this next code, which shows how you could instantiate an instance of this class:

```
// Instantiate a Book using the primary constructor
val book = Book("Animal Farm", 20000000)
```

In the preceding code, an object called `book` is instantiated using the primary constructor and the properties, `title` and `copiesSold`, are initialized to `Animal Farm` and `20000000` (twenty million) respectively.

Just as with functions, you can shape constructors to have any combinations, types, and number of parameters.

The potential downfall of primary constructors is that the properties take their values from the passed in arguments without any flexibility. What if we needed to do some calculations with the passed in values before assigning them to the properties? Fortunately, there are ways we can handle this.

Secondary constructors

A secondary constructor is one that is declared separately from the class declaration, but is still within the class body. A couple of things to note about secondary constructors is that you can't declare properties in the parameters, and you must also call the primary constructor from the code of the secondary constructor. The advantage to a secondary constructor is that you can write some logic (code) to initialize your properties. Look at the following code, which shows this in action. We will also introduce a new keyword at the same time:

```
// Perhaps the user of the class
// doesn't know the time as it
// is yet to be confirmed
class Meeting(val day: String, val person: String) {
    var time: String = "To be decided"
    // The user of the class can
    // supply the day, time and person
    // of a meeting
    constructor(day: String, person: String, time: String)
            :this(day, person ){

        // "this" refers to the current instance
        this.time = time
        // time (the property) now equals time
        // that was passed in as a parameter
    }
}
```

In the preceding code we declare a class called `Meeting`. The primary constructor declares two properties, one called `day` and one called `person`. Next, a property called `time` is declared and initialized to the value of `To be decided`.

What follows is the secondary constructor. Notice that the parameters are preceded by the `constructor` keyword. You will also notice that the secondary constructor contains three parameters, the same two as the primary constructor and one more called `time`.

Note that the `time` parameter is not the same entity as the `time` property that was previously declared and initialized. The secondary constructor contains only "throw-away" parameters, they do not become persistent properties like those of the primary constructor. This allows us to firstly call the primary constructor passing in `day` and `person`, and secondly (in the body of the secondary constructor) assign the value passed in via the `time` parameter to the `time` property.

You can have multiple secondary constructors provided that the signatures are all different. The appropriate secondary constructor will be called by matching the parameters of the calling/instantiating code.

We need to talk about this

Literally, I mean, we need to talk about the `this` keyword. When we use `this` inside a class it has the effect of referring to the current instance - so it acts on itself.

Therefore the `this(day, person)` code calls the primary constructor that initializes the `day` and `person` properties. Furthermore, the `this.time = time` code has the effect of assigning the value passed in via the `time` parameter to the actual `time` property (`this.time`).

Just to mention in case it isn't obvious; the `Meeting` class would need additional functions to make it worthwhile, such as `setTime`, `getMeetingDetails`, and probably others to.

Users of our class can create instances of the `Meeting` class when they don't know the time (via the primary constructor) or when they do know the time (via the secondary constructor).

Using the Meeting class

We would instantiate our instances by calling either of our constructors, as shown in the following code:

```
// Book two meetings
// First when we don't yet know the time
val meeting = Meeting("Thursday", "Bob")

// And secondly when we do know the time
val anotherMeeting = Meeting("Wednesday","Dave","3 PM")
```

In the preceding code, we initialize two instances of the `Meeting` class, one called `meeting` and the other called `anotherMeeting`. With the first instantiation we called the primary constructor because we didn't know the time and with the second, we called the secondary constructor because we did know the time.

We can have more than one secondary constructor if required, provided that they all call the primary constructor.

Init blocks

Kotlin was designed to be a succinct language, and often there is a more succinct way to initialize our properties. If the class is not depending upon multiple different signatures, then we can stick to the more succinct primary constructor and provide any required initialization logic in an `init` block:

```
init{
  // This code runs when the class is instantiated
  // and can be used to initialize properties
}
```

That is probably enough theory; let's use everything we have been talking about in a working app. Next, we will write a small app that uses classes, including a primary constructor and an `init` block.

Basic classes app and using the init block

You can get the completed code for this app in the code download. It is in the `Chapter10/Basic Classes` folder. But it is most useful to read on to create your own working example.

We will create a few different classes using what we have learned throughout this chapter to put the theory in to practice. We will also see our first example of how classes can interact with each other by passing a class as a parameter into the function of another class. We know how to do this in theory already, we just haven't seen it in practice yet.

We will also see another way to initialize our data when the class is first instantiated by using an `init` block.

We will create a small app that plays with the idea of simulating ships, docks, and sea battles.

> The output for the apps in this chapter and the next will be just text to the logcat window. In *Chapter 12, Connecting our Kotlin to the UI and Nullability*, we will bring together everything we learned in the first five chapters (about the Android UI) and everything in the six that followed (about Kotlin) to bring our apps to life.

Create a project with the Empty Activity template. Call the application `Basic Classes`. Now we will create a new class called `Destroyer`:

1. Right-click the `com.gamecodeschool.basicclasses` (or whatever your package name is) folder in the project explorer window.
2. Select **New | Kotlin File/Class**.
3. In the **Name:** field, type `Destroyer`.
4. In the drop-down box, select **Class**.
5. Click the **OK** button to add the new class to the project.
6. Repeat the previous five steps and create two more classes, one called `Carrier` and another called `ShipYard`.

The new classes are created for us with a class declaration and curly brackets ready for our code. The auto-generated code also includes the package declaration, which will be different based on your choices when you created the project. This is what my code looks like at this point.

Inside `Destroyer.kt`:

```
package com.gamecodeschool.basicclasses

class Destroyer {
}
```

Inside `Carrier.kt`:

```
package com.gamecodeschool.basicclasses

class Carrier {
}
```

Inside `ShipYard.kt`:

```
package com.gamecodeschool.basicclasses

class ShipYard {
}
```

Let's start by coding the first part of the Destroyer class. What follows is the constructor, some properties, and an init block. Add the code to the project, study it, and then we will review what we have done:

```
class Destroyer(name: String) {
    // What is the name of this ship
    var name: String = ""
        private set

    // What type of ship is it
    // Always a destroyer
    val type = "Destroyer"

    // How much the ship can take before sinking
    private var hullIntegrity = 200

    // How many shots left in the arsenal
    var ammo = 1
    // Cannot be directly set externally
        private set

    // No external access whatsoever
    private var shotPower = 60

    // Has the ship been sunk
    private var sunk = false

    // This code runs as the instance is being initialized
    init {
        // So we can use the name parameter
        this.name = "$type $name"
    }
```

The first thing to notice is that the constructor receives a String value called name. It is not declared with a val or a var property. Therefore, it is not a property, it is just a regular parameter that will cease to exist after the initialization of the instance. We will see shortly how we can make use of this.

In the preceding code we declared some properties. Notice that most are all mutable var except type, which is a String val type that is initialized to Destroyer. Also notice that most are private access except for two.

The `type` property is public, and therefore fully accessible via an instance of the class. The `name` property is also public but has a `private` setter. This will give access to the instance for getting the value but protect the backing field (value) from being altered by the instance.

The `hullIntegrity`, `ammo`, `shotPower`, and `sunk` properties are all `private` and inaccessible through the instance, at least, inaccessible directly. Be sure to make a mental note of the values assigned to and the types of these properties.

The final section of the preceding code is an `init` block, in which the `name` property is initialized by concatenating the type and name properties with a space in the middle.

Next, add the `takeDamage` function that follows:

```
fun takeDamage(damageTaken: Int) {
    if (!sunk) {
        hullIntegrity -= damageTaken
        Log.i("$name damage taken =","$damageTaken")
        Log.i("$name hull integrity =","$hullIntegrity")

        if (hullIntegrity <= 0) {
            Log.d("Destroyer", "$name has been sunk")
            sunk = true
        }
    } else {
        // Already sunk
        Log.d("Error", "Ship does not exist")
    }
}
```

In the `takeDamage` function, the `if` expression checks that the `sunk` Boolean is not true. If the ship isn't already sunk, then `hullIntegrity` is reduced by subtracting the value of `damageTaken`, which was passed in as a parameter. Therefore, indirectly, the instance will be affecting `hullIntegrity` even though it is `private`. The point is that it can only do so in a manner decided by the programmer of the class; in this case - us. As we will see, all the private properties will eventually be manipulated in some way.

Also, if the ship is not yet sunk, two `Log.i` calls output the damage taken and the remaining hull integrity information to the logcat window. Finally, in the not sunk scenario `(!sunk)`, a nested `if` expression checks whether `hullIntegrity` is less than zero. If it is, then a message is printed indicating the ship has been sunk, and the `sunk` Boolean is set to true.

When the damageTaken function is called and the sunk variable is true, the else block will execute, and a message will be printed that the ship doesn't exist because it has already been sunk.

Next, add the shootShell function, which will work in conjunction with the takeDamage function. Or rather, to be more precise, the takeDamage function of one ship instance will work in conjunction with the shootShell function of other ship instances, as we will see soon:

```
fun shootShell():Int {
  // Let the calling code no how much damage to do
  return if (ammo > 0) {
         ammo--
         shotPower
  }else{
        0
  }
}
```

In the shootShell function, if the ship has any ammo, the ammo property is decreased by one, and the value of shotPower is returned to the calling code. If the ship has no ammo left (ammo is not greater than zero), then the value of 0 is returned to the calling code.

Finally, for the Destroyer class add the serviceShip function, which sets ammo to 10 and hullIntegrity to 100 so that the ship is fully prepared to take damage again (via takeDamage) and deal damage (via shootShell):

```
fun serviceShip() {
    ammo = 10
    hullIntegrity = 100
}
```

Next, we can quickly code the Carrier class because it is so similar. Just make a note of the slight differences in the values assigned to type and hullIntegrity. Also notice that, instead of ammo and shotPower, we use attacksRemaining and attackPower. Furthermore, shootShell has been replaced with launchAerialAttack, which seemed more appropriate for an aircraft carrier. Add the following code to the Carrier class:

```
class Carrier (name: String){
    // What is the name of this ship
    var name: String = ""
        private set

    // What type of ship is it
```

```
// Always a destroyer
val type = "Carrier"

// How much the ship can take before sinking
private var hullIntegrity = 100

// How many shots left in the arsenal
var attacksRemaining = 1
// Cannot be directly set externally
    private set

private var attackPower = 120

// Has the ship been sunk
private var sunk = false

// This code runs as the instance is being initialized
init {
    // So we can use the name parameter
    this.name = "$type $name"
}


fun takeDamage(damageTaken: Int) {
    if (!sunk) {
        hullIntegrity -= damageTaken
        Log.d("$name damage taken =","$damageTaken")
        Log.d("$name hull integrity =","$hullIntegrity")

        if (hullIntegrity <= 0) {
            Log.d("Carrier", "$name has been sunk")
            sunk = true
        }
    } else {
        // Already sunk
        Log.d("Error", "Ship does not exist")
    }
}

fun launchAerialAttack() :Int {
    // Let the calling code no how much damage to do
    return if (attacksRemaining > 0) {
        attacksRemaining--
        attackPower
```

```
            }else{
                0
            }
        }

        fun serviceShip() {
            attacksRemaining = 20
            hullIntegrity = 200
        }
    }
```

The final code before we start using our new classes is the `ShipYard` class. It has two simple functions:

```
    class ShipYard {

        fun serviceDestroyer(destroyer: Destroyer){
            destroyer.serviceShip()
        }

        fun serviceCarrier(carrier: Carrier){
            carrier.serviceShip()
        }
    }
```

The first function, `serviceDestroyer`, takes a `Destroyer` instance as a parameter, and inside that function simply calls the instance's `serviceShip` function. The second function, `serviceCarrier`, has the same effect, but takes a `Carrier` instance as a parameter. While these two functions are short and simple, their later usage will soon reveal some quite interesting nuances to do with classes and their instances.

Now we will create some instances and put our classes to work by simulating a fictional naval battle. Add this code to the `onCreate` function in the `MainActivity` class:

```
val friendlyDestroyer = Destroyer("Invincible")
val friendlyCarrier = Carrier("Indomitable")

val enemyDestroyer = Destroyer("Grey Death")
val enemyCarrier = Carrier("Big Grey Death")

val friendlyShipyard = ShipYard()

// Uh oh!
friendlyDestroyer.takeDamage(enemyDestroyer.shootShell())
```

```
friendlyDestroyer.takeDamage(enemyCarrier.launchAerialAttack())

// Fight back
enemyCarrier.takeDamage(friendlyCarrier.launchAerialAttack())
enemyCarrier.takeDamage(friendlyDestroyer.shootShell())

// Take stock of the supplies situation
Log.d("${friendlyDestroyer.name} ammo = ",
        "${friendlyDestroyer.ammo}")

Log.d("${friendlyCarrier.name} attacks = ",
        "${friendlyCarrier.attacksRemaining}")

// Dock at the shipyard
friendlyShipyard.serviceCarrier(friendlyCarrier)
friendlyShipyard.serviceDestroyer(friendlyDestroyer)

// Take stock of the supplies situation again
Log.d("${friendlyDestroyer.name} ammo = ",
        "${friendlyDestroyer.ammo}")

Log.d("${friendlyCarrier.name} attacks = ",
        "${friendlyCarrier.attacksRemaining}")


// Finish off the enemy
enemyDestroyer.takeDamage(friendlyDestroyer.shootShell())
enemyDestroyer.takeDamage(friendlyCarrier.launchAerialAttack())
enemyDestroyer.takeDamage(friendlyDestroyer.shootShell())
```

Let's review that code. The code begins by instantiating two friendly ships (`friendlyDestroyer` and `friendlyCarrier`) and two enemy ships (`enemyDestroyer` and `enemyCarrier`). In addition, a `Shipyard` instance called `friendlyShipyard` is also instantiated in preparation for the inevitable carnage that will follow:

```
val friendlyDestroyer = Destroyer("Invincible")
val friendlyCarrier = Carrier("Indomitable")

val enemyDestroyer = Destroyer("Grey Death")
val enemyCarrier = Carrier("Big Grey Death")

val friendlyShipyard = ShipYard()
```

Next, the `friendlyDestroyer` object takes damage twice. Once from `enemyDestroyer` and once from `enemyCarrier`. This is achieved by the `takeDamage` function of `friendlyDestroyer` passing in the return value of the `shootShell` and `launchAerialAttack` functions, respectively, of the two enemies:

```
// Uh oh!
friendlyDestroyer.takeDamage(enemyDestroyer.shootShell())
friendlyDestroyer.takeDamage(enemyCarrier.launchAerialAttack())
```

Next, the friendlies fight back by dealing two attacks on the `enemyCarrier` object, one from the `friendlyCarrier` object via `launchAerialAttack`, and one from the `friendlyDestroyer` object via `shootShell`:

```
// Fight back
enemyCarrier.takeDamage(friendlyCarrier.launchAerialAttack())
enemyCarrier.takeDamage(friendlyDestroyer.shootShell())
```

The states of the two friendly ships are then output to the logcat window:

```
// Take stock of the supplies situation
Log.d("${friendlyDestroyer.name} ammo = ",
        "${friendlyDestroyer.ammo}")

Log.d("${friendlyCarrier.name} attacks = ",
        "${friendlyCarrier.attacksRemaining}")
```

Now the appropriate function of the `Shipyard` instance is called on each of appropriate instances in turn. There is no `enemyShipyard` object, so they will not be able to repair and rearm:

```
// Dock at the shipyard
friendlyShipyard.serviceCarrier(friendlyCarrier)
friendlyShipyard.serviceDestroyer(friendlyDestroyer)
```

Next, the stats are printed again so that we can see the difference after a visit to the shipyard:

```
// Take stock of the supplies situation again
Log.d("${friendlyDestroyer.name} ammo = ",
        "${friendlyDestroyer.ammo}")

Log.d("${friendlyCarrier.name} attacks = ",
        "${friendlyCarrier.attacksRemaining}")
```

And then, perhaps inevitably, the friendly forces finish off the enemies:

```
// Finish off the enemy
enemyDestroyer.takeDamage(friendlyDestroyer.shootShell())
enemyDestroyer.takeDamage(friendlyCarrier.launchAerialAttack())
enemyDestroyer.takeDamage(friendlyDestroyer.shootShell())
```

Run the app, and then we can examine the following output in the logcat window:

```
Destroyer Invincible damage taken =: 60
Destroyer Invincible hull integrity =: 140
Destroyer Invincible damage taken =: 120
Destroyer Invincible hull integrity =: 20
Carrier Big Grey Death damage taken =: 120
Carrier Big Grey Death hull integrity =: -20
Carrier: Carrier Big Grey Death has been sunk
Error: Ship does not exist
Destroyer Invincible ammo =: 0
Carrier Indomitable attacks =: 0
Destroyer Invincible ammo =: 10
Carrier Indomitable attacks =: 20
Destroyer Grey Death damage taken =: 60
Destroyer Grey Death hull integrity =: 140
Destroyer Grey Death damage taken =: 120
Destroyer Grey Death hull integrity =: 20
Destroyer Grey Death damage taken =: 60
Destroyer Grey Death hull integrity =: -40
Destroyer: Destroyer Grey Death has been sunk
```

Here is the output again, this time broken up in to parts so that we can clearly see which code produced which lines of output.

The friendly destroyer is attacked, leaving its hull near to breaking point:

```
Destroyer Invincible damage taken =: 60
Destroyer Invincible hull integrity =: 140
Destroyer Invincible damage taken =: 120
Destroyer Invincible hull integrity =: 20
```

The enemy carrier is attacked and sunk:

```
Carrier Big Grey Death damage taken =: 120
Carrier Big Grey Death hull integrity =: -20
Carrier: Carrier Big Grey Death has been sunk
```

The enemy carrier is attacked once more, but because it is sunk, the `else` block in the `takeDamage` function is executed:

```
Error: Ship does not exist
```

The current ammo/available attacks stats are printed, and things are looking bad for the friendly forces:

```
Destroyer Invincible ammo =: 0
Carrier Indomitable attacks =: 0
```

A quick visit to the shipyard, and things will look much better:

```
Destroyer Invincible ammo =: 10
Carrier Indomitable attacks =: 20
```

Fully armed and repaired, the friendly forces finish off the remaining destroyer:

```
Destroyer Grey Death damage taken =: 60
Destroyer Grey Death hull integrity =: 140
Destroyer Grey Death damage taken =: 120
Destroyer Grey Death hull integrity =: 20
Destroyer Grey Death damage taken =: 60
Destroyer Grey Death hull integrity =: -40
Destroyer: Destroyer Grey Death has been sunk
```

Be sure to review the code and the output again if any of it doesn't seem to match up.

Introduction to references

There might be a nagging thought in your mind at this point. Look at the two functions from the `Shipyard` class again:

```
fun serviceDestroyer(destroyer: Destroyer){
        destroyer.serviceShip()
}

fun serviceCarrier(carrier: Carrier){
        carrier.serviceShip()
}
```

When we called those functions and passed the `friendlyDestroyer` and `friendlyCarrier` to their appropriate `service...` function, we saw, from the before and after output, that the values inside the instances were changed. Usually, if we want to keep the result from a function, we need to use the return value. What is happening is that, unlike a function that has regular types as parameters, when we pass an instance of a class, we are really passing a **reference** to the instance itself – not just copies of the values within it, but the actual instance.

Furthermore, all the different ship-related instances were declared with `val`, so how did we change any of the properties at all? The short answer to this conundrum is that we didn't change the reference itself, just the properties within it, but a fuller discussion is clearly necessary.

We will start our exploration of references and then dig deep into other related topics, such as the memory inside an Android device in *Chapter 12, Connecting Our Kotlin to the UI and Nullability*. For now, it is enough to know that, when we pass data to a function, if it is a class type, we are passing a reference that is equivalent (although not actually) to the real actual instance itself.

Summary

We have, at last, written our first class. We have seen that we can implement a class in a file of the same name as the class. The class itself doesn't do anything until we instantiate an object/instance of the class. Once we have an instance of the class, we can use its special variables, called properties, and its non-private functions. As we proved in the Basic Classes app, every instance of a class has its own distinct properties, just as when you buy a car made in a factory, you get your very own steering wheel, satnav, and go-faster stripes. We have also bumped into the concept of references, which means that, when we pass an instance of a class to a function, the receiving function has access to the actual instance.

All this information will raise more questions. OOP is like that. So, let's try and consolidate all this class stuff by taking a much closer look at inheritance in the next chapter.

11
Inheritance in Kotlin

In this chapter, we will get to see inheritance in action. In fact, we have already seen it, but now we will examine it more closely, discuss the benefits, and write classes that we can inherit from. Throughout the chapter, I will show you several practical examples of inheritance, and at the end of the chapter we will improve our naval battle simulation from the previous chapter and show how we could have saved lots of typing and future debugging by using inheritance.

We will cover the following topics in this chapter:

- **Object-oriented programming** (**OOP**) and inheritance
- Using inheritance with open classes
- Overriding functions
- A bit more about polymorphism
- Abstract classes
- Inheritance example app

To get started, let's talk a little more about the theory.

OOP and inheritance

We have seen how we can reuse our own code, and other people's code, by instantiating/creating objects from classes. But this whole OOP thing goes even further than that.

What if there is a class that has loads of useful functionality in it, but is not exactly what we want? Think about when we wrote the `Carrier` class. It was so close to the `Destroyer` class that we could have almost copy-and-pasted it. We can **inherit** from a class, and then further refine or add to how it works and what it does.

You might be surprised to hear that we have done this already. In fact, we have done this with every single app we have created. When we use the `:` syntax, we are inheriting. You may recall this code from the `MainActivity` class:

```
class MainActivity : AppCompatActivity() {
```

Here, we are inheriting from the `AppCompatActivity` class all its functionality - or, more specifically, all the functionality that the designers of the class want us to have access to.

We can even override a function and still rely, in part, on the overridden function in the class we inherit from. For example, we overrode the `onCreate` function every time we inherited the `AppCompatActivity` class. But we also called on the default implementation provided by the class designers when we did this:

```
super.onCreate(...
```

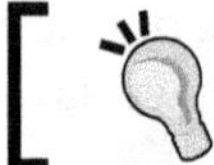

The `super` keyword refers to the super class, which is a class that has been inherited from.

And, in *Chapter 6, The Android Lifecycle*, we overrode many more of the `Activity` class' lifecycle functions. Note that you can have more than one level of inheritance, although good design usually suggests that there are not too many levels. As an example, I have already mentioned that `AppCompatActivity` inherits from `Activity`, and we, in turn, have inherited from `AppCompatActivity`.

With this in mind, let's look at some example classes and see how we can extend them, just to see the syntax, as a first step, and to be able to say we have done it.

Using inheritance with open classes

Some terminology that would be useful to learn at this point is that the class that is inherited from is known as the **super** or **base** class. Other common ways to refer to this relationship is **parent** and **child** class. The child class inherits from the parent class.

By default, a class cannot be inherited from. It is called a **final** class - not open for extending or inheriting from. It is very straightforward, however, to change a class so it can be inherited from. All we need to do is add the `open` keyword to the class declaration.

Basic inheritance examples

Look at this next code, which uses the `open` keyword with the class declaration and enables the class to be inherited from:

```
open class Soldier() {

    fun shoot () {
        Log.i("Action","Bang bang bang")
    }
}
```

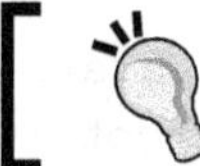

[All the examples from this chapter can be found as completed classes in the `Chapter11/Chapter Examples` folder.]

We can now go ahead and create objects of the `Soldier` type and call the `shoot` function, as in this next code:

```
val soldier = Soldier()
soldier.shoot()
```

The preceding code would still output `Bang bang bang` to the logcat window; we don't have to inherit from it to use it. If we want to refine or specialize our use of the `Soldier` class, however, we could create a specialized type of `Soldier` and inherit the `shoot` function. We could create more classes, perhaps `Special Forces` and `Paratrooper`, and use the `:` syntax to inherit from `Soldier`. What follows is the code for a `SpecialForces` class:

```
class SpecialForces: Soldier(){
    fun SneakUpOnEnemy(){
        Log.i("Action","Sneaking up on enemy")
    }
}
```

Notice the use of the colon to indicate inheritance. It also adds a `sneakUpOnEnemy` function.

Next, consider the following code for a `Paratrooper` class:

```
class Paratrooper: Soldier() {
    fun jumpOutOfPlane() {
        Log.i("Action", "Jump out of plane")
    }
}
```

The preceding code also makes `Paratrooper` inherit from `Soldier`, and it adds a `jumpOutOfPlane` function.

This is how we can use these two new child classes:

```
val specialForces = SpecialForces()
specialForces.shoot()
specialForces.SneakUpOnEnemy()

val paratrooper = Paratrooper()
paratrooper.shoot()
paratrooper.jumpOutOfPlane()
```

In the preceding code, we instantiated a `SpecialForces` instance and a `Paratrooper` instance. The code demonstrates that both instances have access to the `shoot` function in the base class, and both classes have access to their own specialized functions. The output from the code would be as follows:

```
Action: Bang bang bang
Action: Sneaking up on enemy
Action: Bang bang bang
Action: Jump out of plane
```

There is even more to inheritance than this. Let's look at what happens when we need to further refine the functionality of the base/super class.

Overriding functions

Overriding functions is something we have done already, but we need to discuss it further. We have overridden the `onCreate` function in every app we have written, and in *Chapter 6, The Android Lifecycle*, we overrode many more of the functions from the `AppCompatActivity` class.

Consider that we might want to add a `Sniper` class. At first this might seem simple. Just code a class, inherit from `Soldier`, and add a `getIntoPosition` function, perhaps. What if we wanted to make the `Sniper` class shoot differently to the regular `Soldier`? Look at this code for a `Sniper` class, which overrides the `shoot` function and replaces it with a specialized version for the `Sniper` class:

```
class Sniper: Soldier(){
    override fun shoot(){
        Log.i("Action","Steady… Adjust for wind… Bang.")
    }

    fun getIntoPosition(){
```

```
            Log.i("Action","Preparing line of sight to target")
        }
    }
```

You might be tempted to think the job was complete, but this causes a small problem. There is an error in the `Sniper` class, as shown in this next screenshot:

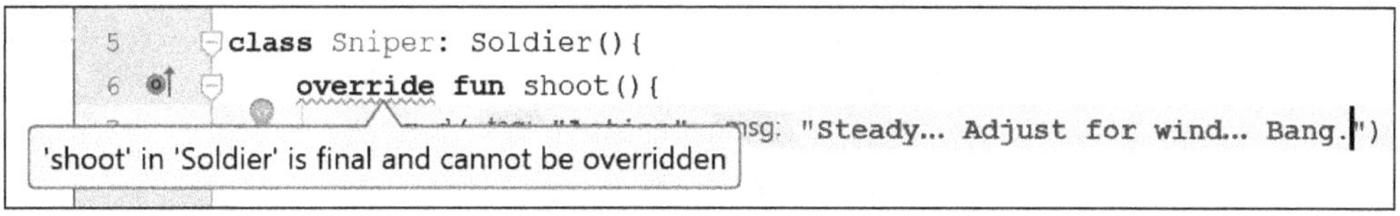

```
5    class Sniper: Soldier(){
6        override fun shoot(){
             msg: "Steady... Adjust for wind... Bang.")
'shoot' in 'Soldier' is final and cannot be overridden
```

The error is because the `shoot` function was not written to be overridden. By default, functions are final, just like classes are. This means that the child class must use it as it is. The solution is to go back to the `Soldier` class and add the `open` keyword in front of the `shoot` function declaration. Here is the updated code for the `Soldier` class with the subtle, but vital, addition highlighted:

```
open class Soldier() {

    open fun shoot () {
        Log.i("Action","Bang bang bang")
    }
}
```

Now we have fixed the error and can write the following code to instantiate the `Sniper` class and use the overridden `shoot` function:

```
val sniper = Sniper()
sniper.shoot()
sniper.getIntoPosition()
```

This produces the following output:

`Action: Steady… Adjust for wind… Bang.`

`Action: Preparing line of sight to target`

We can see that the overridden function has been used. It is also interesting to note that, even though the child class has overridden a function from the parent class, it can still use the function from the parent if it wants to. Consider what might happen if the sniper ran out of ammo for his sniper rifle and needed to switch to his other weapon. Look at this reworked code for the `Sniper` class:

```
class Sniper: Soldier(){
    // He forget to bring enough ammo
```

```
        var sniperAmmo = 3

        override fun shoot(){
            when (sniperAmmo > 0) {
                true -> {
                    Log.i("Action", "Steady… Adjust for wind… Bang.")
                    sniperAmmo--;
                }
                false -> super.shoot()
            }
        }

        fun getIntoPosition(){
            Log.i("Action","Preparing line of sight to target")
        }
    }
```

In the new version of the `Sniper` class, there is a new property called `sniperAmmo`, and it is initialized to `3`. The overridden `shoot` function now uses a `when` expression to check whether `sniperAmmo` is above zero. If it is above zero, then the usual text is printed to the logcat window and `sniperAmmo` is decremented. This means that the expression will only return true three times. The `when` expression also handles what happens when it is false, and calls `super.shoot()`. This line of code calls the version of the `shoot` function from `Soldier` – the super class.

We can now try calling the `shoot` function on a `Sniper` instance four times, like in the following code, and observe what happens:

```
val sniper = Sniper()
sniper.getIntoPosition()
sniper.shoot()
sniper.shoot()
sniper.shoot()
// Damn! where did I put that spare ammo
sniper.shoot()
```

This is the output we get from the preceding code:

```
Action: Preparing line of sight to target
Action: Steady… Adjust for wind… Bang.
Action: Steady… Adjust for wind… Bang.
Action: Steady… Adjust for wind… Bang.
Action: Bang bang bang
```

We can see that the first three calls to `sniper.shoot()` gets output from the overridden `shoot` function in the `Sniper` class, and the fourth still calls the overridden version, but the `false` branch of the `when` expression calls the super class version of `shoot` and we get the output from the `Soldier` class.

A working project based on the examples used so far for inheritance can be found in the `Chapter11` folder of the code download. It is called `Inheritance Examples`.

Summary so far

As if OOP were not useful enough already, we can now model real-world objects. We have also seen that we can make OOP even more useful by subclassing/extending/inheriting from other classes.

As usual, we might find ourselves asking this question about inheritance: why? The reason is something like this: if we write common code in the parent class, then we can update that common code, and all classes that inherit from it will also be updated. Furthermore, we can aid encapsulation with visibility modifiers because a subclass only gets to use public/protected instance variables and functions, and only gets to override open functions. So, designed properly, this also further enhances the benefits of encapsulation.

More polymorphism

We already know that polymorphism means many forms, but what does it mean to us?

Boiled down to its simplest, it means the following:

Any subclass can be used as part of code that uses the super class.

This means that we can write code that is easier to understand, and simpler to change.

Also, we can write code for the super class and rely on the fact that no matter how many times it is subclassed, the code will still work within certain parameters. Let's discuss an example.

Suppose that we want to use polymorphism to help write a zoo management app. We will probably want to have a function, such as `feed`. Let's also say we have `Lion`, `Tiger`, and `Camel` classes, which all inherit from a parent class called `Animal`. We will also probably want to pass a reference to the animal to be fed into the `feed` function. This might seem like we need to write a feed function for each and every type of `Animal`.

Instead, however, we can write polymorphic functions with polymorphic arguments:

```
fun feed(animalToFeed: Animal){
   // Feed any animal here
}
```

The preceding function has `Animal` as a parameter, which means that any object that is built from a class that inherits from `Animal` can be passed into it.

So, you can even write code today and make another subclass in a week, month, or year, and the very same functions and data structures will still work.

Also, we can enforce upon our subclasses a set of rules as to what they can and cannot do, as well as how they do it. So, clever design in one stage can influence it at other stages.

But will we ever really want to instantiate an actual `Animal`?

Abstract classes and functions

An abstract function is a function that is declared with the `abstract` keyword. No problem so far. However, an abstract function also has no body at all. To be clear, an abstract function has no code in it. So, why would we ever want to do this? The answer is that when we write an abstract function, we force any class that inherits from the class with the abstract function to implement/ override that function. Here is a hypothetical abstract function:

```
abstract fun attack(): Int
```

No body, no code, not even empty curly braces. Any class that wants to inherit from that class must implement the `attack` function with precisely the signature of the preceding declaration.

An `abstract` class is a class that cannot be instantiated - cannot be made into an object. So, it's a blueprint that will never be used then? But that's like paying an architect to design your home and then never building it! You might be saying to yourself, "I kind of got the idea of an abstract function, but abstract classes are just silly."

If the designer of a class wants to force the user of a class to inherit before using their class, they can declare a class as `abstract`. Then, we cannot make an object from it; therefore, we must inherit from it first and make an object from the subclass.

Let's look at an example. We make a class `abstract` by declaring it with the `abstract` keyword, like this:

```
abstract class someClass{
   /*
         All functions and properties here.
         As usual!
         Just don't try and make
         an object out of me!
   */
}
```

Yes, but why?

Sometimes we want a class that can be used as a polymorphic type, but we need to guarantee it can never be used as an object. For example, `Animal` doesn't really make sense on its own.

We don't talk about animals, we talk about *types* of animals. We don't say, "Ooh, look at that lovely fluffy, white animal," or, "Yesterday we went to the pet shop and got an animal and an animal bed." It's just too, well, *abstract*.

So, an `abstract` class is kind of like a template to be used by any class that inherits from it.

We might want a `Worker` class and extend this to make `Miner`, `Steelworker`, `OfficeWorker`, and, of course, `Programmer`. But what exactly does a plain `Worker` do? Why would we ever want to instantiate one?

The answer is that we wouldn't want to instantiate one, but we might want to use it as a polymorphic type so that we can pass multiple worker subclasses between functions and have data structures that can hold all types of `Worker`.

We call this type of class an abstract class, and when a class has even one abstract function, it must be declared abstract itself. All abstract functions must be overridden by any class that inherits from it.

This means that the abstract class can give some of the common functionality that would be available in all its subclasses. For example, the `Worker` class might have the `height`, `weight`, and `age` properties.

It might also have the `getPayCheck` function, which is not abstract and is the same in all the subclasses, but a `doWork` function, which is abstract and must be overridden, because all the different types of worker `doWork` very differently.

Classes using the Inheritance example app

We have looked at the way we can create hierarchies of classes to model the system that fits our app. So, let's build a project to improve upon the naval battle we had in the previous chapter.

Create a new project called `Basic Classes with Inheritance Example` using the Empty Activity template. As you have come to expect, the completed code can be found in the `Chapter11` folder.

This is what we are going to do:

- Put most of the functionality of the `Carrier` and `Destroyer` classes into a `Ship` super class.
- Inherit from the `Ship` class for both `Carrier` and `Destroyer`, and therefore save a lot of code maintenance.
- Use polymorphism to adapt the `serviceShip` function in the `Shipyard` class so that it takes `Ship` as a parameter, and can therefore service any instance that inherits from `Ship`, thereby reducing the number of functions in the class.
- We will also see that not only is there less code achieving the same functionality as before, but it is more encapsulated than before as well.

Create a new class called `Ship` and code it as follows. We will then discuss how it compares to the `Destroyer` and `Carrier` classes of the previous project:

```
abstract class Ship(
        val name: String,
        private var type: String,
        private val maxAttacks: Int,
        private val maxHullIntegrity: Int) {

    // The stats that all ships have
    private var sunk = false
    private var hullIntegrity: Int
    protected var attacksRemaining: Int

    init{
```

```
        hullIntegrity = this.maxHullIntegrity
        attacksRemaining = 1
    }

    // Anything can use this function
    fun takeDamage(damageTaken: Int) {
        if (!sunk) {
            hullIntegrity -= damageTaken
            Log.i("$name damage taken =","$damageTaken")
            Log.i("$name hull integrity =","$hullIntegrity")

            if (hullIntegrity <= 0) {
                Log.i(type, "$name has been sunk")
                sunk = true
            }
        } else {
            // Already sunk
            Log.i("Error", "Ship does not exist")
        }
    }

    fun serviceShip() {
        attacksRemaining = maxAttacks
        hullIntegrity = maxHullIntegrity
    }

    fun showStats(){
        Log.i("$type $name",
                "Attacks:$attacksRemaining - Hull:$hullIntegrity")
    }

    abstract fun attack(): Int

}
```

First, you will notice that the class is declared `abstract`, so we know that we must inherit from this class and we cannot use it directly. Scan down to near the end of the code and you will see an abstract function called `attack`. We now know that when we inherit from `Ship`, we will need to override and provide the code for a function called `attack`. This is just what we need, because you might remember that aircraft carriers launch attacks and destroyers shoot shells.

Scan back to the top of the preceding code and you will see that the constructor declares four properties. Two of the properties are new and two have the same uses as the previous project, but how we call the constructor is what is interesting, and we will see that shortly.

The two new properties are `maxAttacks` and `maxHullIntegrity`, so that `Shipyard` restores them back to a level appropriate for the specific type of ship.

In the `init` block, the properties that were not initialized in the constructor are initialized. What follows is the `takeDamage` function, which has the same functionality as the `takeDamage` function from the previous project, except that it is in just the `Ship` class and not both the `Carrier` and `Destroyer` classes.

Finally, we have a `showStats` function for printing the stats related values to the logcat window, meaning that those properties can be private too.

Notice that all the properties are private except for `name` and one protected property called `attacksRemaining`. Remember that `protected` means that it is only visible inside instances that inherit from the `Ship` class.

Now, code the new `Destroyer` class as shown next:

```
class Destroyer(name: String): Ship(
        name,
        "Destroyer",
        10,
        200) {

    // No external access whatsoever
    private var shotPower = 60

    override fun attack():Int {
        // Let the calling code no how much damage to do
        return if (attacksRemaining > 0) {
            attacksRemaining--
            shotPower
        }else{
            0
        }
    }
}
```

Now, code the `Carrier` class that follows, and we can then compare `Destroyer` and `Carrier`:

```
class Carrier (name: String): Ship(
        name,
        "Carrier",
        20,
        100){

    // No external access whatsoever
    private var attackPower = 120

    override fun attack(): Int {
        // Let the calling code no how much damage to do
        return if (attacksRemaining > 0) {
            attacksRemaining--
            attackPower
        }else{
            0
        }
    }
}
```

Notice that both the preceding two classes receive only a `String` value called `name` as a constructor parameter. You will further notice that `name` is not declared with `val` or `var`, so it is not a property, just a throw-away parameter that will not persist. The first thing each of the classes does is inherit from `Ship` and call the constructor of the `Ship` class, passing in `name` along with the values appropriate for either `Destroyer` or `Carrier`.

Both classes have an attack-related property. `Destroyer` has `shotPower` and `Carrier` has `attackPower`. Then they both implement/override the `attack` function to suit the type of attack they will carry out. However, both types of attack will be triggered in the same way with the same function call.

Code the new `Shipyard` class as shown next:

```
class ShipYard {
    fun serviceShip(shipToBeServiced: Ship){
        shipToBeServiced.serviceShip()
        Log.i("Servicing","${shipToBeServiced.name}")
    }
}
```

In the `Shipyard` class, there is now only one function. It is a polymorphic function that takes a `Ship` instance as a parameter. It then calls the `serviceShip` function from the super class, which will restore the ammo/attacks and `hullIntegrity` back to the levels appropriate for the type of ship.

> It is true that the `Shipyard` class is superficial. We could have called `serviceShip` directly without passing the instance to another class. But it neatly demonstrates that we can treat two different classes as the same type because they inherit from the same type. The idea of polymorphism goes even further than this, as we will see in the next chapter when we talk about interfaces. After all, polymorphism means many things, not just two things.

Finally, add code to the `onCreate` function in the `MainActivity` class to put our hard work in to action:

```
val friendlyDestroyer = Destroyer("Invincible")
val friendlyCarrier = Carrier("Indomitable")

val enemyDestroyer = Destroyer("Grey Death")
val enemyCarrier = Carrier("Big Grey Death")

val friendlyShipyard = ShipYard()

// A small battle
friendlyDestroyer.takeDamage(enemyDestroyer.attack())
friendlyDestroyer.takeDamage(enemyCarrier.attack())
enemyCarrier.takeDamage(friendlyCarrier.attack())
enemyCarrier.takeDamage(friendlyDestroyer.attack())

// Take stock of the supplies situation
friendlyDestroyer.showStats()
friendlyCarrier.showStats()

// Dock at the shipyard
friendlyShipyard.serviceShip(friendlyCarrier)
friendlyShipyard.serviceShip(friendlyDestroyer)

// Take stock of the supplies situation
friendlyDestroyer.showStats()
friendlyCarrier.showStats()

// Finish off the enemy
enemyDestroyer.takeDamage(friendlyDestroyer.attack())
enemyDestroyer.takeDamage(friendlyCarrier.attack())
enemyDestroyer.takeDamage(friendlyDestroyer.attack())
```

This code follows exactly the same pattern as the following:

1. Attacking the friendly ship
2. Fighting back and sinking the enemy carrier
3. Printing the stats
4. Visiting the shipyard for repairs and rearming
5. Printing the stats again
6. Finishing off the final enemy

And now we can observe the output:

```
Invincible damage taken =: 60
Invincible hull integrity =: 140
Invincible damage taken =: 120
Invincible hull integrity =: 20
Big Grey Death damage taken =: 120
Big Grey Death hull integrity =: -20
Carrier: Big Grey Death has been sunk
Error: Ship does not exist
Destroyer Invincible: Attacks:0 - Hull:20
Carrier Indomitable: Attacks:0 - Hull:100
Servicing: Indomitable
Servicing: Invincible
Destroyer Invincible: Attacks:10 - Hull:200
Carrier Indomitable: Attacks:20 - Hull:100
Grey Death damage taken =: 60
Grey Death hull integrity =: 140
Grey Death damage taken =: 120
Grey Death hull integrity =: 20
Grey Death damage taken =: 60
Grey Death hull integrity =: -40
Destroyer: Grey Death has been sunk
```

In the preceding output, we can see an almost identical output. However, we achieved it with less code and more encapsulation, and furthermore, if in six months we need a `Submarine` class that attacks with torpedoes, then we can add it without changing any of the preexisting code.

Summary

If you haven't memorized everything, or if some of the code seemed a bit too in-depth, then you have still succeeded.

If you just understand that OOP is about writing reusable, extendable, and efficient code through encapsulation, inheritance, and polymorphism, then you have the potential to be a Kotlin master.

Simply put, OOP enables us to use other people's code, even when those other people were not aware of exactly what we would be doing at the time they did the work.

All you have to do is keep practicing, because we will constantly be using these same concepts over and over again throughout the book, so you do not need to have even begun to master them at this point.

In the next chapter, we will be revisiting some concepts from this one, as well as looking at some new aspects of OOP and how it enables our Kotlin code to interact with our XML layouts.

12
Connecting Our Kotlin to the UI and Nullability

By the end of this chapter, the missing link between our Kotlin code and our XML layouts will be fully revealed, leaving us with the power to add all kinds of widgets and UI features to our layouts as we have done before, but this time we will be able to control them through our code.

In this chapter, we will take control of some simple UI elements, such as `Button` and `TextView`, and, in the next chapter, we will take things further and manipulate a whole range of UI elements.

To enable us to understand what is happening, we need to find out a bit more about the memory in an app, and two areas of it in particular - the **Stack** and the **Heap**.

In this chapter, we will cover the following topics:

- Android UI elements are classes
- Garbage collection
- Our UI is on the Heap
- More polymorphism
- Nullability - val and var revisited
- Casting to different types

Prepare to make your UI come to life.

All the Android UI elements are classes too

When our app is run and the `setContentView` function is called from the `onCreate` function, the layout is **inflated** from the XML UI, and is loaded into memory as usable objects. They are stored in a part of the memory called the Heap.

But where is this Heap place? We certainly can't see the UI instances in our code. And how on earth do we get our hands on them?

The operating system inside every Android device takes care of memory allocation to our apps. In addition, it stores different types of variables in different places.

Variables that we declare and initialize in functions are stored in an area of memory known as the Stack. We already know how we can manipulate variables on the Stack with straightforward expressions. So, let's talk about the Heap some more.

Important fact: all objects of classes are reference type variables and are just references to the actual objects that are stored on the Heap – they are not the actual objects.

Think of the Heap as a separate area of the same warehouse as where our regular variables are stored. The Heap has lots of floor space for odd-shaped objects, racks for smaller objects, lots of long rows with smaller sized cubby holes, and so on. This is where objects are stored. The problem is that we have no direct access to the Heap. Think of it as a restricted access part of the warehouse. You can't actually go there, but you can *refer* to what is stored there. Let's look at what a reference variable really is.

It is a variable that we refer to and use via a reference. A reference can be loosely, but usefully, defined as an address or location. The reference (address or location) of the object is on the Stack.

So, when we use the dot operator, we are asking the OS to perform a task at a specific location, a location that is stored in the reference.

Reference variables are just that – a reference. They are a way to access and manipulate the object (properties and functions), but they are not the actual object itself.

Why would we ever want a system like this? Just give me my objects on the Stack, already! Here is why.

A quick break to throw out the trash

This is what the whole Stack and Heap thing does for us.

As we know, the operating system keeps track of all our objects for us and stores them in a devoted area of our warehouse called the Heap. While our app is running, the operating system will regularly scan the Stack, the regular racks of our warehouse, and match up references to objects that are on the Heap. Any objects it finds without a matching reference, it destroys. Or, in correct terminology, it **garbage collects**.

Think of a very discerning refuse vehicle driving through the middle of our Heap, scanning objects to match up to references (on the Stack). No reference means it is garbage collected.

If an object has no related reference variable, we can't possibly do anything with it anyway because we have no way to access it/refer to it. This system of garbage collection helps our apps run more efficiently by freeing up unused memory.

If this task was left to us, our apps would be much more complicated to code.

So, variables declared inside a function are local, on the Stack, and are only visible within the function where they were declared. A property (of an object) is on the Heap, and can be referenced from anywhere where there is a reference to it, and if the access modifier (encapsulation) allows.

Seven useful facts about the Stack and the Heap

Let's take a quick look at what we have learned about the Stack and the Heap:

- You don't delete objects, but the operating system sends the garbage collector when it thinks it is appropriate. This is usually when there is no active reference to an object.
- Variables are on the Stack, and are local to the specific function within which they were declared.
- Properties are on the Heap (with their object/instance), but the reference to the object/instance (its address) is a local variable on the Stack.
- We control what goes onto the Stack. We can use the objects on the Heap, but only by referencing them.
- The Heap is kept clear and up-to-date by the garbage collector.

- An object is garbage collected when there is no longer a valid reference to it. So, when a reference variable is removed from the Stack, then its related object becomes viable for garbage collection. And, when the operating system decides the time is right (usually very promptly), it will free up the RAM memory to avoid running out.
- If we managed to reference an object that didn't exist, we will get a **NullPointerException** error, and the app will crash. One of the major features of Kotlin is that it protects us from this occurring. In Java, which Kotlin is trying to improve upon, a **NullPointerException error** is the most common cause of an app crashing. We will learn more about how Kotlin helps us avoid **NullPointerException** errors in the section near the end of this chapter called *Nullability –* `val` *and* `var` *revisited.*

Let's move on and see exactly what this information buys us in terms of taking control of our UI.

So, how does this Heap thing help me?

Any UI element that has its `id` attribute set in the XML layout can have its reference retrieved from the Heap and used, just as we can with the classes we wrote and declared ourselves over the previous two chapters.

If we create a project with a Basic Activity template (feel free to do so, but you don't need to), drag a button on to the UI, infer the constraints, and run the app on an emulator. We will then get what we see in this next screenshot:

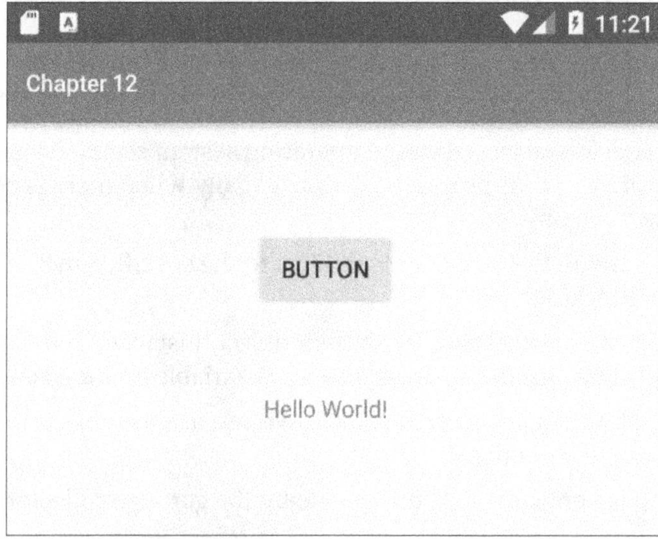

This is what we should expect from what we have already seen in the first five chapters. If we added this line of code to the `onCreate` function, then something interesting will happen:

```
button.text = "WOO HOO!"
```

Run the app again and observe the change in the button:

We have changed the text on the button.

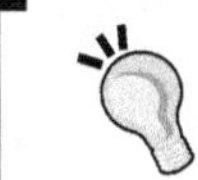

> At this point, if you have previously programmed Android using Java, you might want to lie down for a few minutes and contemplate how easy life will be from now on.

This is quite exciting, because it shows we can grab a reference to a whole bunch of stuff from our layout. We can then start using all the functions and properties that these objects have that are provided by the Android API.

The `button` instance in the code refers to the `id` of the `Button` widget in the XML layout. The `text` instance in our code then refers to the `text` property of the `Button` class, and the `= "WOO HOO!"` text in our code uses the setter of the `text` property to change the value it holds.

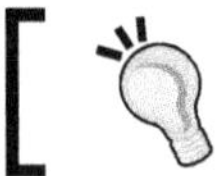

> If the `Button` class (or an other UI element) had a different `id` value, then we would need to adjust our code accordingly.

If you think that after eleven chapters we are finally going to start doing some neat stuff with Android, you would be right!

Let's learn about another aspect of OOP, and then we will be able to build our most functional app so far.

Kotlin interfaces

An interface is like a class. Phew! Nothing complicated here then. But, it's like a class that is always abstract, and only has abstract functions.

We can think of an interface as an entirely abstract class, with all its functions and properties being abstract. When a property is abstract, it does not hold a value. It has no backing field for the property. However, when another class implements (uses) the interface, it must override the property, and therefore provide the backing field for storing a value.

Simply put, interfaces are stateless classes. They provide an implementation template without any data.

OK, so you can just about wrap your head round an abstract class, because at least it can pass on some functionality in its functions and some state in its properties that are not abstract and serve as a polymorphic type.

But, seriously, this interface seems a bit pointless. Let's look at the simplest possible example of an interface, then we can discuss it further.

To define an interface, we type the following:

```
interface SomeInterface {

    val someProperty: String
    // Perhaps more properties

    fun someFunction()
    // Perhaps more functions
    // With or without parameters
    // and return types
}
```

The functions of an interface have no body, because they are abstract, but they can still have return types and parameters.

To use an interface, we use the same `:` syntax after the class declaration:

```
class SomeClass() : SomeInterface{

    // Overriding any properties
    // is not optional
    // It is an obligation for a class
    // that uses the interface
```

```
    override val someProperty: String = "Hello"

    override fun someFunction() {
        // This implementation is not optional
        // It is an obligation for a class
        // that uses the interface
    }
}
```

In the preceding code, the property and the function has been overridden in the class that implements the interface. The compiler forces the user of an interface to do this, or else the code will not compile.

If you are inheriting from a class at the same time as implementing one or more interfaces, then the super class simply goes into the list with the interface(s). It is convention, to make the different relationships clear, to put the super class first in the list. This is, however, not required by the compiler.

This enables us to use polymorphism with multiple different objects that are from completely unrelated inheritance hierarchies. If a class implements an interface, the whole thing can be passed along or used as if it is that thing, because it is that thing. It is polymorphic (many things).

We can even have a class implement multiple different interfaces at the same time. Just add a comma between each interface, and be sure to override all the necessary functions.

In this book, we will use the interfaces of the Android API more often than we write our own. In the next section, one such interface we will use is the `OnClickListener` interface.

Many things might like to know when they are being clicked, such as a `Button` widget or a `TextView` widget. So, using an interface, we don't need different functions for every type of UI element we might like to click.

Let's have a look at an interface in action at the same time as connecting our Kotlin code with the UI.

Using buttons and TextView widgets from our layout with a little help from interfaces

To follow along with this project, create a new Android Studio project, call it `Kotlin Meet UI`, and choose the **Empty Activity** template. You can find the code and the XML layout code in the `Chapter12/Kotlin Meet UI` folder.

First, let's build a simple UI by observing the following steps:

1. In the editor window of Android Studio, switch to `activity_main.xml` and make sure you are on the **Design** tab.
2. Delete the auto-generated `TextView`, the one that reads "Hello world!".
3. Add a **TextView** widget to the top-center of the layout.
4. Set its **text** property to `0`, its `id` property to `txtValue`, and its `textSize` to `40sp`. Pay careful attention to the case of the `id` value. It has an uppercase `V`.
5. Now, drag and drop six buttons on to the layout so that it looks a bit like the following diagram. The exact layout isn't important:

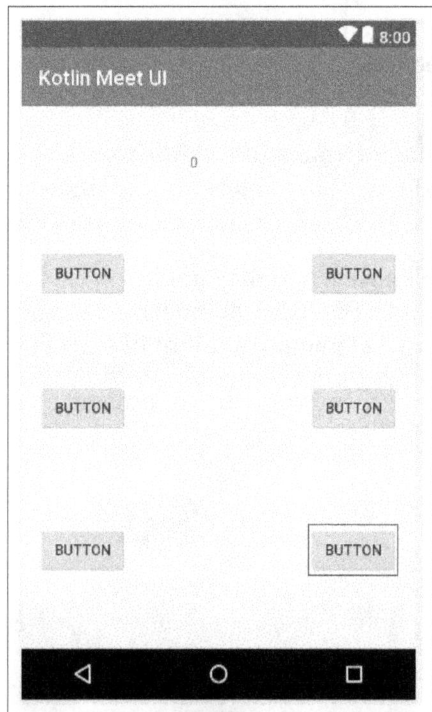

6. When the layout is how you want it, click the **Infer Constraints** button to constrain all the UI items.
7. Double left-click on each button in turn (left-to-right, and then top-to-bottom), and set the `text` and `id` properties, as shown in the following table:

The `text` property	The `id` property
`add`	`btnAdd`
`take`	`btnTake`
`grow`	`btnGrow`
`shrink`	`btnShrink`
`hide`	`btnHide`
`reset`	`btnReset`

When you're done, your layout should look like the following screenshot:

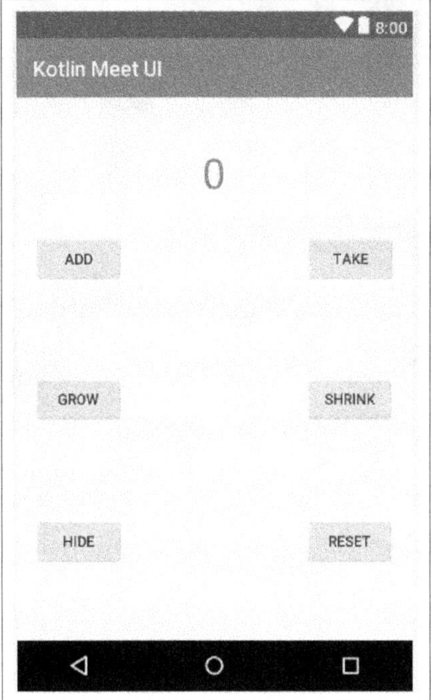

The precise position and text on the buttons are not very important, but the values given to the `id` properties must be the same. The reason for this is that we will be using these `id` values to get a reference to the `Button` instances and the `TextView` instance in this layout from our Kotlin code.

Switch to the **MainActivity.kt** tab in the editor and find the following line:

```
class MainActivity : AppCompatActivity(){
```

Now amend the line of code to the following:

```
class MainActivity : AppCompatActivity,
   View.OnClickListener{
```

As you type, you will get a pop-up list asking you to choose an interface to implement. Choose **OnClickListener (android.view.view)**, as shown in the next screenshot:

```
class MainActivity : AppCompatActivity(), View.OnClickListener {
                                            OnClickListener (android.view.View)
    override fun onCreate(savedInstanceSta  OnContextClickListener (android.view.View)
        super.onCreate(savedInstanceState)  OnLongClickListener (android.view.View)
        setContentView(R.layout.activity_main)
    }
}
```

You will need to import the `View` class. Be sure to do this before continuing with the next step, or you will get confusing results:

```
import android.view.View
```

Notice that the `MainActivity` declaration is underlined in red, showing an error. Now, because we have made `MainActivity` into `OnClickListener` by adding it as an interface, we must implement the abstract function of `OnClickListener`. The function is called `onClick`. When we add the function, the error will be gone.

We can get Android Studio to add it for us by left-clicking anywhere on the code containing the error, and then by using the keyboard combination *Alt* + *Enter*. Left-click **Implement members**, as shown in the following screenshot:

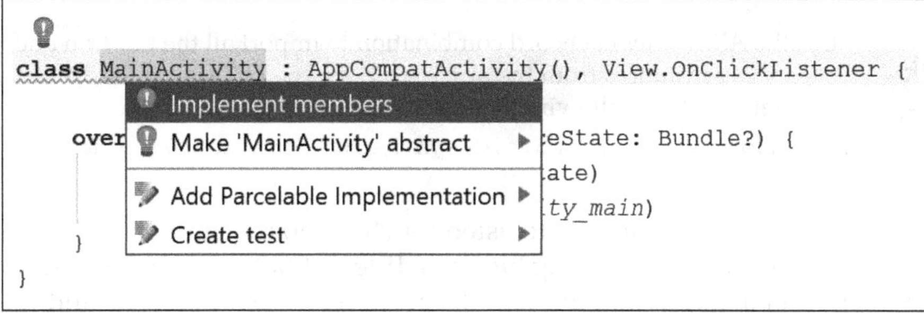

Now, left-click **OK** to confirm we want Android Studio to add the `onClick` method/function. The error is gone, and we can carry on adding code. We also have an `onClick` function, and we will soon see what we will do with that.

A quick note on terminology. A **method** is a function that is implemented in a class. Kotlin allows programmers to implement functions independent of a class, so all methods are functions but not all functions are methods. I chose to refer to all functions/methods throughout this book as functions. There is an argument that method would have been a more precise term, but in the context of this book, either is correct. You can call functions in classes methods if you prefer.

Now, add the following property inside the class declaration but outside/before any functions:

```
class MainActivity : AppCompatActivity(), View.OnClickListener {

    // An Int property to hold a value
     private var value = 0
```

We have declared an `Int` property called `value` and initialized it to `0`. Notice that it is a `var` property because we need to change it.

Next, inside the `onCreate` function, add the following six lines of code:

```
// Listen for all the button clicks
btnAdd.setOnClickListener(this)
btnTake.setOnClickListener(this)
txtValue.setOnClickListener(this)
btnGrow.setOnClickListener(this)
btnShrink.setOnClickListener(this)
btnReset.setOnClickListener(this)
btnHide.setOnClickListener(this)
```

Use the *Alt* + *Enter* keyboard combination to import all the `Button` and `TextView` instances from the `activity_main.xml` layout file. Or, manually add the following import statement:

```
import kotlinx.android.synthetic.main.activity_main.*
```

The preceding code sets up our app to listen for clicks on the buttons in the layout. Each line of code does the same thing but on a different button. For example, `btnAdd` refers to the button in our layout with the `id` property value of `btnAdd`, and `btnTake` refers to the button in our layout with the `id` property value of `btnTake`.

Each button instance then calls the `setOnClickListener` function on itself. The argument passed in is `this`. Remember from *Chapter 10, Object-Oriented Programming*, `this` refers to the current class where the code is written. Therefore, in the preceding code, `this` refers to `MainActivity`.

The `setOnClickListener` function sets up our app to call the `onClick` function of the `OnClickListener` interface. Now, whenever one of our buttons gets clicked, the `onClick` function will be called. All this works because `MainActivity` implements the `OnClickListener` interface.

If you want to verify this, temporarily delete the `View.OnClickListener` code from the end of the class declaration, and our code will suddenly be riddled with a sea of red errors. This is because `this` is no longer of the `OnCLickListener` type, and therefore it cannot be passed to the `setOnClickListener` function of the various buttons, and the `onClick` function will also show an error because the compiler has no idea what we are trying to override. The interface is what makes all this functionality come together.

Replace the `View.OnClickListener` at the end of the class declaration if you previously removed it.

Now, scroll down to the `onClick` function that Android Studio added for us after we implemented the `OnClickListener` interface. Add the `Float size` variable declaration and an empty `when` block inside it so it looks like this next code. The new code to add is highlighted next. There is one more thing to notice and implement in the next code. When the `onClick` function was autogenerated by Android Studio, a question mark was added after the `v: View?` parameter. Remove the question mark, as shown in the following code:

```
override fun onClick(v: View) {
   // A local variable to use later
```

```
        val size: Float

        when (v.id) {

        }
    }
```

Remember that when will check for a matching value to an expression. The when condition is v.id. The v variable is passed to the onClick function, and v.id identifies the id property of whichever button was clicked. It will match the id of one of our buttons in the layout.

> If you are wondering about that curious question mark that we deleted, it will be explained in the next section: *Nullability – val and var revisited.*

What we need to do next is handle what happens for each button. Add this next block of code inside the opening and closing curly brackets of the when expression, and then we will go through and discuss it. Try and work out the code for yourself first, as you will be pleasantly surprised how much we already understand:

```
    R.id.btnAdd -> {
        value++
        txtValue.text = "$value"
    }

    R.id.btnTake -> {
        value--
        txtValue.text = "$value"
    }

    R.id.btnReset -> {
        value = 0
        txtValue.text = "$value"
    }

    R.id.btnGrow -> {
        size = txtValue.textScaleX
        txtValue.textScaleX = size + 1
    }

    R.id.btnShrink -> {
        size = txtValue.textScaleX
```

```
        txtValue.textScaleX = size - 1
    }

    R.id.btnHide ->
        if (txtValue.visibility
                == View.VISIBLE) {
        // Currently visible so hide it
        txtValue.visibility = View.INVISIBLE

        // Change text on the button
        btnHide.text = "SHOW"

    } else {
        // Currently hidden so show it
        txtValue.visibility = View.VISIBLE

        // Change text on the button
        btnHide.text = "HIDE"
    }
```

Here is that first line of code again:

```
override fun onClick(v: View) {
```

`View` is the parent class for `Button`, `TextView`, and more. So, perhaps as we might expect, using `v.id` will return the `id` attribute of the UI widget that has been clicked, and which triggered the call to `onClick` in the first place.

All we need to do then is provide a `when` statement (and an appropriate action) for each of the `Button` id values we want to respond to. Here is that part of the code again for your convenience:

```
when (v.id) {

}
```

Have another look at the next part of the code:

```
R.id.btnAdd -> {
    value++
    txtValue.text = "$value"
}

R.id.btnTake -> {
    value--
    txtValue.text = "$value"
```

```
}

R.id.btnReset -> {
    value = 0
    txtValue.text = "$value"
}
```

The preceding code is the first three `when` branches. They handle `R.id.btnAdd`, `R.id.btnTake`, and `R.id.btnReset`.

The code in the `R.id.btnAdd` branch simply increments the `value` variable, and then it does something new.

It sets the `text` property of the the `txtValue` object. This has the effect of causing this `TextView` to display whatever value is stored in `value`.

The **TAKE** button (`R.id.btnTake`) does exactly the same, only it subtracts one from `value` instead of adding one.

The third branch of the `when` statement handles the **RESET** button, sets `value` to zero, and again updates the `text` property of `txtValue`.

At the end of whichever `when` branch is executed, the entire `when` block is exited, the `onClick` function returns, and life goes back to normal – until the user's next click.

Let's move on to examine the next two branches of the `when` block. Here they are again for your convenience:

```
R.id.btnGrow -> {
    size = txtValue.textScaleX
    txtValue.textScaleX = size + 1
}

R.id.btnShrink -> {
    size = txtValue.textScaleX
    txtValue.textScaleX = size - 1
}
```

The next two branches handle the **SHRINK** and **GROW** buttons from our UI. We can confirm this from the id's `R.id.btnGrow` value and `R.id.btnShrink` value. What is new, and more interesting, are the getter and setter of the `TextView` class that are used on the buttons.

The getter of the `textScaleX` property returns the horizontal scale of the text within the object it is used on. We can see that the object it is used on is our `TextView` `txtValue` instance. The `size =` code at the start of the line of code assigns that returned value to our `Float` variable `size`.

The next line of code in each `when` branch changes the horizontal scale of the text using the setter of the `textScaleX` property. When the **GROW** button is pressed, the scale is set to `size + 1`, and when the **SHRINK** button is pressed, the scale is set to `size - 1`.

The overall effect is to allow these two buttons to grow and shrink the text in `txtValue` by a scale of `1` on each click.

Let's look at the final branch of the `when` code. Here it is again for your convenience:

```
R.id.btnHide ->
    if (txtValue.visibility == View.VISIBLE) {
        // Currently visible so hide it
        txtValue.visibility = View.INVISIBLE

        // Change text on the button
        btnHide.text = "SHOW"

    } else {
        // Currently hidden so show it
        txtValue.visibility = View.VISIBLE

        // Change text on the button
        btnHide.text = "HIDE"
    }
```

The preceding code takes a little bit of explaining, so let's take it a step at a time. First, there is an `if` - `else` expression nested inside the `when` branch. Here is the `if` part again:

```
if (txtValue.visibility == View.VISIBLE)
```

The condition to be evaluated is `txtValue.visibility == View.VISIBLE`. The first part of that, before the `==` operator, uses the `visibility` property's getter to return the value describing whether or not the `TextView` is currently visible. The return value will be one of three possible constant values as defined in the `View` class. They are `View.VISIBLE`, `View.INVISIBLE`, and `View.GONE`.

If `TextView` is visible to the user on the UI, the getter returns `View.VISIBLE`, the condition is evaluated as `true`, and the `if` block is executed.

Inside the `if` block, we use the `visibility` property's setter and make it invisible to the user with the `View.INVISIBLE` value.

In addition to this, we change the text on the `btnHide` object to **SHOW** using the `text` property's setter.

After the `if` block has executed, `txtValue` will be invisible, and we have a button on our UI that says **SHOW**. When the user clicks on it in this state, the `if` statement will be false and the `else` block will execute. In the `else` block, we reverse the situation. We set the `txtValue` object's `visibility` property back to `View.VISIBLE`, and the `text` property on `btnHide` back to **HIDE**.

If this is in any way unclear, just enter the code, run the app, and revisit this last code and explanation once you have seen it in action.

We have the UI and the code in place, so it is now time to run the app and try out all the buttons. Notice that the **ADD** and **TAKE** buttons change the value of `value` by one in either direction, and then display the result in the `TextView`. In this next image, I have clicked the **ADD** button three times:

Notice that the **SHRINK** and **GROW** buttons increase the width of the text, and **RESET** sets the `value` variable to zero and displays it on the `TextView`. In the following screenshot, I have clicked the **GROW** button eight times:

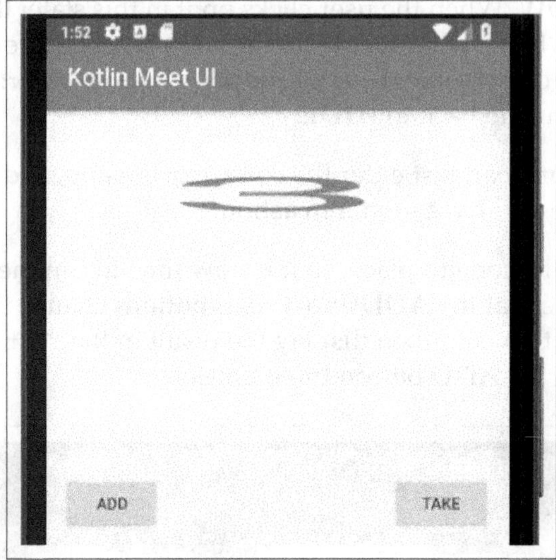

Finally, the **HIDE** button not only hides the `TextView`, but changes its own text to **SHOW**, and will, indeed, re-show the `TextView` if tapped again.

> I will not bother you by showing you an image of something that is hidden. Be sure to try the app in an emulator as well as following along with the book. If you are wondering about the difference between `View.INVISIBLE` and `View.GONE`, `INVISIBLE` simply hides the object, but when `GONE` is used the layout behaves as if the object was never there, so can affect the layout of the remaining UI. Change the line of code from `INVISIBLE` to `GONE` and run the app to observe the difference.

Notice that there was no need for `Log` or `Toast` in this app, as we are finally manipulating the UI using our Kotlin code.

Nullability – val and var revisited

When we declare an instance of a class with `val` it does not mean we cannot change the value held in the properties. What determines whether we can reassign the values held by the properties is whether the properties themselves are `val` or `var`.

When we declare an instance of a class with `val`, it just means we cannot reassign another instance to it. When we want to reassign to an instance, we must declare it with `var`. Here are some examples:

```
val someInstance = SomeClass()
someInstance.someMutableProperty = 1// This was declared as var
someInstance.someMutableProperty = 2// So we can change it

someInstance.someImutableProperty = 1
// This was declared with val. ERROR!
```

In the preceding hypothetical code, an instance called `someInstance` is declared, and it is of the `SomeClass` type. It is declared as `val`. The three lines of code that follow suggest that, if its properties were declared with `var` we can change those properties, but, as we have already learned, when the property is declared with `val` we cannot change it. So, what exactly does declaring an instance with `val` or `var` mean? Look at this next hypothetical code:

```
// Continued from previous code
// Three more instances of the same class
val someInstance2 = SomeClass() // Immutable
val someInstance3 = SomeClass()// Immutable
var someInstance4 = SomeClass() // Mutable

// Let's change these instances around— or try to
someInstance = someInstance2
// Error cannot reassign, someInstance is immutable

someInstance2 = someInstance3 // Error someInstance2 is immutable
someInstance3 = someInstance4 // Error someInstance3 is immutable

// However,
someInstance4 = someInstance
// No problem! someInstance4 and someInstance are now the
// same object— refer to the same object on the heap

// Sometime in the future…
someInstance4 = someInstance3 // No problem
// Sometime in the future…
someInstance4 = someInstance2 // No problem
// Sometime in the future…
// I need a new SomeClass instance

someInstance4 = SomeClass() // No problem
// someInstance4 now uniquely refers
// to a new object on the heap
```

The preceding code makes clear that when an instance is a `val`, it cannot be reassigned to refer to a different object on the heap, but when it is `var` it can. Whether an instance is `val` or `var` does not affect whether its properties are `val` or `var`.

We have already learned when discussing properties that, if we don't need to change a value, it is good practice to declare as `val`. The same is true for objects/instances. If we don't need to reassign an instance, we should declare it as `val`.

Null objects

When we declare an object or property as `var`, we have the option not to initialize it immediately, and sometimes this is what we need. When we don't initialize an object, it is called a **null reference**, because it doesn't refer to anything. We often need to declare an object but not initialize it until our app is running, but this can cause a problem. Look at some more hypothetical code:

```
var someInstance5: SomeClass
someInstance5.someMutableProperty = 3
```

In the preceding code, we have declared a new instance of `SomeClass` called `someInstance5`, but we have not initialized it. Now, look at this screenshot to see what happens when we try to use this instance before we have initialized it:

```
var someInstance5: SomeClass
someInstance5.someMutableProperty = 3
```

Variable 'someInstance5' must be initialized

The compiler will not allow us to do this. When we need to initialize an instance during program execution, we must specifically initialize it as `null` so that the compiler knows it is intentional. Furthermore, when we initialize an instance as `null`, we must use the **nullable operator**. Look at the next hypothetical code that fixes the problem we have just seen:

```
var someInstance5: SomeClass? = null
```

In the preceding code, the nullable operator is used on the end of the `SomeClass?` type, and the instance is initialized to `null`. When we use the nullable operator we can think of the instance as being a different type - *SomeClass nullable* as opposed to just *SomeClass*.

Then, we could initialize the instance whenever we need to in our code. We will see some real examples of this starting in *Chapter 14, Android Dialog Windows*, and throughout the rest of the book, but for now, here is a hypothetical way we might conditionally initialize this null object:

```
var someBoolean = true
// Program execution or user input might change
// the value of someBoolean

if(someBoolean) {
   someInstance5 = someInstance
}else{
   someInstance5 = someInstance2
}
```

We could then proceed to use `someInstance5` as normal.

Safe call operator

Sometimes we need more flexibility. Suppose that we need the value of one of the properties in `someInstance5`, but it is not possible to guarantee that it has been initialized? In this situation we can use the **safe call** `?` operator:

```
val someInt = someInstance5?.someImmutableProperty
```

In the preceding code, if `someInstance5` has been initialized, the value stored in the `someImmutable` property will be used to initialize `someInt`. If it hasn't been initialized, then `someInt` will be initialized with null. Note, therefore, that `someInt` is inferred to be of the `Int` nullable type, not plain `Int`.

Non null assertion

There will arise situations where we cannot guarantee, at compile time, that the instance is initialized, and it is not possible to satisfy the compiler that it will be. When this is the case, we must assert that the object is not null with the **non-null assertion** `!!` operator. Consider the following code:

```
val someBoolean = true
if(someBoolean) {
   someInstance5 = someInstance
}

someInstance5!!.someMutableProperty = 3
```

In the preceding code, it is possible that `someInstance5` might not have been initialized, and we used the non-null assertion operator, or the code would not have compiled.

Also note that, if we write some faulty logic and the instance is still null when we use it, then the app will crash. In fact, the `!!` operator should be used as infrequently as possible, as the safe call operator is preferred.

Nullability in review

There is more to nullability than we have covered so far. It is possible to write many pages discussing the different usages of the different operators, and there are more of these as well. The point is that Kotlin is designed to help us avoid crashes due to null objects whenever possible. It is much more instructive, however, to see nullable types, the safe call operator, and the non-null assertion operator in action than it is to theorize about them. We will bump into all three of them regularly throughout the book, when hopefully their context will be more instructive than their theory.

Summary

In this chapter, we finally had some real interaction between our code and our UI. It turns out that every time we add a widget to our UI, we are adding a Kotlin instance of a class that we can access with a reference in our code. All these objects are stored in a separate area of memory called the Heap - along with any instances of classes of our own.

We are now in a position where we can learn about and do cool things with some of the more interesting widgets. We will look at loads of them in the next chapter, *Chapter 13, Bringing Android Widgets to Life,* and we will also keep introducing new widgets throughout the rest of the book.

13
Bringing Android Widgets to Life

Now that we have a good overview of both the layout and coding of an Android app, as well as our newly acquired insight into **object-oriented programming** (**OOP**) and how we can manipulate the UI from our Kotlin code, we are ready to experiment with more widgets from the Android Studio palette.

At times, OOP is a tricky thing, and this chapter introduces some topics that can be awkward for beginners. However, by gradually learning these new concepts and practicing them repeatedly, they will, over time, become our friend.

In this chapter, we will diversify a lot by going back to the Android Studio palette and looking at half a dozen widgets that we have either not seen at all or have not used fully yet.

Once we have done so, we will put them all into a layout and practice manipulating them with our Kotlin code.

In this chapter, we will cover the following topics:

- Refresh our memories on declaring and initializing layout widgets
- See how to create widgets with just Kotlin code
- Take a look at the `EditText`, `ImageView`, `RadioButton` (and `RadioGroup`), `Switch`, `CheckBox`, and `TextClock` widgets
- Learn how to use lambda expressions
- Make a widget demo mini app using all the preceding widgets and plenty of lambda expressions

Let's start with a quick recap.

Declaring and initializing the objects from the layout

We know that when we call `setContentView` in the `onCreate` function, Android inflates all the widgets and layouts, and turns them into *real* instances on the Heap.

We know that to use a widget from the Heap, we must have an object of the correct type by using its unique `id` property. Sometimes, we must specifically obtain a widget from a layout. For example, to get a reference to a `TextView` class with an `id` property of `txtTitle` and assign it to a new object called `myTextView`, we can do the following:

```
// Grab a reference to an object on the Heap
val myTextView = findViewById<TextView>(R.id.txtTitle)
```

The left-hand side of the declaration of the `myTextView` instance should look familiar to all the instances of other classes that we declared throughout the previous three chapters. What is new here is that we are relying on the return value of a function to supply the instance. The `findViewById` function does indeed return an instance that was created on the Heap when the layout was inflated. The required instance is identified by the function argument that matches the `id` property of the widget in the layout. The curious-looking `<TextView>` syntax is a **cast** or conversion to `TextView` because the function returns the super-class type, `View`.

Now, using our `myTextView` instance variable, we can do anything that the `TextView` class was designed to do; for example, we can set the text to appear as follows:

```
myTextView.text = "Hi there"
```

Then, we can make it disappear like this:

```
// Bye bye
myTextView.visibility = View.GONE
```

Now change its text again and make it reappear, as follows:

```
myTextView.text = "BOO!"

// Surprise
myTextView.visibility = View.VISIBLE
```

It is worth mentioning that we can manipulate any property in Kotlin that we can set using XML code in the previous chapters. Furthermore, we have hinted at, but not actually seen, that we can create widgets from nothing, using just code.

Creating UI widgets from pure Kotlin without XML

We can also create widgets from Kotlin objects that are not a reference to an object in our layout. We can declare, instantiate, and set a widget's attributes, all in code, as follows:

```
Val myButton = Button()
```

The preceding code creates a new `Button` instance. The only caveat is that the `Button` instance must be part of a layout before it can be seen by the user. So, we can either get a reference to a layout element from our XML layout in the same way that we previously did using the `findViewById` function, or we can create a new one in code.

If we assume that we have a `LinearLayout` in our XML with an `id` property equal to `linearLayout1`, we can incorporate our `Button` instance from the preceding line of code in it, as follows:

```
// Get a reference to the LinearLayout
val linearLayout =
   findViewById<LinearLayout>(R.id.linearLayout)

// Add our Button to it
linearLayout.addView(myButton)
```

We can even create an entire layout in pure Kotlin code by first creating a new layout, then all the widgets that we want to add, and finally calling `setContentView` on the layout that has our required widgets in it.

In the following piece of code, we create a layout in pure Kotlin, albeit a very simple one with a single `Button` instance inside a `LinearLayout`:

```
// Create a new LinearLayout
val linearLayout = LinearLayout()

// Create a new Button
val myButton = Button()

// Add myButton to the LinearLayout
linearLayout.addView(myButton)

// Make the LinearLayout the main view of the app
setContentView(linearLayout)
```

It is probably obvious, but it is still worth mentioning that designing a detailed and nuanced layout in Kotlin only is significantly more awkward, harder to visualize, and not the way it is most commonly done. There are times, however, when we will find it useful to do things this way.

We are getting quite advanced now with layouts and widgets. It is evident, however, that there are a lot of other widgets (and UI elements) from the palette that we have not explored or interacted with (other than just dumping them in a layout and not doing anything with them); so, let's fix that.

Exploring the palette – part 1

Let's take a whirlwind tour of some of the previously unexplored and unused items from the palette, and then we can drag a number of them onto a layout and see what useful functions they might have. We can then implement a project to put them all to use.

We have already explored `Button` and `TextView` in the previous chapter. Now let's take a closer look at some more widgets alongside them.

The EditText widget

The `EditText` widget does as its name suggests. If we make an `EditText` widget available to our users, then they will indeed be able to *edit* the *text* in it. We saw this in an earlier chapter, but we didn't achieve anything with it. What we didn't see was how to capture the information from within it, or where we could type this text-capturing code.

The next block of code assumes that we have declared an object of type `EditText` and have used it to get a reference to an `EditText` widget in our XML layout. We might write something similar to the following code for a button click, perhaps a "submit" button for a form, but it can go anywhere we deem it necessary in our app:

```
val editTextContents = editText.text
// editTextContents now contains whatever the user entered
```

We will see an `EditText` widget in a real context in the next app.

The ImageView widget

We have already put an image onto our layout a couple of times so far, but we haven't got a reference to one from our code or done anything with it before. The process of getting a reference to an `ImageView` widget is the same as it is to any other widget:

1. Declare an object.
2. Get a reference using the `findViewById` function and a valid `id` property, as follows:

   ```
   val imageView = findViewById<ImageView>(R.id.imageView)
   ```

Then, we can go on to do some interesting things with our image by using code that is similar to the following:

```
// Make the image 50% TRANSPARENT
imageView.alpha = .5f
```

The odd-looking `f` value simply lets the compiler know that the value is type `Float`, as required by the `alpha` property.

In the preceding code, we use the `alpha` property from `imageView`. The `alpha` property requires a value between 0 and 1. 0 is completely transparent, while 1 indicates no transparency at all. We will use some of the features of `ImageView` in our next app.

RadioButtons and RadioGroups

A `RadioButton` widget is used when there are two or more mutually exclusive options for the user to choose from. This means that when one option is chosen, the other options are not; such as on an old-fashioned radio. Take a look at a simple `RadioGroup` widget with a few `RadioButton` widgets in the following screenshot:

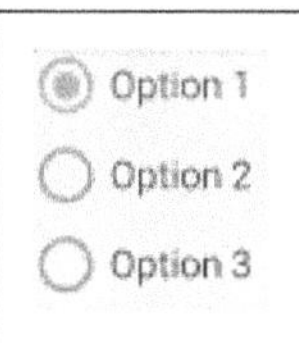

When the user makes a choice, the other options will automatically be deselected. We control `RadioButton` widgets by placing them within a `RadioGroup` widget in our UI layout. We can, of course, use the visual designer to simply drag a bunch of `RadioButtons` onto a `RadioGroup`. When we do, the XML code will look something like this:

```
<RadioGroup
   android:layout_width="match_parent"
   android:layout_height="match_parent"
   android:layout_alignParentTop="true"
   android:layout_alignParentLeft="true"
   android:layout_alignParentStart="true"
   android:id="@+id/radioGroup">

   <RadioButton
         android:layout_width="wrap_content"
         android:layout_height="wrap_content"
         android:text="Option 1"
         android:id="@+id/radioButton1"
         android:checked="true" />

   <RadioButton
         android:layout_width="wrap_content"
         android:layout_height="wrap_content"
         android:text="Option 2"
         android:id="@+id/radioButton2"
         android:checked="false" />

   <RadioButton
         android:layout_width="wrap_content"
         android:layout_height="wrap_content"
         android:text="Option 3"
         android:id="@+id/radioButton3"
         android:checked="false" />


<RadioGroup/>
```

Notice, as highlighted in the previous code, that each `RadioButton` widget and the `RadioGroup` widget has an appropriate `id` attribute set. We can then get a reference to them as we might expect, as shown in the following code:

```
// Get a reference to all our widgets
val radioGroup =
    findViewById<RadioGroup>(R.id.radioGroup)

val rb1 =
    findViewById<RadioButton>(R.id.radioButton1)

val rb2 =
    findViewById<RadioButton> R.id.radioButton2)

val rb3 =
    findViewById<RadioButton>(R.id.radioButton3)
```

In practice, however, we can manage almost everything from the `RadioGroup` reference alone.

You might be thinking how do we know when they have been clicked on, or that keeping track of which one is selected might be awkward? We need some help from the Android API and Kotlin in the form of **lambdas**.

Lambdas

When a `RadioButton` widget is part of `RadioGroup`, the visual appearance of them is coordinated for us. All we need to do is react when any given `RadioButton` widget is pressed. Of course, as with any other button, we need to know when they have been clicked on.

A `RadioButton` widget behaves differently to a regular `Button` widget and simply listening for clicks in `onClick` (after implementing `OnClickListener`) will not work because the `RadioButton` class is not designed that way.

What we need to do is use another Kotlin feature. We need an instance of a special interface, for the sole purpose of listening for clicks on `RadioGroup`. The next block of code assumes that we have a reference to a `RadioGroup` instance called `radioGroup`; here is the code to examine:

```
radioGroup.setOnCheckedChangeListener {
    group, checkedId ->
    // Handle the clicks here
}
```

The preceding code, specifically `setOnChekedChangeListener` from its opening curly brace ({) to the closing curly brace (}), is what is known as a lambda.

Lambdas are a wide-ranging topic and they will be further explored as we progress. They are used in Kotlin to avoid unnecessary typing. The compiler knows that `setOnCheckedChangeListener` requires a special interface as an argument, and it handles this for us behind the scenes. Furthermore, the compiler knows that the interface has one abstract function that we must override. The code that is between the opening and closing curly brackets is where our implementation of the function goes. The curious-looking `group, checkedId ->` parameters are the parameters of this function.

Assume, for the purpose of further discussion, that the preceding code was written in the `onCreate` function. Note that the code within the curly braces does not run when `onCreate` is called; it simply prepares the instance (`radioGroup`) so that it is ready to handle any clicks. We will now discuss this in more detail.

This unseen interface is known as an **anonymous** class.

What we are doing is adding a listener to `radioGroup`, which has very much the same effect as when we implemented `View.OnClickListener` in *Chapter 12, Connecting Our Kotlin to the UI and Nullability*. Only this time, we are declaring and instantiating a listener interface, and preparing it to listen to `radioGroup`, while simultaneously overriding the required function, which, in this case (although we can't see the name), is `onCheckedChanged`. This is like the `RadioGroup` equivalent of `onClick`.

If we use the preceding code to create and instantiate a class that listens for clicks to our `RadioGroup`, in the `onCreate` function, it will listen and respond for the entire life of the Activity. All we need to learn about now is how to handle the clicks in the `onCheckedChanged` function that we are overriding.

Some students find the preceding code straightforward and others find it a little overwhelming. It is not an indication of your intelligence level that determines the way that you perceive it, but a matter of how your brain likes to learn. There are two ways that you can tackle the information in this chapter:

Accept that the code works, move on, and revisit exactly how things work later in your programming career.

Insist on becoming expert on the topics in this chapter and devote a lot of time to mastering them before moving on.

I strongly recommend option 1. Some topics can't be mastered until other topics are understood. But a problem arises when, to move on to the latter, you first need to have an introduction to the former. The problem becomes circular and unsolvable if you insist on complete mastery at all times. Sometimes, it is important to just accept that there is more under the surface. If you can simply accept that the code we just looked at does work behind the scenes, and that the code within the curly braces is what happens when the radio button is clicked on; then, you are ready to proceed. You can now go and do a web search for lambdas; however, be prepared for many hours of theory. We will revisit lambdas again in this chapter and throughout the book while focusing on practical application.

Writing the code for the overridden function

Notice that one of the parameters of this function that is passed in when the `radioGroup` instance is pressed is `checkedId`. This parameter is an `Int` type and it holds the `id` property of the currently selected `RadioButton`. This is just what we need - almost.

It might be surprising that `checkedId` is an `Int` type. Android stores all IDs as `Int`, even though we declare them with alphanumeric characters such as `radioButton1` or `radioGroup`.

All our human-friendly names are converted to `Int` when the app is compiled. So, how do we know which `Int` type refers to an ID such as `radioButton1` or `radioButton2`?

What we need to do is get a reference to the actual object that the `Int` type is an ID for, using the `Int id` property and then ask the object for its human-friendly `id` value. We will do so as follows:

```
val rb = group.findViewById<RadioButton>(checkedId)
```

Now we can retrieve the familiar `id` property that we used for the currently-selected `RadioButton` widget, for which we now have a reference stored in `rb`, with the `id` property's getter function, as follows:

```
rb.id
```

We could, therefore, handle `RadioButton` clicks by using a `when` block with a branch for each possible `RadioButton` that could be pressed, and `rb.id` as the condition.

The following code shows the entire contents of the `onCheckedChanged` function that we have just discussed:

```
// Get a reference to the RadioButton
// that is currently checked
val rb = group.findViewById<RadioButton>(checkedId)

// branch the code based on the 'friendly' id
when (rb.id) {

   R.id.radioButton1->
         // Do something here

   R.id.radioButton2->
         // Do something here

   R.id.radioButton3->
         // Do something here

}
// End when block
```

Seeing this in action in the next working mini-app, where we can press the buttons for real, will make this clearer.

Let's continue with our palette exploration.

Exploring the palette – part 2, and more lambdas

Now that we have seen how lambdas and anonymous classes and interfaces work, specifically with `RadioGroup` and `RadioButton`, we can now continue exploring the palette and look at working with some more UI widgets.

The Switch widget

The `Switch` widget is just like a `Button` widget except that it has two fixed states that can be read and responded to.

An obvious use for the `Switch` widget is to show and hide something. Remember that in our *Kotlin Meet UI* app in *Chapter 12, Connecting Our Kotlin to the UI and Nullability* we used a `Button` to show and hide a `TextView` widget?

Each time we hid or showed the `TextView` widget, we changed the `text` property on the `Button` to make it evident what would happen if it was clicked on again. What might have been more intuitive for the user, and more straightforward for us as programmers, would have been to use a `Switch` widget, as illustrated in the following screenshot:

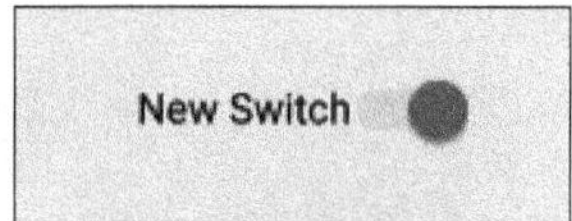

The following code assumes that we already have an object called `mySwitch`, which is a reference to a `Switch` object in the layout. We could show and hide a `TextView` widget just as we did in our *Kotlin Meet UI* app in *Chapter 12*.

To listen for, and respond to, clicks/switching, we again use an anonymous class. This time, however, we use the `CompoundButton` version of `OnCheckedChangeListener`. As before, these details are inferred, and we can use very similar and simple code as when we handled the radio button widgets.

We need to override the `onCheckedChanged` function and that function has a `Boolean` parameter, `isChecked`. The `isChecked` variable is simply false for off and true for on.

This is how we can more intuitively replace this text by hiding or showing code:

```
mySwitch.setOnCheckedChangeListener{
   buttonView, isChecked->
      if(isChecked){
            // Currently visible so hide it
            txtValue.visibility = View.INVISIBLE

      }else{
            // Currently hidden so show it
            txtValue.visibility = View.VISIBLE
      }
}
```

If the anonymous class or lambda code still looks a little odd, don't worry because it will become more familiar the more we use it. And we will do so again now when we look at CheckBox.

The CheckBox widget

With a CheckBox widget, we simply detect its state (checked or unchecked) at a given moment - such as at the moment when a specific button is clicked on. The following code gives us a glimpse of how this might happen, again using an anonymous class and lambda to act as a listener:

```
myCheckBox.setOnCheckedChangeListener{
    buttonView, isChecked->

    if (myCheckBox.isChecked) {
           // It's checked so do something
    } else {
           // It's not checked do something else
    }
}
```

In the previous code, we assume that myCheckBox has been declared and initialized, and then use the same type of anonymous class as we did for Switch to detect and respond to clicks.

The TextClock widget

In our next app, we will use the TextClock widget to show off some of its features. We will need to add the XML code directly to the layout as this widget is not available to drag and drop from the palette. This is what the TextClock widget looks like:

4:28 PM

As an example of using TextClock, this is how we will set its time to the same time as it is in Brussels, Europe:

```
tClock.timeZone = "Europe/Brussels"
```

The previous code assumes that tClock is a reference to a TextClock widget in the layout.

With all this extra information, let's make an app to use the Android widgets more practically than what we have so far.

The widget exploration app

We have just discussed six widgets – `EditText`, `ImageView`, `RadioButton` (and `RadioGroup`), `Switch`, `CheckBox`, and `TextClock`. Let's make a working app and do something practical with each of them. We will also use a `Button` widget and a `TextView` widget again as well.

In this layout, we will use `LinearLayout` as the layout type that holds everything, and within `LinearLayout`, we will use multiple `RelativeLayout` instances.

`RelativeLayout` has been superseded by `ConstraintLayout`, but they are still commonly used and are worth playing around with. You will see as you build layouts within `RelativeLayout` that the UI elements behave very much the same as `ConstraintLayout`, but that the underlying XML is different. It is not necessary to learn this XML in detail, rather, using `RelativeLayout` will allow us to show the interesting way that Android Studio enables you to convert these layouts to `ConstraintLayout`.

Remember that you can refer to the completed code in the download bundle. This app can be found in the `Chapter13/Widget Exploration` folder.

Setting up the widget exploration project and UI

First, we will set up a new project and prepare the UI layout. These steps will get all the widgets on the screen and the `id` properties set, ready to grab a reference to them. It will help to have a look at the target layout up and running, before we get started, and it is shown in the following screenshot:

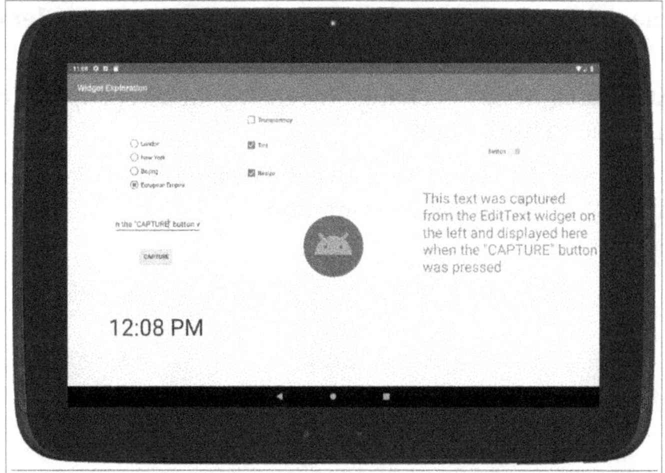

Here is how this app will demonstrate these widgets:

- The radio buttons allow the user to change the time that is displayed on the clock to a choice of four time zones.
- The **Capture** button, when clicked on, will change the `text` property of the `TextView` widget (on the right) to whatever is currently in the `EditText` widget (on the left).
- The three `CheckBox` widgets will add and remove visual effects from the Android robot image. In the previous screenshot, the image is resized (made bigger) and has a color tint applied.
- The `Switch` widget will turn on and off the `TextView` widget that displays information entered in the `EditText` widget (which is captured at the click of a button).

The exact layout positions are not essential, but the `id` properties specified must match exactly. So, let's perform the following steps to set up a new project and prepare the UI layout:

1. Create a new project called `Widget Exploration` and use the **Empty Activity** project template with its usual settings except for one small change. Set the **Minimum API level** option to `API 17: Android 4.2 (Jelly Bean)` and keep all the other settings at their default settings. We are using API 17 because one of the features of the `TextClock` widget requires us to. We still support in excess of 98% of all Android devices.
2. Let's create a new layout file as we want our new layout to be based on `LinearLayout`. Right-click on the `layout` folder in the project explorer and select **New** | **Layout resource file** from the pop-up menu.
3. In the **New resource file** window, enter `exploration_layout.xml` in the **File name** field and then enter `LinearLayout` in the **Root element** field; now click on **OK**.
4. In the **Attributes** window, change the `orientation` property of the `LinearLayout` to **horizontal**.
5. Using the drop-down controls above the design view, make sure you have selected a tablet in landscape orientation.

For a reminder of how to make a tablet emulator, refer to *Chapter 3, Exploring Android Studio and the Project Structure*. For advice on how to manipulate the orientation of the emulator, refer to *Chapter 5, Beautiful Layouts with CardView and ScrollView*.

6. We can now begin to create our layout. Drag and drop three **RelativeLayout** layouts from the **Legacy** category of the palette onto the design to create the three vertical divisions of our design. You will probably find it easier to use the **Component Tree** window for this step.
7. Set the **weight** property for each of the `RelativeLayout` widgets in turn to `.33`. We now have three equal vertical divisions, just like in the following screenshot:

8. Check that the **Component Tree** window looks like the following screenshot:

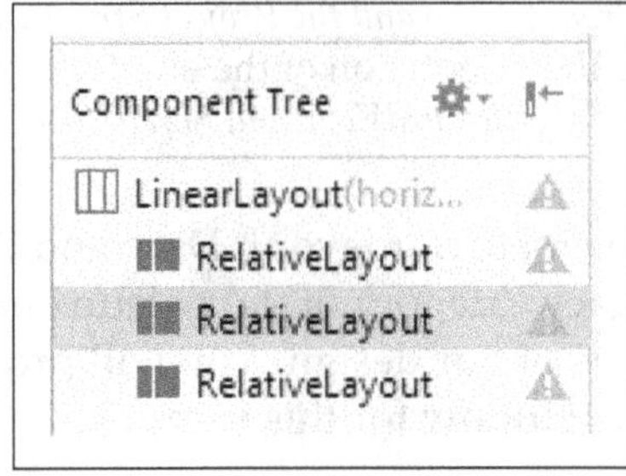

If you want to use `ConstraintLayout` instead of `RelativeLayout`, then the following instructions will be nearly identical. Just remember to set the final position of your UI by clicking the **Infer Constraints** button, or by setting the constraints manually, as discussed in *Chapter 4, Getting Started with Layouts and Material Design*. Alternatively, you can build the layout exactly as detailed in this tutorial and you can use the **Convert to Constraint layout** feature that is discussed later in this chapter. This is excellent for using layouts you have and want to use, but prefer to use the faster-running `ConstraintLayout`.

9. Drag a **Switch** widget near the top-center of the right-hand `RelativeLayout` widget and just below, drag a **TextView** from the palette. The right-hand side of your layout should now look like the following screenshot:

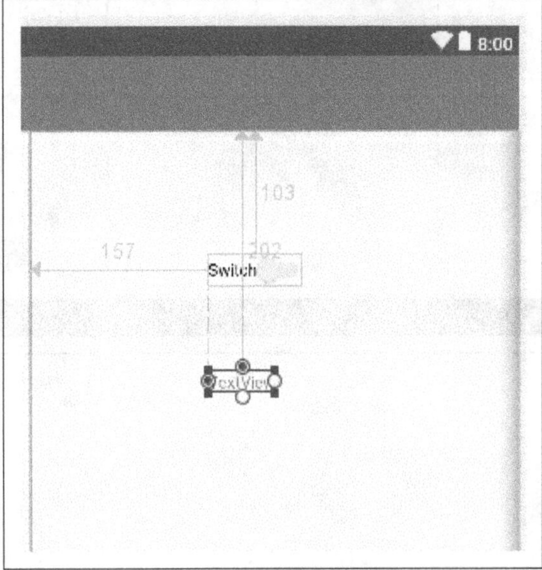

10. Drag three **CheckBox** widgets, one above the other, and then an **ImageView** widget underneath them onto the central `RelativeLayout`. In the resulting pop-up **Resources** dialog window, choose **Project** | **ic_launcher** to use the Android icon as the image for the `ImageView` widget. The central column should now appear as follows:

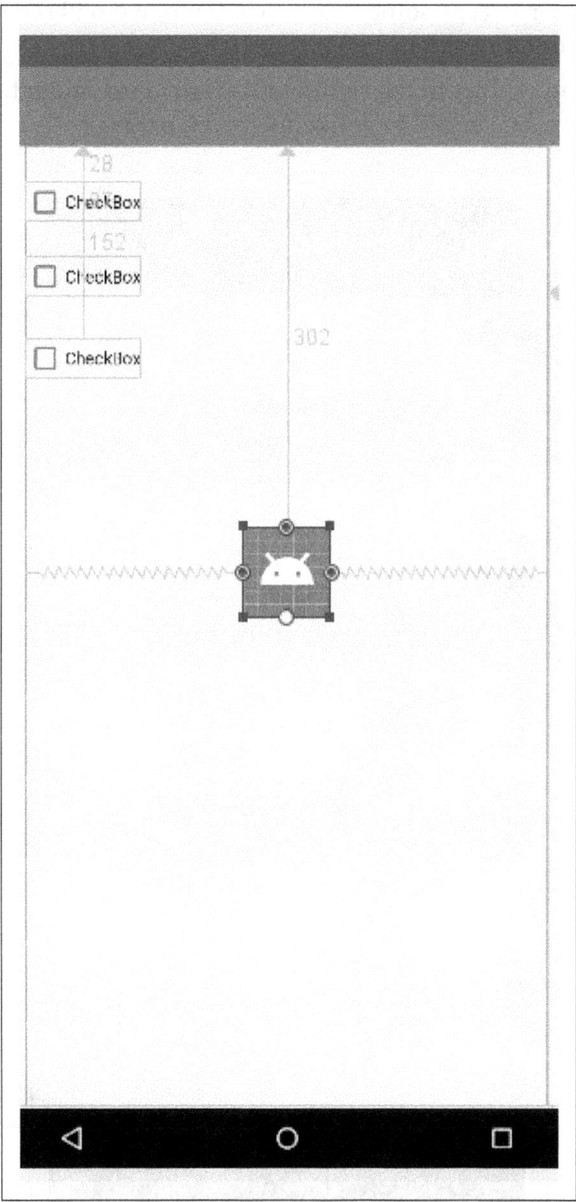

11. Drag a **RadioGroup** widget to the left-hand `RelativeLayout`.
12. Add four **RadioButton** widgets within the **RadioGroup** widget. This step will be easier by using the **Component Tree** window.
13. Underneath the **RadioGroup** widget, drag a **Plain Text** widget from the **Text** category of the palette. Remember, despite its name, that this is a widget that allows the user to type some text into it. Soon, we will see how to capture and use the entered text.
14. Add a **Button** widget to the right of the **Plain Text** widget. Your left-hand `RelativeLayout` should look like this screenshot:

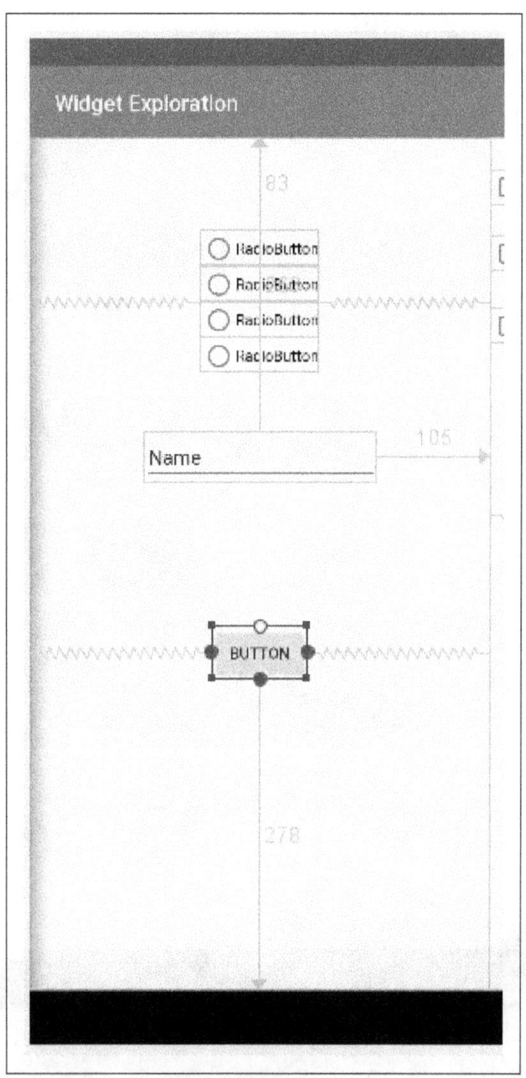

The **Component Tree** window will look like the following screenshot at this stage:

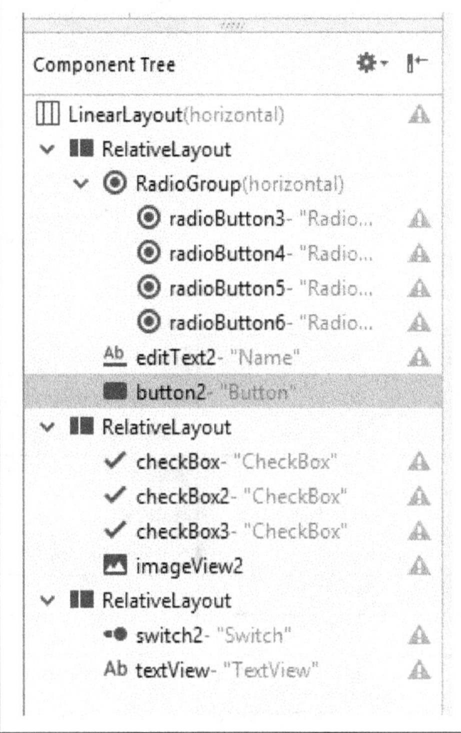

15. Now add the following attributes to the widgets that we have just laid out:

Note that some of the attributes might already be correct by default.

Widget type	Property	Value to set to
RadioGroup	`id`	`radioGroup`
RadioButton (top)	`id`	`radioButtonLondon`
RadioButton (top)	`text`	`London`
RadioButton (top)	`checked`	Select the "tick" icon for true
RadioButton (second)	`id`	`radioButtonBeijing`
RadioButton (second)	`text`	`Beijing`
RadioButton (third)	`id`	`radioButtonNewYork`
RadioButton (third)	`text`	`New York`

Widget type	Property	Value to set to
RadioButton (bottom)	id	`radioButtonEuropeanEmpire`
RadioButton (bottom)	text	`European Empire`
EditText	id	`editText`
Button	id	`button`
Button	text	`Capture`
CheckBox (top)	text	`Transparency`
CheckBox (top)	id	`checkBoxTransparency`
CheckBox (middle)	text	`Tint`
CheckBox (middle)	id	`checkBoxTint`
CheckBox (bottom)	text	`Resize`
CheckBox (bottom)	id	`checkBoxReSize`
ImageView	id	`imageView`
Switch	id	`switch1`
Switch	enabled	Select the "tick" icon for true
Switch	clickable	Select the "tick" icon for true
TextView	id	`textView`
TextView	textSize	`34sp`
TextView	layout_width	`match_parent`
TextView	layout_height	`match_parent`

16. Now switch to the **Text** tab to view the XML code for the layout. Find the end of the first (left-hand) `RelativeLayout` column as shown in the following code listing. I have added an XML comment and highlighted it in the following code:

```
...
...
   </RadioGroup>

   <EditText
         android:id="@+id/editText2"
         android:layout_width="wrap_content"
         android:layout_height="wrap_content"
         android:layout_alignParentTop="true"
         android:layout_alignParentEnd="true"
         android:layout_marginTop="263dp"
```

```
        android:layout_marginEnd="105dp"
        android:ems="10"
        android:inputType="textPersonName"
        android:text="Name" />

    <Button
        android:id="@+id/button2"
        android:layout_width="wrap_content"
        android:layout_height="wrap_content"
        android:layout_alignParentBottom="true"
        android:layout_centerHorizontal="true"
        android:layout_marginBottom="278dp"
        android:text="Button" />

    <!-- Insert TextClock here-->

</RelativeLayout>
```

17. After the `<!--Insert TextClock Here-->` comment, insert the following XML code for the `TextClock` widget. Note that the comment was added by me in the previous listing to show you where to put the code. The comment will not be present in your code. We did things this way because `TextClock` is not available directly from the palette. Here is the code to add after the comment:

```
<TextClock
    android:id="@+id/textClock"
    android:layout_width="wrap_content"
    android:layout_height="wrap_content"
    android:layout_alignParentBottom="true"
    android:layout_centerHorizontal="true"
    android:layout_gravity="center_horizontal"
    android:layout_marginBottom="103dp"
    android:textSize="54sp" />
```

18. Switch to the **Design** tab and tweak your layout to resemble the following reference diagram as closely as possible, but if you have the appropriate types of UI with the correct `id` attributes, then the code will still work even if the layout isn't identical:

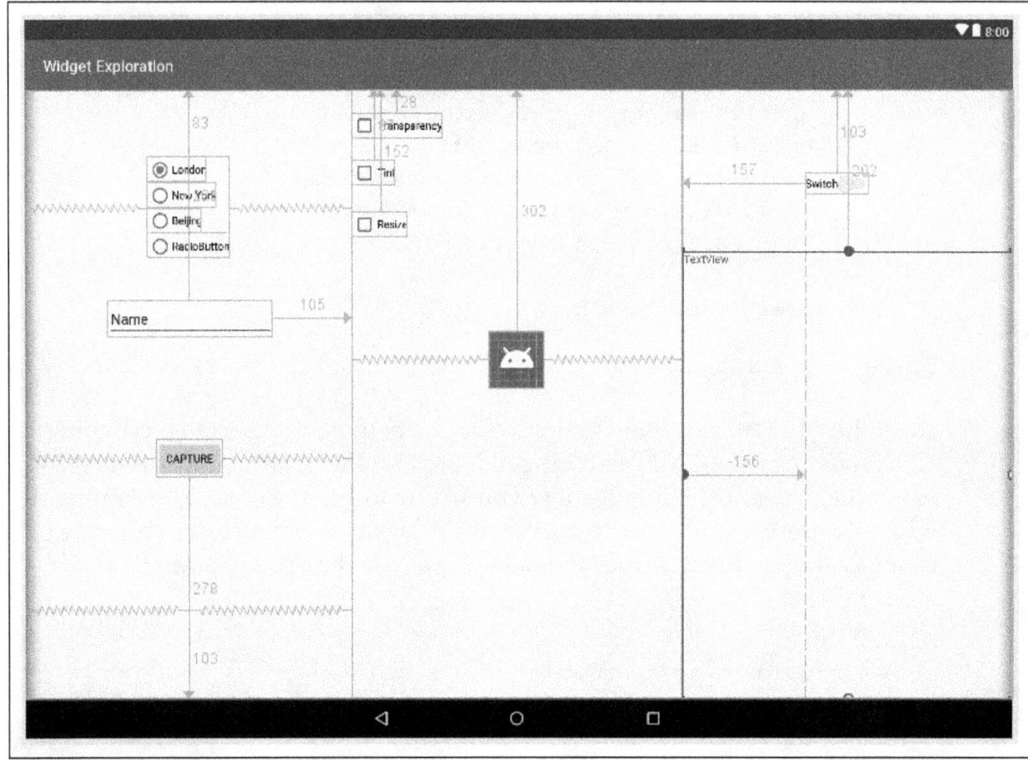

We have just set the required attributes for our layout. There is nothing new that we haven't done before, except that some of the widget types are new to us and the layout is slightly more intricate.

Now we can get on with using all these widgets with our Kotlin code.

Coding the widget exploration app

The first part of the Kotlin code that we need to change is to make sure that our new layout is displayed. We can do so by changing the call to the `setContentView` function in the `onCreate` function to look like this:

```
setContentView(R.layout.exploration_layout)
```

There are many `import` statements that are needed for this app, so let's add them all up front to save us from having to keep mentioning them as we proceed. Add the following `import` statements:

```
import androidx.appcompat.app.AppCompatActivity
import android.graphics.Color
import android.os.Bundle
import android.view.View
import android.widget.CompoundButton
import android.widget.RadioButton
import kotlinx.android.synthetic.main.exploration_layout.*
```

The preceding code also includes the ...`exploration_layout.*` code (as highlighted in the preceding code) to automatically enable us to use the `id` attributes that we have just configured as the instance names in our Kotlin code. This saves us from using the `findViewByID` function multiple times. It will not always be possible to do things this way and knowing how to use the `findViewByID` function as we discussed earlier in the *Declaring and initializing the objects from the layout* section will sometimes be necessary.

Coding the CheckBox widget

Now we can create a lambda to listen for and handle clicks on the checkboxes. The following three blocks of code implement an anonymous class for each of the checkboxes in turn. What is different in each of them, however, is how we respond to a click, and we will discuss each of these in turn.

Changing transparency

The first checkbox is labeled **Transparency** and we use the `alpha` property on the `imageView` instance to change how transparent (that is, see-through) it is. The `alpha` property requires a floating-point value between 0 and 1 as an argument.

0 is invisible and 1 has no transparency at all. So, when this checkbox is checked, we set the `alpha` property to `.1`, so that the image is barely visible; then, when it is unchecked, we set it to `1`, which is completely visible with no transparency. The `Boolean isChecked` parameter of `onCheckedChanged` function contains a true or false value as to whether the checkbox is checked or not.

Add the following code after the call to the `setContentView` function in the `onCreate` function:

```
// Listen for clicks on the button,
// the CheckBoxes and the RadioButtons

// setOnCheckedChangeListener requires an interface of type
// CompoundButton.OnCheckedChangeListener. In turn this interface
// has a function called onCheckedChanged
// It is all handled by the lambda
checkBoxTransparency.setOnCheckedChangeListener({
   view, isChecked ->
      if (isChecked) {
         // Set some transparency
         imageView.alpha = .1f
      } else {
         // Remove the transparency
         imageView.alpha = 1f
      }
})
```

In the next anonymous class, we handle the checkbox labeled **Tint**.

Changing color

In the `onCheckedChanged` function, we use the `setColorFilter` function on `imageView` to overlay a color layer on the image. When `isChecked` is true, we layer a color, and when `isChecked` is false, we remove it.

The `setColorFilter` function takes a color in the **ARGB (alpha, red, green,** and **blue)** format as an argument. The color is provided by the `argb` function of the `Color` class. The four arguments of the `argb` function are values for alpha, red, green, and blue. These four values create a color. In our case, the `150, 255, 0, 0` value creates a strong red tint, while the `0, 0, 0, 0` value creates no tint at all.

To understand more about the `Color` class, check out the Android developer site at `http://developer.android.com/reference/android/graphics/Color.html`, and to understand the RGB color system more, take a look at Wikipedia here: `https://en.wikipedia.org/wiki/RGB_color_model`.

Add the following code after the previous block of code in the `onCreate` function:

```
checkBoxTint.setOnCheckedChangeListener({
    view, isChecked ->
    if (isChecked) {
        // Checked so set some tint
        imageView.setColorFilter(Color.argb(150, 255, 0, 0))
    } else {
        // No tint required
        imageView.setColorFilter(Color.argb(0, 0, 0, 0))
    }
})
```

Now we will see how to scale the UI by playing with the size of the `ImageView` widget.

Changing size

In the anonymous class that handles the **Resize** labeled checkbox, we use the `scaleX` and `scaleY` properties to resize the robot image. When we set `scaleX` to 2 and `scaleY` to 2 on `imageView`, we will double the size of the image, while setting the values to 1 will return the image to its normal size.

Add the following code after the previous block of code in the `onCreate` function:

```
checkBoxReSize.setOnCheckedChangeListener({
    view, isChecked ->
    if (isChecked) {
        // It's checked so make bigger
        imageView.scaleX = 2f
        imageView.scaleY = 2f
    } else {
        // It's not checked make regular size
        imageView.scaleX = 1f
        imageView.scaleY = 1f
    }
})
```

Now we will handle the three radio buttons.

Coding the RadioButton widgets

As they are part of a `RadioGroup` widget, we can handle them much more succinctly than we did with the `CheckBox` objects.

First, we make sure they are clear to start with by calling `clearCheck()` on the `radioGroup` instance. Then, we create our anonymous class of the `OnCheckedChangeListener` type and override the `onCheckedChanged` function with a short and sweet lambda.

This function will be called when any `RadioButton` from the `RadioGroup` widget is clicked on. All we need to do is get the `id` property of the `RadioButton` widget that was clicked on and respond accordingly. We will achieve this by using a `when` statement with three possible paths of execution - one for each `RadioButton` widget.

Remember that when we first discussed `RadioButton`, the `id` property supplied in the `checkedId` parameter of `onCheckedChanged` was an `Int` type. This is why we must first create a new `RadioButton` object from `checkedId`:

```
val rb = group.findViewById<View>(checkedId) as RadioButton
```

Then, we can use the `id` property's getter of the new `RadioButton` object as the condition for `when`, as follows:

```
when (rb.id) {
   ...
```

Then, in each branch, we use the `timeZone` property's setter with the correct Android time zone code as an argument.

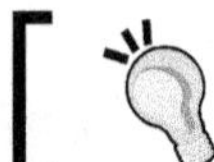

[You can see all the Android time zone codes at `https://gist.github.com/arpit/1035596`.]

Add the following code, which incorporates everything that we have just discussed. Add it in the `onCreate` function after the previous code that we entered for handling the checkboxes:

```
// Now for the radio buttons
// Uncheck all buttons
radioGroup.clearCheck()

radioGroup.setOnCheckedChangeListener {
   group, checkedId ->
```

```
        val rb = group.findViewById<View>(checkedId) as RadioButton

        when (rb.id) {
            R.id.radioButtonLondon ->
                textClock.timeZone = "Europe/London"

            R.id.radioButtonBeijing ->
                textClock.timeZone = "CST6CDT"


            R.id.radioButtonNewYork ->
                textClock.timeZone = "America/New_York"


            R.id.radioButtonEuropeanEmpire ->
                textClock.timeZone = "Europe/Brussels"
        }
    }
```

Now it's time for something a little bit new.

Using a lambda for handling clicks on a regular Button widget

In the next block of code that we will write, we will use a lambda to implement an anonymous class to handle the clicks on a regular `Button` widget. We call `button.setOnclickListener`, as we have done previously. This time, however, instead of passing `this` as an argument, we create a brand-new class of the type `View.OnClickListener` and override the `onClick` function as the argument, just as we did with our other anonymous classes. In the same way as our previous classes, the code is inferred and we have short, snappy code where our code isn't cluttered with too many details.

> This method is preferable in this situation because there is only one button. If we had lots of buttons, then having `MainActivity` implement `View.OnClickListener` and then overriding `onClick` to handle all clicks in one function would probably be preferable, as we have done previously.

In the `onClick` function, we use the `text` property's setter to set the `text` property on `textView`, and then the getter of the `text` property of the `editText` instance to get whatever text (if any) the user has entered in the `EditText` widget.

Add the following code after the previous block of code in the `onCreate` function:

```
/*
   Let's listen for clicks on our "Capture" Button.
   The compiler has worked out that the single function
   of the required interface has a single parameter.
   Therefore, the syntax is shortened (->) is removed
   and the only parameter, (should we have needed it)
   is declared invisibly as "it"
*/
button.setOnClickListener {
   // it... accesses the view that was clicked

   // We want to act on the textView and editText instances
   // Change the text on the TextView
   // to whatever is currently in the EditText
   textView.text = editText.text
}
```

Next, we will handle the Switch widget.

Coding the Switch widget

Next, we create yet another anonymous class to listen for and handle changes to our `Switch` widget.

When the `isChecked` variable is `true`, we show the `TextView` widget, and when it is false, we hide it.

Add the following code after the previous block of code in the `onCreate` function:

```
// Show or hide the TextView
switch1.setOnCheckedChangeListener {
   buttonView, isChecked ->
   if (isChecked) {
      textView.visibility = View.VISIBLE
   } else {
      textView.visibility = View.INVISIBLE
   }
}
```

Now we can run our app and try out all the features.

The Android emulators can be rotated into landscape mode by pressing the *Ctrl* + *F11* keyboard combination on Windows, or *Ctrl* + *fn*+ *F11* on a macOS.

Running the Widget Exploration app

Try checking the radio buttons to see the time zone change on the clock. In the following image, I have photoshopped a few cropped screenshots to show that the time changes when a new time zone is selected:

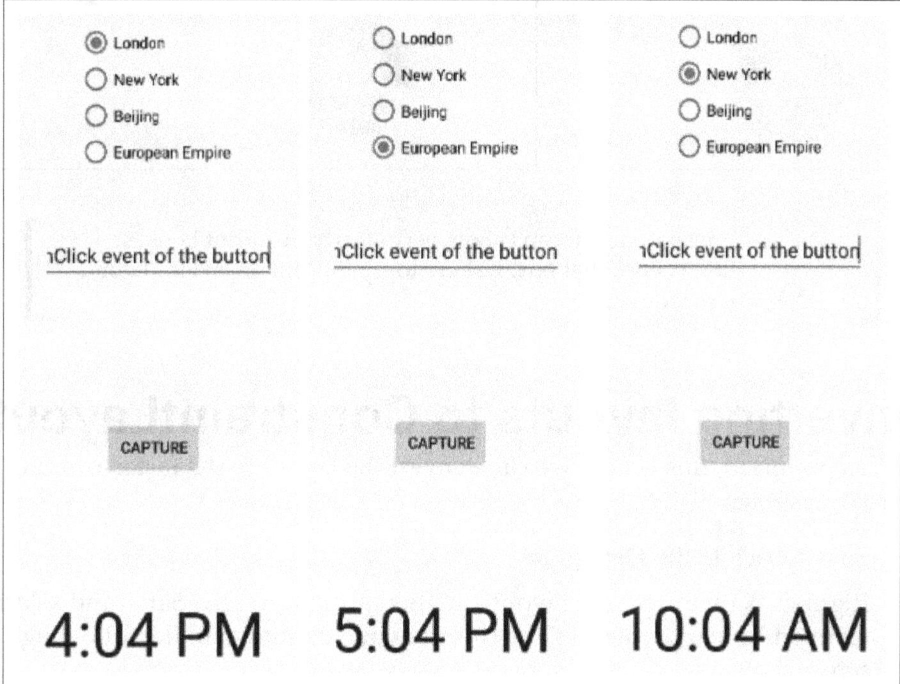

Enter different values into the `EditText` widget, and then click the button to see it grab the text and display it on itself, as demonstrated in the screenshot at the start of this tutorial.

Change what the image in the app looks like with different combinations of checked and unchecked checkboxes and hide and show the `TextView` widget by using the `Switch` widget above it. The following screenshot displays two combinations of the checkboxes and the switch widget photoshopped together for demonstration purposes:

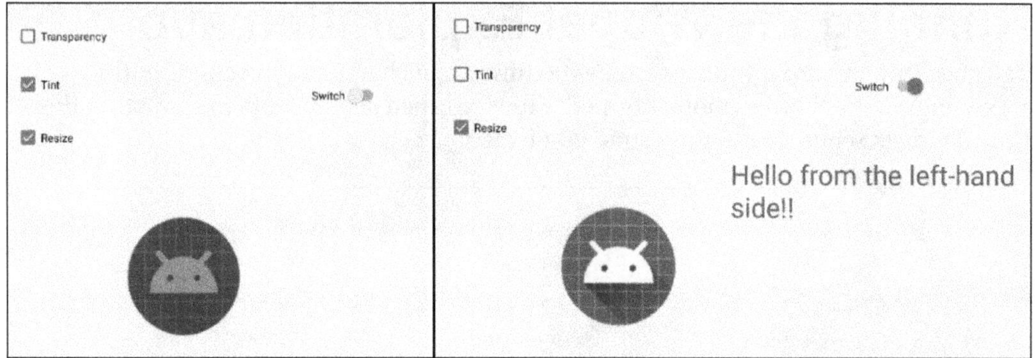

Transparency doesn't show very clearly in a print book, so I didn't check that box. Be sure to try this out on an emulator or real device.

Converting layouts to ConstraintLayout

Finally, as promised, this is how we can convert the layout to the faster-running `ConstraintLayout`:

1. Switch back to the **Design** tab
2. Right-click on the parent layout - in this case, `LinearLayout` - and select **Convert LinearLayout to ConstraintLayout**, as shown in the following screenshot:

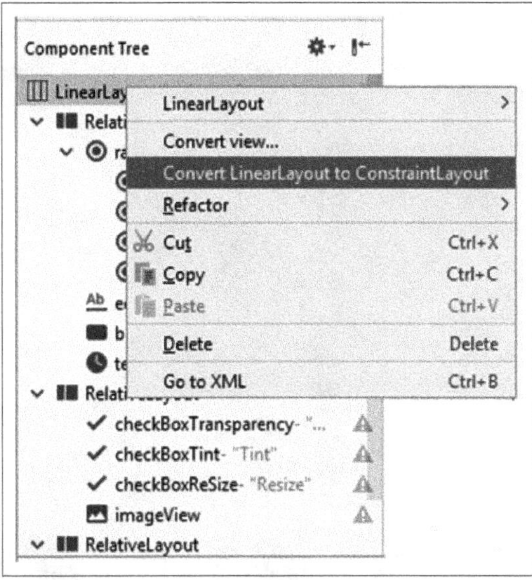

Now you can convert any old `RelativeLayout` layouts to the newer and faster `ConstraintLayout` widget, as well as build your own `RelativeLayout`.

Summary

We have learned a lot in this chapter. As well as exploring a plethora of widgets, we learned how to implement widgets in Kotlin code without any XML, we used our first anonymous classes using short, snappy code in the form of a lambda to handle clicks on a selection of widgets, and we put all our new widget prowess into a working app.

Now let's move on to look at another way that we can significantly enhance our UI.

In the next chapter, we will see a completely new UI element that we can't just drag and drop from the palette, but we will still have plenty of help from the Android API. We will learn about **dialog windows**. We will also make a start on our most significant app to date called Note to self. It is a memo, to-do, and personal note app.

14
Android Dialog Windows

In this chapter, we will learn how to present the user with a pop-up dialog window. We can then put all that we know into the first phase of our first multi-chapter app, *Note to self*. We will then learn about more Android and Kotlin features in this chapter and the four following chapters (up to *Chapter 18*, *Localization*), and then use our newly acquired knowledge to enhance the Note to self app.

In each chapter, we will also build a selection of smaller apps that are separate from this main app. So, what does *Chapter 14*, *Android Dialog Windows*, hold in store for you? The following topics will be covered in this chapter:

- Implement a simple app with a pop-up dialog box
- Learn how to use `DialogFragment` to begin the Note to self app
- Start the Note to self app and learn how to add string resources in our projects instead of hardcoding text in our layouts
- Implement more complex dialog boxes to capture input from the user

So, let's get started.

Dialog windows

Often in our apps, we will want to show the user some information, or perhaps ask for confirmation of an action in a pop-up window. This is known as a **dialog** window. If you quickly scan the palette in Android Studio, you might be surprised to see no mention of dialog windows whatsoever.

Dialog windows in Android are more advanced than a simple widget or even a whole layout. They are classes that can also have layouts and other UI elements of their own.

The best way to create a dialog window in Android is to use the `DialogFragment` class.

Fragments are an extensive and vital topic in Android, and we will spend much of the second half of this book exploring and using them. Creating a neat pop-up dialog (using `DialogFragment`) for our user to interact with is, however, a great introduction to fragments and is not complicated at all.

Creating the dialog demo project

We previously mentioned that the best way to create a dialog window in Android is with the `DialogFragment` class. However, there is another way to create dialogs in Android that is arguably a little bit simpler. The problem with this simpler `Dialog` class is that it is not very well supported in the Activity lifecycle. It is even possible that using `Dialog` could accidentally crash the app.

If you were writing an app with one fixed orientation layout that only needed one simple pop-up dialog, it could be argued that the simpler `Dialog` class should be used. But, as we are aiming to build modern, professional apps with advanced features, we will benefit from ignoring this class.

Create a new project in Android Studio using the **Empty Activity** project template and call it `Dialog Demo`. The completed code for this project is in the `Chapter14/Dialog Demo` folder of the download bundle.

Coding a DialogFragment class

Create a new class in Android Studio by right-clicking on the folder with the name of your package (the one that has the `MainActivity.kt` file). Select **New | Kotlin File/class**, name it `MyDialog`, and choose **Class** in the drop-down selector. Left-click on **OK** to create the class.

The first thing you need to do is to change the class declaration to inherit from `DialogFragment`. Also, let's add all the imports we will need in this class. When you have done so, your new class will look like this:

```
import android.app.Dialog
import android.os.Bundle
import androidx.appcompat.app.AlertDialog
import androidx.fragment.app.DialogFragment

class MyDialog : DialogFragment() {
}
```

Now, let's add code to this class a bit at a time and explain what is happening at each step.

As with so many classes in the Android API, `DialogFragment` provides us with functions that we can override to interact with the different events that will occur with the class.

Add the following highlighted code that overrides the `onCreateDialog` function. Study it carefully, and then we will examine what is happening:

```
class MyDialog : DialogFragment() {

    override
    fun onCreateDialog(savedInstanceState: Bundle?): Dialog {

        // Use the Builder class because this dialog
        // has a simple UI.
        // We will use the more flexible onCreateView function
        // instead of onCreateDialog in the next project
        val builder = AlertDialog.Builder(this.activity!!)

        // More code here soon
    }
}
```

There is one error in the code because we are missing the return statement, which needs to return an object of type `Dialog`. We will add this when we have finished coding the rest of the function shortly.

In the code that we just added, we first add the overridden `onCreateDialog` function, which will be called by Android when we later show the dialog with code from the `MainActivity` class.

Then, inside the `onCreateDialog` function, we get our hands on an instance of a new class. We declare and initialize an object of the `AlertDialog.Builder` type that needs a reference to the `MainActivity` class to be passed into its constructor. This is why we use `activity!!` as the argument; and we are asserting that the instance is not null (!!).

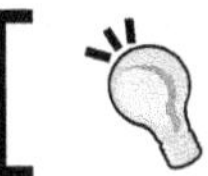

Refer to *Chapter 12, Connecting Our Kotlin to the UI and Nullability*, for a refresher on the not null assertion (`!!`).

The activity property is part of the Fragment class (and, therefore, DialogFragment too) and it is a reference to the Activity class instance that will create the DialogFragment instance. In this case, this is our MainActivity class.

Let's take a look at what we can do with builder now that we have declared and initialized it.

Using chaining to configure the DialogFragment class

Now we can use our builder object to do the rest of the work. There is something slightly odd in the next three blocks of code. If you look ahead and quickly scan them, you will notice that there are three uses of the dot operator, but only one usage is actually placed next to the builder object. This shows that these three apparent blocks of code are, in fact, just one line to the compiler.

We have seen what is going on here before, but in a less pronounced situation. When we create a Toast message and add a .show() call on to the end of it, we are **chaining**. That is, we are calling more than one function, in sequence, on the same object. This is equivalent to writing multiple lines of code; it is just clearer and shorter this way.

Add this code, which utilizes chaining, right after the previous code that we added in onCreateDialog, examine it, and then we will discuss it:

```
// Dialog will have "Make a selection" as the title
builder.setMessage("Make a selection")
    // An OK button that does nothing
    .setPositiveButton("OK", { dialog, id ->
        // Nothing happening here
    })
    // A "Cancel" button that does nothing
    .setNegativeButton("Cancel", { dialog, id ->
        // Nothing happening here either
    })
```

Each of the three parts of code that we added can be explained as follows:

1. In the first of the three blocks that uses chaining, we call builder.setMessage, which sets the main message that the user will see in the dialog box. Also, note that it is fine to have comments in between parts of the chained function calls, as these are ignored entirely by the compiler.

2. Then, we add a button to our dialog with the `setPositiveButton` function and the first argument sets the text on it to `OK`. The second argument is a lambda that implements `DialogInterface.OnClickListener` that handles clicks on the button. Notice that we are not going to add any code to the `onClick` function, but we could, just as we did in the previous chapter. We just want to see this simple dialog and we will take things a step further in the next project.
3. Next, we call yet another function on the same `builder` object. This time, it's the `setNegativeButton` function. Again, the two arguments set `Cancel` as the text for the button and a lambda is used to set up listening for clicks. Again, for the purposes of this demo, we are not taking any action in the overridden `onClick` function.

Next, we will code the `return` statement to complete the function and remove the error. Add the `return` statement to the end (but keep it inside the final curly brace) of the `onCreateDialog` function:

```
    // Create the object and return it
    return builder.create()
}// End of onCreateDialog
```

This last line of code has the effect of returning to `MainActivity` (which will call `onCreateDialog` in the first place) our new, fully configured, dialog window. We will see and add this calling code quite soon.

Now that we have our `MyDialog` class that inherits from `FragmentDialog`, all we have to do is to declare an instance of `MyDialog`, instantiate it, and call its overridden `onCreateDialog` function.

Using the DialogFragment class

Before we turn to the code, let's add a button to our layout, by observing the following steps:

1. Switch to the `activity_main.xml` tab, and then switch to the **Design** tab.
2. Drag a **Button** widget onto the layout and make sure its `id` attribute is set to `button`.
3. Click the **Infer Constraints** button to constrain the button exactly where you place it, but the position isn't important; how we will use it to create an instance of our `MyDialog` class is the key lesson.

Now switch to the `MainActivity.kt` tab and we will handle a click on this new button by using a lambda as we did in *Chapter 13, Bringing Android Widgets to Life* during the Widget exploration app. We do it this way as we only have one button in the layout, and it seems sensible and more compact than doing the alternative (that is, implementing the `OnClickListener` interface and then overriding `onClick` for the entire `MainActivity` class as we did in *Chapter 12, Connecting Our Kotlin to the UI and Nullability*).

Add the following code to the `onCreate` function of `MainActivity` after the call to `setContentView`:

```
val button = findViewById<Button>(R.id.button)
// We could have removed the previous line of code by
// adding the ...synthetic.main.activity_main.* import
// as an alternative

button.setOnClickListener {
   val myDialog = MyDialog()
   myDialog.show(supportFragmentManager, "123")
   // This calls onCreateDialog
   // Don't worry about the strange looking 123
   // We will find out about this in chapter 18
}
```

The following `import` statement is needed for this code:

```
import android.widget.Button;
```

Notice that the only thing that happens in the code is that the `setOnClickListener` lambda overrides `onClick`. This means that when the button is pressed, a new instance of `MyDialog` is created and calls its `show` function, which will show our dialog window just as we configured it in the `MyDialog` class.

The `show` function needs a reference to `FragmentManager`, which we get from the `supportFragmentManager` property. This is the class that tracks and controls all fragment instances for an `Activity` instance. We also pass in an ID (`"123"`).

More details on `FragmentManager` will be revealed when we look more deeply at fragments, starting in *Chapter 24, Design Patterns, Multiple Layouts, and Fragments*.

The reason we use the `supportFragmentManager` property is because we are supporting older devices by extending `AppCompatActivity`. If we simply extended `Activity`, then we could use the `fragmentManager` property. The downside is that the app won't run on many older devices.

Now we can run the app and admire our new dialog window that appears when we click the button in the layout. Notice that clicking either of the buttons in the dialog window will close it; this is the default behavior. The following screenshot shows our dialog window in action on the tablet emulator:

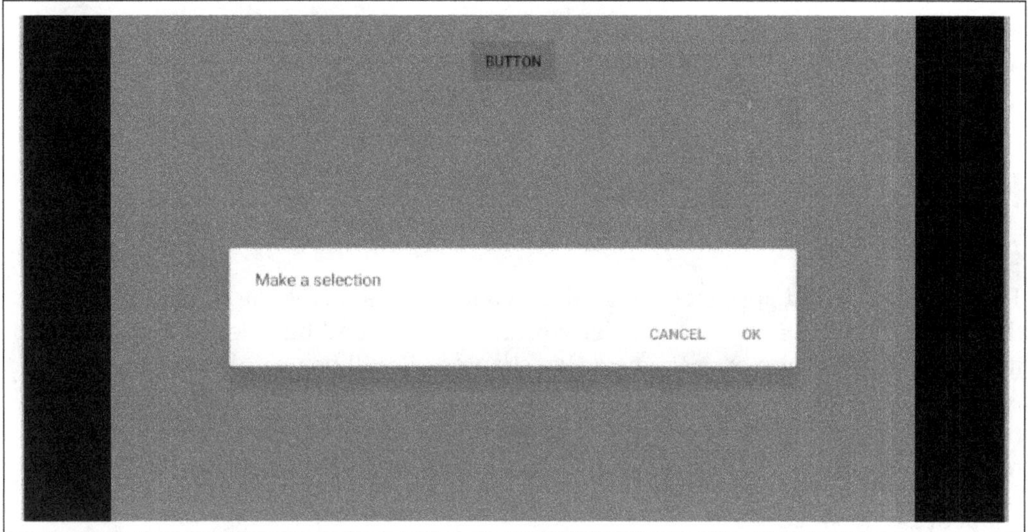

Next, we will make two more classes that implement dialogs as the first phase of our multi-chapter Note to self app. We will see that a dialog window can have almost any layout we choose, and that we don't have to rely on the simple layouts that the `Dialog.Builder` class provided us with.

The Note to self app

Welcome to the first of the multi-chapter apps that we will implement in this book. When we do these projects, we will do them more professionally than we do the smaller apps. In this project, we will use String resources instead of hardcoding the text in the layouts.

Sometimes, these things can be overkill when you are trying to learn a new Android or Kotlin topic, but they are useful and important to start using as soon as possible in real projects. They soon become like second nature and the quality of our apps will benefit from it.

Using String resources

In *Chapter 3, Exploring Android Studio and the Project Structure,* we discussed using String resources instead of hardcoding text in our layout files. There were a few benefits of doing things this way, but it was also slightly long-winded.

As this is our first multi-chapter project, it is a good time to do things the right way. If you want a quick refresher on the benefits of String resources, refer back to *Chapter 3, Exploring Android Studio and the Project Structure.*

How to get the code files for the Note to self app

The fully-completed app, including all the code and resources, can be found in the `Chapter18/Note to self` folder within the download bundle. As we are implementing this app over the next five chapters, it will be useful to see the part-completed, runnable app at the end of every chapter as well. The part-completed, runnable apps and all their associated code and resources can be found in their respective folders:

`Chapter14/Note to self`

`Chapter16/Note to self`

`Chapter17/Note to self`

`Chapter18/Note to self`

There is no Note to self code in *Chapter 15, Handling Data and Generating Random Numbers,* because although we will learn about topics we use in Note to self, we don't make the changes to the app until *Chapter 16, Adapters and Recyclers.*

Be aware that each of these folders contains a separate, runnable project, and is also contained within its own unique package. This is so that you can easily see the app running as it would do after completing a given chapter. When copying and pasting the code, be careful not to include the package name because it will likely be different from your package name and cause the code not to compile.

If you are following along and intend to build Note to self from start to finish, we will build a project simply called `Note to self`. There is still nothing stopping you, however, from dipping into the code files of the projects from each chapter to do a bit of copying and pasting at any time. Just don't copy the package directive from the top of a file. Additionally, be aware that at a couple of points in the instructions, you will be asked to remove or replace the occasional line of code from a previous chapter.

So, even if you are copying and pasting more than you are typing the code, be sure to read the instructions in full and look at the code in the book for extra comments that might be useful.

In each chapter, the code will be presented as if you have completed the last chapter in full, showing code from earlier chapters, where necessary, as context for the new code.

Each chapter will not be solely devoted to the Note to self app. We will learn about other related things and build some smaller and simpler apps as well. So, when we come to the Note to self implementation, we will be technically prepared for it.

The completed app

The following features and screenshots are from the completed app. It will obviously look slightly different to this at the various stages of development. Where necessary, we will look at more images, either as a reminder, or to see the differences throughout the development process.

The completed app will allow the user to tap the floating button icon in the bottom-right corner of the app to open a dialog window to add a new note. The following screenshot shows this highlighted feature:

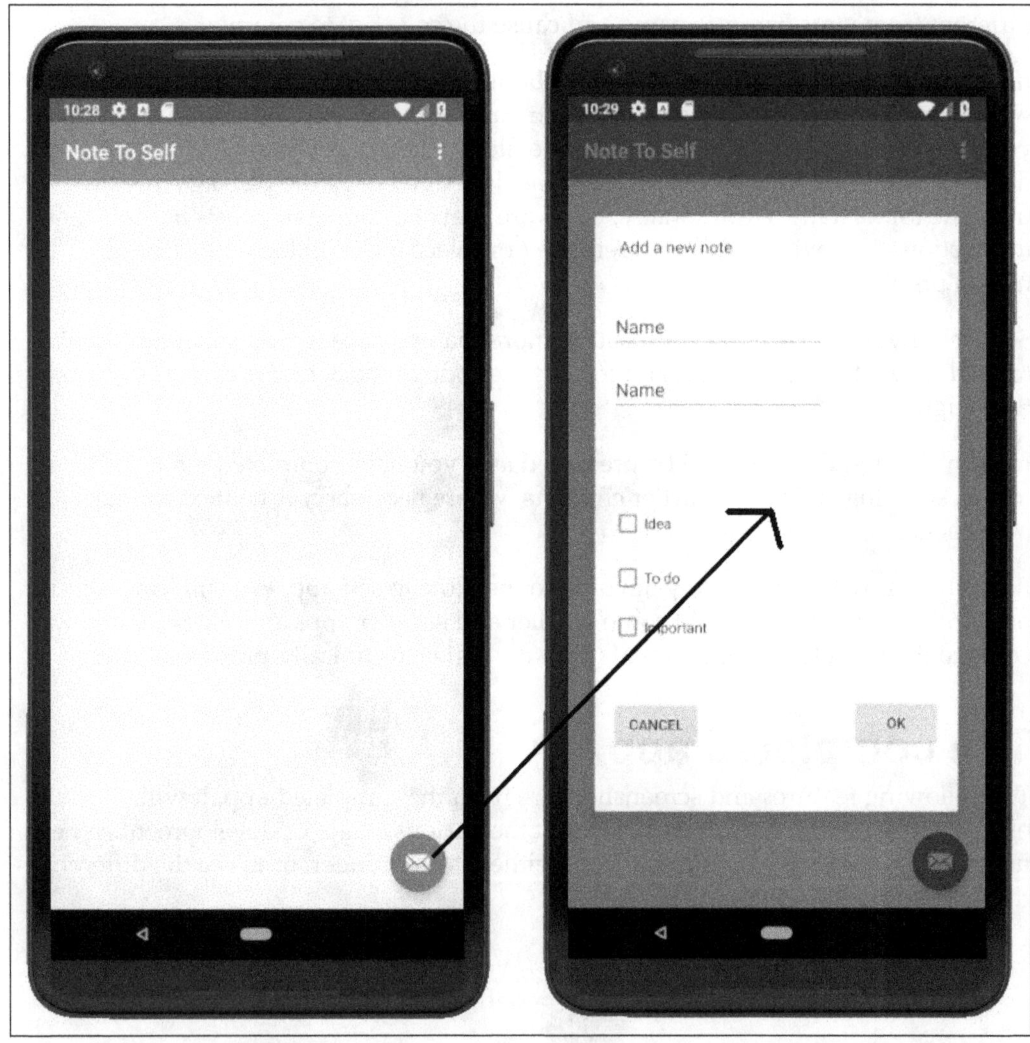

The screenshot on the left shows the button to tap, and the screenshot on the right shows the dialog window where the user can add a new note.

Eventually, as the user adds more notes, they will have a list of all the notes they have added on the main screen of the app, as shown in the following screenshot. The user can select whether the note is **Important**, an **Idea**, and/or a **To do** note:

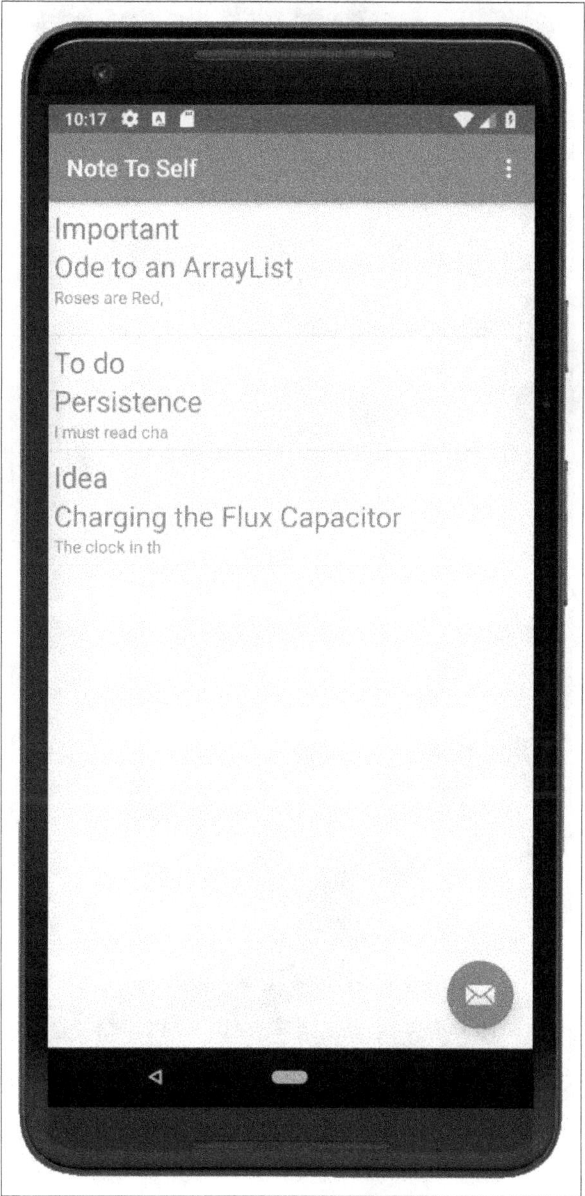

They will be able to scroll the list and tap on a note to see it shown in another dialog window dedicated to that note. Here is that dialog window showing a note:

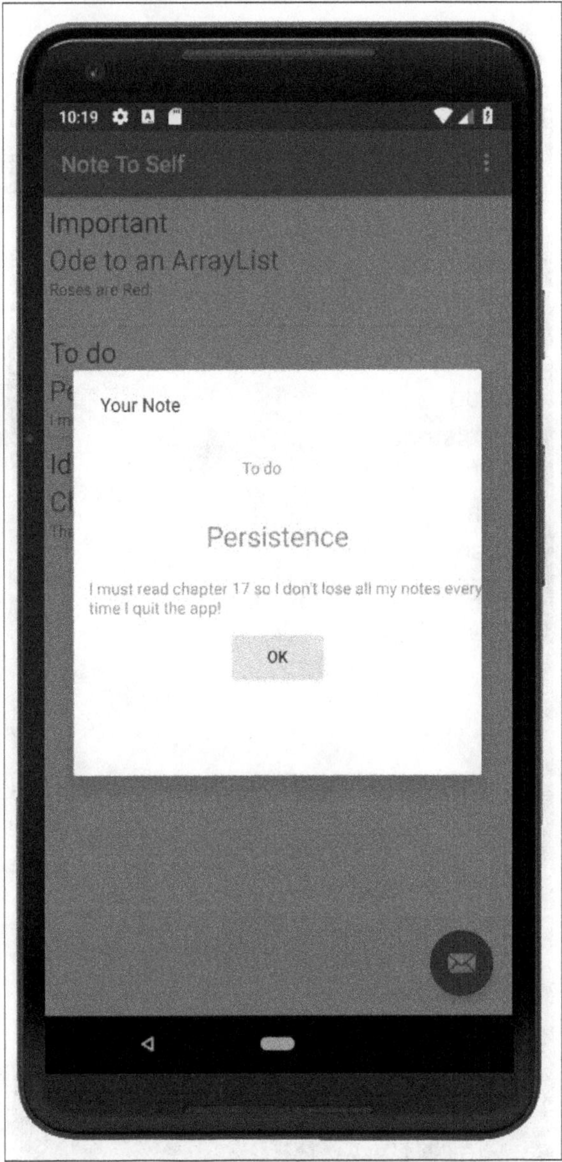

There will also be a simple (very simple) settings screen that is accessible from the menu that will allow the user to configure whether the note list is formatted with a dividing line. Here is the settings menu option in action:

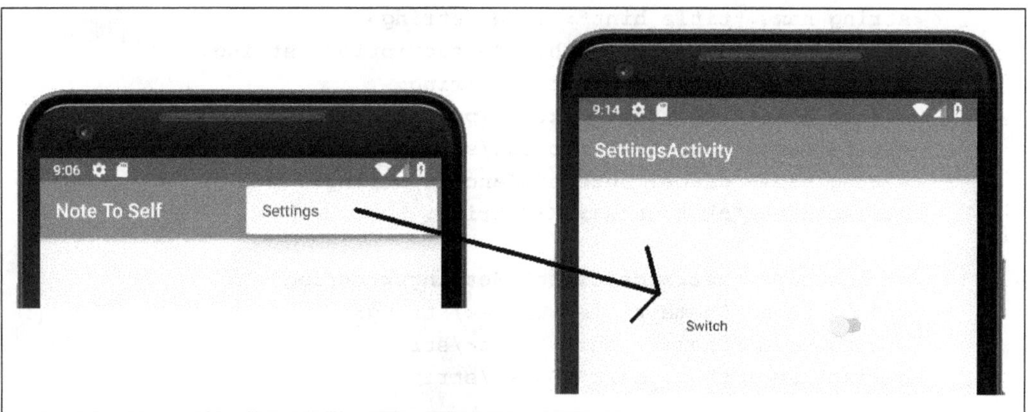

Now we know exactly what we are going to build, we can go ahead and start to implement it.

Building the project

Let's create our new project now. Call the project `Note to Self` and use the **Basic Activity** template. Remember from *Chapter 3, Exploring Android Studio and the Project Structure,* that this template will generate a simple menu and a floating action button, which are both used in this project. Leave the other settings at their default settings.

Preparing the String resources

Here, we will create all the String resources that we will refer to from our layout files instead of hardcoding the `text` property, as we have been doing up until now. Strictly speaking, this is a step that can be avoided. However, if you are looking to make in-depth Android apps, you will benefit from learning to do things this way.

To get started, open the `strings.xml` file from the `res/values` folder in the project explorer. You will see the autogenerated resources. Add the following highlighted String resources that we will use in our app throughout the rest of the project. Add the code before the closing `</resources>` tag:

```
...
<resources>
    <string name="app_name">Note To Self</string>
```

```
    <string name="hello_world">Hello world!</string>
    <string name="action_settings">Settings</string>

    <string name="action_add">add</string>
    <string name="title_hint">Title</string>
    <string name="description_hint">Description</string>
    <string name="idea_text">Idea</string>
    <string name="important_text">Important</string>
    <string name="todo_text">To do</string>
    <string name="cancel_button">Cancel</string>
    <string name="ok_button">OK</string>

    <string name="settings_title">Settings</string>
    <string name="theme_title">Theme</string>
    <string name="theme_light">Light</string>
    <string name="theme_dark">Dark</string>

</resources>
```

Observe in the preceding code that each String resource has a `name` attribute that is unique and distinguishes it from all the others. The `name` attribute also provides a meaningful and, hopefully, memorable clue as to the actual String value it represents. It is these name values that we will use to refer to the String that we want to use from within our layout files.

Coding the Note class

This is the fundamental data structure of the app. It is a class we will write ourselves from scratch and it has all the properties that we need to represent a single user note. In *Chapter 15, Handling Data and Generating Random Numbers,* we will learn some new Kotlin code to gain an understanding of how we can let the user have dozens, hundreds, or even thousands of notes.

Create a new class by right-clicking on the folder with the name as your package – as usual, the one that contains the `MainActivity.kt` file. Select **New** | **Kotlin File/class**, name it `Note`, and select **Class** from the drop-down selector. Left-click on **OK** to create the class.

Add the following code to the new `Note` class:

```
class Note {
    var title: String? = null
    var description: String? = null
    var idea: Boolean = false
    var todo: Boolean = false
    var important: Boolean = false
}
```

We have a simple class with no functions, called `Note`. The class has five `var` properties called `title`, `description`, `idea`, `todo`, and `important`. Their uses are to hold the title of the user's note, the description (or contents) of the note, and to detail whether the note is an idea, a to-do, or an important note, respectively. Let's now design the layout of the two dialog windows.

Implementing the dialog designs

Now we will do something that we have done many times before, but this time, for a different reason. As you know, we will have two dialog windows - one for the user to enter a new note, and one for the user to view a note of their choice.

We can design the layouts of these two dialog windows in the same way that we have designed all our previous layouts. When we come to create the Kotlin code for the `FragmentDialog` classes, we will then learn how to incorporate these layouts.

First, let's add a layout for our "new note" dialog by following these steps:

1. Right-click on the `layout` folder in the project explorer and select **New** | **Layout resource file**. Enter `dialog_new_note` in the **File name:** field and then start typing `Constrai` for the **Root element:** field. Notice that there is a drop-down list with multiple options that start with **Constrai...**. Now select **androidx.constraintlayout.widget.ConstraintLayout**. Left-click on **OK** to generate the new layout file that will have the `ConstraintLayout` type as its root element.

2. Refer to the target design in the following screenshot while following the rest of these instructions. I have photoshopped together the finished layout, including the constraints that we will soon autogenerate, next to the layout, with the constraints hidden for extra clarity:

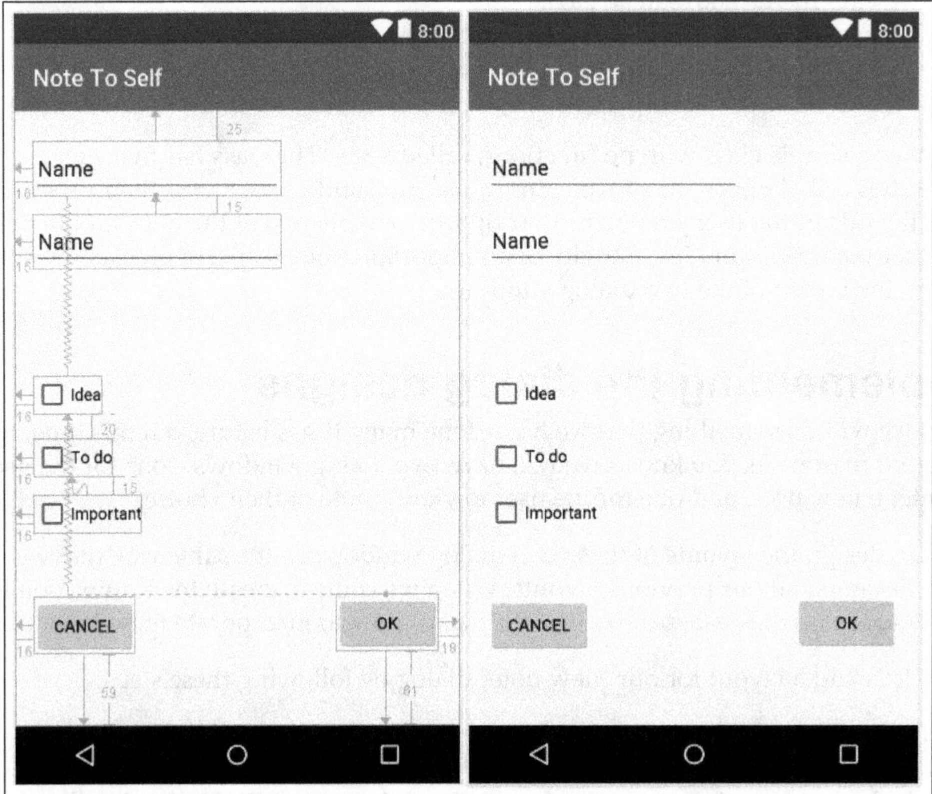

3. Drag and drop a **Plain Text** widget (from the **Text** category) to the very top and left of the layout, and then add another **Plain Text** below it. Don't worry about any of the attributes for now.
4. Drag and drop three **CheckBox** widgets from the **Button** category, one below the other. Look at the previous reference screenshot for guidance. Again, don't worry about any attributes for now.
5. Drag and drop two **Buttons** onto the layout, the first directly below the last **CheckBox** widget from the previous step, and the second horizontally in line with the first **Button** widget, but fully over to the right of the layout.
6. Tidy up the layout so that it resembles the reference screenshot as closely as possible, and then click on the **Infer Constraints** button to fix the positions that you have chosen.

7. Now we can set up all our `text`, `id`, and `hint` properties. You can do so by using the values from this next table. Remember that we are using our String resources for the `text` and `hint` properties.

When you edit the first `id` property, you may be shown a pop-up window asking for confirmation of your changes. Check the box for **Don't ask again during this session** and click on **Yes** to continue, as shown in the following screenshot:

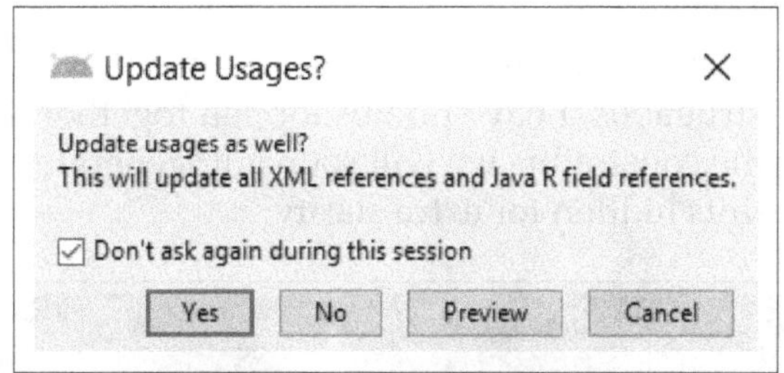

Here are the values to enter:

Widget type	**Property**	**Value to set to**
Plain Text (top)	id	`editTitle`
Plain Text (top)	hint	`@string/title_hint`
Plain Text (bottom)	id	`editDescription`
Plain Text (bottom)	hint	`@string/description_hint`
Plain Text (bottom)	inputType	textMultiLine (uncheck any other options)
CheckBox (top)	id	`checkBoxIdea`
CheckBox (top)	text	`@string/idea_text`
CheckBox (middle)	id	`checkBoxTodo`
CheckBox (middle)	text	`@string/todo_text`
CheckBox (bottom)	id	`checkBoxImportant`
CheckBox (bottom)	text	`@string/important_text`
Button (left)	id	`btnCancel`
Button (left)	text	`@string/cancel_button`
Button (right)	id	`btnOK`
Button (right)	text	`@string/ok_button`

We now have a nice neat layout ready for our Kotlin code to display. Be sure to keep in mind the `id` value of the different widgets because we will see them in action when we write our code. The important thing is that our layout looks nice and has an `id` value for every relevant item, so that we can get a reference to it.

Let's lay out our dialog box to show a note to the user:

1. Right-click on the **layout** folder in the project explorer and select **New | Layout resource file**. Enter `dialog_show_note` for the **File name:** field, and then start typing `Constrai` for the **Root element:** field. Notice that there is a drop-down list with multiple options that start with **Constrai...**. Now select **androidx.constraintlayout.widget.ConstraintLayout**. Left-click on **OK** to generate the new layout file that will have the `ConstraintLayout` type as its root element.
2. Refer to the target design in the next screenshot, while following the rest of these instructions. I have photoshopped together the finished layout including the constraints we will soon autogenerate, next to the layout, with the constraints hidden for extra clarity:

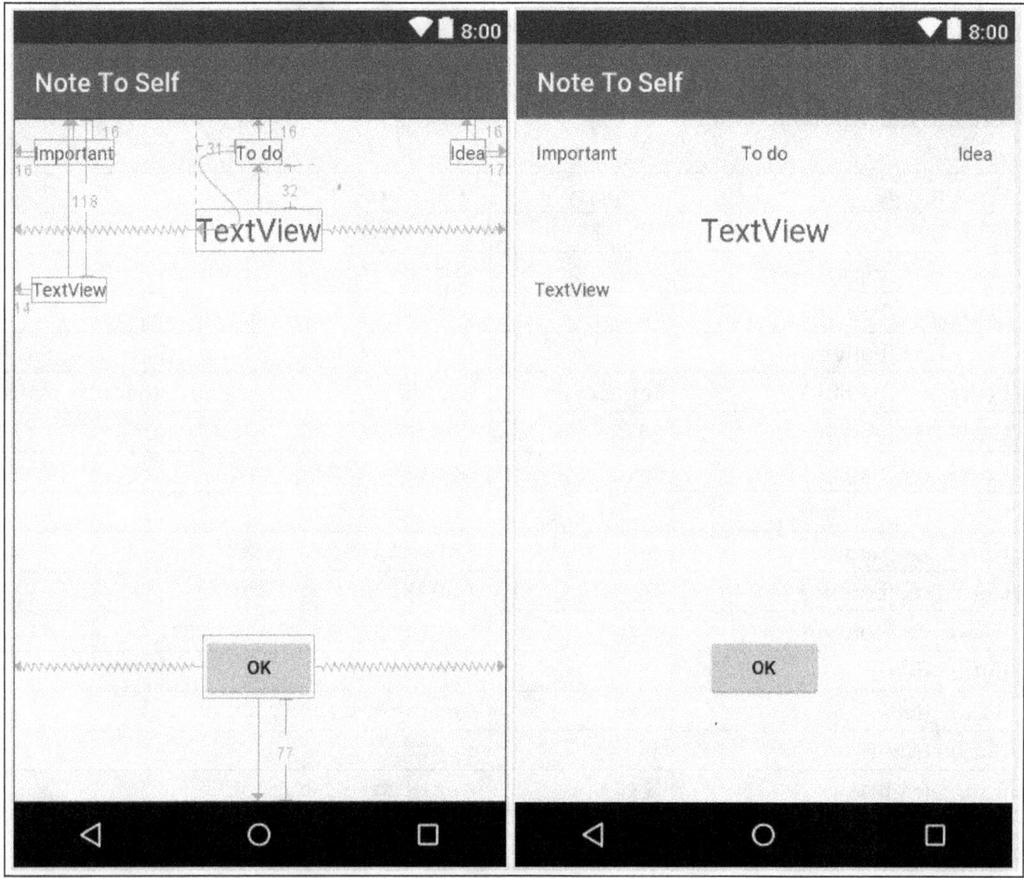

3. First, drag and drop three **TextView** widgets, vertically aligned across the top of the layout.

4. Next, drag and drop another **TextView** widget just below the center of the three previous `TextView` widgets.
5. Add another **TextView** widget just below the previous one, but on the left side.
6. Now add a **Button** horizontally and centrally, and near the bottom of the layout. This is what it should look like so far:

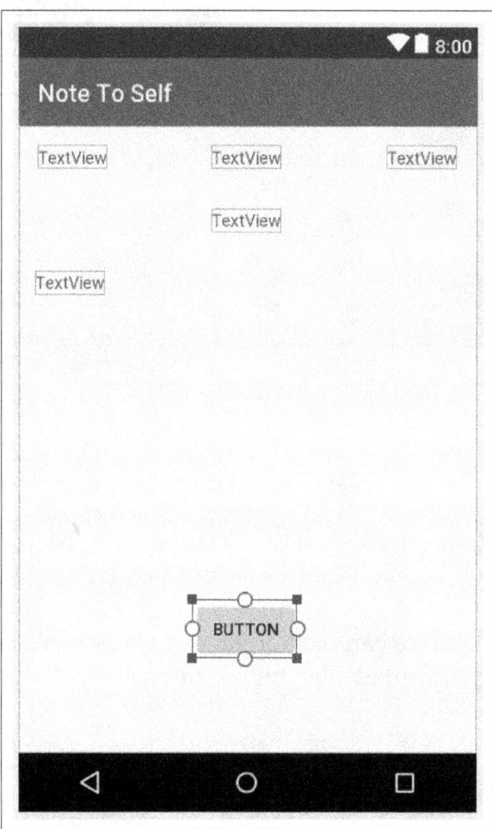

7. Tidy up the layout so that it resembles the reference screenshot as closely as possible, and then click on the **Infer Constraints** button to fix the positions that you have chosen.

8. Configure the attributes from the following table:

Widget type	**Attribute**	**Value to set to**
TextView (top-left)	`id`	`textViewImportant`
TextView (top-left)	`text`	`@string/important_text`
TextView (top-center)	`id`	`textViewTodo`
TextView (top-center)	`text`	`@string/todo_text`
TextView (top-right)	`id`	`textViewIdea`
TextView (top-right)	`text`	`@string/idea_text`
TextView (center, second row)	`id`	`txtTitle`
TextView (center, second row)	`textSize`	`24sp`
TextView (last one added)	`id`	`txtDescription`
Button	`id`	`btnOK`
Button	`text`	`@string/ok_button`

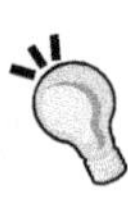

After the preceding changes, you might want to tweak the final positions of some of the UI elements by dragging them around the screen since we have adjusted their size and contents. First, click on **Clear all Constraints**, then tweak the layout to be how you want it, and finally, click on **Infer Constraints** to constrain the positions again.

Now we have a layout that we can use for showing a note to the user. Notice that we get to reuse some string resources. The bigger our apps get, the more beneficial it is to do things this way.

Coding the dialog boxes

Now that we have a design for both of our dialog windows ("show note" and "new note"), we can use what we know about the `FragmentDialog` class to implement a class to represent each of the dialog windows that the user can interact with.

We will start with the "new note" screen.

Coding the DialogNewNote class

Create a new class by right-clicking on the project folder that has the `.kt` files and choose **New** | **Kotlin File/Class**. Name the `DialogNewNote` class and select **Class** in the drop-down selector. Click on **OK** to generate the new class.

First, change the class declaration and inherit from `DialogFragment`. Also, override the `onCreateDialog` function, which is where all the rest of the code in this class will go. Make your code the same as the following in order to achieve this:

```
class DialogNewNote : DialogFragment() {

    override
    fun onCreateDialog(savedInstanceState: Bundle?): Dialog {

        // All the rest of the code goes here

    }
}
```

You will need to add these new imports as well:

```
import androidx.fragment.app.DialogFragment;
import android.app.Dialog;
import android.os.Bundle;
```

We temporarily have an error in the new class because we need a `return` statement in the `onCreateDialog` function, but we will get to that in just a moment.

In the next block of code, which we will add in a moment, first we declare and initialize an `AlertDialog.Builder` object as we have previously done when creating dialog windows. This time, however, we will not use this object as much as we have before.

Next, we initialize a `LayoutInflater` object, which we will use to inflate our XML layout. "Inflate" simply means to turn our XML layout into a Kotlin object. Once this has been done, we can then access all our widgets in the usual way. We can think of `inflater.inflate` replacing the `setContentView` function call for our dialog. And, in the second line, we do just that with the `inflate` function.

Add the three lines of code that we have just discussed:

```
// All the rest of the code goes here
val builder = AlertDialog.Builder(activity!!)

val inflater = activity!!.layoutInflater

val dialogView = inflater.inflate
    (R.layout.dialog_new_note, null)
```

To support the new classes in the previous three lines of code, you will need to add the following `import` statements:

```
import androidx.appcompat.app.AlertDialog
import android.view.View
import android.view.LayoutInflater
```

We now have a `View` object called `dialogView` that has all the UI elements from our `dialog_new_note.xml` layout file.

Now, underneath the previous block of code, we will add the following code.

This code will get a reference to each of the UI widgets. Add this following code just after the previous block of code:

```
val editTitle =
      dialogView.findViewById(R.id.editTitle) as EditText

val editDescription =
      dialogView.findViewById(R.id.editDescription) as
              EditText

val checkBoxIdea =
      dialogView.findViewById(R.id.checkBoxIdea) as CheckBox

val checkBoxTodo =
      dialogView.findViewById(R.id.checkBoxTodo) as CheckBox

val checkBoxImportant =
      dialogView.findViewById(R.id.checkBoxImportant) as
              CheckBox

val btnCancel =
      dialogView.findViewById(R.id.btnCancel) as Button

val btnOK =
      dialogView.findViewById(R.id.btnOK) as Button
```

Be sure to add the following `import` code to make the code you just added error-free:

```
import android.widget.Button
import android.widget.CheckBox
import android.widget.EditText
```

There is a new Kotlin feature in the preceding code that is known as the `as` keyword; for example, `as EditText`, `as CheckBox`, and `as Button`. This feature is used because there is no way for the compiler to infer the specific type of each of the UI widgets. Try deleting one of the `as`... keywords from the code and notice the error that arises. Using the `as` keyword (because we do know the type) overcomes this problem.

In the next code block, we will set the message of the dialog using the `builder` instance. Then, we will write a lambda to handle clicks on `btnCancel`. In the overridden `onClick` function, we will simply call `dismiss()`, which is a function of `DialogFragment`, to close the dialog window. This is just what we need should the user click on **Cancel**.

Add this code that we have just discussed:

```
builder.setView(dialogView).setMessage("Add a new note")

// Handle the cancel button
btnCancel.setOnClickListener {
    dismiss()
}
```

Now we will add a lambda to handle what happens when the user clicks on the **OK** button (`btnOK`).

Inside it, we create a new `Note` called `newNote`. Then, we set each of the properties from `newNote` to the appropriate content of the form.

After this, we use a reference to `MainActivity` to call the `createNewNote` function in `MainActivity`.

Note that we have not written this `createNewNote` function yet, and the function call will show an error until we do so later in this chapter.

The argument sent in this function is our newly initialized `newNote` object. This has the effect of sending the user's new note back to `MainActivity`. We will see what we do with this later in the chapter.

Finally, we call `dismiss` to close the dialog window. Add the code that we have been discussing after the previous block of code that we added:

```
btnOK.setOnClickListener {
    // Create a new note
    val newNote = Note()

    // Set its properties to match the
    // user's entries on the form
    newNote.title = editTitle.text.toString()

    newNote.description = editDescription.text.toString()

    newNote.idea = checkBoxIdea.isChecked
    newNote.todo = checkBoxTodo.isChecked
    newNote.important = checkBoxImportant.isChecked

    // Get a reference to MainActivity
    val callingActivity = activity as MainActivity?

    // Pass newNote back to MainActivity
    callingActivity!!.createNewNote(newNote)

    // Quit the dialog
    dismiss()
}

return builder.create()
```

That's our first dialog window done. We haven't wired it up to appear from `MainActivity` yet, and we need to implement the `createNewNote` function too. We will do this right after we create the next dialog.

Coding the DialogShowNote class

Create a new class by right-clicking on the project folder that contains all the `.kt` files and choose **New | Kotlin File/Class**. Name the `DialogShowNote` class, then choose **Class** in the drop-down selector, and click on **OK** to generate the new class.

First, change the class declaration and inherit from `DialogFragment`, and then override the `onCreateDialog` function. As most of the code for this class goes in the `onCreateDialog` function, implement the signature and empty body as shown in the following code and we will revisit it in a minute.

Notice that we declare a `var` property, `note`, of the `Note` type. In addition, add the `sendNoteSelected` function and its single line of code that initializes `note`. This function will be called by `MainActivity` and it will pass in the `Note` object that the user has clicked on.

Add the code that we have just discussed, and then we can look at the details of `onCreateDialog`:

```
class DialogShowNote : DialogFragment() {

    private var note: Note? = null

    override fun
    onCreateDialog(savedInstanceState: Bundle?): Dialog {

        // All the other code goes here


    }


    // Receive a note from the MainActivity class
    fun sendNoteSelected(noteSelected: Note) {
        note = noteSelected
    }

}
```

At this point, you will need to import the following classes:

```
import android.app.Dialog;
import android.os.Bundle;
import androidx.fragment.app.DialogFragment;
```

Next, we declare and initialize an instance of `AlertDialog.Builder`. Next, as we did for `DialogNewNote`, we declare and initialize `LayoutInflater`, and then use it to create a `View` object that has the layout for the dialog. In this case, it is the layout from `dialog_show_note.xml`.

Finally, in the following block of code, we get a reference to each of the UI widgets and set the `text` properties on `txtTitle` and `textDescription` using the appropriate related properties from `note`, which was initialized in the `sendNoteSelected` function call.

Add the code that we have just discussed within the `onCreateDialog` function:

```
val builder = AlertDialog.Builder(this.activity!!)

val inflater = activity!!.layoutInflater

val dialogView = inflater.inflate(R.layout.dialog_show_note, null)

val txtTitle =
   dialogView.findViewById(R.id.txtTitle) as TextView

val txtDescription =
   dialogView.findViewById(R.id.txtDescription) as TextView

txtTitle.text = note!!.title
txtDescription.text = note!!.description

val txtImportant =
   dialogView.findViewById(R.id.textViewImportant) as TextView

val txtTodo =
   dialogView.findViewById(R.id.textViewTodo) as TextView

val txtIdea =
   dialogView.findViewById(R.id.textViewIdea) as TextView
```

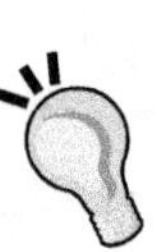

Add the following `import` statements to make all the classes in the previous code available:

```
import android.view.LayoutInflater;
import android.view.View;
import android.widget.TextView;
import androidx.appcompat.app.AlertDialog;
```

This next code is also in the `onCreateDialog` function. It checks whether the note being shown is "important", and then shows or hides the `txtImportant TextView` widget accordingly. We then do the same for the `txtTodo` and `txtIdea` widgets.

Add this code after the previous block of code, while still in the `onCreateDialog` function:

```
if (!note!!.important){
    txtImportant.visibility = View.GONE
}

if (!note!!.todo){
    txtTodo.visibility = View.GONE
}

if (!note!!.idea){
    txtIdea.visibility = View.GONE
}
```

All we need to do now is `dismiss` (that is, close) the dialog window when the user clicks on the **OK** button. This is done with a lambda, as we have seen several times already. The `onClick` function simply calls the `dismiss` function that closes the dialog window.

Add this code to the `onCreateDialog` function after the previous block of code:

```
val btnOK = dialogView.findViewById(R.id.btnOK) as Button

builder.setView(dialogView).setMessage("Your Note")

btnOK.setOnClickListener({
    dismiss()
})

return builder.create()
```

Import the `Button` class with this line of code:

```
import android.widget.Button;
```

We now have two dialog windows ready to roll. We just must add some code to the `MainActivity` class to finish the job.

Showing and using our new dialogs

Add a new temporary property just after the `MainActivity` declaration:

```
// Temporary code
private var tempNote = Note()
```

This code won't be in the final app; it is just so we can test our dialog windows right away.

Now add this function so that we can receive a new note from the `DialogNewNote` class:

```
fun createNewNote(n: Note) {
   // Temporary code
   tempNote = n
}
```

Now, to send a note to the `DialogShowNote` function, we need to add a button with the `button` `id` to the `layout_main.xml` layout file.

So that it is clear what this button is for, we will change its `text` attribute to `Show Note`, as follows:

- Drag a `Button` widget onto `layout_main.xml`, and configure its `id` as `button` and `text` as `Show Note`.
- Click on the **Infer Constraints** button so that the button stays where you put it. The exact position of this button is not important at this stage.

Just to clarify, this is a temporary button for testing purposes and will not be used in the final app. At the end of development, we will click on a note's title from a list.

Now, in the `onCreate` function, we will set up a lambda to handle clicks on our temporary button. The code in `onClick` will do the following:

- Create a new `DialogShowNote` instance that is simply called `dialog`.
- Call the `sendNoteSelected` function on `dialog` to pass in our `Note` object, called `tempNote`, as an argument.
- Finally, it will call `show`, which breathes life into our new dialog.

Add the code described previously to the `onCreate` function:

```
// Temporary code
val button = findViewById<View>(R.id.button) as Button
button.setOnClickListener {
    // Create a new DialogShowNote called dialog
    val dialog = DialogShowNote()

    // Send the note via the sendNoteSelected function
    dialog.sendNoteSelected(tempNote)

    // Create the dialog
    dialog.show(supportFragmentManager, "123")
}
```

Be sure to import the `Button` class with this line of code:

```
import android.widget.Button;
```

We can now summon our `DialogShowNote` dialog window at the click of a button. Run the app and click on the **SHOW NOTE** button to see the `DialogShowNote` dialog with the `dialog_show_note.xml` layout, as demonstrated in the following screenshot:

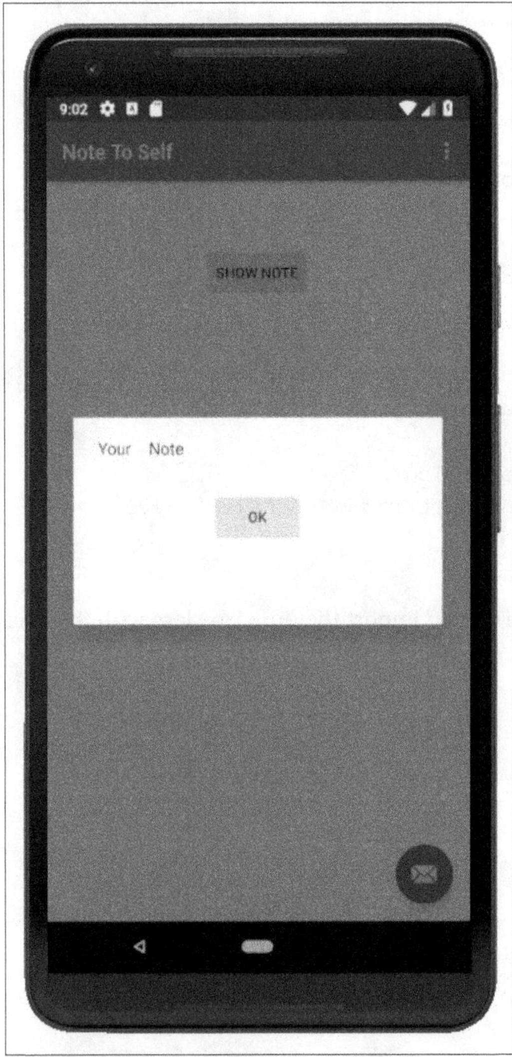

Admittedly, this is not much to look at considering how much coding we have done in this chapter, but when we get the `DialogNewNote` class working, we will see how `MainActivity` interacts and shares data between the two dialogs.

Let's make the `DialogNewNote` dialog useable.

Coding the floating action button

This is going to be easy. The floating action button was provided for us in the layout. By way of a reminder, this is the floating action button:

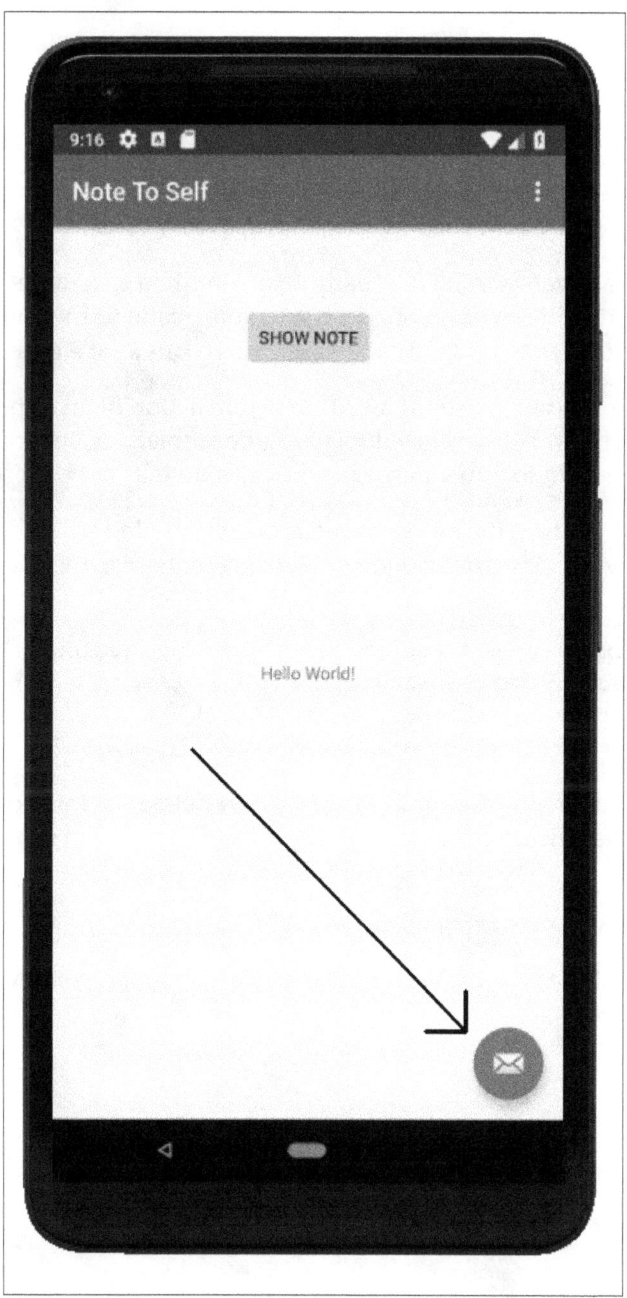

It is in the `activity_main.xml` file. This is the XML code that positions and defines its appearance:

```
<com.google.android.material.floatingactionbutton
    .FloatingActionButton

    android:id="@+id/fab"
    android:layout_width="wrap_content"
    android:layout_height="wrap_content"
    android:layout_gravity="bottom|end"
    android:layout_margin="@dimen/fab_margin"
    app:srcCompat="@android:drawable/ic_dialog_email" />
```

Android Studio has even provided a ready-made lambda to handle clicks on the floating action button. All we need to do is add some code to the `onClick` function of this already provided code and we can use the `DialogNewNote` class.

The floating action button is usually used for a core action of an app. For example, in an email app, it will probably be used to start a new email; or, in a note-keeping app, it will probably be used to add a new note. So, let's do that now.

In `MainActivity.kt`, find the autogenerated code provided by Android Studio in the `MainActivity.kt` class in the `onCreate` function; here is the code in its entirety:

```
fab.setOnClickListener { view ->
    Snackbar.make(view, "Replace with your own action",
            Snackbar.LENGTH_LONG)
            .setAction("Action", null).show()
}
```

In the previous code, note the highlighted line and delete it. Now add the following code in place of the deleted code:

```
val dialog = DialogNewNote()
dialog.show(supportFragmentManager, "")
```

The new code creates a new dialog window of the `DialogNewNote` variety and then shows it to the user.

We can now run the app; tap the floating action button and add a note along the lines of the following screenshot:

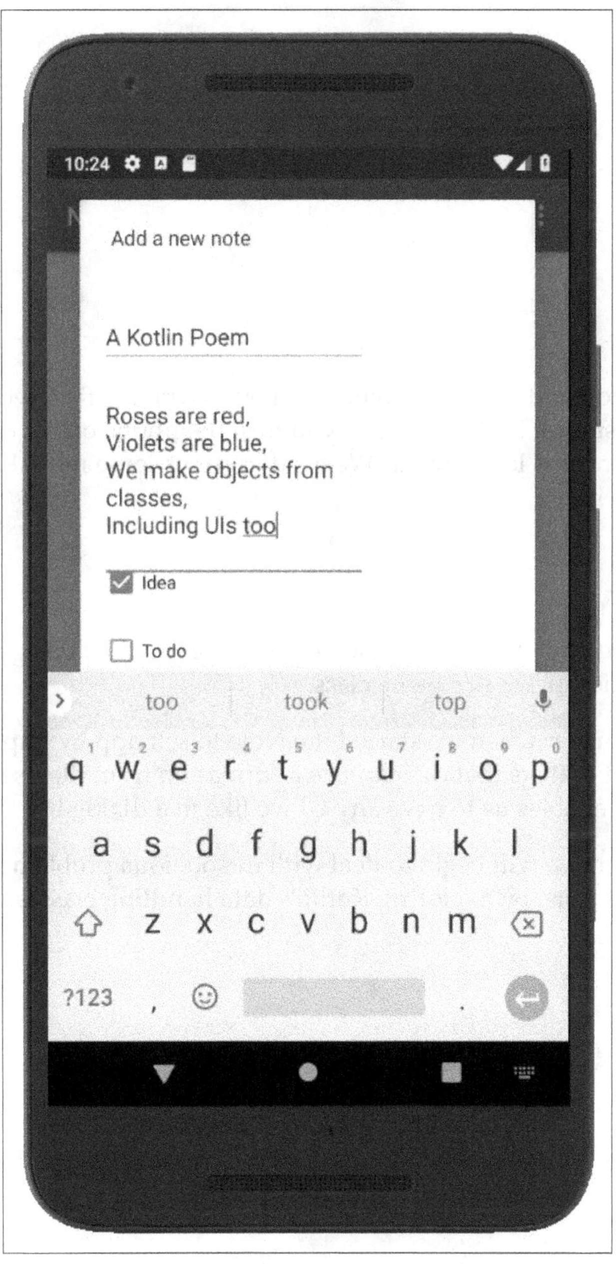

Click on **OK** to save the note and return to the main layout. Next, we can tap the **Show Note** button to see it in a dialog window like the following screenshot:

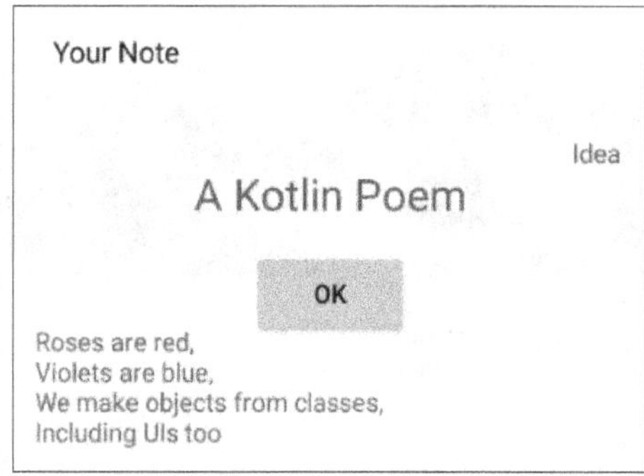

Be aware that if you add a second note, it will overwrite the first because we only have one `Note` instance. Furthermore, if you turn the phone off, or fully shut down the app, then the note is lost forever. We need to cover some more Kotlin in order to solve these problems.

Summary

In this chapter, we have seen and implemented a common UI design with dialog windows using the `DialogFragment` class.

We went a step further when we started the Note to self app by implementing more complicated dialogs that can capture information from the user. We saw that `DialogFragment` enables us to have any UI we like in a dialog box.

In the next chapter, we will begin to deal with the obvious problem whereby the user can only have one note, by exploring Kotlin's data handling classes.

15
Handling Data and Generating Random Numbers

We are making good progress. We have a rounded knowledge of both the Android UI options and the basics of Kotlin. In the previous few chapters, we started bringing these two areas together and we manipulated the UI, including some new widgets, using Kotlin code. However, while building the Note to self app, we have stumbled upon a couple of blanks in our knowledge. In this chapter, we will fill in the first of these blanks, and then, in the next chapter, we will use this new information to progress with the app. We currently have no way of managing large amounts of related data. Aside from declaring, initializing, and managing dozens, hundreds, or even thousands of properties or instances, how will we let the users of our app have more than one note? We will also take a quick diversion to learn about random numbers.

We will cover the following topics in this chapter:

- Random numbers
- Arrays
- A simple array mini-app
- A dynamic array mini-app
- Ranges
- ArrayLists
- Hashmaps

First, let's learn about the `Random` class.

A random diversion

Sometimes, we will want a random number in our apps and, for these occasions, Kotlin provides us with the `Random` class. There are many possible uses for this class, such as if our app wants to show a random tip-of-the-day, or a game that has to choose between scenarios, or a quiz that asks random questions.

The `Random` class is part of the Android API and is fully compatible in our Android apps.

Let's take a look at how to create random numbers. All the hard work is done for us by the `Random` class. First, we need to create a `Random` object, as follows:

```
val randGenerator = Random()
```

Then, we use our new object's `nextInt` function to generate a random number between a certain range. The following line of code generates the random number using our `randGenerator` object and stores the result in the `ourRandomNumber` variable:

```
var ourRandomNumber = randGenerator.nextInt(10)
```

The number that we enter for the range starts from zero. So, the preceding line will generate a random number between 0 and 9. If we want a random number between 1 and 10, we just add the increment operator on the end of the same line of code:

```
ourRandomNumber ++
```

We can also use the `Random` object to obtain other types of random numbers using `nextLong`, `nextFloat`, and `nextDouble`.

Handling large amounts of data with arrays

You might be wondering what happens when we have an app with lots of variables to keep track of. What about our Note to self app with 100 notes, or a high-score table in a game with the top 100 scores? We can declare and initialize 100 separate variables as follows:

```
var note1 = Note()
var note2 = Note()
var note3 = Note()
// 96 more lines like the above
var note100 = Note()
```

Or, by using the high scores example we might use something like the following code:

```
var topScore1: Int
var topScore2: Int
// 96 more lines like the above
var topScore100: Int
```

Immediately, this code can seem unwieldy, but what about when someone gets a new top score, or if we want to let our users sort the order that their notes are displayed in? Using the high scores scenario, we must shift the scores in every variable down one place. This is the beginning of a nightmare, as shown in the following code:

```
topScore100 = topScore99;
topScore99 = topScore98;
topScore98 = topScore97;
// 96 more lines like the above
topScore1 = score;
```

There must be a better way of doing this. When we have a whole array of variables, what we need is a Kotlin **array**. An array is an object that holds up to a predetermined, fixed-maximum number of elements. Each element is a variable with a consistent type.

The following code declares an array that can hold `Int` type variables; such as a high-score table or a series of exam grades:

```
var myIntArray: IntArray
```

We can also declare arrays of other types, as follows:

```
var myFloatArray: FloatArray
var myBooleanArray: BooleanArray
```

Each of these arrays will need to have a fixed-maximum amount of allocated storage space before it is used. Just as we have done with other objects, we must initialize arrays before we use them, and we can do so as follows:

```
myIntArray = IntArray(100)
myFloatArray = FloatArray(100)
myBooleanArray = BooleanArray(100)
```

The preceding code allocates up to a maximum of `100` storage spaces of the appropriate type. Think of a long aisle of 100 consecutive storage spaces in our variable warehouse. The spaces will probably be labeled `myIntArray[0]`, `myIntArray[1]`, and `myIntArray[2]`, with each space holding a single `Int` value. The slightly surprising thing here is that the storage spaces start off at zero, not 1. Therefore, in a 100-*wide* array, the storage spaces will run from 0 to 99.

We can initialize some of these storage spaces as follows:

```
myIntArray [0] = 5
myIntArray [1] = 6
myIntArray [2] = 7
```

However, note that we can only ever put the predeclared type into an array and that the type that an array holds can never change, as demonstrated in the following code:

```
myIntArray [3] = "John Carmack"
// Won't compile String not Int
```

So, when we have an array of `Int` types, what are each of these `Int` variables called and how do we access the values stored in them? The array notation syntax replaces the name of the variable. Additionally, we can do anything with a variable in an array that we can do with a regular variable with a name; this is demonstrated as follows:

```
myIntArray [3] = 123
```

The preceding code assigns the value 123 to the 4th position in the array.

Here is another example of using an array just like a normal variable:

```
myIntArray [10] = myIntArray [9] - myIntArray [4]
```

The preceding code subtracts the value stored in the 5th position of the array from the value stored in the 10th position of the array and assigns the answer to the 11th position of the array.

We can also assign the value from an array to a regular variable of the same type, as follows:

```
Val myNamedInt = myIntArray[3]
```

Note, however, that `myNamedInt` is a separate and distinct variable and any changes to it do not affect the value that is stored in the `IntArray` reference. It has its own space in the warehouse and is otherwise unconnected to the array.

In the previous examples, we did not examine any Strings or objects. Strings, in fact, are objects and when we want to make arrays of objects, we deal with them slightly differently; take a look at the following code:

```
var someStrings = Array<String>(5) { "" }
// You can remove the String keyword because it can be inferred like
// this
var someMoreStrings = Array(5) { "" }

someStrings[0]= "Hello "
someStrings[1]= "from "
someStrings[2]= "inside "
someStrings[3]= "the "
someStrings[4]= "array "
someStrings[5]= "Oh dear "
// ArrayIndexOutOfBoundsException
```

The preceding code declares an array of String objects that can hold up to five objects. Remember that arrays start from 0, so the valid positions are 0 to 4 inclusively. If you attempt to use an invalid position, you will get an **ArrayIndexOutOfBoundsException** error. If the compiler notices the error, then the code will not compile; however, if the compiler cannot spot the error and it happens while the app is executing, then the app will crash.

The only way we can avoid this problem is to know the rule – that arrays start at 0 and go up to their length minus 1. So `someArray[9]` is the tenth position in the array. We can also use clear readable code where it is easy to evaluate what we have done and spot problems more easily.

You can also initialize the contents of an array at the same time as declaring the array, as shown in the following code:

```
var evenMoreStrings: Array<String> =
        arrayOf("Houston", "we", "have", "an", "array")
```

The preceding code uses the `arrayOf` built-in Kotlin function to initialize the array.

The ways in which you can declare and initialize arrays are extremely flexible in Kotlin. We are not close to covering all the ways in which we can use arrays and, even by the end of the book, we still won't have covered everything. Let's dig a little deeper, however.

Arrays are objects

Think of an array variable as an address to a group of variables of a given type. For instance, using a warehouse analogy, `someArray` can be an aisle number. So, `someArray[0]` and `someArray[1]` are the aisle numbers followed by the position number in the aisle.

Because arrays are also objects, they have functions and properties that we can use, as can be seen in the following example:

```
val howBig = someArray.size
```

In the preceding example, we assigned the length (that is, size) of `someArray` to the `Int` variable called `howBig`.

We can even declare an array of arrays. This is an array where another array lurks in each of its positions; this is shown as follows:

```
val cities = arrayOf("London", "New York", "Yaren")
val countries = arrayOf("UK", "USA", "Nauru")

val countriesAndCities = arrayOf(countries, cities)

Log.d("The capital of " +
  countriesAndCities[0][0],
  " is " +
  countriesAndCities[1][0])
```

The preceding `Log` code will output the following text to the logcat window:

```
The capital of UK:  is London
```

Let's use some arrays in a real app to try and gain an understanding of how to use them in real code and what they might be used for.

A simple mini-app array example

Let's make a simple working array example. You can get the completed code for this project in the downloadable code bundle. It can be found in the `Chapter15/Simple Array Example/MainActivity.kt` file.

Create a project with an **Empty Activity** project template and call it `Simple Array Example`.

First, we declare our array, allocate five spaces, and initialize values to each of the elements. Then, we output each of the values to the **logcat** window.

This is slightly different to the earlier examples that we have seen because we declare the size at the same time as we declare the array itself.

Add the following code to the `onCreate` function just after the call to `setContentView`:

```
// Declaring an array
// Allocate memory for a maximum size of 5 elements
val ourArray = IntArray(5)

// Initialize ourArray with values
// The values are arbitrary, but they must be Int
// The indexes are not arbitrary. Use 0 through 4 or crash!

ourArray[0] = 25
ourArray[1] = 50
ourArray[2] = 125
ourArray[3] = 68
ourArray[4] = 47

//Output all the stored values
Log.i("info", "Here is ourArray:")
Log.i("info", "[0] = " + ourArray[0])
Log.i("info", "[1] = " + ourArray[1])
Log.i("info", "[2] = " + ourArray[2])
Log.i("info", "[3] = " + ourArray[3])
Log.i("info", "[4] = " + ourArray[4])
```

Next, we add each of the elements of the array together, just as we do with ordinary `Int` type variables. Notice that when we add the array elements together, we are doing so over multiple lines for clarity. Add the code that we have just discussed to `MainActivity.kt`, as follows:

```
/*
   We can do any calculation with an array element
   provided it is appropriate to the contained type
   Like this:
*/
val answer = ourArray[0] +
      ourArray[1] +
      ourArray[2] +
      ourArray[3] +
      ourArray[4]

Log.i("info", "Answer = $answer")
```

Run the example and note the output in the logcat window. Remember that nothing will happen on the emulator display as all the output will be sent to the logcat window in Android Studio; here is the output:

```
info: Here is ourArray:
info: [0] = 25
info: [1] = 50
info: [2] = 125
info: [3] = 68
info: [4] = 47
info: Answer = 315
```

We declare an array called `ourArray` to hold `Int` values, and then allocate space for up to five values of that type.

Next, we assign a value to each of the five spaces in `ourArray`. Remember that the first space is `ourArray[0]`, and the last space is `ourArray[4]`.

Next, we simply print the value in each array location to the logcat window and, from the output, we can see they hold the value that we initialized them to be in the previous step. Then, we add together each of the elements in `ourArray` and initialize their value to the `answer` variable. We then print `answer` to the logcat window and we can see that indeed, all the values are added together as though they are ordinary `Int` types (which they are), just stored in a different manner.

Getting dynamic with arrays

As we discussed at the beginning of this section, if we need to declare and initialize each element of an array individually, there isn't a huge benefit to using an array over regular variables. Let's take a look at an example of declaring and initializing arrays dynamically.

A dynamic array example

You can get the working project for this example in the download bundle. It can be found in the `Chapter15/Dynamic Array Example/MainActivity.kt` file.

Create a project with an **Empty Activity** template and call it `Dynamic Array Example`.

Type the following code just after the call to `setContentView` in the `onCreate` function. See if you can work out what the output will be before we discuss and analyze the code:

```
// Declaring and allocating in one step
val ourArray = IntArray(1000)

// Let's initialize ourArray using a for loop
// Because more than a few variables is allot of typing!

for (i in 0..999) {

    // Put the value into ourArray
    // At the position decided by i.
    ourArray[i] = i * 5

    //Output what is going on
    Log.i("info", "i = $i")
    Log.i("info", "ourArray[i] = ${ ourArray[i]}")
}
```

Run the example app. Remember that nothing will happen on screen as all the output will be sent to our logcat window in Android Studio; here is the output:

```
info: i = 0
info: ourArray[i] = 0
info: i = 1
info: ourArray[i] = 5
info: i = 2
info: ourArray[i] = 10
```

994 iterations of the loop have been removed for the sake of brevity:

```
info: ourArray[i] = 4985
info: i = 998
info: ourArray[i] = 4990
info: i = 999
info: ourArray[i] = 4995
```

First, we declared and allocated an array called `ourArray` to hold up to 1,000 `Int` values. Notice that this time, we performed the two steps in a single line of code:

```
val ourArray = IntArray(1000)
```

Then, we used a `for` loop that was set to loop 1,000 times:

```
for (i in 0..999) {
```

We initialized the spaces in the array, from 0 to 999, with the value of `i` multiplied by 5, as follows:

```
    ourArray[i] = i * 5
```

Then, to demonstrate the value of `i` and the value held in each position of the array, we output the value of `i` followed by the value held in the corresponding position in the array, as follows:

```
    //Output what is going on
    Log.i("info", "i = $i")
    Log.i("info", "ourArray[i] = ${ ourArray[i]}")
```

All this happened 1,000 times, producing the output that we have seen. Of course, we have yet to use this technique in a real-world app, but we will use it soon to make our Note to self app hold an almost infinite number of notes.

ArrayLists

An `ArrayList` object is like a normal array, but on steroids. It overcomes some of the shortfalls of arrays, such as having to predetermine its size. It adds several useful functions to make its data easy to manage and it is used by many classes in the Android API. This last point means that we need to use `ArrayList` if we want to use certain parts of the API. In *Chapter 16, Adapters and Recyclers*, we will put `ArrayList` to work for real. First the theory.

Let's take a look at some code that uses `ArrayList`:

```
// Declare a new ArrayList called myList
// to hold Int variables
val myList: ArrayList<Int>

// Initialize myList ready for use
myList = ArrayList()
```

In the preceding code, we declared and initialized a new `ArrayList` object called `myList`. We can also do this in a single step, as demonstrated by the following code:

```
val myList: ArrayList<Int> = ArrayList()
```

So far, this is not particularly interesting, so let's take a look at what we can actually do with `ArrayList`. Let's use a `String ArrayList` object this time:

```
// declare and initialize a new ArrayList
val myList = ArrayList<String>()

// Add a new String to myList in
// the next available location
myList.add("Donald Knuth")
// And another
myList.add("Rasmus Lerdorf")
// We can also choose 'where' to add an entry
myList.add(1,"Richard Stallman")

// Is there anything in our ArrayList?
if (myList.isEmpty()) {
   // Nothing to see here
} else {
   // Do something with the data
}

// How many items in our ArrayList?
val numItems = myList.size

// Now where did I put Richard?
val position = myList.indexOf("Richard Stallman")
```

In the previous code, we saw that we can use some useful functions of the `ArrayList` class on our `ArrayList` object; these functions are as follows:

- We can add an item (`myList.add`)
- We can add an entry at a specific location (`myList.add(x, value)`)
- We can check whether the `ArrayList` instance is empty (`myList.isEmpty ()`)
- We can see how big the `ArrayList` instance is (`myList.size`)
- We can get the current position of a given item (`myList.indexOf...`)

There are even more functions in the `ArrayList` class, but what we have seen so far is enough to complete this book.

With all this functionality, all we need now is a way to handle `ArrayList` instances dynamically. This is what the condition of an enhanced `for` loop looks like:

```
for (String s : myList)
```

The previous example will iterate (step through) all the items in `myList` one at a time. At each step, `s` will hold the current `String` entry.

So, this code will print all of our eminent programmers from the previous section's `ArrayList` code sample to the logcat window, as follows:

```
for (s in myList) {
    Log.i("Programmer: ", "$s")
}
```

The way that this works is that the `for` loop iterates through each `String` in the `ArrayList` and assigns the current `String` entry to `s`. Then, for each in turn, `s` is used in the `Log...` function call. The previous loop will create the following output to the logcat window:

```
Programmer:: Donald Knuth
Programmer:: Richard Stallman
Programmer:: Rasmus Lerdorf
```

The `for` loop has output all the names. The reason that Richard Stallman is in between Donald Knuth and Rasmus Lerdof is because we inserted him at a specific position, (1), which is the second position in the `ArrayList`. An `insert` function call does not delete any existing entries but shifts their position instead.

There's an incoming news flash!

Arrays and ArrayLists are polymorphic

We already know that we can put objects into arrays and `ArrayList` objects. However, being polymorphic means that they can handle objects of multiple distinct types as long as they have a common parent type - all within the same array or `ArrayList`.

In *Chapter 10, Object-Oriented Programming,* we learned that polymorphism means many forms. But what does it mean to us in the context of arrays and `ArrayList`?

In its simplest form, it means that any subclass can be used as part of the code that uses the super-class.

For example, if we have an array of `Animals`, we can put any object that is a subclass of `Animal` in the `Animals` array, such as `Cat` and `Dog`.

This means we can write code that is simpler, easier to understand, and easier to change:

```
// This code assumes we have an Animal class
// And we have a Cat and Dog class that
// inherits from Animal
val myAnimal = Animal()
val myDog = Dog()
val myCat = Cat()
val myAnimals = arrayOfNulls<Animal>(10)
myAnimals[0] = myAnimal // As expected
myAnimals[1] = myDog // This is OK too
myAnimals[2] = myCat // And this is fine as well
```

Also, we can write code for the super-class and rely on the fact that no matter how many times it is subclassed, within certain parameters, the code will still work. Let's continue our previous example as follows:

```
// 6 months later we need elephants
// with its own unique aspects
// If it extends Animal we can still do this
val myElephant = Elephant()
myAnimals[3] = myElephant // And this is fine as well
```

All that we have just discussed is true for `ArrayLists` as well.

Hashmaps

Kotlin `HashMaps` are interesting; they are a type of cousin to `ArrayList`. They encapsulate useful data storage techniques that would otherwise be quite technical for us to code successfully ourselves. It is worth looking at `HashMap` before getting back to the Note to self app.

Suppose that we want to store the data of lots of characters from a role-playing game and each different character is represented by an object of the `Character` type.

We could use some of the Kotlin tools that we already know about, such as arrays or `ArrayList`. However, with `HashMap`, we can give a unique key or identifier to each `Character` object, and access any such object using that same key or identifier.

The term "hash" comes from the process of turning our chosen key or identifier into something used internally by the `HashMap` class. The process is called **hashing**.

Any of our `Character` instances can then be accessed with our chosen key or identifier. A good candidate for a key or identifier in the `Character` class scenario is the character's name.

Each key or identifier has a corresponding object; in this case, of the `Character` instance. This is known as a **key-value pair**.

We simply give `HashMap` a key and it gives us the corresponding object. There is no need to worry about which index we stored our characters, such as Geralt, Ciri, or Triss; simply pass the name to `HashMap` and it will do the work for us.

Let's take a look at some examples. You don't need to type any of this code; simply get familiar with how it works.

We can declare a new `HashMap` instance to hold keys and `Character` instances like as follows:

```
val characterMap: Map<String, Character>
```

The previous code assumes that we have coded a class called `Character`. We can then initialize the `HashMap` instance as follows:

```
characterMap = HashMap()
```

We can then add a new key and its associated object as follows:

```
characterMap.put("Geralt", Character())
characterMap.put("Ciri", Character())
characterMap.put("Triss", Character())
```

All the example code assumes that we can somehow give the `Character` instances their unique properties to reflect their internal differences elsewhere.

We can then retrieve an entry from the `HashMap` instance as follows:

```
val ciri = characterMap.get("Ciri")
```

Alternatively, we can use the `Character` class's functions directly:

```
characterMap.get("Geralt").drawSilverSword()

// Or maybe call some other hypothetical function
characterMap.get("Triss").openFastTravelPortal("Kaer Morhen")
```

The previous code calls the hypothetical `drawSilverSword` and `openFastTravelPortal` functions on the `Character` class instance stored in the `HashMap` instance.

Armed with this new toolkit of arrays, `ArrayList`, `HashMap`, and the fact that they are polymorphic, we can move on to learn about some more Android classes that we will soon use to enhance our Note to self app.

The Note to self app

Despite all we have learned, we are not quite ready to apply a solution to the Note to self app. We could update our code to store lots of `Note` instances in an `ArrayList`, but before we do, we also need a way to display the contents of our `ArrayList` in the UI. It won't look good to throw the whole thing in a `TextView` instance.

The solution is **adapters**, and a special UI layout called `RecyclerView`. We will get to them in the next chapter.

Frequently asked questions

Q) How can a computer that can only make real calculations possibly generate a genuinely random number?

A) In reality, a computer cannot create a number that is truly random, but the `Random` class uses a **seed** that produces a number that will stand up as genuinely random under close statistical scrutiny. To find out more about seeds and generating random numbers, look at the following article: `https://en.wikipedia.org/wiki/Random_number_generation`.

Summary

In this chapter, we looked at how to use simple Kotlin arrays to store substantial amounts of data provided that it is of the same type. We also used `ArrayList`, which is like an array with lots of extra features. Furthermore, we discovered that both arrays and `ArrayList` are polymorphic, which means that a single array (or `ArrayList`) can hold multiple different objects as long as they are all derived from the same parent class.

We also learned about the `HashMap` class, which is also a data storage solution, but which allows access in different ways.

In the next chapter, we will learn about `Adapter` and `RecyclerView` to put the theory into practice and enhance our Note to self app.

16
Adapters and Recyclers

We will achieve much in this brief chapter. We will first go through the theory of adapters and lists. We will then look at how we can use a `RecyclerAdapter` instance in Kotlin code and add a `RecyclerView` widget to the layout, which acts as a list for our UI, and then, through the apparent magic of the Android API, bind them together so that the `RecyclerView` instance displays the contents of the `RecyclerAdapter` instance and allows the user to scroll through the contents of an `ArrayList` instance full of `Note` instances. You have probably guessed that we will be using this technique to display our list of notes in the Note to self app.

In this chapter, we will do the following:

- Explore another type of Kotlin class – the **inner class**
- Look at the theory of adapters and examine binding them to our UI
- Implement the layout with `RecyclerView`
- Lay out a list item for use in `RecyclerView`
- Implement the adapter with `RecyclerAdapter`
- Bind the adapter to `RecyclerView`
- Store notes in `ArrayList` and display them in `RecyclerView` via `RecycleAdapter`

Soon, we will have a self-managing layout that holds and displays all our notes, so let's get started.

Inner classes

In this project, we will use a type of class we have not seen yet – an **inner** class. Suppose that we have a regular class called `SomeRegularClass`, with a property called `someRegularProperty`, and a function called `someRegularFunction`, as shown in this next code:

```
class SomeRegularClass{
    var someRegularProperty = 1

    fun someRegularFunction(){
    }
}
```

An inner class is a class that is declared inside of a regular class, like in this next highlighted code:

```
class SomeRegularClass{
    var someRegularProperty = 1

    fun someRegularFunction(){
    }

    inner class MyInnerClass {
       val myInnerProperty = 1

       fun myInnerFunction() {
       }
    }

}
```

The preceding highlighted code shows an inner class called `MyInnerClass`, with a property called `myInnerProperty`, and a function called `myInnerFunction`.

One advantage is that the outer class can use the properties and functions of the inner class by declaring an instance of it, as shown highlighted in the next code snippet:

```
class SomeRegularClass{
    var someRegularProperty = 1

    val myInnerInstance = MyInnerClass()

    fun someRegularFunction(){
        val someVariable = myInnerInstance.myInnerProperty
```

```
        myInnerInstance.myInnerFunction()
    }

    inner class MyInnerClass {
        val myInnerProperty = 1

        fun myInnerFunction() {
        }

    }
}
```

Furthermore, the inner class can also access the properties of the regular class, perhaps from the `myInnerFunction` function. This next code snippet shows this in action:

```
fun myInnerFunction() {
    someRegularProperty ++
}
```

This ability to define a new type within a class and create instances and share data is very useful in certain circumstances and for encapsulation. We will use an inner class in the Note to self app later in this chapter.

RecyclerView and RecyclerAdapter

In *Chapter 5, Beautiful Layouts with CardView and ScrollView*, we used a `ScrollView` widget and we populated it with a few `CardView` widgets so that we could see it scrolling. We could take what we have just learned about `ArrayList` and create a container of `TextView` objects, use them to populate a `ScrollView` widget, and, within each `TextView`, place the title of a note. This sounds like a perfect solution for showing each note so that it is clickable in the Note to self app.

We could create the `TextView` objects dynamically in Kotlin code, set their `text` property to be the title of a note, and then add the `TextView` objects to a `LinearLayout` contained in `ScrollView`. But this is imperfect.

The problem with displaying lots of widgets

This might seem fine, but what if there were dozens, hundreds, or even thousands of notes? We couldn't have thousands of `TextView` objects in memory because the Android device might simply run out of memory, or, at the very least, grind to a halt as it tries to handle the scrolling of such a vast amount of data.

Now, also imagine that we wanted (which we do) each note in the `ScrollView` widget to show whether it was important, a to-do, or an idea. And how about a short snippet from the text of the note as well?

We would need to devise some clever code that loads and destroys `Note` objects and `TextView` objects from `ArrayList`. It can be done - but to do it efficiently is far from straightforward.

The solution to the problem with displaying lots of widgets

Fortunately, this is a problem faced so commonly by mobile developers that the Android API has a solution built in.

We can add a single widget, called `RecyclerView` (like an environmentally friendly `ScrollView`, but with boosters too), to our UI layout. The `RecyclerView` class was designed as a solution to the problem we have been discussing. In addition, we need to interact with `RecyclerView` with a special type of class that understands how `RecyclerView` works. We will interact with it using an **adapter**. We will use the `RecyclerAdapter` class, inherit from it, customize it, and then use it to control the data from our `ArrayList` and display it in the `RecyclerView` class.

Let's find out a bit more about how the `RecyclerView` and `RecyclerAdapter` classes work.

How to use RecyclerView and RecyclerAdapter

We already know how to store almost unlimited notes - we can do so in `ArrayList`, although we haven't implemented it yet. We also know that there is a UI layout called `RecyclerView` that is specifically designed to display potentially long lists of data. We just need to see how to put it all into action.

To add a `RecyclerView` widget to our layout, we can simply drag and drop it from the palette onto our UI in the usual way.

[Don't do it yet. Let's just discuss it for a while first.]

The `RecyclerView` class will look like this in the UI designer:

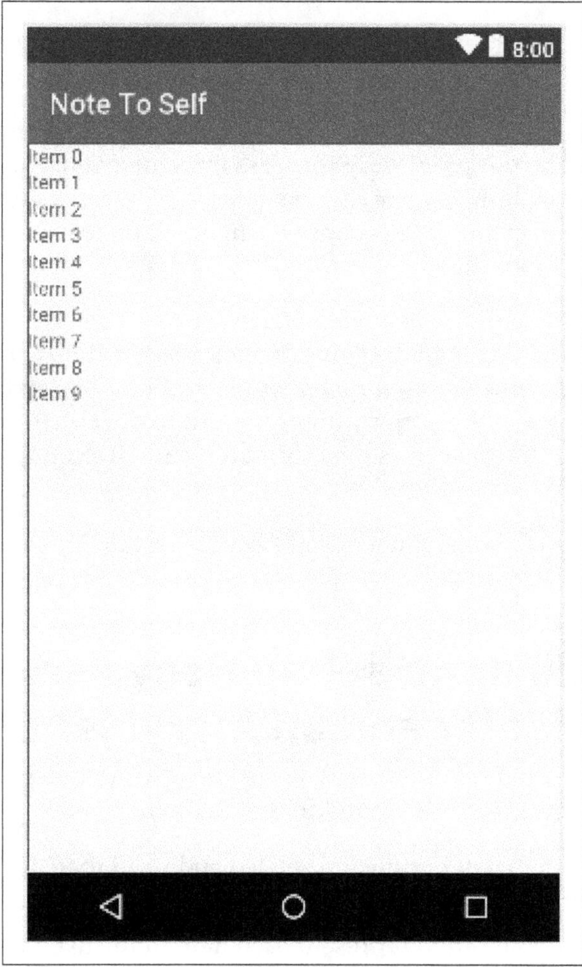

This appearance, however, is more a representation of the possibilities than the actual appearance in an app. If we run the app at once after adding a `RecyclerView` widget, we will just get a blank screen.

The first thing we need to do to make practical use of a `RecyclerView` widget is decide what each item in the list will look like. It could be just a single `TextView` widget, or it could be an entire layout. We will use `LinearLayout`. To be clear and specific, we will use a `LinearLayout` instance that holds three `TextView` widgets for each item in our `RecyclerView` widget. This will allow us to display the note status (important/idea/to-do), the note title, and a short snippet of text from the actual note contents.

A list item needs to be defined in its own XML file, then the `RecyclerView` widget can hold multiple instances of this list item layout.

Of course, none of this explains how we overcome the complexity of managing what data is shown in which list item and how it is retrieved from `ArrayList`.

This data handling is taken care of by our own customized implementation of `RecyclerAdapter`. The `RecyclerAdapter` class implements the `Adapter` interface. We don't need to know how `Adapter` works internally, we just need to override some functions, and then `RecyclerAdapter` will do all the work of communicating with our `RecyclerView` widget.

Wiring up an implementation of `RecyclerAdapter` to a `RecyclerView` widget is certainly more complicated than dragging 20 `TextView` widgets onto a `ScrollView` widget, but once it is done we can forget about it, and it will keep on working and manage itself regardless of how many notes we add to `ArrayList`. It also has built-in features for handling things such as neat formatting and detecting which item in a list was clicked.

We will need to override some functions of `RecyclerAdapter` and add a little code of our own.

What we will do to set up RecyclerView with RecyclerAdapter and an ArrayList of notes

Look at this outline of the required steps so we know what to expect. To get the whole thing up and running, we would do the following:

1. Delete the temporary button and related code and then add a `RecyclerView` widget to our layout with a specific `id` property.
2. Create an XML layout to represent each item in the list. We have already mentioned that each item in the list will be a `LinearLayout` that contains three `TextView` widgets.
3. Create a new class that inherits from `RecyclerAdapter`, and add code to several overridden functions to control how it looks and behaves, including using our list item layout and `ArrayList` full of `Note` instances.
4. Add code in `MainActivity` to use `RecyclerAdapter` and the `RecyclerView` widget and bind it to our `ArrayList` instance.
5. Add an `ArrayList` instance to `MainActivity` to hold all our notes, and update the `createNewNote` function to add any new notes created in the `DialogNewNote` class to this `ArrayList`.

Let's go through and implement each of those steps in detail.

Adding RecyclerView, RecyclerAdapter, and ArrayList to the Note to Self project

Open the Note to self project. As a reminder, if you want to see the completed code and working app based on completing this chapter, it can be found in the `Chapter16/Note to self` folder.

As the required action in this chapter jumps around between different files, classes, and functions, I encourage you to follow along with the files from the download bundle open in your preferred text editor for reference.

Removing the temporary "Show Note" button and adding RecyclerView

These next few steps will get rid of the temporary code we added in *Chapter 14, Android Dialog Windows*, and set up our `RecyclerView` ready for binding to `RecyclerAdapter` later in the chapter:

1. In the `content_main.xml` file, remove the temporary `Button` with an `id` of `button`, which we added previously for testing purposes.
2. In the `onCreate` function of `MainActivity.kt`, delete the `Button` instance declaration and initialization along with the lambda that handles its clicks, as this code now creates an error. We will delete some more temporary code later in this chapter. Delete the code shown next:

```
// Temporary code
val button = findViewById<View>(R.id.button) as Button
button.setOnClickListener {
  // Create a new DialogShowNote called dialog
  val dialog = DialogShowNote()

  // Send the note via the sendNoteSelected function
  dialog.sendNoteSelected(tempNote)

  // Create the dialog
  dialog.show(supportFragmentManager, "123")
}
```

3. Now, switch back to `content_main.xml` in design view and drag a **RecyclerView** widget from the **Common** category of the palette onto the layout.
4. Set its `id` property to `recyclerView`.

Now we have removed the temporary UI aspects from our project, and we have a `RecyclerView` widget complete with a unique `id` attribute ready to be referenced from our Kotlin code.

Creating a list item for RecyclerView

Next, we need a layout to represent each item in our `RecyclerView` widget. As previously mentioned, we will use a `LinearLayout` instance that holds three `TextView` widgets.

These are the steps needed to create a list item for use within `RecyclerView`:

1. Right-click on the `layout` folder in the project explorer and select **New | Layout resource file**. Enter `listitem` in the **Name:** field and make the **Root element:** `LinearLayout`. The default orientation attribute is vertical, which is just what we need.
2. Look at the next screenshot to see what we are trying to achieve with the remaining steps of this section. I have annotated it to show what each part will be in the finished app:

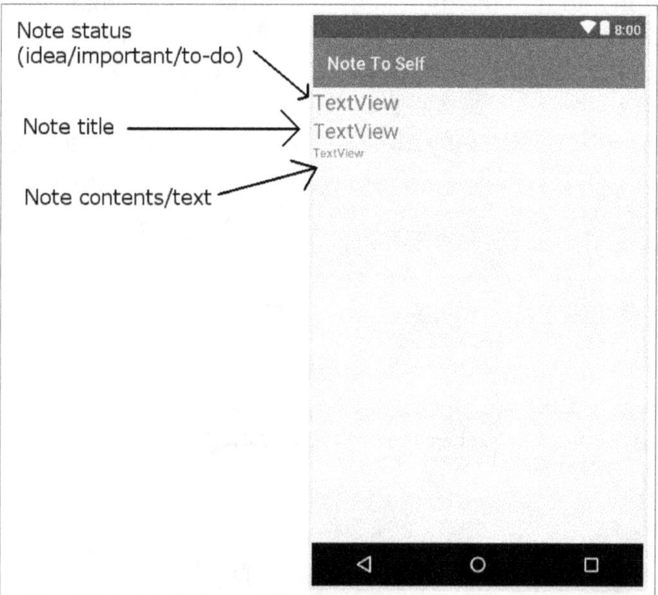

3. Drag three `TextView` instances onto the layout, one above the other, as per the reference screenshot. The first (top) will hold the note status/type (idea/important/to-do), the second (middle) will hold the note title, and the third (bottom) will hold a snippet of the note itself.
4. Configure the various attributes of the `LinearLayout` instance and the `TextView` widgets as shown in the following table:

Widget type	**Property**	**Value to set to**
LinearLayout	`layout_height`	`wrap_contents`
LinearLayout	`Layout_Margin all`	`5dp`
TextView (top)	`id`	`textViewStatus`
TextView (top)	`textSize`	`24sp`
TextView (top)	`textColor`	`@color/colorAccent`
TextView (middle)	`id`	`textViewTitle`
TextView (middle)	`textSize`	`24sp`
TextView (top)	`id`	`textViewDescription`

Now we have a `RecylerView` widget for the main layout and a layout to use for each item in the list. We can go ahead and code our `RecyclerAdapter` implementation.

Coding the RecyclerAdapter class

We will now create and code a brand-new class. Let's call our new class `NoteAdapter`. Create a new class called `NoteAdapter` in the same folder as the `MainActivity` class (and all the other classes) in the usual way.

Edit the code for the `NoteAdapter` class by adding these `import` statements and inheriting from the `RecyclerView.Adapter` class, then add the two properties as shown. Edit the `NoteAdapter` class to be the same as the following code that we have just discussed:

```
import android.view.LayoutInflater
import android.view.View
import android.view.ViewGroup
import android.widget.TextView
import androidx.recyclerview.widget.RecyclerView

class NoteAdapter(
   private val mainActivity: MainActivity,
   private val noteList: List<Note>)
   : RecyclerView.Adapter<NoteAdapter.ListItemHolder>() {

}
```

In the previous code, we declare and initialize two properties of the `NoteAdapter` class using the primary constructor. Notice the parameters of the constructor. It receives a `MainActivity` reference as well as a `List` reference. This implies that, when we use this class, we will need to send in a reference to the main activity of this app (`MainActivity`) as well as a `List` reference. We will see what use we put the `MainActivity` reference to shortly, but we can sensibly guess that the reference to a `List` with a type of `<Note>` will be a reference to our `Note` instances, which we will soon code in the `MainActivity` class. `NoteAdapter` will then hold a permanent reference to all the users' notes.

You will notice, however, that the class declaration and other areas of the code are underlined in red, showing that there are errors in our code.

The first error is because the `RecylerView.Adapter` class (which we are inheriting from) needs us to override some of its abstract functions.

We discussed abstract classes and their functions in *Chapter 11, Inheritance in Kotlin.*

The quickest way to do this is to click the class declaration, hold the *Alt* key, and then tap the *Enter* key. Choose **Implement members,** as shown in the next screenshot:

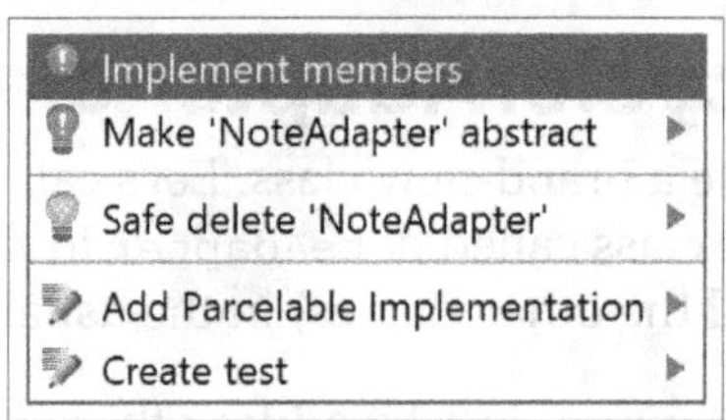

In the window that follows, hold down *Shift* and left-click all three options (functions to add) and then click **OK**. This process adds the following three functions:

- The `onCreateViewHolder` function, which is called when a layout for a list item is required
- The `onBindViewHolder` function, which is called when the `RecyclerAdapter` instance is bound to (connected/associated with) the `RecyclerView` instance in the layout
- The `getItemCount` function, which will be used to return the number of `Note` instances in `ArrayList`

We will soon add code to each of these functions to do the required work at the specific time.

Note, however, that we still have multiple errors in our code, including in the newly autogenerated functions as well as the class declaration. We need to do some work to resolve these errors.

The errors are because the `NoteAdapter.ListItemHolder` class does not exist. `ListItemHolder` was added by us when we extended `NoteAdapter`. It is our chosen class type that will be used as the holder for each list item. Currently, it doesn't exist - hence the error. The two functions that also have the same error for the same reason were autogenerated when we asked Android Studio to implement the missing functions.

Let's solve the problem by making a start on the required `ListItemHolder` class. It is useful to us for `ListItemHolder` instances to share data/variables with `NoteAdapter`; therefore, we will create `ListItemHolder` as an inner class.

Click the error in the class declaration and select **Create class 'ListItemHolder'**, as shown in this next screenshot:

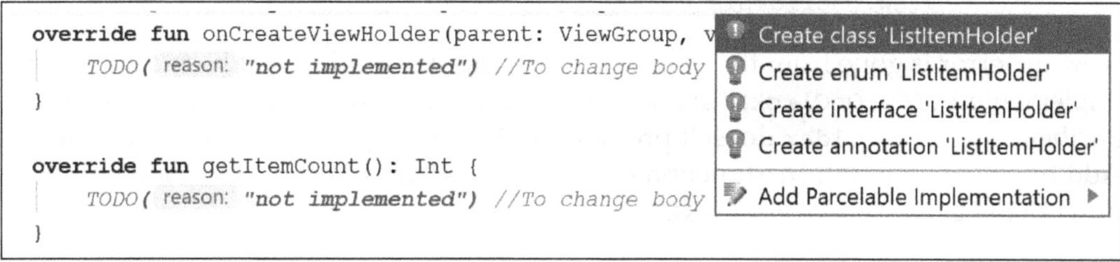

In the pop-up window that follows, choose **NoteAdapter** to generate `ListItemHolder` inside `NoteAdapter`.

The following code has been added to the `NoteAdapter` class:

```
class ListItemHolder {

}
```

But we still have multiple errors. Let's fix one of them now. Hover your mouse over the red-underlined error in the class declaration as shown in the next screenshot:

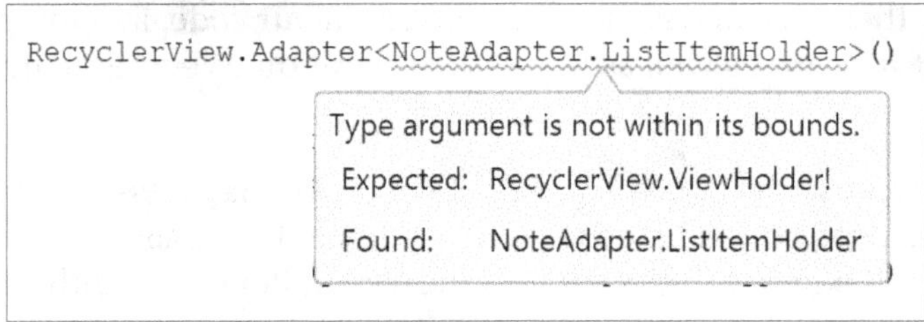

The error message reads **Type argument is not within its bounds. Expected: RecyclerView.ViewHolder! Found: NoteAdapter.ListItemHolder**. The reason for this is because we may have added `ListItemHolder`, but `ListItemHolder` must also implement `RecyclerView.ViewHolder` in order to be used as the correct type.

Amend the declaration of the `ListItemHolder` class to match this code:

```
inner class ListItemHolder(view: View) :
     RecyclerView.ViewHolder(view),
     View.OnClickListener {
```

Now the error is gone from the `NoteAdapter` class declaration, but because we also implemented `View.OnClickListener`, we need to implement the `onClick` function. Furthermore, `ViewHolder` doesn't provide a default constructor, so we need to do it. Add the following `onClick` function (empty for now) and this `init` block (empty for now) to the `ListItemHolder` class:

```
init {
}

override fun onClick(view: View) {
}
```

Be sure you added the code to the inner `ListItemHolder` class and not the `NoteAdapter` class.

Let's clear up the final remaining errors. When the `onBindViewHolder` function was autogenerated, Android Studio didn't add the type for the `holder` parameter. This is causing an error in the function and an error in the class declaration. Update the `onBindViewHolder` function's signature, as shown in the next code:

```
override fun onBindViewHolder(
   holder: ListItemHolder, position: Int) {
```

In the `onCreateViewHolder` function signature, the return type has not been autogenerated. Amend the signature of the `onCreateViewHolder` function, as shown in this next code:

```
override fun onCreateViewHolder(
   parent: ViewGroup, viewType: Int): ListItemHolder {
```

As a last bit of good housekeeping, let's delete the three `// TODO...` comments that were autogenerated but not required. There is one in each of the autogenerated functions. They look like the one highlighted in this next screenshot:

```
override fun onCreateViewHolder(
        parent: ViewGroup, viewType: Int): ListItemHolder {
    TODO( reason: "not implemented") //To change body of created functions use File | Settings | File Templates.
}
```

As you delete the `TODO...` comments, more errors will appear. We need to add `return` statements to some of the autogenerated functions. We will do this as we proceed with coding the class.

After much tinkering and autogenerating, we finally have an almost error-free `NoteAdapter` class, complete with overridden functions and an inner class that we can code to get our `RecyclerAdapter` instance working. In addition, we can write code to respond to clicks (in `onClick`) on each of our `ListItemHolder` instances.

What follows is a complete listing of what the code should look like at this stage (excluding the import statements):

```
class NoteAdapter(
  private val mainActivity: MainActivity,
  private val noteList: List<Note>)
  : RecyclerView.Adapter<NoteAdapter.ListItemHolder>() {


    override fun onCreateViewHolder(
         parent: ViewGroup, viewType: Int):
         ListItemHolder {

    }

    override fun getItemCount(): Int {

    }

    override fun onBindViewHolder(
         holder: ListItemHolder,
```

```
        position: Int) {
    }

    inner class ListItemHolder(view: View) :
            RecyclerView.ViewHolder(view),
            View.OnClickListener {

        init {

        }

        override fun onClick(view: View) {
        }
    }
}
```

> You could have just copy and pasted the preceding code instead of enduring the machinations of the previous pages, but then you wouldn't have experienced the process of implementing interfaces and inner classes so closely.

Now, let's code the functions and get this class operational.

Coding the onCreateViewHolder function

Next, we will adapt the autogenerated `onCreateViewHolder` function. Add the highlighted lines of code to the `onCreateViewHolder` function and study them:

```
override fun onCreateViewHolder(
    parent: ViewGroup, viewType: Int):
    ListItemHolder {

    val itemView = LayoutInflater.from(parent.context)
      .inflate(R.layout.listitem, parent, false)

    return ListItemHolder(itemView)
}
```

This code works by initializing `itemView` using `LayoutInflater` and our newly designed `listitem` layout. It then returns a new `ListItemHolder` instance, complete with an inflated and ready-to-use layout.

Coding the onBindViewHolder function

Next, we will adapt the `onBindViewHolder` function. Add the highlighted code to make the function the same as this code, and be sure to study the code as well:

```
override fun onBindViewHolder(
        holder: ListItemHolder, position: Int) {

    val note = noteList[position]
    holder.title.text = note.title

    // Show the first 15 characters of the actual note
    holder.description.text =
        note.description!!.substring(0, 15)

    // What is the status of the note?
    when {
            note.idea -> holder.status.text =
            mainActivity.resources.getString(R.string.idea_text)

            note.important -> holder.status.text =
            mainActivity.resources.getString(R.string.important_text)

            note.todo -> holder.status.text =
            mainActivity.resources.getString(R.string.todo_text)
    }

}
```

First, the code truncates the text to 15 characters so that it looks sensible in the list. Note that if the user enters a very short note below 15 characters this will cause a crash. It is left as an exercise for the reader to come back to this project and discover a solution to this imperfection.

It then checks what type of note it is (idea/to-do/important) and assigns the appropriate label from the string resources using a `when` expression.

This new code has left some errors in the code with `holder.title`, `holder.description`, and `holder.status`, because we need to add them to our `ListItemHolder` inner class. We will do this very soon.

Coding getItemCount

Amend the code in the `getItemCount` function, as shown next:

```
override fun getItemCount(): Int {
    if (noteList != null) {
          return noteList.size
   }
   // error
   return -1
}
```

This function is used internally by the class, and it supplies the current number of items in `List`.

Coding the ListItemHolder inner class

Now we can turn our attention to the `ListItemHolder` inner class. Adapt the `ListItemHolder` inner class by adding the following highlighted code:

```
inner class ListItemHolder(view: View) :
         RecyclerView.ViewHolder(view),
         View.OnClickListener {

   internal var title =
             view.findViewById<View>(
                          R.id.textViewTitle) as TextView

   internal var description =
             view.findViewById<View>(
                          R.id.textViewDescription) as TextView

   internal var status =
             view.findViewById<View>(
                          R.id.textViewStatus) as TextView

   init {

         view.isClickable = true
         view.setOnClickListener(this)
   }

   override fun onClick(view: View) {
         mainActivity.showNote(adapterPosition)
   }
}
```

The `ListItemHolder` properties get a reference to each of the `TextView` widgets in the layout. The `init` block code sets the whole view as clickable so that the OS will call the next function we discuss, `onClick`, when a holder is clicked.

In `onClick`, the call to `mainActivity.showNote` has an error because the function doesn't exist yet, but we will fix that in the next section. The call will simply show the clicked note using our custom `DialogFragment` instance.

Coding MainActivity to use the RecyclerView and RecyclerAdapter classes

Now, switch over to the `MainActivity` class in the editor window. Add these three new properties to the `MainActivity` class and remove the temporary code:

```
// Temporary code
//private var tempNote = Note()

private val noteList = ArrayList<Note>()
private val recyclerView: RecyclerView? = null
private val adapter: NoteAdapter? = null
```

These three properties are our `ArrayList` instance for all our `Note` instances, our `RecyclerView` instance, and an instance of our `NoteAdapter` class.

Adding code to onCreate

Add the following highlighted code in the `onCreate` function after the code that handles the user pressing on the floating action button (shown again for context):

```
fab.setOnClickListener { view ->
   val dialog = DialogNewNote()
   dialog.show(supportFragmentManager, "")
}

recyclerView =
          findViewById<View>(R.id.recyclerView)
          as RecyclerView

adapter = NoteAdapter(this, noteList)
val layoutManager =
    LinearLayoutManager(applicationContext)

recyclerView!!.layoutManager = layoutManager
```

```
recyclerView!!.itemAnimator = DefaultItemAnimator()

// Add a neat dividing line between items in the list
recyclerView!!.addItemDecoration(
        DividerItemDecoration(this,
                LinearLayoutManager.VERTICAL))

// set the adapter
recyclerView!!.adapter = adapter
```

Here, we initialize `recyclerView` with the `RecyclerView` widget from the layout. Our `NoteAdapter` (`adapter`) instance is initialized by calling the constructor we coded. Note that a reference to `MainActivity` (`this`) and the `ArrayList` instance is passed in, just as required by the class we have coded previously.

Next, we create a new object – a `LayoutManager` object. In the next four lines of code, we configure some properties of `recyclerView`.

The `itemAnimator` property and `addItemDecoration` function make each list item a little more visually enhanced with a separator line between each item in the list. Later, when we build a "Settings" screen, we will give the user the option to add and remove this separator.

The last thing we do is initialize the `adapter` property of `recylerView` with our adapter, which combines our adapter with our view.

Now, we will make some changes to the `createNewNote` function.

Modifying the createNewNote function

In the `createNewNote` function, delete the temporary code we added in *Chapter 14, Android Dialog Windows* (shown commented out). and add the new highlighted code shown next:

```
fun createNewNote(n: Note) {
  // Temporary code
  // tempNote = n
  noteList.add(n)
  adapter!!.notifyDataSetChanged()

}
```

The new highlighted code adds a note to the ArrayList instance instead of simply initializing a solitary Note object, which has now been commented out. Then, we need to call notifyDataSetChanged, which lets our adapter know that a new note has been added.

Coding the showNote function

Add the showNote function, which is called from the NoteAdapter class using the reference to this class that was passed into the NoteAdapter constructor. Or, more accurately, it is called from the ListerItemHolder inner class when one of the items in the RecyclerView widget is tapped by the user. Add the showNote function to the MainActivity class:

```
fun showNote(noteToShow: Int) {
   val dialog = DialogShowNote()
   dialog.sendNoteSelected(noteList[noteToShow])
   dialog.show(supportFragmentManager, "")
}
```

All the errors in the NoteAdapter.kt file are now gone.

The code just added will launch a new instance of DialogShowNote, passing in the specific required note as referenced by noteToShow.

Running the app

You can now run the app and enter a new note, as shown in this next screenshot:

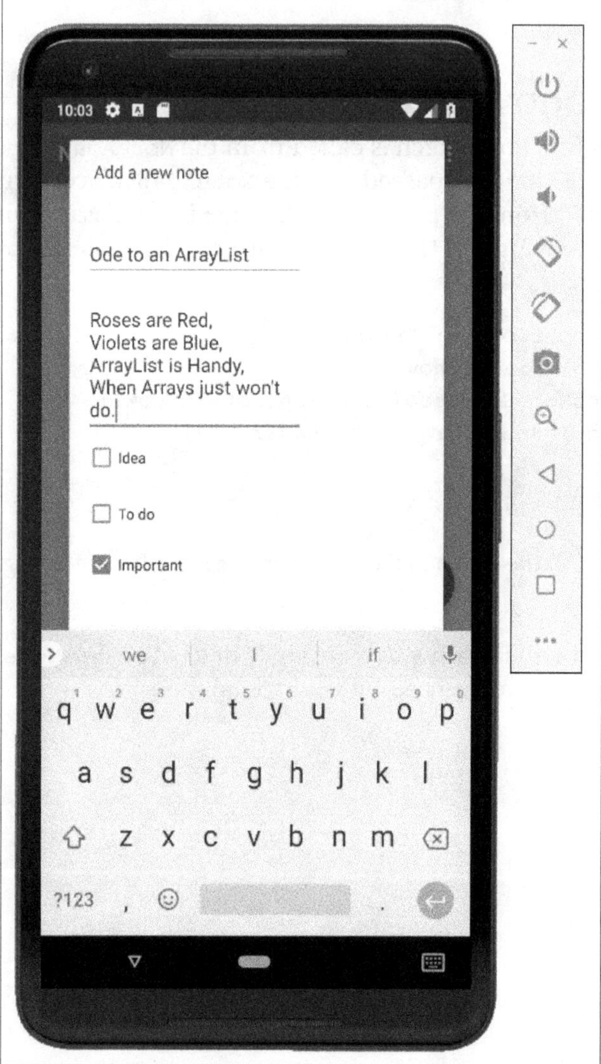

After you have entered several notes of several types, the list (`RecyclerView`) will look something like this next screenshot:

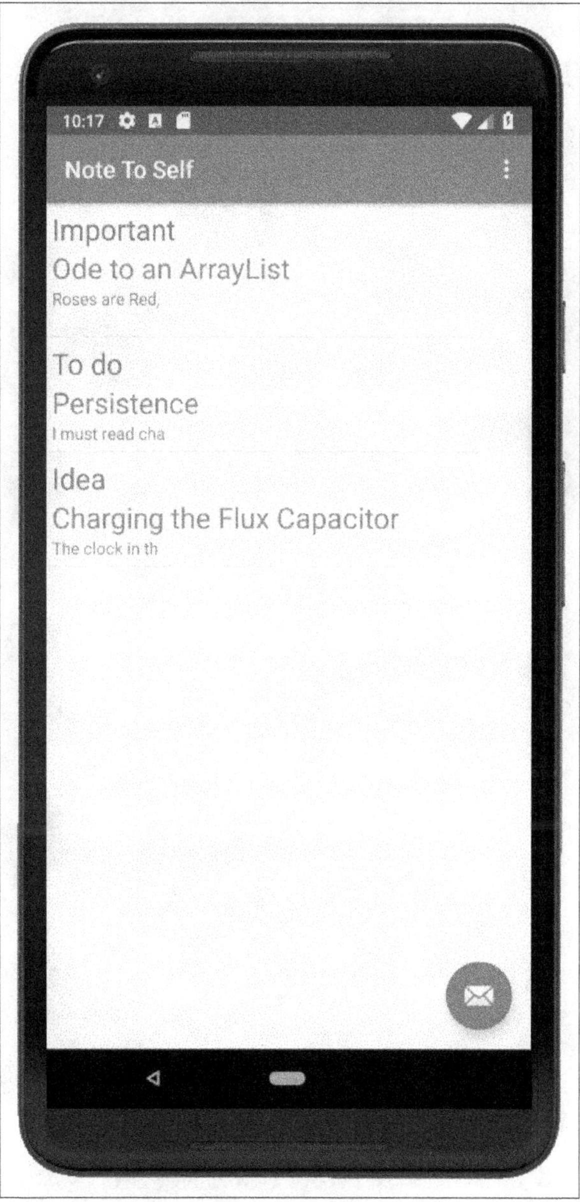

And, if you click to view one of the notes, it will look like this:

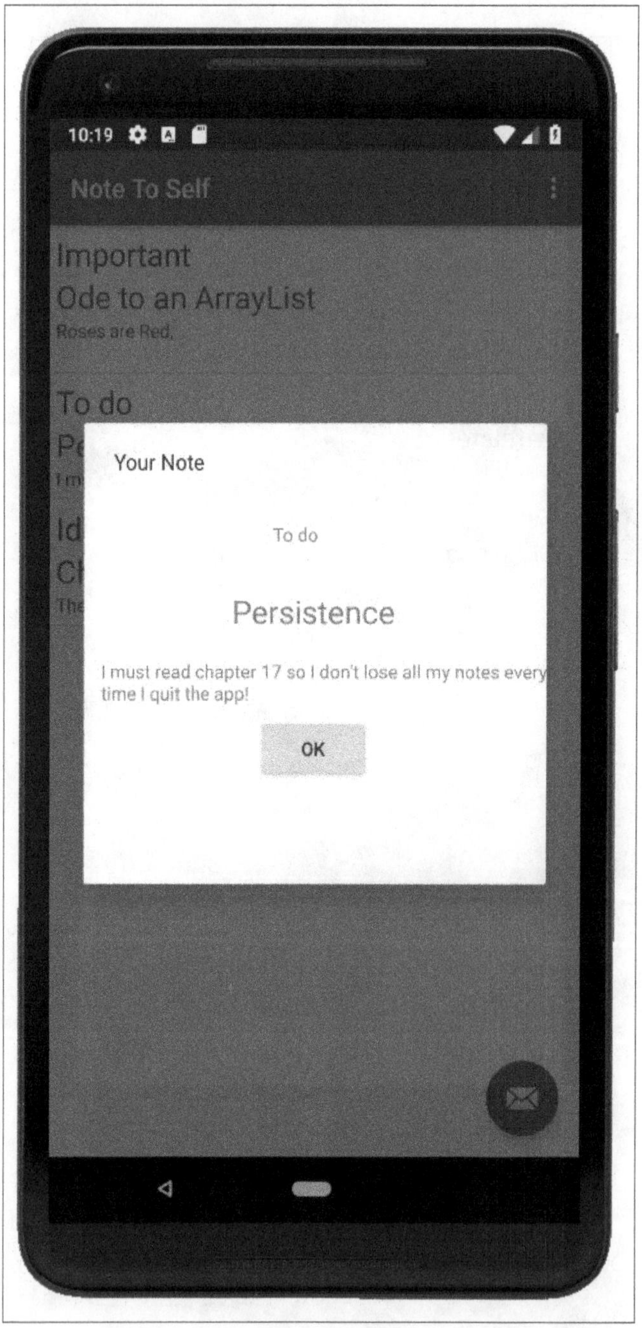

Reader challenge
We could have spent more time formatting the layouts of our two dialog windows. Why not refer to *Chapter 5, Beautiful Layouts with CardView and ScrollView*, as well as the Material Design website, `https://material.io/design/`, and do a better job than this. Furthermore, you could enhance the `RecyclerView` list of notes by using `CardView` instead of `LinearLayout`.

Don't spend too long adding new notes, however, because there is a slight problem: close and restart the app. Uh oh, all the notes are gone!

Frequently asked questions

Q.1) I still don't understand how `RecyclerAdapter` works?

A) That's because we haven't really discussed it. The reason we have not discussed the behind-the-scenes details is because we don't need to know them. If we override the required functions, as we have just seen, everything will work. This is how `RecyclerAdapter` and most other classes we use are meant to be: hidden implementation with public functions to expose the necessary functionality.

Q.2) I feel like I *need* to know what is going on inside `RecyclerAdapter` and other classes as well. How can I do this?

A) It is true that there are more details for `RecyclerAdapter` (and almost every class that we use in this book) that we don't have the space to discuss. It is good practice to read the official documentation of the classes you use. You can read more about it at `https://developer.android.com/reference/android/support/v7/widget/RecyclerView.Adapter`.

Summary

Now we have added the functionality to hold multiple notes and implemented the ability to display them.

We achieved this by learning about and using the `RecyclerAdapter` class, which implements the `Adapter` interface, which allows us to bind together a `RecyclerView` instance and an `ArrayList` instance, allowing for the seamless display of data without us (the programmer) having to worry about the complex code that is part of these classes, and which we don't even see.

In the next chapter, we will start with making the user's notes persist when they quit the app or switch off their device. In addition, we will create a "Settings" screen, and see how we can make the settings persist as well. We will use different techniques to achieve each of these goals.

17
Data Persistence and Sharing

In this chapter, we will look at a couple of different ways to save data to an Android device's permanent storage. Also, for the first time, we will add a second `Activity` instance to our app. It often makes sense when implementing a separate "screen", such as a "Settings" screen, in our app to do so in a new `Activity` instance. We could go to the trouble of hiding the original UI and then showing the new UI in the same `Activity`, as we did in *Chapter 4, Getting Started with Layouts and Material Design*, but this would quickly lead to confusing and error-prone code. So, we will see how to add another `Activity` instance and navigate the user between them.

In this chapter, we will do the following:

- Learn about the Android `Intent` class to switch `Activity` instances and pass data between them
- Create a very simple settings screen in a new `Activity` instance
- Persist the settings screen data using the `SharedPreferences` class
- Learn about **JavaScript Object Notation** (**JSON**) for serialization
- Explore `try-catch-finally`
- Implement saving data in our Note to self app

The Android Intent class

The `Intent` class is appropriately named. It is a class that demonstrates the intent of an `Activity` instance from our app. It makes intent clear and it also facilitates it.

All our apps so far have had just one `Activity` instance but many Android apps comprise more than one.

In perhaps its most common use, an `Intent` object allows us to switch between `Activity` instances. But, of course, `Activity` instances are made from classes. So, what happens to the data when we switch between these classes? The `Intent` class handles this problem for us as well by allowing us to pass data between them.

`Intent` classes aren't just about wiring up the Activities of our app. They also make it possible to interact with other apps, too. For example, we could provide a link in our app for the user to send an email, make a phone call, interact with social media, or open a web page in a browser, and have the email, dialer, web browser, or relevant social media app do all the work.

There aren't enough pages to really dig deep into interacting with other apps, and so we will mainly focus on switching between Activities and passing data.

Switching Activity

Let's say we have an app with two `Activity`-based classes, and we will soon. We can assume that, as usual, we have an `Activity` instance called `MainActivity`, which is where the app starts, and a second `Activity` instance called `SettingsActivity`. This is how we can swap from `MainActivity` to `SettingsActivity`:

```
// Declare and initialize a new Intent object called myIntent
val myIntent = Intent(this,
        SettingsActivity::class.java)

// Switch to the SettingsActivity
startActivity(myIntent)
```

Look carefully at how we initialized the `Intent` object. `Intent` has a constructor that takes two arguments. The first is a reference to the current `Activity` instance, `this`. The second parameter is the name of the `Activity` instance that we want to open, `SettingsActivity::class`. The `class` on the end of `SettingsActivity` makes it the full name of the `Activity` instance as declared in the `AndroidManifest.xml` file, and we will peek at that when we experiment with `Intent` shortly.

The odd-looking `.java` on the end is because all the Kotlin code is turned into Java byte code, and `SettingsActivity::class.java` is its fully qualified name.

The only problem is that `SettingsActivity` doesn't share any of the data of `MainActivity`. In a way, this is a good thing, because if you need all the data from `MainActivity`, then it is a reasonable indication that switching `Activity` instances might not be the best way of proceeding with your app's design. It is, however, unreasonable to have encapsulation so thorough that the two `Activity` instances know absolutely nothing about each other.

Passing data between Activities

What if we have a sign-in screen for the user, and we want to pass the login credentials to each `Activity` instance of our app? We could do so using the `Intent` class.

We can add data to an `Intent` instance like this:

```
// Create a String called username
// and set its value to bob
val username = "Bob"

// Create a new Intent as we have already seen
val myIntent = Intent(this,
        SettingsActivity::class.java)

// Add the username String to the Intent
// using the putExtra function of the Intent class
myIntent.putExtra("USER_NAME", username)

// Start the new Activity as we have before
startActivity(myIntent)
```

In `SettingsActivity`, we could then retrieve the `String` value like this:

```
// Here we need an Intent also
// But the default constructor will do
// as we are not switching Activity
val myIntent = Intent()

// Initialize username with the passed in String
val username = intent.extras.getString("USER_NAME")
```

In the previous two blocks of code, we switched `Activity` instances in the same way as we have already seen. But, before we called `startActivity`, we used the `putExtra` function to load a `String` value into `myIntent`.

We add data using **key-value pairs**. Each piece of data needs to be accompanied by an **identifier** that can be used in the retrieving `Activity` instance to identify and then retrieve the data.

The identifier name is arbitrary, but useful/memorable values should be used.

Then, in the receiving `Activity` instance, we simply create an `Intent` object using the default constructor:

```
val myIntent = Intent();
```

We can then retrieve the data using the `extras.getString` function and the appropriate identifier from the key-value pair.

The `Intent` class can help us send more complex data than this, but the `Intent` class has its limits. For example, we wouldn't be able to send a `Note` object. Once we want to start sending more than a few values, it is worth considering different tactics.

Adding a settings page to Note to self

Now we are armed with all this knowledge about the Android `Intent` class, we can add another screen (`Activity`) to our Note to self app: a "Settings" screen.

We will first create a new `Activity` instance for our new screen and see what effect that has on the `AndroidManifest.xml` file. We will then create a very simple layout for our settings screen and add the Kotlin code to switch from `MainActivity` to the new one. We will, however, defer wiring up our settings screen layout with Kotlin until we have learned how to save the users preferred settings to disk. We will do this later on in this chapter and then come back to the settings screen to make its data persist.

First, let's code that new `Activity` class. We will call it `SettingsActivity`.

Creating the SettingsActivity

SettingsActivity will be a screen where the user can turn on or off the decorative divider between each note in the `RecyclerView` widget. This will not be a very comprehensive settings screen, but it will be a useful exercise, and we will see switching between the two `Activity` instances in action as well as save data to disk. Follow these steps to get started:

1. In the project explorer window, right-click the folder that contains all your `.kt` files and has the same name as your package. From the pop-up context menu, select **New | Activity | Empty Activity**.
2. In the **Activity Name:** field, enter `SettingsActivity`.
3. Leave all the other options at their defaults and left-click **Finish**.

Android Studio has created a new `Activity` class for us and its associated `.kt` file. Let's take a quick peek at some of the work that was done behind the scenes for us, because it is useful to know what is going on.

Open the `AndroidManifest.xml` file from within the `manifests` folder in the project explorer. Notice the following new line of code near the end of this file:

```
<activity android:name=".SettingsActivity"></activity>
```

This is how an `Activity` class is **registered** with the operating system. If an `Activity` class is not registered, then an attempt to run it will crash the app. We could create an `Activity` class simply by creating a class that extends `Activity` (or `AppCompatActivity`) in a new `.kt` file. However, we would then have had to add the preceding code ourselves. Also, by using the new activity wizard, we got a layout XML file (`activity_settings.xml`) automatically generated for us.

Designing the settings screen layout

We will quickly build a user interface for our settings screen; the following steps and screenshot should make this straightforward:

1. Open the `activity_settings.xml` file and switch to the **Design** tab, where we will quickly lay out our settings screen.
2. Use this next screenshot as a guide while following the rest of the steps:

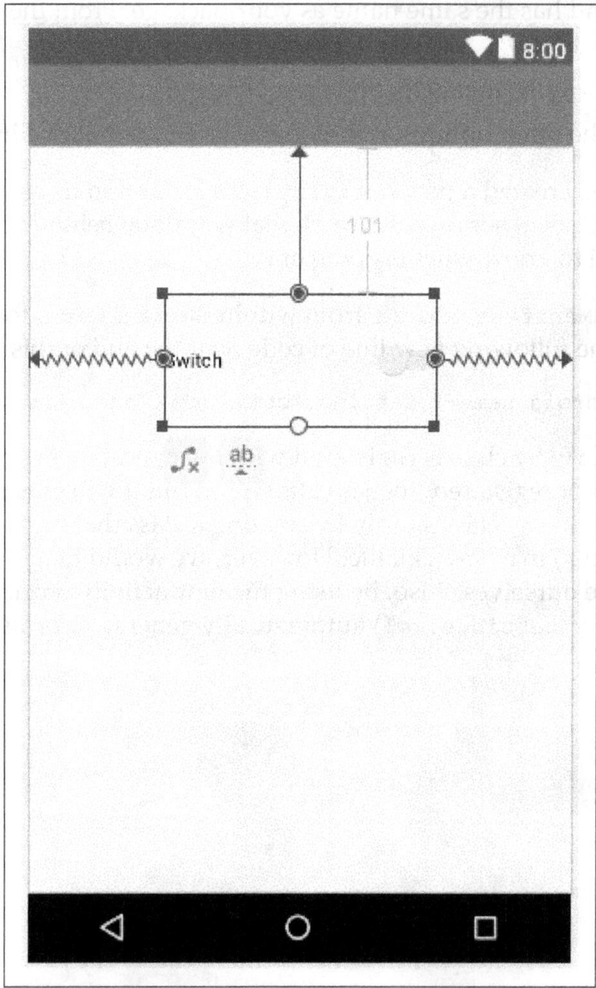

3. Drag and drop a **Switch** widget onto the center-top of the layout. I stretched mine by dragging the edges to make it larger and clearer.

4. Add an `id` attribute of `switch1` (if it isn't already) so that we can interact with it using Kotlin.
5. Use the constraint handles to fix the position of the switch, or click the **Infer Constraints** button to fix it automatically.

We now have a nice (and very simple) new layout for our settings screen, and the `id` property is in place, ready for when we wire it up with our code later in the chapter.

Enabling the user to switch to the "Settings" screen

We already know how to create and switch to a `SettingsActivity` instance. Also, as we won't be passing any data to it or from it, we can get this working with just a few lines of Kotlin code.

You might have noticed in the action bar of our app there is the menu icon. It is indicated in this next screenshot:

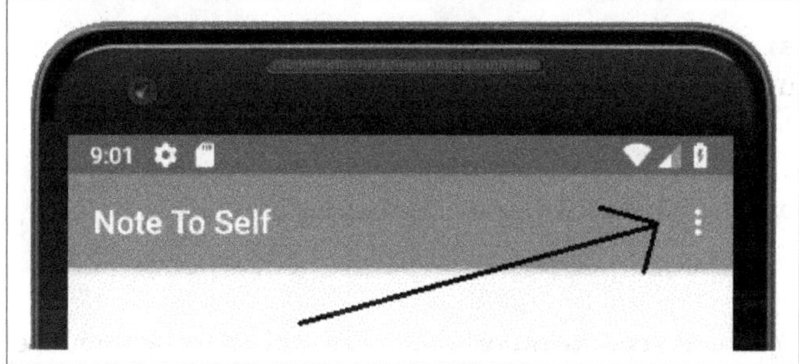

If you tap it, there is already a menu option in there for **Settings**, provided by default when we first created the app. This is what you will see when you tap the menu icon:

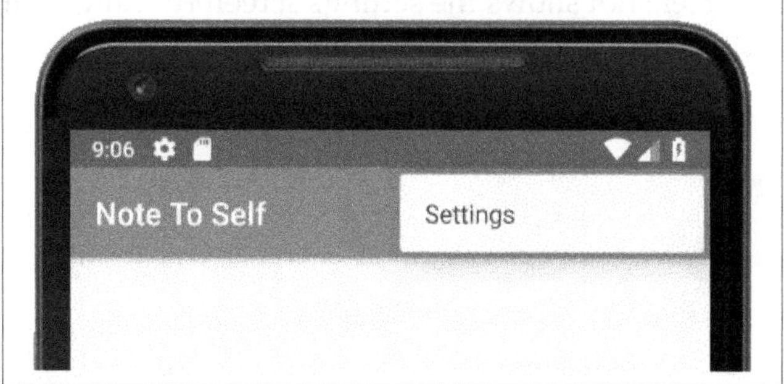

All we need to do is place our code to create and switch to the `SettingsActivity` instance within the `onOptionsItemSelected` function in the `MainActivity.kt` file. Android Studio even provides a `when` block by default for us to paste our code into, on the assumption that we would one day want to add a settings menu. How thoughtful.

Switch to `MainActivity.kt` in the editor window and find the following block of code in the `onOptionsItemSelected` function:

```
return when (item.itemId) {
    R.id.action_settings -> true
    else -> super.onOptionsItemSelected(item)
}
```

Edit the `when` block shown previously to match the following code:

```
return when (item.itemId) {
    R.id.action_settings -> {
            val intent = Intent(this,
                             SettingsActivity::class.java)

            startActivity(intent)
            true
  }

  else -> super.onOptionsItemSelected(item)
}
```

You will need to import the `Intent` class using your preferred technique to add this line of code:

```
import android.content.Intent
```

You can now run the app and visit the new settings screen by tapping the **Settings** menu option. This screenshot shows the settings screen running on the emulator:

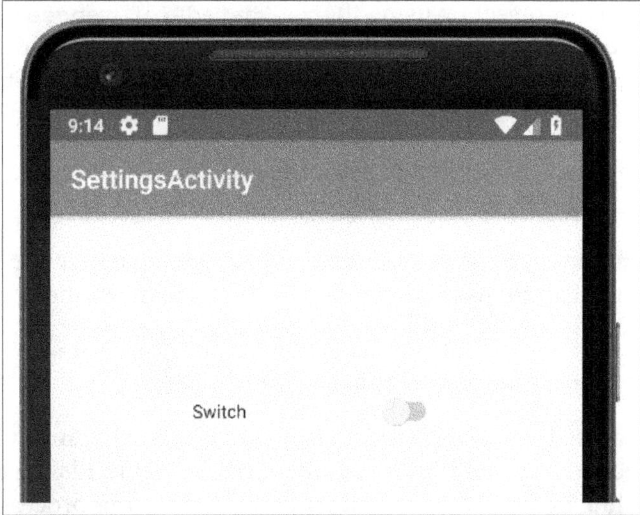

To return from `SettingsActivity` screen to the `MainActivity` screen, you can tap the back button on the device.

Persisting data with SharedPreferences

In Android, there are a few ways to make data persist. By persist, I mean that if the user quits the app, then when they come back to it their data will still be available. Which technique is the correct one to use is dependent upon the app and the type of data.

In this book, we will look at three ways to make data persist. For saving our user's settings, we only need a simple method. After all, we just need to know whether they want the decorative divider between each of the notes in the `RecyclerView` widget.

Let's look at how we can make our apps save and reload variables to the internal storage of the device. We need to use the `SharedPreferences` class. `SharedPreferences` is a class that provides access to data that can be accessed and edited by all the classes of an app. Let's look at how we can use it:

```
// A SharedPreferences instance for reading data
val prefs = getSharedPreferences(
         "My app",
          Context.MODE_PRIVATE)

// A SharedPreferences.Editor instance for writing data
val editor = prefs.edit()
```

We initialized the `prefs` object by using the `getSharedPreferences` function and passing in a `String` value that will be used to refer to all the data read and written using this object. Typically, we could use the name of the app as this String value. In the next code, `Mode_Private` means that any class can access it, but only from this app.

We then used our newly initialized `prefs` object to initialize our `editor` object by calling the `edit` function.

Let's say we wanted to save the user's name, which we have in a `String` instance called `username`. We can then write the data to the internal memory of the device like this:

```
editor.putString("username", username)
```

The first argument used in the `putString` function is a label that can be used to refer to the data, the second argument is the actual variable that holds the data we want to save. The second line in the previous code initiates the saving process. So, we could write multiple variables to disk like this:

```
editor.putString("username", username)
editor.putInt("age", age)
editor.putBoolean("newsletter-subscriber", subscribed)

// Save all the above data
editor.apply()
```

The preceding code demonstrates that you can save other variable types and it, of course, assumes that the `username`, `age`, and `subscribed` variables have previously been declared then initialized with appropriate values.

Once `editor.apply()` has executed, the data is stored. We can quit the app, even turn off the device, and the data will persist.

Reloading data with SharedPreferences

Let's see how we can reload our data the next time the app is run. This code will reload the three values that the previous code saved. We could even declare our variables and initialize them with the stored values:

```
val username  = prefs.getString(
   "username", "new user")

val age  = prefs.getInt("age", -1)

val subscribed = prefs.getBoolean(
    "newsletter-subscriber", false)
```

In the previous code, we load the data from disk using the function appropriate for the data type and the same label we used to save the data in the first place. What is less clear is the second argument to each of the function calls.

The `getString`, `getInt`, and `getBoolean` functions require a default value as the second argument. If there is no data stored with that label, it will then return the default value.

We could then check for these default values in our code and go about trying to obtain the required values or handling an error. For example, see the following code:

```
if (age == -1){
   // Ask the user for his age
}
```

We now know enough to save our user's settings in the Note to self app.

Making the Note to self settings persist

We have already learned how to save data to the device's memory. As we implement saving the user's settings, we will, again, see how we handle the `Switch` widget input and where exactly the code we have just seen will go to make our app work the way we want it to.

Coding the SettingsActivity class

Most of the action will take place in the `SettingsActivity.kt` file. So, click on the appropriate tab and we will add the code a bit at a time.

First, we want a property to represent the user's option on the settings screen - whether they want decorative dividers or not.

Add the following to `SettingsActivity`:

```
private val showDividers: Boolean = true
```

Now, in `onCreate`, add the highlighted code to initialize `prefs`, which is inferred to be a `SharedPreferences` instance:

```
val prefs = getSharedPreferences(
              "Note to self",
               Context.MODE_PRIVATE)
```

Import the `SharedPreferences` class:

```
import android.content.SharedPreferences
```

Next, still in `onCreate`, let's load up the saved data, which represents our user's previous choice for whether to show the dividers. We will set the switch to either on or off, as appropriate:

```
showDividers  = prefs.getBoolean("dividers", true)

// Set the switch on or off as appropriate
switch1.isChecked = showDividers
```

Next, we will create a lambda to handle changes to our `Switch` widget. We simply set the value of `showDividers` to be the same as the `isChecked` variable of the `Switch` widget. Add the following code to the `onCreate` function:

```
switch1.setOnCheckedChangeListener {
   buttonView, isChecked ->

   showDividers = isChecked
}
```

You might have noticed that we did not write any values to the device storage at any point in any of that code. We could have placed it after we detected a change to the switch, but it is much simpler to put it where it is guaranteed to be called - but only once.

We will use our knowledge of the `Activity` lifecycle and override the `onPause` function. When the user leaves the `SettingsActivity` screen, either to go back to the `MainActivity` screen or to quit the app, `onPause` will be called and the settings will be saved. This way, the user can flip the switch as often as they like, and the app will save their final decision. Add this code to override the `onPause` function and save the user's settings. Add the code just before the closing curly brace of the `SettingsActivity` class:

```
override fun onPause() {
   super.onPause()

   // Save the settings here
   val prefs = getSharedPreferences(
            "Note to self",
             Context.MODE_PRIVATE)
```

```
    val editor = prefs.edit()

    editor.putBoolean("dividers", showDividers)

    editor.apply()
}
```

The preceding code declares and initializes a new `SharedPreferences` instance in private mode, using the name of the app. It also declares and initializes a new `SharedPreferences.Editor` instance. Finally, the value is entered into the `editor` object using `putBoolean`, and written to the disk using the `apply` function.

Now, we can add some code to `MainActivity` to load the settings when the app starts, or when the user switches back from the settings screen to the main screen.

Coding the MainActivity class

Add this highlighted code after the `NoteAdapter` declaration:

```
private var adapter: NoteAdapter? = null
private var showDividers: Boolean = false
```

Now we have a `Boolean` property to decide whether to show the dividers. We will override the `onResume` function and initialize our `Boolean` property. Add the overridden `onResume` function, as shown next to the `MainActivity` class:

```
override fun onResume() {
    super.onResume()

    val prefs = getSharedPreferences(
                "Note to self",
                 Context.MODE_PRIVATE)

   showDividers = prefs.getBoolean(
                "dividers", true)
}
```

The user is now able to choose their settings. The app will both save and reload them as necessary, but we need to make `MainActivity` respond to the user's choice.

Find this code in the `onCreate` function and delete it:

```
recyclerView!!.addItemDecoration(
    DividerItemDecoration(this,
          LinearLayoutManager.VERTICAL))
```

The previous code is what set the dividers between each note in the list. Add this new code to the `onResume` function, which is the same line of code surrounded by an `if` statement, to selectively use dividers only when `showDividers` is `true`. Add the code after the previous code in `onResume`:

```
// Add a neat dividing line between list items
if (showDividers)
    recyclerView!!.addItemDecoration(
          DividerItemDecoration(
          this, LinearLayoutManager.VERTICAL))
else {
  // check there are some dividers
  // or the app will crash
  if (recyclerView!!.itemDecorationCount > 0)
        recyclerView!!.removeItemDecorationAt(0)
}
```

Run the app and you'll notice the dividers are gone; go to the settings screen, switch on the dividers, return to the main screen (with the back button), and behold: there are now separators. This next screenshot shows the list with and without separators, photoshopped side by side, to illustrate that the switch works, and that the settings persist between the two `Activity` instances:

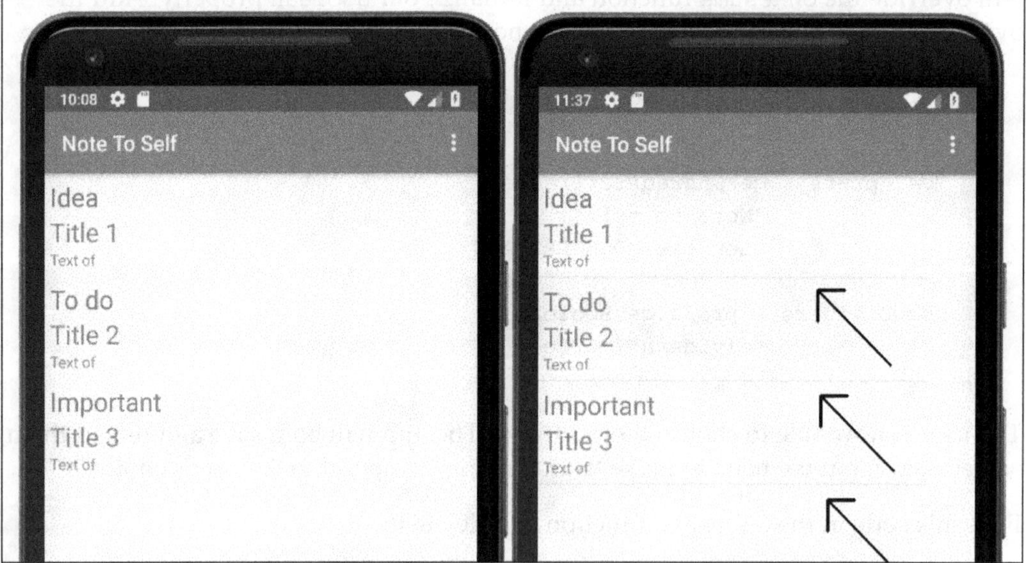

Be sure to try quitting the app and restarting to verify that the settings are saved to disk. You can even turn the emulator off and back on again and the settings will persist.

Now we have a neat settings screen, and we can permanently save the users choices. Of course, the big missing link regarding persistence is that the user's fundamental data, their notes, still does not persist.

More advanced persistence

Let's think about what we need to do. We want to save a bunch of notes to the internal storage. Being more specific, we want to store a selection of Strings and related Boolean values. These Strings and Boolean values represent the user's note title, the text, and whether it is a to-do, important, or an idea.

Given what we already know about the `SharedPreferences` class, at first glance, this might not seem especially challenging - until we dig a little deeper into our requirements. What if the user loves our app and ends up with 100 notes? We would need 100 identifiers for key-value pairs. Not impossible, but starting to get awkward.

Now, imagine that we wanted to enhance the app and give the user the ability to add dates to them. Android has a `Date` class that is perfect for this. It would be reasonably straightforward to then add neat features, such as reminders, to our app. But when it comes to saving data, things suddenly start to get complicated.

How would we store a date using `SharedPreferences`? It wasn't designed for this. We could convert it to a String value when we save it, and then could convert it back again when we load it, but this is far from simple.

And, as our app grows in features and our users get more and more notes, the whole persistence thing becomes a nightmare. What we need is a way to save and load actual Kotlin objects. If we can simply save and load objects, including their internal data (Strings, Booleans, dates, or anything else), our apps can have any kind of data we need to suit our users.

The process of converting data objects into bits and bytes to store on a disk is called **serialization**; the reverse process is called **de-serialization**. Serialization on its own is a vast topic and is far from straightforward. Fortunately, as we are coming to expect, there is a class to handle most of the complexity for us.

What is JSON?

JSON stands for **JavaScript Object Notation**, and it is widely used in fields beyond Android programming. It is perhaps more frequently used for sending data between web applications and servers.

Fortunately, there are JSON classes available for Android that almost entirely hide the complexity of the serialization process. By learning about a few more Kotlin concepts, we can quickly begin to use these classes and start writing entire Kotlin objects to the device storage, rather than worry ourselves about what primitive types make up the objects.

The JSON classes, when compared with other classes we have seen so far, undertake operations that have a higher than normal possibility of failure beyond their control. To find out why this is so and what can be done about it, let's look at **exceptions**.

Exceptions – try, catch, and finally

All this talk of JSON requires us to learn another Kotlin concept: **exceptions**. When we write a class that performs operations that have a possibility of failure, especially for reasons beyond our control, it is advisable to make this plain in our code so that anyone using our class is prepared for the possibility.

Saving and loading data is one such scenario where failure is possible beyond our control. Think about trying to load data when the SD card has been removed or has been corrupted. Another instance where code might fail is perhaps when we write code that relies on a network connection - what if the user goes offline part of the way through a data transfer?

Kotlin exceptions are the solution, and the JSON classes use them, so it is a good time to learn about them.

When we write a class that uses code with a chance of failure, we can prepare the users of our class by using exceptions with `try`, `catch`, and `finally`.

We can write functions in our classes using the `@Throws` annotation before the signature; a bit like this, perhaps:

```
@Throws(someException::class)
fun somePrecariousFunction() {
    // Risky code goes here
}
```

Now, any code that uses `somePrecariousFunction` will need to **handle** the exception. The way that we handle exceptions is by wrapping code in `try` and `catch` blocks; perhaps like this:

```
try {
  ...
  somePrecariousFunction()
  ...

} catch (e: Exception) {
   Log.e("Uh Oh!", "somePrecariousFunction failure", e)
}
```

Optionally, we can also add a `finally` block if we want to take any further action after the `try` and `catch` blocks:

```
finally{
   // More action here
}
```

In our Note to self app, we will take the minimum of necessary action to handle exceptions, and simply output an error to the logcat window, but you could do things such as notify the user, retry the operation, or put into operation some clever back-up plan.

Backing up user data in Note to self

So, with our new-found insight into exceptions, let's modify our Note to self code, and then we can be introduced to `JSONObject` and `JSONException`.

First, let's make some minor modifications to our `Note` class.

Add some more properties that will act as the key in a key-value pair for each aspect of our `Note` class:

```
private val JSON_TITLE = "title"
private val JSON_DESCRIPTION = "description"
private val JSON_IDEA = "idea"
private val JSON_TODO = "todo"
private val JSON_IMPORTANT = "important"
```

Now, add a constructor and an empty default constructor that receives a `JSONObject` reference and throws a `JSONException` error. The body of the first constructor initializes each of the members that define the properties of a single `Note` object by calling the `getString` or `getBoolean` function of the `JSONObject` class, passing in the key as an argument. We also provide an empty constructor, which is required so that we can also create a `Note` object with uninitialized properties:

```
// Constructor
// Only used when created from a JSONObject
@Throws(JSONException::class)
constructor(jo: JSONObject) {

  title = jo.getString(JSON_TITLE)
  description = jo.getString(JSON_DESCRIPTION)
  idea = jo.getBoolean(JSON_IDEA)
  todo = jo.getBoolean(JSON_TODO)
  important = jo.getBoolean(JSON_IMPORTANT)
}

// Now we must provide an empty default constructor for
// when we create a Note to pass to the new note dialog
constructor() {

}
```

You will need to import the `JSONException` and `JSONObject` classes:

```
import org.json.JSONException;
import org.json.JSONObject;
```

The next code we will see will load the property values of a given `Note` object into a `JSONObject` instance. This is where the `Note` object's values are packed up ready for when the actual serialization takes place.

All we need to do is call `put` with the appropriate key and the matching property. This function returns `JSONObject` (we will see where to in a minute) and also throws a `JSONObject` exception. Add the code we have just discussed:

```
@Throws(JSONException::class)
fun convertToJSON(): JSONObject {

  val jo = JSONObject()

  jo.put(JSON_TITLE, title)
```

```
    jo.put(JSON_DESCRIPTION, description)
    jo.put(JSON_IDEA, idea)
    jo.put(JSON_TODO, todo)
    jo.put(JSON_IMPORTANT, important)

    return jo
}
```

Now, let's make a `JSONSerializer` class, which will perform the actual serialization and deserialization. Create a new Kotlin class and call it `JSONSerializer`.

Let's split up the coding into a few chunks and talk about what we are doing as we code each chunk.

First, the declaration and a couple of properties: a `String` instance to hold the filename where the data will be saved, and a `Context` instance, which is necessary in Android for writing data to a file. Edit the `JSONSerializer` class code to be the same as the following:

```
class JSONSerializer(
    private val filename: String,
    private val context: Context) {
    // All the rest of the code goes here

}
```

You will need to import the `Context` class:

```
import android.content.Context
```

Now we can start coding the real guts of the class. The `save` function is next. It first creates a `JSONArray` object, which is a specialized `ArrayList` class for handling JSON objects.

Next, the code uses a `for` loop to go through all the `Note` objects in `notes` and convert them to JSON objects using the `convertToJSON` function from the `Note` class that we added previously. Then, we load these converted `JSONObjects` into `jArray`.

Next, the code uses a `Writer` instance and an `Outputstream` instance combined to write the data to an actual file. Notice that the `OutputStream` instance needed the `Context` object. Add the code we have just discussed:

```
@Throws(IOException::class, JSONException::class)
fun save(notes: List<Note>) {

    // Make an array in JSON format
    val jArray = JSONArray()

    // And load it with the notes
    for (n in notes)
          jArray.put(n.convertToJSON())

   // Now write it to the private disk space of our app
   var writer: Writer? = null
   try {
     val out = context.openFileOutput(filename,
                 Context.MODE_PRIVATE)

     writer = OutputStreamWriter(out)
     writer.write(jArray.toString())

   } finally {
         if (writer != null) {

         writer.close()
      }
   }
}
```

You will need to add the following import statements for these new classes:

```
import org.json.JSONArray
import org.json.JSONException
import java.io.IOException
import java.io.OutputStream
import java.io.OutputStreamWriter
import java.io.Writer
import java.util.List
```

Now for the de-serialization - loading the data. This time, as we might expect, the function has no parameters, but instead returns `ArrayList`. An `InputStream` instance is created using `context.openFileInput`, and our file containing all our data is opened.

We use a `for` loop to append all the data to a `String` object and use our new `Note` constructor, which extracts JSON data to regular properties to unpack each `JSONObject` into a `Note` object and add it to `ArrayList`, which is finally returned to the calling code. Add the `load` function:

```
@Throws(IOException::class, JSONException::class)
fun load(): ArrayList<Note> {
   val noteList = ArrayList<Note>()
   var reader: BufferedReader? = null

   try {

         val `in` = context.openFileInput(filename)
         reader = BufferedReader(InputStreamReader(`in`))
         val jsonString = StringBuilder()

    for (line in reader.readLine()) {
          jsonString.append(line)
    }

    val jArray = JSONTokener(jsonString.toString()).
                 nextValue() as JSONArray

    for (i in 0 until jArray.length()) {
           noteList.add(Note(jArray.getJSONObject(i)))
    }

  } catch (e: FileNotFoundException) {
         // we will ignore this one, since it happens
        // when we start fresh. You could add a log here.

  } finally {
   // This will always run
            reader!!.close()
  }

  return noteList
}
```

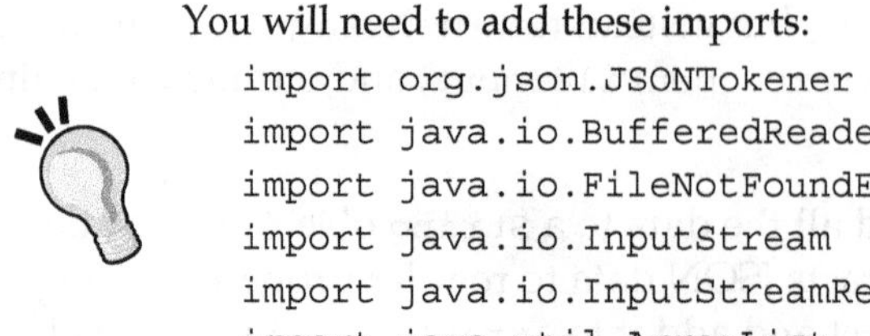

You will need to add these imports:

```
import org.json.JSONTokener
import java.io.BufferedReader
import java.io.FileNotFoundException
import java.io.InputStream
import java.io.InputStreamReader
import java.util.ArrayList
```

Now, all we need to do is put our new class to work in the `MainActivity` class. Add a new property after the `MainActivity` declaration as shown next. Also, remove the initialization of `noteList` to leave just the declaration, as we will now initialize it with some new code in the `onCreate` function. I have commented out the line you need to delete:

```
private var mSerializer: JSONSerializer? = null
private var noteList: ArrayList<Note>? = null
//private val noteList = ArrayList<Note>()
```

Now, in the `onCreate` function, we initialize `mSerializer` by calling the `JSONSerializer` constructor with the filename and `getApplicationContext()`, which is the `Context` instance of the application and is required. We can then use the `JSONSerializer load` function to load any saved data. Add this new highlighted code after the code that handles the floating action button. This new code must come before the code where we initialize the `RecyclerView` instance:

```
fab.setOnClickListener { view ->
   val dialog = DialogNewNote()
   dialog.show(supportFragmentManager, "")
}

mSerializer = JSONSerializer("NoteToSelf.json",
         applicationContext)

try {
   noteList = mSerializer!!.load()
} catch (e: Exception) {
   noteList = ArrayList()
   Log.e("Error loading notes: ", "", e)
}

recyclerView =
         findViewById<View>(R.id.recyclerView)
```

```
        as RecyclerView

adapter = NoteAdapter(this, this.noteList!!)
val layoutManager = LinearLayoutManager(
         applicationContext)
```

I have shown a great deal of context in the previous code because its correct positioning is necessary for it to work. If you are having any problems getting this to work, be sure to compare it to the code in the download bundle in the `Chapter17/Note to self` folder.

Now, add a new function to our `MainActivity` class so that that we can call it to save all our user's data. All that this new function does is call the `save` function of the `JSONSerializer` class, passing in the required list of `Note` objects:

```
private fun saveNotes() {
  try {
        mSerializer!!.save(this.noteList!!)

  } catch (e: Exception) {
        Log.e("Error Saving Notes", "", e)
  }
}
```

Now, we will override the `onPause` function to save our user's data just as we did when saving our user's settings. Be sure to add this code in the `MainActivity` class:

```
override fun onPause() {
   super.onPause()

   saveNotes()
}
```

That's it. We can now run the app and add as many notes as we like. The `ArrayList` instance will store them all in our running app, our `RecyclerAdapter` will manage displaying them in the `RecyclerView` widget, and now JSON will take care of loading them from disk and saving them back to disk as well.

Frequently asked questions

Q.1) I didn't understand everything in this chapter, so am I cut out to be a programmer?

A) This chapter introduced many new classes, concepts, and functions. If your head is aching a little, that is to be expected. If some of the detail is unclear, don't let it hold you back. Proceed with the next couple of chapters (they are much more straightforward), then revisit this one, and especially examine the completed code files.

Q.2) So, how does serialization work in detail?

A) Serialization really is a vast topic. It is possible to write apps your whole life and never really need to understand it. It is the type of topic that would be the subject of a computer science degree. If you are curious to know more, have a look at this article: `https://en.wikipedia.org/wiki/Serialization`.

Summary

At this point in our journey through the Android API, it is worth taking stock of what we know. We can lay out our own UI designs, and can choose from a wide and diverse range of widgets to allow the user to interact. We can create multiple screens, as well as pop-up dialogs, and we can capture comprehensive user data. Furthermore, we can now make this data persist.

Certainly, there is a lot more to the Android API still to learn, even beyond what this book will teach you, but the point is that we know enough now to plan and implement a working app. You could get started on your own app right now.

If you have the urge to start your own project right away, then my advice is to go ahead and do it. Don't wait until you consider yourself "expert" or more ready. Reading this book and, more importantly, implementing the apps will make you a better Android programmer, but nothing will teach you faster than designing and implementing your own app! It is perfectly possible to read this book and work on your own project simultaneously.

In the next chapter, we will add the finishing touches to this app by making it multilingual. This is quite quick and easy.

18
Localization

This chapter is quick and simple, but what we will learn to do can make your app accessible to millions of potential users. We will see how to add additional languages and we will see why adding text the correct way via String resources benefits us when it comes to adding multiple languages.

In this chapter, we will do the following:

- Make the Note to self app multilingual by adding the Spanish and German languages
- Learn how to better use **String resources**

Let's get started.

Making the Note to self app Spanish, English, and German

First, we need to add some folders to our project - one for each new language. The text is classed as a **resource**, and, consequently, needs to go in the `res` folder. Follow these steps to add Spanish support to the project.

While the source files for this project are provided in the `Chapter18` folder, they are just for reference. You need to go through the processes described next to achieve multilingual functionality.

Adding Spanish support

Follow the next steps to add the Spanish language:

1. Right-click on the `res` folder, then select **New** | **Android resource directory**. In the **Directory name** field, type `values-es`.
2. Now we need to add a file in which we can place all our Spanish translations.
3. Right-click on `res`, then select **New** | **Android resource file** and type `strings.xml` in the **File name** field. Type `values-es` in the **Directory name** field.

We now have a `strings.xml` file that any device set to use the Spanish language will refer to. To be clear, we now have two distinct `strings.xml` files.

Adding German support

Follow these steps to add German language support.

1. Right-click on the `res` folder then select **New** | **Android resource directory**. In the **Directory name** field, type `values-de`.
2. Now we need to add a file in which we can place all our German translations.
3. Right-click on `res`, then select **New** | **Android resource file** and type `strings.xml` in the **File name** field. Type `values-de` in the **Directory name** field.

The following screenshot shows what the `strings.xml` folder looks like. You are probably wondering where the `strings.xml` folder came from, as it doesn't correspond to the structure we seemed to be creating in the previous steps.

Android Studio is helping us to organize our files and folders as it is required by the Android operating system in the APK format. You can, however, clearly see the Spanish and German files indicated by their flags as well as their **(de)** and **(es)** postfixes:

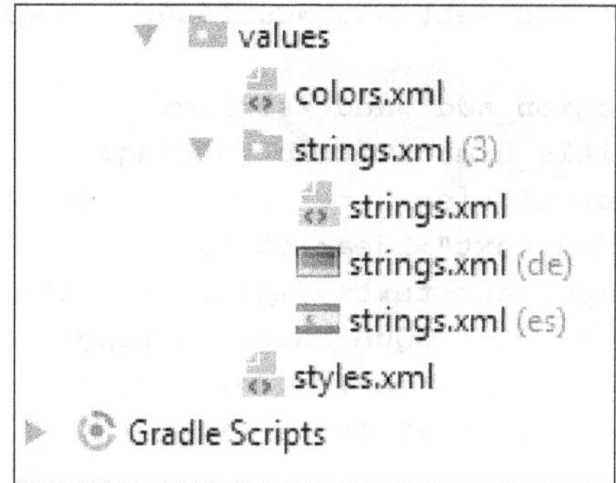

Depending on your Android Studio settings, you might not see the country flag icons. Provided that you can see three `strings.xml` files, one without a postfix, one with **(de)**, and one with **(es)**, then you are ready to continue.

Now we can add the translations to the files we just created.

Adding the String resources

As we know, the `strings.xml` file contains the words that the app will display, words such as important, to-do, and idea. By having a `strings.xml` file for each language we want to support, we can then leave Android to choose the appropriate text depending upon the language settings of the user.

As you go through the following, notice that, although we place the translation of whatever word we are translating as the value, the `name` attribute remains the same. If you think about it, this is logical, because it is the `name` attribute that we refer to in our layout files.

Let's provide the translations, see what we have achieved, and then come back and discuss what we will do about text in our Kotlin code.

The simplest way to achieve this code is to copy and paste the code from the original `strings.xml` file and then edit the values of each of the `name` attributes:

1. Open the `strings.xml` file by double-clicking it. Be sure to choose the one next to the Spanish flag or **(es)** postfix. Edit the file to look like this:

```
<?xml version="1.0" encoding="utf-8"?>
<resources>
<string name="app_name">Nota a sí mismo</string>
```

```
<string name="action_settings">Configuración</string>

<string name="action_add">add</string>
<string name="title_hint">Título</string>
<string name="description_hint">Descripción</string>
<string name="idea_text">Idea</string>
<string name="important_text">Importante</string>
<string name="todo_text">Que hacer</string>
<string name="cancel_button">Cancelar</string>
<string name="ok_button">Vale</string>

<string name="settings_title">Configuración</string>
<string name="title_activity_settings">Configuración</string>

</resources>
```

2. Open the `strings.xml` file by double-clicking it. Be sure to choose the one next to the German flag or **(de)** postfix. Edit the file to look like this:

```
<?xml version="1.0" encoding="utf-8"?>
<resources>
<string name="app_name">Hinweis auf selbst</string>
<string name="action_settings">Einstellungen</string>

<string name="action_add">add</string>
<string name="title_hint">Titel</string>
<string name="description_hint">Beschreibung</string>
<string name="idea_text">Idee</string>
<string name="important_text">Wichtig</string>
<string name="todo_text">zu tun</string>
<string name="cancel_button">Abbrechen</string>
<string name="ok_button">Okay</string>

<string name="settings_title">Einstellungen</string>
<string name="title_activity_settings">Einstellungen</string>
</resources>
```

If you don't provide all the string resources in the extra (Spanish and German) `strings.xml` files, then the missing resources will be taken from the default file.

What we have done is provided two translations. Android knows which translation is for which language because of the folders they are placed in. Furthermore, we have used a **String identifier** (the `name` attribute) to refer to the translations. Look back at the previous code and you will see that the same identifier is used for both translations as well as in the original `strings.xml` file.

You can even localize to different versions of a language, such as US or United Kingdom English. The complete list of codes can be found at `http://stackoverflow.com/questions/7973023/what-is-the-list-of-supported-languages-locales-on-android`. You can even localize resources such as images and sound. Find out more about this at `http://developer.android.com/guide/topics/resources/localization.html`.

The translations were copy and pasted from Google translate, so it is very likely that some of the translations are far from correct. Doing translation on the cheap like this can be an effective way to get an app with a basic set of String resources onto devices of users who speak different languages to yourself. Once you start having any depth of translation needed, perhaps for the lines of a story-driven game or social media app, you will certainly benefit from having the translation done by a human professional.

The purpose of this exercise is to show how Android works, not how to translate.

My sincere apologies to any Spanish or German speakers who are likely to be able to see the limitations of the translations provided here.

Now that we have the translations, we can see them in action - up to a point.

Running Note to self in German or Spanish

Run the app to see whether it is working as expected. Now, we can change the localization settings to see it in Spanish. Different devices vary slightly in how to do this, but the Pixel 2 XL emulator can be changed by clicking on the **Custom Locale** app:

Next, select **es-ES** and then click the **SELECT 'ES'** button in the bottom-left of the screen, as shown in the next screenshot:

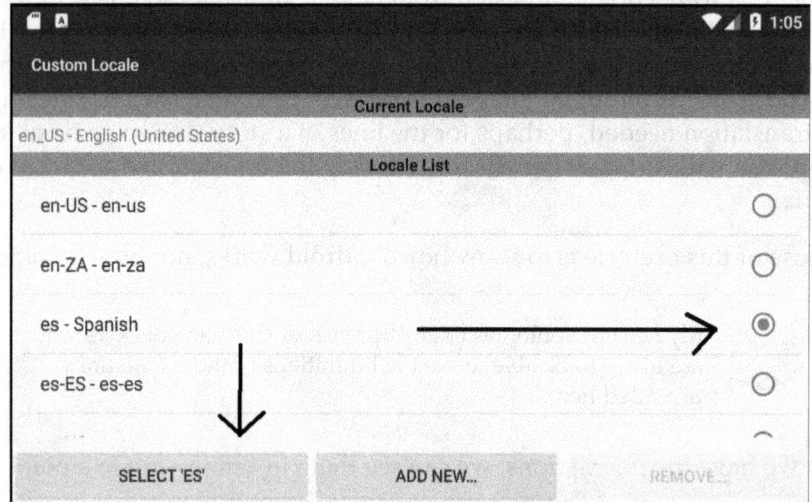

Now you can run the app in the usual way. Here is a screenshot showing the app running in Spanish. I have photoshopped a few images side by side to show a few different screens of the Note to self app:

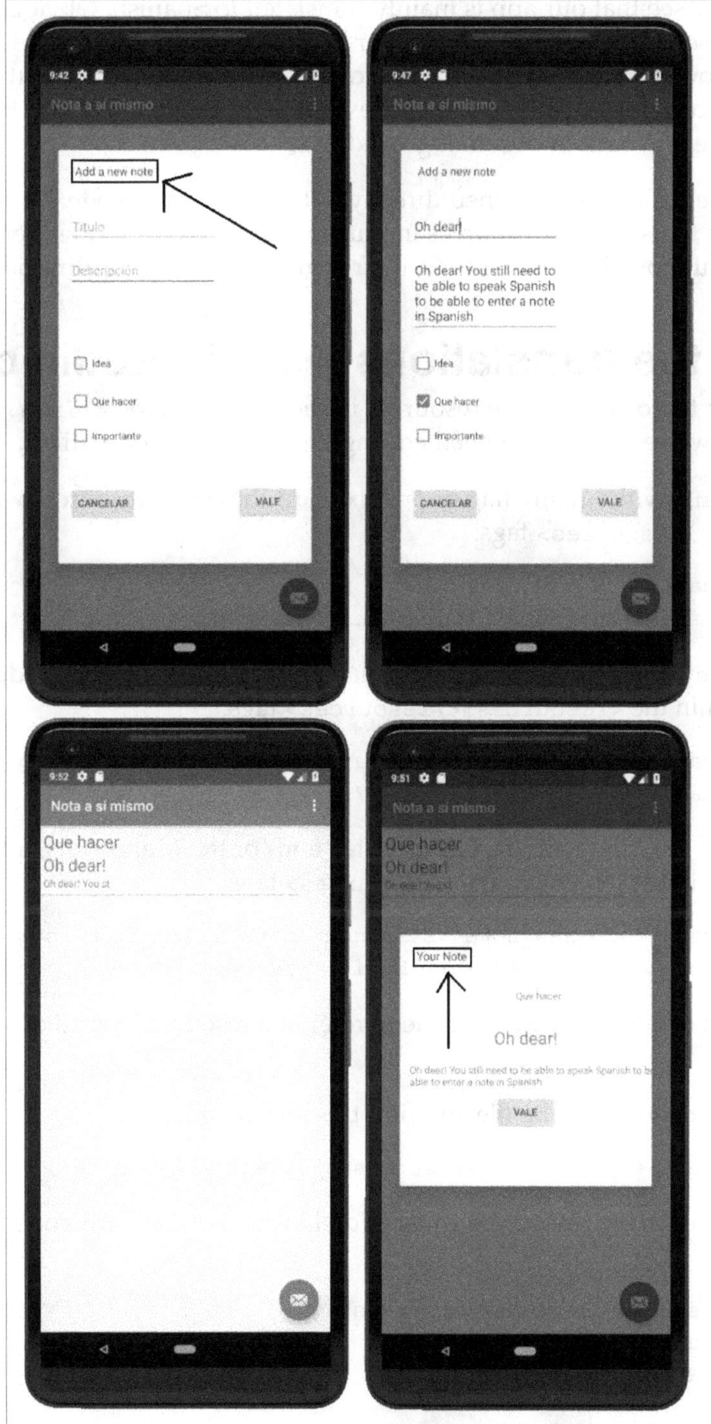

Nota a sí mismo
Add a new note
Titulo
Descripción
Idea
Que hacer
Importante
CANCELAR
VALE
Oh dear
Oh dear! You still need to be able to speak Spanish to be able to enter a note in Spanish
Que hacer
Oh dear!
Your Note

You can clearly see that our app is mainly translated to Spanish. Obviously, the text that the user enters will be in whatever language they speak – that is not a flaw of our app. However, look at the images closely and you will notice that I have pointed out a couple of places where the text is still in English. We still have some untranslated text in each of our dialog windows.

This is because the text is contained directly within our Kotlin code. As we have seen, it is easy to use String resources in multiple languages and then refer to them in our layouts, but how do we refer to String resources from our Kotlin code?

Making the translations work in Kotlin code

The first thing to do is create the resources in each of the three `strings.xml` files. Here are the two resources that need adding to the three different files.

In `strings.xml` (without any flag or postfix), add these two resources within the `<resources></resources>` tags:

```
<string name="add_new_note">Add a new note</string>
<string name="your_note">Your note</string>
```

In the `strings.xml` file with the Spanish flag and/or the **(es)** postfix, add these two resources within the `<resources></resources>` tags:

```
<string name="add_new_note">Agregar una nueva nota</string>
<string name="your_note">Su nota</string>
```

In the `strings.xml` file with the German flag and/or the **(de)** postfix, add these two resources within the `<resources></resources>` tags:

```
<string name="add_new_note">Eine neue Note hinzufügen</string>
<string name="your_note">Ihre Notiz</string>
```

Next, we need to edit some Kotlin code to refer to a resource instead of a hard-coded String.

Open the `DialogNewNote.kt` file and find this line of code:

```
builder.setView(dialogView).setMessage("Add a new note")
```

Edit it to use the String resource we just added instead of the hard-coded text as shown next:

```
builder.setView(dialogView).setMessage(
      resources.getString(
         R.string.add_new_note))
```

The new code uses the chained `setView`, `setMessage`, and `resources.getString` functions to replace the previously hard-coded `"Add a new note"` text. Look closely, and you will see that the argument sent to `getString` is the String `R.string.add_new_note` identifier.

The `R.string` code refers to the String resources in the `res` folder, and `add_new_note` is our identifier. Android will then be able to decide which version (default, Spanish, or German) is appropriate based upon the locale of the device on which the app is running.

We have one more hard-coded String resource to change.

Open the `DialogShowNote.kt` file and find this line of code:

```
builder.setView(dialogView).setMessage("Your Note")
```

Edit it to use the String resource we just added instead of the hard-coded text as shown next:

```
builder.setView(dialogView).setMessage(
        resources.getString(R.string.your_note))
```

The new code again uses the chained `setView`, `setMessage`, and `resources.getString` functions to replace the previously hard-coded `"Your note"` text. And, again, the argument sent to `getString` is the String identifier, in this case `R.string.your_note`.

Android can now decide which version (default, Spanish, or German) is appropriate based upon the locale of the device on which the app is running. The next screenshot shows that the new note screen now has the opening text in the appropriate language:

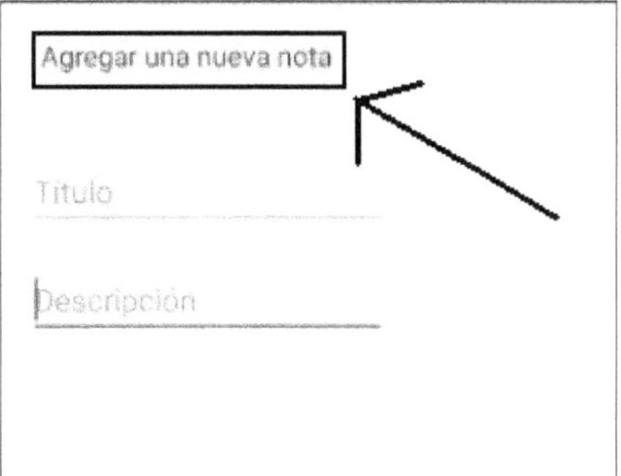

You can add as many String resources as you like. As a reminder from *Chapter 3, Exploring Android Studio and the Project Structure,* note that using String resources is the recommended way to add all text to all projects. The tutorials in this book (apart from Note to Self) will tend to hard-code them to make a more compact tutorial.

Summary

We can now go global with our apps, as well as add the more flexible String resources instead of hard-coding all the text.

In the next chapter, we will see how we can add cool animations to our layouts using animations and interpolators.

19
Animations and Interpolations

Here, we will see how we can use the `Animation` class to make our UI a little less static and a bit more interesting. As we have come to expect, the Android API will allow us to do some quite advanced things with relatively straightforward code, and the `Animation` class is no different.

This chapter can be approximately divided into these parts:

- An introduction to how animations in Android work and are implemented
- An introduction to a UI widget that we haven't explored yet, the `SeekBar` class
- A working animation app

First, let's explore how animations work in Android.

Animations in Android

The normal way to create an animation in Android is through XML. We can write XML animations, and then load and play them through our Kotlin code on a specified UI widget. So, for example, we can write an animation that fades in and out five times over three seconds, then play that animation on an `ImageView` or any other widget. We can think of these XML animations as a script, as they define the type, order, and timing.

Let's explore some of the different properties we can assign to our animations, how to use them in our Kotlin code, and finally, we can make a neat animations app to try it all out.

Designing cool animations in XML

We have learned that XML can be used to describe animations as well as UI layouts, but let's find out exactly how. We can state values for properties of an animation that describe the starting and ending appearance of a widget. The XML can then be loaded by our Kotlin code by referencing the name of the XML file that contains the animation and turning it into a usable Kotlin object, again, not unlike a UI layout.

Many animation properties come in pairs. Here is a quick look at some of the animation property pairs we can use to create an animation. Straight after we have looked at some XML, we will see how to use it.

Fading in and out

Alpha is the measure of transparency. So, by stating the starting `fromAlpha` and ending `toAlpha` values, we can fade items in and out. A value of `0.0` is invisible, and `1.0` is an object's normal appearance. Steadily moving between the two makes a fading-in effect:

```
<alpha
   android:fromAlpha = "0.0"
   android:toAlpha = "1.0" />
```

Move it, move it

We can move an object within our UI by using a similar technique; `fromXDelta` and `toXDelta` can have their values set as a percentage of the size of the object being animated.

The following code would move an object from left to right a distance equal to the width of the object itself:

```
<translate
android:fromXDelta = "-100%"
android:toXDelta = "0%"/>
```

In addition, there are the `fromYDelta` and `toYDelta` properties for animating upward and downward movement.

Scaling or stretching

The `fromXScale` and `toXScale` properties will increase or decrease the scale of an object. As an example, the following code will change the object running the animation from normal size to invisible:

```
<scale
android:fromXScale = "1.0"
android:fromYScale = "0.0"/>
```

As another example, we could shrink the object to a tenth of its usual size using `android:fromYScale = "0.1"`, or make it 10 times as big using `android:fromYScale = "10.0"`.

Controlling the duration

Of course, none of these animations would be especially interesting if they just instantly arrived at their conclusion. To make our animations more interesting, we can therefore set their duration in milliseconds. A millisecond is one thousandth of a second. We can also make timing easier, especially in relation to other animations, by setting the `startOffset` property, which is also in milliseconds.

The next code would begin an animation one third of a second after we started it (in code), and it would take two thirds of a second to complete:

```
android:duration = "666"
android:startOffset = "333"
```

Rotate animations

If you want to spin something around, just use the `fromDegrees` and `toDegrees` properties. This next code, probably predictably, will spin a widget around in a complete circle because, of course, there are 360 degrees in a circle:

```
<rotate android:fromDegrees = "360"
        android:toDegrees = "0"
/>
```

Repeating animations

Repetition might be important in some animations, perhaps a wobble or shake effect, so we can add a `repeatCount` property. In addition, we can specify how the animation is repeated by setting the `repeatMode` property.

The following code would repeat an animation 10 times, each time reversing the direction of the animation. The `repeatMode` property is relative to the current state of the animation. What this means is that if you rotated a button from 0 to 360 degrees, for example, the second part of the animation (the first repeat) would rotate the other way, from 360 back to 0. The third part of the animation (the second repeat) would, again, reverse and rotate from 0 to 360:

```
android:repeatMode = "reverse"
android:repeatCount = "10"
```

Combining an animation's properties with sets

To combine groups of these effects, we need a `set` of properties. This code shows how we can combine all the previous code snippets we have just seen into an actual XML animation that will compile:

```
<?xml version="1.0" encoding="utf-8"?>
<set xmlns:android="http://schemas.android.com/apk/res/android"
     ...All our animations go here
</set>
```

We still haven't seen any Kotlin with which to bring these animations to life. Let's fix that now.

Instantiating animations and controlling them with Kotlin code

This next snippet of code shows how we would declare an object of the `Animation` type, initialize it with an animation contained in an XML file named `fade_in.xml`, and start the animation on an `ImageView` widget. We will soon do this in a project and also see where we can put the XML animations:

```
// Declare an Animation object
var animFadeOut: Animation? = null

// Initialize it
animFadeIn = AnimationUtils.loadAnimation(
                this, R.anim.fade_in)

// Start the animation on the ImageView
// with an id property set to imageView
imageView.startAnimation(animFadeIn)
```

We already have quite a powerful arsenal of animations and control features for things such as timing. But the Android API gives us a little bit more than this as well.

More animation features

We can listen for the status of animations much like we can listen for clicks on a button. We can also use **interpolators** to make our animations more life-like and pleasing. Let's look at listeners first.

Listeners

If we implement the `AnimationListener` interface, we can indeed listen to the status of animations by overriding the three functions that tell us when something has occurred. We could then act based on these events.

`OnAnimationEnd` announces the end of an animation, `onAnimationRepeat` is called each time an animation begins a repeat, and - perhaps predictably - `onAnimationStart` is called when an animation has started animating. This might not be the same time as when `startAnimation` is called if a `startOffset` is set in the animations XML:

```
override fun onAnimationEnd(animation: Animation) {
   // Take some action here

}

override fun onAnimationStart(animation: Animation) {

   // Take some action here

}

override fun onAnimationRepeat(animation: Animation){

   // Take some action here

}
```

We will see how `AnimationListener` works in the Animations demo app, and we'll also put another widget, `SeekBar`, into action.

Animation interpolators

If you can think back to high school, you might remember exciting lessons about calculating acceleration. If we animated something at a constant speed, at first glance, things might seem OK. If we then compared the animation to another that uses gradual acceleration, then the latter would almost certainly be more pleasing to watch.

It is possible that if we were not told the only difference between the two animations was that one used acceleration and the other didn't, we wouldn't be able to say *why* we preferred it. Our brains are more receptive to things that conform to the norms of the world around us. Therefore, adding a bit of real-world physics, such as acceleration and deceleration, improves our animations.

The last thing we want to do, however, is start doing a bunch of mathematical calculations just to slide a button onto the screen or spin some text in a circle.

This is where **interpolators** come in. They are animation modifiers that we can set in a single line of code within our XML.

Some examples of interpolators are `accelerate_interpolator` and `cycle_interpolator`:

```
android:interpolator="@android:anim/accelerate_interpolator"
android:interpolator="@android:anim/cycle_interpolator"/>
```

We will put some interpolators, along with some XML animations and the related Kotlin code, into action next.

You can learn more about interpolators and the Android `Animation` class on the Android developer website here: `http://developer.android.com/guide/topics/resources/animation-resource.html`.

Animations demo app – introducing SeekBar

That's enough theory, especially with something that should be so visible. Let's build an animation demo app that explores everything we have just discussed, and a bit more as well.

This app involves small amounts of code in lots of different files. Therefore, I have tried to make it plain what code is in what file, so you can keep track of what is going on. This will make the Kotlin we write for this app more understandable as well.

The app will demonstrate rotations, fades, translations, animation events, interpolations, and controlling duration with a `SeekBar` widget. The best way to explain what `SeekBar` does is to build it and then watch it in action.

Laying out the animation demo

Create a new project called `Animation Demo` using the **Empty Activity** template, leaving all the other settings at their usual settings. As usual, should you wish to speed things up by copying and pasting the layout, the code, or the animation XML, it can all be found in the `Chapter19` folder.

Use the following reference screenshot of the finished layout to help guide you through the next steps:

Here is how you can lay out the UI for this app:

1. Open `activity_main.xml` in the design view of the editor window.
2. Delete the default **Hello world!** `TextView`.

3. Add an **ImageView** to the top-center portion of the layout. Use the previous reference screenshot to guide you. Use the `@mipmap/ic_launcher` to show the Android robot in `ImageView` when prompted to do so by selecting **Project | ic_launcher** in the pop-up **Resources** window.
4. Set the `id` property of the `ImageView` to `imageView`.
5. Directly below the `ImageView`, add a `TextView`. Set the `id` to `textStatus`. I made my `TextView` a little bigger by dragging its edges (not the constraint handles) and changed its `textSize` attribute to `40sp`. The layout so far should look something like this next screenshot:

6. Now we will add a large selection of **Button** widgets to the layout. Exact positioning is not vital, but the exact `id` property values we add to them later in the tutorial will be. Follow this next screenshot to lay out 12 buttons in the layout. Alter the `text` attribute so that your buttons have the same text as those in the next screenshot. The `text` attributes are detailed specifically in the next step in case the screenshot isn't clear enough:

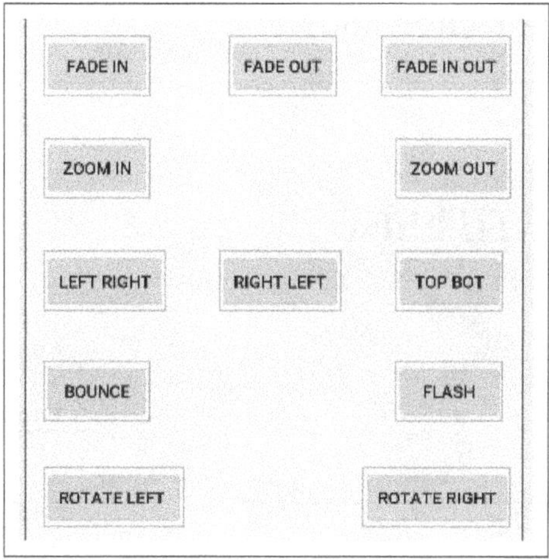

To make the process of laying out the buttons quicker, lay them out just approximately at first, then add the `text` attributes from the next step, and then fine-tune the button positions to get a neat layout.

7. Add the `text` values as they are in the screenshot; here are all the values from left to right and top to bottom: `FADE IN`, `FADE OUT`, `FADE IN OUT`, `ZOOM IN`, `ZOOM OUT`, `LEFT RIGHT`, `RIGHT LEFT`, `TOP BOT`, `BOUNCE`, `FLASH`, `ROTATE LEFT`, and `ROTATE RIGHT`.
8. Add a `SeekBar` widget from the **Widgets** category of the palette, on the left, below the buttons. Set the `id` property to `seekBarSpeed` and the `max` property to `5000`. This means that `SeekBar` widget will hold a value between 0 and 5,000 as it is dragged by the user from left to right. We will see how we can read and use this data soon.

9. We want to make the `SeekBar` widget much wider. To achieve this, you use the exact same technique as with any widget; just drag the edges of the widget. However, as the `SeekBar` widget is quite small, it is hard to increase its size without accidentally selecting the constraint handles. To overcome this problem, zoom into the design view by holding the *Ctrl* key and rolling the middle mouse wheel forward. You can then grab the edges of the `SeekBar` widget without touching the constraint handles. I have shown this in action in the next screenshot:

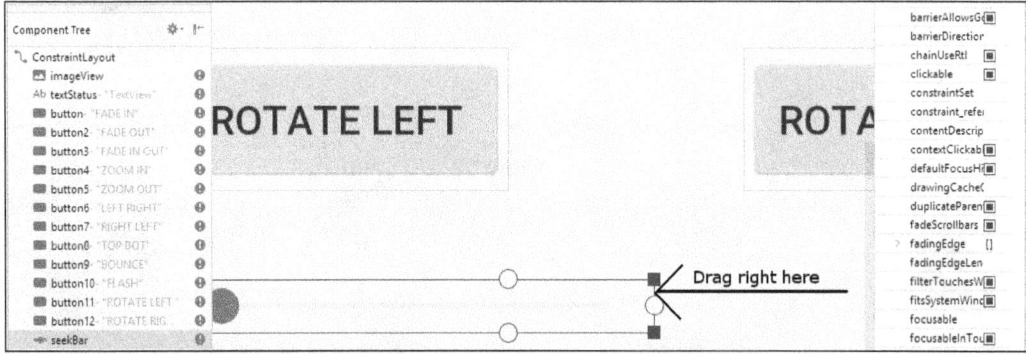

10. Now, add a `TextView` widget just to the right of the `SeekBar` widget and set its `id` property to `textSeekerSpeed`. This step, combined with the previous two, should look like this screenshot:

11. Tweak the positions to look like the reference screenshot at the start of these steps, and then click the **Infer Constraints** button to lock the positions. Of course, you can do this manually if you want the practice. Here is a screenshot with all the constraints in place:

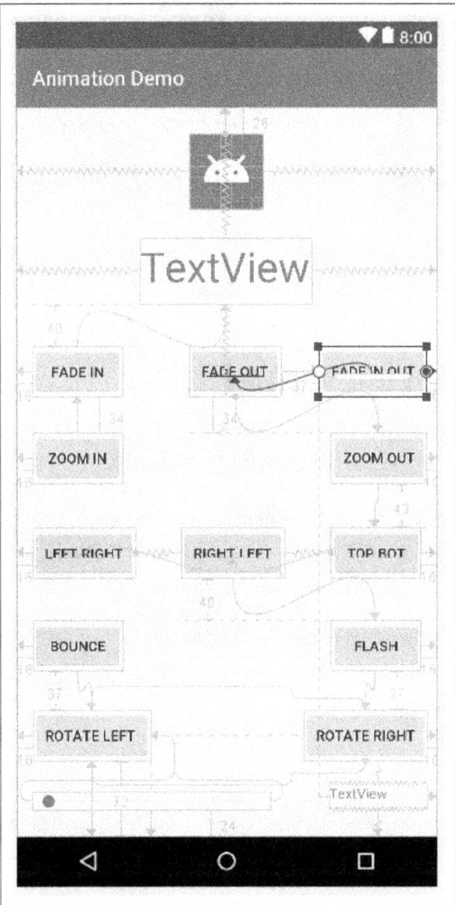

12. Next, add the following `id` properties to the buttons, as identified by the text property that you have already set. If you are asked whether you want to **Update usages...** as you enter these values, select **Yes**:

Existing text property	**Value of id property to set**
Fade In	`btnFadeIn`
Fade Out	`btnFadeOut`
Fade In Out	`btnFadeInOut`
Zoom In	`btnZoomIn`
Zoom Out	`btnZoomOut`
Left Right	`btnLeftRight`
Right Left	`btnRightLeft`
Top Bot	`btnTopBottom`

Existing text property	Value of id property to set
Bounce	btnBounce
Flash	btnFlash
Rotate Left	btnRotateLeft
Rotate Right	btnRotateRight

We will see how to use this newcomer to our UI (`SeekBar`) when we get to coding the `MainActivity` class in a few sections time.

Coding the XML animations

Right-click on the **res** folder and select **New | Android resource directory**. Enter `anim` in the `Directory name:` field and left-click **OK**.

Now right-click on the new **anim** directory and select **New | Animation resource file**. In the **File name:** field, type `fade_in` and then left-click **OK**. Delete the contents and add this code to create the animation:

```
<?xml version="1.0" encoding="utf-8"?>
<set xmlns:android="http://schemas.android.com/apk/res/android"
   android:fillAfter="true" >

   <alpha
   android:fromAlpha = "0.0"
   android:interpolator =
              "@android:anim/accelerate_interpolator"

   android:toAlpha="1.0" />
</set>
```

Right-click on the **anim** directory and select **New | Animation resource file**. In the `File name:` field, type `fade_out` and then left-click **OK**. Delete the contents and add this code to create the animation:

```
<?xml version="1.0" encoding="utf-8"?>
<set xmlns:android="http://schemas.android.com/apk/res/android"
   android:fillAfter = "true" >

   <alpha
         android:fromAlpha = "1.0"
         android:interpolator =
              "@android:anim/accelerate_interpolator"

   android:toAlpha = "0.0" />
</set>
```

Right-click on the **anim** directory and select **New | Animation resource file**. In the `File name:` field, type `fade_in_out` and then left-click **OK**. Delete the contents and add this code to create the animation:

```
<?xml version="1.0" encoding="utf-8"?>
<set xmlns:android="http://schemas.android.com/apk/res/android"
    android:fillAfter = "true" >

    <alpha
          android:fromAlpha="0.0"
          android:interpolator =
          "@android:anim/accelerate_interpolator"

          android:toAlpha = "1.0" />

    <alpha
       android:fromAlpha = "1.0"
          android:interpolator =
         "@android:anim/accelerate_interpolator"

         android:toAlpha = "0.0" />
</set>
```

Right-click on the **anim** directory and select **New | Animation resource file**. In the `File name:` field, type `zoom_in` and then left-click **OK**. Delete the contents and add this code to create the animation:

```
<set xmlns:android="http://schemas.android.com/apk/res/android"
    android:fillAfter = "true" >

    <scale
        android:fromXScale = "1"
        android:fromYScale = "1"
        android:pivotX = "50%"
        android:pivotY = "50%"
        android:toXScale = "6"
        android:toYScale = "6" >
    </scale>
</set>
```

Right-click on the **anim** directory and select **New | Animation resource file**. In the `File name:` field, type `zoom_out` and then left-click **OK**. Delete the contents and add this code to create the animation:

```
<?xml version="1.0" encoding="utf-8"?>
<set xmlns:android="http://schemas.android.com/apk/res/android">
    <scale
        android:fromXScale = "6"
        android:fromYScale = "6"
        android:pivotX = "50%"
        android:pivotY = "50%"
        android:toXScale = "1"
        android:toYScale = "1" >
    </scale>
</set>
```

Right-click on the **anim** directory and select **New | Animation resource file**. In the `File name:` field, type `left_right` and then left-click **OK**. Delete the contents and add this code to create the animation:

```
<?xml version="1.0" encoding="utf-8"?>
<set xmlns:android="http://schemas.android.com/apk/res/android">
    <translate

        android:fromXDelta = "-500%"
        android:toXDelta = "0%"/>
</set>
```

Again, right-click on the **anim** directory and select **New | Animation resource file**. In the **File name:** field, type `right_left` and then left-click **OK**. Delete the entire contents and add this code to create the animation:

```
<?xml version="1.0" encoding="utf-8"?>
<set xmlns:android="http://schemas.android.com/apk/res/android">
    <translate
        android:fillAfter = "false"
        android:fromXDelta = "500%"
        android:toXDelta = "0%"/>
</set>
```

As before, right-click on the **anim** directory and select **New | Animation resource file**. In the **File name:** field, type `top_bot` and then left-click **OK**. Delete the entire contents and add this code to create the animation:

```
<?xml version="1.0" encoding="utf-8"?>
<set xmlns:android="http://schemas.android.com/apk/res/android">
```

```
    <translate
        android:fillAfter = "false"
        android:fromYDelta = "-100%"
        android:toYDelta = "0%"/>
</set>
```

You guessed it; right-click on the **anim** directory and select **New | Animation resource file**. In the **File name:** field, type `flash` and then left-click **OK**. Delete the contents and add this code to create the animation:

```
<?xml version="1.0" encoding="utf-8"?>
<set xmlns:android="http://schemas.android.com/apk/res/android">
    <alpha android:fromAlpha = "0.0"
        android:toAlpha = "1.0"
        android:interpolator =
           "@android:anim/accelerate_interpolator"

        android:repeatMode = "reverse"
        android:repeatCount = "10"/>
</set>
```

Just a few more to go – right-click on the **anim** directory and select **New | Animation resource file**. In the **File name:** field, type `bounce` and then left-click **OK**. Delete the contents and add this code to create the animation:

```
<?xml version="1.0" encoding="utf-8"?>
<set xmlns:android="http://schemas.android.com/apk/res/android"
    android:fillAfter = "true"
    android:interpolator =
         "@android:anim/bounce_interpolator">

    <scale
        android:fromXScale = "1.0"
        android:fromYScale = "0.0"
        android:toXScale = "1.0"
        android:toYScale = "1.0" />

</set>
```

Right-click on the **anim** directory and select **New | Animation resource file**. In the **File name:** field, type `rotate_left` and then left-click **OK**. Delete the contents and add this code to create the animation. Here we see something new, `pivotX="50%"` and `pivotY="50%"`. This makes the rotate animation central on the widget that will be animated. We can think of this as setting the *pivot* point of the animation:

```
<?xml version="1.0" encoding="utf-8"?>
<set xmlns:android="http://schemas.android.com/apk/res/android">
    <rotate android:fromDegrees = "360"
        android:toDegrees = "0"
        android:pivotX = "50%"
        android:pivotY = "50%"
        android:interpolator =
           "@android:anim/cycle_interpolator"/>
</set>
```

Right-click on the **anim** directory and select **New | Animation resource file**. In the **File name:** field, type `rotate_right` and then left-click **OK**. Delete the contents and add this code to create the animation:

```
<?xml version="1.0" encoding="utf-8"?>
<set xmlns:android="http://schemas.android.com/apk/res/android">
    <rotate android:fromDegrees = "0"
        android:toDegrees = "360"
        android:pivotX = "50%"
        android:pivotY = "50%"
        android:interpolator =
             "@android:anim/cycle_interpolator"/>

</set>
```

Phew! Now we can write the Kotlin code to add our animations to our UI.

Wiring up the Animation demo app in Kotlin

Open the `MainActivity.kt` file. Now, following the class declaration, we can declare the following properties for animations:

```
var seekSpeedProgress: Int = 0

private lateinit var animFadeIn: Animation
private lateinit var animFadeOut: Animation
private lateinit var animFadeInOut: Animation

private lateinit var animZoomIn: Animation
```

```
private lateinit var animZoomOut: Animation

private lateinit var animLeftRight: Animation
private lateinit var animRightLeft: Animation
private lateinit var animTopBottom: Animation

private lateinit var animBounce: Animation
private lateinit var animFlash: Animation


private lateinit var animRotateLeft: Animation
private lateinit var animRotateRight: Animation
```

You will need to add the following `import` statement at this point:

```
import android.view.animation.Animation;
```

In the preceding code, we used the `lateinit` keyword when declaring the `Animation` instances. This will mean that Kotlin will check that each instance is initialized before it is used. This avoids us using `!!` (null checks) each time we use a function on one of these instances. For a refresher on the `!!` operator, refer to *Chapter 12, Connecting Our Kotlin to the UI and Nullability*.

We also added an `Int` property, `seekSpeedProgress`, which will be used to track the current value/position of `SeekBar`.

Now, let's call a new function from `onCreate` after the call to `setContentView`:

```
override fun onCreate(savedInstanceState: Bundle?) {
    super.onCreate(savedInstanceState)
    setContentView(R.layout.activity_main)

    loadAnimations()
}
```

At this point, the new line of code will have an error until we implement the new function.

Now we will implement the `loadAnimations` function. Although the code in this function is quite extensive, it is also very straightforward. All we are doing is using the `loadAnimation` function of the `AnimationUtils` class to initialize each of our `Animation` references with one of our XML animations. You will also notice that, for the `animFadeIn Animation`, we also call `setAnimationListener` on it. We will write the functions to listen for events shortly.

Add the `loadAnimations` function:

```
private fun loadAnimations() {

    animFadeIn = AnimationUtils.loadAnimation(
                 this, R.anim.fade_in)
    animFadeIn.setAnimationListener(this)
    animFadeOut = AnimationUtils.loadAnimation(
                 this, R.anim.fade_out)
    animFadeInOut = AnimationUtils.loadAnimation(
                 this, R.anim.fade_in_out)

    animZoomIn = AnimationUtils.loadAnimation(
                 this, R.anim.zoom_in)
    animZoomOut = AnimationUtils.loadAnimation(
                 this, R.anim.zoom_out)

    animLeftRight = AnimationUtils.loadAnimation(
                  this, R.anim.left_right)
    animRightLeft = AnimationUtils.loadAnimation(
                  this, R.anim.right_left)
    animTopBottom = AnimationUtils.loadAnimation(
                  this, R.anim.top_bot)

    animBounce = AnimationUtils.loadAnimation(
                  this, R.anim.bounce)
    animFlash = AnimationUtils.loadAnimation(
                  this, R.anim.flash)

    animRotateLeft = AnimationUtils.loadAnimation(
                  this, R.anim.rotate_left)
    animRotateRight = AnimationUtils.loadAnimation(
                  this, R.anim.rotate_right)
}
```

You will need to import one new class at this point:

```
import android.view.animation.AnimationUtils
```

Now, we will add a click-listener for each button. Add this code immediately before the closing curly brace of the `onCreate` function:

```
btnFadeIn.setOnClickListener(this)
btnFadeOut.setOnClickListener(this)
btnFadeInOut.setOnClickListener(this)
btnZoomIn.setOnClickListener(this)
btnZoomOut.setOnClickListener(this)
btnLeftRight.setOnClickListener(this)
btnRightLeft.setOnClickListener(this)
btnTopBottom.setOnClickListener(this)
btnBounce.setOnClickListener(this)
btnFlash.setOnClickListener(this)
btnRotateLeft.setOnClickListener(this)
btnRotateRight.setOnClickListener(this)
```

The code we just added creates errors in all the lines of code. We can ignore them for now, as we will fix them shortly and discuss what happened.

Now, we can use a lambda to handle the `SeekBar` interactions. We will override three functions, as it is required by the interface when implementing `OnSeekBarChangeListener`:

- A function that detects a change in the position of the `SeekBar` widget, called `onProgressChanged`
- A function that detects the user starting to change the position, called `onStartTrackingTouch`
- A function that detects when the user has finished using the `SeekBar` widget, called `onStopTrackingTouch`

To achieve our goals, we only need to add code to the `onProgressChanged` function, but we must still override them all.

All we do in the `onProgressChanged` function is assign the current value of the `SeekBar` object to the `seekSpeedProgress` member variable, so it can be accessed from elsewhere. Then, we use this value along with the maximum possible value of the `SeekBar` object, obtained by using `seekBarSpeed.max`, and output a message to the `textSeekerSpeed TextView`.

Add the code we have just discussed before the closing curly brace of the `onCreate` function:

```
seekBarSpeed.setOnSeekBarChangeListener(
        object : SeekBar.OnSeekBarChangeListener {

    override fun onProgressChanged(
                seekBar: SeekBar, value: Int,
                fromUser: Boolean) {

        seekSpeedProgress = value
        textSeekerSpeed.text =
             "$seekSpeedProgress of $seekBarSpeed.max"
    }

    override fun onStartTrackingTouch(seekBar: SeekBar) {}

    override fun onStopTrackingTouch(seekBar: SeekBar) {}
})
```

Now, we need to alter the `MainActivity` class declaration to implement two interfaces. In this app, we will be listening for clicks and for animation events, so the two interfaces we will be using are `View.OnClickListener` and `Animation.AnimationListener`. You will notice that to implement more than one interface, we simply separate the interfaces with a comma.

Alter the `MainActivity` class declaration by adding the highlighted code we have just discussed:

```
class MainActivity : AppCompatActivity(),
        View.OnClickListener,
        Animation.AnimationListener {
```

At this stage, we can add and implement the required functions for those interfaces. First, the `AnimationListener` functions, `onAnimationEnd`, `onAnimationRepeat`, and `onAnimationStart`. We only need to add a little code to two of these functions. In `onAnimationEnd`, we set the `text` property of `textStatus` to `STOPPED`, and in `onAnimationStart`, we set it to `RUNNING`. This will demonstrate our animation listeners are indeed listening and working:

```
override fun onAnimationEnd(animation: Animation) {
   textStatus.text = "STOPPED"
}

override fun onAnimationRepeat(animation: Animation) {
```

```
}

override fun onAnimationStart(animation: Animation) {
   textStatus.text = "RUNNING"
}
```

The onClick function is quite long, but nothing complicated. Each option of the when block handles each button from the UI, sets the duration of an animation based on the current position of the SeekBar widget, sets up the animation so it can be listened to for events, and then starts the animation.

You will need to use your preferred technique to import the View class:

```
import android.view.View;
```

Add the onClick function we have just discussed, and we have then completed this mini app:

```
override fun onClick(v: View) {
when (v.id) {
  R.id.btnFadeIn -> {
        animFadeIn.duration = seekSpeedProgress.toLong()
        animFadeIn.setAnimationListener(this)
        imageView.startAnimation(animFadeIn)
  }

  R.id.btnFadeOut -> {
        animFadeOut.duration = seekSpeedProgress.toLong()
        animFadeOut.setAnimationListener(this)
        imageView.startAnimation(animFadeOut)
  }

  R.id.btnFadeInOut -> {

        animFadeInOut.duration = seekSpeedProgress.toLong()
        animFadeInOut.setAnimationListener(this)
        imageView.startAnimation(animFadeInOut)
  }

  R.id.btnZoomIn -> {
        animZoomIn.duration = seekSpeedProgress.toLong()
        animZoomIn.setAnimationListener(this)
```

```
        imageView.startAnimation(animZoomIn)
    }

    R.id.btnZoomOut -> {
        animZoomOut.duration = seekSpeedProgress.toLong()
        animZoomOut.setAnimationListener(this)
        imageView.startAnimation(animZoomOut)
    }


    R.id.btnLeftRight -> {
        animLeftRight.duration = seekSpeedProgress.toLong()
        animLeftRight.setAnimationListener(this)
        imageView.startAnimation(animLeftRight)
    }

    R.id.btnRightLeft -> {
        animRightLeft.duration = seekSpeedProgress.toLong()
        animRightLeft.setAnimationListener(this)
        imageView.startAnimation(animRightLeft)
    }

    R.id.btnTopBottom -> {
        animTopBottom.duration = seekSpeedProgress.toLong()
        animTopBottom.setAnimationListener(this)
        imageView.startAnimation(animTopBottom)
    }

    R.id.btnBounce -> {
        /*
        Divide seekSpeedProgress by 10 because with
        the seekbar having a max value of 5000 it
        will make the animations range between
        almost instant and half a second
        5000 / 10 = 500 milliseconds
        */
        animBounce.duration =
              (seekSpeedProgress / 10).toLong()
        animBounce.setAnimationListener(this)
        imageView.startAnimation(animBounce)
    }

    R.id.btnFlash -> {
        animFlash.duration = (seekSpeedProgress / 10).toLong()
```

```
            animFlash.setAnimationListener(this)
            imageView.startAnimation(animFlash)
        }

        R.id.btnRotateLeft -> {
            animRotateLeft.duration = seekSpeedProgress.toLong()
            animRotateLeft.setAnimationListener(this)
            imageView.startAnimation(animRotateLeft)
        }

        R.id.btnRotateRight -> {
            animRotateRight.duration = seekSpeedProgress.toLong()
            animRotateRight.setAnimationListener(this)
            imageView.startAnimation(animRotateRight)
        }
    }

    }
```

Now, run the app and move the `SeekBar` widget to roughly the center so that the animations run for a reasonable amount of time:

Click the **ZOOM IN** button:

Notice how the text on the Android robot changes from **RUNNING** to **STOPPED** at the appropriate time. Now, click one of the **ROTATE** buttons:

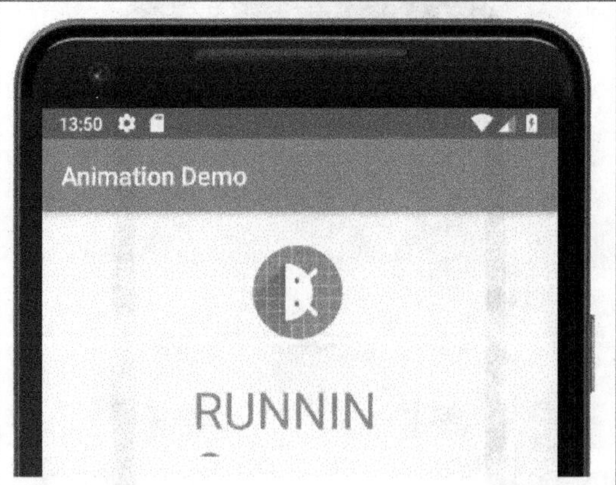

Most of the other animations don't do themselves justice in a screenshot, so be sure to try them all out for yourself.

Frequently asked questions

Q.1) We know how to animate widgets now, but what about shapes or images that I create myself?

A) An `ImageView` widget can hold any image you like. Just add the image to the `drawable` folder and then set the appropriate `src` attribute on the `ImageView` widget. You can then animate whatever image is being shown in the `ImageView` widget.

Q.2) But what if I want more flexibility than this, more like a drawing app or even a game?

A) To implement this kind of functionality, we will need to learn about another general computing concept known as **threads**, as well as some more Android classes (such as `Paint`, `Canvas`, and `SurfaceView`). We will learn how to draw anything from a single pixel to shapes, and then move them around the screen, starting in the next chapter, *Chapter 20, Drawing Graphics*.

Summary

Now we have another app-enhancing trick up our sleeves. In this chapter, we saw that animations in Android are quite straightforward. We designed an animation in XML and added the file to the `anim` folder. Next, we got a reference to the animation in XML with an `Animation` object in our Kotlin code.

We then used a reference to a widget in our UI, set an animation to it using `setAnimation`, and passed in the `Animation` object. We commenced the animation by calling `startAnimation` on the reference to the widget.

We also saw that we can control the timing of animations and listen for animation events.

In the next chapter, we will learn about drawing graphics in Android. This will be the start of several chapters on graphics, where we will build a kid's-style drawing app.

20
Drawing Graphics

This entire chapter will be about the Android `Canvas` class and some related classes, such as `Paint`, `Color`, and `Bitmap`. When combined, these classes bring great power when it comes to drawing on the screen. Sometimes, the default UI provided by the Android API isn't what we need. If we want to make a drawing app, draw graphs, or perhaps make a game, we need to take control of every pixel that the Android device has to offer.

In this chapter, we will cover the following topics:

- Gain an understanding of the `Canvas` class and some related classes
- Write a `Canvas`-based demo app
- Look at the Android coordinate system so that we know where to do our drawing
- Learn about drawing and manipulating bitmap graphics
- Write a bitmap graphics-based demo app

So, let's get drawing!

Understanding the Canvas class

The `Canvas` class is part of the `android.graphics` package. In the next two chapters, we will be using all the following `import` statements from the `android.graphics` package and one more from the now familiar `View` package. They give us access to some powerful drawing functions from the Android API:

```
import android.graphics.Bitmap
import android.graphics.Canvas
import android.graphics.Color
import android.graphics.Paint
import android.widget.ImageView
```

First, let's talk about `Bitmap`, `Canvas`, and `ImageView`, as highlighted in the previous code.

Getting started drawing with Bitmap, Canvas, and ImageView

As Android is designed to run all types of mobile apps, we can't immediately start typing our drawing code and expect it to work. We need to do a bit of preparation (that is, more coding) to consider the specific device that our app is running on. It is true that some of this preparation can be slightly counterintuitive, but we will go through this one step at a time.

Canvas and Bitmap

Depending on how you use the `Canvas` class, the term can be slightly misleading. While the `Canvas` class *is* the class that you draw your graphics to, such as a painting canvas, you still need a **surface** to transpose the canvas on.

The surface, in this case (and in our first two demo apps), will be from the `Bitmap` class.

Note that a bitmap is a type of image and Android has a `Bitmap` class. The `Bitmap` class can be used to draw bitmap images to the screen but, as we will see, it also has other uses as well. When talking about bitmap images and the `Bitmap` class I will try and be as clear as possible, so the distinction is as clear as possible.

We can think of the process as follows: we get a `Canvas` object and a `Bitmap` object, and then set the `Bitmap` object as the part of the `Canvas` object to draw on.

This is slightly counterintuitive if you take the word "canvas" in its literal sense, but once it is all set up, we can forget about it and concentrate on the graphics that we want to draw.

The `Canvas` class supplies the *ability* to draw. It has all the functions for doing things such as drawing shapes, text, lines, and image files (such as other bitmaps), and even supports plotting individual pixels.

The `Bitmap` class is used by the `Canvas` class and is the surface that gets drawn on. You can think of the `Bitmap` instance as being inside a picture frame on the `Canvas` instance.

Paint

In addition to `Canvas` and `Bitmap`, we will be using the `Paint` class. This is much easier to understand; `Paint` is the class that is used to configure specific properties, such as the color that we will draw on the `Bitmap` instance (within the `Canvas` instance).

There is, however, still another piece of the puzzle before we can start drawing things.

ImageView and Activity

The `ImageView` class is the class that the `Activity` class will use to display output to the user. The reason for this third layer of abstraction is that, as we have seen throughout the book, the `Activity` class needs to pass a `View` reference to the `setContentView` function to display something to the user. Throughout the book, this has been a layout that we created in the visual designer or in XML code.

This time, however, we don't want a UI - instead, we want to draw lines, pixels, images, and shapes.

There are multiple classes that inherit from `View` that enable all different types of apps to be made, and they will all be compatible with the `Activity` class, which is the foundation of all regular Android apps (including drawing apps and games).

It is, therefore, necessary to associate the `Bitmap` class that gets drawn on (through its association with `Canvas`) with the `ImageView` class, once the drawing is done. The last step will be to tell the `Activity` class that our `ImageView` represents the content for the user to see by passing it to `setContentView`.

Canvas, Bitmap, Paint, and ImageView – a quick summary

If the theory of the code structure that we need to set up doesn't appear simple, then you will breathe a sigh of relief when you see the relatively simple code later.

Here is a quick summary of what we've covered so far:

- Every app needs an `Activity` class to interact with the user and the underlying operating system. Therefore, we must conform to the required hierarchy if we want to succeed.
- We will use the `ImageView` class, which inherits from the `View` class. The `View` class is what `Activity` needs to display our app to the user.

- The `Canvas` class supplies the *ability* to draw lines, pixels, and other graphics. It has all the functions for doing things, such as drawing shapes, text, lines, and image files, and even supports plotting individual pixels.
- The `Bitmap` class will be associated with the `Canvas` class, and it is the surface that gets drawn on.
- The `Canvas` class uses the `Paint` class to configure details, such as the color that is drawn.
- Finally, once the `Bitmap` instance has been drawn on, we must associate it with the `ImageView` class, which, in turn, is set as the view for the `Activity` instance.

The result will be that what we draw on the `Bitmap` instance in the `Canvas` instance will be displayed to the user through the `ImageView` instance via the call to `setContentView`. Phew!

It doesn't matter if this isn't 100% clear. It is not you that isn't seeing things clearly - it simply isn't a clear relationship. Writing the code and using the techniques over and over will cause things to become clearer. Take a look at the code, perform the demo apps in this chapter and the next, and then re-read this section.

Let's take a look at how to set up this relationship in code - don't worry about typing the code; we will just study it first.

Using the Canvas class

Let's take a look at the code and the different stages that are required to get drawing, then we can quickly move on to drawing something, for real, with the `Canvas` demo app.

Preparing the instances of the required classes

The first step is to turn the classes that we need into usable instances.

First, we declare all the instances that we require. We can't initialize the instances right away, but we can make sure that we initialize them before they are used, so we use `lateinit` in the same way we did in the Animation demo app:

```
// Here are all the objects(instances)
// of classes that we need to do some drawing
lateinit var myImageView: ImageView
lateinit var myBlankBitmap: Bitmap
lateinit var myCanvas: Canvas
lateinit var myPaint: Paint
```

The previous code declares references of the `ImageView`, `Bitmap`, `Canvas`, and `Paint` types. They are named `myImageView`, `myBlankBitmap`, `myCanvas`, and `myPaint`, respectively.

Initializing the objects

Next, we need to initialize our new objects before using them:

```
// Initialize all the objects ready for drawing
// We will do this inside the onCreate function
val widthInPixels = 800
val heightInPixels = 600

// Create a new Bitmap
myBlankBitmap = Bitmap.createBitmap(widthInPixels,
        heightInPixels,
        Bitmap.Config.ARGB_8888)

// Initialize the Canvas and associate it
// with the Bitmap to draw on
myCanvas = Canvas(myBlankBitmap)

// Initialize the ImageView and the Paint
myImageView = ImageView(this)
myPaint = Paint()
// Do drawing here
```

Notice the following comment in the previous code:

```
// Do drawing here
```

This is where we will configure our color and draw our graphics. Additionally, notice at the top of the code that we declare and initialize two `Int` variables, called `widthInPixels` and `heightInPixels`. When we code the `Canvas` demo app, I will go into greater detail about some of those lines of code.

We are now ready to draw; all we need to do is assign the `ImageView` instance to the `Activity` via the `setContentView` function.

Setting the Activity content

Finally, before we can see our drawing, we tell Android to use our `ImageView` instance, called `myImageView`, as the content to display to the user:

```
// Associate the drawn upon Bitmap with the ImageView
myImageView.setImageBitmap(myBlankBitmap);
// Tell Android to set our drawing
// as the view for this app
// via the ImageView
setContentView(myImageView);
```

As you have already seen in every app so far, the `setContentView` function is part of the `Activity` class, and this time we pass in `myImageView` as an argument, instead of an XML layout as we have been doing throughout the book. That's it – all we have to learn now is how to actually draw on the `Bitmap` instance.

Before we do some drawing, it will be useful to start a real project. We will copy and paste the code that we have just discussed, one step at a time, into the correct place, and then actually see something drawn on the screen.

So, let's do some drawing.

The Canvas Demo app

First, create a new project to explore the topic of drawing with `Canvas`. We will reuse what we have learned and, this time, we will also draw to the `Bitmap` instance.

Creating a new project

Create a new project and call it `Canvas Demo`, and make sure that you choose the **Empty Activity** template option.

In this app, we will make a change that we have not seen before. We will be using the vanilla version of the `Activity` class. Therefore, `MainActivity` will inherit from `Activity` instead of `AppCompatActivity`, as has been the case previously. We are doing this because we are not using a layout from an XML file, and so we have no need for the backward compatibility features of `AppCompatActivity` as we did in all the previous projects.

You should edit the class declaration as follows.

```
class MainActivity : Activity() {
```

You will also need to add the following import statement:

```
import android.app.Activity
```

The complete code for this app can be found in the download bundle in the `Chapter20/Canvas Demo` folder.

Coding the Canvas demo app

Next, delete all the contents of the `onCreate` function, except the declaration/signature, call to super.onCreate, and the opening and closing curly braces.

Now, we can add the following highlighted code after the class declaration, but before the `onCreate` function. This is what the code will look like after this step:

```
// Here are all the objects(instances)
// of classes that we need to do some drawing

lateinit var myImageView: ImageView
lateinit var myBlankBitmap: Bitmap
lateinit var myCanvas: Canvas
lateinit var myPaint: Paint


override fun onCreate(savedInstanceState: Bundle?) {
   super.onCreate(savedInstanceState)
}
```

Notice in Android Studio that the four new classes are underlined in red. This is because we need to add the appropriate `import` statements. You could copy them from the first page of this chapter, but it will be much quicker to place the mouse cursor on each error in turn, and then hold the *ALT* key and tap the *Enter* key. If prompted from the pop-up options, select **Import class**.

Once you have done this for `ImageView`, `Bitmap`, `Canvas`, and `Paint`, all the errors will be gone, and the relevant `import` statements will have been added to the top of the code.

Now that we have declared instances of the required classes, we can initialize them. Add the following code to the `onCreate` function after the call to `super.onCreate`..., as shown in the following code:

```
override fun onCreate(savedInstanceState: Bundle?) {
    super.onCreate(savedInstanceState)

    // Initialize all the objects ready for drawing
    // We will do this inside the onCreate function
    val widthInPixels = 800
    val heightInPixels = 600

    // Create a new Bitmap
    myBlankBitmap = Bitmap.createBitmap(widthInPixels,
                heightInPixels,
                Bitmap.Config.ARGB_8888)

    // Initialize the Canvas and associate it
    // with the Bitmap to draw on
    myCanvas = Canvas(myBlankBitmap)

    // Initialize the ImageView and the Paint
    myImageView = ImageView(this)
    myPaint = Paint()
}
```

This preceding code is the same as the code that we saw when we were discussing `Canvas` in theory. However, it is worth exploring the `Bitmap` class initialization a little more as it is not straightforward.

Exploring the Bitmap initialization

Bitmaps, more typically in graphics-based apps and games, are used to represent objects, such as different brushes to paint with, a player character, backgrounds, game objects, and more. Here, we are simply using it to draw on. In the next project, we will use bitmaps to represent the subject of our drawing and not just the surface to draw on.

The function that requires explaining is the `createBitmap` function. The parameters from left to right are as follows:

- Width (in pixels)
- Height (in pixels)
- The bitmap configuration

`Bitmap` instances can be configured in several different ways; the `ARGB_8888` configuration means that each pixel is represented by four bytes of memory.

There are a number of bitmap formats that Android can use. This one is perfect for a good range of color and will ensure that the bitmaps we use and the color that we request will be drawn as intended. There are higher and lower configurations, but `ARGB_8888` is a good fit for this book.

Now, we can do the actual drawing.

Drawing on the screen

Add the following highlighted code after the initialization of `myPaint` and inside the closing curly brace of the `onCreate` function:

```
// Draw on the Bitmap
// Wipe the Bitmap with a blue color
myCanvas.drawColor(Color.argb(255, 0, 0, 255))

// Re-size the text
myPaint.textSize = 100f
// Change the paint to white
myPaint.color = Color.argb(255, 255, 255, 255)
// Draw some text
myCanvas.drawText("Hello World!",100f, 100f, myPaint)

// Change the paint to yellow
myPaint.color = Color.argb(255, 212, 207, 62)
// Draw a circle
myCanvas.drawCircle(400f, 250f, 100f, myPaint)
```

The previous code uses:

- `myCanvas.drawColor` to fill the screen with color
- The `myPaint.textSize` property defines the size of the text that will be drawn next
- The `myPaint.color` property determines what color any future drawing will be
- The `myCanvas.drawText` function actually draws the text to the screen.

If we analyze the arguments passed into `drawText`, we can see that the text will say "Hello World!", and that it will be drawn 100 pixels from the left and 100 pixels from the top of our `Bitmap` instance (`myBitmap`).

Next, we use the `color` property again to change the color that will be used for drawing. Finally, we use the `drawCircle` function to draw a circle that is 400 pixels from the left, and 100 pixels from the top. The circle will have a radius of 100 pixels.

I have refrained from explaining the `Color.argb` function until now.

Explaining Color.argb

The `Color` class, unsurprisingly, helps us to manipulate and represent color. The `argb` function returns a color that is constructed using the **a**lpha (for opacity and transparency), **r**ed, **g**reen, **b**lue model. This model uses values ranging from 0 (no color) to 255 (full color) for each element. It is important to note - although, it might seem obvious - that the mixed colors are intensities of different colored light, and the results are quite different to what happens when we mix paint, for example.

To devise an ARGB value and explore this model further, take a look at this handy website: `https://www.rapidtables.com/web/color/RGB_Color.html`. The website helps you to pick the RGB values; you can then experiment with the alpha values.

The values used to clear the drawing surface were `255`, `0`, `0`, and `255`. These values mean full opacity (that is, solid color), no red, no green, and full blue. This makes a blue color.

The next call to the `argb` function is in the first call to `setColor`, where we are setting the required color for the text. The `255`, `255`, `255`, and `255` values mean full opacity, full red, full green, and full blue. When you combine light with these values, you will get white.

The final call to `argb` is in the final call to `setColor`, where we are setting the color to draw the circle; `255`, `21`, `207`, and `62` makes a sun-yellow color.

The last step that we need to perform before we can run the code is to add the call to the `setContentView` function, which places our `ImageView` instance (`myImageView`) as the view to be set as the content for this app. Here are the final lines of code for after the code that we have already added, but before the closing curly brace of `onCreate`:

```
// Associate the drawn upon Bitmap with the ImageView
myImageView.setImageBitmap(myBlankBitmap);
// Tell Android to set our drawing
// as the view for this app
// via the ImageView
setContentView(myImageView);
```

Finally, we tell the `Activity` class to use `myImageView` by calling `setContentView`.

The following screenshot illustrates what the Canvas demo app looks like when you run it. We can see an 800 by 800-pixel drawing. In the next chapter, we will use more advanced techniques to utilize the entire screen, and we will also learn about threads to make the graphics move in real time:

It will help you to understand the result of the coordinates that we use in our `Canvas` drawing functions if you know more about the Android coordinate system.

The Android coordinate system

As you will see, drawing a bitmap graphic is trivial. However, the coordinate system that we use to draw our graphics on requires a brief explanation.

Plotting and drawing

When we draw a bitmap graphic on the screen, we pass in the coordinates that we want to draw the object to. The available coordinates of a given Android device depend upon the resolution of its screen.

For example, the Google Pixel phone has a screen resolution of 1,920 pixels (across) by 1,080 pixels (down) when held in landscape orientation.

The numbering system of these coordinates starts in the top left-hand corner at 0,0, and proceeds downward and to the right until the bottom-right corner is pixel 1919, 1079. The apparent 1-pixel disparity between 1,920/1,919 and 1,080/1,079 is because the numbering starts at 0.

So, when we draw a bitmap graphic or anything else on the screen (such as `Canvas` circles and rectangles), we must specify an *x*, *y* coordinate.

Furthermore, a bitmap graphic (or `Canvas` shape), of course, comprises many pixels. So, which pixel of a given bitmap graphic is drawn at the *x*, *y* screen coordinate that we will be specifying?

The answer is the top-left pixel of the bitmap graphic. Take a look at the next diagram, which should clarify the screen coordinates using the Google Pixel phone as an example. As a graphical means for explaining the Android coordinate drawing system, I will use a cute spaceship graphic:

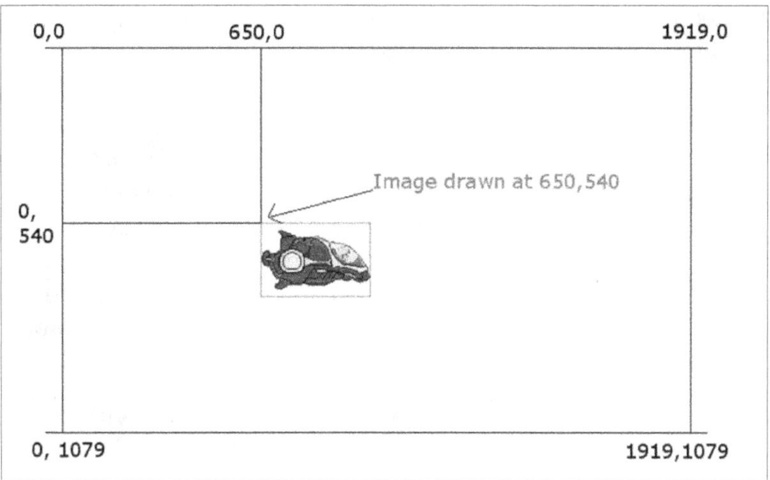

Furthermore, the coordinates are relative to what you draw on. So, in the `Canvas` demo that we just coded and in the next demo, the coordinates are relative to the `Bitmap` object (`myBitmap`). In the next chapter, we will use the entire screen, and the previous diagram will be a more accurate representation of what is happening.

Let's do some more drawing - this time with bitmap graphics (and the `Bitmap` class again). We will use the same starting code as we have seen in this app.

Creating bitmap graphics with the Bitmap class

Let's examine a bit of theory before we dive into the code and consider exactly how we are going to draw images to the screen. To draw a bitmap graphic, we will use the `drawBitmap` function of the `Canvas` class.

First, we will need to add a bitmap graphic to the project in the `res/drawable` folder - we will do this in reality in the Bitmap demo app later. For now, assume that the graphics file/bitmap has a name of `myImage.png`.

Next, we will declare an object of the `Bitmap` type in the same way that we did for the `Bitmap` object that we used for our background in the previous demo.

Next, we will need to initialize the `myBitmap` instance using our preferred image file, which we previously added to the project's `drawable` folder:

```
myBitmap = BitmapFactory.decodeResource
                (resources, R.drawable.myImage)
```

The `decodeResource` function of the `BitmapFactory` class is used to initialize `myBitmap`. It takes two parameters; the first is the `resources` property that is made available by the `Activity` class. This function, as the name suggests, gives access to the project resources, and the second parameter, `R.drawable.myImage`, points to the `myImage.png` file in the `drawable` folder. The `Bitmap` (`myBitmap`) instance is now ready to be drawn by the `Canvas` class.

You can now draw the bitmap graphic via the `Bitmap` instance with the following code:

```
// Draw the bitmap at coordinates 100, 100
canvas.drawBitmap(myBitmap,
                100, 100, myPaint);
```

Here is what the spaceship graphic from the previous section looks like when drawn on the screen (just for reference when we talk about rotating bitmaps):

Manipulating bitmaps

Quite often, however, we need to draw bitmaps in a rotated or otherwise altered state. It is quite easy to use Photoshop, or whatever your favorite image editing software happens to be and create more bitmaps from the original bitmap to face other directions. Then, when we come to draw our bitmap, we can simply decide which way and draw the appropriate pre-loaded bitmap.

However, I think it will be much more interesting and instructive if we work with just the one single source image and learn about the class that Android provides to manipulate images with our Kotlin code. You will then be able to add rotating and inverting graphics to your app developer's toolkit.

What is a bitmap?

A bitmap is called a bitmap because that is exactly what it is: a *map of bits*. While there are many bitmap formats that use different ranges and values to represent colors and transparency, they all amount to the same thing. They are a grid or map of values and each value represents the color of a single pixel.

Therefore, to rotate, scale, or invert a bitmap, we must perform the appropriate mathematical calculation on each pixel or bit of the image, grid, or map of the bitmap. The calculations are not terribly complicated, but they are not especially simple either. If you took math to the end of high school, you will probably understand the math without too much difficulty.

Unfortunately, understanding the math isn't enough. We will also need to devise efficient code as well as understand the bitmap format, and then modify our code for each format; this is not trivial. Fortunately (as we have come to expect), the Android API has done it all for us - meet the `Matrix` class.

The Matrix class

The class is named `Matrix` because it uses the mathematical concept and rules to perform calculations on a series of values known as matrices - the plural of matrix.

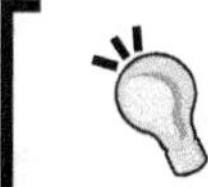

The Android `Matrix` class has nothing to do with the movie series of the same name. However, the author advises that all aspiring app developers take the **red** pill.

You might be familiar with matrices, but don't worry if you're not, because the `Matrix` class hides all the complexity away. Furthermore, the `Matrix` class not only allows us to perform calculations on a series of values, but it also has some pre-prepared calculations that enable us to do things such as rotate a point around another point by a specific number of degrees. We get all this without knowing anything about trigonometry.

If you are intrigued by how the math works behind the scenes of the `Matrix` class and want an absolute beginner's guide to the mathematics of rotating game objects, then look at this series of Android tutorials on my website, which ends with a flyable and rotatable spaceship. These tutorials are in Java, but should be quite straightforward to follow:

`http://gamecodeschool.com/essentials/calculating-heading-in-2d-games-using-trigonometric-functions-part-1/`

`http://gamecodeschool.com/essentials/rotating-graphics-in-2d-games-using-trigonometric-functions-part-2/`

`http://gamecodeschool.com/android/2d-rotation-and-heading-demo/`

This book will stick to using the Android `Matrix` class, but we will do slightly more advanced math when we create a particle system in the next chapter.

Inverting a bitmap to face the opposite direction

First, we need to create an instance of the `Matrix` class. The following line of code does so in a familiar way by calling the default constructor:

```
val matrix = Matrix()
```

Note that you don't need to add any of this code to a project right now; it will all be shown again shortly with much more context. I just thought it would be easier to see all the `Matrix`-related code on its own beforehand.

Now we can use one of the many neat functions of the `Matrix` class. The `preScale` function takes two parameters; one for the horizontal change and one for the vertical change. Take a look at the following line of code:

```
matrix.preScale(-1, 1)
```

What the `preScale` function will do is loop through every pixel position and multiply all the horizontal coordinates by `-1`, and all the vertical coordinates by `1`.

The effect of these calculations is that all the vertical coordinates will remain the same, because if you multiply by one, then the number doesn't change. However, when you multiply by minus one, the horizontal position of the pixel will be inverted. For example, horizontal positions 0, 1, 2, 3, and 4 will become 0, -1, -2, -3, and -4.

At this stage, we have created a matrix that can perform the necessary calculations on a bitmap. We haven't actually done anything to the bitmap yet. To use the `Matrix` instance, we call the `createBitmap` function of the `Bitmap` class, as in the following line of code:

```
myBitmapLeft = Bitmap
    .createBitmap(myBitmapRight,
          0, 0, 50, 25, matrix, true)
```

The previous code assumes that `myBitmapLeft` is already initialized along with `myBitmapRight`. The parameters to the `createBitmap` function are explained as follows:

- `myBitmapRight` is a `Bitmap` object that has already been created and scaled and has the image (facing to the right) loaded into it. This is the image that will be used as the source for creating the new `Bitmap` instance. The source `Bitmap` object will not be altered at all.
- `0, 0` is the horizontal and vertical starting position that we want the new `Bitmap` instance to be mapped to.
- The `50, 25` parameters are values that set the size that the bitmap is scaled to.
- The next parameter is our pre-prepared `Matrix` instance, `matrix`.
- The final parameter, `true`, instructs the `createBitmap` function that filtering is required to correctly handle the creation of the `Bitmap` type.

This is what `myBitmapLeft` will look like when drawn to the screen:

We can also create the bitmap facing up and down using a rotation matrix.

Rotating the bitmap to face up and down

Let's take a look at rotating a `Bitmap` instance and then we can build the demo app. We already have an instance of the `Matrix` class, so all we have to do is call the `preRotate` function to create a matrix that is capable of rotating every pixel by a specified number of degrees in the single argument to `preRotate`. Take a look at the following line of code:

```
// A matrix for rotating
matrix.preRotate(-90)
```

How simple was that? The `matrix` instance is now ready to rotate any series of numbers (map of bits) we pass to it, anti-clockwise (`-`), by `90` degrees.

The following line of code has the same parameters as the previous call to `createBitmap` that we dissected, except that the new `Bitmap` instance is assigned to `myBitmapUp`, and the effect of `matrix` is to perform the rotate instead of the `preScale` function:

```
mBitmapUp = Bitmap
    .createBitmap(mBitmap,
            0, 0, 25, 50, matrix, true)
```

This is what `myBitmapUp` will look like when drawn:

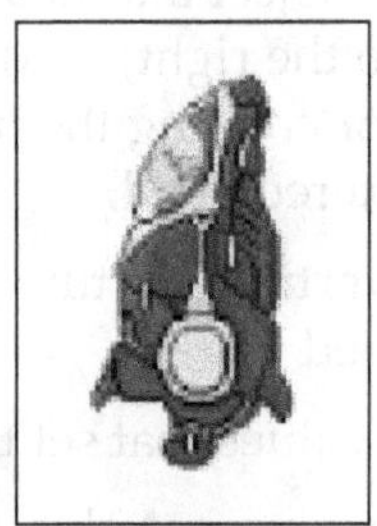

You can also use the same technique, but with a different value, in the argument to `preRotate` to face the bitmap downward. Let's get on with the demo app to see all this stuff in action.

The Bitmap manipulation demo app

Now that we have studied the theory, let's draw and spin some bitmaps. First, create a new project and call it `Bitmap manipulation`. Choose the **Empty Activity** option with all the other settings as they have been throughout the book.

Adding the Bob graphic to the project

Right-click and select **Copy** to copy the `bob.png` graphics file from the download bundle in the `Chapter20/Bitmap Manipulation/drawable` folder. Bob, represented by `bob.png`, is a simple, static video game character.

In Android Studio, locate the `app/res/drawable` folder in the project explorer window and paste the `bob.png` image file into it. The following screenshot makes it clear where this folder is located and what it will look like with the `bob.png` image in it:

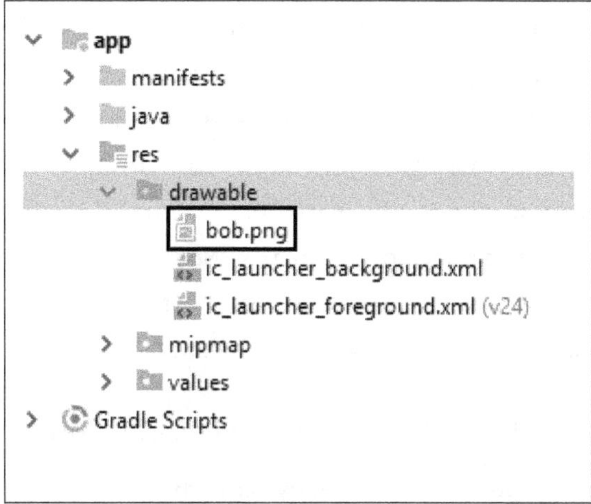

Right-click on the `drawable` folder and select **Paste** to add the `bob.png` file to the project. Click on **OK** twice to confirm the default options for importing the file into the project.

In this app, we will make the same change that we did in the previous app. We will be using the vanilla version of the `Activity` class. Therefore, `MainActivity` will inherit from `Activity` instead of `AppCompatActivity`, as has been the case previously. We are doing this because, again, we are not using a layout from an XML file, and so we have no need for the backward compatibility features of `AppCompatActivity` as we did in all the previous projects.

You should edit the class declaration as follows.

```
class MainActivity : Activity() {
```

You will also need to add the following import statement:

```
import android.app.Activity
```

Add the following required properties to the `MainActivity` class, after the class declaration and before the `onCreate` function, ready to do some drawing:

```
// Here are all the objects(instances)
// of classes that we need to do some drawing
lateinit var myImageView: ImageView
```

```
lateinit var myBlankBitmap: Bitmap
lateinit var bobBitmap: Bitmap
lateinit var myCanvas: Canvas
lateinit var myPaint: Paint
```

Add the following imports after the package declaration:

```
import android.graphics.Bitmap
import android.graphics.BitmapFactory
import android.graphics.Canvas
import android.graphics.Color
import android.graphics.Matrix
import android.graphics.Paint
import android.widget.ImageView
```

Now, we can initialize all the instances in `onCreate`, as follows:

```
// Initialize all the objects ready for drawing
val widthInPixels = 2000
val heightInPixels = 1000

// Create a new Bitmap
myBlankBitmap = Bitmap.createBitmap(widthInPixels,
         heightInPixels,
         Bitmap.Config.ARGB_8888)

// Initialize Bob
bobBitmap = BitmapFactory.decodeResource(
          resources, R.drawable.bob)

// Initialize the Canvas and associate it
// with the Bitmap to draw on
myCanvas = Canvas(myBlankBitmap)

// Initialize the ImageView and the Paint
myImageView = ImageView(this)
myPaint = Paint()

// Draw on the Bitmap
// Wipe the Bitmap with a blue color
myCanvas.drawColor(Color.argb(
         255, 0, 0, 255))
```

Next, we add calls to three functions that we will write soon and set our new drawing as the view for the app:

```
// Draw some bitmaps
drawRotatedBitmaps()
drawEnlargedBitmap()
drawShrunkenBitmap()

// Associate the drawn upon Bitmap
// with the ImageView
myImageView.setImageBitmap(myBlankBitmap)
// Tell Android to set our drawing
// as the view for this app
// via the ImageView
setContentView(myImageView)
```

Now, add the `drawRotatedBitmap` function, which performs the bitmap manipulation:

```
fun drawRotatedBitmaps() {
   var rotation = 0f
   var horizontalPosition = 350
   var verticalPosition = 25
   val matrix = Matrix()

   var rotatedBitmap: Bitmap

   rotation = 0f
   while (rotation < 360) {
         matrix.reset()
         matrix.preRotate(rotation)
         rotatedBitmap = Bitmap
                       .createBitmap(bobBitmap,
                       0, 0, bobBitmap.width - 1,
                       bobBitmap.height - 1,
                       matrix, true)

        myCanvas.drawBitmap(
                     rotatedBitmap,
                     horizontalPosition.toFloat(),
                     verticalPosition.toFloat(),
                     myPaint)

        horizontalPosition += 120
        verticalPosition += 70
```

```
            rotation += 30f
        }
    }
```

The previous code uses a loop to iterate through 360 degrees, 30 degrees at a time. The value (at each pass through the loop) is used in the `Matrix` instance to rotate the image of Bob, and he is then drawn to the screen using the `drawBitmap` function.

Add the final two functions, as follows:

```
fun drawEnlargedBitmap() {
  bobBitmap = Bitmap
              .createScaledBitmap(bobBitmap,
                          300, 400, false)
  myCanvas.drawBitmap(bobBitmap, 25f, 25f, myPaint)

}

fun drawShrunkenBitmap() {
  bobBitmap = Bitmap
             .createScaledBitmap(bobBitmap,
                         50, 75, false)
  myCanvas.drawBitmap(bobBitmap, 250f, 25f, myPaint)
}
```

The `drawEnlargedBitmap` function uses the `createScaledBitmap` function, enlarging the bitmap graphic to 300 by 400 pixels. The `drawBitmap` function then draws it to the screen.

The `drawShrunkenBitmap` function uses the exact same technique, except that it scales and then draws a 50 x 75 pixel image.

Finally, run the app to see Bob grow, shrink, and then spin around through 360 degrees at 30-degree intervals, as shown in the following screenshot:

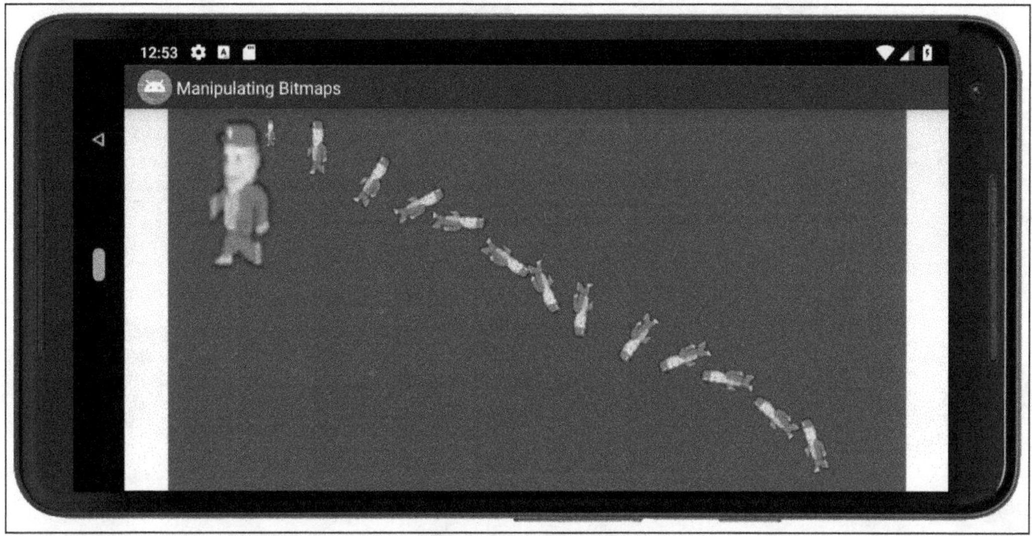

The only thing missing from our drawing repertoire is the ability to watch all this activity as it happens. We will fix this gap in our knowledge next.

Frequently asked question

Q 1) I know how to do all this drawing, but why can't I see anything move?

A) To see things move, you need to be able to regulate when each part of the drawing occurs. You need to use animation techniques. This is not trivial, but it is not beyond the grasp of a determined beginner, either. We will study the required topics in the next chapter.

Summary

In this chapter, we saw how to draw custom shapes, text, and bitmaps. Now that we know how to draw and manipulate both primitive shapes, text, and bitmaps, we can take things up a level.

In the next chapter, we will start our next multi-chapter app, which is a kid's-style drawing app that comes to life at the tap of a button.

21
Threads and Starting the Live Drawing App

In this chapter, we will get started on our next app. This app will be a kid's-style drawing app where the user can draw on the screen using their finger. The drawing app that we create will be slightly different, however. The lines that the user draws will be comprised of particle systems that explode into thousands of pieces. We will call the project *Live Drawing*.

To achieve this, we will cover the following topics in this chapter:

- Getting started with the Live Drawing app
- Learning about real-time interaction, sometimes referred to as a **game loop**
- Learning about **threads**
- Coding a real-time system that is ready to draw in

Let's get started!

Creating the Live Drawing project

To get started, create a new project in Android Studio and call it `Live Drawing`. Use the **Empty Activity** project and leave the rest of the settings at their defaults.

Similar to the two drawing apps from the previous chapter, this app consists of Kotlin files only, and no layout files. The Kotlin files and all the code up to the end of this chapter can all be found in the `Chapter21` folder of the download bundle. The complete project can be found in the `Chapter22` folder of the download bundle.

Next, we will create empty classes that we will code throughout the project over the next two chapters. Create a new class called `LiveDrawingView`, a new class called `ParticleSystem`, and a new class called `Particle`.

Looking ahead at the Live Drawing app

As this app is more in-depth and needs to respond in real time, it is necessary to use a slightly more in-depth structure. At first, this may seem like a complication, but in the long run, it will make our code simpler and easier to understand.

We will have four classes in the Live Drawing app, as follows:

- `MainActivity`: The `Activity` class provided by the Android API is the class that interacts with the **operating system** (**OS**). We have already seen how the OS interacts with `onCreate` when the player clicks on the app icon to start an app. Rather than have the `MainActivity` class that does everything, this `Activity`-based class will just handle the startup and shutdown of our app, and offer some assistance with initialization by calculating the screen resolution. It makes sense that this class will be of the `Activity` type and not `AppCompatActivity`. However, as you will soon see, we will delegate interaction through touches to another class, that is, the same class that will also handle almost every aspect of the app. This will introduce us to a number of new and interesting concepts.
- `LiveDrawingView`: This is the class that will be responsible for doing the drawing and creating the real-time environment that allows the user to interact at the same time as their creations are moving and evolving.
- `ParticleSystem`: This is the class that will manage up to thousands of instances of the `Particle` class.
- `Particle`: This class will be the simplest of them all; it will have a location on screen and a heading. It will update itself about 60 times per second when prompted to by the `LiveDrawingView` class.

Now, we can start coding.

Coding the MainActivity class

Let's get started with coding the `Activity`-based class. As usual, the class is called `MainActivity`, and it was autogenerated for us when we created the project.

Edit the class declaration and add the first part of the code for the `MainActivity` class:

```
import android.app.Activity
import android.os.Bundle
import android.graphics.Point

class MainActivity : Activity() {

    private lateinit var liveDrawingView: LiveDrawingView

    override fun onCreate(savedInstanceState: Bundle?) {
        super.onCreate(savedInstanceState)

        val display = windowManager.defaultDisplay
        val size = Point()
        display.getSize(size)

        liveDrawingView = LiveDrawingView(this, size.x)

        setContentView(liveDrawingView)

    }
}
```

The preceding code shows several errors that we will talk about shortly. The first thing to note is that we are declaring an instance of our `LiveDrawingView` class. Currently, this is an empty class:

```
private lateinit var liveDrawingView: LiveDrawingView
```

The next code gets the number of pixels (horizontally and vertically) for the device in the following way:

```
val display = windowManager.defaultDisplay
```

We create an object of the `Display` type, called `display`, and initialize it with `windowManager.defaultDisplay`, which is part of the `Activity` class.

Then, we create a new object, called `size`, of the `Point` type. We send `size` as an argument to the `display.getSize` function. The `Point` type has an `x` and `y` property and, therefore, so does the `size` object, which, after the third line of code, now holds the width and height (in pixels) of the display. Now, we have the screen resolution in the `x` and `y` properties tucked away in the `size` object.

Next, in `onCreate`, we initialize `liveDrawingView` as follows:

```
liveDrawingView = LiveDrawingView(this, size.x)
```

What we are doing is passing two arguments to the `LiveDrawingView` constructor. We have obviously not coded a constructor yet and, as we know, the default constructor takes zero arguments. Therefore, this line will cause an error until we fix this.

The arguments that are passed in are interesting. First, `this`, which is a reference to `MainActivity`. The `LiveDrawingView` class will need to perform actions (use some functions) that it needs this reference for.

The second argument is the horizontal screen resolution. It makes sense that our app will need these to perform tasks, such as scaling the other drawing objects to an appropriate size. We will discuss these arguments further when we get to coding the `LiveDrawingView` constructor.

Now, take a look at the even stranger line that follows:

```
setContentView(liveDrawingView)
```

This is where, in the Canvas Demo app, we set `ImageView` as the content for the app. Remember that the `Activity` class's `setContentView` function must take a `View` object, and `ImageView` is a `View` object. This preceding line of code seems to be suggesting that we will use our `LiveDrawingView` class as the visible content for the app? But `LiveDrawingView`, despite its name, isn't a `View` object. That is, at least not yet.

We will fix the constructor and the not-a-`View` problem after we add a few more lines of code to `MainActivity`.

Add these two overridden functions and then we will talk about them. Add them underneath the closing curly brace of `onCreate`, but before the closing curly brace of `MainActivity`:

```
override fun onResume() {
   super.onResume()

   // More code here later in the chapter
}

override fun onPause() {
   super.onPause()

  // More code here later in the chapter
}
```

What we have done here is override two more of the functions of the `Activity` class. We will see why we need to do this and what we will do inside these functions. The point to note is that by adding these overridden functions, we are giving the OS the opportunity to notify us of the user's intentions in two more situations, in the same way as we did when saving and loading our data in the Note to self app.

It makes sense at this point to move on to the `LiveDrawingView` class, which is the most significant class of this app. We will come back to `MainActivity` toward the end of the chapter.

Coding the LiveDrawingView class

The first thing we will do is solve the problem of our `LiveDrawingView` class not being of the `View` type and having the wrong constructor. Update the class declaration as follows:

```
class LiveDrawingView(
        context: Context,
        screenX: Int)
    : SurfaceView(context){
```

You will be prompted to import the `android.view.SurfaceView` class, as shown in the following screenshot:

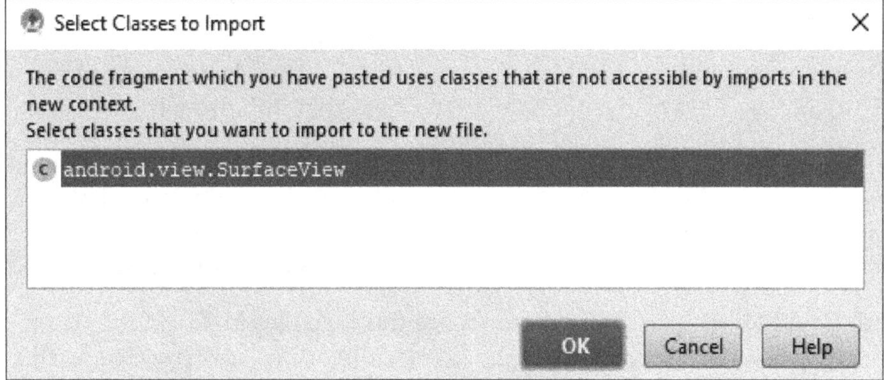

Click on **OK** to confirm.

`SurfaceView` is a descendant of `View` and now `LiveDrawingView` is, by inheritance, also a type of `View`. Look at the `import` statement that has been added. This relationship is made clear, as highlighted in the following code:

```
android.view.SurfaceView
```

Remember that it is because of polymorphism that we can send descendants of `View` to the `setContentView` function in the `MainActivity` class, and that it is because of inheritance that `LiveDrawingView` is now a type of `SurfaceView`.

There are quite a few descendants of `View` that we could have extended to fix this initial problem, but we will see as we continue that `SurfaceView` has some very specific features that are perfect for real-time interactive apps and make this the right choice for us. We have also provided a constructor that matches the arguments called from `MainActivity`.

To import the `Context` class, follow these steps:

1. Place the mouse cursor on the red-colored `Context` text in the new constructor's signature.
2. Hold the *Alt* key and tap the *Enter* key. Choose **Import Class** from the pop-up options.

The previous steps will import the `Context` class. Now, we have no errors in our `LiveDrawingView` class or the `MainActivity` class that initializes it.

At this stage, we could run the app and see that using `LiveDrawingView` as the `View` argument in `setContentView` has worked and that we have a beautiful blank screen, which is ready to draw our particle systems on. You can try this if you wish to, but we will be coding the `LiveDrawingView` class so that it does something next.

Remember that `LiveDrawingView` cannot see the variables in `MainActivity`. By using the constructor, `MainActivity` is providing `LiveDrawingView` with a reference to itself (`this`) as well as the screen resolution in pixels contained in `size.x`.

We will be returning to this class constantly over the course of this project. What we will do right now is get the fundamentals set up ready to add the `ParticleSystem` instances after we have coded them in the next chapter.

To achieve this, we will first add a number of properties. Following this, we will get to code the `draw` function, which will reveal the new steps that we need to take to draw on the screen 60 times per second. Additionally, we will see some familiar code that uses our old friends, `Canvas`, `Paint`, and `drawText`, from the previous chapter.

At this point, we will need to discuss some more theory; items such as how we will time the animations of the particles, and how we can lock these timings without interfering with the smooth running of Android. These last two topics, that is, the **game loop** and **threads,** will then allow us to add the final code of the chapter and witness our particle system painting app in action, albeit with just a bit of text.

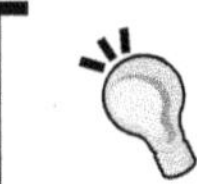

A game loop is a concept that describes allowing virtual systems to update and draw themselves at the same time as allowing them to be altered and interacted with by the user.

Adding the properties

Add the properties after the `LiveDrawingView` declaration and constructor that we have coded, as demonstrated in the following code block:

```
// Are we debugging?
private val debugging = true

// These objects are needed to do the drawing
private lateinit var canvas: Canvas
private val paint: Paint = Paint()

// How many frames per second did we get?
private var fps: Long = 0
// The number of milliseconds in a second
private val millisInSecond: Long = 1000

// How big will the text be?
// Font is 5% (1/20th) of screen width
// Margin is 1.5% (1/75th) of screen width
private val fontSize: Int = mScreenX / 20
private val fontMargin: Int = mScreenX / 75

// The particle systems will be declared here later
```

Make sure that you study the code, and then we will talk about it. Notice that all the properties are declared `private`. You can happily delete all the `private` access specifiers and the code will still work but, as we have no need to access any of these properties from outside of this class, it is sensible to guarantee that this can never happen by declaring them `private`.

The first property is `debugging`. We will use this so that we can manually switch between printing debugging information and not printing debugging information.

The following two classes that we declared instances of will handle the drawing on the screen:

```
// These objects are needed to do the drawing
private lateinit var canvas: Canvas
private val paint: Paint = Paint()
```

The following two properties will give us a bit of insight into what we need to achieve our smooth and consistent animation:

```
// How many frames per second did we get?
private var fps: Long = 0
// The number of milliseconds in a second
private val millisInSecond: Long = 1000
```

Both properties are of the `long` type because they will be holding a large number that we will use to measure time. Computers measure time based on the number of milliseconds since 1970. We will discuss this more when we learn about the game loop; however, for now, we need to know that monitoring and measuring the speed of each frame of animation is how we will make sure that the particles move exactly as they should.

The first variable, `fps`, will be reinitialized in every frame of animation at approximately 60 times per second. It will be passed into each of the `ParticleSystem` objects (every frame of animation) so that they know how much time has elapsed, and can then calculate how far to move or not.

The `millisInSecond` variable is initialized to `1000`. There are indeed `1000` milliseconds in a second. We will use this variable in calculations as it will make our code clearer than if we used the literal value, 1,000.

The next part of the code that we just added is shown here for convenience:

```
// How big will the text be?
// Font is 5% (1/20th) of screen width
// Margin is 1.5% (1/75th) of screen width
private val fontSize: Int = screenX / 20
private val fontMargin: Int = screenX / 75
```

The `fontSize` and `marginSize` properties will be initialized, based on the screen resolution in pixels that were passed in through the constructor (`screenX`). They will hold a value in pixels to make the formatting of our text neat and more concise, rather than constantly doing calculations for each bit of text.

Before we move on, we should make clear that these are the `import` statements that you should currently have at the top of the `LiveDrawingView.kt` code file:

```
import android.content.Context
import android.graphics.Canvas
import android.graphics.Paint
import android.view.SurfaceView
```

Now, let's get ready to draw.

Coding the draw function

Add the `draw` function immediately after the properties that we just added. There will be a couple of errors in the code. We will deal with them first, and then we will go into detail about how the `draw` function will work in relation to `SurfaceView` because there are a number of alien-looking lines of code in there, as well as some familiar ones. Add the following code:

```
// Draw the particle systems and the HUD
private fun draw() {
   if (holder.surface.isValid) {
         // Lock the canvas (graphics memory) ready to draw
         canvas = holder.lockCanvas()

         // Fill the screen with a solid color
         canvas.drawColor(Color.argb(255, 0, 0, 0))

         // Choose a color to paint with
         paint.color = Color.argb(255, 255, 255, 255)

         // Choose the font size
         paint.textSize = fontSize.toFloat()

         // Draw the particle systems

         // Draw the HUD

         if (debugging) {
               printDebuggingText()
         }
```

```
            // Display the drawing on screen
            // unlockCanvasAndPost is a
            // function of SurfaceHolder
            holder.unlockCanvasAndPost(canvas)
        }
    }
```

We have two errors - one error is that the `Color` class needs importing. You can fix this in the usual way or add the next line of code manually. Whatever method you choose, the following extra line needs to be added to the code at the top of the file:

```
import android.graphics.Color;
```

Let's now deal with the other error.

Adding the printDebuggingText function

The second error is the call to `printDebuggingText`. The function doesn't exist yet; so, let's add that now. Add the code after the `draw` function, as follows:

```
private fun printDebuggingText() {
    val debugSize = fontSize / 2
    val debugStart = 150
    paint.textSize = debugSize.toFloat()
    canvas.drawText("fps: $fps",
            10f, (debugStart + debugSize).toFloat(), paint)

}
```

The previous code uses the local `debugSize` variable to hold a value that is half that of the `fontSize` property. This means that as `fontSize` (which is used for the **HUD**) is initialized dynamically based on the screen resolution, `debugSize` will always be half of that.

HUD stands for Heads Up Display and is a fancy way of referring to the buttons and text that overlays the other objects in the app.

The `debugSize` variable is then used to set the size of the font before we start drawing the text. The `debugStart` variable is a guess at a tidy vertical position to start printing the debugging text with a bit of padding so that it isn't squashed too close to the edge of the screen.

These two values are then used to position a line of text on the screen that shows the current frames per second. As this function is called from `draw`, which, in turn, will be called from the game loop, this line of text will be constantly refreshed up to 60 times per second.

> It is possible that on very high- or very low-resolution screens, you might need to experiment with this value to find something that works for your screen.

Let's explore these new lines of code in the `draw` function and examine exactly how we can use `SurfaceView`, from which our `LiveDrawingView` class is derived, to handle all our drawing requirements.

Understanding the draw function and the SurfaceView class

Starting in the middle of the function and working outward for a change, we have a few familiar things, such as the calls to `drawColor`, and then we set the color and text size as we have before. We can also see the comment that indicates where we will eventually add the code to draw the particle systems and the HUD:

- The `drawColor` code clears the screen with a solid color.
- The `textSize` property of `paint` sets the size of the text for drawing the HUD.
- We will code the process of drawing the HUD once we have explored particle systems a little more. We will let the player know how many particles and systems their drawing is comprised of.

What is completely new, however, is the code at the very start of the `draw` function, as shown in the following code block:

```
if (holder.surface.isValid) {
        // Lock the canvas (graphics memory) ready to draw
        canvas = holder.lockCanvas()
```

The `if` condition is `holder.surface.isValid`. If this line returns true, it confirms that the area of memory that we want to manipulate to represent our frame of drawing is available, and then the code continues inside the `if` statement.

This is necessary because all our drawing and other processing (such as moving the objects) will take place asynchronously with the code that detects the user input and listens to the OS for messages. This wasn't an issue in the previous project because our code simply sat there waiting for input, drew a single frame, and then sat there waiting again.

Now that we want to continuously execute the code 60 times per second, we are going to need to confirm that we have access to the memory where the graphics are drawn to, before we access it.

This raises another question about how this code runs asynchronously. But that will be answered when we discuss threads shortly. For now, just know that the line of code checks whether another part of our code, or Android itself, is currently using the required portion of memory. If it is free, then the code inside the `if` statement executes.

Furthermore, the first line of code to execute inside the `if` statement calls `lockCanvas`, so that if another part of the code tries to access the memory while our code is accessing it, it won't be able to - and then we do all our drawing.

Finally, in the `draw` function, the following line of code (plus comments) appears right at the end:

```
// Display the drawing on screen
// unlockCanvasAndPost is a
// function of SurfaceHolder
holder.unlockCanvasAndPost(canvas)
```

The `unlockCanvasAndPost` function sends our newly decorated `Canvas` object (`canvas`) for drawing to the screen and releases the lock so that other areas of code can use it, albeit very briefly, before the whole process starts again. This process happens for every single frame of animation.

We now understand the code in the `draw` function. However, we still don't have the mechanism that calls the `draw` function over and over. In fact, we don't even call the `draw` function once. Next, we will discuss game loops and threads.

The game loop

So, what is a game loop anyway? Almost every live drawing, graphics-based app, and game has a game loop. Even games that you might not expect, such as turn-based games, still need to synchronize player input with drawing and AI, while following the rules of the underlying OS.

There is a constant need to update the objects in the app, such as by moving them and drawing everything in its current position while simultaneously responding to user input:

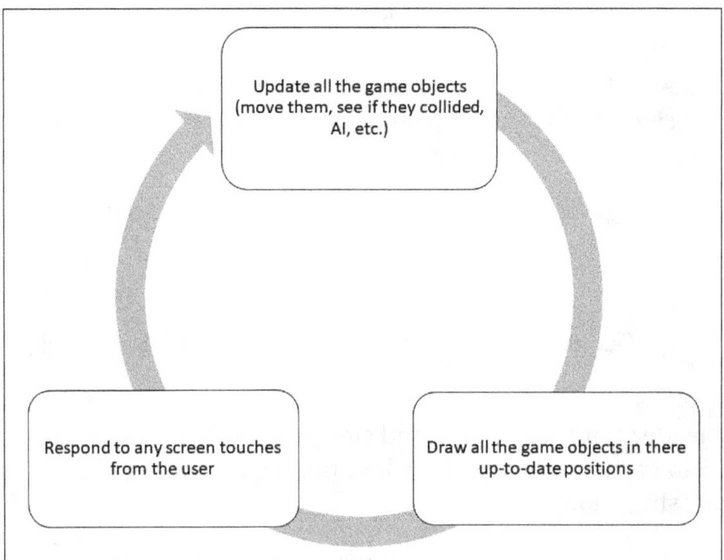

Our game loop comprises three main phases:

1. Update all game and drawing objects by moving them, detecting collisions, and processing the AI, such as particle movements and state changes
2. Based on the data that has just been updated, draw the frame of animation in its latest state
3. Respond to screen touches from the user

We already have a `draw` function for handling this part of the loop. This suggests that we will have a function to do all the updating as well. We will soon code the outline of an `update` function. In addition, we know that we can respond to screen touches, although we will need to adapt slightly from all the previous projects because we are no longer working inside an `Activity` class or using conventional UI widgets from a layout.

There is a further issue in that (as I briefly mentioned) all the updating and drawing happens asynchronously to detect screen touches and listen to the OS.

Just to be clear, asynchronous means that it does not occur at the same time. Our code will work by sharing execution time with Android and the UI. The CPU will very quickly switch back and forth between our code and Android or user input.

But how exactly will these three phases be looped through? How will we code this asynchronous system, from which `update` and `draw` can be called, and how will we make the loop run at the correct speed (or frame rate)?

As you can probably guess, writing an efficient game loop is not as simple as a `while` loop.

Our game loop will, however, also contain a `while` loop.

We need to consider timing, starting, and stopping the loop, in addition to not causing the OS to become unresponsive because we are monopolizing the entire CPU within our single loop.

But when and how do we call our `draw` function? How do we measure and keep track of the frame rate? With these things in mind, our finished game loop is probably better represented by the following diagram – notice the introduction to the concept of **threads**:

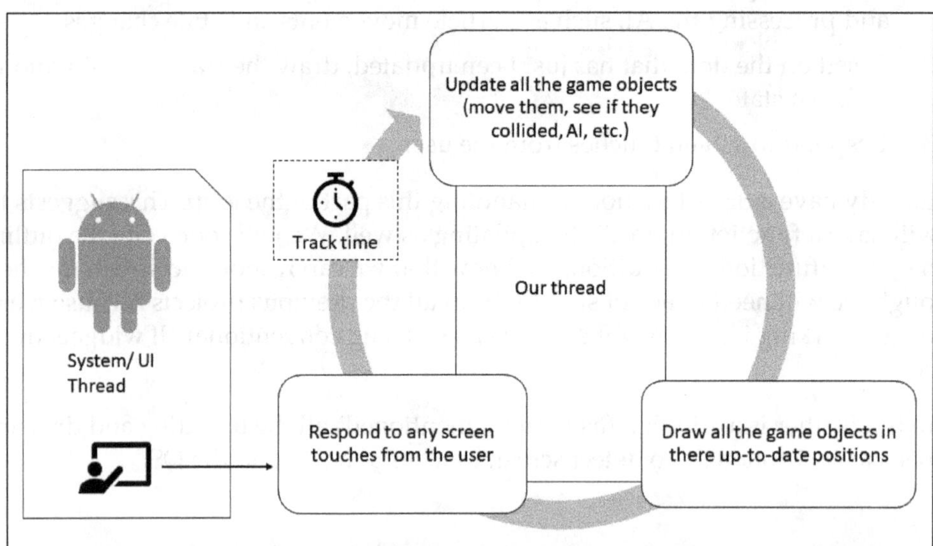

Now that we know what we want to achieve, let's learn about threads.

Threads

So, what is a thread? You can think of threads in programming in the same way as you do threads in a story. In one thread of a story, we might have the primary character battling the enemy on the frontline, while in another thread, the soldier's family are living, day to day. Of course, a story doesn't have to have only two threads - we could introduce a third thread. For instance, the story also tells of the politicians and military commanders making decisions, and these decisions then subtly, or not so subtly, affect what happens in the other threads.

Programming threads are just like this. We create parts or threads in our program that control different aspects for us. In Android, threads are especially useful when we need to ensure that a task does not interfere with the main (UI) thread of the app, or if we have a background task that takes a long time to complete and must not interrupt the main thread of execution. We introduce threads to represent these different aspects for the following reasons:

- They make sense from an organizational point of view
- They are a proven way of structuring a program that works
- The nature of the system we are working on forces us to use them anyway

In Android, we use threads for all three reasons simultaneously - because it makes sense, it works, and we must use threads since the design of the Android system requires it.

Often, we use threads without knowing it. This happens because we use classes that use threads on our behalf. All the animations that we coded in *Chapter 19, Animations and Interpolations,* were all running in threads. Another such example in Android is the `SoundPool` class, which loads sound in a thread. We will see, or rather hear, `SoundPool` in action in *Chapter 23, Android Sound Effects and the Spinner Widget*. We will see again that our code doesn't have to handle the aspects of threads that we are about to learn about because it is all handled internally by the class. In this project, however, we need to get a bit more involved.

In real-time systems, think about a thread that is receiving the player's button taps for moving left and right at the same time as listening for messages from the OS, such as calling `onCreate` (and other functions that we will see later) as one thread, and another thread that draws all the graphics and calculates all the movements.

Problems with threads

Programs with multiple threads can have problems associated with them, such as the threads of a story; if proper synchronization does not occur, then things can go wrong. What if our soldier went into battle before the battle or the war even existed?

Consider that we have a variable, `Int x`, that represents a key piece of data that three threads of our program use. What happens if one thread gets slightly ahead of itself and makes the data "wrong" for the other two? This problem is the problem of **correctness** caused by multiple threads racing to completion while remaining oblivious - because, after all, they are just dumb code.

The problem of correctness can be solved by close oversight of the threads and locking. **Locking** means temporarily preventing execution in one thread to make sure that things are working in a synchronized manner; this is similar to preventing a soldier from boarding a ship to war until the ship has docked and the gangplank has been lowered, thereby avoiding an embarrassing splash.

The other problem with programs with multiple threads is the problem of **deadlock**. Here, one or more threads become locked, waiting for the "right" moment to access `Int x`; however, that moment never comes and, eventually, the entire program grinds to a halt.

You might have noticed that it was the solution to the first problem (correctness) that is the cause of the second problem (deadlock).

Fortunately, the problem has been solved for us. In the same way that we use the `Activity` class and override `onCreate` to know exactly when we need to create our app, we can also use other classes to create and manage our threads. For example, with `Activity,` we only need to know how to use them, not how they work.

So, why did I tell you about threads when you don't need to know about them, you rightly ask? This is simply because we will be writing code that looks different and is structured in an unfamiliar manner. We can then achieve the following goals:

- Understand the general concept of a thread in that it is the same as a story thread that happens almost simultaneously
- Learn the few rules of using a thread

By doing so, we will have no difficulty in writing our Kotlin code to create and work within our threads. There are a few different Android classes that handle threads, and different thread classes work best in different situations.

All we need to remember is that we will be writing parts of our program that run at *almost* the same time as each other.

What do you mean by almost? What is happening is that the CPU switches between threads in turn/asynchronously. However, this happens so fast that we will not be able to perceive anything but simultaneity/synchrony. Of course, in the story thread analogy, people do act entirely synchronously.

Let's take a glimpse of what our thread code will look like. Don't add any code to the project just yet. We can then declare an object of the `Thread` type, as follows:

```
private lateinit var thread: Thread
```

You can then initialize and start it as follows:

```
// Initialize the instance of Thread
thread = Thread(this)

// Start the thread
thread.start()
```

There is one more conundrum to threads; take another look at the constructor that initializes the thread. Here is the line of code again for your convenience:

```
thread = Thread(this)
```

Take a look at the argument that is passed to the constructor; we pass in `this`. Remember that the code is going inside the `LiveDrawingView` class, not `MainActivity`. We can, therefore, surmise that `this` is a reference to a `LiveDrawingView` class (which extends `SurfaceView`).

It seems very unlikely that when the engineers at Android HQ wrote the `Thread` class, they would have been aware that one day, we would be writing our `LiveDrawingView` class. So, how can this work?

The `Thread` class needs an entirely different type to be passed into its constructor. The `Thread` constructor needs a `Runnable` object.

You can confirm this fact by referring to the `Thread` class on the Android developer's website here: `https://developer.android.com/reference/java/lang/Thread.html#Thread(java.lang.Runnable)`.

Do you recall that we discussed interfaces in *Chapter 12, Connecting Our Kotlin to the UI and Nullability*? As a reminder, we can implement an interface by adding the interface name after the class declaration.

We must then implement the abstract functions of the interface. `Runnable` has just one; it is the `run` function.

You can confirm this preceding fact by looking at the `Runnable` interface on the Android developer's website here: `https://developer.android.com/reference/java/lang/Runnable.html`.

We can then use the `override` keyword to change what happens when the OS allows our thread object to run its code:

```
override fun run() {
        // Anything in here executes in a thread
        // No skill needed on our part
        // It is all handled by Android, the Thread class
        // and the Runnable interface
}
```

Within the overridden `run` function, we will call two functions, one that we have started already, `draw`, and the other is `update`. The `update` function is where all our calculations and AI will go. The code will be similar to the following block, but don't add it yet:

```
override fun run() {
    // Update the drawing based on
    // user input and physics
    update()

    // Draw all the particle systems in their updated locations
    draw()
}
```

When appropriate, we can also stop our thread as follows:

```
thread.join()
```

Now, everything that is in the `run` function is executing in a separate thread, leaving the default or UI thread to listen for touches and system events. We will see how the two threads communicate with each other in the drawing project shortly.

Note that precisely where all these parts of the code will go in our app has not been explained, but it is so much easier to show you in the real project.

Implementing the game loop with a thread

Now that we have learned about the game loop and threads, we can put it all together to implement our game loop in the Living Drawing project.

We will add the entire code for the game loop, including writing code in two functions in the `MainActivity` class to start and stop the thread that will control the loop.

Reader challenge

Can you work out for yourself how the `Activity`-based class will start and stop the thread in the `LiveDrawingView` class?

Implementing Runnable and providing the run function

Update the class declaration by implementing `Runnable`, as shown in the following highlighted code:

```
class LiveDrawingView(
        context: Context,
        screenX: Int)
    : SurfaceView(context), Runnable {
```

Notice that we have a new error in the code. Hover the mouse cursor over the word `Runnable`, and you will see a message informing you that we need to implement the `run` function just as we discussed during the discussion on interfaces and threads in the previous section. Add the empty `run` function, including the `override` label.

It doesn't matter where you add it, provided that it is within the `LiveDrawingView` class's curly braces and not inside another function. Add the empty `run` function, as follows:

```
// When we start the thread with:
// thread.start();
// the run function is continuously called by Android
// because we implemented the Runnable interface
// Calling thread.join();
// will stop the thread
override fun run() {

}
```

The error is gone and now we can declare and initialize a `Thread` object.

Coding the thread

Declare some variables and instances underneath all our other members in the `LiveDrawingView` class, as follows:

```
// Here is the Thread and two control variables
private lateinit var thread: Thread
// This volatile variable can be accessed
// from inside and outside the thread
@Volatile
private var drawing: Boolean = false
private var paused = true
```

Now, we can start and stop the thread - take a moment to think about where we might do this. Remember that the app needs to respond to the OS that is starting and stopping the app.

Starting and stopping the thread

Now, we need to start and stop the thread. We have seen the code that we need, but when and where should we do it? Let's add code to two functions - one to start and one to stop - and then we can consider when and where to call these functions. Add these two functions inside the `LiveDrawingView` class. If their names sound familiar, it is not by chance:

```
// This function is called by MainActivity
// when the user quits the app
fun pause() {
   // Set drawing to false
   // Stopping the thread isn't
   // always instant
   drawing = false
   try {
         // Stop the thread
         thread.join()
  }  catch (e: InterruptedException) {
     Log.e("Error:", "joining thread")
  }

}
```

```
// This function is called by MainActivity
// when the player starts the app
fun resume() {
    drawing = true
    // Initialize the instance of Thread
    thread = Thread(this)

    // Start the thread
    thread.start()
}
```

What is happening is slightly given away by the comments. We now have a `pause` and `resume` function that stop and start the `Thread` object using the same code we discussed previously.

Notice that the new functions are `public`, and therefore, they are accessible from outside the class to any other class that has an instance of `LiveDrawingView`. Remember that `MainActivity` holds the fully declared and initialized instance of `LiveDrawingView`.

Let's use the Android Activity lifecycle to call these two new functions.

Using the Activity lifecycle to start and stop the thread

Update the overridden `onResume` and `onPause` functions in `MainActivity`, as shown in the following highlighted lines of code:

```
override fun onResume() {
  super.onResume()

  // More code here later in the chapter
  liveDrawingView.resume()
}

override fun onPause() {
   super.onPause()

   // More code here later in the chapter
   liveDrawingView.pause()
}
```

Now, our thread will be started and stopped when the OS is resuming and pausing our app. Remember that `onResume` is called after `onCreate` the first time that an app is started, not just after resuming from a pause. The code inside `onResume` and `onPause` uses the `liveDrawingView` object to call its `resume` and `pause` functions, which, in turn, has the code to start and stop the thread. This code then triggers the thread's `run` function to execute. It is in this `run` function (in `LiveDrawingView`) that we will code our game loop. Let's do that now.

Coding the run function

Although our thread is set up and ready to go, nothing happens because the `run` function is empty. Code the `run` function, as follows:

```
override fun run() {
    // The drawing Boolean gives us finer control
    // rather than just relying on the calls to run
    // drawing must be true AND
    // the thread running for the main
    // loop to execute
    while (drawing) {

            // What time is it now at the
            // start of the loop?
            val frameStartTime =
                    System.currentTimeMillis()

           // Provided the app isn't paused
           // call the update function
           if (!paused) {
                 update()
           }

           // The movement has been handled
           // we can draw the scene.
           draw()

           // How long did this frame/loop take?
           // Store the answer in timeThisFrame
           val timeThisFrame = System.currentTimeMillis()
                - frameStartTime

        // Make sure timeThisFrame is
        // at least 1 millisecond
```

```
        // because accidentally dividing
        // by zero crashes the app
        if (timeThisFrame > 0) {
            // Store the current frame rate in fps
            // ready to pass to the update functions of
            // of our particles in the next frame/loop
            fps = millisInSecond / timeThisFrame
        }
    }
}
```

Notice that there are two errors in Android Studio. This is because we have not written the `update` function yet. Let's quickly add an empty function (with a comment) for it; I added mine after the `run` function:

```
private fun update() {
    // Update the particles
}
```

Now, let's discuss in detail how the code in the `run` function achieves the aims of our game loop by looking at the entire thing one step at a time.

This first part initiates a `while` loop with the `drawing` condition, and then wraps the rest of the code inside `run` so that the thread will need to be started (for `run` to be called) and `drawing` will need to be true for the `while` loop to execute:

```
override fun run() {
    // The drawing Boolean gives us finer control
    // rather than just relying on the calls to run
    // drawing must be true AND
    // the thread running for the main
    // loop to execute
    while (drawing) {
```

The first line of code inside the `while` loop declares and initializes a local variable, `frameStartTime`, with whatever the current time is. The `currentTimeMillis` function of the `System` class returns this value. If we later want to measure how long a frame has taken, then we need to know what time it started:

```
// What time is it now at the
// start of the loop?
val frameStartTime =
  System.currentTimeMillis()
```

Next, still inside the `while` loop, we check whether the app is paused, and only if the app is not paused does this next code get executed. If the logic allows execution inside this block, then `update` is called:

```
// Provided the app isn't paused
// call the update function
if (!paused) {
   update()
}
```

Outside of the previous `if` statement, the `draw` function is called to draw all the objects in the just-updated positions. At this point, another local variable is declared and initialized with the length of time that it took to complete the entire frame (updating and drawing). This value is calculated by getting the current time, once again with `currentTimeMillis`, and subtracting `frameStartTime` from it, as follows:

```
// The movement has been handled
// we can draw the scene.
draw()

// How long did this frame/loop take?
// Store the answer in timeThisFrame
val timeThisFrame = System.currentTimeMillis()
  - frameStartTime
```

The next `if` statement detects whether `timeThisFrame` is greater than zero. It is possible for the value to be zero if the thread runs before the objects are initialized. If you look at the code inside the `if` statement, it calculates the frame rate by dividing the elapsed time by `millisInSecond`. If you divide by zero, the app will crash, which is why we perform the check.

Once `fps` gets the value assigned to it, we can use it in the next frame to pass to the `update` function, which updates all the particles that we will code in the next chapter. They will use the value to make sure that they move by precisely the correct amount based on their target speed and the length of time the frame of animation that has just ended has taken:

```
// Make sure timeThisFrame is
// at least 1 millisecond
// because accidentally dividing
// by zero crashes the app
if (timeThisFrame > 0) {
   // Store the current frame rate in fps
```

```
        // ready to pass to the update functions of
        // of our particles in the next frame/loop
        fps = millisInSecond / timeThisFrame
    }
```

The result of the calculation that initializes `fps` in each frame is that `fps` will hold a fraction of one. As the frame rate fluctuates, `fps` will hold a different value and supply the particle systems with the appropriate number to calculate each move.

Running the app

Click on the play button in Android Studio and the hard work and theory of the chapter will come to life:

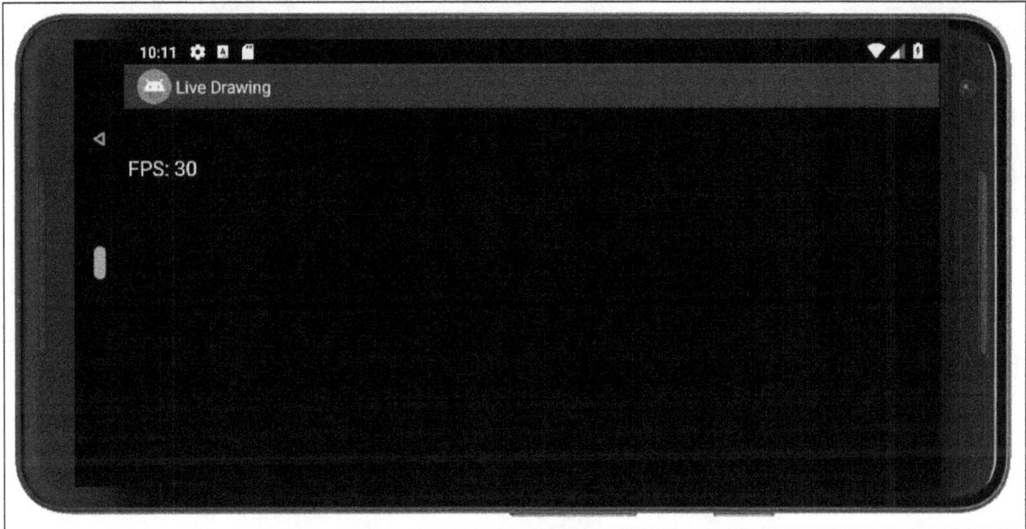

You can see that we now have a real-time system created with our game loop and a thread. If you run this on a real device, you will easily achieve 60 frames per second at this stage.

Summary

This was probably the most technical chapter so far. We explored threads, game loops, timing, using interfaces, and the `Activity` lifecycle – it's a very long list of topics to cram in.

If the exact interrelationship between these things is still not entirely clear, it is not a problem. All you need to know is that when the user starts and stops the app, the `MainActivity` class will handle starting and stopping the thread by calling the `LiveDrawingView` class's `pause` and `resume` functions. It achieves this through the overridden `onPause` and `onResume` functions, which are called by the OS.

Once the thread is running, the code inside the `run` function executes alongside the UI thread that is listening for user input. As we call the `update` and `draw` functions from the `run` function at the same time as keeping track of how long each frame is taking, our app is ready to rock and roll.

We just need to allow the user to add some particles to their artwork, which we can then update in each call to `update` and draw in each call to `draw`.

In the next chapter, we will be coding, updating, and drawing both the `Particle` and `ParticleSytem` classes. In addition, we will be writing code for the user to interact (do some drawing) with the app.

22
Particle Systems and Handling Screen Touches

We already have our real-time system that we implemented in the previous chapter using a thread. In this chapter, we will create the entities that will exist and evolve in this real-time system as if they have a mind of their own.

We will also look at how the user can draw these entities to the screen by learning how to set up the ability to interact with the screen. This is different than interacting with a widget in a UI layout.

Here is what is coming up in this chapter:

- Adding custom buttons to the screen
- Coding the `Particle` class
- Coding the `ParticleSystem` class
- Handling screen touches

We will start by adding a custom UI to our app.

Adding custom buttons to the screen

We need to let the user control when to start another drawing and clear the screen of their previous work. We also need the user to be able to decide whether or when to bring the drawing to life. To achieve this, we will add two buttons to the screen, one for each of these tasks.

Add these new properties to the code after the other properties in the `LiveDrawingView` class:

```
// These will be used to make simple buttons
private var resetButton: RectF
private var togglePauseButton: RectF
```

We now have two `RectF` instances. These objects hold four `Float` coordinates each, one coordinate for each corner of our two proposed buttons.

We will now add an `init` block to the `LiveDrawingView` class and initialize the positions when the `LiveDrawingView` instance is first created, as follows:

```
init {
   // Initialize the two buttons
   resetButton = RectF(0f, 0f, 100f, 100f)
   togglePauseButton = RectF(0f, 150f, 100f, 250f)
}
```

Now we have added actual coordinates for the buttons. If you visualize the coordinates on screen, then you will see that they are in the top left-hand corner, with the pause button just below the reset/clear button.

Now we can draw the buttons. Add the following two lines of code to the `draw` function of the `LiveDrawingView` class. The preexisting comment shows exactly where the new highlighted code should go:

```
// Draw the buttons
canvas.drawRect(resetButton, paint)
canvas.drawRect(togglePauseButton, paint)
```

The new code uses an overridden version of the `drawRect` function, and we simply pass our two `RectF` instances straight in alongside the usual `Paint` instance. Our buttons will now appear on the screen.

We will see how the user can interact with these slightly crude buttons later in the chapter.

Implementing a particle system effect

A particle system is a system that controls particles. In our case, `ParticleSystem` is a class we will write that will spawn instances (lots of instances) of the `Particle` class (also a class we will write) that together will create a simple explosion-like effect.

Here is a screenshot of some particles controlled by a particle system as it may appear by the end of this chapter:

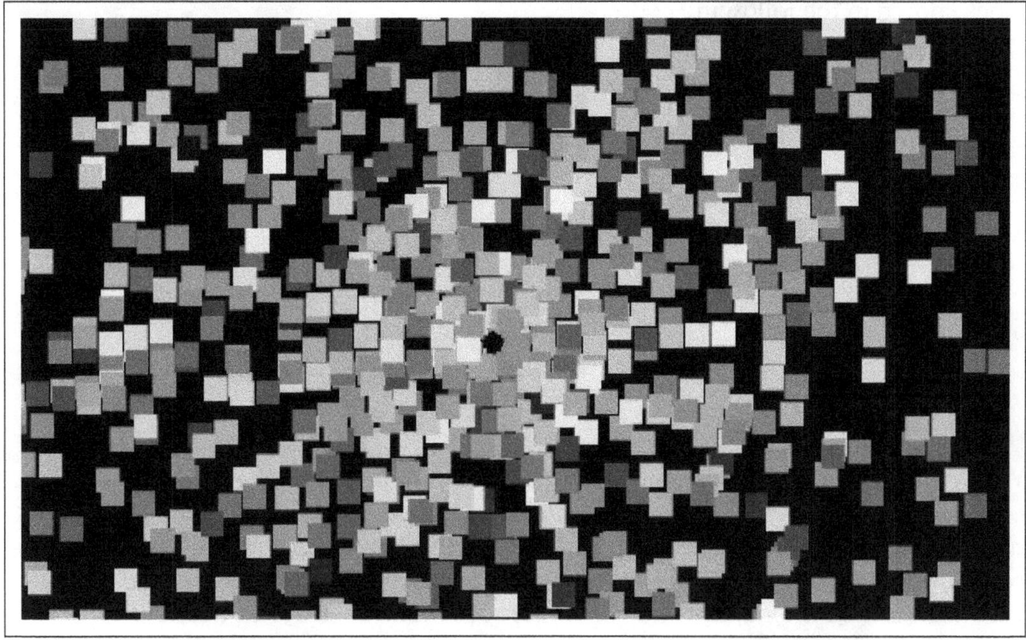

Just for clarification, each of the colored squares is an instance of the `Particle` class, and all the `Particle` instances are controlled and held by the `ParticleSystem` class. In addition, the user will create multiple (hundreds) of `ParticleSystem` instances by drawing with their finger. The particle systems will appear as dots or blocks until the user taps the Pause button and they come to life. We will examine the code closely enough that you will be able to amend in code the size, color, speed, and quantities of `Particle` and `ParticleSystem` instances.

> It is left as an exercise for the reader to add additional buttons to the screen to allow the user to change these properties as a feature of the app.

We will start by coding the `Particle` class.

Coding the Particle class

Add the `import` statement, the member variables, the constructor, and the `init` block shown in the following code:

```
import android.graphics.PointF

class Particle(direction: PointF) {

    private val velocity: PointF = PointF()
    val position: PointF = PointF()

    init {
          // Determine the direction
          velocity.x = direction.x
          velocity.y = direction.y
    }
```

We have two properties—one for velocity and one for position. They are both `PointF` objects. `PointF` holds two `Float` values. The position of a particle is simple: it is just a horizontal and vertical value. The velocity is worth explaining a little more. Each of the two values in the `velocity` object `PointF` will be a speed, one horizontal and the other vertical. It is the combination of these two speeds that will create a direction.

Next, add the following `update` function; we will look at it in more detail in a moment:

```
fun update() {
    // Move the particle
    position.x += velocity.x
    position.y += velocity.y
}
```

Each `Particle` instance's `update` function will be called for each frame of the app by the `ParticleSystem` object's `update` function, which, in turn, will be called by the `LiveDrawingView` class (again in the `update` function), which we will code later in the chapter.

Inside the `update` function, the horizontal and vertical values of `position` are updated using the corresponding values of `velocity`.

Note that we don't bother using the current frame rate in the update. You could amend this if you want to be certain that your particles will all fly at exactly the correct speed, but all the speeds are going to be random anyway. There is not much to gain from adding this extra calculation (for every particle). As we will soon see, however, the `ParticleSystem` class will need to take account of the current number of frames per second to measure how long it should run for.

Now we can move on to the `ParticleSysytem` class.

Coding the ParticleSystem class

The `ParticleSystem` class has a few more details than the `Particle` class, but it is still reasonably straightforward. Remember what we need to achieve with this class: hold, spawn, update, and draw a bunch (quite a big bunch) of `Particle` instances.

Add the following constructor, properties, and import statements:

```
import android.graphics.Canvas
import android.graphics.Color
import android.graphics.Paint
import android.graphics.PointF

import java.util.*

class ParticleSystem {

    private var duration: Float = 0f
    private var particles:
          ArrayList<Particle> = ArrayList()

    private val random = Random()
    var isRunning = false
```

We have four properties: first, a `Float` called `duration` that will be initialized to the number of seconds we want the effect to run for; the `ArrayList` instance called `particles`, holds `Particle` instances and will hold all the `Particle` objects we instantiate for this system.

The `Random` instance called `random` is created because we need to generate so many random values that creating a new object each time would slow us down a bit.

Finally, the `Boolean` called `isRunning` will track whether the particle system is currently being shown (updating and drawing).

Now we can code the `initParticles` function. This function will be called each time we want a new `ParticleSystem`. Note that the one and only parameter is an `Int` called `numParticles`.

When we call `initParticles`, we can have some fun initializing crazy amounts of particles. Add the `initParticles` function as follows and then we will look more closely at the code:

```
fun initParticles(numParticles:Int){

    // Create the particles
    for (i in 0 until numParticles) {
          var angle: Double = random.nextInt(360).toDouble()
          angle *= (3.14 / 180)

          // Option 1 - Slow particles
          val speed = random.nextFloat() / 3

          // Option 2 - Fast particles
          //val speed = (random.nextInt(10)+1);

          val direction: PointF

          direction = PointF(Math.cos(
                      angle).toFloat() * speed,
                      Math.sin(angle).toFloat() * speed)

          particles.add(Particle(direction))

     }
}
```

The `initParticles` function consists of just one `for` loop that does all the work. The `for` loop runs from zero to `numParticles`.

First, a random number between 0 and 359 is generated and stored in `Float angle`. Next, there is a little bit of math where we multiply `angle` by `3.14/180`. This turns the angle in degrees to radian-based measurements, which are required by the `Math` class that we will use in a moment.

Then we generate another random number between 1 and 10 and assign the result to a `Float` variable called `speed`.

Note that I have added comments to suggest different options for values in this part of the code. I do this in several places in the `ParticleSystem` class, and when we get to the end of the chapter, we will have some fun altering these values and see what effect this has on the drawing app.

Now that we have a random angle and speed, we can convert and combine them into a vector that can be used inside the `update` function in each frame.

A vector is a value that determines both the direction and speed. Our vector is stored in the `direction` object until it is passed into the `Particle` constructor. Vectors can be of many dimensions. Ours consists of two dimensions, and therefore defines a heading between 0 and 359 degrees and a speed between 1 and 10. You can read more about vectors, headings, sine and cosine on my website at `http://gamecodeschool.com/essentials/calculating-heading-in-2d-games-using-trigonometric-functions-part-1/`.

I have decided not to explain the single line of code that uses `Math.sin` and `Math.cos` to create a vector in full because the magic occurs partly in the following formulas:

- Cosine of an angle x `speed`
- Sine of an angle x `speed`

The rest of the magic takes place in the hidden calculations within the cosine and sine functions provided by the `Math` class. If you want to know their full details, then you can look at the previous tip.

Finally, a new `Particle` is created and then added to the `particles ArrayList`.

Next, we will code the `update` function. Note that the `update` function needs the current frame rate as a parameter. Code the `update` function as follows:

```
fun update(fps: Long) {
    duration -= 1f / fps

    for (p in particles) {
            p.update()
   }

    if (duration < 0) {
            isRunning = false
   }
}
```

The first thing that happens inside the `update` function is that the elapsed time is taken off `duration`. Remember that `fps` means frames per second, so `1/fps` gives a value of a fraction of a second.

Next, there is a `for` loop, which calls the `update` function for every `Particle` instance in the `particles ArrayList`.

Finally, the code checks whether the particle effect has run its course with `if(duration < 0)` and if it has then `isRunning` is set to `false`.

Now we can code the `emitParticles` function, which will set each `Particle` instance running, and which is not to be confused with `initParticles`, which creates all the new particles and gives them their velocities. The `initParticles` function will be called once before the user gets to interact with the screen, whereas the `emitParticles` function will be called each time the effect needs to be started as the user draws on the screen.

Add the `emitParticles` function using the following code:

```
fun emitParticles(startPosition: PointF) {
    isRunning = true

    // Option 1 - System lasts for half a minute
    duration = 30f

    // Option 2 - System lasts for 2 seconds
    //duration = 3f

    for (p in particles) {
          p.position.x = startPosition.x
          p.position.y = startPosition.y
    }
}
```

First, note that a `PointF` where all the particles will start is passed in as a parameter. All the particles will start at the same position and then fan out every frame, based on their individual random velocities.

The `isRunning` `Boolean` is set to `true` and `duration` is set to `30f`, so the effect will run for 30 seconds and the `for` loop will set the position of every particle to the starting coordinates.

The final function for our `ParticleSysytem` is the `draw` function, which will reveal the effect in all its glory. The function receives a reference to `Canvas` and `Paint` so it can draw to the same `Canvas` instance that `LiveDrawingView` has just locked in its `draw` function.

Add the `draw` function as follows:

```
fun draw(canvas: Canvas, paint: Paint) {

    for (p in particles) {

            // Option 1 - Colored particles
            //paint.setARGB(255, random.nextInt(256),
            //random.nextInt(256),
            //random.nextInt(256))

            // Option 2 - White particles
            paint.color = Color.argb(255, 255, 255, 255)
            // How big is each particle?

            // Option 1 - Big particles
            //val sizeX = 25f
            //val sizeY = 25f

            // Option 2 - Medium particles
            //val sizeX = 10f
            //val sizeY = 10f

            // Option 3 - Tiny particles
            val sizeX = 12f
            val sizeY = 12f

            // Draw the particle
            // Option 1 - Square particles
            canvas.drawRect(p.position.x, p.position.y,
                        p.position.x + sizeX,
                        p.position.y + sizeY,
                        paint)

           // Option 2 - Circular particles
           //canvas.drawCircle(p.position.x, p.position.y,
           //sizeX, paint)
    }
}
```

In the preceding code, a `for` loop steps through each of the `Particle` instances in `particles`. Each `Particle`, in turn, is drawn using `drawRect` after the size and color of the rectangle are set.

Note again how I have suggested different options for code changes so that we can have some fun when we have finished coding.

We can now start to put the particle system to work.

Spawning particle systems in the LiveDrawingView class

Add an `ArrayList` instance full of systems and some more members to keep track of things. Add the highlighted code in the following code to the positions indicated by the existing comments:

```
// The particle systems will be declared here later
private val particleSystems = ArrayList<ParticleSystem>()

private var nextSystem = 0
private val maxSystems = 1000
private val particlesPerSystem = 100
```

We can now keep track of up to 1,000 particle systems with 100 particles in each. Feel free to play with these numbers. On a modern device, you can run particles into the millions without any trouble, but on the emulator, it will begin to struggle with just a few hundred thousand.

Initialize the systems in the `init` block by adding the following highlighted code:

```
init {

  // Initialize the two buttons
  resetButton = RectF(0f, 0f, 100f, 100f)
  togglePauseButton = RectF(0f, 150f, 100f, 250f)

  // Initialize the particles and their systems
  for (i in 0 until maxSystems) {
    particleSystems.add(ParticleSystem())
    particleSystems[i]
          .initParticles(particlesPerSystem)
  }
}
```

The code loops through the `ArrayList`, calling the constructor followed by `initParticles` on each of the `ParticleSystem` instances.

Now we can update the systems on each frame of the loop by adding the highlighted code to the `update` function:

```
private fun update() {
  // Update the particles
  for (i in 0 until particleSystems.size) {
        if (particleSystems[i].isRunning) {
              particleSystems[i].update(fps)
        }
  }
}
```

The previous code loops through each of the `ParticleSystem` instances, first checking whether they are active and then calling the `update` function and passing in the current frames per second.

Now we can draw the systems in each frame of the loop by adding the highlighted code in the following snippet to the `draw` function:

```
// Choose the font size
paint.textSize = fontSize.toFloat()

// Draw the particle systems
for (i in 0 until nextSystem) {
  particleSystems[i].draw(canvas, paint)
}

// Draw the buttons
canvas.drawRect(resetButton, paint)
canvas.drawRect(togglePauseButton, paint)
```

The previous code loops through `particleSystems`, calling the `draw` function on each. Of course, we haven't actually spawned any instances yet; for that, we will need to learn how to respond to screen interactions.

Handling touches

To get started with screen interaction, add the `OnTouchEvent` function to the `LiveDrawingView` class as follows:

```
override fun onTouchEvent(
   motionEvent: MotionEvent): Boolean {

   return true
}
```

This is an overridden function, and it is called by Android every time the user interacts with the screen. Look at the one and only parameter of `onTouchEvent`.

It turns out that `motionEvent` has a whole bunch of data tucked away inside it, and this data contains the details of the touch that just occurred. The operating system sent it to us because it knows we will probably need some of it.

Note that I said *some of it*. The `MotionEvent` class is quite extensive; it contains within it dozens of functions and properties.

For now, all we need to know is that the screen responds at the precise moment that the player's finger moves, touches the screen, or is removed.

Some of the variables and functions contained within `motionEvent` that we will use include the following:

- The `action` property, which, unsurprisingly, holds the action that was performed. Unfortunately, it supplies this information in a slightly encoded format, which explains the need for some of these other variables.
- The `ACTION_MASK` variable, which provides a value known as a mask, which, with the help of a little bit more Kotlin trickery, can be used to filter the data from `action`.
- The `ACTION_UP` variable, which we can use to see whether the action performed (such as removing a finger) is the one we want to respond to.
- The `ACTION_DOWN` variable, which we can use to see whether the action performed is the one we want to respond to.
- The `ACTION_MOVE` variable, which we can use to see whether the action performed is a move/drag action.
- The `x` property holds a horizontal floating-point coordinate where the event happened.
- The `y` property holds a vertical floating-point coordinate where the event happened.

As a specific example, say we need to filter the data in `action` using `ACTION_MASK` and see whether the result is the same as `ACTION_UP`. If it is, then we know that the user has just removed their finger from the screen, perhaps because they just tapped a button. Once we are sure that the event is of the correct type, we will need to find out where it happened using `x` and `y`.

There is one final complication. The Kotlin trickery I referred to is the `&` bitwise operator, not to be confused with the logical `&&` operator we have been using in conjunction with the `if` keyword.

The `&` bitwise operator checks to see whether each corresponding part in two values is true. This is the filter that is required when using `ACTION_MASK` with `action`.

Sanity check: I was hesitant to go into detail about `MotionEvent` and bitwise operators. It is possible to complete this entire book and even make a professional-quality interactive app without ever needing to fully understand them. If you know that the line of code we will write in the next section determines the event type the player triggers, then that is all you need to know. I just thought that a discerning reader such as your would like to know the ins and outs of how the system works. In summary, if you understand bitwise operators, then great; you are good to go. If you don't, it doesn't matter; you are still good to go. If you are curious about bitwise operators (there are quite a few), you can read more about them at `https://en.wikipedia.org/wiki/Bitwise_operation`.

Now we can code the `onTouchEvent` function and see all the `MotionEvent` stuff in action.

Coding the onTouchEvent function

Respond to the user moving their finger on the screen by adding the highlighted code in the following snippet inside the `onTouchEvent` function to the code we already have:

```
// User moved a finger while touching screen
if (motionEvent.action and MotionEvent.
                        ACTION_MASK ==
                        MotionEvent.ACTION_MOVE) {

  particleSystems[nextSystem].emitParticles(
            PointF(motionEvent.x,
                        motionEvent.y))

  nextSystem++
  if (nextSystem == maxSystems) {
        nextSystem = 0
  }
}

return true
```

The `if` condition checks to see whether the type of event was the user moving their finger. If it was, then the next particle system in `particleSystems` has its `emitParticles` function called. Afterward, the `nextSystem` variable is incremented and a test is performed to see whether it was the last particle system. If it was, then `nextSystem` is set to zero, ready to start reusing existing particle systems the next time one is required.

We can move on to making the system respond to the user pressing one of the buttons by adding the highlighted code in the following snippet right after the previous code we just discussed and before the `return` statement we have already coded:

```
// Did the user touch the screen
if (motionEvent.action and MotionEvent.ACTION_MASK ==
        MotionEvent.ACTION_DOWN) {

  // User pressed the screen so let's
  // see if it was in the reset button
  if (resetButton.contains(motionEvent.x,
                          motionEvent.y)) {

    // Clear the screen of all particles
    nextSystem = 0
  }

  // User pressed the screen so let's
  // see if it was in the toggle button
  if (togglePauseButton.contains(motionEvent.x,
                                motionEvent.y)) {

        paused = !paused
  }
}

return true
```

The condition of the `if` statement checks to see whether the user has tapped the screen. If they have, then the `contains` function of the `RectF` class is used in conjunction with `x` and `y` to see whether that press was inside one of our custom buttons. If the reset button was pressed, then all the particles will disappear when `nextSystem` is set to zero. If the paused button is pressed, then the value of `paused` is toggled causing the `update` function to stop/start being called inside the thread.

Finishing the HUD

Edit the code in the `printDebuggingText` function to appear as follows:

```
canvas.drawText("Systems: $nextSystem",
        10f, (fontMargin + debugStart +
        debugSize * 2).toFloat(), paint)

canvas.drawText("Particles: ${nextSystem *
        particlesPerSystem}",
        10f, (fontMargin + debugStart
        + debugSize * 3).toFloat(), paint)
```

The preceding code will just print some interesting statistics to the screen to tell us how many particles and systems are currently being drawn.

Running the app

Now we get to see the live drawing app in action and play with some of the different options we left commented out in the code.

Run the app with small, round, colorful, fast particles. The following screenshot shows a screen that has been tapped in several places:

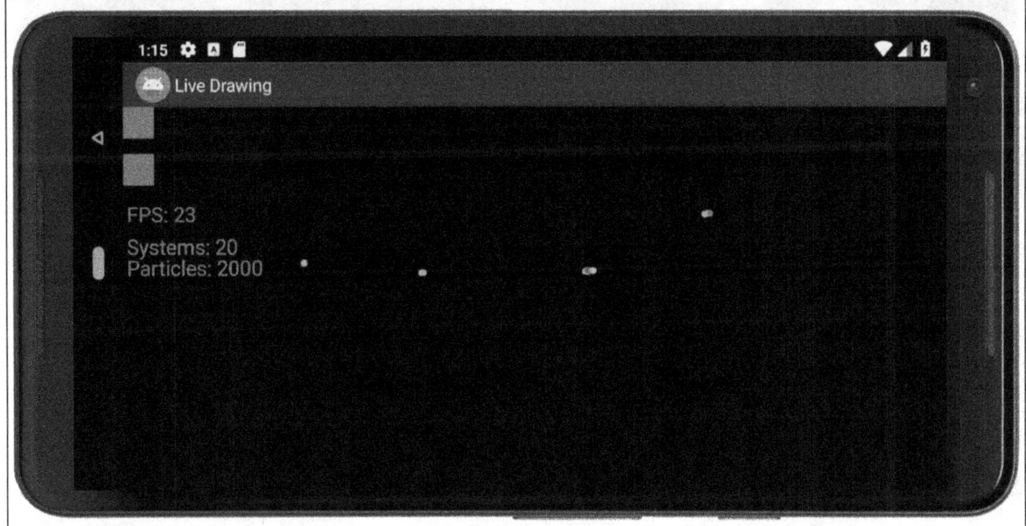

Then resume the drawing, as shown in the following screenshot:

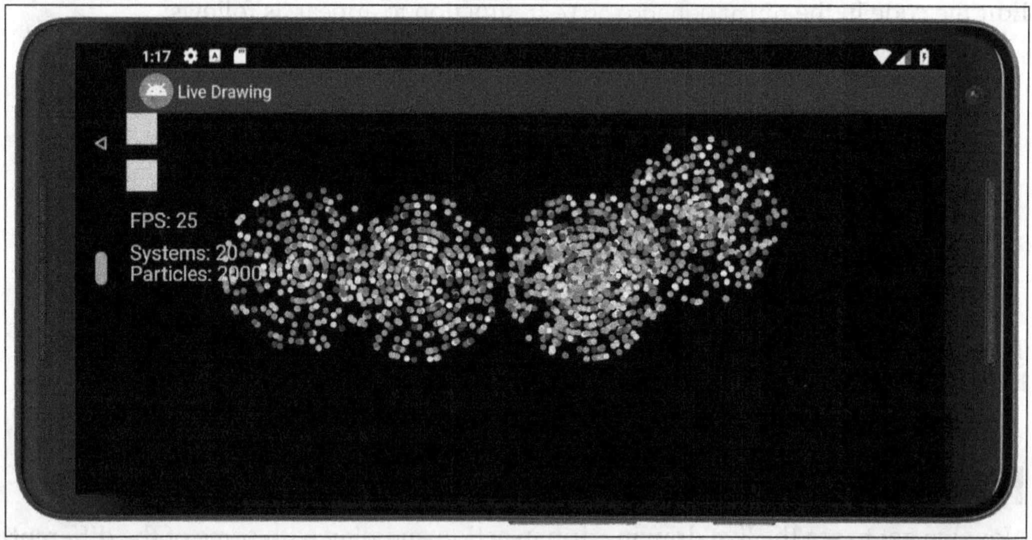

Make a kid-style drawing with particles that are small, white, square, slow, and of a long duration, as shown in the following screenshot:

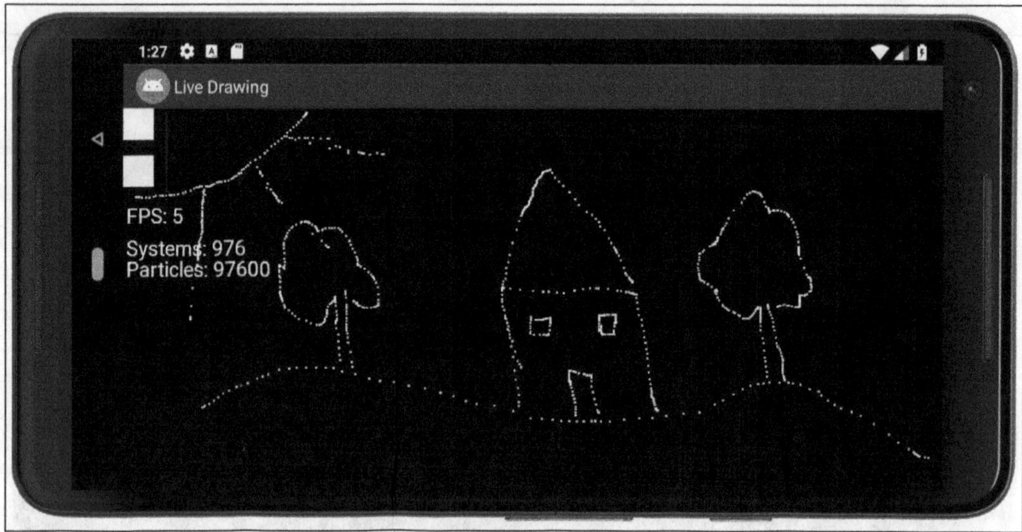

Then resume the drawing and wait for 20 seconds while the drawing comes to life and changes:

Summary

In this chapter, we learned how we can add thousands of self-contained entities to our real-time system. The entities were controlled by the `ParticleSystem` class, which, in turn, interacted with, and was controlled by, the game loop. As the game loop was running in a thread, we learned that the user can still interact seamlessly with the screen and the operating system will send us the details of these interactions via the `onTouchEvent` function.

In the next chapter, our apps will finally get a bit noisier when we explore how to play sound effects.

23
Android Sound Effects and the Spinner Widget

In this chapter, we will study the `SoundPool` class and the different ways we can use it depending on whether we just want to play sounds or go further and keep track of the sounds we are playing. Then, we will put everything we will have learned into action by producing a cool sound demo app, which will also introduce us to a new UI widget: the **spinner**.

In this chapter, we will do the following:

- Learn how to use the Android `SoundPool` class
- Code a sound-based app using `SpinnerView`

Let's get started.

The SoundPool class

The `SoundPool` class allows us to hold and manipulate a collection of sound effects: literally, a pool of sounds. The class handles everything from decompressing a sound file, such as a `.wav` or a `.ogg` file, keeping an identifying reference to it via an integer ID, and, of course, playing the sound. When the sound is played, it is played in a non-blocking manner (using a thread behind the scenes) that does not interfere with the smooth running of our app or our user's interaction with it.

The first thing we need to do is add the sound effects to a folder called `assets` in the `main` folder of the game project. We will do this shortly.

Next, in our Kotlin code, we declare an object of the `SoundPool` type and an `Int` identifier for each sound effect we intend to use, as shown in the following code. We will also declare another `Int` called `nowPlaying`, which we can use to track which sound is currently playing; we will see how we do this shortly:

```
var sp: SoundPool
var idFX1 = -1
nowPlaying = -1
volume = .1f
```

Now, we will look at the way we initialize a `SoundPool`.

Initializing SoundPool

We will use an `AudioAttributes` object to set the attributes of the pool of sound we want.

The first block of code uses chaining, and calls four separate functions on one object that initializes our `AudioAttributes` object (`audioAttributes`), as shown in the following code:

```
val audioAttributes = AudioAttributes.Builder()
          .setUsage(AudioAttributes.
                        USAGE_ASSISTANCE_SONIFICATION)
          .setContentType(AudioAttributes.
                        CONTENT_TYPE_SONIFICATION)
          .build()

sp = SoundPool.Builder()
          .setMaxStreams(5)
          .setAudioAttributes(audioAttributes)
          .build()
```

In the preceding code, we used the `Builder` function of this class to initialize an `AudioAttributes` instance to let it know that it will be used for user interface interaction with `USAGE_ASSISTANCE_SONIFICATION`.

We also used `CONTENT_TYPE_SONIFICATION`, which lets the class know that it is for responsive sounds, for example, button clicks, a collision, or similar.

Now, we can initialize the SoundPool (sp) itself by passing in the AudioAttributes object (audioAttributes) and the maximum number of simultaneous sounds we are likely to want to play.

The second block of code chains another four functions to initialize sp, including a call to setAudioAttributes that uses the audioAttributes object that we initialized in the earlier block of chained functions.

Now, we can go ahead and load up (decompress) the sound files into our SoundPool.

Loading sound files into memory

Like our thread control, we are required to wrap our code in try-catch blocks. This makes sense because reading a file can fail for reasons beyond our control, but we also do this because we are forced to, as the function that we use throws an exception and the code we write will not compile otherwise.

Inside the try block, we declare and initialize objects of the AssetManager and AssetFileDescriptor types.

The AssetFileDescriptor is initialized by using the openFd function of the AssetManager object that decompresses the sound file. We then initialize our ID (idFX1) at the same time that we load the contents of the AssetFileDescriptor instance into our SoundPool.

The catch block simply outputs a message to the console to let us know whether something has gone wrong, as shown in the following code:

```
try {
    // Create objects of the 2 required classes
    val assetManager = this.assets
    var descriptor: AssetFileDescriptor

    // Load our fx in memory ready for use
    descriptor = assetManager.openFd("fx1.ogg")
    idFX1 = sp.load(descriptor, 0)

}  catch (e: IOException) {
    // Print an error message to the console
    Log.e("error", "failed to load sound files")
}
```

Now, we are ready to make some noise.

Playing a sound

At this point, there is a sound effect in our `SoundPool`, and we have an ID that we can use to refer to it.

This is how we play the sound. Note that in the following line of code, we initialize the `nowPlaying` variable with the return value from the same function that plays the sound. The following code therefore simultaneously plays a sound and loads the value of the ID that is being played into `nowPlaying`:

```
nowPlaying = sp.play(idFX2,
  volume, volume, 0, repeats, 1f)
```

It is not necessary to store the ID in `nowPlaying` in order to play a sound, but it has its uses, as we will now see.

The parameters of the `play` function are as follows, from left to right:

- The ID of the sound effect
- The left and right speaker volumes
- The priority over other sounds that might be playing/played
- The number of times the sound is repeated
- The rate/speed it is played at (1 being the normal rate)

There's just one more thing we need to cover before we make the sound demo app.

Stopping a sound

It is also very easy to stop a sound when it is still playing by using the `stop` function, as shown in the following code. Note that there might be more than one sound effect playing at any given time, so the `stop` function needs the ID of the sound effect that you want to stop:

```
sp.stop(nowPlaying)
```

When you call `play`, you only need to store the ID of the currently playing sound if you want to track it so that you can interact with it later. Now, we can make the Sound demo app.

Sound demo app introducing the Spinner widget

Of course, with all this talk of sound effects, we need some actual sound files. You can make you own with BFXR (as explained in the next section) or use the ones supplied. The sound effects for this app are in the download bundle, and can be found in the `assets` folder of the `Chapter23/Sound Demo` folder.

Making sound effects

There is an open source app called BFXR that allows us to make our own sound effects. Here is a very fast guide to making your own sound effects using BFXR. Grab a free copy from `www.bfxr.net`.

Note that the sound effects for the Sound demo app are supplied to you in the `Chapter23/assets` folder. You don't have to create your own sound effects unless you want to, but it is still worth getting this free software and learning how to use it.

Follow the simple instructions on the website to set it up. Try out a few of these things to make cool sound effects:

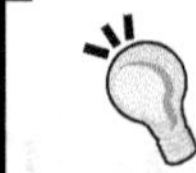

> This is a seriously condensed tutorial. You can do so much with BFXR. To learn more, read the tips on the website at the URL we mentioned previously.

1. Run `bfxr`. You should see a screen similar to the one shown in the following screenshot:

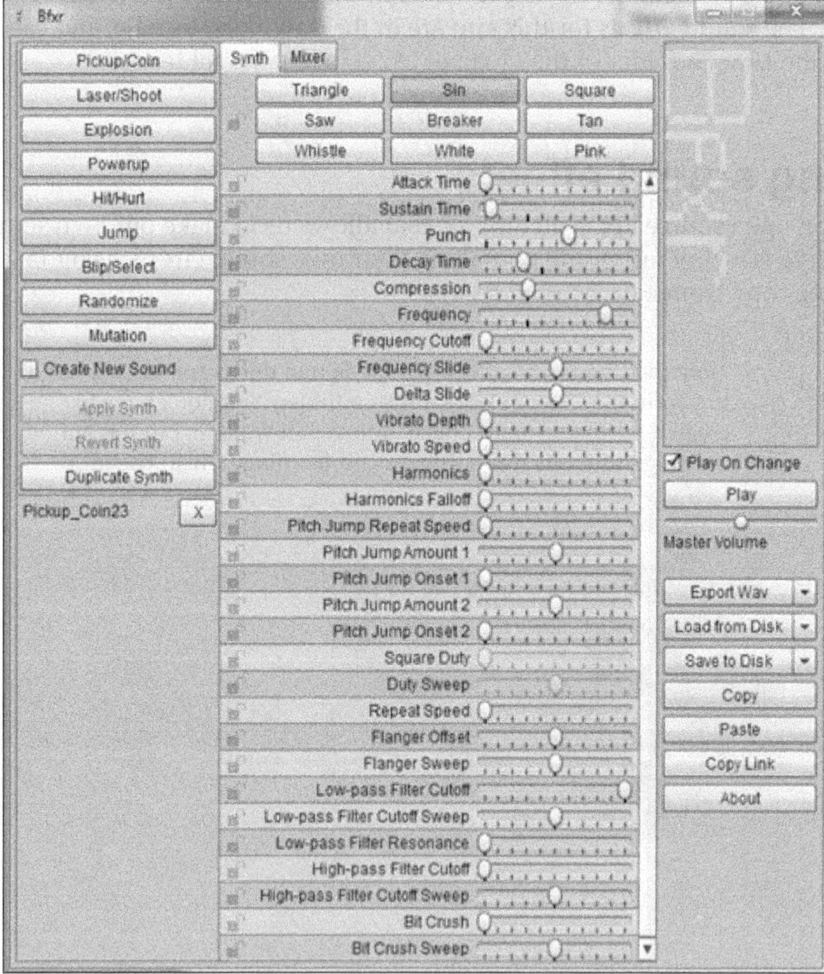

2. Try out all the preset types that generate a random sound of that type, as shown in the following screenshot. When you have a sound that is close to what you want, move on to the next step:

3. Use the sliders to fine-tune the pitch, duration, and other aspects of your new sound, as shown in the following screenshot:

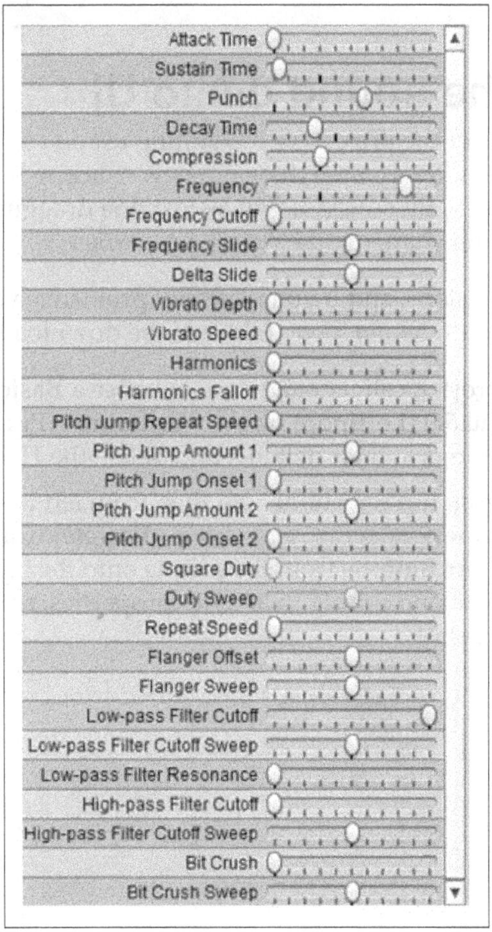

4. Save your sound by clicking the **Export Wav** button, as shown in the following screenshot. Despite the text of this button, as we will see, we can also save in formats other than `.wav`:

5. Android works very well with sounds in OGG format, so when asked to name your file, use the `.ogg` extension at the end of the filename.
6. Repeat steps 2 to 5 to create three cool sound effects. Name them `fx1.ogg`, `fx2.ogg`, and `fx3.ogg`. We use the `.ogg` file format as it is more compressed than formats such as WAV.

When you have your sound files ready, we can proceed with the app.

Laying out the sound demo UI

I will describe the parts of the project we are getting used to a little more briefly than I did in previous projects. Every time there is a new concept, however, I will be sure to explain it in full. I guess by now you will be just fine dragging a few widgets onto a `ConstraintLayout` and changing their `text` properties.

Complete the following steps, and if you have any problems, you can copy or view the code in the `Chapter23/Sound Demo` folder of the download bundle:

1. Create a new project, call it `Sound Demo`, choose a **Basic Activity**, and choose **API 21: Android 5.0 (Lollipop)** on the **Minimum API level** option, but leave all the other settings at their defaults and delete the **Hello world!** `TextView`.
2. In this order, from top to bottom, and then from left to right, drag a **Spinner** from the **Containers** category, a **SeekBar (discrete)** from the **Widgets** category, and four **Buttons** from the palette onto the layout while arranging and resizing them and setting their `text` properties, as shown in the following screenshot:

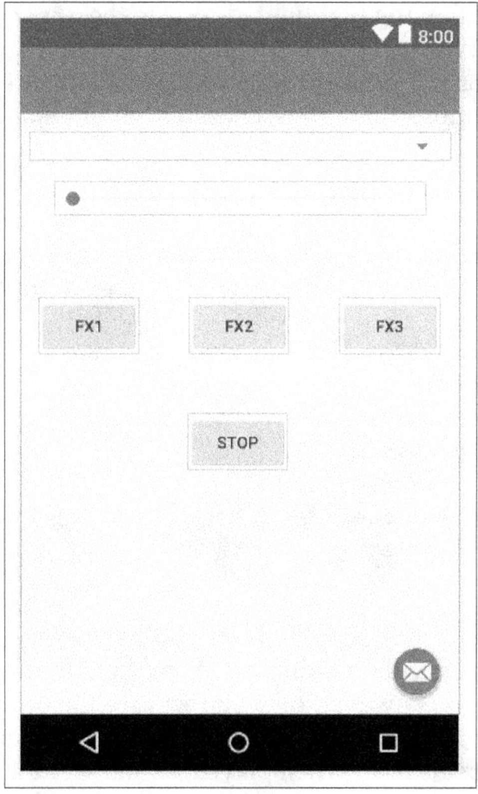

3. Click the **Infer Constraints** button.
4. Use the following table to set their attributes:

Widget	**Property to change**	**Value to set**
Spinner	id	`spinner`
Spinner	spinnerMode	`dropdown`
Spinner	entries	`@array/spinner_options`
SeekBar	id	`seekBar`
SeekBar	max	`10`
Button (**FX 1**)	id	`btnFX1`
Button (**FX 2**)	id	`btnFX2`
Button (**FX 3**)	id	`btnFX3`
Button (**STOP**)	id	`btnStop`

5. Next, add the following highlighted code to the `strings.xml` file in the `values` folder. We used this array of String resources, which is named `spinner_options`, for the `options` property in the previous step. It will represent the options that can be chosen from our spinner:

```
<resources>
    <string name="app_name">Sound Demo</string>

    <string name="hello_world">Hello world!</string>
    <string name="action_settings">Settings</string>

    <string-array name="spinner_options">
      <item>0</item>
      <item>1</item>
      <item>3</item>
      <item>5</item>
      <item>10</item>
    </string-array>

</resources>
```

Run the app now and you will not initially see anything that you haven't seen before. If you click on the spinner, however, then you will see the options from our String array called `spinner_options`. We will use the spinner to control the number of times a sound effect repeats itself when played, as shown in the following image:

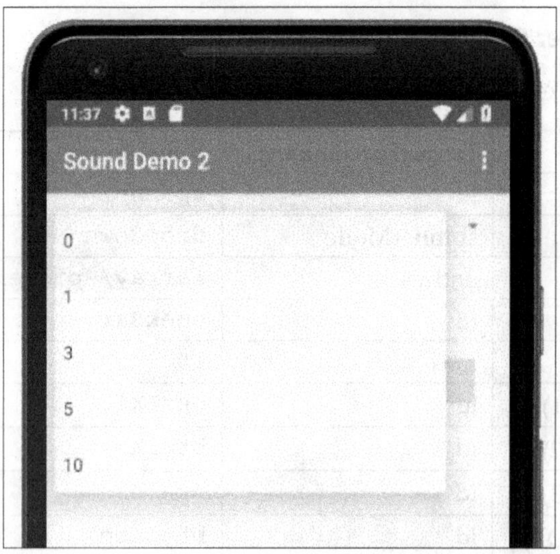

Let's write the Kotlin code to make this app work, including how we interact with our spinner.

Using your operating system's file browser, go to the `app\src\main` folder of the project and add a new folder called `assets`.

There are three sound files ready-made for you in the `Chapter23/Sound Demo/assets` folder of the download bundle. Place these three files into the `assets` directory you just created or use the ones you created yourself. The important thing is that their filenames must be `fx1.ogg`, `fx2.ogg`, and `fx3.ogg`.

Coding the Sound demo

First, we will change the class declaration so that we can handle interaction with all our widgets efficiently. Edit the declaration to implement `View.OnClickListener`, as highlighted in the following code:

```
class MainActivity : AppCompatActivity(),
  View.OnClickListener {
```

We will add the required `onClick` function shortly.

Now, we will add some properties for our `SoundPool` instance, sound effect IDs, and a `nowPlaying Int` property, as we discussed previously, and we will also add a `Float` to hold a value for a volume between 0 (silent) and 1 (full volume, based on the current volume of the device). We will also add an `Int` property called `repeats`, which, unsurprisingly, holds the value of the number of times we will repeat a given sound effect:

```
var sp: SoundPool


private var idFX1 = -1
private var idFX2 = -1
private var idFX3 = -1

var nowPlaying = -1
var volume = .1f
var repeats = 2

init{

  val audioAttributes = AudioAttributes.Builder()
        .setUsage(AudioAttributes.
              USAGE_ASSISTANCE_SONIFICATION)
        .setContentType(AudioAttributes.
              CONTENT_TYPE_SONIFICATION)
```

```
            .build()

    sp = SoundPool.Builder()
            .setMaxStreams(5)
            .setAudioAttributes(audioAttributes)
            .build()
}
```

In the preceding code, we also added an `init` block where we initialized our `SoundPool` instance.

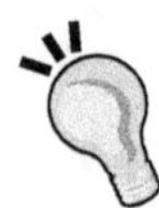

Add the following `import` statements for the previous code to work using your preferred method:

```
import android.media.AudioAttributes
import android.media.AudioManager
import android.media.SoundPool
import android.os.Build

import android.view.View
import android.widget.Button
```

Now, in the `onCreate` function, we can set a click listener for our buttons in the usual way, as follows:

```
btnFX1.setOnClickListener(this)
btnFX2.setOnClickListener(this)
btnFX3.setOnClickListener(this)
btnStop.setOnClickListener(this)
```

Be sure to add the following `import` to make the preceding code work:

```
import kotlinx.android.synthetic.main.content_main.*
```

Next, we load each of our sound effects in turn and initialize our IDs with a value that matches the related sound effect that we load into the `SoundPool`. The whole thing is wrapped in a `try-catch` block, as required, as shown in the following code:

```
try {
    // Create objects of the 2 required classes
    val assetManager = this.assets
    var descriptor: AssetFileDescriptor

    // Load our fx in memory ready for use
```

```
        descriptor = assetManager.openFd("fx1.ogg")
        idFX1 = sp.load(descriptor, 0)

        descriptor = assetManager.openFd("fx2.ogg")
        idFX2 = sp.load(descriptor, 0)

        descriptor = assetManager.openFd("fx3.ogg")
        idFX3 = sp.load(descriptor, 0)


    }   catch (e: IOException) {
        // Print an error message to the console
        Log.e("error", "failed to load sound files")
    }
```

Add the following `import` statements for the previous code using your preferred method:

```
import android.content.res.AssetFileDescriptor
import android.content.res.AssetManager
import android.util.Log
import java.io.IOException
```

Next, we will look at how we are going to handle the `SeekBar`. As you have probably come to expect, we will use a lambda. We will use `OnSeekBarChangeListener` and override the `onProgressChanged`, `onStartTrackingTouch`, and `onStopTrackingTouch` functions.

We only need to add code to the `onProgressChanged` function. Within this function, we simply change the value of our `volume` variable and then use the `setVolume` function on our `SoundPool` object, passing in the currently playing sound effect and the volume of the left and right channels of sound, as shown in the following code:

```
seekBar.setOnSeekBarChangeListener(
        object : SeekBar.OnSeekBarChangeListener {

    override fun onProgressChanged(
        seekBar: SeekBar, value: Int, fromUser: Boolean) {

        volume = value / 10f
        sp.setVolume(nowPlaying, volume, volume)
    }

    override fun onStartTrackingTouch(seekBar: SeekBar) {}
```

```
    override fun onStopTrackingTouch(seekBar: SeekBar) {

    }
})
```

Add the following `import` statements for the previous code using your preferred method:

```
import android.widget.SeekBar
```

After the `SeekBar` comes the `Spinner` and another lambda to handle user interaction. We will use the `AdapterView.OnItemSelectedListener` to override the `onItemSelected` and `onNothingSelected` functions.

All our code goes in to the `onItemSelected` function, which creates a temporary `String` named `temp`, and then uses the `Integer.ValueOf` function to convert the `String` in to an `Int`, which we can use to initialize the `repeats` property, as shown in the following code:

```
spinner.onItemSelectedListener =
        object : AdapterView.OnItemSelectedListener {

    override fun onItemSelected(
            parentView: AdapterView<*>,
            selectedItemView: View,
            position: Int, id: Long) {

            val temp = spinner.selectedItem.toString()
            repeats = Integer.valueOf(temp)
    }

    override fun onNothingSelected(
            parentView: AdapterView<*>) {
    }
}
```

Add the following `import` statements to the previous code using your preferred method:

```
import android.widget.AdapterView
import android.widget.Spinner
```

That's everything for the `onCreate` function.

Now, implement the `onClick` function, which is required because this class implements the `View.OnClickListener` interface. Quite simply, there is a `when` option for each button. Note that the return value for each call to `play` is stored in `nowPlaying`. When the user presses the **STOP** button, we simply call `stop` with the current value of `nowPlaying`, causing the most recently started sound effect to stop, as shown in the following code:

```
override fun onClick(v: View) {
  when (v.id) {
        R.id.btnFX1 -> {
              sp.stop(nowPlaying)
              nowPlaying = sp.play(idFX1, volume,
                          volume, 0, repeats, 1f)
   }

        R.id.btnFX2 -> {
              sp.stop(nowPlaying)
              nowPlaying = sp.play(idFX2,
                          volume, volume, 0, repeats, 1f)
   }

        R.id.btnFX3 -> {
              sp.stop(nowPlaying)
              nowPlaying = sp.play(idFX3,
                          volume, volume, 0, repeats, 1f)
   }

        R.id.btnStop -> sp.stop(nowPlaying)
  }
}
```

We can now run the app. Make sure that the volume on your device is turned up if you can't hear anything.

Click the appropriate button for the sound effect you want to play. Change the volume and the number of times it is repeated and, of course, try stopping it with the **STOP** button.

Also note that you can repeatedly tap multiple play buttons when a sound effect is already playing, and the sounds will be played simultaneously up to the maximum number of streams that we set (five).

Summary

In this chapter, we looked closely at how to use `SoundPool`, and we used all this knowledge to complete the Sound demo app.

In the next chapter, we will learn about how to make our apps work with multiple different layouts.

24
Design Patterns, Multiple Layouts, and Fragments

We have come a long way since the start, when we were just setting up Android Studio. Back then, we went through everything step by step, but as we have proceeded, we have tried to show you not just how to add x to y or feature A to app B, but to enable you to use what you have learned in your own way in order to bring your own ideas to life.

This chapter is more focused on your future apps than any other chapter in this book has been so far. We will look at a few features of Kotlin and Android that you can use as a framework or template to make even more exciting and complex apps while keeping the code manageable. Furthermore, I will suggest areas of further study that are barely touched on in this book, given its limited scope.

In this chapter, we will learn about the following:

- Patterns and the model-view-controller
- Android design guidelines
- Getting started with real-world designs and handling multiple different devices
- An introduction to fragments

Let's get started.

Introducing the model-view-controller pattern

The phrases model, view, and **controller** reflect the separation of the different parts of our app into distinct sections, called **layers**. Android apps commonly use the model-view-controller **pattern**. A pattern is simply a recognized way to structure code and other application resources, such as layout files, images, and databases.

Patterns are useful to us because, by conforming to a pattern, we can be more confident that we are doing things right, and will be less likely to have to undo lots of hard work because we have coded ourselves into an awkward situation.

There are many patterns in computer science, but just an understanding of the MVC pattern will be enough to create some professionally built Android apps.

We have been partly using MVC already, so let's look at each of the three layers in turn.

Model

The model refers to the data that drives our app and any logic/code that specifically manages it and makes it available to the other layers. For example, in our Note to self app, the `Note` class, along with its JSON code, was the data and logic.

View

The view of the Note to self app was all the widgets in all the different layouts. Anything the user can see or interact with on the screen is typically part of the view. You probably also remember that the widgets came from the `View` class hierarchy of the Android API.

Controller

The controller is the bit between the view and the model. It interacts with both and keeps them separate. It contains what is known as the **application logic**. If a user taps a button, the application layer decides what to do about it. When the user clicks **OK** to add a new note, the application layer listens for the interaction on the view layer. It captures the data contained in the view and passes it to the model layer.

> Design patterns are a huge topic. There are many different design patterns, and if you want a beginner-friendly introduction to the topic in general, I would recommend *Head First Design Patterns*. Even though this book's examples are described in another language, Java, it will still be very useful to you. If you want to really dive into the world of design patterns, then you can try *Design Patterns: Elements of Reusable Object-Oriented Software*, which is recognized as a kind of design pattern oracle, but is a much harder read.

As this book progresses, we will also begin to utilize more of the object-oriented programming features we have discussed but not fully benefited from so far. We will do so step by step.

Android design guidelines

App design is a vast topic - so vast that it could only begin to be taught in a book dedicated solely to the topic. Also, like programming, you can only start to get good at app design with constant practice, review, and improvement.

So, what exactly do I mean by design? I am talking about where you put the widgets on the screen, which widgets, what color they should be, how big they should be, how to transition between screens, the best way to scroll a page, when and which animation interpolators to use, what screens your app should be divided into, and much more besides this.

This book will hopefully leave you well-qualified to be able to *implement* all your chosen answers to these questions and many more besides. Unfortunately, it does not have the space, and the author probably doesn't have the skill to teach you how to *make* those choices.

> You might be wondering, "What should I do?". Keep making apps and don't let a lack of design experience and knowledge stop you! Even release your apps to the app store. Keep in mind, however, that there is a whole other topic – design – that needs some attention if your apps are going to truly be world class.

In even medium-sized development companies, the designer is rarely also the programmer, and even very small companies will often outsource the design of their app (or designers might outsource the coding).

Designing is both an art and a science, and Google has demonstrated that it recognizes this with high-quality support for both existing and aspiring designers.

I highly recommend you visit and bookmark the web page `https://developer.android.com/design/`. It is quite detailed and comprehensive, is totally Android focused, and has a ton of digital resources in the form of images, color palettes, and guidelines.

Make understanding design principles a short-term goal. Make improving your actual design skills an ongoing task. Visit and read design-focused websites and try and implement the ideas that you find exciting.

Most important of all, however, don't wait until you are a design expert before you start to make apps. Keep bringing your ideas to life and publishing them. Make a point of making the design of each app a little better than the last.

We will see in the up coming chapters, and have seen to a certain extent already, that the Android API makes a whole bunch of super-stylish UIs available to us that we can then take advantage of with very little code or design skill. These UIs go a long way to making your apps look like they have been designed by a professional.

Real-world apps

So far, we have built a dozen or more apps of various complexity. Most were designed and tested on a phone.

Of course, in the real world, our apps need to work well on any device, and must be able to handle what happens when in either portrait or landscape view (on all devices).

Furthermore, it is often not enough for our apps to just work and look "OK" on different devices. Often, our apps will need to behave differently and appear with a significantly different UI based on whether the device is a phone, a tablet, or has landscape/portrait orientation.

Android supports apps for large screen TVs, smart watches via the wear API, virtual and augmented reality, and "things" for the internet of things. We will not be covering the latter two aspects in this book, but by the end of it, it is the author's hope that you will be sufficiently prepared to venture into these topics should you choose to.

Look at the following screenshot of the BBC News app running on an Android phone in portrait orientation. Look at the basic layout, but also note that the categories of news (**Top Stories**, **World**, **UK**) are all visible and allow the user to scroll to see more categories or to swipe left and right between the stories within each category:

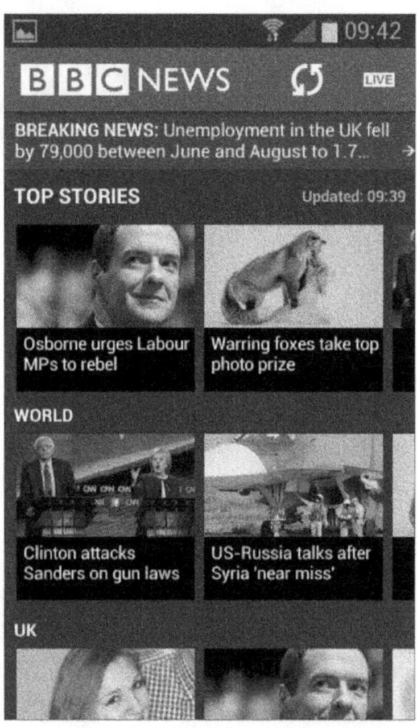

We will see how we can implement a swiping/paging UI using the `ImagePager` and `FragmentPager` classes in the next chapter, but before we can do that, we need to understand some more fundamentals, which we will explore in this chapter. For now, the purpose of the previous screenshot is not so much to show you the specific UI features, but to allow you to compare it to the following screenshot. Look at the exact same app running on a tablet in landscape orientation:

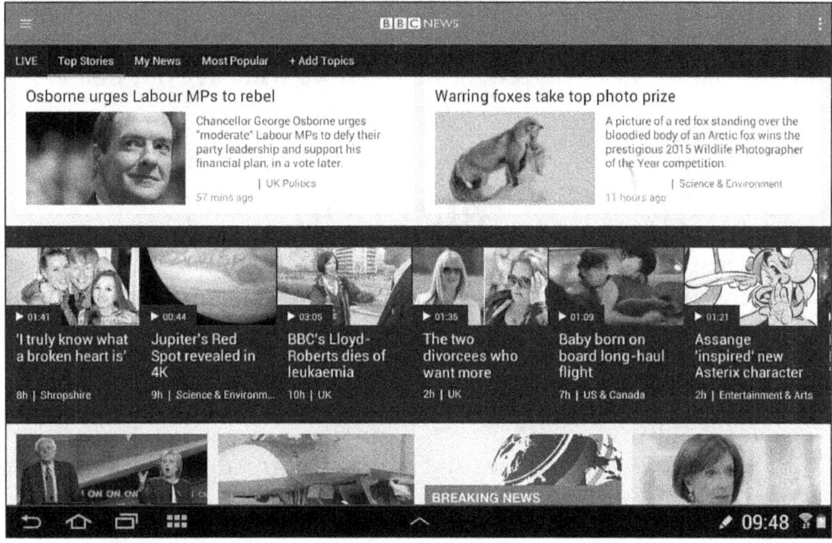

Note that the stories (the data layer) are identical, but that the layout (the view layer) is very different. The user is not only given the option to select categories from a menu of tabs at the top of the app, but they are also invited to add their own tabs through the **Add Topics** option.

Again, the point of this image is to show you not so much the specific UI, or even how we might implement one like it, but that they are so different that they could easily be mistaken for totally different apps.

Android allows us to design real-world apps like this where not only the layout is different for varying device types/orientations/sizes, but so is the behavior, that is, the application layer. Android's secret weapon that makes this possible is the `Fragment` class.

Google says:

"A Fragment represents a behavior or a portion of user interface in an Activity. You can combine multiple fragments in a single activity to build a multi-pane UI and reuse a fragment in multiple activities.

You can think of a fragment as a modular section of an activity, which has its own lifecycle, receives its own input events, and which you can add or remove while the activity is running (sort of like a "sub activity" that you can reuse in different activities).

A fragment must always be embedded in an activity, and the fragment's lifecycle is directly affected by the host activity's lifecycle."

We can design multiple different layouts in different XML files, and will do so soon. We can also detect things such as device orientation and screen resolution in code so that we can then make decisions about layout dynamically.

Let's try this out using device detection, and then we will have our first look at fragments.

Device detection mini app

The best way to learn about detecting and responding to devices and their varying attributes (screens, orientations, and so on) is to make a simple app. Let's do this by going through the following steps:

1. Create a new **Empty Activity** project and call it `Device Detection`. Leave all the other settings as their defaults.
2. Open the `activity_main.xml` file in the **Design** tab and delete the default **Hello world!** `TextView`.

3. Drag a **Button** to the top of the screen and set its **onClick** property to `detectDevice`. We will code this function in a minute.
4. Drag two **TextView** widgets onto the layout, one below the other, and set their **id** properties to `txtOrientation` and `txtResolution`, respectively.
5. Check that you have a layout that looks something like the following screenshot:

I have stretched my widgets (mainly horizontally) and increased the `textSize` attributes to `24sp` to make them clearer on the screen, but this is not required for the app to work correctly.

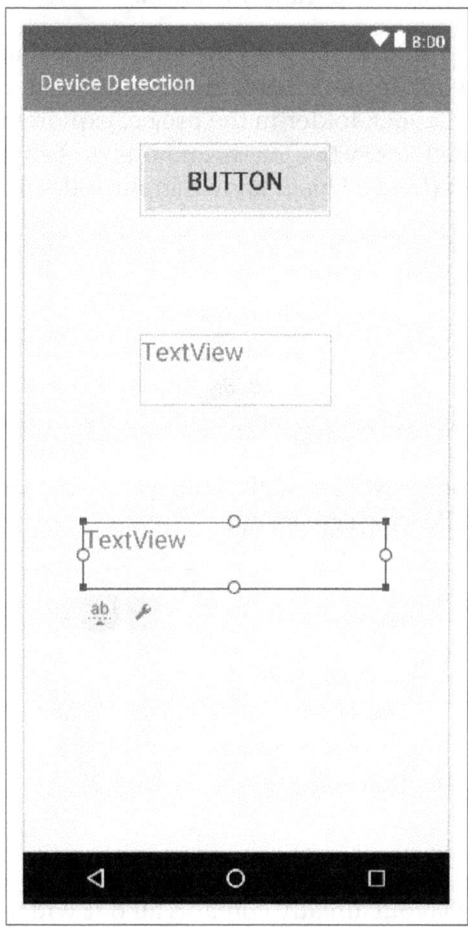

6. Click the **Infer Constraints** button to secure the positions of the UI elements.

Now, we will do something new: we will build a layout specifically for landscape orientation.

In Android Studio, make sure that the `activity_main.xml` file is selected in the editor and locate the **Orientation for preview** button, as shown in the following screenshot:

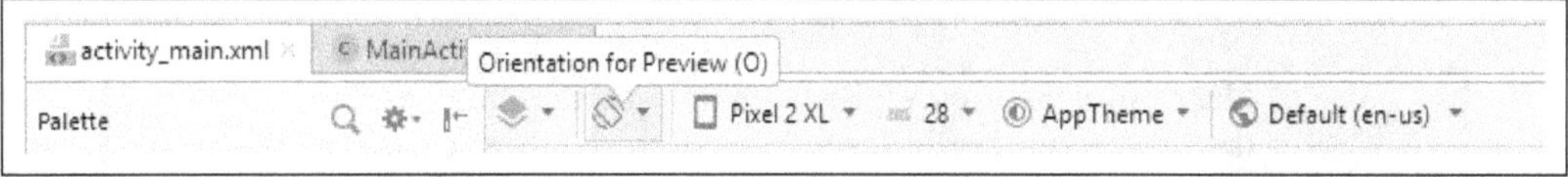

Click it and then select **Create landscape variation**.

You now have a new layout XML file with the same name, but orientated in landscape mode. The layout appears blank in the editor, but as we will see, this is not the case. Look at the `layout` folder in the project explorer and note that there are indeed two files named `activity_main`, and one of them (the new one we just created) is postfixed with **(land)**. This is shown in the following screenshot:

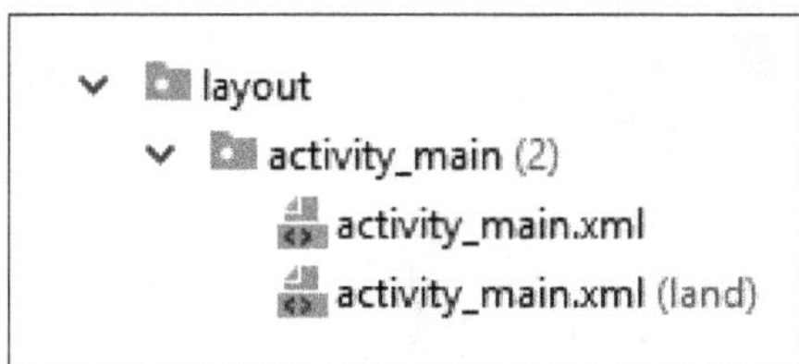

Select this new file (the one postfixed with **(land)**) and now look at the component tree. It is shown in the following screenshot:

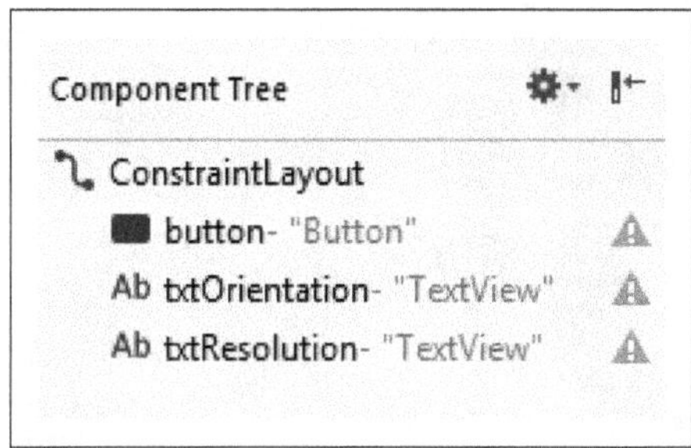

It would appear that the layout already contains all our widgets—we just cannot see them in the design view. The reason for this anomaly is that when we created the landscape layout, Android Studio copied the portrait layout, including all the constraints. The portrait constraints rarely match the landscape constraints.

To solve this problem, click the **Remove all constraints** button; it's the button to the left of the **Infer constraints** button. The UI is now unconstrained. This is what mine looks like:

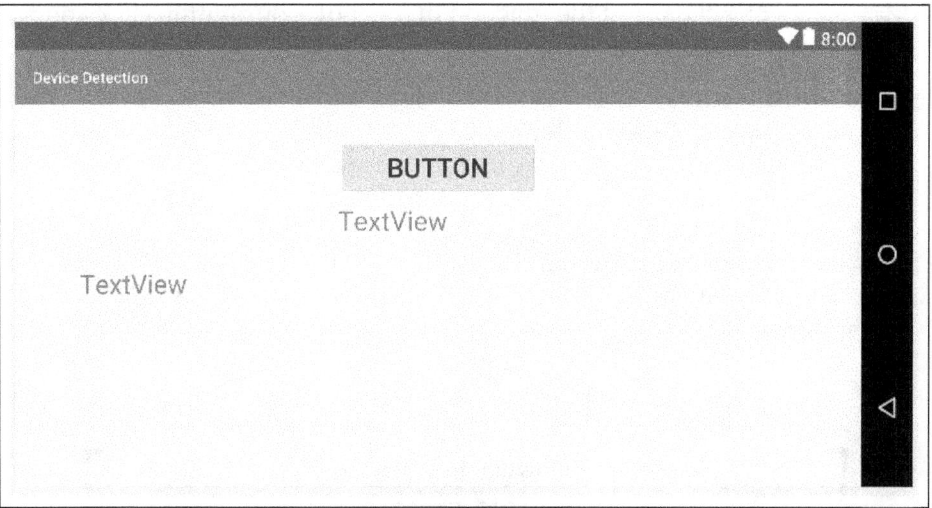

The layout is a bit jumbled up, but at least we can see it now. Rearrange it to make it look neat and tidy. This is how I rearranged mine:

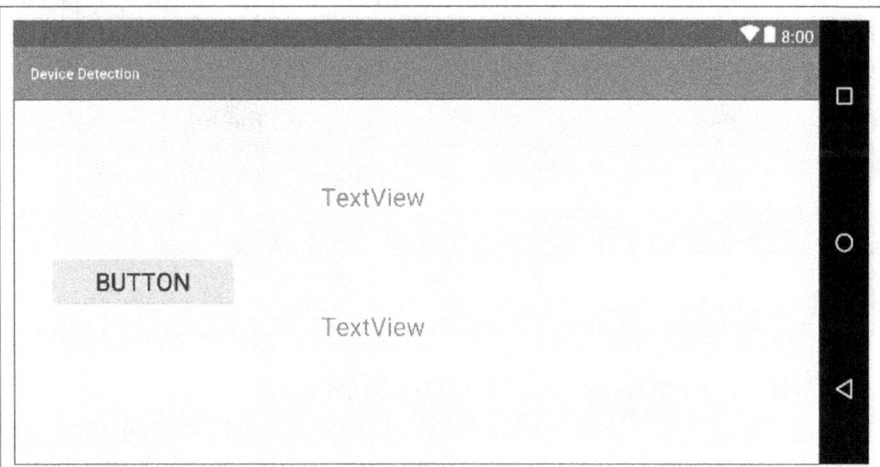

Click the **Infer constraints** button to lock the layout in the new positions.

Now that we have a basic layout for two different orientations, we can turn our attention to our Kotlin code.

Coding the MainActivity class

We already have a mechanism that calls a function called `detectDevice`, and all we need to do to make this demo app is code that function. After the `onCreate` function in the `MainActivity` class, add the function that handles our button click and runs our detection code, as follows:

```
fun detectDevice(v: View) {
   // What is the orientation?
   val display = windowManager.defaultDisplay
   txtOrientation.text = "${display.rotation}"

   // What is the resolution?
   val xy = Point()
   display.getSize(xy)
   txtResolution.text = "x = ${xy.x} y = ${xy.y}"
}
```

Import the following three classes:

```
import android.graphics.Point
import android.view.Display
import android.view.View
```

This code works by declaring and initializing an object of the `Display` type called `display`. This object (`display`) now holds a whole bunch of data about the specific display properties of the device.

The value stored in the `rotation` property is output into the top `TextView` widget.

The code then initializes an object of the `Point` type called `xy`. The `getSize` function then loads up the screen resolution into `xy`. The results are then used to output the horizontal (`xy.x`) and vertical (`xy.y`) resolution into the `TextView`.

Each time the button is clicked, the two `TextView` widgets will be updated.

Unlocking the screen orientation

Before we run the app, we want to make sure that the device isn't locked in portrait mode (most new phones are, by default). From the app drawer of the emulator (or the device you will be using), tap the **Settings** app and choose **Display**, and then use the switch to set **Auto-rotate screen** to on. I have shown this setting in the following screenshot:

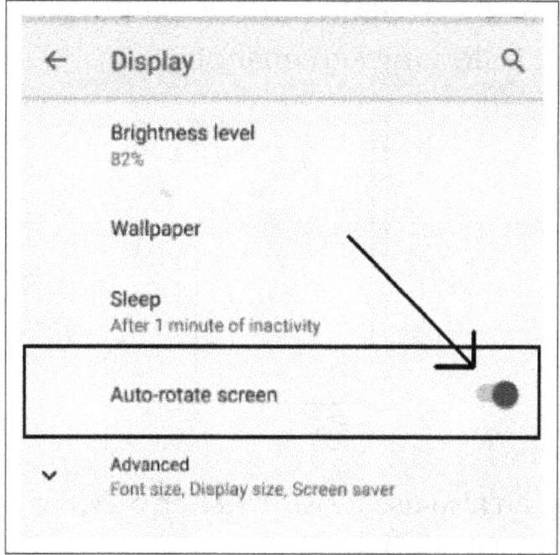

Running the app

Now, you can run the app and click the button, as shown in the following image:

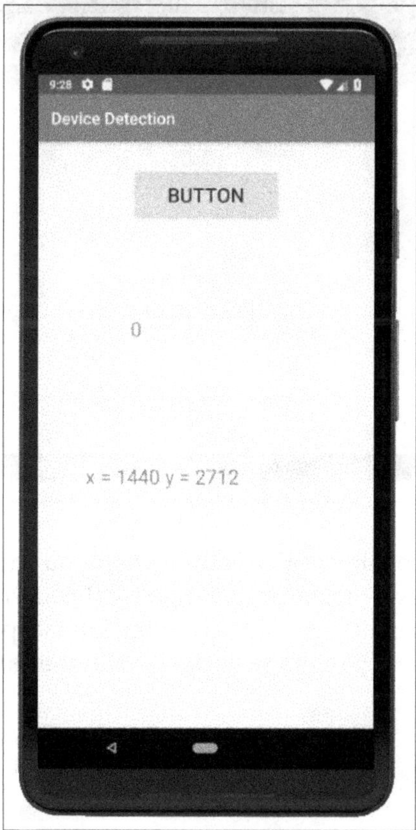

Rotate the device using one of the rotate buttons on the emulator control panel to landscape, as shown in the following screenshot:

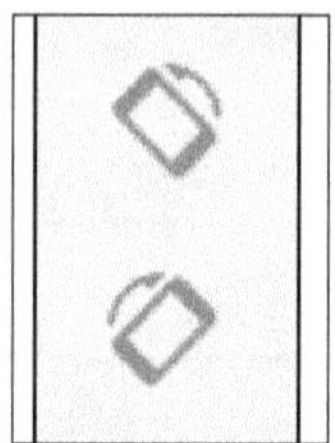

You can also use *CTRL* + *F11* on a PC, or *CTRL* + *FN* + *F11* on a macOS device.

Now, click the button again and you will see the landscape layout in action, as shown in the following image:

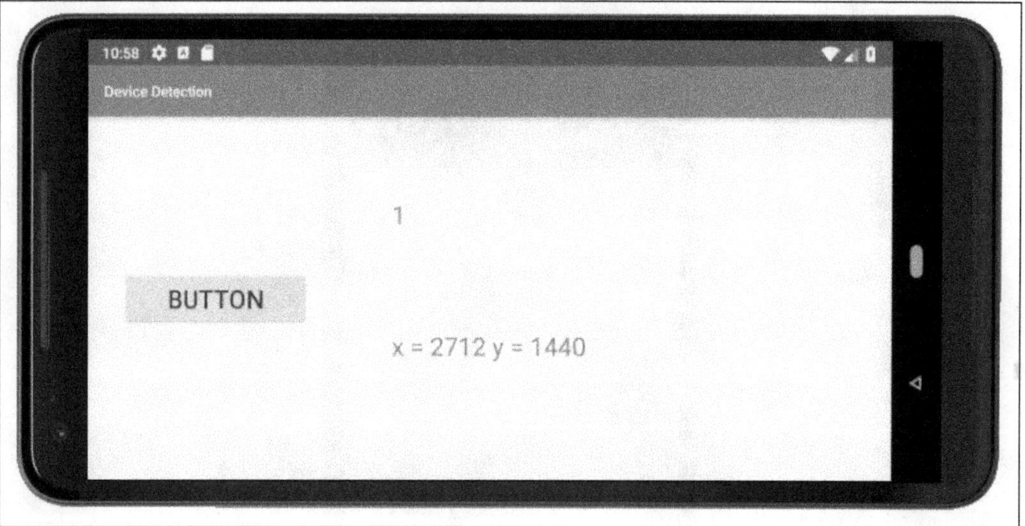

The first thing you will probably notice is that when you rotate the screen, it briefly goes blank. This is the activity restarting and going through `onCreate` again. This is just what we need. It calls `setContentView` on the landscape version of the layout, and the code in `MainActivity` refers to widgets with the same ID, so the exact same code works.

Just for a moment, consider how we might handle things if we needed different behavior as well as layouts between the two orientations. Don't spend too long pondering this because we will discuss it later on in this chapter.

If the `0` and `1` results are less than obvious to you, they refer to `public const` variables of the `Surface` class, where `Surface.ROTATION_0` equals zero and `Surface.ROTATION_180` equals one.

Note that if you rotated the screen to the left, then your value will be `1`, the same as mine, but if you rotated it to the right, you would have seen the value `3`. If you rotate the device to portrait mode (upside down), you will get the value `4`.

We could use a `when` block and execute different code based on the results of these detection tests and load up different layouts. But as we have just seen, Android makes things simpler than this by allowing us to add specific layouts to folders with configuration qualifiers, such as **land**.

Configuration qualifiers

We have already seen configuration qualifiers, such as `layout-large` or `layout-xhdpi`, in *Chapter 3, Exploring Android Studio and the Project Structure*. Here, we will refresh and expand our understanding of them.

We can begin by alleviating our reliance on the controller layer to influence app layout by using configuration qualifiers. There are configuration qualifiers for size, orientation, and pixel density. To take advantage of a configuration qualifier, we simply design a layout in the usual way, optimized for our preferred configuration, and then place that layout in a folder with a name that Android recognizes as being for that particular configuration.

For example, in the previous app, putting a layout in the `land` folder tells Android to use that layout when the device is in landscape orientation.

It is likely that the preceding statement seems slightly ambiguous. This is because the Android Studio project explorer window shows us a file and folder structure that doesn't exactly correspond to reality – it is trying to simplify things and "help" us. If you select the **Project Files** option from the drop-down list at the top of the project explorer window and then examine the project's contents, you will indeed see that there is a layout and `layout-land` folder, as shown in the following screenshot:

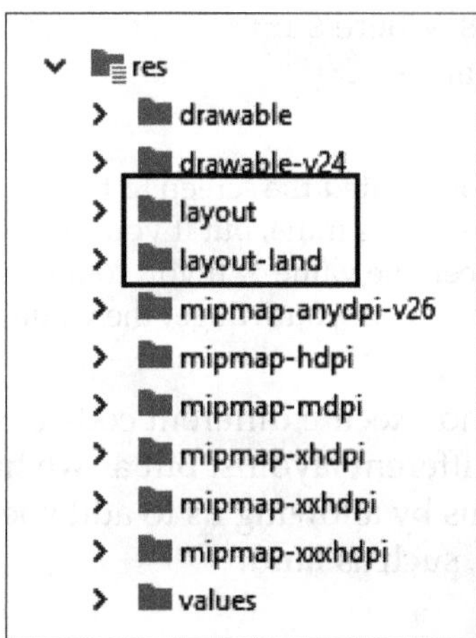

Switch back to the **Android** layout or leave it on the **Project Files** view, whichever you prefer.

If we want to have a different layout for landscape and portrait, we can create a folder called `layout-land` in the `res` folder (or use the shortcut we used in the previous app) and place our specially designed layout within it.

When the device is in portrait orientation, the regular layout from the `layout` folder will be used, and when it is in landscape orientation, the layout from the `layout-land` folder will be used.

If we are designing for different sizes of screen, we place layouts into folders with the following names:

- `layout-small`
- `layout-normal`
- `layout-large`
- `layout-xlarge`

If we are designing for screens with different pixel densities, we can place XML layouts into folders with names such as these:

- `layout-ldpi` for low-DPI devices
- `layout-mdpi` for medium-DPI devices
- `layout-hdpi` for high-DPI devices
- `layout-xhdpi` for extra-high-DPI devices
- `layout-xxhdpi` for extra-extra-high-DPI devices
- `layout-xxxhdpi` for extra-extra-extra-high-DPI devices
- `layout-nodpi` for devices with a DPI you have not otherwise catered for
- `layout-tvdpi` for TVs

What exactly qualifies as low, high, or extra-high DPI and so on can be found at the link in the following information box. The point being made here is simply where to store the layouts.

It is worth mentioning that what we have just discussed is a long way from the whole story regarding configuration qualifiers, and that, as with design, it is worth putting this on your list of things to study further.

As is so often the case, the Android developer site has lots of detailed information on handling layouts for different devices. Go to `https://developer.android.com/guide/practices/screens_support` for more information.

The limitation of configuration qualifiers

What the previous app and our discussion on configuration qualifiers have shown us is certainly very useful in a number of situations. Unfortunately, however, configuration qualifiers and detecting attributes in code only solves the problem in the view layer of our MVC pattern.

As we've discussed, our apps sometimes need to have different *behaviors*, as well as layouts. This perhaps implies multiple branches of our Kotlin code in the controller layer (`MainActivity`, in our previous app) and might summon nightmarish visions of having huge great `if` or `when` blocks with specific code for each different scenario.

Fortunately, this is not how it's done. For such situations—in fact, for most apps—Android has **fragments**.

Fragments

Fragments will likely become a staple of almost every app you make. They are so useful, there are so many reasons to use them, and—once you get used to them—they are so simple, that there is almost no reason not to use them.

Fragments are reusable elements of an app, just like any class, but, as we mentioned previously, they have special features—such as the ability to load their own view/layout, as well as their very own lifecycle functions—which make them perfect for achieving the goals we discussed in the *Real-world apps* section.

Let's dig a bit deeper into fragments, one feature at a time.

Fragments have a life cycle too

We can set up and control fragments, very much like we do with activities, by overriding the appropriate lifecycle functions.

The onCreate function

In the `onCreate` function, we can initialize variables and do almost all the things we typically do in the `Activity` `onCreate` function. The big exception to this is initializing our UI.

The onCreateView function

In the `onCreateView` function, we will, as the name suggests, get a reference to any of our UI widgets, set up lambdas to listen for clicks, and more besides, as we will soon see.

The onAttach and onDetach functions

The `onAttach` and `onDetach` functions are called just before the `Fragment` instance is put into use/taken out of use.

The onStart, onPause, and onStop functions

In the `onStart`, `onPause`, and `onStop` functions, we can take certain actions, such as creating or deleting objects or saving data, just like we did with their activity-based counterparts.

There are other fragment lifecycle functions as well, but we know enough to start using fragments already. If you want to study the details of the fragment lifecycle, you can do so on the Android developer website at `https://developer.android.com/guide/components/fragments`.

This is all fine, but we need a way to create our fragments in the first place and configure them to respond to these functions.

Managing fragments with FragmentManager

The `FragmentManager` class is part of the `Activity` class. We use it to initialize a `Fragment` instance, add `Fragment` instances to the layout, and end a `Fragment`. We briefly saw `FragmentManager` before when we initialized our `FragmentDialog` instances in the Note to self app.

It is very hard to learn much about Android without bumping into the `Fragment` class, just as it is tough to learn much about Kotlin without constantly bumping into OOP, classes, and so on.

The highlighted code in the following code snippet is a reminder of how we used the `FragmentManager` (which is already a part of the `Activity` class) that's being passed in as an argument to create the pop-up dialog:

```
button.setOnClickListener {
    val myDialog = MyDialog()
    myDialog.show(supportFragmentManager, "123")
    // This calls onCreateDialog
    // Don't worry about the strange looking 123
    // We will find out about this in Chapter 18
}
```

At the time, I asked you not to concern yourself with the arguments of the function call. The second argument of the call is an ID for the `Fragment`. We will soon see how we can use `FragmentManager` and the `Fragment` ID more extensively.

The `FragmentManager` does exactly what its name suggests. What is important here is that an `Activity` only has one `FragmentManager`, but it can take care of many `Fragment` instances. This is just what we need in order to have multiple behaviors and layouts within a single app.

The `FragmentManager` also calls the various lifecycle functions of the fragments it is responsible for. This is distinct from the `Activity` lifecycle functions, which are called by Android, yet it is also closely related because the `FragmentManager` calls many of the `Fragment` lifecycle functions *in response to* the `Activity` lifecycle functions being called. As usual, we don't need to worry too much about when and how it does this, provided we respond appropriately in each situation.

Our first fragment app

Let's build a fragment in its simplest possible form so that we can understand what is going on, before we start producing `Fragment` objects all over the place that are of genuine use.

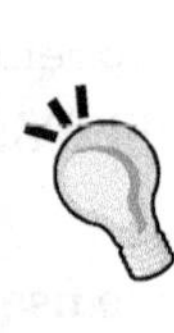

I urge all readers to go through and build this project. There is a lot of jumping around from file to file, and just reading the instructions alone can make it seem more complex than it really is. Certainly, you can copy and paste the code from the download bundle, but please also follow the steps, and create your own projects and classes. Fragments are not too tough, but their implementation, like their name suggests, is a little fragmented.

Create a new project called `Simple Fragment` using the **Empty Activity** template and leave the rest of the settings at their defaults.

Note that there is the option to create a project with a fragment, but we will learn more by doing things ourselves from scratch.

Switch to `activity_main.xml` and delete the default **Hello world!** `TextView`.

Now, make sure that the root `ConstraintLayout` is selected by left-clicking it in the **Component tree** window, and then change its **id** property to `fragmentHolder`. We will now be able to get a reference to this layout in our Kotlin code, and, as the **id** property implies, we will be adding a fragment to it.

Now, we will create a layout that will define our fragment's appearance. Right-click the `layout` folder and choose **New | Layout resource file**. In the **File name:** field, type `fragment_layout` and left-click **OK**. We have just created a new layout of the `LinearLayout` type.

Add a single **Button** widget anywhere on the layout and make its **id** property `button`.

Now that we have a simple layout for our fragment to use, let's write some Kotlin code to make the actual fragment.

Note that you can create a `Fragment` instance by simply dragging and dropping one from the palette, but doing things that way is much less flexible and controllable, and flexibility and control are the big benefits of using fragments, as we will see throughout this and the next three chapters. By creating a class that extends `Fragment`, we can make as many fragments from it as we like.

In the project explorer, right-click the folder that contains the `MainActivity` file. From the context menu, create a new Kotlin class called `SimpleFragment`.

In our new `SimpleFragment` class, change the code to inherit from `Fragment`. As you type the code, you will be asked to choose the specific `Fragment` class to import, as shown in the following screenshot:

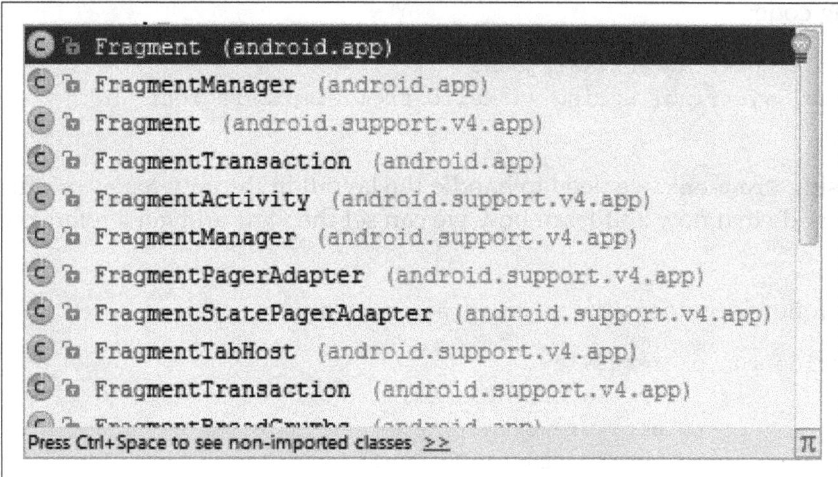

Choose the top option (as shown in the preceding screenshot), which is the regular `Fragment` class.

We will need all of the following import statements in this class:

```
import android.app.Fragment
import android.os.Bundle
import android.view.LayoutInflater
import android.view.View
import android.view.ViewGroup
import android.widget.Button
import android.widget.Toast
```

This is what the code looks like at this stage:

```
class SimpleFragment: Fragment() {
}
```

Now, add a single `String` property called `myString` and initialize it, as shown in the following code:

```
class SimpleFragment: Fragment() {
    val myString: String = "Hello from SimpleFragment"
}
```

When using `Fragment`, we need to handle the layout in the `onCreateView` function. Let's override that now and learn how we can set the view and get a reference to our `Button`.

Add the following code to the `SimpleFragment` class:

```
override fun onCreateView(
          inflater: LayoutInflater,
          container: ViewGroup?,
          savedInstanceState: Bundle?)
          : View? {

  val view = inflater.inflate(
              R.layout.fragment_layout,
              container,
              false)

  return view
}
```

To understand the previous block of code, we must first look at the `onCreateView` signature. Note that in the first instance, the signature states that it must return an object of the `View` type, as shown in the following code:

```
….:View?
```

Next, we have the three parameters. Let's look at the first two:

```
(inflater: LayoutInflater, container: ViewGroup?...
```

We need a `LayoutInflater`, as we cannot call `setContentView` because `Fragment` provides no such function. In the body of `onCreateView`, we use the `inflate` function of `inflater` to inflate our layout contained in `fragment_layout.xml` and initialize `view` (an object of the `View type`) with the result.

We use `container`, which was passed into `onCreateView`, as an argument in the `inflate` function as well. The `container` variable is a reference to the layout in `activity_main.xml`.

It might seem obvious that `activity_main.xml` is the containing layout, but, as we will see later in this chapter, the `ViewGroup container` argument allows *any* `Activity` with *any* layout to be the container for our fragment. This is exceptionally flexible and makes our `Fragment` code reusable to a significant extent.

The third argument we pass into `inflate` is `false`, which means that we don't want our layout added immediately to the containing layout. We will do this ourselves soon from another part of the code.

The third parameter of `onCreateView` is `Bundle savedInstanceState`, which is there to help us maintain the data that our fragments hold.

Now that we have an inflated layout contained in `view`, we can use this to get a reference to our `Button` widget from the layout and listen for clicks.

Finally, we use `view` as the return value to the calling code, as required. We can set this up as follows:

```
return view
```

Now, we can add a lambda to listen for clicks on our button in the usual manner. In the `onClick` function, we display a pop-up `Toast` message to demonstrate that everything is working as expected.

Add this code just before the `return` statement in `onCreateView`, as shown in the following code:

```
val button = view.findViewById(R.id.button) as Button

button.setOnClickListener(
  {
        Toast.makeText(activity,
              myString, Toast.LENGTH_SHORT).show()
  }
)
```

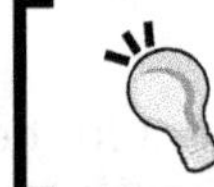

Note the use of the `activity` property in `makeText`, which is a reference to the `Activity` that contains the `Fragment`. This is required to display a `Toast` message.

We can't run our app just yet; it will not work because there is one more step required. We need to create an instance of `SimpleFragment` and initialize it appropriately. This is where `FragmentManager` will get introduced.

The following code uses the `supportFragmentManager` property of `Activity`. It creates a new `Fragment`, based on our `SimpleFragment` class, using the `findFragmentByID` function, and passes in the ID of the layout (within the `Activity`) that will hold it.

Add this code to the `onCreate` function of `MainActivity.kt`, just after the call to `setContentView`:

```
// Create a new fragment using the manager
var frag = supportFragmentManager
        .findFragmentById(R.id.fragmentHolder)

// Check the fragment has not already been initialized
if (frag == null) {
   // Initialize the fragment based on our SimpleFragment
   frag = SimpleFragment()
         supportFragmentManager.beginTransaction()
               .add(R.id.fragmentHolder, frag)
               .commit()
}
```

Now, run the app and gaze in wonder at our clickable button that displays a message with the `Toast` class, and which took two layouts and two whole classes to create:

If you remember doing this way back in *Chapter 2, Kotlin, XML, and the UI Designer*, and with far less code, then it is clear that we need a fragment reality check to answer the question, "Why?"!

Fragment reality check

So, what does this fragment stuff really do for us? Our first fragment mini-app would have the same appearance and functionality had we not bothered with the fragment at all.

In fact, using the fragment has made the whole thing more complicated! Why would we want to do this?

We kind of know the answer to this already; it just isn't especially clear based on what we have seen so far. We know that a fragment, or fragments, can be added to the layout of an activity.

We know that a fragment not only contains its own layout (view), but also its very own code (controller), which, although hosted by an activity, is virtually independent.

Our quick app only showed one fragment in action, but we could have an activity that hosts two or more fragments. We then effectively have two almost independent controllers displayed on a single screen. This sounds like it could be useful.

What is most useful about this, however, is that when the activity starts, we can detect attributes of the device our app is running on, perhaps a phone or tablet, in portrait or landscape mode. We can then use this information to decide to display either just one or two of our fragments simultaneously.

This not only helps us achieve the kind of functionality we discussed in the *Real- world apps* section, at the start of this chapter, but it also allows us to do so using the exact same fragment code for both possible scenarios!

This really is the essence of fragments. We create a whole app by pairing up both functionality (controller) and appearance (view) into a bunch of fragments that we can reuse in different ways, almost without a care.

The missing link is that if all these fragments are fully-functioning, independent controllers, then we need to learn a bit more about how we can implement our model layer.

It is, of course, possible to foresee a few stumbling blocks, so take a look at the following frequently asked question.

Frequently asked question

Q) If we simply have an `ArrayList`, as we did with the Note to self app, where will it go? How would we share it between fragments (assuming both/all fragments need access to the same data)?

A) There is an entirely more elegant solution we can use to create a model layer (both the data itself and the code to maintain the data). We will see this when we explore `NavigationDrawer` in *Chapter 26, Advanced UI with Navigation Drawer and Fragments*, and Android databases in *Chapter 27, Android Databases*.

Summary

Now that we have a broad understanding of what fragments are meant for and how we can begin to use them, we can start to go deeper into how they are used. In the next chapter, we will make a couple of apps that use multiple fragments in different ways.

25
Advanced UI with Paging and Swiping

Paging is the act of moving from page to page, and, on Android, we do this by swiping a finger across the screen. The current page then transitions in a direction and speed to match the finger movement. It is a useful and practical way to navigate around an app, but perhaps even more than this, it is an extremely satisfying visual effect for the user. Also, like `RecyclerView`, we can selectively load just the data required for the current page and perhaps the data for the previous and following pages in anticipation.

The Android API, as you would have come to expect, has a few solutions for achieving paging in a quite simple manner.

In this chapter, we will learn to do the following:

- Achieve paging and swiping with images like you might find in a photo gallery app
- Implement paging and swiping with `Fragment`-based layouts, giving the potential to offer our users the ability to swipe their way through a selection of entire user interfaces

First, let's look at a swiping example.

The Angry Birds classic swipe menu

Here, we can see the famous Angry Birds level selection menu showing swiping/paging in action:

Let's build two paging apps: one with images, and one with `Fragment` instances.

Building an image gallery/slider app

Create a new project in Android Studio called `Image Pager`. Use the **Empty Activity** template and leave the remainder of the settings at their defaults.

These images are located in the download bundle in the `Chapter25/Image Pager/drawable` folder. The following diagram shows them in Windows Explorer:

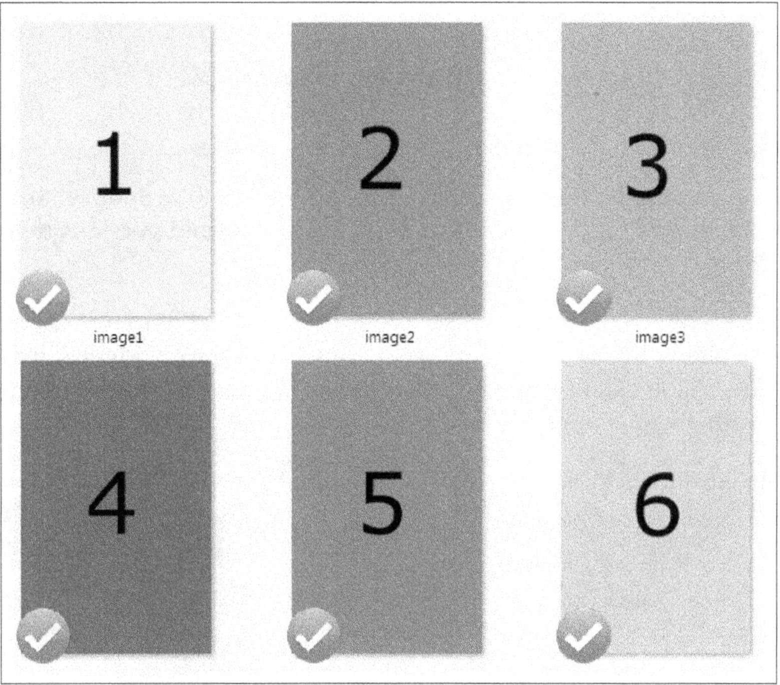

Add the images to the drawable folder in the project explorer or, of course, you could add more interesting images, perhaps some photos you have taken.

Implementing the layout

For a simple image paging app, we use the PagerAdapter class. We can think of this as being like RecyclerApater but for images, as it will handle the display of an array of images in a ViewPager widget. This is much like RecyclerAdapter, which handles the display of the content of an ArrayList in a RecyclerView. All we need to do is override the appropriate functions.

To implement an image gallery with PagerAdapter, we first need a ViewPager widget in our main layout. So, you can see precisely what is required; here is the actual XML code for activity_main.xml. Edit layout_main.xml to look exactly like this:

```
<RelativeLayout xmlns:android=
   "http://schemas.android.com/apk/res/android"
    android:layout_width="fill_parent"
    android:layout_height="fill_parent" >

    <androidx.viewpager.widget.ViewPager
```

```
            android:id="@+id/pager"
            android:layout_width="wrap_content"
            android:layout_height="wrap_content" />

</RelativeLayout>
```

The slightly unusually named class, `androidx.ViewPager.widget.ViewPager`, is the class that makes this functionality available in Android versions that were released prior to `ViewPager`.

Next, a bit like where we needed a layout to represent a list item, we need a layout to represent an item, in this case an image, in our `ViewPager` widget. Create a new layout file in the usual way, and call it `pager_item.xml`. It will have a single `ImageView` with an `id` property of `imageView`.

Use the visual designer to achieve this, or copy the following XML into `pager_item.xml`:

```
<RelativeLayout xmlns:android=
   "http://schemas.android.com/apk/res/android"
    android:layout_width="fill_parent"
    android:layout_height="fill_parent" >

    <androidx.viewpager.widget.ViewPager
        android:id="@+id/pager"
        android:layout_width="wrap_content"
        android:layout_height="wrap_content" />

</RelativeLayout>
```

Now, we can make a start on our `PagerAdapter` class.

Coding the PagerAdapter class

Next, we need to inherit from `PagerAdapter` to handle images. Create a new class called `ImagePagerAdapter` and make it inherit from `PagerAdapter`. This is what the code should look like at this point:

```
class ImagePagerAdapter: PagerAdapter() {
}
```

Add the following imports to the top of the `ImagePagerAdapter` class. We normally rely on using the shortcut *Alt* + *Enter* to add imports. We are doing things slightly differently this time because there are some very similarly named classes in the Android API that will not suit our objectives.

Add the following imports to the `ImagePagerAdapter` class:

```
import android.content.Context
import android.view.LayoutInflater
import android.view.Vie
import android.view.ViewGroup
import android.widget.ImageView
import android.widget.RelativeLayout

import androidx.viewpager.widget.PagerAdapter
import androidx.viewpager.widget.ViewPager
```

Next, add a constructor to the class to get a `Context` object and an array of `Int` (that refers to the image resource IDs) from `MainActivity` when the instance is created:

```
class ImagePagerAdapter(
        var context: Context,
        private var images: IntArray)
        : PagerAdapter() {

}
```

Now, we must override the required functions of `PagerAdapter`. Inside the body of the `ImagePagerAdapter` class, add the overridden `getCount` function, which simply returns the number of image IDs in the array. This function is used internally by the class:

```
override fun getCount(): Int {
   return images.size
}
```

Now, we must override the `isViewFromObject` function, which just returns a `Boolean`, depending on whether the current `View` is the same or associated with the current `Object` that was passed in as a parameter. Again, this is a function that is used internally by the class. Immediately after the previous code, add this overridden function:

```
override fun isViewFromObject(
         view: View, `object`: Any)
       : Boolean {
   return view === `object`
}
```

Now, we must override the `instantiateItem` function, and this is where we do most of the work that concerns us. First, we declare a new `ImageView` object, and then we initialize a `LayoutInflater`. Next, we use `LayoutInflater` to declare and initialize a new `View` from our `pager_item.xml` layout file.

After this, we get a reference to the `ImageView` inside the `pager_item.xml` layout. We can now add the appropriate image as the content of the `ImageView` widget based on the `position` parameter of the `instantiateItem` function and the appropriate ID from the `images` array.

Finally, we add the layout to the `PagerAdapter` with `addView` and return from the function.

Now, add the code we have just discussed:

```
override fun instantiateItem(
        container: ViewGroup,
        position: Int)
        : View {

  val image: ImageView
  val inflater: LayoutInflater =
        context.getSystemService(
        Context.LAYOUT_INFLATER_SERVICE)
        as LayoutInflater

  val itemView =
        inflater.inflate(
              R.layout.pager_item, container,
              false)

     // get reference to imageView in pager_item layout
     image = itemView.findViewById<View>(
           R.id.imageView) as ImageView

  // Set an image to the ImageView
  image.setImageResource(images[position])

  // Add pager_item layout as
  // the current page to the ViewPager
  (container as ViewPager).addView(itemView)

  return itemView
}
```

The last function we must override is `destroyItem`, which the class can call when it needs to remove an appropriate item based on the value of the `position` parameter.

Add the `destroyItem` function after the previous code and before the closing curly brace of the `ImagePagerAdapter` class:

```
override fun destroyItem(
  container: ViewGroup,
  position: Int,
  `object`: Any) {

  // Remove pager_item layout from ViewPager
  (container as ViewPager).
        removeView(`object` as RelativeLayout)
}
```

As we saw when coding `ImagePagerAdapter`, there is very little to this. It is just a case of properly implementing the overridden functions that the `ImagePagerAdapter` class uses to help make things work smoothly behind the scenes.

Now, we can code the `MainActivity` class, which will use the `ImagePagerAdapter`.

Coding the MainActivity class

Finally, we can code our `MainActivity` class. As with the `ImagePagerAdapter` class, for clarity, add the following import statements manually to the `MainActivity` class before the class declaration, as shown in the following code:

```
import android.view.View
import androidx.viewpager.widget.ViewPager
import androidx.viewpager.widget.PagerAdapter
```

All the code goes in the `onCreate` function. We initialize our `Int` array with each of the images that we added to the `drawable-xhdpi` folder.

We initialize a `ViewPager` widget in the usual way with the `findViewByID` function. We also initialize our `ImagePagerAdapter` instance by passing in a reference of `MainActivity` and the `images` array, as required by the constructor that we coded previously. Finally, we bind the adapter to the pager with `setAdapter`.

Code the `onCreate` function to look just like the following code:

```
override fun onCreate(savedInstanceState: Bundle?) {
   super.onCreate(savedInstanceState)

   setContentView(R.layout.activity_main)

   // Grab all the images and stuff them in our array
   val images: IntArray = intArrayOf(
         R.drawable.image1,
         R.drawable.image2,
         R.drawable.image3,
         R.drawable.image4,
         R.drawable.image5,
         R.drawable.image6)

  // get a reference to the ViewPager in the layout
  val viewPager: ViewPager =
        findViewById<View>(R.id.pager) as ViewPager

  // Initialize our adapter
  val adapter: PagerAdapter =
        ImagePagerAdapter(this, images)

  // Binds the Adapter to the ViewPager
  viewPager.adapter = adapter

}
```

Now, we are ready to run the app.

Running the gallery app

Here, we can see the first image from our `int` array:

Swipe to the left and right a little to see the pleasing manner in which the images transition smoothly:

Now, we will build an app with almost identical functionality, except that each page in the pager will be a `Fragment` instance, which could have any of the functionality a regular `Fragment` can have, because they are regular `Fragments`.

Before we implement this, let's learn some more Kotlin, which will help us achieve this.

Kotlin companion objects

A companion object is similar in syntax to an inner class because we declare it inside a regular class, but note we refer to it as an object, not a class. This implies it is in itself an instance as opposed to a blueprint for an instance. This is exactly what it is. When we declare a companion object inside a class, its properties and functions are shared by all instances of the regular class. It is perfect when we want a bunch of regular classes to share one set of related data. We will see a companion object in action in the next app, and also in the Age database app in the penultimate chapter.

Building a Fragment Pager/slider app

We can put whole `Fragment` instances as pages in a `PagerAdapter`. This is quite powerful because, as we know, a `Fragment` instance can have a large amount of functionality - even a fully-fledged UI.

To keep the code short and straightforward, we will add a single `TextView` to each `Fragment` layout, just to demonstrate that the pager is working. When we see how easy it is to get a reference to the `TextView`, however, it should be obvious how we could easily add any layout we have learned so far and then let the user interact with it.

In the next project, we will see yet another way to display multiple `Fragment` instances, `NavigationView`, and we will actually implement multiple coded `Fragment` instances.

The first thing we will do is build the content for the slider. In this case, of course, the content is an instance of `Fragment`. We will build one simple class called `SimpleFragment`, and one simple layout called `fragment_layout`.

You might think this implies that each slide will be identical in appearance, but we will use the ID that was passed in by the `FragmentManager` at instantiation time as the text for the `TextView`. This way, when we flip/swipe through the `Fragment` instances, it will be clear that each is a new distinct instance.

When we see the code that loads `Fragment` instances from a list, it will be easy to design completely different `Fragment` classes, as we have done before, and use these different classes for some or all of the slides. Each of these classes could, of course, also use a different layout as well.

Coding the SimpleFragment class

As with the Image Pager app, it is not exactly straightforward which classes need to be auto-imported by Android Studio. We use the classes that we do because they are all compatible with each other, and it is possible that if you let Android Studio suggest which classes to import, it will get it "wrong." The project files are located in the `Chapter25/Fragment Pager` folder.

Create a new project called `Fragment Slider` using the **Empty Activity** template, and leave all the settings at the defaults.

Now, create a new class called `SimpleFragment`, inherit from `Fragment`, and add the `import` statements, as shown in the following code:

```
import android.view.LayoutInflater
import android.view.View
import android.view.ViewGroup
import android.widget.TextView

import androidx.fragment.app.Fragment

class SimpleFragment: Fragment() {
}
```

We must add two functions, the first of which is `newInstance` and will be contained inside a companion object, which we will call from `MainActivity` to set up and return a reference to the `Fragment`. The following code creates a new instance of the class, but it also puts a `String` into the `Bundle` object that will eventually be read from the `onCreateView` function. The `String` that is added to the `Bundle`, which is passed in as the one and only parameter of this `newInstance` function.

Add the `newInstance` function inside the companion object to the `SimpleFragment` class, as follows:

```
class SimpleFragment: Fragment() {
// Our companion object which
// we call to make a new Fragment

companion object {
```

```
    // Holds the fragment id passed in when created
    val messageID = "messageID"

    fun newInstance(message: String)
                : SimpleFragment {
        // Create the fragment
        val fragment = SimpleFragment()

        // Create a bundle for our message/id
        val bundle = Bundle(1)
        // Load up the Bundle
        bundle.putString(messageID, message)
        fragment.arguments = bundle
        return fragment
    }
}
```

The final function for our `SimpleFragment` class needs to override `onCreateView` where, as usual, we will get a reference to the layout that's passed in and load up our `fragment_layout` XML file as the layout.

Then, the first line of code unpacks the `String` from the `Bundle` using `getArguments.getString` and the `MESSAGE` identifier of the key-value pair.

Add the `onCreateView` function we have just discussed:

```
override fun onCreateView(
         inflater: LayoutInflater,
         container: ViewGroup?,
         savedInstanceState: Bundle?)
         : View? {

    // Get the id from the Bundle
    val message = arguments!!.getString(messageID)

    // Inflate the view as normal
    val view = inflater.inflate(
              R.layout.fragment_layout,
              container,
              false)

    // Get a reference to textView
    val messageTextView = view
          .findViewById<View>(R.id.textView)
```

```
                as TextView

        // Display the id in the TextView
        messageTextView.text = message


        // We could also handle any UI
        // of any complexity in the usual way
        // And we will over the next two chapters
        // ..
        // ..

        return view
    }
```

Let's also make a super-simple layout for the `Fragment`, which will, of course, contain the `TextView` we have just been using.

The fragment_layout

The `fragment_layout` is the simplest layout we have ever made. Right-click on the `layout` folder and choose **New | Resource layout file**. Name the file `fragment_layout`, and left-click **OK**. Now, add a single `TextView` and set its `id` property to `textView`.

We can now code the `MainActivity` class, which handles the `FragmentPager` and brings our `SimpleFragment` instances to life.

Coding the MainActivity class

This class consists of two main parts; first, the changes we will make to the overridden `onCreate` function, and second, the implementation of an inner class and its overridden functions of `FragmentPagerAdapter`.

First, add the following imports:

```
import java.util.ArrayList

import androidx.appcompat.app.AppCompatActivity
import androidx.fragment.app.Fragment
import androidx.fragment.app.FragmentManager
import androidx.fragment.app.FragmentPagerAdapter
import androidx.viewpager.widget.ViewPager
```

Next, in the `onCreate` function, we create an `ArrayList` for `Fragment` instances, and then create and add three instances of `SimpleFragment`, passing in a numerical identifier to be packed away in the `Bundle`.

We then initialize `SimpleFragmentPagerAdapter` (which we will code soon), passing in our list of fragments.

We get a reference to the `ViewPager` with `findViewByID` and bind our adapter to it with `setAdapter`.

Add this code to the `onCreate` function of `MainActivity`:

```
public override fun onCreate(savedInstanceState: Bundle?) {
  super.onCreate(savedInstanceState)
  setContentView(R.layout.activity_main)

  // Initialize a list of three fragments
  val fragmentList = ArrayList<Fragment>()

  // Add three new Fragments to the list
  fragmentList.add(SimpleFragment.newInstance("1"))
  fragmentList.add(SimpleFragment.newInstance("2"))
  fragmentList.add(SimpleFragment.newInstance("3"))

  val pageAdapter = SimpleFragmentPagerAdapter(
            supportFragmentManager, fragmentList)

  val pager = findViewById<View>(R.id.pager) as ViewPager
  pager.adapter = pageAdapter

}
```

Now, we will add our `inner` class, `SimpleFragmentPagerAdapter`. All we do is add an `ArrayList` for `Fragment` instances in the constructor that initializes it with the passed-in list.

Then, we override the `getItem` and `getCount` functions, which are used internally, in the same way we did in the last project. Add the following `inner` class that we have just discussed to the `MainActivity` class:

```
private inner class SimpleFragmentPagerAdapter
   // A constructor to receive a fragment manager
   (fm: FragmentManager,
   // An ArrayList to hold our fragments
   private val fragments: ArrayList<Fragment>)
```

```
    : FragmentPagerAdapter(fm) {

    // Just two methods to override to get the current
    // position of the adapter and the size of the List
    override fun getItem(position: Int): Fragment {
            return this.fragments[position]
    }

   override fun getCount(): Int {
            return this.fragments.size
   }
}
```

The last thing we need to do is add the layout for `MainActivity`.

The activity_main layout

Implement the `activity_main` layout by copying the following code. It contains a single widget, a `ViewPager`, and it is important that it is from the correct hierarchy so that it is compatible with the other classes that we use in this project.

Amend the code in the `layout_main.xml` file that we have just discussed:

```
<RelativeLayout xmlns:android=
      "http://schemas.android.com/apk/res/android"
      xmlns:tools="http://schemas.android.com/tools"
      android:layout_width="match_parent"
      android:layout_height="match_parent"
      tools:context=".MainActivity">

      <androidx.viewpager.widget.ViewPager
      android:id="@+id/pager"
      android:layout_width="wrap_content"
      android:layout_height="wrap_content" />

</RelativeLayout>
```

Let's see our fragment slider in action.

Running the fragment slider app

Run the app, and then you can swipe your way, left or right, through the fragments in the slider. The following screenshot shows the visual effect produced by `FragmentPagerAdapter` when the user tries to swipe beyond the final `Fragment` in the `List`:

Summary

In this chapter, we saw that we can use pagers for simple image galleries or for swiping through complex pages of an entire UI, although we demonstrated this by means of a very simple `TextView`.

In the next chapter, we will look at another really cool UI element that is used in many of the latest Android apps, probably because it looks great and is a real pleasure, as well as extremely practical to use. Let's take a look at `NavigationView`.

26
Advanced UI with Navigation Drawer and Fragment

In this chapter, we will see what is (arguably) the most advanced UI. The `NavigationView`, or navigation drawer (because of the way it slides out its content), can be created simply by choosing it as a template when you create a new project. We will do just that, and then we will examine the auto-generated code and learn how to interact with it. We will then use everything we know about the `Fragment` class to populate each of the "drawers" with different behaviors and views. Then, in the next chapter, we will learn about databases to add some new functionality to each `Fragment`.

In this chapter, the following topics will be covered:

- Introducing the `NavigationView` widget
- Getting started with the Age Database app
- Implementing a `NavigationView` using the project template
- Adding multiple `Fragment` instances and layouts to `NavigationView`

Let's take a look at this extremely cool UI pattern.

Introducing the NavigationView

What's so great about the `NavigationView`? Well the first thing that might catch your eye is that it can be made to look extremely stylish. Look at this following screenshot, which shows off a `NavigationView` in action in the Google Play app:

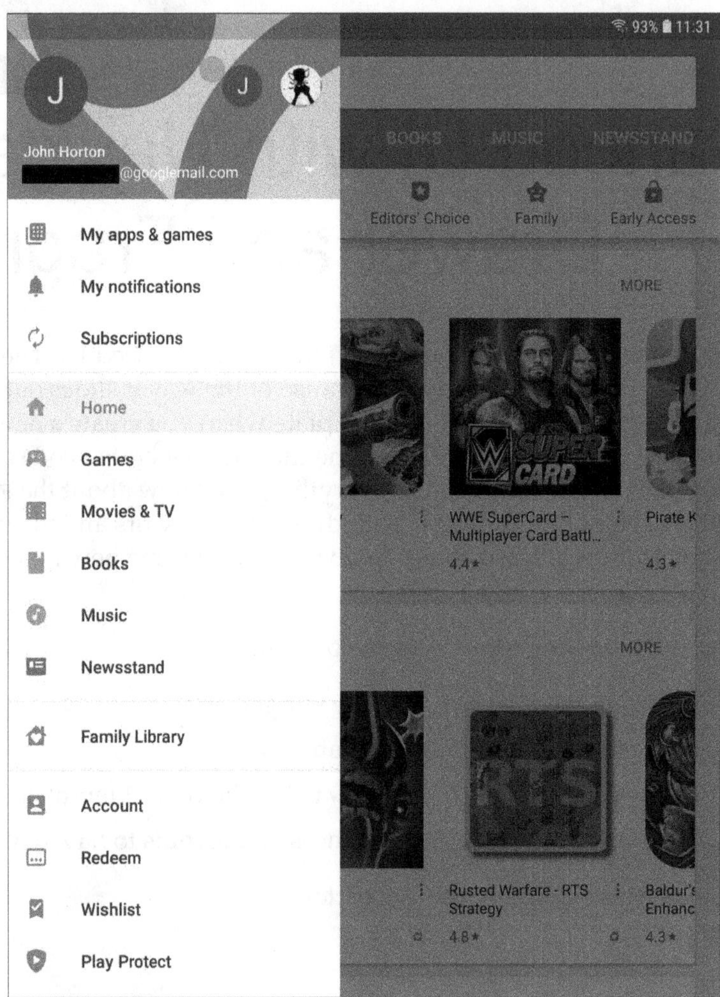

To be honest, right from the outset, ours is not going to be as fancy as the one in the Google Play app. However, the same functionality will be present in our app.

What else is neat about this UI is the way that it slides to hide or reveal itself when required. It is because of this behavior that it can be a significant size, making it extremely flexible regarding the options that can be added to it and, when the user is finished with it, it completely disappears—like a drawer.

I suggest trying the Google Play app now and seeing how it works, if you haven't already.

You can slide your thumb or finger from the left-hand edge of the screen and the drawer will slowly slide out. You can, of course, slide it away again in the opposite direction.

While the navigation drawer is open, the rest of the screen is slightly dimmed (as seen in the previous screenshot), helping the user to focus on the navigation options offered.

You can also tap anywhere off the navigation drawer while it is open, and it will slide itself away, leaving the entire screen clear for the rest of the layout.

The drawer can also be opened by tapping on the menu icon in the top-left corner.

We can also tweak and refine the behavior of the navigation drawer, as we will see toward the end of the chapter.

Examining the Age Database app

In this chapter, we will focus on creating the `NavigationView` and populating it with four `Fragment` classes and their respective layouts. In the next chapter, we will learn about, and implement, the database functionality.

Here is what our `NavigationView` looks like in all its glory. Note that many of the options, and most of the appearance and decoration, is provided by default when using the `NavigationView` Activity template:

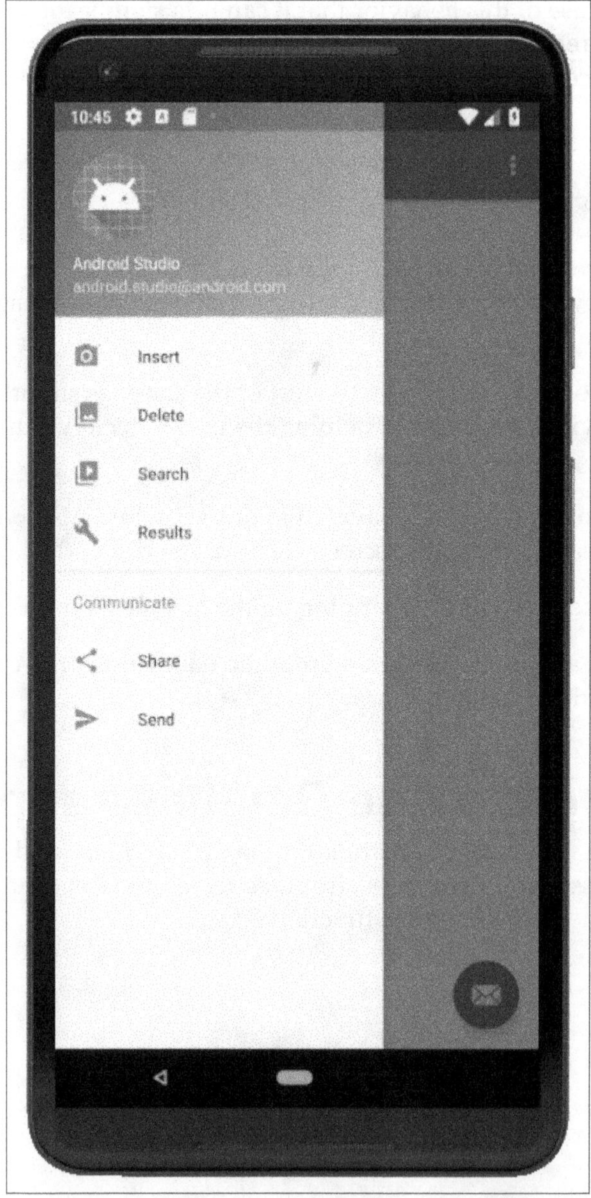

The four main options are what we will add to the UI. They are **Insert**, **Delete**, **Search**, and **Results**. The layouts are shown, and their purposes described, next.

Insert

The first screen allows the user to insert a person's name and their associated age into the database:

This simple layout has two `EditText` widgets and a button. The user will enter a name and an age, and then click the **INSERT** button to add them to the database.

Delete

This screen is even simpler. The user will enter a name in the `EditText` widget and click the button:

If the name entered is present in the database, then the entry (name and age) will be deleted.

Search

This layout is much the same as the previous layout, but has a different purpose:

The user will enter a name into the `EditText` and then click the button. If the name is present in the database, then it will be displayed along with the matching age.

Results

This screen shows all the entries in the entire database:

Let's get started with the app and the navigation drawer.

Starting the Age Database project

Create a new project in Android Studio. Call it `Age Database`, use the **Navigation Drawer Activity** template, and leave all the other settings as we have throughout the book. Before we do anything else, it is well worth running the app on an emulator to see how much has been auto-generated as part of this template, as can be seen in the following screenshot:

At first glance, it is just a plain old layout with a `TextView`. But, swipe from the left edge, or press the menu button, and the navigation drawer reveals itself:

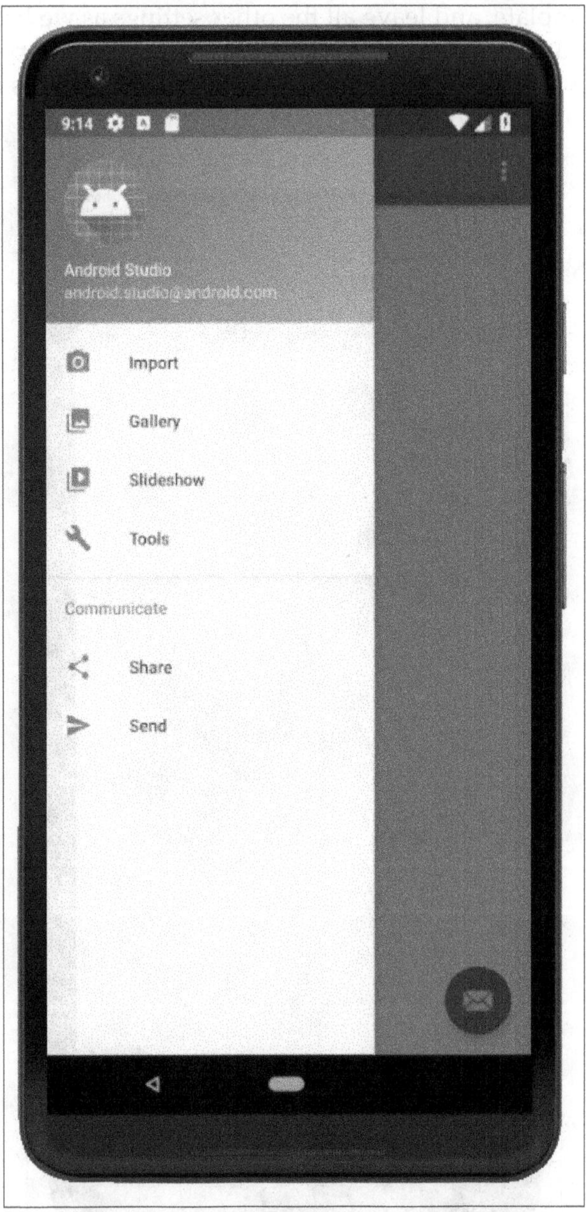

Now, we can modify the options and insert a `Fragment` instance (with a layout) for each option. To understand how it works, let's examine the auto-generated code.

Exploring the auto-generated code and assets

In the `drawable` folder, there are some icons, as shown in the following screenshot:

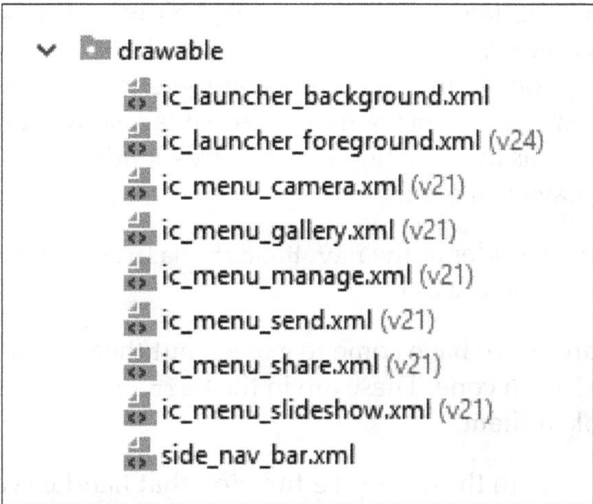

These are the usual icons, but also the ones that appear in the menu of the navigation drawer. We will not take the trouble to change these, but if you want to personalize the icons in your app, it should be plain by the end of this exploration how to do so.

Next, open the `res/menu` folder. Notice that there is an extra file titled `activity_main_drawer.xml`. This next code is an excerpt from this file, so we can discuss its contents:

```
<group android:checkableBehavior="single">
   <item
         android:id="@+id/nav_camera"
         android:icon="@drawable/ic_menu_camera"
         android:title="Import" />
   <item
         android:id="@+id/nav_gallery"
         android:icon="@drawable/ic_menu_gallery"
         android:title="Gallery" />
   <item
         android:id="@+id/nav_slideshow"
         android:icon="@drawable/ic_menu_slideshow"
         android:title="Slideshow" />
```

```
    <item
          android:id="@+id/nav_manage"
          android:icon="@drawable/ic_menu_manage"
          android:title="Tools" />
</group>
```

Notice there are four `item` tags within a `group` tag. Now, notice how the `title` tags from top to bottom (`Import`, `Gallery`, `Slideshow`, and `Tools`) exactly correspond to the first four text options in the menu of the auto-generated navigation drawer. Also, notice that within each `item` tag there is an `id` tag, so we can refer to them in our Kotlin code, as well as an `icon` tag, which corresponds to one of the icons in the `drawable` folder we have just seen.

Also, look in the `layout` folder at the `nav_header_main.xml` file, which contains the layout for the header of the drawer.

The rest of the files are as we have come to expect, but there are a few more key points to note in the Kotlin code. These are in the `MainActivity.kt` file. Open it up now and we will look at them.

The first is the extra code in the `onCreate` function that handles various aspects of our UI. Look at this additional code, and then we can discuss it:

```
val toggle = ActionBarDrawerToggle(
        this, drawer_layout,
        toolbar,
        R.string.navigation_drawer_open,
        R.string.navigation_drawer_close)

drawer_layout.addDrawerListener(toggle)

toggle.syncState()

nav_view.setNavigationItemSelectedListener(this)
```

The code gets a reference to a `DrawerLayout`, which corresponds to the layout we have just seen. The code also creates a new instance of `ActionBarDrawerToggle`, which allows the controlling or toggling of the drawers. The final line of code sets a listener on the `NavigationView`. Now, Android will call a special function every time the user interacts with the navigation drawer. This special function I refer to is `onNavigationItemSelected`. We will see this auto-generated function in a minute.

Next, look at the `onBackPressed` function:

```
override fun onBackPressed() {
   if (drawer_layout.isDrawerOpen(GravityCompat.START)) {
```

```
            drawer_layout.closeDrawer(GravityCompat.START)
        } else {
            super.onBackPressed()
        }
    }
```

This is an overridden function of the `Activity` class and it handles what happens when the user presses the back button on their device. The code closes the drawer if it is open and, if it is not, simply calls `super.onBackPressed`. This means that the back button will close the drawer if it is open or use the default behavior if it was already closed.

Now, look at the `onNavigationItemSelected` function, which is key to the functionality of this app:

```
override fun onNavigationItemSelected(
    item: MenuItem)
    : Boolean {

    // Handle navigation view item clicks here.
    when (item.itemId) {
        R.id.nav_camera -> {
            // Handle the camera action
        }
        R.id.nav_gallery -> {

        }
        R.id.nav_slideshow -> {

        }
        R.id.nav_manage -> {

        }
        R.id.nav_share -> {

        }
        R.id.nav_send -> {

        }
    }

    drawer_layout.closeDrawer(GravityCompat.START)
    return true
}
```

Notice that the `when` block branches correspond to the `id` values contained in the `activity_main_drawer.xml` file. This is where we will respond to the user selecting options in our navigation drawer menu. Currently, the `when` code does nothing. We will change it to load a specific `Fragment`, along with its related layout, into the main view. This will mean that our app will have entirely separate functionality and a separate UI, depending on the user's choice from the menu – as described when we discussed the MVC pattern in *Chapter 24, Design Patterns, Multiple Layouts, and Fragments*.

Let's code the `Fragment` classes and their layouts, and then we can come back and write the code to use them in the `onNavigationItemSelected` function.

Coding the Fragment classes and their layouts

We will create the four classes, including the code that loads the layout as well as the actual layouts, but we won't put any of the database functionality into the Kotlin code until we have learned about Android databases in the next chapter.

Once we have our four classes and their layouts, we will see how to load them from the navigation drawer menu. By the end of the chapter, we will have a fully working navigation drawer that lets the user swap between fragments, but the fragments won't do anything until the next chapter.

Creating the empty files for the classes and layouts

Create four layout files with vertical `LinearLayout` as their parent view by right-clicking on the `layout` folder and selecting **New | Layout resource file**. Name the first file `content_insert`, the second `content_delete`, the third `content_search`, and the fourth `content_results`. All the other options can be left at their defaults.

You should now have four new layout files containing `LinearLayout` parents, as shown in the following screenshot:

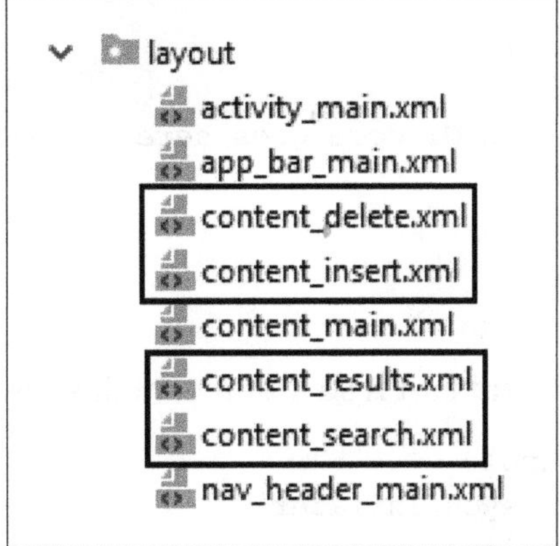

Let's code the Kotlin classes.

Coding the classes

Create four new classes by right-clicking the folder that contains the `MainActivity.kt` file and selecting **New | Kotlin File/Class**. Name them `InsertFragment`, `DeleteFragment`, `SearchFragment`, and `ResultsFragment`. It should be plain from the names which fragments will show which layouts.

Next, let's add some code to each class to make the classes inherit from `Fragment` and load their associated layout.

Open `InsertFragment.kt` and edit it to contain the following code:

```
import android.os.Bundle
import android.view.LayoutInflater
import android.view.View
import android.view.ViewGroup

import androidx.fragment.app.Fragment

class InsertFragment : Fragment() {
    override fun onCreateView(
          inflater: LayoutInflater,
          container: ViewGroup?,
          savedInstanceState: Bundle?)
          : View? {

          val view = inflater.inflate(
                 R.layout.content_insert,
```

```
                container,
                false)

        // Database and UI code goes here in next chapter

        return view
    }
}
```

Open `DeleteFragment.kt` and edit it so that it contains the following code:

```
import android.os.Bundle
import android.view.LayoutInflater
import android.view.View
import android.view.ViewGroup

import androidx.fragment.app.Fragment

class DeleteFragment : Fragment() {
    override fun onCreateView(
         inflater: LayoutInflater,
        container: ViewGroup?,
        savedInstanceState:
        Bundle?)
        : View? {

        val view = inflater.inflate(
               R.layout.content_delete,
               container,
               false)

        // Database and UI code goes here in next chapter

        return view
    }
}
```

Open `SearchFragment.kt` and edit it so that it contains the following code:

```
import android.os.Bundle
import android.view.LayoutInflater
import android.view.View
import android.view.ViewGroup
```

```
import androidx.fragment.app.Fragment

class SearchFragment : Fragment() {
    override fun onCreateView(
         inflater: LayoutInflater,
        container: ViewGroup?,
        savedInstanceState: Bundle?)
        : View? {

         val view = inflater.inflate(
               R.layout.content_search,
               container,
               false)

        // Database and UI code goes here in next chapter

        return view
    }
}
```

Open `ResultsFragment.kt` and edit it so that it contains the following code:

```
import android.os.Bundle
import android.view.LayoutInflater
import android.view.View
import android.view.ViewGroup

import androidx.fragment.app.Fragment

class ResultsFragment : Fragment() {

    override fun onCreateView(
         inflater: LayoutInflater,
        container: ViewGroup?,
        savedInstanceState: Bundle?)
         : View? {

        val view = inflater.inflate(
               R.layout.content_results,
               container,
               false)

        // Database and UI code goes here in next chapter

        return inflater.inflate(R.layout.content_results,
```

```
                        container,
                        false)
        }
    }
```

Each class is completely devoid of functionality, except that in the `onCreateView` function, the appropriate layout is loaded from the associated layout file.

Let's add the UI to the layout files we created earlier.

Designing the layouts

As we saw at the start of the chapter, all the layouts are simple. Getting your layouts identical to mine is not essential but, as always, the `id` attribute values must be the same or the Kotlin code we write in the next chapter won't work.

Designing content_insert.xml

Drag two **Plain Text** widgets from the **Text** category of the palette onto the layout. Remember that **Plain Text** widgets are `EditText` instances. Now, drag a **Button** onto the layout after the two **EditText/Plain Text** widgets.

Configure the widgets according to this table:

Widget	**Attribute and value**
Top edit text	id = `editName`
Top edit text	text = `Name`
Second edit text	id = `editAge`
Second edit text	text = `Age`
Button	id = `btnInsert`
Button	text = `Insert`

This is what your layout should look like in the design view in Android Studio:

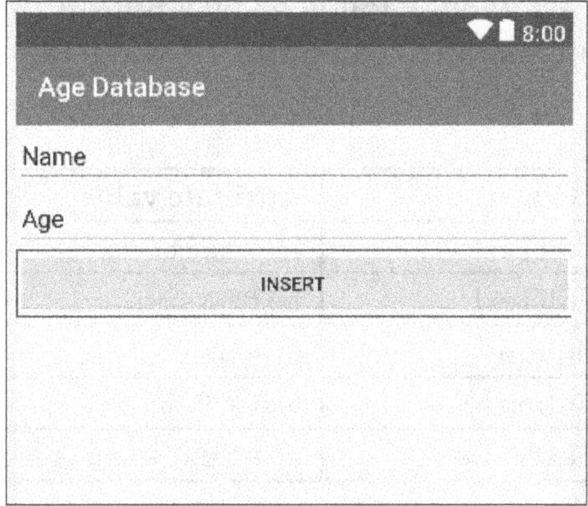

Designing content_delete.xml

Drag a **Plain Text/EditText** widget onto the layout with a **Button** below it. Configure the widgets according to the following table:

Widget	**Attribute value**
EditText	id = `editDelete`
EditText	text = `Name`
Button	id = `btnDelete`
Button	text = `Delete`

This is what your layout should look like in the design view in Android Studio:

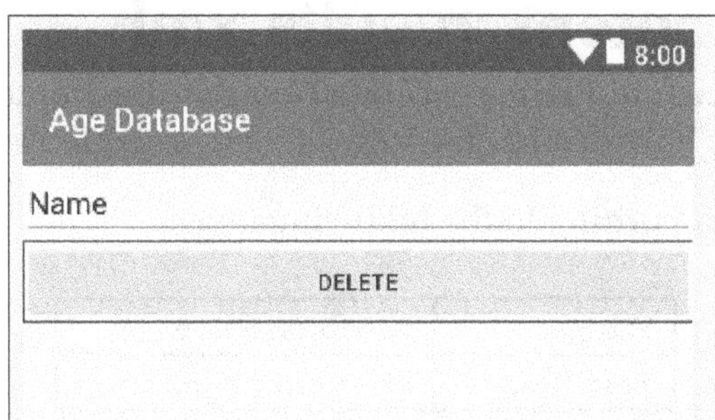

Designing content_search.xml

Drag a **Plain Text/EditText** widget, followed by a **Button** and then a regular **TextView**, onto the layout, and then configure the widgets according to the following table:

Widget	**Attribute value**
EditText	id = `editSearch`
EditText	text = `Name`
Button	id = `btnSearch`
Button	text = `Search`
TextView	id = `textResult`

This is what your layout should look like in the design view in Android Studio:

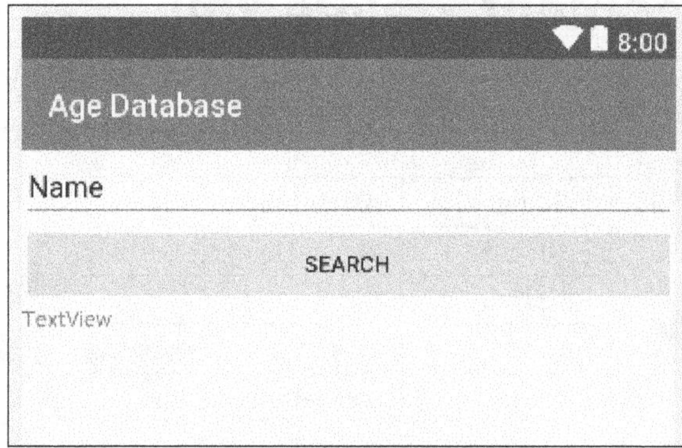

Designing content_results.xml

Drag a single `TextView` (not **Plain Text/EditText** this time) onto the layout. We will see in the next chapter how to add an entire list to this single `TextView`.

Configure the widget according to the following table:

Widget	**Attribute value**
TextView	id = `textResults`

This is what your layout should look like in the design view in Android Studio:

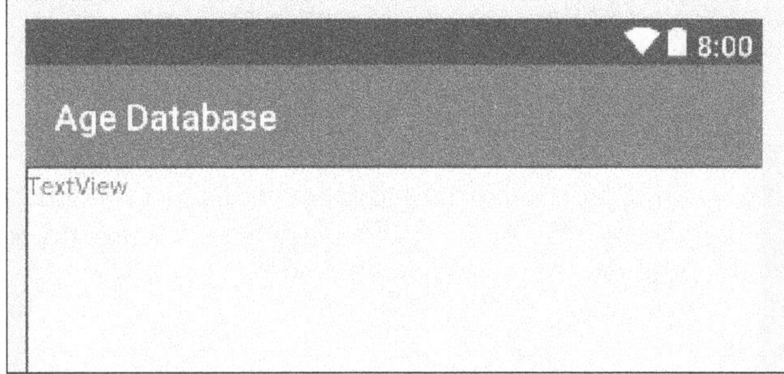

Now, we can use the classes based on the `Fragment` class, and their layouts.

Using the Fragment classes and their layouts

This stage has three steps. First, we need to edit the menu of the navigation drawer to reflect the options the user has. Next, we need a `View` instance in the layout to hold whatever the active `Fragment` instance is, and finally, we need to add code to `MainActivity.kt` to switch between the different `Fragment` instances when the user taps on the menu of the navigation drawer.

Editing the navigation drawer menu

Open the `activity_main_drawer.xml` file in the `res/menu` folder of the project explorer. Edit the code within the `group` tags that we saw earlier to reflect our menu options of **Insert**, **Delete**, **Search**, and **Results**:

```
<group android:checkableBehavior="single">
   <item
         android:id="@+id/nav_insert"
         android:icon="@drawable/ic_menu_camera"
         android:title="Insert" />
   <item
         android:id="@+id/nav_delete"
         android:icon="@drawable/ic_menu_gallery"
         android:title="Delete" />
   <item
         android:id="@+id/nav_search"
         android:icon="@drawable/ic_menu_slideshow"
         android:title="Search" />
```

```
    <item
          android:id="@+id/nav_results"
          android:icon="@drawable/ic_menu_manage"
          android:title="Results" />
</group>
```

Now would be a good time to add new icons to the `drawable` folder and edit the preceding code to refer to them if you wanted to use your own icons.

Adding a holder to the main layout

Open the `content_main.xml` file in the layout folder and add this highlighted XML code just before the closing tag of the `ConstraintLayout`:

```
<FrameLayout
    android:id="@+id/fragmentHolder"
    android:layout_width="0dp"
    android:layout_height="0dp"
    app:layout_constraintBottom_toBottomOf="parent"
    app:layout_constraintEnd_toEndOf="parent"
    app:layout_constraintStart_toStartOf="parent"
    app:layout_constraintTop_toTopOf="parent">
</FrameLayout>

</androidx.constraintlayout.widget.ConstraintLayout>
```

Now, we have a `FrameLayout` with an `id` attribute of `fragmentHolder` that we can get a reference to and load all our `Fragment` instance layouts into.

Coding the MainActivity.kt file

Open the `MainActivity` file and edit the `onNavigationItemSelected` function to handle all the different menu options the user can choose from:

```
override fun onNavigationItemSelected(
  item: MenuItem):
  Boolean {

  // Create a transaction
  val transaction =
        supportFragmentManager.beginTransaction()

  // Handle navigation view item clicks here.
```

```
    when (item.itemId) {
          R.id.nav_insert -> {
                // Create a new fragment of the appropriate type
                val fragment = InsertFragment()
                // What to do and where to do it
                transaction.replace(R.id.fragmentHolder, fragment)
      }
      R.id.nav_search -> {
                val fragment = SearchFragment()
                transaction.replace(R.id.fragmentHolder, fragment)
      }
      R.id.nav_delete -> {
                val fragment = DeleteFragment()
                transaction.replace(R.id.fragmentHolder, fragment)
      }
      R.id.nav_results -> {
        val fragment = ResultsFragment()
        transaction.replace(R.id.fragmentHolder, fragment)
      }

    }

     // Ask Android to remember which
     // menu options the user has chosen
     transaction.addToBackStack(null);

    // Implement the change
    transaction.commit();

     drawer_layout.closeDrawer(GravityCompat.START)
     return true
  }
```

Let's go through the code we just added. Most of the code should look familiar. For each of our menu options, we create a new `Fragment` instance of the appropriate type and insert it into our `FrameLayout` with an `id` value of `fragmentHolder`.

The `transaction.addToBackStack` function call means that the chosen `Fragment` will be remembered in order with any others. The result of this is that if the user chooses the **Insert** fragment, then the **Results** fragment and then taps the back button, the app will return the user to the **Insert** fragment.

You can now run the app and use the navigation drawer menu to flip between all our different `Fragment` instances. They will look just as they did in the images at the start of this chapter, but they don't have any functionality yet.

Summary

In this chapter, we saw how straightforward it is to have an attractive and pleasing UI and, although our `Fragment` instances don't have any functionality yet, they are set up ready to go once we have learned about databases.

In the next chapter, we will learn about databases in general, and the specific database that Android apps can use, before we add the functionality to our `Fragment` classes.

27 Android Databases

If we are going to make apps that offer our users significant features, then almost certainly we are going to need a way to manage, store, and filter significant amounts of data.

It is possible to efficiently store very large amounts of data with JSON, but when we need to use that data selectively rather than simply restricting ourselves to the options of "save everything" and "load everything", we need to think about which other options are available.

A good computer science course would probably teach the algorithms necessary for handling the sorting and filtering our data, but the effort involved would be quite extensive, and what are the chances of us coming up with a solution that is as good as the people who provide us with the Android API?

So often, it makes sense to use the solutions provided in the Android API. As we have seen, `JSON` and `SharedPreferences` classes have their place but at some point, we need to move on to using real databases for real-world solutions. Android uses the SQLite database management system and, as you would expect, there is an API to make it as easy as possible.

In this chapter, we will do the following:

- Find out exactly what a database is
- Learn what SQL and SQLite are
- Learn the basics of the SQL language
- Take a look at the Android SQLite API
- Code the Age Database app that we started in the previous chapter

Database 101

Let's answer a whole bunch of those database-related questions, and then we can get started making apps that use SQLite.

So, what is a database?

What is a database?

A **database** is both a place of storage and the means to retrieve, store, and manipulate data. It helps to be able to visualize a database before learning how to use it. The actual structure of the internals of a database varies greatly depending upon the database in question. SQLite actually stores all its data in a single file.

It will aid our comprehension greatly however if we visualize our data as if it were in a spreadsheet, or sometimes, multiple spreadsheets. Our database, like a spreadsheet, will be divided into multiple columns that represent different types of data, and rows that represent entries into the database.

Think about a database with names and exam scores. Take a look at this visual representation of this data for how we could imagine it in a database:

_ID	name	score
1	Bart	23
2	Lisa	100
3	Jim	66

Notice, however, that there is an extra column of data—an **ID** column. We will talk more about this as we proceed. This single spreadsheet-like structure is called a **table**. As mentioned before, there might be, and often are, multiple tables in a database. Each column of the table will have a name that can be referred to when speaking to the database. When we ask the database questions, we say that we are **querying** the database.

What is SQL?

SQL stands for **Structured Query Language**. It is the syntax that is used to get things done with the database.

What is SQLite?

SQLite is the name of the entire database system that is favored by Android, and it has its own version of SQL. The reason the SQLite version of SQL needs to be slightly different to some other versions is because the database has different features.

The SQL syntax primer that follows will focus on the SQLite version.

The SQL syntax primer

Before we can learn how to use SQLite with Android, we need to first learn the basics of how to use SQLite in general, in a platform-neutral context.

Let's look at some example SQL code that could be used on an SQLite database directly, without any Kotlin or Android classes, and then we can more easily understand what our Kotlin code is doing later on.

SQLite example code

SQL has keywords, much like Kotlin, that cause things to happen. Here is a flavor of some of the SQL keywords we will soon be using:

- `INSERT`: Allows us to add data to the database
- `DELETE`: Allows us to remove data from the database
- `SELECT`: Allows us to read data from the database
- `WHERE`: Allows us to specify the parts of the database that match specific criteria we want to `INSERT`, `DELETE`, or `SELECT` from
- `FROM`: Used for specifying a table or column name in a database

There are many more SQLite keywords than this and, for a comprehensive list, take a look at this link: `https://sqlite.org/lang_keywords.html`.

In addition to keywords, SQL has **types**. Some examples of SQL types are as follows:

- **integer**: Just what we need for storing whole numbers
- **text**: Perfect for storing a simple name or address
- **real**: For large floating-point numbers

There are many more SQLite types than this and, for a comprehensive list, take a look at this link: `https://www.sqlite.org/datatype3.html`.

Let's look at how we can combine those types with keywords to create tables, and add, remove, modify, and read data, using full SQLite statements.

Creating a table

It would be a perfectly decent question to ask why we don't first create a new database. The reason for this is that every app has access to an SQLite database by default. The database is private to that app. Here is the statement we would use to create a table within that database. I have highlighted a few parts to make the statement clearer:

```
create table StudentsAndGrades
   _ID integer primary key autoincrement not null,
   name text not null,
   score int;
```

The previous code creates a table called `StudentsAndGrades` with an **integer** row **id** that will be automatically increased (incremented) each time a row of data is added.

The table will also have a `name` column that will be of the `text` type and cannot be blank (`not null`).

It will also have a `score` column that will be of the `int` type. Also, notice that the statement is completed by a semicolon.

Inserting data into the database

Here is how we might insert a new row of data into that database:

```
INSERT INTO StudentsAndGrades
   (name, score)
   VALUES
   ("Bart", 23);
```

The previous code added a row to the database. After the preceding statement, the database will have one entry with the values (1, "Bart", 23) for the columns (_ID, name, and score).

Here is how we might insert another new row of data into that database:

```
INSERT INTO StudentsAndGrades
   (name, score)
   VALUES
   ("Lisa", 100);
```

The previous code added a new row of data with the values (2, "Lisa", 100) for the columns (_ID, name, and score).

Our spreadsheet-like structure would now look like the following diagram:

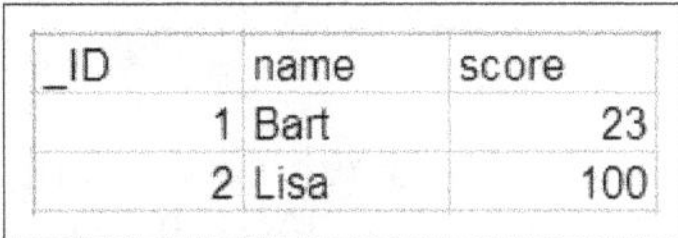

_ID	name	score
1	Bart	23
2	Lisa	100

Retrieving data from the database

Here is how we would access all the rows and columns from our database:

```
SELECT * FROM StudentsAndGrades;
```

The previous code asks for every row and column. The `*` symbol can be read as **all**.

We can also be a little more selective, as the following code demonstrates:

```
SELECT score FROM StudentsAndGrades
   where name = "Lisa";
```

The previous code would only return `100`, which, of course, is the score associated with the name Lisa.

Updating the database structure

We can even add new columns after the table has been created and the data added. This is simple as far as the SQL is concerned, but can cause some issues with regard to a user's data on already-published apps. The next statement adds a new column called `age` that is of the `int` type:

```
ALTER TABLE StudentsAndGrades
            ADD
     age int;
```

There are many more data types, keywords, and ways to use them than we have seen so far. Next, let's look at the Android SQLite API, and we will begin to see how we can use our new SQLite skills.

The Android SQLite API

There are a number of different ways in which the Android API makes it fairly easy to use our app's database. The first class we need to get familiar with is `SQLiteOpenHelper`.

SQLiteOpenHelper and SQLiteDatabase

The `SQLiteDatabase` class is the class that represents the actual database. The `SQLiteOpenHelper` class, however, is where most of the action takes place. This class will enable us to get access to a database and initialize an instance of `SQLiteDatabase`.

In addition, the `SQLiteOpenHelper` class, which we will inherit from in our *Age database* app, has two functions to override. First, it has an `onCreate` function, which is called the first time a database is used, and it therefore makes sense that we would incorporate our SQL in which to create our table structure.

The other function we must override is `onUpgrade`, which, you can probably guess, is called when we upgrade our database (`ALTER` its structure).

Building and executing queries

As our database structures become more complex and as our SQL knowledge grows, our SQL statements will get quite long and awkward. The potential for syntax errors or typos is high.

The way we will help overcome the problem of this complexity is to build our queries from parts into a `String`. We can then pass that `String` to the function (we will see this soon) that will execute the query for us.

Furthermore, we will use `String` instances to represent things such as table and column names, so we can't get in a muddle with them.

For example, we could declare the following `String` instances in a `companion` object, which would represent the table name and column names from the fictitious example from earlier. Note that we will also give the database itself a name and have a `String` for that too:

```
companion object {
    /*
    Next, we have a const string for
    each row/table that we need to refer to both
```

```
    inside and outside this class
    */

    const val DB_NAME = "MyCollegeDB";
    const val TABLE_S_AND_G = "StudentsAndGrades";

    const val TABLE_ROW_ID = "_id";
    const val TABLE_ROW_NAME = "name";
    const val TABLE_ROW_SCORE = "score";

}
```

We could then build a query like this in the next example. The following example adds a new entry to our hypothetical database and incorporates Kotlin variables into the SQL statement:

```
val name = "Smit";
val score = 95;

// Add all the details to the table
val query = "INSERT INTO " + TABLE_S_AND_G + " (" +
         TABLE_ROW_NAME + ", " +
         TABLE_ROW_SCORE +
         ") " +
         "VALUES (" +
         "'" + name + "'" + ", " +
         score +
         ");"
```

Notice that in the previous code, the regular Kotlin variables, `name` and `score`, are highlighted. The previous `String` called `query` is now the SQL statement, exactly equivalent to this:

```
INSERT INTO StudentsAndGrades (
   name, score)
   VALUES ('Smit',95);
```

It is not essential to completely grasp the previous two blocks of code in order to proceed with learning Android programming. But, if you want to build your own apps and construct SQL statements that do exactly what you need, it *will* help to do so. Why not study the previous two blocks of code in order to discern the difference between the parts of the `String` joined together with the pairs of single quote marks, `'`, that are part of the SQL syntax?

Throughout the typing of the query, Android Studio prompts us as to the names of our variables, making the chances of an error much less likely, even though it is more verbose than simply typing the query.

Now, we can use the classes we introduced previously to execute the query:

```
// This is the actual database
private val db: SQLiteDatabase

// Create an instance of our internal CustomSQLiteOpenHelper class
val helper = CustomSQLiteOpenHelper(context)

// Get a writable database
db = helper.writableDatabase

// Run the query
db.execSQL(query)
```

When adding data to the database, we will use `execSQL`, as in the previous code, and when getting data from the database, we will use the `rawQuery` function, demonstrated as follows:

```
Cursor c = db.rawQuery(query, null)
```

Notice that the `rawQuery` function returns an object of `Cursor` type.

There are several different ways in which we can interact with SQLite, and they each have their advantages and disadvantages. We have chosen to use raw SQL statements as it is entirely transparent as to what we are doing, at the same time as reinforcing our knowledge of the SQL language.

Database cursors

In addition to the classes that give us access to the database, and the functions that allow us to execute our queries, there is the issue of exactly how the results we get back from our queries are formatted.

Fortunately, there is the `Cursor` class. All our database queries will return objects of the `Cursor` type. We can use the functions of the `Cursor` class to selectively access the data returned from the queries, as in the following code:

```
Log.i(c.getString(1), c.getString(2))
```

The previous code would output to the logcat window the two values stored in the first two columns of the result that the query returned. It is the `Cursor` object itself that determines which row of our returned data we are currently reading.

We can access various functions of the `Cursor` object, including the `moveToNext` function, which, unsurprisingly, would move the `Cursor` to the next row ready for reading:

```
c.moveToNext()

/*
   This same code now outputs the data in the
   first and second column of the returned
   data but from the SECOND row.
*/

Log.i(c.getString(1), c.getString(2))
```

On certain occasions, we will be able to bind a `Cursor` to a part of our UI (such as `RecyclerView`), as we did with an `ArrayList` in the *Note to self* app, and just leave everything to the Android API.

There are many more useful functions in the `Cursor` class, some of which we will see soon.

> This introduction to the Android SQLite API really only scratches the surface of its capabilities. We will bump into a few more functions and classes as we proceed further. It is, however, worth studying further if your app idea requires complex data management.

Now, we can see how all this theory comes together and how we will structure our database code in the Age Database app.

Coding the database class

Here, we will put into practice everything we have learned so far and finish coding the Age database app. Before our `Fragment` classes from the previous section can interact with a shared database, we need a class to handle interaction with, and creation of, the database.

We will create a class that manages our database by implementing `SQLiteOpenHelper`. It will also define some `String` variables in a `companion object` to represent the names of the table and its columns. Furthermore, it will supply a bunch of helper functions we can call to perform all the necessary queries. Where necessary, these helper functions will return a `Cursor` object that we can use to show the data we have retrieved. It would be trivial then to add new helper functions should our app need to evolve:

Create a new class called `DataManager` and add the companion object, the constructor, and the `init` block:

We discussed the `companion object` in *Chapter 25, Advanced UI with Paging and Swiping*

```
class DataManager(context: Context) {

    // This is the actual database
    private val db: SQLiteDatabase

    init {
        // Create an instance of our internal
        // CustomSQLiteOpenHelper class
        val helper = CustomSQLiteOpenHelper(context)
        // Get a writable database
        db = helper.writableDatabase
    }

    companion object {
        /*
        Next, we have a const string for
        each row/table that we need to refer to both
        inside and outside this class
        */

        const val TABLE_ROW_ID = "_id"
        const val TABLE_ROW_NAME = "name"
        const val TABLE_ROW_AGE = "age"

        /*
        Next, we have a private const strings for
        each row/table that we need to refer to just
```

```
        inside this class
        */


        private const val DB_NAME = "address_book_db"
        private const val DB_VERSION = 1
        private const val TABLE_N_AND_A = "names_and_addresses"
    }
}
```

I named the database and the table as it could evolve to be an address book app that also keeps track of ages and perhaps birthdays.

The previous code gives us all our handy `String` instances for building our queries, and it also declares and initializes our database and helper class.

Now, we can add the helper functions we will access from our `Fragment` classes; first, the `insert` function, which executes an `INSERT` SQL query based on the `name` and `age` parameters passed into the function.

Add the `insert` function to the `DataManager` class:

```
// Insert a record
fun insert(name: String, age: String) {
  // Add all the details to the table
  val query = "INSERT INTO " + TABLE_N_AND_A + " (" +
              TABLE_ROW_NAME + ", " +
              TABLE_ROW_AGE +
              ") " +
              "VALUES (" +
              "'" + name + "'" + ", " +
              "'" + age + "'" +
              ");"

  Log.i("insert() = ", query)

  db.execSQL(query)
}
```

This next function, called `delete`, will delete a record from the database if it has a matching value in the `name` column to that of the passed-in `name` parameter. It achieves this using the SQL `DELETE` keyword.

Add the `delete` function to the `DataManager` class:

```
// Delete a record
fun delete(name: String) {

    // Delete the details from the table
    // if already exists
    val query = "DELETE FROM " + TABLE_N_AND_A +
                " WHERE " + TABLE_ROW_NAME +
                " = '" + name + "';"

    Log.i("delete() = ", query)

    db.execSQL(query)

}
```

Next, we have the `selectAll` function, which also does as the name suggests. It achieves this with a `SELECT` query using the `*` parameter, which is equivalent to specifying all the columns individually. Also, note that the function returns a `Cursor`, which we will use in some of the `Fragment` classes.

Add the `selectAll` function to the `DataManager` class as follows:

```
// Get all the records
fun selectAll(): Cursor {
    return db.rawQuery("SELECT *" + " from " +
                TABLE_N_AND_A, null)
}
```

Now, we add a `searchName` function, which has a `String` parameter for the name the user wants to search for. It also returns a `Cursor` object, which will contain all the entries that were found. Notice that the SQL statement uses `SELECT`, `FROM`, and `WHERE` to achieve this:

```
// Find a specific record
fun searchName(name: String): Cursor {
     val query = "SELECT " +
                 TABLE_ROW_ID + ", " +
                 TABLE_ROW_NAME +
                 ", " + TABLE_ROW_AGE +
                 " from " +
                 TABLE_N_AND_A + " WHERE " +
                 TABLE_ROW_NAME + " = '" + name + "';"
```

```
        Log.i("searchName() = ", query)

        return db.rawQuery(query, null)
    }
```

Finally, for the DataManager class, we create an inner class that will be our implementation of SQLiteOpenHelper. It is a barebones implementation.

We have a constructor that receives a Context object, the database name, and the database version.

We also override the onCreate function, which has the SQL statement that creates our database table with _ID, name, and age columns.

The onUpgrade function is left intentionally blank for this app, but still needs to be present because it is part of the contract when we inherit from SQLiteOpenHelper.

Add the inner CustomSQLiteOpenHelper class to the DataManager class:

```
    // This class is created when
    // our DataManager class is instantiated
    private inner class CustomSQLiteOpenHelper(
             context: Context)
        : SQLiteOpenHelper(
              context, DB_NAME,
              null, DB_VERSION) {

      // This function only runs the first
      // time the database is created
      override fun onCreate(db: SQLiteDatabase) {

            // Create a table for photos and all their details
            val newTableQueryString = ("create table "
                  + TABLE_N_AND_A + " ("
                  + TABLE_ROW_ID
                  + " integer primary key autoincrement not null,"
                  + TABLE_ROW_NAME
                  + " text not null,"
                  + TABLE_ROW_AGE
                  + " text not null);")

            db.execSQL(newTableQueryString)
      }

      // This function only runs when we increment DB_VERSION
      override fun onUpgrade(db: SQLiteDatabase,
```

```
                        oldVersion: Int,
                        newVersion: Int) {

    }

}
```

Now, we can add code to our `Fragment` classes to use our new `DataManager` class.

Coding the Fragment classes to use the DataManager class

Add this highlighted code to the `InsertFragment` class to update the `onCreateView` function, as follows:

```
val view = inflater.inflate(
        R.layout.content_insert,
        container,
        false)

// Database and UI code goes here in next chapter
val dm = DataManager(activity!!)

val btnInsert = view.findViewById(R.id.btnInsert) as Button
val editName = view.findViewById(R.id.editName) as EditText
val editAge = view.findViewById(R.id.editAge) as EditText

btnInsert.setOnClickListener(
        {
          dm.insert(editName.text.toString(),
                editAge.text.toString())
        }
)

return view
```

In the code, we get an instance of our `DataManager` class and a reference to each of our UI widgets. Then, in the `onClick` function of the button, we use the `insert` function to add a new name and age to the database. The values to insert are taken from the two `EditText` widgets.

Add this highlighted code to the `DeleteFragment` class to update the `onCreateView` function:

```
val view = inflater.inflate(
        R.layout.content_delete,
        container,
        false)

// Database and UI code goes here in next chapter
val dm = DataManager(activity!!)

val btnDelete =
   view.findViewById(R.id.btnDelete) as Button
val editDelete =
   view.findViewById(R.id.editDelete) as EditText

btnDelete.setOnClickListener(
  {
         dm.delete(editDelete.text.toString())
  }
)

return view
```

In the `DeleteFragment` class, we create an instance of our `DataManager` class, and then get a reference to the `EditText` and the `Button` from our layout. When the button is clicked, the `delete` function is called, passing in the value of any text from the `EditText`. The delete function searches our database for a match and, if one is found, it deletes it.

Add this highlighted code to the `SearchFragment` class to update the `onCreateView` function:

```
val view = inflater.inflate(R.layout.content_search,
        container,
        false)

// Database and UI code goes here in next chapter
val btnSearch = view.findViewById(R.id.btnSearch) as Button
val editSearch = view.findViewById(R.id.editSearch) as EditText
val textResult = view.findViewById(R.id.textResult) as TextView

// This is our DataManager instance
```

```
val dm = DataManager(activity!!)

btnSearch.setOnClickListener(
  {
          val c = dm.searchName(editSearch.text.toString())

          // Make sure a result was found
          // before using the Cursor
          if (c.count > 0) {
                c.moveToNext()
                textResult.text =
                "Result = ${c.getString(1)} - ${c.getString(2)}"
    }
  }
)

return view
```

As we do for all our different `Fragment` classes, we create an instance of `DataManager` and get a reference to all the different UI widgets in the layout. In the `onClick` function of the button, the `searchName` function is used, passing in the value from the `EditText`. If the database returns a result in the `Cursor`, then the `TextView` uses its `text` property to output the results.

Add this highlighted code to the `ResultsFragment` class to update the `onCreateView` function:

```
val view = inflater.inflate(R.layout.content_results,
        container,
        false)

// Database and UI code goes here in next chapter
// Create an instance of our DataManager
val dm = DataManager(activity!!)

// Get a reference to the TextView
// to show the results in
val textResults =
  view.findViewById(R.id.textResults) as TextView

// Create and initialize a Cursor
// with all the results in
val c = dm.selectAll()

// A String to hold all the text
```

```
var list = ""

// Loop through the results in the Cursor
while (c.moveToNext()) {
   // Add the results to the String
   // with a little formatting
   list += c.getString(1) + " - " + c.getString(2) + "\n"
}

// Display the String in the TextView
textResults.text = list

return view
```

In this class, the `Cursor` object is loaded up with data using the `selectAll` function before any interactions take place. The contents of the `Cursor` are then output into the `TextView` by concatenating the results. The `\n` in the concatenation is what creates a new line between each result in the `Cursor`.

Running the Age Database app

Let's run through some of the functions of our app to make sure it is working as expected. First, I added a new name to the database using the **Insert** menu option:

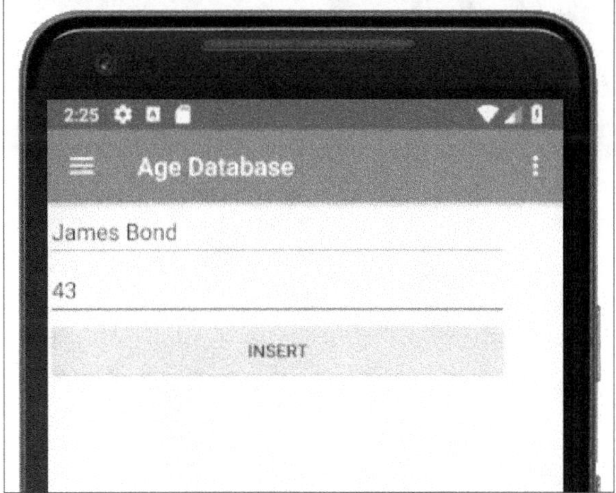

And then, I confirmed it was there by viewing the **Results** option:

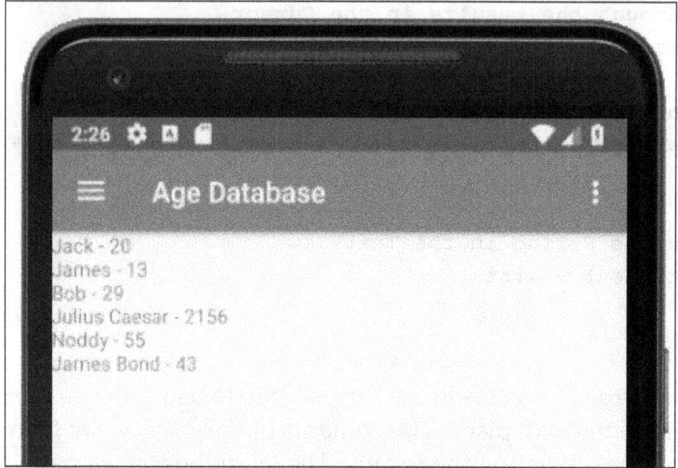

Then, I used the **Delete** menu option and looked at the **Results** option again to check that my chosen name was, in fact, removed:

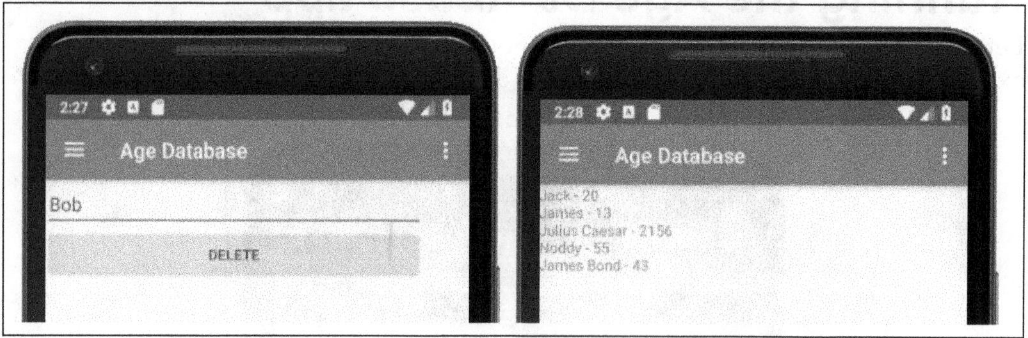

Next, I searched for a name that I knew existed to test the **Search** function:

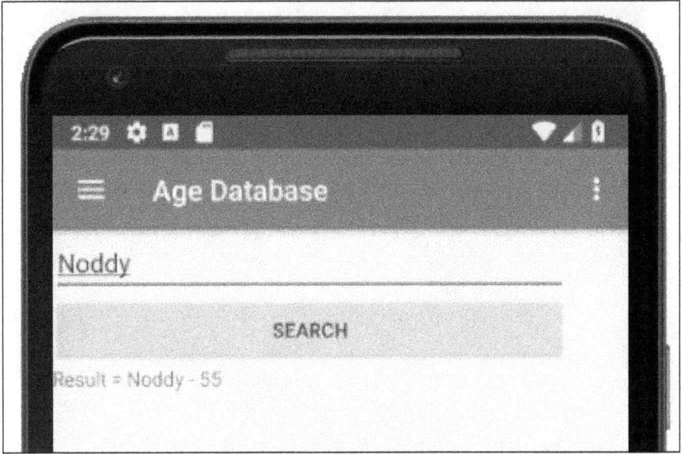

Let's review what we have done in this chapter.

Summary

We have covered a lot in this chapter. We have learned about databases and, in particular, the database of Android apps, SQLite. We have practiced the basics of communicating with and querying a database using the SQL language.

We have seen how the Android API helps us use an SQLite database, and have implemented our first working app with a database.

That is just about it, but please look at the brief final chapter that follows.

28

A Quick Chat Before You Go

We are just about done with our journey. This chapter is just a few ideas and pointers that you might like to look at before rushing off and making your own apps:

- Publishing
- Making your first app
- Carrying on learning
- Thanks

Publishing

You easily know enough to design your own app. You could even just make some modifications and add lots of new features to one of the apps from the book.

I decided not to do a step-by-step guide to publishing on Google's Play store because the steps are not complicated. They are, however, quite in-depth and a little laborious. Most of the steps involve entering personal information and images about you and your app. Such a tutorial would read something like the following:

1. Fill this text box.
2. Now, fill that text box.
3. Upload this image.
4. And so on.

Not much fun or use.

To get started, you just need to visit `https://play.google.com/apps/publish` and pay a modest fee (around $25) depending on your region's currency. This allows you to publish apps for life.

> If you want a checklist for publishing, take a look at the following URL: `https://developer.android.com/distribute/best-practices/launch/launch-checklist.html`. You will find the process intuitive (if very drawn out).

Making an app!

You could ignore everything else in this chapter if you just put this one thing into practice:

> Don't wait until you are an expert before you start making apps!

Start building your dream app, the one with all the features that's going to take Google Play by storm. A simple piece of advice, however, is this: do some planning first! Not too much though, and then get started.

Have some smaller and more easily achievable projects on the sidelines; projects you will be able to show to friends and family and that explore areas of Android that are new to you. If you are confident about these apps, you could upload them to Google Play. If you are worried about how they might be received by reviewers, then make them free and put a note in the description about it being "just a prototype," or something similar.

If your experience is anything like mine, you will find that as you read, study, and build apps, you will discover that your dream app can be improved in many ways and you will probably be inspired to redesign it or even start again.

When you do this, I can guarantee that the next time you build it, you will do it in half the time and twice as good, at least!

Carrying on learning

If you feel like you have come a long way, you are right. There is always more to learn, however.

Carrying on reading

You will find that as you make your first app, you suddenly realize that there is a gap in your knowledge that needs to be filled to make some feature come to life. This is normal and guaranteed; don't let it put you off. Think of how to describe the problem and search for the solution on Google.

You might also find that specific classes in a project will grow beyond the practical and maintainable size. This is a sign that there is a better way to structure things and there is probably a ready-made design pattern out there somewhere that will make your life easier.

To pre-empt this almost-inevitability, why not study some patterns right away? One great source is `https://proandroiddev.com/kotlin-design-patterns-8e152540ee2c`.

GitHub

GitHub allows you to search and browse code that other people have written and see how they have solved problems. This is useful, because seeing the file structure of classes, and then dipping into them, often shows how to plan your apps from the start and prevent you from starting off on the wrong path. You can even get a GitHub app that allows you to do this from the comfort of your phone or tablet.

You can even configure Android Studio to save and share your projects to GitHub. For example, search for "Android fragment" on the homepage, `www.github.com`, and you will see more than 1,000 related projects that you can snoop through, as demonstrated in the following:

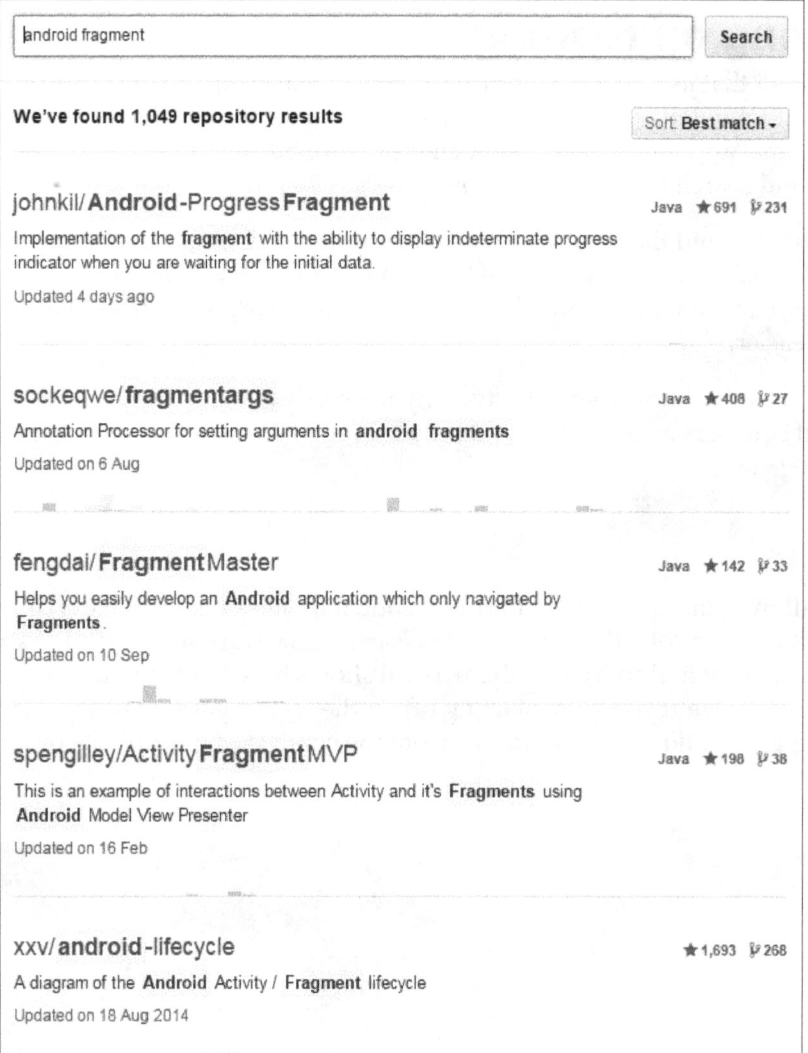

StackOverflow

If you get stuck, have a weird error, or an unexplained crash, often the best place to turn is Google. Do this, and you will be surprised how often StackOverflow seems to be prominent in the search results; and for good reason.

StackOverflow allows users to post a description of their problem, along with sample code, so the community can respond with answers. In my experience however, it is rarely necessary to post a question because there is almost always somebody who has had the exact same problem.

StackOverflow is especially good for bleeding-edge issues. If a new Android Studio version has a bug, or a new version of the Android API seems to not be doing what it should, then you can be almost certain that a few thousand other developers around the world are having the same problem as you. Then, some smart coder, often from the Android development team itself, will be there with an answer.

StackOverflow is also good for a bit of light reading. Go to the `www.stackoverflow.com` homepage, type "Android" in the search box, and you will see a list of all the latest problems that the StackOverflow community are having:

I am not suggesting that you dive in and start trying to answer them all just yet, but reading the problems and the suggestions will teach you a lot and you will probably find that, more often than not, you have the solution, or at least an idea of the solution.

Android user forums

Also, it is well worth signing up to some Android forums and visiting occasionally to find out what the hot topics and trends are from a user's perspective. I don't list any here because a quick web search is all that is required.

If you're serious, then you can attend some Android conferences where you can rub shoulders with thousands of other developers and attend lectures. If this interests you, do a web search for Droidcon, Android developer Days, or GDG DevFest.

Higher-level study

You can now read a wider selection of other Android books. I mentioned at the start of this book that there were very few, arguably no, books that taught Android programming to readers with no Kotlin experience. That was the reason I wrote this book.

Now you have a good understanding of OOP and Kotlin, as well as a brief introduction to app design and the Android API, you are well-placed to read the Android "beginner" books for people who already know how to program in Kotlin, just like you do now.

These books are packed full of good examples that you can build or just read about to reinforce what you have learned in this book, use your knowledge in different ways, and, of course, learn some completely new stuff too.

It might also be worth reading some pure Kotlin books. It might be hard to believe, having just waded through around 750 pages, but there is a whole lot more to Kotlin than there was time to cover here.

I could name a number of titles, but the books with the largest number of positive reviews on Amazon tend to be the ones worth exploring.

My other channels

Please keep in touch:

- `www.gamecodeschool.com`
- `www.facebook.com/gamecodeschool`
- `www.twitter.com/gamecodeschool`
- `www.youtube.com/channel/UCY6pRQAXnwviO3dpmV258Ig/videos`
- `www.linkedin.com/in/gamecodeschool`

Goodbye and thank you

I had a lot of fun writing this book. I know that's a cliché, but it's also true. Most importantly though, I hope you managed to take something from it and use it as a stepping stone for your future in programming.

You are perhaps reading this for a bit of fun or the kudos of releasing an app, a stepping stone to a programming job, or maybe you actually will build that app that takes Google Play by storm.

Whatever the case, a big thank you from me for buying this book and I wish you all the best in your future endeavors.

I think that everybody has an app inside of them, and all you need do is work hard enough to get it out of you.

Other Book You May Enjoy

If you enjoyed this book, you may be interested in these other books by Packt:

Android 9 Development Cookbook - Third Edition

Rick Boyer

ISBN: 978-1-78899-121-6

- Develop applications using the latest Android framework while maintaining backward-compatibility with the support library
- Create engaging applications using knowledge gained from recipes on graphics, animations, and multimedia
- Work through succinct steps on specifics that will help you complete your project faster
- Add location awareness to your own app with examples using the latest Google Play services API
- Utilize Google Speech Recognition APIs for your app

Kotlin Programming Cookbook

Aanand Shekhar Roy, Rashi Karanpuria

ISBN: 978-1-78847-214-2

- Understand the basics and object-oriented concepts of Kotlin Programming
- Explore the full potential of collection frameworks in Kotlin
- Work with SQLite databases in Android, make network calls, and fetch data over a network
- Use Kotlin's Anko library for efficient and quick Android development
- Uncover some of the best features of Kotlin: Lambdas and Delegates
- Set up web service development environments, write servlets, and build RESTful services with Kotlin
- Learn how to write unit tests, integration tests, and instrumentation/ acceptance tests

Leave a review - let other readers know what you think

Please share your thoughts on this book with others by leaving a review on the site that you bought it from. If you purchased the book from Amazon, please leave us an honest review on this book's Amazon page. This is vital so that other potential readers can see and use your unbiased opinion to make purchasing decisions, we can understand what our customers think about our products, and our authors can see your feedback on the title that they have worked with Packt to create. It will only take a few minutes of your time, but is valuable to other potential customers, our authors, and Packt. Thank you!

Index

A

B

E

F

G

H

I

J

K

L

M

N

O

P

Q

R

S

T

U

V

W

X

www.ingramcontent.com/pod-product-compliance
Lightning Source LLC
Chambersburg PA
CBHW060633060326
40690CB00020B/4388

* 9 7 8 1 7 8 9 6 1 5 4 0 1 *